Nonpareil
Jack Dempsey

ALSO BY JOSEPH S. PAGE

*Pro Football Championships Before the Super Bowl:
A Year-by-Year History, 1926–1965*
(McFarland, 2011)

*Primo Carnera: The Life and Career
of the Heavyweight Boxing Champion*
(McFarland, 2011)

Nonpareil Jack Dempsey

Boxing's First World Middleweight Champion

JOSEPH S. PAGE

Foreword by TRACY CALLIS

McFarland & Company, Inc., Publishers
Jefferson, North Carolina

LIBRARY OF CONGRESS CATALOGUING-IN-PUBLICATION DATA

Names: Page, Joseph S., author. | Callis, Tracy, author of foreword.
Title: Nonpareil Jack Dempsey : boxing's first world middleweight champion / Joseph S. Page ; foreword by Tracy Callis.
Description: Jefferson, North Carolina : McFarland & Company, Inc., Publishers, 2019 | Includes bibliographical references and index.
Identifiers: LCCN 2019017454 | ISBN 9781476677644 (paperback : acid free paper) ∞
Subjects: LCSH: Dempsey, Jack, 1862–1895. | Boxers (Sports)—United States—Biography. | Boxing—United States—History—19th century.
Classification: LCC GV1132.D4 P34 2019 | DDC 796.83092 B—dc23
LC record available at https://lccn.loc.gov/2019017454

BRITISH LIBRARY CATALOGUING DATA ARE AVAILABLE

ISBN (print) 978-1-4766-7764-4
ISBN (ebook) 978-1-4766-3669-6

© 2019 Joseph S. Page. All rights reserved

No part of this book may be reproduced or transmitted in any form or by any means, electronic or mechanical, including photocopying or recording, or by any information storage and retrieval system, without permission in writing from the publisher.

Front cover: Nonpareil Jack Dempsey, circa 1885

Printed in the United States of America

McFarland & Company, Inc., Publishers
Box 611, Jefferson, North Carolina 28640
www.mcfarlandpub.com

A Dedication to a Friend Without Compare

To Lenny—my oldest and dearest friend for over 43 years. Always a smile and the first to make everyone feel welcome. As much brother as friend. Through years of change, you were a constant—our friendship never failed. I miss our visits and I'll always wish I could still pick up the phone and it would be you on the other end of the line. You are truly a friend "nonpareil!" I love you, pal...

Leonard Ambrose Lepore, Jr.—
July 2, 1961–January 7, 2011

Joe (left) and Lenny—Madison, New Jersey, July, 2006

Table of Contents

Acknowledgments	ix
Foreword by Tracy Callis	1
Introduction	3
The Evolution of Rules and Equipment	13
1862 to 1882—From Athgarvan to Brooklyn	27
1883—The Cooper Enters the Ring	32
1884—On the Rise	51
1885—A Full Dance Card	81
1886—The Nonpareil Emerges	108
1887—Breaks and Gashes, but Still on Top	146
1888—Professor Mike Donovan and a Chink in the Armor	176
1889—The Nonpareil Is Brought to Earth	210
1890—In Search of the Marine	238
1891—At the Hands of Ruby Robert	264
1892—Convalescence	287
1893—The Road Back	294
1894—The Slowing Champion	312
1895—Tommy Ryan and the End	324
Immortal Nonpareil	342
"Jack Dempsey's Grave"	349
Appendix: Dempsey's Professional Bouts, 1883–1895	350
Notes	361
Bibliography	376
Index	379

Acknowledgments

This is now my third book and I am still amazed by the goodness and generosity of so many who have gone out of their way to assist me in the preparation of this book. Librarians, fellow authors and researchers, and friends and family have all played varying, but important, roles in the research and writing of this book.

A huge thank you goes out to boxing historians Arly Allen, Tracy Callis, Jim Curl, Mark Dunn, Chris Klein, Clay Moyle and Tony Triem, whose collective archive of boxing photographs is second to none. These fine gentlemen shared a treasure trove of knowledge, ideas, newspaper clippings and photographs from their personal collections, and gave lots of encouragement. The lengths to which they each went out of their way are truly amazing and I am fully in their debt.

Librarian Jessica Jones, Rare Books Cataloger in the Special Collections section of the Tulane University Library, was of invaluable assistance in my hunt for a copy of Richard Fox's 1888 book on Dempsey, the only other biography of the Nonpareil. Librarians Nancy Woods, Deborah May and Tracey Howerton from the Nashville Public Library have now assisted me on all three books with a smile and a great deal of help. Myriad other librarians from Buffalo to Chicago to San Francisco to Pittsburgh to New York have been a tremendous help, whether they guided me to the microfiche or researched a bout and sent me an e-copy of a newspaper article on a fight from more than a century ago.

My family and friends always get a tremendously large thank you. My mother does not like seeing less of me, nor do my friends, but they all seem to understand. Karen sees me across the room, but at times I might as well be somewhere else and in a sense, I am. Brian and Kevin have to read sections and give feedback, which they don't seem to mind, but they're good eggs who would not tell me if they did. Brian has also acted as my copy editor on this book and for that I am very grateful. Also, a big thank you goes out to my wife Karen and to Sandy Reagan of Sandra Reagan Photography for their excellent photography cleanup—a task for which they both really shine. Both ladies, terrific photographers in their own right, are able to clean up many old photographs by eliminating scratches, worn spots, water stains, etc., and making them look like new. Kate, Chloe and Ritz frequently try to help, but my writing seems to take longer as I often find myself typing with one hand while cradling a cat in the other arm, or have a cat lying in front of the keyboard or swatting at the screen as the cursor darts back and forth. Their interest in my work and their companionship, however, are unfailing.

This book has taken much longer than I ever anticipated. It started as a chapter in a compilation book on a number of fighters, but I saw that the Nonpareil's chapter kept getting longer because there was simply so much information. With a great deal of support and encouragement from Tracy Callis, I put the compilation book on hold and concentrated on Dempsey. Tracy continually stressed to me that the Nonpareil deserved his own book and to that point Tracy is correct. The more I looked, the more information I found. There is so much material on this man and it has been forgotten about in the 120 years since his premature death. I'm delighted to bring it to you in this book.

To all, a hearty and sincere thank you!

Foreword
by Tracy Callis

I was flattered when Joe Page asked me to write a foreword to his book. While working with him, the excellent research he does and the keen eye he possesses for detail and accuracy was observed. He writes well, presents the material in an interesting and informative manner and places events in the proper perspective.

Today, it seems that sports writers and analysts are eager to describe modern athletes in glowing terms of "all time" greatness. Comments about their wonderful skills flow easily and frequently. In many instances, these men are called the best ever and placed at the top of any lists of achievements. However, descriptions and praises for great athletes of the past are noticeably lacking.

One such athlete is Jack Dempsey, a pugilist from the early years of modern boxing. He was a man of outstanding ability who built an excellent record for himself in the fistic ring. Furnished with the nickname "Nonpareil" by sportswriters of the day, Dempsey was recognized by many as the first world middleweight champion, a position he held for a number of years. Unbeaten during his first six years in the ring, he held the title until he fell victim to a dreaded disease of the day—consumption (tuberculosis). As his health declined, he lost his strength as well as his exceptional quickness and stamina, but never did he lose his will to fight. Jack Dempsey never lost his courage and gameness, two components that enabled him to be the great fighter that he was.

He was a sociable, friendly type of man who enjoyed the company of his friends and colleagues. He frequently visited with them in local hotels and lounges, engaging in sessions of drink and dialogue. This habit was one of his weaknesses. He much preferred it to a rigorous training ritual and it sometimes affected his conditioning. His other major weakness, as humorous as it sounds, was his great talent as a fighter. It led him to not prepare as thoroughly as he might for particular encounters. However, with his rare natural skills, he came out victorious in the vast majority of his contests. As stated earlier, Dempsey's only two indisputable ring losses came during his period of declining health.

Dempsey tangled with many of the most talented lightweights and middleweights of his era. In addition, he often fought much larger men, some as much as 20 to 30 pounds heavier. Many in the boxing community felt that if he weighed just a little more, he could defeat the great John L. Sullivan. In fact, some thought he could beat him just as he was.

In my opinion, Dempsey and "Sugar" Ray Robinson rank as the two best welterweight fighters of all time. They also rank among the greatest middleweights ever. In fact, more research and study into Dempsey's early career as a lightweight may show that he deserves to rank among the best ever in this group as well.

The author, Joe Page, has done the same thing for himself, first as an athlete in his younger days, then as a manager throughout his life in various business endeavors and now as a writer of sports biographies and organizations. His willingness to undertake difficult tasks accompanied by his disciplined dedication, keen insight and determination has enabled him to complete these efforts in remarkable fashion. His work is highly commendable.

In summary, Dempsey was an immortal, one of the very best pugilists who ever graced the ring. It is, therefore, altogether fitting and proper that one of today's best sports writers presents us with an account of the life and battles of Jack Dempsey, the "Nonpareil."

Tracy Callis is the director of historical research for www.cyberboxingzone.com, an elector to the International Boxing Hall of Fame, and a member of the executive board of directors of the International Boxing Research Organization. He is the author of A Brief History of the Heavyweights, 1881–2010 *(2013).*

Introduction

I found no marble monolith,
No broken shaft, or stone,
Recording sixty victories,
This vanquished victor won;
No rose, no shamrock could I find,
No mortal here to tell,
Where sleeps in this forsaken spot
Immortal Nonpareil.[1]

In the last two decades of the nineteenth century a middleweight prize fighter named Jack Dempsey was one of the most popular sports figures in America. Baseball had yet to reach the height of its popularity, football was in its infancy and golf was still a country club sport, but boxing, while illegal in many locations, was—along with horse racing—the most popular sport in America. Arguably, only heavyweight champion John L. Sullivan was more famous than Dempsey, who was known universally as "The Nonpareil," a French noun that translates to "an individual of unequalled excellence."[2]

To many observers, Dempsey is one of the greatest pound-for-pound fighters in ring history. Inside the ropes, he was poised, quick, agile and had terrific punching power with both hands. Jack originally fought as a lightweight, but throughout his career he regularly fought men ten and twenty pounds heavier. Ultimately, he moved up in weight class and in a short time he won the middleweight championship. Even with his move to the heavier weight classes Dempsey regularly continued to fight larger opponents, including heavyweights, despite the fact that he rarely weighed more than a middleweight.[3]

Part of Dempsey's ring appeal was that he was more than just a slugger. While he had the ability to punch with power and proved this by knocking out better than a third of his adversaries, he regularly engaged his opponents by employing science and technique. "To a generation of American boxing followers, he was a fighter who first demonstrated that boxing can be performed as art, with style, grace and athleticism. Where Sullivan vanquished foes with brute strength, Dempsey was a craftsman who employed technique, strategy and guile."[4] William Brady observed in 1916 that Jim Corbett had introduced the practice of jabbing. "He used his left hand. Up to that time, no pugilist ever had the free use of his left arm that Corbett had. This of itself was of immense value."[5] Brady was absolutely correct that the use of a left jab is of immense value and that Gentleman Jim used it to his advantage, but he was dead wrong when he stated that up until Corbett no pugilist ever used it regularly. Corbett himself spoke of how he had learned to both feint and use the jab from his friend Dempsey who used it regularly throughout his career.

In eulogizing the former champion in 1895, the *San Francisco Call* stated, "The Nonpareil's fighting qualities were never called into question. Whenever he entered the ring a high classed exhibition was insured. Cleverness and gameness, two of the essential attributes of a champion, he abundantly possessed." The *Call* added that "his popularity was of a national character. Excepting John L. Sullivan, perhaps, no man ever commanded such a following. Particularly was this true of him in and around New York. His manly conduct, together with his staying powers, made for him a legion of admirers."[6] In the same vein, the *National Police Gazette* stated that "Jack Dempsey was second only to Sullivan as one of the most popular pugilistic idols of this or any other time in the history of the ring. Bob Fitzsimmons often spoke of him as being the nerviest and best man he ever met in this country and it is a well-known fact that Dempsey was not in his best form when he met Lanky Bob."[7]

Dempsey first climbed into the prize ring in the spring of 1883 and was unbeaten until late August 1889. Over the course of his fourteen-year career, Dempsey lost only three times. There was a questionable loss to his bitter rival George La Blanche and later, there were brutal and decisive losses at the hands of ring greats Bob Fitzsimmons and Tommy Ryan. The losses to Fitzsimmons and Ryan came "when Dempsey was well past his peak and in a dissipated physical condition [due to a losing battle against tuberculosis]."[8] A great many people—including this author—have argued that Jack should never have entered the ring with either Fitzsimmons or Ryan due to size and health considerations.

Nonpareil Jack Dempsey.

Many claim that Dempsey's record should have another victory or at least show one less defeat due to the suspect nature of his loss to La Blanche in 1889. "In the battle with George La Blanche, the Marine, in San Francisco, the claim has often been made that Dempsey was not defeated, but that at a certain stage of the fight, when the betting was 50 to 1 on Dempsey, and La Blanche was virtually a defeated man, the latter wheeled suddenly about and accidentally caught Dempsey on the point of the jaw with his elbow and knocked him out."[9] The backhand pivot punch, whether "accidental" or a final, calculated act of desperation by La Blanche, was viewed as dirty fighting by most and was considered illegal in many states. The referee in this fight, however, let it stand and ruled that La Blanche had won the bout by way of knockout. This put the first blemish on the Nonpareil's record. Despite his "win," La Blanche was not eligible for the middleweight crown since he weighed in over the 154-pound limit, so Dempsey retained the title, but the loss affected Jack's psyche for the rest of his life. In short order, action was taken in many jurisdictions to officially outlaw the pivot punch or, as it became known, "The La Blanche Swing."

In addition to the questionable loss to La Blanche, a number of the "draw" decisions on his record muddy the understanding of his true greatness and were a result of peculiarities of the era. One reason for frequent draws was that in the signed agreements for some contests, Dempsey was held to a higher standard than his opponents—he was the superior fighter and he had to win by knockout. In some of these cases, Jack thoroughly defeated his opponent in the ring, but because the man was still on his feet at the end of the appointed number of rounds, a draw was declared and the purse split evenly. A second reason draws were fairly common is due to the aforementioned "outlaw" status of prizefighting. In many localities police interference during contests was common, regularly causing bouts to be broken up prior to their natural conclusion. In these cases, draws were often the result. Since prizefighting was illegal in so many localities fight backers and promoters generally went to great lengths to keep the locations, dates and times of contests a secret in order to keep the police away. One inherent problem with no police presence at a fight is crowd control. If the secret got out and uninvited fans showed up at a bout, there was no way to keep the peace among the throngs outside of the squared circle. This set up a final reason for many draws being called by the referee—the problem of unruly fight fans who might be tempted to disrupt a bout to protect their bet if their man was losing. Suffice to say, draws in prizefights in the latter part of the nineteenth century were fairly common.

The police interference with prizefights during Dempsey's time was chiefly due to the mores of the nineteenth century, which did not favor the sport. Well-heeled citizens, civic groups and many newspapers railed against boxing, frequently using terms such as "brutal" and "desperate" to describe prizefights. In one article from 1883 the *Brooklyn Eagle* called for an end to the sport. "The *Eagle* does not believe that General Jordan or Superintendent Campbell approves of prizefighting; they are both gentlemen, and as such must hold this brutal and abominable business in proper abhorrence." The newspaper went on to speak of the high status and general respect enjoyed by local officials Jordan and Campbell in the community, but warned that "if they are desirous of retaining that confidence and respect they must put a stop, once and forever, to prize fighting."[10] It is worth noting, however, that a touch of hypocrisy was evident as that same newspaper would run lengthy coverage of some of these fights at the same time it was calling for the sport's abolishment.[11]

Some descriptions of Jack Dempsey from those who knew him and saw him fight are illuminating. After a bout early in Jack's career, the *Brooklyn Eagle* stated, "Dempsey had three things to favor him: the legs of a champion collar and elbow wrestler; the arms of a Donnelly[12]—long in the reach; and the head of a lawyer. He was cool and fought like a general who knew the value of brains and superiority of tactics over brute force."[13]

As early as 1884, Richard K. Fox, the longtime editor of the *National Police Gazette*, noted after Jack's bout with Canadian George Fulljames that "Dempsey fully confirmed the high opinion entertained of him as a boxer, showing himself to be a clever two-handed fighter and a punishing hitter. Cool and collected, he was ever ready to take advantage of any mistake or opening presented by his antagonist, while his courage was undisputable."[14] Two years later Fox wrote of Dempsey, "His style and method of boxing has a neatness about it which is completely new and unknown. He stops blows aimed by his adversaries with so much skill, and hits his antagonist with such terrific force and comparative ease that he astonishes and terrifies his opponents beyond measure, and those ambitious to win and wear the title of middleweight champion are soon convinced of his superior knowledge and athletic prowess, and only face him to be vanquished."[15] Fox added that "his agility and quickness on his legs and his thorough knowledge of pedal motion, handicaps any boxer he faces in the roped arena, no matter what rules govern."

One reporter went so far with his praise of Jack that he stated in November 1884, "If Dempsey weighed thirty pounds more he could whip John L. Sullivan with ease. He is the champion light weight fighter of America and I believe he could whip any man in the world of his weight. There are very few pugilists of his age who can point to sixteen victories, undimmed by a single defeat."[16]

The Nonpareil did not come across as the typical pugilist. Meeting Jack away from the ring one might not even know that he was a boxer. Physically he was not an imposing figure. Jack was slender, "handsome, well-spoken and mannerly. Also, he was quite personable and made friends easily. On most occasions, after trouncing an opponent in the ring, he was calm and rather indifferent towards the praise being heaped upon him."[17]

The *National Police Gazette* wrote of Dempsey's pleasing face, refined manners and gentlemanly demeanor, "which almost dispel all thought of his being the dreaded pugilist that he is," and continued by stating that "he is quite unassuming, he is not a boaster."[18]

Chicago journalist Bill Nye travelled across the Pacific Northwest and the Great Plains with Jack in 1886 and described him as follows. "Mr. Dempsey is not a man who would be picked out as a great man. You might pass him by two or three times without recognizing his eminence, and yet at a scrapping matinee or swatting recital he seems to hold his audience at his own sweet will—also his antagonist." Nye continued, "Mr. Dempsey does not crave notoriety. He seems rather to court seclusion. This is characteristic of the man. His logic, however, is wonderful. Though quiet and unassuming in his manner, his arguments are powerful and generally make a large protuberance wherever they alight."[19]

Richard K. Fox, publisher of the *National Police Gazette*.

Journalist Charley White commented many years after the Nonpareil's untimely death that

"Dempsey was very proud, as honest as the day is long, and as for gameness, that word doesn't begin to do him justice. He has left a name in the annals of the ring that stands to this day as a synonym for squareness and gameness. He is one of the most popular men that ever held the title."[20]

Sullivan commented after Jack's defeat at the hands of Fitzsimmons in 1891 that he was both shocked and devastated by the news. He stated that he was not upset about losing several hundred dollars on wagers, but rather for the mere fact that his friend Jack had lost the bout. "I admired Dempsey as a fighter and a gentleman. I always regarded him as one of my best friends. Then again, I considered him the best middleweight on earth."[21] When asked how he accounted for the Nonpareil's loss to Fitzsimmons, Sullivan responded, "How do I account for it? You might as well ask me to account for the spots on the sun. It is one of those things that can't be accounted for."[22] In a prediction haunting in its accuracy, Sullivan forecast correctly that "he'll never recover from this licking. The poor fellow's heart must be broken."[23]

Dempsey was one of the "Three Jacks," a trio of prominent fighters of the 1880s and 1890s made up of the Nonpareil, Jack McAuliffe and Jack Skelly, two of his boyhood mates from Brooklyn. All three went on to notable ring careers. In describing Dempsey and McAuliffe, one columnist for the *Brooklyn Eagle* stated that their home borough of Brooklyn should be proud of the two pugilists. "They do all their fighting in the ring, and they fight fairly when they are there. To their fellow citizens who are not looking for a fight they are as pleasant, agreeable and respectable a pair of young men as can be found anywhere. They eschew the company of loafers and blackguards, and their presence anywhere with their friends is neither a menace nor a nuisance. In their own localities they are highly esteemed. They both have a hearty contempt for barroom 'bad men.'"[24] This was all high praise from a newspaper and public who did not officially support boxing as a respectable pastime given the sport's "illegal" status during the 1880s. Remember that as late as 1885 the *Eagle* had referred to prizefighting as "this brutal and abominable business" which must be held "in proper abhorrence" and had regularly called on local officials to put an end to it.[25]

Former middleweight champion and boxing trainer Professor Mike Donovan commented on the day after Jack thoroughly defeated opponent Dominick McCaffrey that "Jack Dempsey is the most scientific fighter that ever appeared with bare knuckles or gloves."[26] Noted fighter, trainer and manager Billy Madden who was an enthusiastic supporter of Jack's throughout the Nonpareil's career stated, "In all

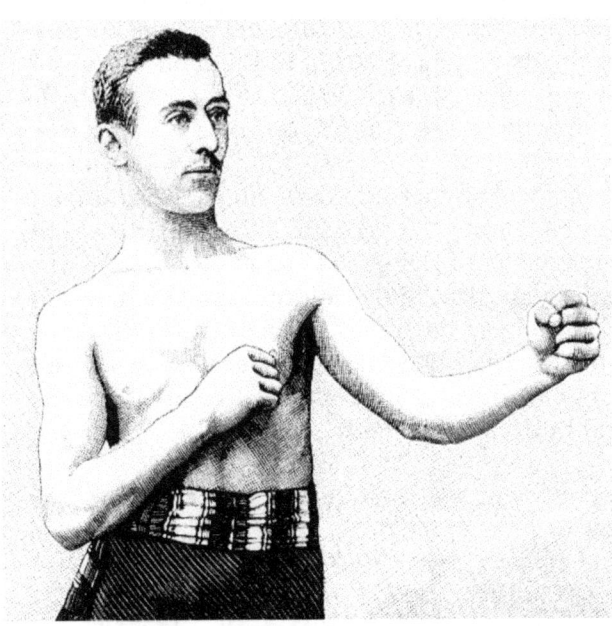

Jack Skelly, one of Dempsey's longtime friends.

my experience among pugilists I never saw such a cool-headed and calculating man in the ring as Dempsey."[27]

In 1886 the *National Police Gazette* commented that Dempsey "carries an intellect which, coupled with his natural and acquired physical superiority and excellent prize ring education gives him a powerful advantage over others in the profession and gives him an even balance against many who are very much more powerful physically." The *Gazette* continued, stating that Dempsey was "just as great a general and tactician in the ring as any champion that preceded him except Jem Mace."[28]

Pope Gooding stated in an 1889 interview that "Dempsey, with skin-tight gloves, in good condition, I think can whip any man of his weight in the world and a good many heavy-weights, but it is well known that he is not what is termed a knocker-out, his forte being to jab a man to death and get away. Four or five-ounce gloves are not as effective in this style of fighting as bare knuckles or skin-tight gloves." Gooding went on to say of the Nonpareil that "he represents the old style of ring tactics brought to the highest state of development."[29]

His old pal Jack Skelly commented, "I wish the boys who are boxing today could have seen Dempsey perform in his prime. They would see a master of the art of boxing. A man not only wonderful with his two hands, but with his two feet also. I readily believe the Nonpareil was the first man to introduce the skillful footwork that revolutionized boxing and made it more scientific and speedy."[30]

Physically Dempsey was at best an average sized man for his era. He stood five feet and eight inches tall and his weight ran from about 125 pounds when he began his ring career in 1883 to roughly 150 pounds as he filled out and his career progressed. "Jack was slender, muscular, quick and agile. He had fast hands and a stiff right-hand punch. He was crafty and elusive and utilized feints accompanied by a sharp, accurate left jab. Fight after fight, his opponents were battered, bruised, and cut up while he scarcely had any marks at all."[31] Author John McCallum noted that "Dempsey brought polished boxing skill and an appreciation of the finer points of ringsmanship to the modern ring."[32] Another report states that "he is a slim and supple little fellow, and he doesn't care to do anything, but fight. He is like Mr. Sullivan in that respect; he had rather be a pugilist than a president."[33]

Jack's close friend Dr. Harry Lane, a noted physician in Portland, Oregon, initially met the Nonpareil when Jack made his first journey to Oregon in 1885. The two became good friends and remained so for the remainder of Dempsey's life. It was Dr. Lane who treated Dempsey during the final months of his fatal battle with consumption. Dr. Lane commented on Dempsey's small hands during an interview in October 1895. "Did you ever notice Jack's hands? It is so small that his wife's gloves are too large for him, and she wears a 6½. It is a shapely hand, too, not at all like a prizefighter's. I secured a plaster cast of it when he was in his prime, and I prize it very highly."[34]

While the Nonpareil had unquestioned success regardless of fight conditions, he was at his best in finish fights—unlimited by rounds, and preferably using the old London prize ring rules under which he could employ his well-honed grappling skills. In that scenario he could wear opponents down round by round—even much larger men. Under Queensbury rules his knowledge, skills and ring generalship still prevailed, but if limited by rounds he faced a greater challenge.

Patrick F. Sheedy, a Chicago gambler and one-time manager of John L. Sullivan, had this to say about Jack in 1887: "You asked me just now if I thought Sullivan to be the greatest fighter in the world. Well, I don't. I think him to be the biggest, but the greatest fighter I ever saw or heard of is Jack Dempsey, and he is the greatest in general, too." After pointing out that Dempsey had fought dozens of bouts against larger men and still triumphed, Sheedy added, "If he weighed ten pounds more—that is, if he scaled 160 pounds—I think he could beat anybody under the London prize ring rules."[35]

Dempsey's longtime friend and fellow pugilist Jack McAuliffe did not believe that it mattered a whit under which prize ring rules the Nonpareil was fighting—he was skilled and dangerous and could beat anyone. "Jack Dempsey in his prime was an ideal fighter. He knew as much about the game under London or Queensberry rules as any man in the ring today, and probably a little more." McAuliffe went on to say that Dempsey cleverly adapted his style throughout a fight to keep his opponents off guard. "This is where Jack Dempsey excelled. His opponents never knew how he was going to fight as Dempsey's style would change as round succeeded round. Sometimes he would fight in close and the next round found him away off, skipping around the ring like a grasshopper."[36]

An 1886 newspaper report described Dempsey's pugilistic style as follows: "His fighting position is unlike that of any other boxer that I know of. He stands with his left foot well to the front, his right side thrown considerably to the back, presenting only his left side to his opponent. He holds his terrible left straight out from his shoulder and his right rather high so as to cover his face." The writer went on to credit much of Dempsey's success to his strong and sturdy legs. "They are the best pair of fighting supports I've ever seen on a pugilist." The report continued, "In his manner of fighting he is what you'd call a 'wheeler,' that is he keeps continually on the move, circling around his opponent, seeking for an opening." In summation the reporter commented that "Jack is quick as lightning with his left" and added that "as a strategist he is unequaled."[37] Such high praise was not at all uncommon in reports on the Nonpareil.

An 1888 article made a similar observation. "Dempsey is undoubtedly the greatest ring general of all American boxers. Before an antagonist he is the personification of coolness and remains so under any and all circumstances." The writer added, "His reach is long and in attitude he stands with the left well out, the right foot being so far back that he presents almost a side view, the best of all defensive positions. Being a left-handed fighter [Dempsey was a righty, but the writer alludes to his wildly effective, leading left] he has a decided advantage over men who depend on their right."[38]

Veteran San Francisco timekeeper George Harting, who held the watch in countless ring battles in the Bay area, described the Nonpareil's style as follows: "Jack Dempsey was a square boxer. He was the most remarkably clever man in the ring. I have seen him box quite frequently and always noticed that he never used his right save when he knew that his opponent was through fighting." Harting felt this was a major ingredient in Dempsey's success. "It was practically impossible to get by that wonderful left." Harting added that it was a fluke when George La Blanche dropped Dempsey in San Francisco in 1889. He noted "that La Blanche got by Dempsey by accident was no sign that he had solved his [Dempsey's] defense. As I have said, that was an accident and might have happened to any boxer."[39]

Another article that ran in Indiana's *Logansport Journal* in December 1888 compared various fighters and styles from the era. The report spoke of Dempsey's coolness in the ring, his damaging left jab and his patience. "Like a successful general, Dempsey maps out his plan of battle after a careful study of his man."[40] The story discussed his long reach and his ability to both defend and jab with his long and terribly quick portside appendage. The article also pointed out Dempsey's capacity to follow his jab with a damaging and lightning-fast right. In summation, the article points out that "Dempsey's style is original, his mode effective, his generalship supreme, for without doubt he is the greatest middleweight the prize ring has seen."[41]

Dempsey once discussed the frequent use of his left jab with a reporter from the *St. Louis Post-Dispatch*. "The great mistake with most fighters is their over anxiety to swing their right. I seldom use my right at the outset of a fight. I wait until my man is a little tired and winded. Then he can't get away so quick and when I swing it, I stand double the chance of getting it in that I would if he were fresh and on alert for it." The reporter then noted that Jack's logic was sound and commented, "Dempsey is the best general of a fighter I ever met and can give the most conclusive reasons for his way of fighting."[42]

For all of the praise heaped on Dempsey's much heralded skills, Jack in turn was also very quick to praise his opponents, particularly an antagonist who provided him with a strong challenge in the ring. Dempsey was once asked by an interviewer which of all of his fights was the hardest one. After thinking for a few moments, Jack said, "Well you can rest assured that the hardest battle I ever had was with Jack Fogarty, of Philadelphia, in which I won in twenty-seven rounds, lasting one hour and fifty-one minutes, for $6,000. Then came the La Blanche fight of thirteen rounds in fifty-two minutes."[43] Dempsey, however, perhaps simply caught up in a moment, regularly pointed to great fights and the skills of his opponents.

Once, when asked how he remained so calm and cool in the ring, Dempsey responded, "I never got in the ring that I wasn't nervous. Take it when I fought Fulljames. I could feel myself trembling from head to foot until the fight began. As soon as I got a clip it straightened out my nerve." Dempsey continued by saying that "the tremble was all over" and "I don't settle down to business until the business has begun and it always seemed to me that I have got to get a good punch at the start to steady me."[44]

In short, Jack Dempsey—the Nonpareil—was a fascinating man. Obviously, he was a highly skilled prize fighter who used his personal popularity to help gain a broader acceptance for the sport of boxing during a time when it was still illegal, a societal pariah and fights had to be held clandestinely to avoid police interference. But some more general observations I have made after years of study of his life are as follows. He was a generous, honest and fair man both inside the ring and out—sometimes to his own detriment. The Nonpareil was well-grounded and refused to let his fame or popularity go to his head. Dempsey was noted as being a quiet but clever and intelligent man who could hold his own in a debate or when sharing his opinions with others. Jack was a gentleman, a trusted friend, a good son and brother and a devoted husband and father.

Through much of his career Jack was torn between his love of his life as a prizefighter and a strong desire to retire from the ring and pursue some other line of business that would allow him to stay at home with his young family. It was an understandable quandary. Dempsey moved easily in boxing circles where he was well-known, respected and almost universally well thought of. The idea of leaving the comfort of something he knew so well was a bit intimidating. He also needed the large sums of money that his name brought in the ring and on the stage in exhibitions because he was a very poor manager of his finances. He spent far too freely and was constantly in need of the next big payday. He spent lavishly during his constant travels, staying in fine hotels, resorts and train berths, dining in fine restaurants and spending on his friends. Jack's marriage to Margaret Brady helped a bit in this area as his wife and in-laws were able to instill a level of investment and financial stability in him, but even with the Bradys' encouragement, Jack was never very responsible with his money.

The Nonpareil stated on more than one occasion that he was in the ring for the money. He told a reporter from the *Brooklyn Eagle* in 1886, "Now the truth of the matter is that I am heartily sick of fighting. I would like to stop and go away somewhere for a rest." But exhibiting the internal tug-of-war he fought for years, he immediately noted that despite his desire to leave the squared circle behind, he kept himself in good condition and always ready for the next challenger. While a part of him loved the world of boxing, Jack repeatedly acknowledged that the lure of the ring for him was the money, the sum of which he could not match in any other profession. Dempsey then stated flatly, "…and consequently I fight."[45]

Despite his myriad good traits, Dempsey certainly had his demons. In addition to his poor financial habits and certainly adding to them, Jack drank too often and too much. Dempsey's love of the bottle was one of the few dark spots on the Nonpareil's history and it would haunt him throughout his career. According to boxing historian Tracy Callis, "Perhaps his greatest weakness as a fighter was his inclination to consume too much alcohol." Callis also points to Dempsey's tendency to underestimate his opposition. "The result was that sometimes he did not train well. However, his great skills usually overcame these problems."[46]

Jack suffered from a weak chest that caused him significant health issues throughout his career and ultimately contributed to his contracting tuberculosis and the consumption that killed him at an early age. Dempsey also seems to have suffered from some level of depression and perhaps anxiety. He could be fine one moment, but seemingly dark and depressed or acting erratically the next. All of this was only exacerbated by his love of the bottle. Add his many years of taking punches to the head and body and this once strong and virile young man became a physical and emotional wreck at a still early age. Each of these issues would help to explain his periodic bouts with what were described as "chest colds," periods of seclusion and his occasional habit of disappearing for days on end, as well as his sometimes odd and erratic behavior. Dozens of newspaper articles referred to these issues and while Dempsey, his friends and managers all did their best to cover them up, in many cases their excuses only added to the rumors and speculation as to the real causes of his troubles.

In all, Jack Dempsey was a great fighter and a good but troubled person who regrettably has been far too long in the shadows of boxing history. This is true I believe for several reasons. First, his long period of illness and premature death in 1895 at age 33 robbed him of at least several more years in the ring while at the top of his game. His heavy drinking, periods of depression and occasionally erratic behavior no doubt intensified this erosion of skills. His premature death caused him to lose years of additional ring battles, newspaper interviews and the ability to opine and be quoted on boxing events well into his golden years.

The second and perhaps greatest reason that Jack Dempsey has been too often forgotten over the past century is Jack Dempsey. The Nonpareil has been long overshadowed by the Manassa Mauler. William Harrison Dempsey took the nickname "Jack" somewhat in tribute to the Nonpareil whom he admired, but in doing so he unwittingly helped to diminish the Nonpareil's memory.

Through size, chronology and longevity, the second Jack Dempsey had advantages over the first. Typically, heavyweights garner a larger share of the press than do the lighter weight classes. The sheer fact that his career came some thirty years after the Nonpareil's helped. Boxing had become a popular, legal and mainstream sport by the time the Manassa Mauler entered the prize ring. A sports culture had developed in North America—indeed in much of the Western world— enabling the second Dempsey to benefit from even greater press coverage and eventually from radio broadcasts as well. The Nonpareil's tragically short life extinguished his voice and press early on whereas the Manassa Mauler lived well into his 80s and continued to be interviewed, photographed, seen around town, asked his opinion about fighters and so on for many years after he retired from the ring. He was a restaurateur, columnist, referee and served in the military in World War II. In short, from the mid–1910s to the early 1980s the second Jack Dempsey was never far from the public's eye.

While writing this book I became more and more aware of just how well forgotten the Nonpareil has become and how well-known the Manassa Mauler still is. Over the past couple of years, when asked the topic of my current project I would respond that I was writing a biography of the boxer Jack Dempsey. Invariably my questioner assumed it was the Manassa Mauler and would begin speaking about him. I would then have to correct them and explain that my subject was the middleweight champion from the 1880s and 1890s of whom most had absolutely no knowledge. In time, I began to preempt their misconception by adding that I was writing a biography of the boxer Jack Dempsey, but not the one they were thinking of. I then began to joke—somewhat seriously—that I would name the book, "Not Him, the Other Guy."

This biography has been a developing project. As mentioned, I began writing a book with mini-biographies of multiple fighters, one of whom happened to be the Nonpareil. As I researched and wrote, Dempsey's chapter kept getting longer as I found a plethora of information on him in old newspapers and magazines. Despite the abundance of material, the only biography ever written about the first Jack Dempsey was published by Richard K. Fox's *National Police Gazette* in 1888, while Jack was still in the middle of his career. This great boxer from the early days of the prize ring, who in equal measure with his friend, the great and well-known John L. Sullivan, did so much to popularize the sport, needs to be remembered. The dust and cobwebs that have hidden this legend of the ring need to be swept away and his story told. It was high time that this gaping hole in the fabric of boxing's history was closed.

Nonpareil Jack Dempsey's story is a rich one full of amazing highs and terrible lows. He was a poor immigrant Irish boy who scaled great heights to become one of the nation's first sports celebrities. He became a household name, wealthy and popular. He married the love of his life and had two beautiful little girls. He loved his family and wanted to be devoted to them only, but his other love was boxing, and the lure of the ring, with its fame and fortune, continually pulled him away. He was a gifted athlete, strong, rugged, and fearless, but in time his violent profession and his passion for the bottle began to wear his body down. Mental illness and the contraction of tuberculosis helped the process along until there was little left to recognize of the valiant hero of so many battles. He died from the wasting effects of consumption a broken man and a physical wreck just a month short of his thirty-third birthday. It was a tragic end to a complicated story. "Ernest Hemingway once said 'Every true story ends in death.' Well, this is a true story."[47]

The Evolution of Rules and Equipment

One of the challenges in writing a book about a fighter from the nineteenth century is helping today's reader understand the world of boxing as it was in that time. It was a different era with different equipment and different rules of the ring. Bare knuckles or gloves, two- and four-ounce kid gloves or modern padded gloves and, of course, the London Rules or the Marquess of Queensberry Rules.

In addition to the variations in rules and equipment, there were differences in the skills the fighters needed to possess in order to succeed. The men who engaged in prizefighting in the early days of the sport certainly needed to know how to punch and defend themselves, but they also needed to know how to grapple. One report on the evolution of the sport stated that "the warriors of the London ring were skilled in wrestling, as the rules allowed throwing on holds above the waist." The report noted that "Jack Dempsey was a collar and elbow wrestler in his younger days when he worked in a Brooklyn Cooper shop."[1]

As I began writing, I continued to come across events that needed explaining to a twenty-first-century audience. As I thought about it, it seemed that the place to start was undoubtedly with an introduction to the differences in the world of boxing then and now. Without this, the story of the Nonpareil's career might well prove confusing to the average modern reader.

Boxing traces its history back to ancient times. The Etruscans, Egyptians, Greeks, Romans and other early civilizations became fans of the sport and the Greeks eventually added it to the ancient Olympic games. The sport, while somewhat recognizable to today's fan, was also quite different. The term sport could be at times a misnomer. In ancient times, boxing was more of a no holds barred gladiator contest which might well end in death for one or both men. The combatants engaged in brutal and merciless combat that makes today's bloodiest battles look almost tame by comparison. Fighters were encouraged to battle until one or both men could not go on. Men such as Tisander, Theagenes and Cleitomachus were some of the most notable Olympic champions of that earlier era.

Early equipment was different and its use inconsistent. Some fighters wore headgear and even leather gum guards, but the most notable difference may have been the earliest form of boxing gloves. Leather straps known as "cestus" were sometimes wrapped around the combatants' knuckles with much the same hand-protecting purpose as the gauze and tape wraps worn by today's fighters under their gloves. By the days of the Roman Empire however, blades and spikes were often introduced into the wrappings, turning the cestus' protective purpose into a deadly one. With the fall of the Roman Empire, boxing too retreated into obscurity, not to be seen again on any notable level until early eighteenth-century England.

According to boxing historian Arly Allen, "The word 'Prizefighting' originally described sword-fighting. It grew out of Medieval Battles when 'prizes' were fought for with swords. Prizes were the only rewards of battle and often the only payment that the winning side received. The word 'box' originally meant a blow and usually a blow from a sword, but by the middle 1500s a 'box' came to mean a blow from a fist." Allen points out that "by the late 1500s 'boxers' or 'ruffians,' 'roisters' or 'bruisers' were fist fighters who fought in the streets and in public places. By 1681 these boxers had attracted the attention of the nobility. The first championship boxing match was fought in London between a butcher and a footman of the second Duke of Albemarle. According to reports, the butcher won 'as he had done many times before.'" Allen adds, "In 1734 James Figg, the foremost sword-prizefighter in England, organized a series of boxing matches, showing that boxing was taking over the locations and the basic rules of prizefighting. By 1813 boxing had supplanted sword-prizefighting in England and now carried the name 'prizefighting' by which it was introduced to America."[2]

During the early eighteenth century bare-knuckle fighting began to gain popularity. In addition to prizefights, bouts between men trying to settle general disagreements became more common. This is confirmed by the Swiss author Cesar de Saussure who wrote about his observations of the aspects of life in England from 1725 to 1729. De Saussure wrote, "The insolence of the populace is so great that as soon as an honest man has any disagreement with one of their kind, he is at once invited to strip and fight."[3]

Prizefighting at this time often resembled more of a street brawl, with the fighters not only landing punches but also attempting to send their opponents to the ground—rarely a padded canvas—by a variety of other means including tripping, grappling and throw downs. In this way contests somewhat resembled a present-day Mixed Martial Arts contest, except that when a fighter landed on the ground, the round ended. After a short rest period—usually between thirty seconds and a minute—the fighters were called back to the center ring by the referee to "come to scratch" and resume their battle.

"Whilst Figg could be said to have brought the sport into prominence initially, it is Jack Broughton who is generally credited with being its true founder."[4] Broughton was the first person known to have written down rules for boxing. While Broughton was the first to capture the rules in print, this did not mean that boxing had no rules before 1743 when Broughton put pen to paper. In fact, the rules of boxing were established much earlier and were well-known to the public, so much so that one observer noted in 1775 that "the *London* Mob will not suffer in boxing the least foul play; as, for instance, two to fall upon one."[5] According to Allen, these generally accepted, but unwritten rules were derived from wrestling and included the following:

    1. Two men, and only two men, might box each other at one time. No one else was allowed within the ring.
    2. No weapons might be used. The fight must be with fists or arms or heads and feet. No artificial weapons such as canes or swords or knives could be used.
    3. The men must strip to their waists before beginning the fight to demonstrate that they had no weapons.

4. The men must shake hands before the fight to demonstrate that there was no animosity between them. This was important from the standpoint of law. Shaking hands demonstrated that they had both agreed to the fight and there was no malice intended.

5. While the men fought primarily with fists, they could also use their arms to wrestle their opponent down. They might also charge their opponent with their head to knock him down. Bringing your opponent to the ground was the objective of the fight whether it was done by knocking him down with your fists, by a wrestling throw, such as a cross-buttock, or by a headbutt.

6. When one man went down, his opponent might hit him once with his fist and no more. Although it was not strictly legal, it might occur that the standing man would fall on his opponent when he was down, as was common in wrestling, before he got up. But the standing man was not allowed to stay on top of the down man, nor was the objective to pin him down as it was in wrestling.

7. In wrestling, once a man was on the ground, he was ruled to have lost the fall. There might be three falls to a match. But in boxing, once a man was down, he might get up and fight again after a brief period. (How long he might remain down before he was considered to have lost the fight was uncertain and was a source of dispute.)

8. When one man went down it was allowed for members of the ring to help him up, dust him off and encourage him to get back in the battle. It is not clear how far this help might go. This too was a source of dispute.

As stated, one of the early attempts to put forth a satisfactory set of rules around prizefighting was undertaken in 1743 by Englishman Jack Broughton, who when not engaged in bare-knuckle prizefights ferried passengers as a waterman or boatman back and forth across the Thames River. When he opened his own amphitheater in 1743 Broughton decided that a set of rules should be affirmed to govern all battles held at his venue.

Broughton's rules were designed to eliminate areas of controversy which often sprang up during a match. Broughton's rules were a short list of measures intended to bring a greater level of standardization and a degree of civility to the prize ring. Broughton's seven rules were the first attempt at changing boxing's image from the brutal and often deadly battles waged in the ancient world. The rules read as follows:

I. That a square of a yard be chalked in the middle of the stage, and on every fresh set-to after a fall, or being parted from the rails, each second is to bring his man to the side of the square, and place him opposite to the other, and till they are fairly set-to at the lines, it shall not be lawful for one to strike at the other.

II. That, in order to prevent any disputes, the time a man lies after a fall, if the second does not bring his Man to the side of the square, within the space of half a minute, he shall be deemed a beaten Man.

III. That in every main battle, no person whatever shall be upon the stage, except the principals and their seconds, the same rule to be observed in bye-battles, except that in the latter, Mr. Broughton is allowed to be upon the stage to keep decorum, and to assist gentlemen in getting to their places, provided always he does not interfere in the Battle; and whoever pretends to infringe these rules to be turned immediately out of the house. Everybody is to quit the stage as soon as the champions are stripped, before the set-to.

IV. That no champion be deemed beaten, unless he fails coming up to the line in the limited time, or that his own second declares him beaten. No second is to be allowed to ask his man's adversary any questions or advise him to give out.

V. That in bye-battles, the winning man to have two-thirds of the money given, which shall be publicly divided upon the stage, notwithstanding any private agreements to the contrary.

VI. That to prevent disputes, in every main battle the principals shall, on coming on the stage, choose from among the gentlemen present two umpires, who shall absolutely decide all disputes that may arise about the battle; and if the two umpires cannot agree, the said umpires to choose a third, who is to determine it.

VII. That no person is to hit his adversary when he is down, or seize him by the hair, the breeches, or any part below the waist: a man on his knees to be reckoned down.[6]

Due to its brutal reputation and allegations of fight fixing, boxing was driven out of London around 1754. It was reestablished in the countryside where Broughton continued to teach young boxers and bouts were often held outdoors. The sport was still of interest to many in the upper classes who looked to men such as Broughton and John Jackson to teach them how to box. Due to its broad appeal during this period, the need for additional rules became evident and twenty-three new dictates were set down that built upon and added to Jack Broughton's existing seven. These became known as the London Rules of 1838.

Bouts held under these guidelines were generally contested with bare knuckles. The rules also allowed for a broad range of fighting techniques including holds and throws of the opponent. Spiked shoes were within limits—they were allowed because the contests were so often staged outdoors on grass, sand or dirt surfaces. The matches were also often held overnight or in the very early morning when dew on the ground could make it slippery and cleated athletic shoes were helpful in providing traction and stability.

In contrast to today's rules, in which a professional round ends either after three minutes or when one of the contestants is unable to continue, London Rules rounds ended when a fighter was downed by punch or a throw, "whereupon he was given 30 seconds to rest and eight additional seconds to 'come to scratch' or return to the center of the ring where a 'scratch line' was drawn, and square off with his opponent once more. Consequently, there were most often no round limits to fights." When a man could not rise and come to scratch, his opponent would be declared the winner and the fight would be brought to a halt. Under the London Rules, a fighter's seconds could enter the ring at the end of a round and assist the fallen man to his feet and back to his corner. "It was also fairly common for a bout to be ended by crowd riot, police interference or if both men were willing to accept that the contest was a draw." The lack of set three-minute rounds, fights to the finish and the granting of a stoppage of thirty-eight seconds each time a man was downed were the reasons that so many old-time contests lasted for an enormous number of rounds. While fights could have thirty, forty or more rounds, "the rounds in practice could be quite short with fighters pretending to go down from minor blows to take advantage of the 30-second rest period."[7] By way of example, if a forty-seven-round bout was fought under today's rules with three-minute rounds each separated by a one-minute break, it would last 187 minutes, whereas under the London Rules it might well last less than an hour.

Over the next fifteen years the new rules helped to further popularize the sport, but by 1853 it was determined that the London Rules were insufficient to address all circumstances that occurred concerning prizefighting. A committee was established to review the existing rules and make recommendations for changes and additions. The revision committee was made up of members of the Pugilistic Benevolent Association. The revised London Rules of 1853 were a twenty-nine-statute canon that built upon the rules laid down in 1838 but added clarifying wording to several existing ordinances and added six new ones. Rule 5 from 1838 dealt with protective cups and footwear. This was split into two separate statutes in 1853, one dealing specifically with each equipment issue. Other minor changes dealt with the removal of the umpire from wording around decisions, therefore giving the referee virtually complete control of the fight. Rule 22 from 1838 dealt with fights not settled on the day scheduled whether through postponement, pending darkness, police interference or other. The 1853 version became rule number 23 and dealt with the same topic, but in much greater detail. The five new rules addressed forfeits, foul calls, the use of hard substances in fighters' fists and choking an opponent. The rules also addressed how to resolve wagers in case of interference by the law, darkness or when cancellations occurred. Below is a quick review of the London Rules of 1853:

Rule one shows a major difference from today's rules when it starts out by saying that, "the ring shall be made on turf, and shall be four and twenty feet square, formed of eight stakes and ropes, the latter extending in double lines, the uppermost line being four feet from the ground, and the lower two feet from the ground."[8] In the center of the ring a chalked mark was formed and it was called the "Scratch." So immediately we have a call for an outdoor venue and a ring with eight posts and two strands of ropes versus three.

Rule two stated that each fighter would be attended by two "seconds" and a bottle holder. Rule three then stated that after the men all shook hands, the seconds would meet and toss a coin to decide which corner each would take. While not a major factor today, this had an impact at the time as many, if not most, bouts were held outdoors and much like in an American football game, wind and sun could have a tremendous impact on the fighters, so having the elements at your back between rounds could make a real difference. After the toss, the winner chose the most advantageous corner for his fighter and the loser would take his place in the opposite diagonal corner.

Rule four was concerned with the fighters' colors, which were handkerchiefs of their own choosing that were tied to one of the center stakes or posts (remember that there were eight posts, not today's four). The colors would fly during the fight and at the conclusion; the winner was entitled to collect his opponent's colors or handkerchief as a token of victory.

The fifth rule was concerned with the selection of umpires and the referee. Each man would be represented by one umpire who was selected by his seconds or backers. The umpires would keep time and watch the progress of the fight and take exception with any rule violations he saw. The referee would be selected by the umpires, unless agreed upon by the fighters and their teams. All disputes would be referred to the referee and his decision on the matter would be final and binding.

Rule six had the seconds inspect the fighters' "drawers" or trunks to be certain that no illegal substances had been inserted (i.e., a cup, which was at the time considered an unfair and unnecessary tool). Were something to be found, the umpires would rule on admissibility and direct what alteration, if any, needed to be made.

Rule seven dealt with the spikes on the fighters' shoes. As mentioned earlier when discussing rule two, many bouts were held outdoors and often on grass, dirt, sand or even gravel at hours when frost or dew was common and could make the fighting surface slippery. As such, fighters would wear cleated shoes to improve their footing. The rule reads as follows: "That the spikes in the lighting boots shall be confined to three in number, which shall not exceed three-eighths of an inch from the sole of the boot, and shall not be less than one-eighth of an inch broad at the point; two to be placed in the broadest part of the sole and one in the heel; and that in the event of a man wearing any other spikes either in the toes or elsewhere, he shall be compelled either to remove them or provide other boots properly spiked, the penalty for refusal to be a loss of the stakes."[9]

Rule eight stated that the seconds needed to leave the ring before the start of any round and remain outside the ropes until the end of each round. Rule eight continues by stating that at the conclusion of a round when their fighter is down, the seconds should step into the ring and carry or otherwise assist their man back to his corner where they were to administer whatever aid was necessary to return their man to the fight for the next round. That is certainly quite a difference from today's boxing, wherein the inability to rise unaided and resume the bout or to make it back to his corner means a knockout loss for the prostrate fighter.

Rule nine stated that the time between rounds would be thirty seconds and that when the appointed umpire yelled "Time," each fighter was to come to the scratch under his own power within eight seconds.

Rule ten discussed that no one other than the fighters, their seconds and the referee were allowed inside the ring at any time during the course of the fight and that if unauthorized persons did interfere either by entering the ring or by disturbing the posts or ropes, the referee was within his rights to end the fight and call it a draw or award the decision to the fighter he thought was winning. This rule was sometimes taken advantage of by backers of a fighter who seemed to be losing a bout. Not anxious to see their man lose the fight or, maybe more importantly, not anxious to lose their wagers, the backers of the losing pugilist would occasionally attempt to disrupt the bout, often by storming the ring and intimidating the referee into calling the contest a draw.

Rules eleven and twelve instructed the seconds to not interfere with their principal's opponent either physically or verbally. They also instructed them to conduct themselves with order and decorum.

Rule thirteen stated that a fighter who drops himself to the ground intentionally to avoid a punch could be deemed to have lost the fight unless the referee determines that he slipped while avoiding. Rule fourteen instructed against head-butting, rule fifteen dealt with hitting a man while he is down and rule sixteen forbade hitting below the waist. Rules seventeen and eighteen dealt with gouging, biting, scratching, kneeing and kicking. Each was of course a foul.

Rule nineteen stated that all bets should be paid promptly upon the conclusion of the battle. Rule twenty addressed the positioning of the referee and umpires and rule twenty-one discussed the stakeholder's responsibilities for paying out the purse to those designated by the referee whose decision is final.

Rule twenty-two specifically addressed "magisterial" or other interference, a.k.a. the police. It also addresses impending darkness—again a reminder that bouts were often staged outdoors. In the case of any of these types of interference with the bout, the referee has the power to name the time and place of the resumption of the contest, preferably on the same day or as soon thereafter as possible.

Rule twenty-three sorted out the manner in which bets and stakes money should be handled by the stakeholder. The stake money was to be retained by the stakeholder until a fight was decided, a draw was agreed upon or if one of the fighters was absent from the ring at the appointed time and place, in which case the fighter who was present was declared the winner.

Rule twenty-four stated that if a fighter withdraws during the contest, the referee will declare that the man withdrawing has lost the fight and his opponent is the winner of the bout.

Rule twenty-five said that if either an umpire or the seconds claim a foul has been committed, both fighters must return to their corners until the referee has made his decision. If a foul is determined, the bout is ended and decided in favor of the victim. If no foul is found, "Time" will be called and the fighters must again meet at the scratch within eight seconds.

Rule twenty-six made it clear that if a fighter leaves the ring during the bout "to escape punishment or for any other purpose" without the permission of the referee—unless involuntarily forced out by his opponent—he has forfeited the battle.

Rule twenty-seven stated that the use of any hard substance held in the hands, such as a stone, stick or other item, is illegal and can be the cause for a disqualification.

Rule twenty-eight discussed using the ropes or stakes in the course of the bout. A fighter hugging the ropes to avoid going down was deemed guilty of a foul. Using the ropes or stakes to prop up your opponent to inflict more punishment or to squeeze him between the ropes was a disqualification foul. Finally, a fighter whose opponent has fallen or dropped to his knees against the ropes must immediately release him and step away or risk being disqualified.

Rule twenty-nine stated simply that all glove fights or those staged indoors must conform as nearly as possible to the previous twenty-eight rules. In all, a review of the twenty-nine rules shows some to be very familiar while some are very different from today's rules.

Seeing the need for further civilization of the sport, in 1865 a new set of rules was written by a Welshman and boxing enthusiast named John Graham Chambers. These rules were the first to set three-minute rounds with one-minute rest intervals in between as well as the first to require the use of gloves versus bare knuckles. The statutes also forbade wrestling and throwing an opponent. Because the rules were publicly endorsed by John Sholto Douglas, the ninth Marquess of Queensberry, the new set of rules were named after him. First published in 1867, the new code was meant to supersede the Revised London Prize Ring Rules of 1853, which had themselves replaced the earlier set of London Prize Ring Rules. The sport's supporters hoped that the changes in the rules would help civilize the sport and quiet the rhetoric of boxing's detractors. The Queensberry Rules are as follows:

Rule one was concerned with the size and shape of the ring, calling for a twenty-four-foot ring or one as near to that size as was practical.

Rule two specifically forbade wrestling and hugging (i.e., clinching).

Rule three set the length of each round at three minutes and the rest period between rounds at one minute.

Rule four stated that if a man is knocked down or falls through weakness, he must rise, unaided, within ten seconds. It also made clear that as soon as the stricken fighter fell, his opponent must return to his corner—not yet a neutral corner—until the fight was continued or ruled over. When the stricken fighter reached his feet and the referee instructed the men to fight, the round would continue until the remainder of the three minutes had elapsed.

Rule five stated that a fighter leaning on or propped up by the ropes and whose toes were off the mat was considered down.

Rule six stated that no seconds or any other persons were to be allowed in the ring during any round.

Rule seven addressed the event of unavoidable stoppages from external interference. It empowered the referee to name a place—as soon as possible—to finish the contest.

Rules eight and nine dealt with gloves. They were to be of good quality, but if they were damaged during the bout, they were to be replaced to the referee's satisfaction.

Rule ten stated that a man on one knee is considered down and that if a man is hit when he is down, he is the winner by disqualification and is entitled to the stakes.

Rule eleven stated, "No shoes or boots with springs allowed."[10] I don't entirely understand this statement, however, this was enough of a problem in 1865 that Chambers felt it needed to be addressed.

Rule twelve declared that all other aspects of a bout were to be governed by the Revised London Prize Ring Rules.

Ultimately changes were made to the original Queensberry Rules and the *National Police Gazette* took the lead. On March 25, 1884, Richard K. Fox, through the publication, issued a set of rules "hereafter to be known as the '*Police Gazette* Revised Queensberry Rules.'"[11] In 1887 Fox's journal stated that

> *Police Gazette* or Queensberry rules are preferred, for then a battle can be brought off in any convenient room and privacy can be secured, while under the London Rules the ring must be pitched on the turf, and if the mob can once get on to the tip, they cannot be prevented from being present at the fight; and with a mob at ring side there is always danger of the fight being broken up in a row, if nothing worse happens, where the losing man has the most friends present.[12]

The *Police Gazette* revisions contained sixteen rules, many of which mirrored existing regulations, but other points were set as well:

Rule one set weights for four classes. These were heavyweight, over 158 pounds; middleweight, under 158 pounds and over 140 pounds; lightweight, under 140 pounds but over 115 pounds; and featherweight, under 115 pounds.

Rule two reestablished the twenty-four-foot ring. Rule three reestablished that wrestling, throw downs and hugging were not allowed, and that rounds of three minutes divided by one-minute rest periods were the norm.

Rule four was consistent with the previous rules, stating that had each side chose an umpire, the two of whom would select a referee, and rule five stated that two timekeepers would also be chosen. Rule five also stated clearly that the referee should never be in charge of the clock.

Rule six echoed rule four of the Queensberry Rules in that a fighter who had fallen by punch or through weakness must rise by his own power before the referee reached the count of ten. It also directed the upright opponent to retire to his corner until further instructed by the referee. If the stricken man was unable to rise by the count of ten, the referee was instructed to award the fight to the fighter who was still standing.

Rule seven combined Queensberry rules five and six.

Rule eight echoed Queensberry rule seven concerning outside interference with the bout, fight stoppages and continuances.

Rule nine repeated rule six but added that if a fighter should fall within ten seconds of the end of a round he could not be counted out—the original "saved by the bell" instance.

Rule ten covered Queensberry rules two and three and rule eleven covered Queensberry rules eight and nine and went on to specifically forbid spiked shoes in the ring.

Rule twelve followed London rule twenty-six and stated that stakes should not be awarded to either fighter until the referee had made a clear determination as to the winner of the bout. It also stated that should a fighter leave the ring under his own power for any reason without the referee's express permission, he would forfeit the battle to his opponent. Rule thirteen reiterated this point.

Rule fourteen instructed the fighters' seconds not to interfere with, advise or direct the man's opponent. They also were told to refrain from offensive and irritating expression. Instead they should conduct themselves with honor and decorum as they discharged their duties.

Rule fifteen stated that if a man went down by choice to avoid a punch, he shall be deemed to have lost the fight.

Rule sixteen stated that the referee was in charge of the bout, and that he had full power to instruct the men to fight, break and to make outcome decisions.

The *Police Gazette* commented that their revised Queensberry Rules were more than sufficient to meet any question that arose in the ring. "The *Police Gazette* and London prize ring rules lack nothing, but the only trouble is that one half of the referees lack either the courage to see them enforced or they are ignorant of the rules. If rules are not to be enforced what is the use of competing or contending by them?" They go on to say that "the *Police Gazette* rules are the only rules that govern all questions in dispute, and if referees would give them careful perusal and study the many disputes and wrangles in prize ring encounters that have been contested in the Puritan, California, Granite, and Coney Island athletic clubs would not have occurred."[13]

Both sets of rules had their advocates. While the rules varied a good deal in form, the successful pugilists were capable of fighting under both styles and simply adapted their fighting method to whichever rules were governing their current battle. Dempsey was fine with both sets of rules but felt that championships should be decided under the London Rules. Burly, legendary heavyweight champion John L. Sullivan shared his feelings about the differences between the London and Queensberry rules this way: "There's not much difference. I'd like to see a man lick me by throwing me. I'd let him do all the throwing he was able to and punch his head off while he was trying to do it." Sullivan summed up by adding, "Give me a good puncher, and the deuce take the wrestling."[14]

The *Cincinnati Commercial Tribune* commented on the changes in the sport in an 1890 article,

> Before Sullivan opened up his knocking out career it was seldom that putting of a man to sleep was heard of. This is doubtless due to the fact that in former years London prize ring rules governed most battles. In these wrestling is permitted, and rounds are often quickly ended by a throw of one of the contestants to the ground before there is much opportunity for stand-off, square hitting, as there is under the Queensberry rules, under which John L. made his name.[15]

In addition to the rules variations there was also a bit of difference in the weight classes from the London to Queensberry rules. In each case there were only four weight classes. Under the London Rules the brackets were as follows—featherweight, up to and including 112 pounds; lightweight, 133 pounds; middleweight, 154 pounds; and heavyweight, over 154 pounds. Under the Queensberry Rules the weights for the four classes were up to 115 pounds, 140 pounds, 158 pounds and over 158 pounds, respectively.[16]

In the eighteenth and nineteenth centuries prizefighting had more than its share of detractors who disliked the sport and its participants, whom they thought of as nothing more than brutes. At the time when Dempsey became a professional in the early 1880s, prizefighting was illegal in every state in the Union. Although many in positions of authority turned a blind eye and the sport would begin to gain a broader acceptance by the 1890s, it continued to have a great many detractors. In an editorial titled "Extinguish the Pugs" published in December 1896 the *Los Angeles Times* called for the abolishment of prizefighting. The piece called on the incoming state legislature to "suppress pugilism" in California. In less than flattering terms, the newspaper denigrated the "local press" for covering and elevating fighters and their backers to "heroic positions" in the public eye. The article said that if this gang of thieves and vagrants "want to keep on at their villainous methods of getting a precarious livelihood, let them go elsewhere."[17] The article went on to say that in a hundred fighters, perhaps a half dozen might not be "thieves and toughs," but even they were surrounded by hangers on. In a nod to the Nonpareil, however, the *Times* stated that "Jack Dempsey was as honest a man as could be found in any one of a dozen states, but he always had a gang of vagabond leeches at his heels."[18] After adding a few unflattering lines about these "alleged gladiators" living off the earnings of "fallen women" and their being "pests and eyesores to decent people" the article again called for legislative action. It's safe to say that in some corners, boxing was still quite unwelcome.

Until the twentieth century, boxing or prizefighting remained outlawed in much of England, the United States and Canada and much of the rest of the Western world. To avoid detection, bouts were often held in barns, stables, on the shores of rivers, in gambling venues and in a variety of other clandestine locations. As stated earlier, bouts were often prevented or broken up by local constabularies.

While local laws often forbade prizefighting, officials would sometimes consider allowing a sparring session if "scientific" boxing techniques for points alone were employed. Needless to say, many fights were allowed under these auspices, but the "scientific" sparring sessions quickly devolved into pitched battles to the finish. At times, local police attended the fights and allowed the bouts to continue unless they deemed them too one-sided or too violent. The threat of police raids on fights was a constant in the late nineteenth century. If permission for a scientific bout was given, the local constabularies were evident at the event.

Brawling fans were also a common problem, and fights among these unruly fans were fairly typical occurrences. Alcohol, wagering and rampant emotions were most often the causes that fueled these "side bouts." Occasionally, as stated earlier, there was also the problem of fans rushing the ring when their man, on whom they may have wagered heavily, was at risk of losing the fight. To avoid the loss and in hopes of a draw being declared by the referee, they would swarm the ring.

Keeping fight locations secret was a commonplace measure in an effort to keep both the police and the unruly fans away. Often these attempts came in the form of false leads as to the fight's whereabouts. "The tip was extended only to the eminent members of the most aristocratic sporting circles, and objectionable persons were given what is known in technical parlance as the 'rapid trail,' i.e., they were informed in the strictest confidence that the fight was to be in some place where it was not." As a result, "undesirables" would be "rapid trailed" to various parts of the city and surrounding counties. Sometimes, however, word of the true location leaked out and scores would descend upon the fight pitch. The *New York Times* spoke of how the crowd would often gather "in the vain hope that something might interfere with the intentions of the Police Department to make the fight a 'scientific' one instead of a slugging match."

One story from the *New York Sun* reported on the prefight secrecy game as follows: "Four sets of men in this city have the entree to prize fights and the other manly sports where policemen and crowds are not wanted. First, the wealthy men of sporting proclivities, who give financial aid and encouragement to the art; next, the fighters—the artists themselves; third, the go-betweens, who bring the men together and run around smoothing over difficulties; and fourth, the newspaper men, who reward the brave by publishing the details of their deeds."[19]

It was common for back up plans to be considered even in the contracts signed by fighters before bouts. Here is an example from the contractual agreement for the Dempsey-Fulljames bout from July 1884: "In case of magisterial interference, the referee, if appointed, or the stakeholder, if not, shall name the next time and place of meeting, if possible on the same day or in the same week, and either party failing to appear at the time and place specified by that official, to lose the battle money."[20]

Regardless of these difficulties, throughout this period there arose some notable bare-knuckle champions who developed fairly sophisticated fighting tactics even as they avoided police and unruly fans.

Another difference in the prizefighting of the 1880s and 1890s was the equipment used. Gloves and rings were different, as were the togs the fighters wore. The original boxing ring was a crowd gathered around two men who chose to fight. Noted boxing historian Arly Allen sent me a quote from Henri de Valbourg Misson who was visiting England in 1718. The statement sums this point about impromptu rings up nicely: "If two little Boys quarrel in the Street, the Passengers stop, make a Ring round them in a Moment, and set them against one another, that they may come to Fisticuffs"[21] Allen added, "This showed the natural tendency to create a ring to isolate the boxers and protect them from interference while they fought. This concept of the Ring was a holdover (as much of boxing was) from wrestling."

In 1613 Michael Drayton, in his poem *Poly-Olbion*, describes a Cornish wrestling match:

> When stript into their shirts, each other they invade
> Within a spacious ring by the beholders made.[22]

This observation on the forming of the boundaries during ring contests is confirmed by Cesar de Saussure in his book, *A Foreign View of England in the Reigns of George I and George II*. Writing from London in 1727 he described a boxing match between two men of the lower class.

> Should two men of this class have a disagreement which they cannot end up amicably, they retire to some quiet place and strip from their waists upwards. Everyone who sees them preparing for a fight surrounds them, not in order to separate them, but on the contrary to enjoy the fight, for it is great sport to the lookers-on, and they judge the blows and also help to enforce certain rules in use for this mode of warfare. The spectators sometimes get so interested that they lay bets on the combatants and form a big circle around them. The two champions shake hands before commencing, and then attack each other courageously with their fists, and sometimes also with their heads, which they use like rams. Should one of the men fall, his opponent may, according to the rules, give him a blow with his fist, but those who have laid their bets on the fallen man generally encourage him to continue till one of the combatants is quite knocked up and says he has had enough.[23]

When James Figg, the early eighteenth-century English bare-knuckle boxing champion, introduced boxing at his amphitheater, the boxers fought on the raised platform, just as the earlier sword wielding prizefighters had done. Stage fights lasted until boxing was driven out of London in 1754. As noted, earlier boxing was reestablished in the countryside and most matches were moved outdoors "on the turf." This change in venue led to the revised London Prize Ring Rules of 1838 which, among other things, took into account that fights were now often contested outdoors. By way of review, the first rule states "that in the center of the ring a mark be formed, to be termed a scratch; and that at two opposite corners, as may be selected, spaces enclosed by other marks sufficiently large for the reception of the seconds and bottle holders, to be entitled 'the corners.'"[24]

Until the turn of the twentieth century, rings typically had eight posts rather than today's four. The squared circle was still a square, but in between each pair of corner posts was an additional stake in the middle. Rings varied in size and were typically set up outside in the grass, dirt, sand or occasionally on wooden boards as in the classic 1810 bout between Tom Cribb and Tom Molineaux. Their construction was often poor and last minute as the fight locations were kept secret and often changed like the wind. When bouts were held indoors they were often in barns or basements with dirt or tan bark floor coverings. In time it became more and more common for contests to be held in saloons and theaters in which—at most—canvas was laid upon hard wooden floors and, more often than not, no padding lay between. More than one fighter suffered greater damage from hitting the floor than from the punch that sent him down on his way. The best a fighter could hope for was that he would do battle in an athletic club or a true arena such as Madison Square Garden in New York or the Mechanics' Pavilion in San Francisco.

Rather than the satin and nylon trunks of today, fighters wore knicker-length woolen tights or some wore the equivalent of breech cloths. While crude leather gum shields and protective cups were occasionally used by Hellenic fighters, these mostly disappeared until after the turn of the twentieth century. After the demise of the cestus, hand gear was seldom worn again until the 1880s. Boxing gloves have evolved over time from what originally amounted to cudgels strapped to the fighters' hands to bare knuckles to something akin to driving gloves and finally, to the heavily padded mitts we know today.

As stated earlier, the first gloves recorded from the days of the ancient Greeks and Etruscans were simply hard leather straps wrapped around the gladiator's knuckles and they often damaged the man being hit much more than a bare fist might, but in most cases, that was intentional. "In pugilistic encounters in ancient times, those who followed boxing as a means to settle disputes and to prove the question of superiority, according to historians, used the cestus, which was a formidable gauntlet of various patterns, composed of thongs of rawhide, with a woolen glove covering the hand with a wellus or fringe. It was a brutal and dangerous weapon."[25]

Boxing historian Arly Allen notes that "the first development of English boxing gloves that I have found were those introduced by Jack Broughton in 1743 to convince the aristocracy to take up boxing. Young aristocrats hesitated to engage in bare-knuckle fighting, so Broughton introduced what he called 'Mufflers' or boxing gloves to eliminate the cuts and bruises which bare-knuckles left on faces."[26] Broughton wrote, "And that Persons of Quality and Distinction may not be deterr'd from entering into a Course of these Lectures, they will be given with the utmost Tenderness and Regard to the Delicacy of the Frame and Constitution of the Pupil; for which Reason, Mufflers are provided that will effectually secure them from the Inconveniency of black Eyes, broken Jaws, and bloody Noses."[27] Aristocracy aside, the ultimate reason for the use of boxing gloves was not to protect the face, but rather to protect the hands. Damaged hands could ruin a boxing career.

The first modern-day boxing gloves became popular during the late nineteenth century and were most often used to curb police interference. "Originally, they were worn solely for the purpose of avoiding breaking the law, which nearly everywhere expressly forbade bare knuckle fights…." While gloves might lessen the punishment to the hands from landing blows, experience showed that those blows proved more damaging to the opponent's face. "The glove covered hand cuts like a razor, especially if the blow is glancing. The bloodiest battles are now with skin-tight gloves."[28] Originally the most popular gloves, skin-tights were made to fit the hand snugly and were laced up. Half of the fingers on each glove were cut off to permit the fists to close naturally and without restriction. These resembled driving gloves or those used by weight lifters in the gym.

Middleweight legend Tommy Ryan wrote in 1911 that "the boxing gloves of those days and the gloves of today are entirely different things, though known by the same name. The boxing glove of 1885 was a skin-tight leather glove that was devised more for the protection of the hand of the boxer wearing it than for the protection of the many upon whom it was to be used."[29]

In time, padding in the gloves was introduced and by the 1880s it had become common. The *National Police Gazette* observed in 1889 that "pugilists of our day contest themselves with gloves of which there are six regular sizes—skin tights, 2-, 4-, 6-, and 8-ounce, and slappers, 15 inches long, used in theatrical exhibitions." The eight-ounce gloves were the most popular in gymnasiums and for friendly sparring, while the six-ounce variety were used in some gyms and in most amateur contests. Two- and four-ounce gloves were the most common with many club room and finish fights, "but the skin-tights are the popular hand coverings for real battlers."[30] Various changes to padding were tried and enhancements made to the gloves over the next few years, all with the goal of protecting both the hands of the puncher and the face of the recipient of the blow. These enhancements were clear attempts at improving the safety of the sport as well as an effort at increasing societal acceptance of boxing.

Also, as mentioned above, boxing footwear is quite an interesting story unto itself. Boots made from canvas or leather were typically worn much as they are today, but in the outdoor fights on turf or loose soil and sand, pugilists often wore cleats on their boxing shoes to avoid slipping on the wet grass or loose surface. This type of spiked boot would play a role in Dempsey's 1886 bout with Johnny Reagan.

Another difference in the sport in the late 1800s and early 1900s was the regular practice of exhibition matches or sparring exhibitions. These came in several forms. One was touring exhibitions that were held on stage in theatres and were often a part of traveling vaudeville troupes or were inserted into scenes in plays. After the audience was regaled with comedy, music, wrestlers, weight lifters and more, popular prizefighters would enter a makeshift ring pitched on the stage and spar for three or four rounds. Occasionally, a challenge would go out from one of the troupe fighters to the men in the audience to see if anyone thought they could last three or four rounds in the ring and offered a cash prize to the intrepid soul if he could do so. Also popular at the time were "benefits" held in a fighter's honor. These benefits were an evening of sparring interspersed with music, wrestling and dancing. They were benefits in the sense that the bulk of the gate receipts went to a notable boxer or one who was down on his luck.

In each case, the sparring exhibitions differed little from actual prizefights and since there were no official sanctioning bodies in those days, it is often difficult to determine today which of these was an official fight versus an exhibition. As such, I have included all fights in Dempsey's overall record in this book, but I have indicated which appear to be exhibitions and which were clearly actual prizefights.

It is now time to look at the life, times and career of Nonpareil Jack Dempsey. "Seconds out!"

1862 to 1882—From Athgarvan to Brooklyn

Jack Dempsey, the champion middleweight prizefighter who would become known the world over as the "Nonpareil," was born John Edward Kelly on December 15, 1862, near the Curragh in the rural town of Athgarvan in County Kildare, Ireland. Fittingly, the future Nonpareil's birthplace was a mere stone's throw from the spot where in 1815 what is arguably the most celebrated prizefight in Irish history took place. That year, on the thirteenth of December, Irishman Dan Donnelly defeated Englishman George Cooper by knockout in eleven rounds.

In a bout that went back and forth by round, Donnelly finished Cooper in the eleventh with a thundering right to the jaw that laid the Englishman out. It was a victory of more than just pride for Donnelly. It was also a victory of national pride for the Irish people to have one of their own beat an Englishman and leave him lying unconscious with his jaw broken on Irish soil. To this day, "a squat, weather-beaten, gray obelisk surrounded by a short iron fence marks the exact site, which has been called Donnelly's Hollow since the bout. The inscription on the monument reads: Dan Donnelly beat George Cooper on this spot 13th Dec. 1815."[1]

This bright event in Irish history was highly important to many Irishmen including Jack's father, who frequently took his sons to see the monument erected at the spot where the ring had been laid. There, he relayed the story of the pitched battle to the young men. More than fifteen years after the Nonpareil's death, sportswriter Charley White recounted that he

> often heard Dempsey tell of how his father, to whom Donnelly was a hero, as he was to most of the Irish, used to take Jack as a small boy out for a long walk across country with him and together they would visit the scene of the greatest pugilistic battle ever fought on Irish soil. Jack's father would recount to him the achievements and glories of the great Donnelly, and they would go to visit the hero's grave. These recitals and visits were a great treat to the little Irish lad and bred in him the desire to become a worthy representative of his race in the prize ring.[2]

Jack was the son of Martin and Alicia Lennon Kelly. Martin Kelly passed away when Jack was still a young boy. Martin was reportedly thirty-four years old and died of consumption—an eerie premonition of Jack's own end.[3] Martin was reportedly a caring and proud father who loved to spend time with his children and share with them stories of great Irish heroes and Celtic lore. Jack had two brothers, Martin, Jr., older than he, and Thomas, younger. He also had a younger sister. After the death of Martin, Alicia was in time remarried to Patrick Dempsey of neighboring Walshetown, Newbridge.

By all accounts, the family was close and Jack loved his mother very much. The two maintained a close bond with each other for the rest of their lives. Alicia was described in later years as a strong-willed woman and the one person who could still keep the middleweight champion in line. "She is a middle-aged woman of large frame, and when Jack goes to his old home, on Fourth Street, she makes him mind his manners even yet."[4]

Some research has suggested that Jack might have been thirteen months older than is commonly asserted. According to the County Kildare Online Electronic History Journal, a part of the Kildare County Library and Arts Services, a John Kelly was born to John Kelly and Alicia Lennon Kelly in the town of Athgarvan on November 11, 1861. The records go on to report that John Senior passed away when his son was a small boy. John Senior's widow was eventually married to Patrick Dempsey of Walshetown, Newbridge, on August 7, 1865. According to this account, John Kelly, Jr., took the name of John Dempsey.[5] Vital records were not kept as precisely as they are today and either story could be correct. Whether this is the same John Kelly that became the noted middleweight boxer is difficult to be certain, but Dempsey himself claimed both December 15, 1862, and Curragh, and "John Kelly" is hardly an uncommon name in Ireland, so there is little reason to doubt what the Nonpareil claimed.

The points that are agreed upon are that Jack was born in either late 1861 or late 1862 in Athgarvan, that his birth father (whether Martin or John or perhaps John Martin or Martin John) died when he was young; that his birth mother Alicia Lennon Kelly remarried to Patrick Dempsey of Walshetown, Newbridge; and that the family emigrated to New York around 1867 and settled in the Williamsburg section of northeastern Brooklyn's famous Fourteenth Ward.

I was curious as to whether I could research and determine the exact date, and possibly even the ship, on which Jack's family arrived in America. In researching passenger manifests from the mid– to late 1860s, I was able to find a few that might list Jack and his family, but the notoriously inaccurate and incomplete passenger lists from immigrant ships from that time make it difficult to be certain. One, however, was by far the closest. The ship, the S.S. *Virginia*, sailed from Liverpool to Queenstown and docked in New York on April 25, 1868. Listed as Irish immigrants in steerage were a family named Dempsey that included three-year-old Thomas, two-year-old Martin and one-year-old Bridget, but that was all—no five-year-old John (a.k.a. Jack) and no Alicia or Patrick. It is certainly possible that Patrick traveled ahead to secure work and a place to live, but no listing for Jack or Alicia is either a concern or just an incomplete manifest. Also, Jack's brother Martin would have been about six or seven, not two, but it is possible that the names and ages of children were transposed by careless record keeping. While I have no way of being certain that this is the ship that brought the Kelly and Dempsey family across the Atlantic, it is certain that they traveled around this time in a vessel such as the *Virginia* and under similar conditions.

Life onboard an immigrant ship was generally unpleasant for the travelers. The crossing could be difficult due to overcrowding and tight quarters in steerage. The journey was invariably uncomfortable and often disease ridden. Cholera in particular could be a serious problem. Food was sparse and of poor quality and drink was not much better. Rough seas did nothing to improve the list of potential woes for the passengers. To halt the spread of possible diseases at the border, the host countries required all immigrants to be quarantined for anywhere from a week to sixteen days at all ports of entry.

Jack and his family were a part of the large wave of Irish immigrants that came to the American shores between 1820 and 1900. The problems faced by the Irish in their home country during the nineteenth century were legion. A burgeoning population and high unemployment rates had led to endemic poverty. A heavy anti–Catholic prejudice also made it difficult for the bulk of the population to find meaningful work. The Act of Union of 1801 established the United Kingdom, incorporating Ireland into the British state, but nothing about the act served to ease the island's problems. In time, many of the Irish decided to leave their homeland for better opportunities in the Americas. In the four decades between 1820 and the beginning of the American Civil War, the Irish were never less than a third of all annual immigrants coming to the United States. The already heavy rush of Irish immigration became a tidal wave in 1845 with the beginning of the great potato rot. For a full five years, the potato crop, the sole subsistence for millions of Irish peasants, failed. There was nothing to harvest and little to eat. Many thousands perished and many who did not were still starving, impoverished and only wanted to get away from this land of misery and start anew. Estimates put the number of Irish immigrants who came to the United States between 1820 and 1880 at three and a half million.

For these waves of immigrants, a new start in North America provided hope, but it was no guaranteed path to success, and much hard work lay ahead. Most were poor, not particularly well educated and faced anti-immigrant, anti–Irish and anti–Catholic sentiments upon their arrival in America. While many who arrived had been farmers in Ireland, most did not have the capital to start farms on this side of the ocean. Many took positions as laborers working on the burgeoning infrastructure projects of a flourishing new land—building railroads, canals, roads, subways and streetcar lines. Others found work in the cities. Many were employed in factories and shops and a good number as police officers and firemen. Regardless of the type of work found, the Irish, like most immigrants, began to form communities where the members of each new wave of immigrants from the home country would also settle. In these communities, Catholic churches were built, Irish pubs and shops were opened and many Irish customs survived for generations.

The new world in which the Dempsey family found themselves was a bustling and rapidly changing place. The American Civil War was barely over and the wounds to the nation inflicted by that national tragedy were still fresh. The nation's political scene was in an uproar. As the war was ending, President Abraham Lincoln had been assassinated during a loosely conceived and badly enacted plot orchestrated by a handful of Confederate sympathizers. His successor, Andrew Johnson, had been impeached by the U.S. House of Representatives and had narrowly been acquitted by the Senate, after being tried on unreasonable charges that the president rightly claimed to be unconstitutional. In 1868, Northern war hero General Ulysses S. Grant was elected to succeed Johnson and bring a firmer hand to the reins of government and the affairs of the still reeling nation. The secessionist states of the South were being administered by Union military forces and politically appointed magistrates. It was a time of great change as newly emancipated black citizens, protected by Federal troops, were exercising their newly granted voting rights, with some even being elected to state assemblies and to the national congress in Washington. Most in the defeated Confederacy rejected the intrusions by the northern troops. They saw laws viewed as oppressive being pushed on the South by what many of them believed were the occupational forces of a foreign government. As a result, the Ku Klux Klan and other groups who were openly anti-black, anti-immigrant, anti–Catholic and anti–Jewish grew to have a large following and notable political influence in various parts of the country. In New York, Brooklyn and other cities of the Northeast, however, Irish Catholics were finding themselves in ever increasing positions of influence.

On the economic side of the equation, the Industrial Revolution that had begun before the war was now back in full force. Consumer demand for products grew and to meet this demand, new technology and more workers were required, making factory jobs more plentiful. This would mean more opportunities for new immigrants looking for work—a perfect scenario for the many individuals and young families who had just arrived from Europe. Patrick Dempsey soon secured work and the family began to settle in. The children attended public schools and Alicia kept house and took in laundry to help make ends meet.

The first generations of Irishmen often worked at unskilled and semiskilled occupations, but their children often found themselves working at increasingly skilled trades. The children of Alicia Kelly Dempsey were no different. At the age of fourteen, Jack ended his formal schooling and took a position as a cooper—or barrel maker—at the Lorin M. Palmer Cooper Shop at the foot of North Fifth Street in Brooklyn's Eastern District. Not a common trade today, a cooper is a maker and repairer of barrels, buckets, tubs, casks, butter churns or any other wooden vessel bound together with hoops. In that day the placing and hammering of the hoops around barrels was done by hand. "That ten years of passing around a barrel, with a hammer in each hand, pounding, pounding, pounding, was an exercise curiously designed to develop just the muscles that are most needed by a pugilist."[6] It was during his time at the cooperage that Dempsey met and became fast friends with Jack Skelly and Jack McAuliffe who were also cooper's apprentices. The three future pugilists would remain lifelong friends and as their ring successes mounted, they would become known in sporting circles as "The Three Jacks."

When not engaged in their work, the Dempsey brothers could often be found swimming or playing at some sport or another. From his youngest days Jack was extremely interested in physical activities. "He was very fond of all kinds of athletic sports and spent his leisure time in wrestling, running, baseball playing, but wrestling was his favorite hobby and he made his mark in the arena, winning matches at New York, Boston and elsewhere." This was the beginning of Jack's athletic career. His older brother Martin taught him a great deal about wrestling. "Martin himself was an expert collar and elbow wrestler and at one time held the lightweight championship in that sport."[7] Jack commented that his brother "needed a partner, so he taught me how to wrestle and though I never was great at it, I was able to go on at Harry Hill's or anywhere else where we could make $5 or $10 and fake up a good exhibition."[8]

Collar-and-elbow wrestling is a grappling or ground fighting contest in which sheer size and power are not the key to victory and it is the smaller man who often excels. In this sport, participants utilize balance and speed to achieve positioning so that strength can be applied towards the leverage gained and, in this manner, points are scored.

Jack wrestled periodically in the New York City area while in his late teens and early twenties. As he continued to hone his skills, he became more in demand and began to receive moderate pay for his matches. His first recorded collar-and-elbow style match was held at Harry Hill's Place in early January 1883.[9] There is also a report from the *Boston Traveler* claiming Dempsey made his first wrestling appearance in Boston in the early 1880s, "in the old Concert Hall, which stood at the corner of Green and Chardon Streets. He was then a smooth-faced, boyish-looking chap and appeared in a wrestling exhibition. He wrestled collar and elbow style against an expert from Vermont named

Johnson, who was a wonder. Dempsey was a wonderful collar and elbow wrestler, but he gave up the business, claiming there was no money in it."[10] Jack was soon ready to leave the wrestling ring and the cooper's shop and embark on what would quickly become a hugely successful prizefighting career.

While Jack began actively wrestling in his late teens, he had already developed a love of boxing. "Of course, I saw lots of sparring at those places and I took a lively interest in it," said Jack. "A lot of young fellows of my age, who lived near me in Williamsburg, had a set of gloves and we used to put them on and bang away at each other as best we could."[11] While Dempsey continued to wrestle, spar with his friends and work in the cooper shop, it would still be a few years before he first stepped in the prize ring. In the meantime, however, "Dempsey attended all the boxing exhibitions and had a burning desire to enter the magic circle. He decided to give up wrestling in 1883 and try his fortune in the prize ring arena."[12]

Although Jack was always strong and in good condition, he never possessed great size. As an adult he stood only 5'8" tall and at heaviest weighed just 150 pounds in fighting trim. While Jack was slight in physical stature, he had tremendous heart, quickness, skill and ring knowledge. Charley White once said, "Dempsey possessed one of the best fighting brains I have ever seen and could figure out a battle better than any other man of his time. He never let the stature or weight of his opponent bother him and what he lacked in brawn he made up and more than made up in brain and heart."[13] According to numerous reports, Jack had small hands and as a result preferred to wear small, two-ounce kid gloves in the ring because he believed that they complimented his hands and gave him an advantage.

Dempsey was almost fanatical about his weight. In an effort to control it, he often wore heavy clothes and shoes to work out during pre-fight training. Jack also said that he liked to train in heavier shoes because they built up his legs and made them feel light when he actually climbed into the ring with his opponents. Given Jack's already small size, men such as White and Denny Costigan would often plead with Dempsey to avoid the heavy clothing and excessive weight loss and fight at a heavier weight. Given Jack's level of success in the ring, they eventually decided to leave him alone and let him train as he saw fit.

Details of Dempsey's life and boxing career can be sketchy at times. The newspaper accounts of the day were often meager and mistakes in the spelling of names and the relaying of second hand details can leave the door open for factual errors. Many events are widely and accurately documented, while other events are barely noted. Some of these inaccuracies have led to speculation about events and dates. While it is accepted as general knowledge today that Dempsey's first "prizefight" was against Ed "Rug" McDonald in April 1883, the *Brooklyn Eagle* newspaper reported in December 1887 that "he first gained fistic fame by knocking out a bruiser in Frank White's saloon in the Bowery. His first ring fight was with Ned McCann, near Pittsburgh, Pennsylvania in 1881."[14] While it is certainly possible that both of these events occurred, I've found no other evidence of these fights. Jack was a fighter and a wrestler so it is possible that the affair at Frank White's saloon in Brooklyn was simply a bar fight in which Dempsey laid out a local tough and nothing more. If the "ring fight" with Ned McCann in 1881 is valid, it is possible that it was a collar-and-elbow wrestling affair and not a prizefight. It is also possible that someone with the same or a similar name was engaged in the contests and the future Nonpareil got the credit.

1883—The Cooper Enters the Ring

According to the *National Police Gazette* Jack "made his first appearance in public as a collar and elbow wrestler at New York sportsman Harry Hill's infamous saloon and sporting club on January 1, 1883."[1]

It is important to take a few moments and introduce Harry Hill at this time. Hill, along with Richard Fox, Parson Davies and several other sporting men, were critical to the growth, public acceptance and general demand for boxing in the latter half of the nineteenth century. Hill and his sports and entertainment venues became the stuff of legend and infamy in New York during that time. Dempsey and many other pugilists of the era cut their boxing teeth at Hill's emporium, and Harry would play a large role in Dempsey's and a great many other fighters' careers.

Hill was born in England in 1827 and grew up near the Epsom Downs Racetrack with his uncle who was a noted local gambler and betting commissioner. After moving to New York, Hill became a successful horse dealer and eventually opened a sporting house and saloon at Houston and Crosby streets, on the western edge of the Bowery in Manhattan. Hill proved to be a successful businessman. His personal fortune was a matter of speculation, but at one point he was reportedly worth over a million dollars.

Hill's establishment quickly became a popular haunt for a cross section of society. On any evening, you could find a mix of stage and sport personalities, businessmen, literary and political figures, gamblers, sportsmen, ladies of the evening and underworld figures. Many patrons saw the saloon as a social club that provided entertainment and relaxation to hard working citizens, but not everyone agreed. "Moral reformers considered Hill's saloon a hotbed of vice and debauchery—a portal to the gates of Hell and a well-known resort for criminals and prostitutes." The truth lay somewhere in between.[2] While Hill's was certainly a den of gambling, drunkenness and prostitution, it was also a relatively safe place of entertainment and relaxation for a wide swathe of New York's Victorian-era society.

Hill kept an eye on his patrons' best interests while they were in his club—it was in *his* best interest to do so. Harry stated that he had a number of solemn rules in his establishment. While he made sure that patrons knew that the club was open to all segments of society, he demanded strict adherence to his rules. Signs on the walls stated what was and was not allowed and Hill was not afraid to get tough with those who disregarded these guidelines. No fighting among patrons or other unruly behavior would be tolerated. He insisted that "no one violating decency will be permitted to remain in the room and his provision of a private room in which to sober up, lest they be waylaid by thugs outdoors." Hill was firm in insisting that his customers be safe within the confines of his establishment and that "no victim must be snared while at Harry Hill's; any crime to be committed must take place elsewhere."[3]

Harry Hill, the event promoter, club owner and sportsman.

The police—mostly through payoffs—turned a blind eye to all but the most egregious illegalities and even served as protectors of the patrons. Society's most virtuous saw nothing but sin and iniquity, but a growing majority was willing to ignore a little bit of immorality in exchange for what they saw as harmless amusement. The firm Victorian-era grip on Western society had begun to loosen its hold and many Americans began to accept establishments like Hill's. Still, some of the old guard held on. When Harry died in August 1896, his obituary in the New York Times described Hill's saloon as a club frequented by "the most desperate and criminal persons of the city."[4]

By all accounts, Hill was scrupulously honest and was especially known to be so when it came to finances, both his and others'. He was often asked to hold large sums of cash that had been collected as purses for prizefights. In 1870, he was the stakeholder for the $5,000 prizefight between Joe Coburn and Jem Mace. In the 1882 prizefight between John L. Sullivan and Paddy Ryan, Hill held the $25,000 purse. Hill's scrupulous financial honesty also applied to his resort where he would often deposit money and valuables from intoxicated patrons and return their property when they eventually sobered up. One of the best known examples of Harry's caring oversight was an incident in 1884 when a drunken customer left $84,000 to Hill for safekeeping. The following morning when the man sobered up, he was summoned to return to Hill's place. The man had absolutely no recollection of leaving the money with the proprietor. Hill then gave the surprised man his money and kindly "advised him to leave New York before taking another drink."[5]

Despite having a good deal of success in wrestling, the future Nonpareil gave up grappling and switched exclusively to boxing after John Kelly, the young Irish immigrant barrel-maker, went to watch boxing matches on the night of April 6, 1883. Jack was a regular attendee of local prizefights and he was an avid fan. He had frequently expressed to his friends a desire to participate in a bout. On this occasion, he would get his chance. Edward Norton, a.k.a. Ed "Rug" McDonald, a self-styled and self-proclaimed pugilistic "champion" of New York, was scheduled to participate in an exhibition of boxing skills under the London Rules in Staten Island. When McDonald's opponent failed to show up for the bout, Jack volunteered to replace the absent fighter. Jack weighed a mere 130 pounds while McDonald came in at a robust 160 pounds. While registering before the bout, John Kelly gave his name as "Jack Dempsey."

Before the bout, McDonald reportedly offered Jack $25 to spar easily for a few rounds

Harry Hill's Theatre in New York.

and then drop his guard and allow McDonald to knock him out in the sixth. When Jack objected, McDonald raised the offer to $40. Although Jack never agreed, McDonald was still under the impression that Dempsey would go down early. Jack had other ideas. He was after the entire $100 in prize money that was being offered to the winner. McDonald thought the young cooper foolish, but he determined that after he had beaten the brash young man, he would send the $25 his way anyhow.

When the two men finally climbed into the ring, McDonald looked calm and seemed assured that he would win. Jack was seconded by boxer and champion walker and runner Martin Murphy of Dublin, while McDonald had Bob Mace at his side. The referee for the bout was veteran trainer Bob Smith.

As the first round commenced, the men began to spar and in short order some of

McDonald's assuredness began to disappear. After moving around the ring and gaining a level of comfort, Jack began to land a few solid and well-placed blows and to show the mental and physical quickness that he would become known for. A suddenly somewhat concerned McDonald decided that he had better teach his young opponent a lesson. McDonald changed his tactics and elected to rush Dempsey and finish him quickly, but when he did, Jack was too quick and he countered with a smashing left to McDonald's right eye. Jack then rolled away smoothly, each thrust and parry, helping to build his confidence. The men then fell into close quarters, trading jabs at a rapid pace.

In the second round, both men traded heavy blows, with McDonald landing several times on Jack's ribs and Dempsey responding with attacks to the head. As the round ended, Dempsey used his wrestling skills and threw McDonald down amid loud cheering. The crowd, sensing that McDonald had finally met a fighter with superior skills who refused to lie down, began to root for Jack.

The Nonpareil (right) in his first fight, fought against Ed "Rug" McDonald.

Dempsey was the first man to the mark as the third round began. Showing his quickness, he deposited several sound blows on his opponent's face and another squarely on McDonald's already battered right eye. Routinely after landing a punch, Jack would step back and away to avoid retaliation. This technique, which Jack would employ throughout his ring career, was clearly instinctive for Dempsey and not a trained skill. Not able to strike the faster and smaller man with any regularity, McDonald continued to try to rush and catch Jack and wear him out while wrestling and throwing him down. During one rush, McDonald attempted to throw his opponent to the ground, but instead both men went down in a heap with Jack on top.

By the fourth round it was beginning to look as if Dempsey might win the bout. Jack was showing the natural skills and comfort of a much more experienced ring veteran. He was clearly having fun and was indisputably outfighting his opponent. "He landed his left on McDonald's right jaw, drove his right against his adversary's neck, which sent him staggering down in his corner."[6]

McDonald came to the mark looking a bit dazed in the fifth round. Jack forced the fighting and clearly had the advantage as the round came to an end. Over the first five rounds, the men had sparred lightly with the experienced McDonald unable to land any significant blow against Dempsey. As the fighting came to an end in the fifth round, McDonald was becoming frustrated. "He had been surprised to find the unknown, innocent appearing youth able to elude his blows."[7] While he had not gone all out yet, McDonald was mildly concerned that he had barely been able to lay a glove on Dempsey. During the break between rounds he determined to end the bout as soon as the sixth began.

At the beginning of the sixth round, McDonald squared up and let go a powerful right aimed directly at Dempsey's chin. The crowd gasped as they believed the knockout was coming. At the last second, however, Jack astonished his opponent and the crowd by moving his head and avoiding the missile. McDonald tried again and again, but Jack ducked each blow. The crowd cheered and McDonald felt it must be a fluke. He tried again, firing another right-handed mortar shot, but again, Dempsey just smiled as he moved away and avoided the big blow of his opponent. A now clearly exasperated McDonald sprang at Jack and began to attack with full force. At one point Dempsey threw McDonald, but this time McDonald got as good as he gave. He was, however, becoming winded. "At the end of the round McDonald was glad to seek his corner. He was puffing with exertion, but not yet fully alarmed."[8] He decided on a strategy to wear down his opponent with his superior weight.

The seventh round saw McDonald exhausted, but still game. He tried to force the fighting, but Dempsey repeatedly deflected his best blows. In return, Jack landed heavily to his opponent's nose and left eye. Again, Jack clearly got the best of the round.

Over the next dozen rounds, McDonald tried to wear Dempsey down, but when he threw punches, Jack continued to flick them away. When he tried to clinch and lean on Jack to tire him out, Dempsey would land uppercuts and force McDonald away.

By the twentieth round, it was only McDonald who was visibly tired while Jack still looked fresh. At one point McDonald, wrestling on the ropes with Dempsey, fell through the ropes and had to be pushed back through by Dempsey's seconds. As he climbed back through and was trying to right himself, the bell rang, ending the round. Some actually claimed that McDonald's exit from the ring was intentional and planned out of desperation.

As the twenty-first round began, the two fighters sprang to the center of the ring and began the attack on each other. The men stood facing each other "and slammed and slugged like demons." Dempsey, however, became the aggressor, pounding away at his opponent and opening up cuts on his face. "The blood flowed in streams from the anguished McDonald."[9] Jack got the better of the bigger man, hammering and chopping at him like a lumberjack at a large tree and finally felled McDonald with a powerful right in the twenty-second round.

The bout continued with Jack regularly getting the better of his opponent. Finally, in the twenty-seventh round, seeing no other avenue to winning, McDonald "seized Dempsey by the legs and attempted to throw him through a window, but did not succeed. Having seen McDonald try the same illegal tactics before, the referee, Bob Smith, awarded the fight and purse to Dempsey."[10] The *National Police Gazette* called the fight "a rattling mill" and one of the "gamest and most stubborn fights witnessed in many years."[11]

Regardless of the fact that he won the bout by disqualification, the reports on the fight all agree that Dempsey whipped McDonald soundly and that after a round or two, Jack looked more like a seasoned veteran than a novice pugilist. The variation in reports on the bout comes not in any dispute over who won, but rather in the length of the bout. Reports claim anywhere from 21 to 27 to 34 rounds fought over 36 to 38 to 40 minutes. The pertinent point was that Jack soundly defeated McDonald and a new star was on the rise on the fistic horizon.

Dempsey enjoyed his prizefighting experience and before the year was out, he decided to forget all about his wrestling aspirations and instead became a professional boxer. He was already showing huge promise. He was quick and light on his feet. He could use both fists and hit alternately with power and science. He used his left with great precision and he kept his cool in the ring. Jack was undefeated in his first fifty-five fights over the next six years.

In general, the official stance on prizefighting in 1883 was unfavorable. While there was a strong interest in and following of the sport, it was illegal to engage in it in practically every location in North America and many officials and newspapers railed against it. Some papers refused to report on bouts, yet others such as the *New York Times* would occasionally send a reporter to cover a pugilistic event. These reports varied in content, sometimes reporting on the fight round by round and sometimes dedicating considerably more column space to reporting on the assembled crowd. These reports almost invariably acknowledged the illegal nature of the assemblage, but often referred to the event as a "scientific" sparring match or exhibition which was seen as "gentlemanly" instead of a prizefight or boxing match.

While it's difficult to be certain to whom the reporter is referring, the *Brooklyn Eagle* of April 7, 1883, ran an article about two prizefights that occurred the previous day describing them as "brutal and desperate" contests. The bouts were reported as having "occurred within a few miles of the Brooklyn City Hall yesterday, one in New York and the other in the suburbs of our own city."[12]

The *Eagle* dismissed the New York event as Gotham's problem and shame on them if they were unable or unwilling to prevent such events. The Brooklyn bout was, however, a different matter. The people of Brooklyn, stated the paper, were steadfast in their intolerance of boxing and, if driven to it, would "see to it that those who are responsible for fights would pay dearly for their contempt of popular rights."[13] The article goes on to describe the bout from secondhand sources as "one of the most brutal exhibitions that has ever disgraced the city." They also chastised the local police for not knowing enough about what was going on to prevent such meetings.

The paper stated that the preliminaries were believed to have been arranged in Brooklyn and that at least one of the men engaged in the fight was from that borough (Dempsey?). One man was described as "a notorious negro who has no other business on hand but fighting."

The *Eagle* called for the city authorities to bring an immediate end to prizefighting in the city and recommended that a first and proper step would be to "arrest the pair of brutes who pounded each other, one of whom was knocked senseless by the other. This should be followed up by the apprehension of the backers of the men and the promoters of the fight."[14] Clearly boxing had not yet come of age.

Brooklyn was not alone in its "official" distaste for prizefighting. In 1882, the *Milwaukee Sentinel* commented after one bout, "Why a man who can bruise another with skill should be hailed with enthusiasm is not clear. Any healthy mule can use his heels with more skill and effect than the best of the professional bruisers. If there must be a belt for this sort of thing, give the mule a show."[15]

Regardless of how some viewed pugilism, boxing was still popular with a large segment of society. Dempsey's performance against McDonald had gained some notice by other pugilists and their backers. On May 21 local fighter Bob Turnbull, frustrated in his efforts to lure fellow middleweight Jimmy Murray into the ring, visited the *National Police Gazette* offices in New York. While Jack had not yet officially announced that he intended to continue with pugilistic endeavors, Turnbull offered to make a match with Dempsey for something between $200 and $500. His backer left $50 as earnest money with representatives of the *Gazette* and stated that if Dempsey was willing to cover that amount, they would have no trouble in arranging a match.[16] When Jack had not yet responded by July, Turnbull repeated his offer.

On May 24, the Brooklyn Bridge was opened after thirteen years of construction. The structure was at the time it opened, the longest suspension bridge in the world and twice as long as its closest rival. Thousands attended the opening ceremony to celebrate the span connecting Manhattan with Brooklyn.

Jack's next bout was a hard-glove contest in August versus Jack Boylan on the turf at Harry Hill's Pavilion in Flushing, New York. Boylan was a sturdy young pugilist from England who had settled in New York. He had made a bit of a name for himself around Gotham by participating in gloved exhibitions throughout the city. When Boylan challenged Dempsey to fight, he did so through a letter placed in the *New York Daily News* by fellow pugilist Tom "Soap" McAlpine. Dempsey instructed his friend and backer John Shanley to arrange a meeting with Boylan and his backers. The two sides met on August 6 at the *Police Gazette* offices and agreed to a match.

It was determined that the fight would be a glove contest, according to the London Rules, and the date was set for August 14. The bout was to be in New York State, but the final location would be determined by the winner of a coin toss. The winner would choose a spot for the battle and relay its location to his opponent no later than August 11. The men would fight for $250 per side with no weight limits in place. In case of "magisterial interference" either the referee or the stakeholder (if no referee had yet been named), would choose an alternate time, date and location for the fight. In an almost quaint reminder of the much simpler time in boxing the *Police Gazette* noted that in addition to the other items in the articles of agreement, "the expenses of the ropes and stakes shall be borne share and share alike."[17] John Shanley of Williamsburg posted the money for Dempsey and Barney McGuire and Jack Curley both of New York posted the stakes for Boylan.

In preparing for the fight, Jack was trained by Shanley near Hicksville, New York, in west central Long Island. Boylan set up his training headquarters at Stryker's Bay on the East River near Eighty-Seventh Street.

The bout was held in the early morning hours of August 14 in the yard outside of Harry Hill's Pavilion near Flushing Bay. The pavilion was another of Hill's locations set up to provide entertainment such as music, wrestling and prizefighting. The ring was pitched on a level, grassy lawn near the pavilion. Those in attendance each paid two dollars' admission. The *New York Sun* reported that "the Village of Flushing was disturbed just after daybreak yesterday morning by the influx of a throng of sporting men who had come from this city [New York] and Brooklyn to witness a prizefight between John Dempsey of Williamsburg, aged 22, standing 5 feet 8 inches high and weighing 131 pounds, and Jack Boylan of Manchester, England, a shoemaker, 21 years old, 5 feet, 5½ inches high, weighing 138 pounds."[18]

The referee for the contest was Billy O'Brien, and former British heavyweight Jem Mace was chosen as timekeeper. Dempsey was seconded by Jack Davis of England and his umpire was Andy Hanley. Boylan's seconds were Tom McAlpine and lightweight fighter Jimmy Murray.

In keeping with the times, the fight was held in the wee hours of the morning and the location was minimally publicized. Still, as was often the case, the word got out and a crowd assembled. The *New York Sun* described the event as follows: "Shortly after 4 o'clock a.m. the ring was pitched in a grove where nearly 300 persons were assembled. The turf was in good condition."[19] At 5:15 a.m. Boylan entered the ring followed soon after by Dempsey who vaulted over the ropes and chose the southwest corner of the ring, leaving Boylan the lower ground.

When time was called, the two men hurried to the middle of the ring and shook hands. They then took their positions and the contest began. Boylan looked sharp and many thought he stood a good chance of besting Dempsey, but Jack was not among them. Early on Boylan was the aggressor as he pressed the attack and looked for an opening. Jack

Dempsey drops Jack Boylan.

was patient as he waited for his opponent to make a mistake and soon enough, the cobbler did. "Boylan made a sudden blow at Dempsey's chest, but he had miscalculated his distance and the movement brought his head within range of Dempsey's left, which delivered a stinging blow on the jaw of the Englishman."[20] The sting of the blow made Boylan angry. He quickly righted himself and was back at Dempsey in seconds. The round was called and both men were helped back to their corners.

After a half minute of rest, the men returned to center ring and began to "spar for wind"—the parlance of the time meaning that the men lay back from hard fighting, restoring energy reserves and resting a bit. When Boylan regained his breath, he went on the attack, but Jack was ready for him, skillfully defending himself by sidestepping, moving his head and knocking away Boylan's best shots. Boylan's activity paid off eventually, however, when he feinted with his left, causing Dempsey to put out his right in an attempt to block the phantom blow. As soon as he did, Boylan let go a straight right that caught Dempsey flush on the nose, splitting it open, bringing blood and knocking Jack off his feet. Dempsey was up in an instant, but the round was just ending.

In the third round, neither man showed the same spark they had in the first two. They sparred cautiously at first, but after Boylan made several efforts to land on his opponent's head and body, Dempsey moved in and clinched, preferring to wrestle and wrangle with Boylan to wear him down a bit. Boylan had done his best to avoid this, knowing full well that he could not compete with Dempsey's well-honed grappling skills. The round ended when the two men fell to the ground with Dempsey landing on top of Boylan.

As the fourth round was called, Boylan came to scratch looking battered and tired. Dempsey's punches and the grappling of the previous round were beginning to take their toll. Boylan managed to strike Dempsey twice, but with minimal effect. Once he misjudged his distance on a hard swing so badly that he stumbled forward and fell into Jack's arms. "In a twinkling Dempsey threw the Englishman and managed to fall heavily upon his chest and stomach. Boylan was heavily winded by the wrestling and badly bruised, but he came up pluckily for the fifth round."[21] As could happen under the London Rules, the fourth round lasted less than ten seconds.

In the fifth round, both men sparred for wind at first, but began to mix it up after about thirty seconds. Dempsey made another attempt to wrestle with his opponent, moving in and trying to lock him up. Suddenly Boylan pulled away and as he turned, fell down. The round was called after one minute. The sixth lasted twice as long, but ended when the two men, who were once again grappling, went down in the middle of the ring.

For much of the bout, Dempsey fought on the defensive, "and although badly punished, succeeded in winding Boylan by frequently throwing and falling on him."[22]

The ensuing rounds were much the same, with Boylan attempting to force the fighting and keep Dempsey from either landing punches or grappling and Jack playing a waiting game and looking for openings to exploit. "Boylan fought with his usual vehemence and resolution" and though battered, still looked to be in the fight until Jack began landing terrific blows which completely stunned Boylan. At one point Dempsey struck his opponent with a thunderous left that landed flush on Boylan's right temple and "reduced him to a complete state of stupor."[23]

Although he was now wobbly and clearly overmatched, Boylan continued to return to scratch at the beginning of each session. "After fighting twenty-three rounds in twenty-six minutes, Boylan, who was in the act of falling simply to avoid punishment, was caught by Dempsey on his hip, and thrown with terrific force. When his seconds picked him up he was unconscious, and could not come to in time, so Dempsey was proclaimed the victor."[24] Dempsey and Shanley called at the *Police Gazette* offices later that day and received the stakes for the victory.

Dempsey and Boylan were scheduled to meet again on September 20, but the police arrested both parties prior to the event for participating in a prizefight. They were sent to jail in default of $1,000 bail. Fox's attorney, representing Dempsey and Boylan, pointed out during the ensuing hearing that as no fight had begun, there was no evidence that a prizefight had occurred. The judge saw the wisdom in the defense's argument and the case was dismissed for lack of sufficient evidence to convict. The men would meet again on October 15, with Jack taking the return bout in six rounds over twenty-three minutes.

It was not only the local police who interfered with a scheduled fight. In 1888, the *Newburgh Daily News* reported that the city of Poughkeepsie was closed to pugilism. "The manager of the Casino Rink, at Poughkeepsie, has declined to allow Jack Dempsey and Frank White and other boxers and pugilists to give an exhibition here on Thursday night of this week, although the exhibition has been advertised and tickets sold. Father Nilan of St. Peter's Church and the local press denounced the affair so vigorously that the manager of the rink has now notified Frank White that he cannot allow the entertainment to be held in the building."[25] Pressure against prizefighting, whether legal or societal, was still heavy in the 1880s.

Dempsey was building a good reputation as a pugilist and thereby building demand for his services in the ring. The *Brooklyn Eagle* mentioned this when discussing Jack's contest with Henry Joyce [sic] (Harry Force?). Referring to Jack by his given name of John, the *Eagle* noted on September 4 that "Dempsey has recently obtained notoriety as a hard hitter by his fight with 'Cockey' Turnbull [sic] [Jack Boylan?] in the ring at Harry Hill's hotel on Flushing Bay. He knocked out his man on that occasion and his friends have since been trying to make a match for him with several aspiring New York and Brooklyn pugilists."[26]

Shortly after his decisive victory over Boylan, a well-known sportsman by the name of Captain James C. Daly offered to make a match against Dempsey with one of several fighters whom he backed. He suggested a match with Harry Force. On August 25, the parties met in the *Police Gazette* offices and agreed to a glove bout for $50 a side to be held on September 3. "Captain J.C. Daly was sponsor for Force and Gus Tuthill represented Dempsey. After some little discussion the backers of the men each posted $25 for their favorites, selected Richard K. Fox as the final stakeholder and agreed that he should appoint the referee."[27] The *Police Gazette* report from 1883 stated that Thomas "Soap" McAlpine was at the meeting representing Dempsey but did not mention Tuthill. There's no clear evidence that Tuthill became involved with Dempsey until a couple of years later, so the mention of him being present in 1883 might be an honest error in recollection by Fox, who made that note some five years later. Referring to Dempsey as John, the articles of agreement called for the men "to fight a fair stand-up boxing match with kid gloves, according to the Queensbury rules."[28]

The Dempsey-Force bout was well documented by the *New York Times* and *New York Sun* and helps spell out how much the fight game has changed since the days when pugilism was typically frowned upon and generally against the law.

The original plan was to hold the bout at Harry Hill's Pavilion, but no precautions were taken to cloak this fight in the normal secrecy. As such, publicity for the fight was so great that Hill refused to let the contest go on at his place. Both sides met again on September 1 and agreed that the contest would be held at Alex T. Maguire's resort in the Blissville section of Long Island City, in the Borough of Queens.

Backers raised a reported $250 purse and the bout was scheduled for the early morning hours in the upstairs ballroom of Maguire's. "Maguire has a ball-room in the upper story of his house, and in that ball-room on Sunday a lot of planks were laid on the floor and about them was stretched a clothes line. This formed a square ring 20 by 20 [sic] feet, and Maguire and a few choice spirits who inspected it pronounced it 'a daisy' and 'good enough for a slaughter-house.'"[29]

Shortly after 5:00 a.m., Tom McAlpine woke Dempsey, who had been sleeping over at Maguire's, and proceeded to get him ready for the bout.

Mr. William E. Harding was selected to act as referee for the contest. At about 5:30 a.m., as the contest was about to begin, Maguire's patrons began to fill the ballroom, each eager to pay a couple of dollars to witness the bout. A large and vocal crowd today is a fight promoter's dream, but not so in 1883. So great and noisy was the gathering crowd that morning that the local police were alerted. Within minutes, several police officers appeared on the scene to prevent the prizefight.

The police led their investigation of the building and found the twenty-four-foot ring that had been set up in an upstairs ballroom. They also found the pugilists and their backers in side rooms where they were preparing for battle. The police conducted interviews and "took the word of several delegates to the convention who assured them that no one was going to fight, box, spar, wrestle, or do anything contrary to the law, or which could be considered into bringing disrepute upon Blissville."[30] While it was clear that a fight was about to be conducted, the officers were not anxious to press the matter further. "On being assured that the goals would not be disturbed the police took beer all around and also a mild cigar each and returned to Hunter's Point. The fight was postponed by order of the referee."[31]

As the constables told the assembled crowd to move on, tempers began to flare, shoving matches broke out and soon the spectators became the pugilists. "Policemen O'Brien, Welch, Carroll, and Waddle of Blissville, jumped into the room and began to lay about them. Wherever their clubs fell they left their marks."[32] Many in the crowded rooms escaped out the back doors. Soon enough, peace was restored and the crowd disseminated.

Attempts to dissuade the police from interfering having failed, Dempsey, Force and their parties were smuggled away. As they left Maguire's resort, the pugilists and their parties agreed to meet up at Elliot's Hotel on Coney Island in an hour. When the group reunited at the hotel, they discussed several options to enable the bout to proceed. No one was interested in further delay, so viable local venues were considered. A large room in the hotel was considered, but when the crowd gathered, they were met by proprietor Mike Keenan, who made the following address, "Gentlemen, this fight cannot come off in my house as I do not want to break the law and I have refused to allow the pugilists to fight."[33]

The group then attempted to secure the use of the theater adjacent to Elliot's, but it was found to be occupied. The church group meeting in the theater was well engaged in their meeting and not at all interested in giving it up. Other nearby locations were also found to be unavailable.

Undeterred, and having nowhere else to turn, they settled for a vacant lot. Dempsey and Force attempted to settle the question of ring superiority on a partially fenced clearing in the middle of a swampy, four-acre lot within one hundred yards of the hotel, in view of a long row of houses and almost under the Coney Island Elevated Railroad.

A rudimentary ring with no posts or ropes was quickly marked off on the spongy turf as the fighters and their seconds readied themselves. An estimated 300 to 500 spectators gathered around the hastily pitched ring. The passengers on the elevated trains that stopped on the tracks overlooking the lot and the guests who had gathered on the balconies of the Elliott had the best view of the fight. Other people watched from the windows and rooftops of surrounding buildings. The absence of a roped ring allowed the spectators at ringside to crowd in and encroach upon the fighters periodically during the contest.

Harding was again selected as the referee, Casper Hauck and Andy Hanley were selected as judges and George Redmond (also mentioned as Frank and Andy) of Boston acted as the timekeeper. James Daley and Jack Clurnan were in Force's corner while Dempsey was seconded by Tom McAlpine and Joe Fowler.

"Dempsey was the first to enter the ring. He was dressed in the regulation prize ring costume, wearing white trunks and stockings and having the upper portion of his body bare. Force followed him, clad in green trunks and yellow stockings."[34] The fighters wore light leather gloves and fought under the Queensberry Rules, going nine three-minute rounds. At quarter of eleven, Harding called the fighters to the scratch, called time and the men began to fight.

The first round was fairly uneventful as the two men sparred and moved about the ring in the usual effort to size up their opponent. Once they got going, the men each landed multiple lightning blows on the other. Jack landed sharply on Force's eye and "at one time, in a clinch, Dempsey beat a tattoo on Force's ribs."[35]

When time was called for the second round, both men came out promptly and provided three minutes of hard fighting. Dempsey caught Force with a solid left shot to the right eye that stunned his opponent and soon blackened and bruised the eye. This was clearly Dempsey's round as he fought Force "all over the ring."

Dempsey drew the first blood in the third round with blows to Force's nose and mouth. One reporter described it this way: "When the men came to scratch for the third time Dempsey again led and cut Force's face in several places until the man's breast and neck were covered with blood."[36] Not ready to roll over, Force caught Dempsey with several heavy blows to the head and the ear late in the round.

During the fourth round, Dempsey took command of the bout. Force's face was cut in several places and bleeding freely. During the action, a lone off-duty police officer, John McGrady, who had heard the commotion, appeared on the scene and tried to stop the fight, but he was hurried away by several in the crowd.

At the start of the fifth round, Deputy Sheriff H.L. Johnson and Constable Joseph Morris appeared on the scene, climbed into the ring and attempted to stop the fight. In short order Johnson and his associate were subdued; they were then promptly run off the field by the crowd, who had had enough of police interference this day and who weren't in the mood to put up with more. The officers were sent away, but they would be back.

During the commotion, both fighters caught their wind and went hard at it when the bout resumed. During the fifth round, Dempsey landed heavily on Force's nose, but was immediately met with a sharp counter to the stomach. The men continued to mix it up until time was called, ending the round.

The sixth and seventh rounds were commanded by Dempsey, but Force remained in the fight, landing periodic heavy blows in response to the bombardment he was receiving. By the eighth round, the crowd had closed in so tightly due to the lack of posts and ropes that the fighters had limited room to work. "They did the best they could, hitting each other whenever opportunity offered. Dempsey, getting in the most effective blows and getting away from Force's heaviest counters."[37]

By the ninth round, the men only had about ten feet in which to fight. They met at mid-ring and although Force's face was cut up, bruised and bleeding, he was game and the two mixed it up soundly. Force landed several heavy blows to Dempsey's nose and body, but the round was still Dempsey's. Towards the end of the round (according to the *Police Gazette* it was 11 a.m.) the police returned in force. Coney Island Police Chief John Y. McKane arrived on the scene with a party of burly officers. The police entered the ring and arrested both fighters. Referee Harding quickly declared the fight a draw and headed off and into the nearest open door, making good his escape. The crowd also scattered quickly in all directions and by any route available to them to be certain of avoiding arrest. The *Police Gazette* described the mass exodus as follows: "A general stampede followed as spectators climbed over and broke through a fence, tumbling pell-mell over each other in their efforts to escape."[38]

The scene outside Elliot's Hotel in Coney Island, where Dempsey met Harry Force.

While the constables were busy arresting the fighters, Tom McAlpine was arguing with Chief McKane that no "fight" had occurred at all, just a friendly and scientific boxing exhibition between friends. He showed McKane the men's gloves and argued that given their "softness," neither man could have been seriously injured. McKane did not buy McAlpine's argument and the men were taken to the jail at Gravesend to await arraignment and for bail to be set.

A warrant was issued for the arrest of referee Harding as well. He was found that afternoon in his Manhattan office by Constable William Bennett, Chief McKane's right hand man, and accompanied to Gravesend by *National Police Gazette* editor Richard K. Fox. "Harding was taken before Justice Williams, who committed him to appear on September 7, for aiding and abetting a prize fight, fixing bail at $500. Richard K. Fox furnished the bail, and he was liberated. Force and Dempsey were also bailed out in $500 each to appear."[39]

The hearing for all the men finally began on September 11 before Justice Williams. Assistant District Attorney Bussing of Kings County represented the people while Chief McKane acted as prosecutor. Harding, Dempsey and Force were represented by Fox's friend and associate, Colonel Charles S. Spencer. District Attorney Bussing called as witness officers John McGrady and Augustus A. Conway and Captain John S. Hinman of the Coney Island police. McGrady, the first officer on the scene, testified that on the morning of September 3 he came upon a commotion that he determined to be a prizefight. He heard someone call "time" and then waded into the crowd he estimated at around two hundred. He stated that he saw two men with gloves on engaged in a prizefight and committing a breach of the peace. He then left the scene and returned to police headquarters where he reported the situation. McGrady, now accompanied by Captain Hinman and officers Conway, Sullivan and Morris, returned to the scene of the battle and arrested the participants. The other policemen testified to the same. Colonel Spencer then cross-examined the officers and, in a masterful performance, he gained the officer's admission that "they did not know whether the gloves were hard or soft, that they did not know the difference between boxing and fighting, and that they were not posted as to what constituted a prizefight." Bussing then asked for an adjournment, but Spencer argued that "no evidence had been adduced to show that there had been a prizefight or a referee, and that all the elements necessary for a prizefight were lacking the referee, the prize, and even the gloves." The court then adjourned for two weeks.[40]

The hearing resumed on September 25 but "after hearing the opening of the case Justice Williams adjourned until Tuesday October 9."[41]

When the hearing resumed in October, Spencer called each of the policemen involved in the raid to the stand, had them recount their stories from that day and masterfully called their accounts into question. The men knew little about prizefighting or how it differed from street fighting. They could not claim for certain that it had been Harding who called time in the ring. They could not even agree whether gloves had been worn or not. Certain that the case against the pugilists was falling apart, Bussing stepped in and asked the justice for a week's recess to regroup. Spencer objected, pointing out that no evidence had yet been produced to indicate that there had even been a prizefight, gloves or a referee and asked that the charges be thrown out. Williams agreed and the men were acquitted of all charges.

In the contest—or lack of contest, according to Colonel Spencer—Dempsey punished Force badly throughout the thirty-one minutes of fighting (according to the *Police Gazette* it was fifty minutes). Still, Harding, citing the sudden and inconclusive finish, declared the bout a draw, even though it was clear to virtually everyone present that the Nonpareil was the victor.

In an interesting but confusing bit of data, the *Brooklyn Eagle* carried the report of a prizefight that occurred on September 2, 1883. There is clearly no doubt that on September 3, 1883, Jack fought Harry Force. That fact is confirmed by multiple newspaper reports and even a

Dempsey (left) in his match against Harry Force.

half-page illustration that ran in the *Police Gazette*. The *Brooklyn Eagle*, however, also has complete and detailed coverage of a fight between Jack Dempsey and a Henry Joyce that they report occurred on September 2, 1883, at Elliott's Theatre, Brighton Beach, Brooklyn. Aspects of the two reports are similar, but not exactly the same. It appears that the *Eagle* simply mixed up the date and name—certainly not uncommon in the day, although it is hard to be completely certain. It's not inconceivable that Dempsey could have fought two bouts in two days—he did several times—but I find absolutely no other references to the Joyce bout, nor any other record of a Henry Joyce participating in any prizefight before or after. The *Eagle* makes no direct mention of the Dempsey-Force bout until September 12 when it reports that Dempsey, Force and Harding, "who were arrested on September 3, at Coney Island for prize fighting ... were arraigned before Justice Williams, at Coney Island, yesterday afternoon, for examination."[42]

Mention of a prizefight in Coney Island appeared in the *Eagle's* editorial page on September 4. The only names directly cited were William Harding and Richard Fox, but the *Eagle* took them and all persons involved in the event to task. Dempsey and Force were referred to as "a couple of young roughs, already seasoned to the business of prize fighting, were pitted against one another for a stake by a crowd of blackguards...."[43] The *Eagle* continued the attack, stating,

> While the stupid animals who pummeled each other yesterday for a few dollars, their trainers, backers and umpires and referee Harding are all liable to a heavy fine and imprisonment, they do not constitute the only offenders against law and decency. Behind them is a still greater offender, the promoter, stakeholder and encourager of prize fights throughout the country, the proprietor of a publishing establishment especially equipped for the business of encouraging prize fights and the acknowledged protector of those who violate the law."[44]

The proprietor of the publishing establishment was clearly Richard Fox of the *National Police Gazette* and the editors of the *Eagle* called for his indictment as well. In time, the *Eagle* would change its tune, but for now the official position of the editorial board was firmly anti-prizefighting.

The unfinished fight left a bad taste in everyone's mouth so a determination was made to find a time and place in which Dempsey and Force could meet again and bring matters to a more suitable conclusion. They were soon added to a fight card being set for September 17. The rematch was part of a benefit to honor Thomas "Soap" McAlpine and was to be held at Harry Hill's Place at One Hundred and Thirtieth Street and Third Avenue in New York. An evening of bouts was scheduled, with Hill acting as referee for each match. Once again, however, something stood in the way of the conclusion of the bout. While Dempsey and Force were planning to finish their suspended fight from two weeks earlier, come fight time, Force was nowhere to be seen. Conflicting stories were told explaining the pugilist's absence. According to some sources Force was again under arrest and as such, unable to be present. It was reported by the *New York Sun* that "Captain James Daly would not let Force spar until after he had stood his trial."[45] Other sources claimed that he was a free man, but a miscommunication caused him to be absent. The *Police Gazette* commented, "On September 17 they were to finish their fight, but Force, through an apparent misunderstanding, did not appear."[46] Whichever the case, he was not at Harry Hill's at the appointed time and a large crowd was on hand and anxious to see Dempsey fight.[47]

Suddenly in need of an opponent, the evening's honoree Tom McAlpine was tapped to climb into the ring with Dempsey.[48] A fifty-dollar purse was quickly gathered and after a short delay while McAlpine readied himself, the two climbed into the ring for their hastily arranged bout. Again, there were conflicting reports regarding the outcome. Most of those present believed that Dempsey had prevailed easily, but Hill apparently did not want to put a damper on McAlpine's big night and ruled the contest a draw. The *New York Sun* reporter toed the official line reporting the fight as even. "They had four slashing rounds, in which both were badly punished, and Harry Hill declared the contest a draw."[49] Other observers were sure that Dempsey had the clear edge, but Hill, possibly in a nod to McAlpine on the day of his benefit, decided things were considerably more even than that. The *Police Gazette* commented on the decision with a bit of cynicism, stating that "after sparring four rounds, in which Dempsey knocked Soap through the ropes twice, the referee [Harry Hill] decided it a draw."[50] The crowd booed the decision as Jack clearly led throughout, but given Hill's popularity and his reputation for exceeding honesty, the decision was not challenged.

On September 20, Harry Hill's Place was again packed with an assortment of more than eight hundred sporting men who had gotten a tip that Dempsey was supposed to meet Jack Boylan in a return match just a month after they had met at Hill's in August. The two were to meet in a finish fight with hard gloves and the crowd was anxious to see the contest. Hill was determined, however, to give those present "a first-class variety and boxing exhibition before Boylan and Dempsey entered the arena."[51] Those who came out to see the main event were disappointed, however, when soon after several preliminary bouts had taken place, including a rattling encounter between lightweights Johnny Saunders and Tommy Costello a police sergeant and several officers entered the building to investigate rumors of a prizefight. A frustrated Harry Hill accompanied by Jem Mace immediately headed to the police station and told Captain Kelly that all fights that day would be scientific sparring sessions fought with soft gloves and that no laws would be broken. The men then returned to Hill's pavilion and, given Hill's mostly positive relationship with the police, supposed their explanation would suffice to keep the constabulary at bay. But it was not so.

The bouts soon continued, but after another hard-fought contest between lightweights George Taylor and Harry Woodson, "Detective Brennan of the Fourteenth Precinct police entered the hall at the head of a detachment of police and arrested both Dempsey and Boylan on the charge of being about to participate in a prize-fight."[52]

The excitement caused by the police presence and the arrests was intense and the crowd expressed their displeasure as the men were led away. Despite the arrests, the remainder of the evening's bouts went on as scheduled. In a hastily arranged contest, Johnny Saunders reentered the ring with Steve Taylor to fill the places of the arrested pugilists and provided "a very interesting set-to." The bouts were good ones, mollifying the restless crowd to some extent.

Upon their arrests, Dempsey and Boylan were immediately taken to the Mulberry Street station, processed and transferred to the New York City Halls of Justice and House of Detention, known colloquially as the Tombs. Hill, accompanied by pugilist Charlie Norton and William E. Harding of the *Police Gazette*, made the trek down to the Mulberry Street station house to demand the pugilists' release. Upon arriving, however, the desk sergeant refused to listen to their argument, instead directing them to find a judge and procure bail bonds. Bail, which was paid by Harry Hill, was set at $500 each. The men were instructed to appear before Justice Kilbreth at the Tombs Police Court the following morning.

At the hearing the arresting officers, detectives Brennan and Hart, told of how they came to learn of the impending match and how they intervened. An indignant Hill objected strenuously to the arrest of the two pugilists and expressed outrage that anything illegal was to take place in his establishment. Justice Kilbreth, however, not only did not dismiss the charges, he assigned the matter to be adjudicated before Justice Ford and had the fighters returned to their cells, their bail set at $1,000, pending trial.

Richard Fox returned from a trip to New Orleans on September 24 and, learning that the men were still in police custody, went immediately to the Tombs with his attorney, Colonel Charles S. Spencer, and arranged for their release.

Jack's legal troubles continued, however, as he, Harry Force and William Harding were to be on trial the next day in front of Justice Williams of the Coney Island Court on charges stemming from their September 3 bout. Again, Fox provided Colonel Spencer as counsel for the men. After brief opening arguments, the hearing was adjourned by Justice Williams until October 9.[53]

In what may have been a nod to a growing tolerance of prizefighting, the judges in both cases dismissed the charges and Dempsey, Force, Boylan and Harding were acquitted of all charges. The decisions may have also been a result of Fox and Spencer citing a New York State Supreme Court ruling from the previous year acquitting Jem Mace and Slade on similar charges. In that ruling Justice Charles Donohue, presiding justice for the City and County of New York, determined that there was no cause to arrest someone on the suspicion that they might be preparing to engage in a prizefight and therefore the arrests were "illegal and uncalled for." While prizefighting was still illegal in much of the country, it was clearly gaining a much greater degree of acceptance by many state and local officials as well as the justice system. The pugilists were fortunate to have their legal troubles behind them for now. Harry Force's good fortune would soon get even better as it was reported in December that he inherited $80,000 from a recently deceased relative.[54]

After his two brushes with the law, Dempsey would lay low for a few weeks but was soon looking for his next ring opponent. He would fight an exhibition at Harry Hill's at a benefit for pugilist Jack Davis on October 4. This benefit, originally scheduled for Freeman's Hall in College Point on Long Island, is noteworthy for the fact that Davis was black and when the town authorities heard this, they ordered the show cancelled and the Hall padlocked. Upon hearing this, Harry Hill intervened and agreed to host the event at his pavilion. In one of several bouts, Dempsey met Young Nixey of Liverpool, England. Nixey was an experienced fighter who "was too clever for his youthful opponent, but notwithstanding Dempsey showed to good advantage."[55] The three-round exhibition was ruled a draw.

With the charges against them dropped, Dempsey and Boylan agreed to try once again and the pair was finally able to meet on October 15. With no police interference this time, Dempsey defeated Boylan in six rounds over twenty-three minutes.

Dempsey met Billy Frazier in New York on November 10 and won the bout in six rounds. By the end of the decade, Frazier had quit the ring and found a new calling. According to the Sacramento Daily Record Union, "Billy Frasier, the well-known lightweight pugilist, who fought Jack Dempsey, Jack McAuliffe and a number of other noted fighters, is now preaching."[56] Frazier, who stood only 5'2" and weighed but 126 pounds in top condition, regularly fought larger men. He was a smart and scientific ringsman with fast hands. He learned to fight while he was a sailor in the 1870s and turned professional upon returning from sea. By the end of the 1880s he left the ring for the pulpit but by 1892 was growing restless and migrated back to the gym. The lifelong New Englander continued to fight at a busy pace through 1893 and then retired from fighting to begin training students in physical fitness and boxing. He held instructor positions at Williston Seminary, Exeter and Andover Academies and Amherst, Williams, Wesleyan and Harvard colleges.[57] Frazier, his wife, a daughter and one son made their home in Somerville, Massachusetts, where Billy resided for the rest of his life.

Billy Frazier.

After several attempts to meet in the ring, Jack squared off with Bob Turnbull on November 25 at New York's Clarendon Hall located at 114 East 13th Street. "After fighting eight rounds in thirty-three minutes, the referee stopped the fight and declared it a draw, although it was plain to everybody that Dempsey had the best of the fight from beginning to end, having knocked Turnbull down several times."[58] While referee Billy Edwards called the fight a draw, the decision was met with boos and catcalls by the crowd who believed that Dempsey was the clear victor. Jack had the best of his opponent. In addition to flooring Turnbull several times, Dempsey struck his opponent at will from beginning to end.

When several New York athletic clubs offered purses for a rematch with generous terms for both fighters win, lose or draw, Turnbull refused. Days later a $300 purse was arranged by the New York Athletic Club, but again Turnbull declined a return bout with Dempsey. Turnbull got the draw in Clarendon Hall, but he knew, like so many others present that November night, that he was no match for Dempsey. He displayed courage and fought eight well-contested three-minute rounds, but even after Dempsey offered to split the purse evenly, win, lose or draw, Turnbull decided not to have a second go at Jack at this time.

Dempsey then offered Jimmy Murray a chance to fight for the purse under London Rules, but Murray declined the offer, stating that he would only meet Dempsey under the Queensberry Rules. Spurned by Murray and Turnbull and in an effort to remain active and visible in the pugilistic world, Jack left an open invitation to fight any lightweight pugilist who was willing to meet him for $250 a side under the London Prize Ring Rules. On November 26 Dempsey seconded fellow Brooklyn fighter Sam McDonald during an evening of bouts in that city's Eastern District. McDonald met Dave Williams of Greenpoint in a six-round glove match in which the smaller McDonald held his own and "did the better fighting."[59]

1884—On the Rise

In January 1884, Dempsey would make the acquaintance of a man with whom he would remain friends with for the remainder of his life—Denny Costigan of Providence, Rhode Island. Costigan, an aspiring pugilist with just a few bouts under his belt, decided to challenge Dempsey. Challenges and counter-challenges were made until Jack settled the matter by offering to fight Costigan for anywhere from $50 to $100 a side under London Rules and allow Costigan a ten-pound advantage in weight at 140 pounds to Jack's 130 pounds. The fight was the talk of the sporting circles for a time, but eventually, the idea fizzled. Regardless of the outcome of the negotiations, through their interactions the two men so thoroughly enjoyed each other that they became close friends.

In time, Costigan, in addition to being Jack's friend, would also serve as his trainer and manager. He was described as "the chubby, black mustached young gentleman who travels with and trains Jack Dempsey and keeps himself good and fat that he may the better stand the punching he gets when he and Dempsey spar in Billy Madden's play, *Around New York*."[1]

On January 7, Jack was in Boston to fight on a card in a benefit for Frank White, at Revere Hall. Following three three-round battles to warm up the crowd, Jack entered the ring with Professor J.J. Bagley of Boston. The title "professor" in this instance has no educational reference. The unofficial title was often given to pugilists of the era who became boxing instructors at gymnasiums and athletic clubs.

Jack opened the bout on the offensive with several rushes at Bagley, but they proved to be of little use as Bagley's greater size enabled him to easily fend off Dempsey's attacks. Dempsey then changed tactics and became a bit more cautious but was winded, still unable to break through Bagley's defenses and proved powerless to do much until the last round.

By the final round, Jack was rested and he came out ready to fight. Anxious to take the advantage, he pressed too hard and hurried one right-handed shot at Bagley's midsection that only grazed the Bostonian and allowed Bagley to counter with a right of his own that landed flush on the left side of Dempsey's head. This only served to irritate Jack all the more and almost immediately, he began to employ his always reliable left. The professor responded and he landed on Dempsey's ribs, then delivered a strong, right-left combination to the face. The two men grew more cautious, each looking for an opening and trading occasional punches. Suddenly, Jack rushed Bagley and the two met and began to scuffle and wrestle. When they broke, the pair engaged in light sparring until time was called. Bagley's size and experience enabled him to stand toe to toe with the less experienced and smaller Dempsey and the event ended in a draw.

However, Jack's night was not over. He would make a brief return to his collar-and-elbow wrestling roots. After six more bouts, White determined to offer $25 to any 130-pound wrestler who could throw Dempsey. The challenge was accepted by John McMahon on behalf of a man who was introduced as Young Meehan of Fairfield, Vermont. Apparently in addition to the $25 that White put up for the prize money, he had also wagered a larger amount with McMahon and others that Dempsey would not be thrown in the span of five minutes.

When the bout started, Jack took a defensive position as Meehan kept moving around him looking for a way to get an inside hold. "Dempsey feinted with his right, recovering just in time to receive an admonition from Frank White to keep up the defensive tactics."[2] The first round was called after a minute and a half.

In the second round, the men grappled with each angling for an inside hold which Meehan was able to achieve, but he still found himself unable to throw Dempsey.[3] In the end, Meehan was awarded the $25 for his gameness, but Dempsey and White divided the wager money collected after White won his bets that Jack could not be thrown.

While Costigan and Dempsey were countering offers, Jack accepted a fight with Billy Mahoney who had offered to fight him for $50 a side. The two met in New York on January 15. The fight was little more than a tune up for Jack as "Mahoney was a regular chopping block for Dempsey, who put him to sleep in three rounds, lasting eight minutes, 45 seconds."[4]

The very day he defeated Mahoney, Jack agreed to fight Joe Hennessey for a $100 purse under the Queensberry Rules. The contest was scheduled for January 26. Jack was beginning to make believers out of many people as he again had no trouble dispatching his opponent. He beat Hennessey in four one-sided rounds.

Dempsey met Joe Heiser, Jr., at Brooklyn's Williamsburg Athletic Club, on February 10, defeating him in eight rounds. The *Brooklyn Eagle* commented that Heiser, the former amateur lightweight champion, "took lessons in sparring from Jack Dempsey."[5]

On February 14, Dempsey met British heavyweight Jim Fell at Billy Madden's Athletic Hall on East Thirteenth Street in New York. Fell, who arrived in America in 1881, was a former coal miner who "was a plucky, scrappy fighter who traveled extensively and compiled a lengthy record" in the ring.[6] Accounts from the time agree that Dempsey defeated Fell in two rounds but are split as to whether the win came by knockout or decision.

On February 28, Jack fought at Billy Madden's again, where a benefit was given in his honor. As stated earlier, benefits of the era were often events held to raise money for individuals and or clubs. This benefit was typical of the time as it featured music, skits, comedy routines, wrestling and of course, several boxing matches. During the benefit, Jack offered Jim Barry $25 if he could stand up in the ring against him for four three-minute rounds. Barry, a local club fighter, figured that he could stay on his feet for twelve minutes with anyone and with visions of a $25 prize in his head, agreed to toe the scratch.

The boxing portion of the evening began with a heavyweight tilt between Pete Maguire and Barney Langdon, who fought a punishing four-round match. "They were like two bulls and knocked each other down as fast as they could be set up." Both men finished on their feet, but Langdon emerged much the worse for wear—propped against the ropes and barely able to raise his fists.[7] At the conclusion of the Maguire-Langdon bout, Dempsey and Barry stepped into the squared circle.

The large crowd gathered around the ring to watch the event. Bob Smith was named referee and he called the men to center ring where they shook hands and came out fighting.[8] The men sparred cautiously for the first half-minute, but the crowd soon encouraged the fighters to mix it up a bit. Dempsey then led off with a powerful right that clipped Barry on the jaw and sent him to the ground. Not to be defeated, Barry was quickly back on his feet. The two continued to trade jabs until time was called, concluding the first round.

Returning for the second, Barry received a good deal of punishment. Dempsey was busy, using his superior reach to land multiple heavy blows to Barry's face. A straight left found its mark on Barry's right eye. The bruising and swelling were almost immediate. By the beginning of the next round, Barry's eye was nearly closed and his face was bruised, cut and bleeding.

In the third round, Dempsey led off the action by landing several shots to his opponent's head and ear, but Barry, still game, responded vigorously with heavy returns to Dempsey's mouth and ribs. Jack braced himself and fired back with a tremendous blow on Barry's neck, which sent him to the floor for a second time. Barry struggled back to his feet, but when he got there, the welcome was not warm. Jack greeted him with a vicious right-handed blow to the stomach that doubled Barry up. Barry had taken tremendous punishment for three rounds and he was finished. When referee Smith called the fighters to center ring to start the fourth round, Barry was unable to come to scratch and Dempsey was declared the winner.[9]

March 2 found Dempsey in New York, where he met wrestler and sometimes pugilist Joe Hennessey. Jack knocked out the grappler in the fourth chapter of a scheduled four-round bout. The bout took just fifteen minutes.[10]

On March 4, pugilist Tom Sullivan visited Billy Madden's Athletic Hall "and offered to box anybody for $100. Billy Madden, not believing Sullivan was any good, agreed to put John Dempsey against him. The battle was fought and in the second-round Dempsey knocked him out."[11]

After reeling off thirteen straight victories, Dempsey decided to widen his net in search of his next series of opponents. In a challenge, or "defi," carried in the *National Police Gazette*, Dempsey offered to meet any man in America at 130 pounds for a stake of $500 to $1,000 a side. The challenge was the subject of much discussion in sporting circles as the sporting men speculated who might step forward to accept. They did not have to wait long.

The open challenge was quickly accepted by Billy Dacey of Greenpoint, who agreed to meet Dempsey in a hard-glove contest at Campbell's Hotel in the Coney Island section of Brooklyn for what was advertised as a battle for the lightweight championship. Dacey was a courageous and scrappy young man who moved well in the ring and combined a hard punch with fast hands. While he still had much to learn, Dacey saw a match with Dempsey as a positive step for his pugilistic career. Dacey was clearly a believer in the philosophy that win, lose or draw, all publicity is good publicity.

The articles of agreement were signed on February 7 when the men agreed to a glove fight in accordance with the Queensberry Rules for $100 to $200 a side. The date for the contest was set for March 6, and the location would be set on February 29 at a mutually agreed upon location within 100 miles of New York City. "Dempsey, with Harry Force, Frank Stevenson and Tom McAlpine covered Dacey's money...."[12]

"On March 3, the pugilists and their backers met at the *Police Gazette* office to settle the details of the fight. Richard K. Fox had the honor of selecting of the referees and he chose William E. Harding and Frank Stevenson, a noted New York sporting man."[13] Stevenson was appointed to serve as the backup. It was also agreed that the fighters would be in the ring somewhere between the hours of 10:00 p.m. and 4:00 a.m., the absent man forfeiting the stake money.

March 6 was a cold, breezy, late winter day. A recent snowstorm had blanketed the city with several inches of snow and being on the shore only made the wind stronger and colder. In the romantic prose of the period's news reporting, the scene was described as follows:

> Within sound of the billows of the Atlantic as they dashed on the sea girt shore of Long Island, a company of three or four hundred men assembled at an early hour yesterday morning for the purpose of witnessing the glove fight between Jack Dempsey of Williamsburg and Billy Dacey of Greenpoint, who were, according to articles of agreement, to fight for the sum of $300 under the Queensbury rules.[14]

Dacey, who was mistakenly referred to as "Gracey" throughout the *Brooklyn Eagle*'s report on the bout and as "Tracey" in others, was a twenty-year-old Greenpoint resident who at 5'6" was an inch and a half shorter than Dempsey, but was stouter, outweighing him by ten pounds at 148 pounds. While he had only one known bout to his record, George Fulljames, who saw some promise in the young man, was training Dacey for this bout and great speculation arose as to his future in the ring.

Billy Dacey.

The cold and wind kept many of the usual professionals and sporting men set away, and the 3:00 a.m. starting time of the contest certainly did not help draw a crowd. This of course was a positive in those days of clandestine bouts. "When the *Herald* reporter reached the scene of action at midnight, he looked for a long time in vain for a sight at the face of a ringside frequenter." The barroom was described as well filled but having the aroma of a stable and those in attendance as having an undesirable appearance. "Two or three females made themselves very much at home in the barroom but did not add anything to the respectability of the place."[15]

Those attending the fight did their best to keep its location a secret to inhibit police interference, but inevitably, the great migration of men in carriages traveling towards one location at a late hour did raise some attention. One policeman walking his beat on Bedford Avenue "remarked that there was a midnight funeral of some kind, as he had never before seen so many carriages on Bedford Avenue at such an hour and on such an unpleasant night."[16]

Dempsey, Dacey and their seconds arrived at Campbell's Hotel early in the evening to make preparations and let the fighters rest. The spectators began to arrive shortly after midnight—the local toughs by wagonloads and the gentry and professional class by private carriage. Upon their arrival, "they kept as much aloof from the rabble as possible and drank alone in small knots while discussing the merits of the pugilists."[17] Word of the bout had begun to circulate and the crowd had grown larger. By 1:00 a.m., about three hundred hardy souls were said to be present.

By 3:20 a.m., all was ready for the bout to begin and the doors to the hall attached to the hotel were opened. Some of the toughs trying to save the $2.50 admission pushed past the doorman, causing a surge at the door which enabled many to gain entrance for free.

According to the *Galveston Daily News*, "one hundred sons including leading sporting men and eminent politicians at 3 o'clock this morning witnessed a fight at a well-known resort on Coney Island between Billy Tracey [sic] and Jack Dempsey of New York. The fight was for the championship with $400 stakes and the gate money."[18] In the 1800s, each fighter and his backers had to produce an agreed upon sum of money and the winner kept it all. Backers often helped cover fighters' side bets, which was another common practice that helped fighters earn more than the agreed upon purse.

Inside the hall, the ring was pitched on the stage and men pushed forward to get as close to the action as possible. The hall was lit by two large kerosene lamps suspended from the ceiling.

Starting at a quarter to three in the morning, the fighters and their seconds began to appear and were cheered loudly. The first to arrive was Dacey, who was wrapped up in a heavy overcoat as a barrier to the cold. Underneath he sported white trunks. He nimbly jumped over the ropes at 2:55 a.m. and took a chair in the northwest corner of the ring. He was attended to by his seconds, George Fulljames and Tim Driscoll of Jersey City. Dempsey would not enter the ring until well past three as he waited for the appointed referee William E. Harding to arrive. When both Harding and his designated replacement Frank Stevenson failed to appear, a new man was chosen to serve as arbiter. As a note that not all those in official capacity were opposed to prizefighting; George Giddings, the deputy sheriff and constable of Gravesend, was chosen to serve as the referee. Giddings was referred to by some reports as "Jemmy Glidden," possibly as a ruse to prevent Giddings' name from being associated with a prizefight. A Mr. Plummer was selected as the timekeeper. Finally, at 3:15 a.m., Dempsey, wearing blue trunks, climbed through the ropes with his corner men Frank White and Dan Dougherty.

As the fighters readied themselves, Dacey's size advantage was apparent and many in the hall determined at that point to place bets on him to win. As usual, the cool and confident Nonpareil was unfazed by the size disparity or the whims of the sports at ring side. As the momentary wave of excitement over Dacey passed, the betting turned again in favor of Dempsey.

Referee Giddings soon called time and the men advanced to center ring, shook hands and went to work. After sizing each other up for a few seconds, Dacey took a swing at Dempsey, landing a timid right which the Nonpareil countered with a number of hard lefts. The men then fell into a clinch and continued grabbing and holding for much of the round. After the break, Dacey landed hard on Jack's cheek, but Dempsey fired back with a hard blow to the throat. After receiving the punch, Dacey lashed back, rushing Dempsey and reeling off blows. While the Nonpareil fended off most of the punches, one got through and landed hard on Jack's forehead. Dempsey retaliated, firing several more lefts, the last of which knocked Dacey off his feet. The remainder of the round continued to be busy, with both men trading blows and coming out about even.

The second round was as action packed as the first, with both men going to the body. Dempsey's forehead was noticeably flushed and swollen from Dacey's blow in the first round. Still, he led off with a left to the body that caused Dacey to recoil and then to grab Dempsey and fall into a clinch. At one point after taking a sharp left Dacey spun into the ropes, where the Nonpareil hammered away at him until the referee broke them up. Dacey went down during the round, but he was up in a second and it was ruled a slip. The pair then returned to the center of the ring where they traded body blows for the remainder of the round.

In the third round, both men were breathing heavily from the brisk pace of the first two rounds. After a good deal of light sparring, Jack took the lead, forcing Dacey back with a powerful missile to the Greenpoint man's stomach that landed him in the corner. Jack followed this up with a left that found its mark flush on Dacey's nose. From there, however, Dacey recovered and came out swinging with both hands, forcing Jack to back up and catching him at least once with a sharp left to Dempsey's face. Toward the end of the round, the men sparred lightly as they caught their wind.

In the fourth round, the fighting was intense. Jack was slow out of his corner at the timekeeper's bell and an impatient Dacey made his way over to find his opponent. He came in swinging, but Jack was ready for him. Dempsey knocked his opponent down twice with blows to the midsection and he opened a bad cut just under Dacey's ear that bled profusely. Towards the end of the round, the men came together and traded blows at mid-ring, but Jack did the most damage as he landed a number of heavy right uppercuts to Dacey's body. There was general agreement that this was Dempsey's round.

In the fifth round, Dacey knew that he needed to show something now or the fight would get away from him. As such he forced the fighting, but still wound up on the short end, getting dropped in the corner by Dempsey in the middle of the round. He quickly regained his feet and rained counter blows on his antagonist, but to no effect, as "Dempsey began to assert his superiority by his coolness and judgment in attacking and defending." By the end of the round, Dacey's mouth was bleeding. It soon became clear that Dacey was game yet overmatched.

The sixth round was all action, as Dacey continued to work on his opponent, hoping against hope for a break. Dempsey was in command, but he did show a few battle marks. In addition to his forehead, Jack had a slight cut on the cheekbone under his left eye and blood was also trickling from a cut on his nose. Still Dempsey kept landing blow after blow on Dacey's arms, face and body, causing scrapes, contusions and a broken nose that bled heavily. After one hard combination to the ribs, neck and mouth, Jack fired a right-handed missile that opened a deep cut on the Greenpoint man's ear. One account stated that by the end of the round Dacey began to look like a piece of raw beef. Dempsey was again considered the winner of the round.

The seventh session opened with both men moving slowly. After some brief and meaningless sparring, which both fighters seemed to need, Dacey went to work in earnest as he attempted to turn things around. He knew that he had to strike now if he was to have any chance to win. He pursued Dempsey as he landed multiple punches throughout the round. Dempsey looked tired and landed only a few punches of any consequence, and he returned to his corner for the break looking tired. Those scoring in the hall believed that Billy took the round with considerable ease.

Building on his success in the seventh round, Dacey came out swinging to start the eighth. He again believed that he could pull this fight out. At the starting bell, Dacey rushed toward Dempsey with every intention of finishing him. As the two met at mid-ring, however, caution seemed to take over and both men began to spar with only light shots landing periodically. Once again, Jack landed very few meaningful blows, but one that did land caught Dacey in the ribs, causing him to recoil and cover up. From then on, both men fought with passion.

The fighting throughout the round was fierce and at one point Dacey cornered Jack and hammered away at him with both hands, bringing the crowd to their feet. Dacey landed a "stinging left hander" on Jack's stomach that clearly registered on Jack's face. Many in the hall believed that Dacey might finish Dempsey here, but he ran out of gas and could not keep the punishment up. Jack maneuvered out of the trap and stayed away from his winded opponent long enough to shake off the effects of Dacey's attack. Allowing Dempsey to recover was a huge tactical error on Dacey's part. Once Jack righted himself, he retaliated, coming in hard on the attack and forcing Dacey into the corner. The round continued in this see-saw fashion, with Dacey eventually turning the tables on Dempsey again and forcing him into the ropes in the final seconds of the round.

As the ninth round began, Dempsey knew that he was in a tough fight, but he had cleared his head and was fresh. He was cautious coming out of his corner, but he then forced the fighting on his opponent, firing several fierce rights that landed flush and hard on Dacey's chin as well as a left to the jaw. Jack showed quickness in closing fast, landing a few blows and then jumping back out of harm's way before Dacey could counter. "After a couple of rallies, Dacey tried with his left, but was hotly countered on the mouth, the blow completely staggering him."[19] At this point, Jack simply followed Billy around the ring looking for openings and delivering withering punishment each time he caught him. Dacey's defense was breaking down and his counter attacks were weak and slow.

As the round ended, Dacey returned to his corner much the worse for wear. His eyes were dazed and his bruised and swollen face was covered with blood that was flowing from his broken nose, torn ear and the multiple scrapes and cuts he bore. He was exhausted, and when the referee signaled for the fighters to come to center ring for the tenth round, Dacey, too tired to rise, remained on his chair. Pulling off his gloves he told his seconds that he had had enough. With that his seconds threw in the sponge. Fulljames crossed the ring and confirmed to Dempsey that it was over. Immediately, Jack went over to his opponent and shook hands. The time of the fight was thirty-five minutes and forty-five seconds.[20]

One post-fight report observed that "the men were very evenly matched and punished each other severely."[21] While those on hand almost unanimously agreed that Dacey had fought well and been more than willing to mix it up throughout the fight, Dempsey was the clear victor. Dacey showed by far the greater punishment with many scrapes and bruises, the nasty cut on his right ear and his bruised, bloodied and broken nose, while Jack showed only a slight cut on the cheekbone under his left eye, and a few minor scrapes and scratches. Giddings announced to the crowd that Jack was the winner by technical knockout and awarded him the purse.

Dempsey was carried by his friends from the hall in triumph. Neither man, however, stayed near the hall long for fear of the police coming around. Dacey, still in his fighting clothes, embarked for Greenpoint in a light coach. "He was badly punished; his nose being swelled and many claimed broken."[22] Jack also wasted little time in heading home. The next day, in a visit to Fox's *National Police Gazette* office, Dempsey had a few visible bruises and his left eye was black and swollen, but overall, he was not badly damaged.

The contest had been a good one and many believed that it deserved a sequel. The pair would meet again in October 1887 when the Nonpareil again defeated Dacey, this time in four rounds. Dacey characteristically put on a good show in the ring and therefore was a frequently sought-after opponent. He would continue to fight as late as 1902.

On March 10, Dempsey and his backers met at the *Police Gazette* office to arrange a glove contest with Patrick McCausland, known in fistic circles as "Young English." The articles stated that "the said fight shall be for the sum of $100 a side, to take place on Monday, April 7, 1884, at Clarendon Hall." The men were to be in the ring by 9:00 p.m. and if either man failed to appear, they would forfeit the stake money. Despite the signed agreement, the fight never occurred.

After taking a few weeks off to rest from his hard-won victory over Dacey, Jack fought a couple of exhibition matches with Mike Mallory and Jim Sweeney. He fought Mallory in Brooklyn for three rounds on April 2 and the exhibition with Sweeney was a four-rounder at a benefit for Jack's brother and noted wrestler Martin Dempsey. The latter event was held on April 14 at Tom Kearns' Champion's Rest located at 283 Bowery in Manhattan. The sessions were live tune-ups for his upcoming rematch with Joe Heiser, Jr., on April 25.

Like Dempsey, Heiser hailed from Brooklyn. While it was agreed that Jack had soundly defeated him in their previous bout, Heiser was an effective hitter who had won the amateur lightweight championship and many were anxious to see him try his hand with the professionals. The bout was fought in a small room in Manhattan. Fewer than a dozen men were present. The fighters agreed to fight with small, soft gloves for six three-minute rounds. In an unusual move, Tom McAlpine seconded both fighters, and a Captain Tuttle acted as the timekeeper. The only mention of the referee was that he was "a well-known New York sporting man."[23]

The men met at center ring and at the call to box, they moved cautiously about the ring, circling each other and looking for an opening. After some light sparring and feinting, they came together and engaged in some spirited infighting of which Dempsey got full marks. Heiser then landed a stinging shot on Dempsey's jaw. Jack returned fire, pulling the trigger on a powerful left that caught his shorter opponent on the shoulder hard enough to turn Heiser completely around. Joe quickly righted himself and the pair traded several short, quick blows until the round ended.

The second round started off well for Heiser as he was able to connect with multiple one-two-three combinations to Jack's body. But Jack would not be cowed. Dempsey made a strong comeback in the second half of the chapter, working his way in close and pelting Heiser repeatedly, controlling him and driving him all over the ring. While Dempsey may have shown better overall, due to Heiser's strong early work, the round was judged as fairly even.

In the third round, Heiser came out fighting hard. He attempted to land an early right, which Dempsey blocked, and in return detonated a powerful left-hander that landed flush on Heiser's nose, causing it to bleed. First blood was called for Dempsey. The men then came to close quarters and fought actively for the remainder of the round.

After light sparring for well over a minute, Dempsey began to force the fighting in the fourth round, landing several blows with each hand on Heiser's face. Heiser fought back, landing several blows but doing little damage to his opponent. Heiser then slowed his attack and hesitated for a second. Reflexively and instantly, Jack let go his right hand and dropped a mortar round on Heiser's mouth that staggered him. Heiser's recovery was quick, however, and he refused to give in. After righting himself, Heiser led the action for the remainder of the round, following Dempsey around the ring and landing a good number of solid body blows.

The break between rounds provided insufficient rest and the start of the fifth round saw both men winded and looking for a quick break. They sparred lightly for the first two minutes, neither landing a solid blow. By the final minute, the fighters had caught their respective breaths and the action picked up, with each man landing a flurry of punches—Heiser to Jack's neck and body and Dempsey to Heiser's forehead and jaw.

As the sixth and final round began, Heiser rushed Dempsey and forced him into a corner where he proceeded to land a series of vicious body shots that clearly registered with Dempsey. After absorbing a good deal of punishment, Jack turned and worked his way clear of the corner, buying a precious few seconds to catch his breath. Anxious not to let Heiser press the advantage, Dempsey turned and was on his opponent like a cat, delivering a short, fierce blow on Heiser's eye and another to the neck. Heiser responded by backing away momentarily, but then he stopped and stepped into a powerful right that landed on Dempsey's stomach, causing Jack to wince in pain. At this point, the exhausted men fell together and engaged in infighting until time was called. It had been a good match and to the satisfaction of virtually everyone present, the referee decided that the bout was a draw.[24]

Dempsey was matched against Canadian Jimmy Hurst in a May 1 battle for a purse and gate receipts at New York's Clarendon Hall. Hurst was a resident of Montreal who was backed by fellow Canadian George Fulljames. When Hurst decided to skip town and head to Boston for a bout with George La Blanche, Fulljames notified Richard Fox, who was holding the stakes, not to pay Dempsey since the fight would not be held. Fox laughed at Fulljames and immediately paid the $200 stake to Jack when he arrived at the appointed time.

After being paid and informed that Hurst was a no-show, Dempsey appeared on the Clarendon stage, informed the audience of the situation and offered $50 to any lightweight in the audience who could best him over six rounds. The offer was immediately accepted by British lightweight Jack Bowles. There was some discussion as to whether or not Bowles was actually a lightweight, but after $25 more was put up by sportsmen anxious to see the bout, all concerns were put aside and a six-round bout agreed upon.

The bout was a spirited one. Over the first five rounds, both men engaged in a great deal of scientific sparring instead of slugging. While both fought well, Jack was readily acknowledged as having control in each round.

"In the sixth round, the fighting became hot, and Dempsey showed his superior qualities as a fighter. His blows fell indiscriminately on Bowles' jaw, face, ear and eye and with the exception of a few returns Dempsey had things his own way."[25] Jack landed a straight left that smashed into Bowles's nose, covering the Englishman's already bruised face with blood. When the round ended, referee George Taylor declared Dempsey the clear winner. The next day, Fox awarded the remainder of the purse and gate receipts to the Nonpareil.

On the evening of May 12, Jack sparred on the undercard of the Charley Mitchell–Harry Edwards bout at Madison Square Garden. By half past eight in the evening, the bouts began with two young fighters named Chrysler and Williams in a three-rounder followed by Joe Denning and Young Shine and then Denny Costigan and someone named Nixey. Shortly after 9:00 p.m., Master of Ceremonies Bob Smith announced Dempsey and his opponent Mike Mallory of Providence, Rhode Island. "Like all those who proceeded them they were stripped to the waist. Dempsey elicited much applause by his science."[26] This is the second time the men had sparred in the past month. When the men finished their three-round exhibition, English grappling champion James Faulkner and Billy Oliver, a Harlem boat builder, provided entertainment with a spirited wrestling match won by Faulkner.

In the main event, Mitchell defeated Edwards after delivering great punishment to his opponent throughout the brief match. After being slow to leave his corner at the start of the final chapter Edwards was barely able to fend of the Englishman's blows and now all but helpless, he went down a final time. Captain Williams of the local police stepped in and ended the bout after twenty-seven seconds in the third round.[27]

In July 1884, Dempsey had several run-ins with the law for engaging in prizefighting. On July 9, Jack met Tom Henry in Far Rockaway just east of Jamaica Bay on Long Island. The *New York Times* covered the event and opened their story on the fight this way: "The ethics of our effete social and criminal codes being unfavorable to public prizefighting, those two eminent exponents of the exact science of pugilism, Messrs. Jack Dempsey, of Williamsburg, America, and Tom Henry, of Manchester, England, were put to the inconvenience of going to Rockaway Beach on Tuesday in order to decide the ownership of $200 and the survival of the fittest yesterday morning."[28]

Henry started his boxing career in his native England around 1882. His first known bout was a victory over Jack Dodd. The scrappy competitor soon came to the United States where he met Professor James Haley in Hoosick Falls, New York, in December 1883. The two fought a four-round draw. Henry stood at nearly 5'8" tall and weighed 144 pounds.

Estimates vary, but somewhere between two and four hundred people made their way to "the green hotel of Herr Hammel" and waited for the activities to commence. It was agreed by the participants and their seconds that the best place to pitch the ring was just south of the hotel on the extreme western end of the beach. The posts and ropes were then pitched and the crowd assembled. At 4:30 in the morning, the fighters were each driven by coach from the hotel to the ring.

The men "fought for $100 a side and an equal division of 'tip money' which at $10 a ticket amounted to quite a handsome sum."[29] The papers recorded in a circumspect way that the referee selected for the bout was a "prominent ex-official of Brooklyn."

As the men climbed through the ropes at 5:00 a.m., they were each given "hard gloves" that "afforded about as much protection from the knuckles as ordinary kid or doe skin gloves." After shaking hands, the two pugilists began to spar. Dempsey rapped

Henry on the jaw with his right and at almost the same instant that Henry landed a smashing blow to Jack's nose. The two then fell into fighting at close quarters until Dempsey let loose a powerful right hand that landed flush on the Briton's left ear, causing him to stagger forward and drop to the sand some four feet away.

In the second round, Dempsey again dropped Henry to the sand with several hard blows, but Henry got the better of the fighting in the third round, pummeling Jack all over the ring.

Tom Henry.

The fourth round began with Henry once again getting the better of Jack. Just as Dempsey was returning fire, local law enforcement began to appear on the beach, scattering the crowd and ending the fight. The referee, as he was fleeing the scene, explained that he had already been to jail once for being involved with a prizefight, and quickly ruled the bout a draw. Henry and his entourage were indignant with the ruling, insisting that their man had won over the Nonpareil. While Henry had made a good account of himself, few of the others in attendance agreed. Perhaps adding insult to injury, Jack told Henry that he might have licked the Briton in the first round, "only he wanted to practice on him for his upcoming match with Fulljames."[30]

In October, the pair would meet again at the Eighth Street Theatre in Manhattan, with Dempsey winning by way of decision in six rounds. Henry would serve time in jail in 1885 for fighting Jimmy Murray prior to a third contest in the Germania Assembly Rooms in New York, where Jack took another decision in four rounds.

On May 5, Dempsey accepted a challenge to meet British and Canadian lightweight George Fulljames for a $1,000 purse and the middleweight championship of the Americas. Fulljames, who was born in London, England, on February 13, 1852, was already in training at Oak Point on the U.S.–Canadian border, and had been anxious to meet Jack for quite some time. Fulljames, a very clever and scientific fighter, reportedly grew up around fighters in his father's saloon in England. According to boxing historian Tracy Callis, the saloon, called "Old Horseshoe," was frequented by such noted pugilists as Tom Sayers, John Heenan, Tom King and Jem Mace.

The fighters, their backers and various sporting men met on that day at the offices of the *Police Gazette* to discuss details of the contest. A $100 deposit had already been posted with Richard Fox by Eddy Hanley of the Fulton Market and each side deposited an additional $250 that day. It was agreed that the two would meet at catch weights on July 14 within 250 miles of New York City. The bout would be conducted under the Queensberry Rules with hard gloves. The number of rounds was still unspecified. Another $500 was to be deposited with Fox by each side on June 16 and the final $250 by 4:00 p.m. on July 7.

Canadian fighter George Fulljames.

In the ensuing weeks, Fox determined that the bout would be held within 100 miles of Baltimore and he appointed Charles Carroll of Baltimore as referee. This fight was scheduled and rescheduled several times before it finally came off. Somewhere in all of this the rules governing the bout changed from Queensbury to London Rules.

The bout was to be held on July 14. The location originally chosen for the contest was a spot near Baltimore, Maryland, known as Porter's Bar on the Back River. The fighters and their backers made their way to Baltimore and all seemed ready to go, but at 11:00 p.m. on the night before the bout, authorities heard rumors of a prizefight being organized in their jurisdiction and intervened, preventing the contest from taking place. "Deputy Marshal Frey with a squad of one hundred policemen surrounded the Pimlico House in Baltimore, where the principles and their seconds in the proposed contest were stopping."[31] After the police forced their way in, Marshal Frey informed Charles Carroll, one of the referees, that he had bench warrants for the arrest of Dempsey, Fulljames and their backers and he would enforce them if the bout took place. He warned the referee "that the contest must not occur on Maryland soil."[32]

There was some confusion after the police left and Dempsey's and Fulljames's backers met to determine what to do next. Despite Frey's threat of arrest, it was suggested that the fight be held at Porter's Bar sometime between 4:00 and 10:00 a.m. Whether the Fulljames men actually agreed or not, when the meeting broke up, the Dempsey backers believed that they had a deal and had their man at Porter's at nine o'clock, the appointed time. Dempsey and company waited until 10:00 a.m. and then claimed a forfeit by Fulljames. Richard K. Fox had been chosen to hold the $2,000 stakes and while he had every right to award Dempsey the purse, when he was asked about it, said that he would not hand them over to either man until they were fought for. As an inducement to the two men to reschedule the bout, Fox added another $500 to the purse.

Fulljames had reportedly shown up at Porter's earlier in the evening. As he observed the gathering crowd he determined that it was too pro–Dempsey and chose not to fight for fear of an unfair advantage to the New Yorker. Leaving a hand-written note to designate his appearance, he departed well before 9:00 a.m. and therefore before Dempsey and the fight officials arrived.

Later that morning, Dempsey, Fulljames and their backers returned to New York in hopes of securing an agreeable location for the bout. "In the meantime, both men went back into training, Dempsey at Madden's Ocean House, Rockaway, in care of Alfred Powers, and Fulljames at Ravenhall's, Coney Island, under the care of Barney Aaron and John Flood."[33]

While the men continued to train, backers tried to find a suitable location for the bout—one in which the police would not interfere and the crowd could be controlled. Rockaway Beach and Harry Hill's Pavilion in Flushing were considered, but each fell by the wayside, Hill's Pavilion just hours before a possible July 23 reschedule was to begin.

Police departments throughout the New York City region continued to get tips on where and when the fight might take place. They heard one rumor on the morning of July 24 that the bout was underway in the woods bordering the Brighton Railroad track, south of Parkville. The police arrived in full force but looked foolish as they found absolutely no trace of a prizefight.

The fight contingent, determined to press on, agreed that a ring would be pitched in the nearby William's Woods and the preparations soon began for a July 25 contest. Again, word of the fight began to circulate among the sports and a crowd began to assemble, which the Fulljames camp was not comfortable with. They again backed out at the last minute, reportedly due to the overwhelmingly pro–Dempsey crowd on hand. Fulljames and his party claimed that they feared that the unruly crowd would interfere with the fight if Dempsey were losing. At 4:00 a.m., the Fulljames party climbed into their carriages and headed for Manhattan. Dempsey and his supporters headed for Brooklyn.

As the disappointed crowd continued to drink and began to discuss the merits of the two fighters, fierce differences of opinion emerged as to whether or not Fulljames was a coward and afraid to engage Jack. Some argued that he had avoided Dempsey twice in the ring in the past couple of weeks by either not showing up or by backing out at the last minute. Others defended the Canadian, saying that Fulljames and his backers had simply misunderstood the agreement about Porter's Bar in Baltimore and were only trying to go by the agreed upon rules of ten supporters a side at William's Woods. With the argument heated, the liquor liberally flowing and general agreement that it was a shame to have a pitched ring with no fight, many in the crowd arranged a substitute bout between Jack Howard and Tom Donnelly for a $250 purse. Billy O'Brien was chosen as referee and Joe Howard the timekeeper. The fight was vicious, lasting fifteen long and bloody rounds, but Howard won and claimed the prize money.

Richard Fox, unwilling to have this proposed bout fall through, "appointed E.F. Mallahan referee and instructed him, if it was possible, to bring the men together."[34] On July 25 it was agreed that each man would take five men and travel to a location chosen by Mallahan to settle the affair. Finally, after four attempts, Dempsey and Fulljames would meet at Crooke's Point at Great Kills on New York's Staten Island in the early hours of July 30. The Point is a barrier beach that separates Great Kills Harbor from the Lower New York Bay. Fulljames and his party headed for Staten Island on July 28 and Dempsey and his seconds took the ferry the following day.

While the contest eventually did take place on July 30, another change of venue occurred. The original location of the bout scheduled for July 30 was to be the Silver Lake House, a hostelry on Staten Island, but a large crowd, hearing rumors that the bout was to come off there, gathered and made it necessary to change locations once again. The men had met as instructed at the Eastern Hotel on Whitehall Street, but due to the change in locations, "Dempsey was hastily and secretly sent up to the Rochester Hotel at 110 Bleecker Street, and Fulljames took the 1:00 o'clock boat to Staten Island, and landing at Stapleton, was at once transported to the Silver Lake House."[35] There was a bit of a stir at the respective hotels when the pugilists and their seconds arrived. The proprietor of the Silver Lake House sensed that something was about to occur and was pleased that his hostelry was to be the site of such a contest, but he was prevailed upon to keep it quiet. Several sporting types who saw the Nonpareil enter the lobby of the Rochester gathered at the bar and waited for a sign of activity or some clue as to where the bout might occur. Dempsey's people were able to scatter most of the crowd by starting a rumor that Jack was in lower Manhattan to mourn the death of a close relative and that due to his bereavement, the bout with Fulljames was off until September. While most of those gathered fell for the ruse, the wisest and most cynical of the bunch continued to adorn the bar, but they waited in vain.

"At 10:00 o'clock at night, Dempsey secretly left by the back door of the hotel and went through a tenement house into Greene Street, where a carriage was waiting, in which were Referee Mallahan, Mr. Arthur Chambers of Philadelphia, and Professor Watson of Providence."[36] About forty others who had received the latest tip as to Dempsey's movements sat waiting in carriages at the Battery. The group still had no idea whether the contest would be waged in New Jersey, Staten Island or Long Island. In keeping with the secretive nature of prizefighting at the time, a secret signal was devised to inform those in the know where the fight would be. "Their instructions were, if a carriage came by and one of the occupants lost his hat and got out to pick it up, to follow that carriage." As the carriage carrying Dempsey took off, Ned Mallahan's hat came out the window and he immediately climbed out of the cab and retrieved it. The other waiting carriages quickly fell in line and followed the leader onto the eleven o'clock ferry to Stapleton. The ferryman, noting the sudden surge of late night travelers on his normally quiet vessel, asked if this was a wedding. "Naw," replied Mallahan. "It's a funeral." When the gatekeeper inquired as to the whereabouts of the hearse, Dempsey's friend John Conroy stuck his head out of the carriage window and responded, "Say, young feller, there ain't no hearse, because the corpse was havin' so much fun to the wake that he couldn't tear hisself away to git buried, see?"[37]

When the ferry docked in Stapleton, Dempsey's carriage took him immediately to his hotel, where he was put to bed for the evening. He was awoken early and driven to the once again relocated site of the bout. Mallahan, on hearing of the large crowd now gathered at the Silver Lake Hotel, ordered the latest venue change during the night. The new location was another hostelry on Gifford's Lane in Great Kills. The place selected at Crooke's Point was so remote that the fight went undetected. A ring was hurriedly pitched by Mallahan and Hial Stoddard. The wet, sandy soil was so loose that the stakes almost fell over, but they were quickly firmed up and, being anxious to finally bring this bout off, no one complained.

Fulljames was secreted out of the Silver Lake House to keep the milling crowd at that establishment from following him. He was immediately conveyed by wagon to the ring at Gifford's Lane.

At 5:15 a.m., Fulljames climbed into the ring wearing white shorts with no sash. He was soon followed by Dempsey, who sported his customary deep blue tights and white stockings and dark fighting shoes. Fulljames's seconds were John Flood and Ramsey Aaron while Dempsey was attended to by his friends retired lightweight champion Arthur Chambers and Walter Watson of England. As the men readied themselves for the contest, bets were being laid down by the assembled parties.

In an uncommon twist, Jack, standing at 5 feet 8 and one-half inches, was actually taller—by four inches—and outweighed his opponent by a good seven pounds, weighing in at a solid 137 pounds. According to Fox, "The disparity in the size of Dempsey and Fulljames was really astonishing as they faced each other, Dempsey being much taller and heavier than his antagonist, beside whom he appeared a giant."[38]

Referee Ned Mallahan wasted no time in calling the men to center ring and finally getting this nomadic event under way. Mallahan instructed the pair to fight and Henry J. Rice (referred to in some accounts as Price), the appointed timekeeper, started the clock.

The bout began at 5:25 in the morning, just as the sun was beginning to rise. "Mr. Fulljames and Mr. Dempsey, who wore kid gloves, shook hands with the utmost courtesy." In a moment, the men were fully engaged, with Fulljames throwing the first punch, which was short, and Dempsey landing a return blow on the Englishman's forehead. Fulljames responded with a blow to Jack's nose. After another exchange, the fighters fell into a clinch from which Dempsey threw Fulljames, landing hard on him. Somewhere in the exchange, Dempsey landed a hard blow on Fulljames's cheek which resulted in a gash to the face, causing Dempsey's corner to claim first blood. In the early days of prizefighting—both with swords and with fists—the first drawing of blood in a contest was considered to provide an initial advantage over an opponent. Given that many times a fighter who claimed first blood wound up losing the fight, the custom of claiming first blood eventually died out. With Fulljames being thrown to the ground and Dempsey lying on his opponent's chest, the round was ended by Mallahan at the three minute and fifty-six second mark.

Fulljames started the second round much as he had the first. He was active and reeling off multiple punches, but most fell short and those that had the proper range landed with minimal effect. Conversely, Dempsey was generally on target and his blows quite damaging. Fulljames pressed his attack and began hammering Dempsey's body while Jack returned fire, landing several stingers on the Canadian's right eye. "Both fought like savages in the next round, which ended like the first by Fulljames being thrown. In the third round there was some terrific hitting on both sides, and Dempsey finally knocked his opponent clear off his feet by a tremendous left-handed blow, amid wild applause."[39]

In the fourth round, Fulljames realized that he was taking a tremendous beating and if he were going to win it needed to be soon. He fought the round full-out and showed his superior ring knowledge, but he was simply outgunned. Dempsey skillfully swept away Fulljames's blows. The round ended in just under two minutes as Dempsey landed an uppercut.

In the fifth round, Jack continued to punish the Canadian, hitting him on the body, mouth and nose. Fulljames was still short on most of his punches. He was fighting from too far back and given Dempsey's longer reach, he had to rethink his approach lest the fight get completely away from him. The veteran ring man determined that since his arms weren't going to grow, he needed to get in closer and in the sixth round, he did just that. All through the minute and a half, Fulljames stayed close and crouched low, hammering away at Dempsey's midsection. This worked well for that round, but by the seventh Jack had adjusted to his opponent's new strategy and it wasn't long before Fulljames found himself in the sand after the Nonpareil caught him flush on the nose with another powerful right hand.

Fulljames fought on in the eighth and ninth rounds, and while Dempsey landed more often, Fulljames was able to answer back numerous times. Even so, both rounds went to the Nonpareil. Dempsey continued to keep up the pressure during the ninth, at one point landing a hard left that opened a cut over the Canadian's eye. The blood from this gash flowed freely for the rest of the fight.

In the tenth round, "Dempsey planted his left all over Fulljames' face, but never used his right, as it had been disabled in the first round by one of Fulljames' blows."[40] The cause of the damage to Dempsey's right hand is still open to debate. It was probably from a blow by Fulljames or from Jack landing on the Canadian.

Rounds eleven through fourteen were all short and played out the same. Fulljames was again fighting defensively by keeping back and, consequently, again had trouble finding the right distance to land on Dempsey. Jack's punches, on the other hand, generally found their mark and Fulljames was becoming well acquainted with the sandy surface of the ring.

It was becoming clear to all that the Canadian was overmatched. Dempsey was landing punches at will and was either knocking or throwing Fulljames down during nearly every round. His backer Mart Malone recommended at several points that he give it up, but Fulljames would have none of it.

In the fifteenth round, Dempsey again had the advantage and knocked his opponent down at the one-minute mark with a sharp and straight left. Fulljames, unable to get any traction on the sand, decided to remove his shoes to try to improve the situation.

Rounds sixteen through eighteen were short in duration and again Dempsey's, as he landed repeated hard blows and sent the now shoeless Fulljames to the ground several times. By the end of the eighteenth, the Canadian was bleeding badly from cuts over both eyes. In the nineteenth, Fulljames tried to lead the fighting, but he was disoriented and having a hard time seeing. Once he even fell from the force of his own swing as he missed Dempsey. The round lasted only forty seconds.

By the twentieth round, Dempsey was hitting Fulljames whenever and wherever he wanted. He tagged him on the chin and dropped him, ending the round in thirty-nine seconds and in three blows—to the nose, chest and ear. He sent Fulljames down in the twenty-first round about as quickly.

Fulljames fought determinedly in the twenty-second round. Jack, however, opened the round with a strong left to the Canadian's nose and another to his chest, sending Fulljames down in a heap. At this point, his corner had seen enough and Barney Aaron threw in the sponge. "Fulljames' face was battered out of shape and was covered with blood, but he was very indignant at his second's action and said: 'I'm not beat. I can fight an hour yet.'"[41] Fulljames protested that he wanted to go on, but his backers assured him he was through and helped the beaten fighter to his corner.

"Fulljames' left eye was swollen and blackened, his face swollen and his body bruised. He took his medicine like a Spartan and displayed great courage from the start to the finish."[42] Dempsey was virtually unmarked. Even immediately following the bout he showed a minimum of bruising and swelling.

The whole fight lasted only thirty-nine minutes. "As soon as the referee gave his verdict, Dempsey walked over to his defeated antagonist and presented him with a fifty-dollar bill."[43] This and the ensuing warm handshake were surely nice gestures to make towards his defeated foe. Both fighters and their backers immediately took carriages back to the ferry landing and proceeded at once back to Manhattan.

The press was beginning to take full notice of the talented young pugilist from Brooklyn. The *Police Gazette* commented after the fight that "Dempsey fully confirmed the high opinion entertained of him as a boxer, showing himself to be a clever two-handed fighter and a punishing hitter. Cool and collected, he was ever ready to take advantage of any mistake of or opening presented by his antagonist, while his courage was indisputable."[44]

The next day, Jack went to the Russian Baths for a massage, a steam and to let a warm bath soothe his tired muscles. A reporter who was present noted that he looked in fine shape and that he had not a mark on his face; the only traces of the previous night's event were several marks and bruises on his chest and rib cage where Fulljames landed the bulk of his punches. After the contest concluded, Fulljames immediately headed north to Boston and then over the Canadian border to visit friends in Toronto and Barrie, Ontario.

Though Fulljames skipped town, Jack was still within the grasp of the local constabulary. Once again, the police got wind of what had occurred and took action, in this case after the fact. The police on Staten Island soon issued arrest warrants for the participants. Dempsey was arrested on the afternoon of August 8 in the Bowery section of Manhattan by New York City Detective Sergeant Rogers and a Staten Island police officer. He was taken to Richmond, Staten Island, where he was once again charged with engaging in a prizefight, booked and jailed for the night.

On the morning of August 9, Jack was in a Staten Island courtroom pleading "not guilty" to the charge of participating in a prizefight. Richmond County District Attorney Gallagher and Police Captain Blake were in attendance along with a number of local politicians. Justice John L. Young set bail at $700 which Eddy Hanley, a Fulton Market butcher and one of Dempsey's backers, paid at once and within minutes, Jack was free. He immediately headed back to Brooklyn.

On August 13, Dempsey was in court with his lawyer, Schools Commissioner Frean. Jack's trainers James Collins and Taylor were on hand to testify on Jack's behalf. This session was procedural as D.A. Gallagher conducted the prosecution and produced into evidence the gloves worn by the fighters and it was decided which of the various witnesses were to be called when the trial was resumed on August 21. This time Henry Ockerhause became Dempsey's bondsman.

On August 22, the *New York Times* reported that Dempsey "failed to appear yesterday for examination before Justice Young at Richmond. Dempsey's bondsmen were also absent. The case was adjourned until Wednesday next."[45] The *New York Sun* reported that if Dempsey failed to appear at the next appointed hearing date, "summary steps will be taken against him."[46]

Jack was back in court on August 27 for what was for all intents and purposes not a trial, but a show. At least five witnesses for the prosecution described the scene of the match and even the bout itself, but one by one each stated that somehow, they simply could not identify the men who participated. One man, Edward Fitzgerald, testified that he saw nothing more than a light sparring match between friends—nothing that could be construed as a prizefight. Seeing that he was getting nowhere, Richmond County District Attorney Gallagher declared the case closed. At this point, Dempsey's attorney requested that the charges be dismissed for lack of evidence. After receiving a brief lecture from Justice Young on the evils of prizefighting, Dempsey was discharged "and left the court amid the noisy congratulations of his sporting friends."[47]

It is somewhat amazing that even with being arrested and jailed for prizefighting and all of the legal wrangling and courtroom drama that ensued, nineteenth-century fighters seldom seemed to be dissuaded from continuing to box. As a case in point, during the court proceedings regarding the Fulljames battle, Dempsey's backer Gus Tuthill was petitioning in the press for a bout between his man and "any 135-pound pugilist in America."[48] It is almost as if the legal proceedings were nothing more than a minor distraction—just a part of business as usual.

As stated earlier, Fulljames left New York immediately after the bout and headed to Boston and then on to Canada, thereby avoiding arrest by the Richmond County authorities. He would continue to fight sporadically for the next four years, but Fulljames's life came to a tragic end on September 22, 1888. Fulljames died from injuries sustained in a bout at Grand Forks, Dakota Territory, when he was knocked out in the first round. According to the *New York Times*, "A dispatch from Grand Forks, Dakota, says: 'Late on Friday night a brutal prize fight took place in the barn of Frank Church. Barrett and George Fulljames, champion lightweight of Manitoba, were the principals. Barrett had the best of the fight from the start and punished his opponent so badly that he was rendered unconscious and died last evening. Barrett is in jail, and witnesses will be arrested.'"[49] The bout was actually scheduled for 2:00 a.m. on Saturday morning in the barn, but the start time was moved up by several hours. Reportedly the two men shook hands at mid-ring and almost immediately, Barrett "struck Fulljames a blow to the temple, which knocked him to the floor. He soon recovered and staggering to his feet started to continue to fight. The men went at each other viciously, and Fulljames received several hard blows on the face. The fight was a brutal one throughout...."[50] Before the round was over Barrett launched one final blow that landed hard over Fulljames' heart. The Canadian sank to the floor and would not rise. "He was left unattended on the barn floor until 7:00 o'clock Saturday morning. At that time a doctor called and had him removed, but it was too late to save his life. He gradually grew worse and died during the afternoon."[51]

The police began an investigation, arresting Barrett and several witnesses to the bout, but each was allowed out of jail and little ever came of the inquiry into Fulljames's death. The identity of "Barrett" is still uncertain. After his escape from the Grand Forks jail, he disappeared and was certainly in no hurry to claim to be the opponent who killed Fulljames. It has been speculated that his real name was Tom Bannon or even that he was Jack "Young" Barrett of Baltimore. Another story emerged the following April when a man named Brown, who was in jail for murder in Moorhead, Dakota Territory, claimed that the man he shot and killed in late September, a Boston Casey, "admitted that he had killed a man with his fist a week before, and that this man was Fulljames."[52]

The coroner's jury ultimately ruled the death an accident and—in a bizarre note—possibly caused not from Barrett's blows to Fulljames' temple, but by a rock launched from a spectator's slingshot.

On August 2, Jack traveled to Philadelphia to meet British pugilist Professor Walter Watson in a four-round glove match at Arthur Chambers' Champion's Rest.[53] Watson was described as possessing "exceptional acumen and extraordinary skills in the ring, he could easily best boxers half his age."[54]

On August 5, the cornerstone for the Statue of Liberty was laid on Bedloe's Island in New York Harbor. The statue and its pedestal will take more than two years to complete, with the formal unveiling being held on October 28 at a ceremony attended by President Grover Cleveland. In celebration of the event, New York City held its first ticker tape parade to honor the statue and its designer Frèdèric-Auguste Bartholdi.

In late August, Dempsey announced that he was willing to fight either Paddy Lee or Tom Henry in New York with gloves over six rounds. The winner was to take a sixty-forty split of the gate receipts.[55] Jack's opponent in that late October bout was determined on October 9 and wound up being Tom Henry, whom he met at Jack Thompson's Eighth-Street Theatre, where an overflow crowd would see referee Al Smith award Jack a six-round decision.

It was over the summer of 1884 that Dempsey became acquainted with the New York–based owner of the Rochester House, Gus Tuthill. Tuthill, ostensibly a stockbroker, was better known as a bookmaker, fight promoter and backer of pugilists. The title of stockbroker was often argued to be more symbolic than real as many colleagues at the Consolidated Exchange stated that they rarely saw him attending to his work there.[56] Tuthill was clearly more involved with his fight promotion and, with Dempsey's reputation on the rise, Tuthill began to take an interest in the young Brooklyn man. He would begin to financially back Dempsey's bouts that summer and their friendship and business relationship continued through the rest of the Nonpareil's life. It was also about that time that assertions were made on Dempsey's behalf for his claim to the lightweight championship.

Dempsey had created such a name for himself in sporting circles that he was in demand as an official as well as a fighter. On August 29, Jack was called upon to adjudicate what turned out to be a hard-hitting bout between Joe Martin, better known as Sheeny Joe, and Jim Collins at Manhattan's Champion's Rest located on the Bowery corner of Houston Street. Collins was a well-muscled bricklayer from the Greenpoint section of Brooklyn who weighed in at a sturdy 165 pounds. Martin on the other hand was described as bearing "a close resemblance, in comparison, to a consumptive lamp-post." As a stunned crowd watched, however, Martin knocked the bricklayer out at the end of the third round and received the purse.[57] On September 3, he, along with Billy Madden, seconded Jim McHugh in his draw with Dave Fitzgerald. For their efforts, the fighters and their backers were all indicted by the Queens County Grand Jury for having participated in a prizefight.[58] As usual, the charges were soon dropped.

Jack met Mike Dempsey of Cincinnati on the morning of September 4 at Rockaway Beach in a fight that was more of a footnote to the bout that preceded it. The Dempsey-Dempsey bout followed a much longer and bloodier affair between Dave Fitzgerald and Jim McHugh. That contest was listed as being for the lightweight championship of Canada and was fought for $250 a side and gate money. The bout was described as a "disgraceful affair" and one in which friends and backers of Fitzgerald stormed the ring in the twenty-sixth round to claim a foul against their man. In the twenty-ninth, after another foul was claimed, the referee called the fight. The seconds then declared the bout a draw and the two badly punished pugilists split the purse and the gate money.

This wild affair was a hard act to follow, but the crowd actually saw a better contest. When the two Dempseys entered the ring, the men fought seven hard-hitting rounds in twenty-eight minutes, with Jack defeating Mike by a stoppage. For their efforts, the men received just $5 a side.[59]

On September 15, Jack fought Philadelphia middleweight Jimmy Ryan to a draw over seven rounds at the Club Theater in Philadelphia. The glove contest was fought under Queensberry Rules. Jack Welch of Philadelphia and Tommy Ray of New York were chosen as referees and Thomas O'Neil as the timekeeper.

The first two minutes of the first round looked more like a dance contest than a prizefight as the pair waltzed around each other, neither one throwing a punch until Ryan, breaking the stalemate, finally landed the first blow. Dempsey quickly swung back, striking Ryan in the neck. The round ended quickly and was judged a draw. The next five rounds were also fairly even and equally tame. At the end of the sixth, the combatants determined to pick up the pace and fight to the finish.

In the seventh round, Ryan caught Dempsey with several hard blows that rocked Jack. Many observers felt that the Philadelphian could have knocked Dempsey out if he had pressed his advantage, but he did not and Jack recovered quickly. Dempsey countered with several good shots as the round ended, doing just enough to earn another draw.

The men went to their respective corners to prepare for the eighth round, but it was not to be. Once again, the police intervened and called a halt to the match. Johnny Clark announced to the audience that Captain Emory of the Philadelphia police would not permit the fight to go any further. The disappointed crowd groaned, hissed and booed the constabulary, but nothing could be done, so, disappointedly, they left the theater. While many present felt that Jack should be declared the winner, the bout was ruled a draw and the men split a purse of $1,200 and the gate receipts.[60]

On September 23, Jack refereed a scheduled six-round glove bout between Tommy Barnes of Sheffield and Jem Mace's fighter known as the "Stiff Un." The match was to be fought under Queensberry Rules at Mike Cleary's Bowery Sporting house. After a rattling affair, this bout was stopped in the sixth round by Police Captain Murphy who believed that the "scientific sparring match" had gotten too physical. At this point Dempsey declared the contest a draw.[61]

After having now served as both referee and second in several bouts, Dempsey determined that he would prefer to work the corner in the future. Upon reflection, Jack stated, "I would not stand as referee for a glove contest again for $100. You cannot please both sides if you give a square decision."[62]

On October 6, Jack was on hand for the undercard at the Turn Halle on Fourth Street. The auditorium "was filled with spectators who were anxiously awaiting the advent of John L. Sullivan, who was to appear at the benefit tendered to Steve Taylor of New Jersey."

After an initial three-rounder between George Young and Joe Fowler, Dempsey met Tom Ferguson of Philadelphia. The fight was a hot one from the opening bell. In the first round, Jack was not expecting the hard fighting and firm rushes by Ferguson, who brought the battle to his opponent. Failing to adjust quickly enough, Jack simply fought on the defensive and the round went to the Philadelphian. During the break, however, he determined his plan of attack for the next chapter.

"In the second-round Dempsey made the boxing hot, letting go right and left handers on Ferguson, which staggered him and made him wince. The third one was a heavy one and when finished the honors were about equally divided."[63]

After five more bouts, including one that featured Denny Costigan and Pete McCoy, and a long wait, Master of Ceremonies Bob Smith told the crowd, "Gentlemen, Mr. John Sullivan promised Steve Taylor that he would appear positively tonight, but he is not here and therefore Mike Cleary will wind up with him." The crowd was disappointed in Sullivan's no-show, but thoroughly enjoyed the Cleary-Taylor bout.

Dempsey was now a red-hot commodity and his backers were determined to schedule a return match with Bob Turnbull. Turnbull had gained a favorable reputation as a fighter and had expressed great interest in meeting Dempsey again. Several sporting clubs offered to promote the fight, including the New York Athletic Club, who offered to put up a purse. Ultimately the bout was scheduled for October 8 at Billy Madden's Athletic Hall on Thirteenth Street in New York. Madden took swift action to book the bout, figuring that a match featuring Dempsey and the up-and-coming Turnbull would be a popular draw, and quickly arranged for the meeting to be held at his establishment.

According to the signed agreement, the men were to fight for a purse of $125 over eight rounds with soft gloves under the *Police Gazette* Revised Queensberry Rules. Ed Plummer was named referee and John Stack as timekeeper. Dempsey was the heavy favorite in the early betting. When the men entered the ring, all were reminded that Dempsey was taller, heavier and more muscular than his opponent. Dempsey was seconded by Tommy Ferguson and in an interesting twist his friend and sparring partner Denny Costigan was across the ring in Turnbull's corner.

Having met before, the men needed no time to size each other up and immediately went to work. Dempsey rushed Turnbull early in the first round and landed blows—a left to the stomach and a right to the ear that forced Turnbull against the ropes. Jack kept at his opponent like a man possessed and it appeared that he might finish Turnbull inside of the first round. Turnbull began to return punches, landing on Dempsey's midsection, but his blows did little damage. By the end of the round Turnbull's left eye was almost closed and twice he was saved from being knocked down by catching himself and leaning against the wall at the back of the stage.

Dempsey continued the onslaught as the second round began, firing a straight right mortar shot that exploded on Turnbull's nose, opening a free flow of blood that continued throughout the remainder of the fight. "Turnbull's time during the succeeding rounds was principally occupied in getting out of the way. Once in a while he got in some telling blows with his left, but Dempsey scarcely minded them."[64]

Dempsey completely dominated the first three rounds by staying active and clearly outfighting his opponent, but fighting at such an accelerated pace can have its demons. Dempsey found himself tired and winded as the referee called the men to fight in the fourth round, giving Turnbull and his supporters some hope that their man might stand a chance after all. Turnbull attempted to take advantage of Dempsey's exhaustion and make a showing, but he was simply too tired from the battering he had received to be effective. As a result, the fourth round was devoid of much action as Dempsey looked to catch an in-round breather and Turnbull tried and failed to press any advantage. The fighters circled and occasionally jabbed at each other, but that was all.

As the fifth round began both men sparred for wind, but Dempsey would periodically rush his opponent and drive him to the ropes. Turnbull absorbed terrific punishment, but his strong legs never failed him. He stayed upright throughout the Nonpareil's withering attacks, but few in attendance could understand how. Dempsey was fully in command but had pretty well fought himself out and was becoming so tired that Turnbull was able to duck and weave enough to avoid some of the blows and return a few punches on the slowing Dempsey.

By the end of the seventh round Turnbull was so tired and had absorbed so much punishment that he could hardly get to the stool in his corner. Much to the amazement of those in the hall, however, he recovered during the minute's rest—not enough to fight back, but enough to rise and take more punishment.

In the eighth and final round, Dempsey delivered blows that could be heard in the far corners of the hall. He played a drumbeat on Turnbull's head and stomach, landing when and where he chose. Still, Turnbull managed to stay on his feet until the final bell mercifully tolled the end of the one-sided affair. Referee Plummer immediately raised Dempsey's arm and declared him the winner.

As they left the ring, "both men were covered with blood which Turnbull alone had shed, and the nose and the mouth of the latter were swollen out of all shape, while Dempsey's only visible punishment was a broken tooth and a cut lip."[65] Though battered, bloody and bruised, Turnbull had proven to be a game competitor and a collection was taken up for him, "which netted $43."[66]

Turnbull would continue to fight professionally for a number of years to come. In addition to his two battles with Dempsey he "traveled over the country with John L. Sullivan, meeting all comers in short battles." Several reports about Turnbull having died during that tour came out in May 1887, but they proved to be erroneous.[67] The *New York Sun* reported that "Robert Turnbull, the clever middleweight boxer and sporting reporter, who has been traveling with the John L. Sullivan combination of athletes, did not die, as reported in Logansport, Indiana. He reached this city yesterday morning only the worse by an injured hand. The Sullivan party, he says, is doing a good business."[68]

His fighting career closed after his defeat by (Johnny) Reagan at Rochester.[69] After he left the ring, Turnbull made one of the more successful and noteworthy transitions from boxing to life after the ring. He became a sportswriter, boxing instructor for the Boston Athletic Association and then entered the real estate business. All things appeared to be going well for the former prize fighter when suddenly, tragedy struck.

Turnbull's life came to an unfortunate end when he shot himself at his Brooklyn home on August 6, 1908, in what was determined to be "a fit of insanity, due to the intense heat of the last three days." According to a statement from business partner Joseph A. Wheelock, "he had no reason for taking his life. He was in his forty-fifth year and enjoyed excellent health."[70] We may never know the reason for Bob choosing to end his own life, but something was clearly and desperately wrong with the former fighter.

On October 21, Jack met Tommy Ferguson on a mixed undercard in the Germania Assembly Rooms in Manhattan's Bowery section. The headliner of the evening was a bout between Jack Burke and Charley Mitchell in which referee John Scanlan claimed that Burke drew with Mitchell over four rounds despite the fact that Burke clearly got the better of the Englishman. Mitchell refused to fight the fifth round and Scanlan called the fight over and even, but Burke and his corner and most of the three thousand on hand protested this decision. Due to the limited size of the stage, the ring that evening was restricted to an extremely tight twelve-by-fifteen feet in size.

Regardless of the cozy ring, "the entertainment preceding the great event was much better than usual at such matches and included collar and elbow wrestling between Joe Ryan and his protégé Carroll, the lifting of 500-pound dumb-bells by Loennenwein, the "Swiss giant," and another Switzer, boxing by Bob Turnbull and Billy Gregg, Jack Dempsey and Tommy Ferguson, George Taylor and Eddy Grohan and Greco-Roman wrestling between the middleweight champion James Faulkner and the lightweight champion Benny Jones who defeated the Jap Sorahichi."[71]

On October 24, Dempsey climbed back into the ring for a return bout with Tom Henry for a scheduled six-round glove contest at Jack Thompson's Eighth Street Theatre in New York. Each side was set to receive a purse of $1,000 and the winner would also take the gate receipts. A large and diverse crowd assembled at the theatre, "from swell young men about town who wore evening dress, crush hats, and opera coats, down to dance hall bouncers" and "Bowery roughs and prize fighters from the dives" who tried to slip in unnoticed or begged admission from the doormen.[72]

The fight was scheduled to take place after the theatre's evening performance, but the crowd arrived early, filling the theatre beyond capacity. Men with nowhere to sit filled the lobby, the galleries and stood in the aisles.

"Women in gorgeous attire looked over the rails of the boxes, gamblers, men about town, police court clerks, dudes, merchants, and brokers occupied the orchestra chairs, and throngs of waiters forced a passage between them and did a heavy business in liquors and cigars, while an unprepossessing crowd of ruffians circulated between the bar, to the left of the auditorium, and the lobbies and galleries."[73]

The crowd was animated but in a good mood and they grew restless for the fight to begin. Liquor exacerbated their impatience and they made the performers' jobs difficult. A tenor was booed off the stage while a lovely young woman in a very short skirt and blue tights was encored several times until she finally wore out. A gentleman attempting a dramatic recitation was ridiculed and drowned out with shouts and boos. When the leading lady in the evening's main skit made her entrance, she was cheered repeatedly and was frequently forced to stop her lines and acknowledge the audience. In short order, an exasperated John Thompson, the proprietor of the theatre, announced that the performance was concluded. This news was greeted with general shouts of "Good!" and shortly after 10:00 p.m., preparations for the bout were begun.

The ring was quickly set up on the stage and shortly before 10:30 p.m., the fighters appeared. They were met with wild shouts and applause. The fight was a scheduled six-rounder to be fought with gloves under Queensberry Rules; the winner would take sixty-five percent of the gate and the loser the remaining thirty-five. Al Smith was chosen as the referee for the bout and William E. Harding, the sporting editor of the *Police Gazette*, and Mike McDonald, a noted banker and political operative from Chicago, were named timekeepers. Noted British pugilist Walter Watson seconded Dempsey and Mike Cleary seconded Henry.

As the fight began, Henry astonished the crowd by putting the Nonpareil on the floor early. While this early success emboldened Henry, the net result was to prove a disadvantage for the Englishman. The shock of the blow angered Dempsey, who quickly gathered himself and returned fire, landing hard combinations to his opponent's body and head and one squarely on Henry's nose to draw first blood. Overall the first round was fairly even with perhaps a slight nod to the Briton. And while Jack made a solid showing of himself after the knock-down, many in the crowd were convinced that Dempsey could not stand up to the larger man for a full six rounds.

From the second round on there was little for Henry or his backers to feel good about. Dempsey wasted little time in taking command by knocking his opponent down thrice. Those who questioned Dempsey were shocked when he came out at the start of the second round and connected powerfully to Henry's head, sending the Briton staggering and leaving him wobbly for most of the rest of the round. Dempsey took full advantage of his opponent's weakness and hammered away at both body and head with heavy blows. One reporter may have put it best when he commented that "the remaining rounds were a repetition of the disasters to Henry"[74]

During the break Henry righted himself and at the start of the third round showed resilience, looking confident and fresher than Dempsey, who had done virtually all of the work in the previous round. The two sparred briefly, with Henry landing a few tepid blows, when suddenly Dempsey waded into Henry and threw a punch that landed to the body. As Henry attempted to counter, he fell short of his mark and, losing his balance, landed on the floor. As Henry scrambled to his feet, the Nonpareil launched a beautiful straight missile from his shoulder that knocked his opponent flat. Henry rose again, but once more, Dempsey set him down, this time with "a blow under the chin that made Henry's teeth chatter, after which he drew blood from the Englishman's nose and drove him all about the stage, while the spectators went wild with enthusiasm."[75]

The fourth round saw Dempsey force the fighting, driving his opponent all over the ring and eventually knocking Henry down near the stage footlights. The Briton was only stopped from falling off the stage and into the orchestra pit by the presence of mind of the gentleman who played the bass violin. Again, Henry returned to the ring and again Jack went on the attack, leaving Henry's face terribly swollen, bruised and bloody by the end of the round.

The fifth round was virtually all Dempsey as Jack landed blow after punishing blow on the British fighter. Again and again Jack would land a combination and jump back, leaving Henry short on his returns. Jack scored repeatedly on Henry's nose, ears and mouth, staggering his opponent and leaving him groggy, but not quite knocking him off his feet.

The last round was no better for Henry. While he came out looking fresh and landed a few strong blows, it was far too little to make any impact on the outcome of the fight. The action was fast, with Dempsey delivering the more gruesome punishment on his opponent and leaving absolutely no doubt as to who the victor of the bout would be. When time was called, Jack was tired only from beating on his opponent, while Henry was a bruised, swollen and bloody mess. Referee Smith raised Jack's hand in victory and awarded him the fight. He had, in the words of one newspaper, "pummeled Henry for six rounds beyond all recognition."[76]

The two men would soon become close friends and would continue to climb into the ring with each other over the next few years, once more in a competitive bout and several more times in exhibitions.

On November 4, after a particularly nasty, mudslinging presidential campaign, New York's Democratic Governor Grover Cleveland defeated Republican James G. Blaine by a paper-thin margin of just 23,005 popular votes. New York decided the election, with Cleveland carrying the Empire State by barely 1,000 votes of the nearly 1.2 million cast. New York's thirty-six electoral votes went to Cleveland, enabling him to win the all-important Electoral College vote and the first of his two non-consecutive terms.

On November 6, Jack met New York lightweight Tommy Ferguson at Harry Hill's Theatre for a token city championship. The bout had been promoted in the *National Police Gazette* in the weeks leading up to the contest. "At Harry Hill's theatre on Thursday afternoon November 6 there will be a series of glove contests for a beautiful trophy and open to all the lightweight champion pugilists. The conditions will be four rounds, Queensberry rules. It is expected Jimmy Murray, Tom Henry, Paddy Lee, Jack Dempsey, Tommy Ferguson and a host of other lightweights will compete for the trophy. By permission of Richard K. Fox, Alf Greenfield will be referee."[77]

The contest was agreed to be fought under Queensberry Rules for the local lightweight championship, $200 and a *Police Gazette* champion gold medal.[78] Rather than Greenfield, the host Harry Hill was selected as the referee. Greenfield, the noted British pugilist, and William Harding of the *Police Gazette* acted as timekeepers.

The bout was set for four rounds and lasted just fifteen minutes. According to the *Police Gazette* report, Ferguson was selected to box Dempsey due to his high level of skill. During the fight, "Ferguson displayed good science and in the first three rounds divided the honors equally with his game and clever antagonist. In the last round Dempsey's long reach, cool tactics and ability to use both hands with equal skill, gave him the advantage."[79]

The two would meet again just four days later in an exhibition at Madison Square Garden, where 8,000 fans watched the pair spar four rounds.

On November 20, Jack met Billy Frazier of Boston in a bare-knuckle contest to the finish. Frazier, who taught boxing and self-defense in Cambridge, Massachusetts, at Harvard University, claimed the New England middleweight championship and had been after a fight with Jack for a while. The Racquet Club of New York was anxious to sponsor the match and put up the initial $500 purse for the bout, which was arranged just three days before the fight was to be held. The fight was to adhere to the Queensberry Rules, but it was agreed that no gloves would be used.

Frazier was accompanied to New York by Colonel Tom Early "and their errand was ostensibly to witness the Sullivan-Greenfield match, but in reality, to see if Boston's lightweight couldn't beat Dempsey, who has fought fifteen battles without ever being defeated."[80]

In the days before the bout, Frazier, either supremely confident that he would beat Jack or engaging in a bit of 1880s trash-talk, wrote Dempsey a letter in which he recommended that the Nonpareil take out an accident insurance policy.

The bout was kept a secret until the day of the fight. Rumors circulated that a prize-fight would take place, but when, where and even who the pugilists would be was kept as quiet as possible. In speaking of the fight's financial backers, the sports, and the newspaper men who wanted to be present, one news report stated, "For three days past these men have all been worked up. They knew that $250 had been subscribed by members of the Racquet Club, and that two lightweights were to fight to a finish for the money, the winner to take $175 and the loser $75. But only a few knew who was to fight or where it was to be. The match was finally set down for early yesterday morning, and happy faces were to be seen late on Wednesday night strung along on various corners of Sixth Avenue waiting for the tip."[81]

Armed with the information of the fight's whereabouts, the men descended on the Alhambra Theatre. The *New York Times* reported the scene as follows: "There is a pleasant little roadhouse on a secluded thoroughfare in the western part of the city which is a favorite resort of the sporting fraternity. Very early yesterday morning numbers of carriages, coupes, and cabs drove up to this hostelry, and men of various descriptions descended from them."[82] It was a cold, wet night, but the lucky fans that each paid the ten-dollar admission did not seem to mind. Reports state that between eighty and one hundred persons attended, including John L. Sullivan, Professor Mike Donovan, Denny Costigan and lightweight champion Frank White.

Inside the west side venue, beer, wine and liquor flowed freely. The attendees were repeatedly warned to keep the noise down for fear of rousing the suspicion of the guileless policemen patrolling the streets outside. "Hush, hush, gentlemen: if you will make a noise the entertainment won't take place."[83]

Dempsey and Frazier were present on an upstairs balcony where they mixed with a large delegation from the Racquet Club and other notables, including Sullivan.

At twenty minutes past midnight the fighters and their seconds entered the ring. Jack was wearing his familiar blue tights with blue socks while Frazier was clad in white. Al Power, Frank White, and George Tuttle were in Dempsey's corner while Nobby Clark and Tom Early seconded Frazier. Although it had been agreed upon earlier that no gloves would be used, the *New York Sun* reported that small, hard gloves were then put on each man's hands. The hardware was calculated to make the men hit harder as they feared less damage to their hands. The pugilists were described by the *Sun* reporter as follows: "Frazier is short and stout, with heavy calves and a deep chest. He wore a light moustache and smiled confidently. Dempsey, on the other hand, is slender and taller than his opponent, but he has long, powerful arms, well knitted into his shoulders, and his smooth face wore a determined look that meant business."[84]

After announcing to the crowd that the fight would follow the Queensberry Rules and that the men would fight "until one of them was unable to fight any more," referee Ed Plummer signaled timekeeper Walter De Braun as he called time at 1:00 o'clock.

Frazier, after a little sparring between the two men, struck out, landing a solid blow to Dempsey's stomach. Jack responded in kind, landing a terrific left to Frazier's upper cheek and opening up a cut under the left eye that drew first blood. The blood angered Frazier, who let go a flurry of wild punches while charging Dempsey. Frazier continued to take the initiative throughout the round, rushing Jack and trying to land, but Dempsey still controlled the action. "The left was used by Dempsey continually with great force; every blow he gave with it seeming to make his opponent's head swim."[85] Frazier launched a hard punch at Dempsey's face, but Jack deftly blocked the missile with his right arm while countering with his left and striking a vicious blow to his opponent's neck that sent Frazier staggering and the small crowd cheering as the first round came to an end. The men had both fought viciously.

After the break, Frazier seemed sharp and rested. He was warier as the round began, looking for an opening and waiting more patiently than he had in the first round. Jack was less cautious and Frazier caught Dempsey twice in rapid succession with severe blows to the head that left the New Yorker dazed for a few seconds. But it was only a temporary setback as Jack quickly shook off the cobwebs and lit out against his foe, pummeling him with hard combinations that drew blood from Frazier's nose and opened a second cut on his cheek.

"Frazier made a 'Sullivan Rush' when time was called for the third round, but Dempsey threw up his guard and seized him about the neck to save himself from falling, and as they separated he struck Frazier a fearful blow in the face that landed him against the ropes."[86]

Showing the signs of wear, Frazier began the fourth round cautiously. Dempsey fired off a shot aimed at the New Englander's head, which Frazier dodged. Frazier countered with several heavy blows to Dempsey's face, but that was really all he had left. Jack shook off the punches and launched a right uppercut that landed squarely on his opponent's nose. He then began a concentrated attack on Frazier's body that so wore Frazier down that he was clearly spent and the New Englander staggered back to his corner at the break. According to a *New York Sun* reporter, Frazier told his second, Nobby Clark, in his corner after the fourth round, "He's too big for me. I've got to give up."[87]

Frazier "was scarcely able to stand at the beginning of the fifth round and gave up the fight after receiving one or two more blows, which he was powerless to return."[88] Clark then determined to stop the fight and threw in the sponge. Plummer waived his arms signifying an end to the bout and Clark entered the ring to assist his exhausted and badly beaten fighter back to his stool. The *Police Gazette*, while describing it as a "slashing glove contest," noted that the entire bout last just over ten minutes.[89]

After the bout ended, the spectators crowded around Dempsey, who showed no visible signs of a fight on his face or body. They congratulated him as they filed out and quietly dispersed into the night air. "Old time ring-goers say it was one of the best glove fights they ever saw in this country."[90]

The fighters quickly dressed and exited the Alhambra Theatre. Frazier, his face badly cut and bruised, went to his hotel for a short rest and then was on the first train back to Boston with his trainer Tom Early. "Dempsey looked himself over carefully in the glass after the fight and turning to his backer Gus Tuthill, he said with a smile, 'I fought carefully, as I did not want to get a black eye, as I have got an engagement to take my intended wife to a ball tonight.'"[91] Jack then slipped out of the side door and left for Brooklyn by carriage with Tuthill and Frank White.

Jack was in demand and had a full dance card by the end of 1884. He finished out the year with several sparring exhibitions and two bouts, the first on November 30 in Philadelphia versus Mike Mallon. The match was billed as a gloved fight under Queensberry Rules for the lightweight championship of Philadelphia. Mallon had reportedly won that championship in a recent sparring tournament promoted by local boxing instructor Professor John Clark.[92] The purse for this bout was set at $150 a side and the winner would also take the collected gate receipts. The contest was scheduled for the middle of the night and the specific location was only mentioned as "a well-known sporting house in the eastern part of the city"[93] and "the second story of a building in [Philadelphia] last night."[94]

The fighters entered the ring at five minutes to 1:00 a.m. and referee Henry Rice instructed the men to fight just minutes later. Dempsey wasted little time in claiming the prize as he got the better of his opponent early and often, the whole bout taking fewer than ten minutes. The first round opened slowly with each fighter cautiously eyeing his opponent and waiting for an opening. Dempsey finally led with his left and landed hard upon Mallon's stomach, causing the Philadelphian to gasp. Jack followed up with a series of effective blows to Mallon's ribs and stomach. Soon Mallon looked tired and began to clinch as long as the referee would allow. By the end of the round, Mallon had landed only one clean and solid blow and he had to be helped to his corner.[95] The round was entirely in Dempsey's favor.

As time was called for the second round, Mallon struggled to his feet and came to scratch clearly shaken. He complained of a queasy stomach from the punishment he took in the first round and probably from swallowing blood, but his backers pushed him back into the ring. Jack picked up where he left off in the first by working his opponent's body and landing heavily on his ribs and stomach. Mallon could do nothing on the offensive and could barely defend himself. Dempsey began slugging and punished Mallon terribly. "The round had lasted a minute only when Dempsey struck his opponent a powerful blow in the mouth, knocking him down." The round ended and Mallon was helped to his feet by his backers, but as he was woozy and could barely stand, it was doubtful that he could fight on.[96]

His seconds did all they could to ready their man to resume fighting, but after receiving a terrible pounding for two rounds, a dazed Mallon commented that he was not in condition to fight and could not answer the referee's call for the third chapter. Still standing in his corner, but propped up by the ropes, Mallon asked Jack if he would consent to fight some other time. "Dempsey replied in the affirmative and the men shook hands, and Mallon was helped out. The fight was given to Dempsey."[97]

Richard Fox tells a funny story about Dempsey's encounter with a New Yorker named Charles E. Baker, who met Jack in Manhattan one day and mistook him for an out-of-town visitor from the country and offered to show him around the city. Jack, who had a mischievous side and always enjoyed a good joke, introduced himself as "Josiah Ripton" of Wappingers Falls, New York, a scenic town on the east side of the Hudson River just south of Poughkeepsie. The pair had several drinks which Jack paid for by pulling out the wad of bills he won in Philadelphia by defeating Mallon.

Baker began showing his friend "Mr. Ripton" around town and in the course of conversation Baker mentioned that he was a fan of prizefighting and quite a good boxer at that. Jack knew that things were about to get very funny when Baker asked if he had ever seen the *Police Gazette* offices. "Ripton" replied that he had not and the pair proceeded on. When they arrived, Baker began showing Jack pictures of Sullivan and other fighters and explaining the finer points of the sport. When they encountered several men who knew Dempsey, Jack whispered to them to keep quiet as Baker introduced the men to his friend "Ripton."

The two then proceeded to Brooklyn where "Ripton" said he had to meet a friend. Baker asked to borrow some money. When they reached Williamsburg, they proceeded to Joe Heiser's saloon where they again spoke of boxing. The faux countryman told Heiser that Baker was anxious to give him a boxing lesson. Heiser, playing along, told the two to go upstairs to his gym and have Baker teach "Ripton" how to box. Several other men gathered in the gymnasium to watch—and laugh along. Jack pretended to be baffled at first and let Baker land a few punches. Jack played along but could barely contain his smile. Suddenly, "Ripton" put up his fists and planted a driving left into Baker's stomach followed by a rapid right to the lower jaw, knocking his friend to the floor. "When Baker came to his senses he was surprised to learn that the man he was trying to teach how to box was Jack Dempsey, and he left Williamsburg a sadder and wiser man."[98] Apocryphal or not, it is a great story and one quite true to the playful spirit of the champ.

On December 9, Jack engaged in the first of many sparring sessions with Denny Costigan. As mentioned, Costigan had been trying to meet Dempsey in the ring for the past year and during this time the two had begun what would remain a lifelong friendship, but this would be their first meeting in the ring. The event was set as a four-round session in New York City in front of a large audience at the Alhambra at 108 West Eighteenth Street. The exhibition was the main event at a benefit tendered in Costigan's honor and was described in the *Police Gazette* as a "treat" and "a rattling set-to."[99]

On the evening of December 15, Dempsey was back in Philadelphia, this time at the theater at Arthur Chambers's Champion's Rest on Ridge Avenue. The evening was billed as a benefit for Dempsey. "The noted sporting house was packed" as news spread that Dempsey would be in the ring that night. Jack was set to face England's George Wilson in a four-round battle for a $200 prize and gate receipts. To win, Jack had to knock Wilson out or win by stoppage. Jack was never a good short-fight man and although he fought quite well, he could not finish his opponent in the allotted four rounds and the bout was decided as a draw. Reports on Jack's inability to finish his opponent that night stated that "Dempsey was unable to fill the contract. Wilson proved he was a hummer."[100] Some reports indicate that at the end of the fourth round Philadelphia Police Captain Emory brought a halt to the bout which was then declared a draw, but as the bout was only scheduled for four, that would have seemed unnecessary unless the fourth round ended early. It was also reported that the purse and the gate receipts were evenly divided, but that Wilson only came away with $30 to $36 from the purse.[101] Wilson was a nephew of Tug Wilson, notable British pugilist from Leicestershire.

Also on the night's card was a bout between Bill Gabig, "The Mysterious Fighter" from Pittsburgh, and Denny Kelliher. Gabig was referred to in some reports as George Gobig, but this was actually Gabig in one of his early bouts. The heavyweights administered some tremendous punishment on each other for two savage rounds, but again Captain Emory intervened and ended the bout prematurely.[102]

Back in Brooklyn the next evening, Dempsey spoke about the fight as he played pool with Thomas Maher in John C. Eagan's billiards parlor on North Second and Sixth streets. Jack expressed frustration with the draw. "I was pained," commented Dempsey. "I am able to best Wilson just as I did best him last night, and just as the Philadelphia papers report that I did."[103]

Dempsey was beginning to make his forays into life outside of the prize ring and was endeavoring to invest his winnings wisely. On December 18 the *Boston Globe* reported that Jack bought Billy Madden's "sporting resort" at 120 East Thirteenth Street in Manhattan "and will endeavor to become expert in mixing drinks."[104] A grand opening was set for January 12.

On December 19, Harry Hill's place hosted a benefit for champion wrestler Steve O'Donnell. Several wrestling and boxing matches were held, including one in which

Jack's brother Martin competed. Jack also participated, sparring three "hot" exhibition rounds with Tommy Ferguson.[105]

As the year began to grind to a close it had to be considered a great success for Dempsey, who had proven himself an able, tough and durable fighter who had begun to garner the attention of the sporting community. Jack's backer Gus Tuthill continually published offers to match him against "any lightweight pugilist in the world"[106] and sportswriters were now not only reporting on the results of Jack's fights in their columns but previewing his upcoming engagements and speculating on outcomes. Comments such as one regarding a potential bout between Dempsey and Canadian pugilist George La Blanche talked about the conditions of the contest. La Blanche, nicknamed "The Marine," was taller and almost twenty pounds heavier than Jack, but most observers believed that Dempsey would be able to conquer him. One reporter from the *Police Gazette* wrote, "Dempsey will have to give away nearly twenty-pounds avoirdupois for his fighting weight is 133 pounds while in condition. La Blanche will weigh 149 pounds. I think Dempsey will win, but it will be the hardest battle he ever fought."[107] This was the first time that La Blanche's name would be linked to Dempsey's, but it would not be the last. The Marine and the Nonpareil would be connected for the rest of their lives.

1885—A Full Dance Card

Jack opened 1885 with a series of exhibitions in New York. On January 12 Jack hosted a card of fights at Athletic Hall, his recently purchased Manhattan club. During the evening, the host sparred two four-round exhibitions with Billy Frazier and Jimmy Ryan. The event was to celebrate the re-opening of what had been Billy Madden's Athletic Hall, located at 120 East Thirteenth Street in Manhattan, which he had just bought from Madden in December. A large crowd paid the one-dollar admission and came out to drink, see the bouts and to help christen the newly re-launched establishment. Dempsey would put on several evenings of fight cards in January, during which the Nonpareil played a variety of roles, from host to referee to timekeeper to pugilist.

After several preliminaries on January 12, Master of Ceremonies Joe Murphy introduced Jack and Billy Frazier, the lightweight champion of New England whom Dempsey had recently defeated on November 24. "Both were cheered when they mounted the stage." The men had a "hot, but very scientific set-to" over the four rounds and although Frazier was the acknowledged weaker of the two at the finish, referee Billy Madden called the bout a draw. The *Police Gazette* reported that "four rounds were boxed and both pugilists hit quick and hard, but at the conclusion the contest was considered about even."[1] After this contest—their second in as many months—Dempsey had this to say about the boxing instructor from Harvard College: "[He] is the best boxer I ever met. He is quick as a flash and a hard hitter. He is the only man I have stood before who could hit me and get away without a return blow." Referring to their first bout the previous November, Dempsey said, "He just beat a tattoo on my face until I could see about a dozen Billy Fraziers before me, but in the fourth round I got him into a corner and would not let him come out."[2]

After several more bouts, Dempsey entered the ring again to contend with Pennsylvania middleweight champion Jimmy Ryan. It was now well after midnight so the official date was January 13. The two pugilists had previously met in September in Philadelphia, battling tooth and nail in a police-interrupted, seven-round draw. A fair number in the crowd believed that Dempsey would have a difficult time with Ryan after he had already fought four taxing rounds with Frazier. Others knew better than to doubt Dempsey's skill and stamina even as he entered into his second bout of the evening.

The bout began around 1:00 a.m. at a hot pace as the men "fairly slaughtered each other" over the first three minutes.[3] The second round was largely uneventful as the pair sparred lightly. Jack had apparently hurt his right hand in the earlier bout with Frazier and hardly used it during most of those two chapters, but "in the third round he hit Ryan a counter blow with his right on the nose so vigorously that Ryan's head went back and

Billy Madden called time." Dempsey repeated this blow in the fourth round, knocking Ryan backwards against the wall of the saloon, "and when time was called it was evident that Ryan would presently have been a beaten man if time had not been called."[4] While this bout was technically ruled a draw, it was clear to those present that Dempsey was the winner.

The evening's entertainment was given an official okay by the local constabulary. After the last contest, New York City Police Captain McCullough, who was on hand throughout the evening, commented that he enjoyed the contests and especially Dempsey's two bouts. "I never saw any boxing matches that I liked better than those two and I saw nothing that was in violation of law."[5] Each fight netted Jack $200 plus he received the gate receipts.

Dempsey (right) in his bout against Jimmy Ryan.

Throughout early and mid–January, there was a great deal of rumor that John L. Sullivan and his backer Pat Sheedy were endeavoring to set up a tour of England, Scotland, Wales and Ireland in the spring and summer. Dempsey and Pete McCoy were also rumored to be traveling with the tour, sparring and giving boxing demonstrations. They would then sail for Australia for a similar tour and return to the United States sometime in late December or early January. Like so many other rumored events and tours, this one was just talk and it never came off.

Dempsey did attend a meeting between John L. Sullivan and Paddy Ryan in New York's Madison Square Garden on January 19. Dempsey was on hand along with a host of dignitaries that included Richard Fox, Harry Hill, Mike Donovan, Pete McCoy, Parson Davies and other boxing lights. Pete McCoy and Mike Gillespie opened the evening with an exciting three-round match. Thousands of fight fans continued to pour into the Garden as late as 9:00 p.m., each with the anticipation of seeing a first-class bout. They were to be disappointed, though, for no more than a minute into the first round, "Inspector Thorne jumped over the ropes, followed by Captain Williams and the two with uplifted clubs, separated the combatants." The men were forced to their respective corners and their gloves stripped off. No arrests were made, but the crowd was dispersed and no prizefighting would occur that evening.[6]

Dempsey chalked up a win versus John Banks on January 21 and he scored another victory over Jim Fell in four rounds the next day. A tremendous crowd had assembled at Dempsey's place to see Fell meet Bill Glynn, but when Glynn failed to show up, Jack agreed to stand in. Fell, who outweighed Dempsey by almost thirty-five pounds, was described as "a large muscular man, five feet eight inches tall and weighing about 180 pounds."[7] Fell claimed the middleweight championship of Canada. The two fought a soft-glove contest with Billy Madden acting as the referee. The bout was a fierce one with both men giving it their all for four rounds. "In the last round Fell dashed at Dempsey and planted several blows on the ribs. Dempsey got home with the left and right, the latter's fist landing on Fell's ear." The men then began to grapple, with Fell trying to throw Jack with a hip-lock, but Dempsey wriggled away from his larger opponent. During the struggle the men crashed together to the ground. Rising quickly, they immediately resumed the melee. After a sharp exchange of blows Dempsey rushed Fell and was able to throw the larger man to the mat. Madden then called the fight in favor of Dempsey saying, "It was a fierce contest and while Fell showed himself to be a gamey fighter, Dempsey outmatched him in science."[8] In being awarded the decision, Jack pocketed a $200 purse.

On January 26, Dempsey defeated an aspiring fighter named Jack Fay in a glove contest at his new venue. Fay, of Rockville, Connecticut, was a tall, powerful man who had shown some athletic promise, but still had little experience in prizefighting. He was being groomed by backers and had been sent to New York for a trial with Billy Madden to see if he stood any chance in a match against Madden's former pupil, John L. Sullivan. Madden figured that if the Connecticut man could stand up to Dempsey, he might stand a chance against Sullivan. Dempsey quickly disposed of the New Englander, showing that at least for the present, John L. had no reason to fear Jack Fay.[9] Fay squared off with Jim Fell a few days after meeting Dempsey and again lost in three rounds, with Fell dropping Fay to the floor twice during the contest. Fay would fight for a couple more years, meeting such men as Mike Cleary and George Godfrey, but his luck never got much better. Sullivan could rest easy.

On the January 30, Dempsey once again hosted a number of bouts at his saloon in New York. The loosely arranged evening started out with several amateur contests, but it was headlined by a one-sided, four-round contest in which colored lightweight champion Tommy Banks manhandled Jimmy Connors; a rousing six rounder between Jim McHugh and Joe Wannop which ended in a draw even after a seventh round was added; and a final bout between Jim Fell and Tommy Banks, who, in an encore match, put on the gloves at the request of the crowd who was clamoring to see another bout. In what was described as a desperate fight, the bout ended in the second round after Banks, twenty pounds lighter than his opponent, forced the fighting and knocked Fell down. Fell then withdrew, claiming that his wrist had been injured when he landed. Since he could not continue, Banks was declared the winner and took the purse. The Nonpareil acted not only as the host, but also as the referee and timekeeper for all bouts.[10]

On February 10, Jack met Joe Heiser in Brooklyn for the second time in a year. The pair had met the previous April, when they fought to an eight-round draw. The *Boston Globe* reported on the rematch as follows: "The last number on the programme was a scientific set-to for points between Jack Dempsey and Joe Heiser, the amateur champion of that city. It was an eight-round contest and is said to have been one of the finest and most scientific exhibitions of boxing ever seen in that section. The fighting was lively throughout and at long range Dempsey had the best of it, while in short arm work, Heiser did some remarkably fine work."[11] The decision was awarded to the Nonpareil.

In February, Dempsey decided to expand his already growing reputation by taking his show on the road. He spent the month traveling from north to south and from coast to coast making and accepting challenges from lightweights and middleweights all across the country. On February 26, Jack left Brooklyn on his way to New Orleans. He was accompanied by Jake Stearns, his manager. This trip would have a profound and permanent effect on Jack's life as he was to fall in love with both the West Coast and the enchanting Margaret Brady, the woman who would become his wife.

Before leaving for the Crescent City, Jack and Billy Madden hosted a tournament for amateur lightweight fighters at his Athletic Hall on February 19 and 20. His intention was to support and promote amateur pugilism with a contest of fighters and award the winner with a gold medal valued at $150. The event attracted sixteen boxers who each fought four rounds under Queensberry Rules. Dempsey served as both referee and timekeeper for all bouts. The most notable bouts of the two-evening event involved a young Jack McAuliffe, who out-landed his opponent Harry Isaacs by a lopsided eighteen punches on the first night and controlled fellow Brooklynite John Ruddy from start to finish on the second night. Dempsey called the fight in favor of McAuliffe, who took home the gold medal.[12] Isaacs and Ruddy were both game, but it was clear that McAuliffe was something special, a point that he would prove repeatedly as a professional and lightweight champion for many years to come.

Dempsey and Stearns left Brooklyn on February 26 but detoured through Chicago on their way to New Orleans. The two men arrived in the Windy City on the last day of February and were in town to put out feelers for fights for Jack. A possible bout with Johnny Files was talked about and, in a letter to prominent Chicago fight promoter Parson Davies, Jack stated that he was anxious to meet Files, Tommy Chandler or any reputable lightweight or middleweight in a five- or six-round glove contest.

On March 2, Dempsey seconded Frank Glover, "an ambitious and strong young boxer of the South Side," in his bout with Chicago middleweight Tommy Chandler.[13] During this era promising young prizefighters on their way up took every opportunity to make their names known and to catch the eye of fight promoters and managers. Dempsey was no exception. In these early years Jack was well known in the Northeast, but he was still building his name and reputation as a fighter beyond. Boxing historian Mark Dunn commented,

> It is helpful to see who he associated with and where he was at various times. These fighters were often on the move and would need to show up at the biggest fights because that is where the managers and promoters were and where the planning for future matches often began. Using these fighters to work in a corner was a way for the promoters to pay the traveling expenses for up and coming fighters and to get them in front of the public.[14]

In a testament to prizefighting's growing popularity, a crowd of eight thousand packed Chicago's Battery "D" Armory on the night of the Glover-Chandler fight, while an estimated two thousand more were turned away. In the fourth round, Glover delivered a powerful combination that stunned his opponent. As the *Chicago Tribune* reported, "When struck Chandler stiffened as though electrified and the next moment crashed to the floor and lay perfectly motionless." Referee C.C. Corbett of Philadelphia immediately declared Glover the victor.[15]

Jack and Stearns left Chicago for New Orleans by train on the evening of March 3.

After two days of travel they reached the Crescent City. Dempsey immediately found it to his liking. Shortly after his arrival, he and Stearns went about setting up fights. A bout with noted local ring man Charles Bixamos was quickly arranged as were tentative plans for a bout with Tom Dougherty. Jack also was anxious to meet Jack Burke, the "Irish Lad," if it could be arranged. In a letter to the editor of the *Chicago Herald* dated March 13, Dempsey stated that he would gladly meet the much larger Burke, winner take all, for a four- to eight-round glove contest under Queensberry Rules.[16] Many thought it unwise of Jack as the twenty-pound weight disadvantage he would have might prove too much to overcome. Ultimately, plans for the bout were set aside for at least another year and a half, when the pair would fight a ten-round draw at the Mechanics' Pavilion in San Francisco.

Jack met Bixamos on March 19 at Sportsman's Park in New Orleans in a gloved bout fought under the Queensberry Rules. As prizefighting was accepted by most officials in New Orleans, the city had become a popular destination for the boxing fraternity. Since there was virtually no fear of police interference, fights were very well publicized, producing larger crowds and gate receipts. Publicity and the fact that this bout was set to begin at the civilized hour of five in the evening made it a popular ticket. The match was for $500 a side and a split of the gate receipts. With roughly a thousand spectators in attendance, the receipts looked to be high. The betting before the fight was running in favor of Dempsey at 4 to 1.

Charley Bixamos, who resided in the Crescent City, was a locally noted wrestler who engaged periodically and somewhat successfully in prizefights. He had met J.G. Scott twice in the past four weeks, defeating him in four rounds each time. He had also lost on a foul to Ned Lester the previous February when after two warnings for hitting his opponent while down, referee Jere Dunn called a halt to the fight and awarded Lester the win. Bixamos stood about 5'9" and weighed between 155 and 165 pounds when in fighting trim.

Bixamos was the first man in the ring that evening and Dempsey soon followed. As was common in the day, each man had their own timekeeper, Tom Dougherty and John Duffy for Dempsey and Bixamos, respectively. Jack weighed in at 142 pounds before the fight and Bixamos eleven pounds more.

Jere Dunn was chosen as referee and Arthur Chambers as timekeeper. Dunn announced the rules and conditions of the contest and then introduced the fighters to the large and excited audience, who cheered loudly. After the introductions, the fighters prepared for the bout, each stripping to the waist and wearing tights and fighting shoes. Charley was outfitted in flesh-colored tights and black boxing shoes with Jack wearing his customary dark blue tights. Both men appeared to be in excellent condition. Many in the crowd unfamiliar with the Brooklyn man felt that Bixamos would defeat Dempsey simply due to the size differential. Bob Steele, a lightweight out of Philadelphia, was Bixamos's second while George Rooke filled that role for Dempsey.

As referee Dunn called a start to the bout, the men moved toward center, shook hands and then squared off. They moved cautiously, sparring a little and feeling each other out. Suddenly, Dempsey moved forward and landed a hard left to Bixamos's chest then moved back out of range as quickly as he had advanced. The Nonpareil was trying to lure Charley into rushing him, but Bixamos, sensing a trap, was not taking the bait. Jack began to work his way back in, but this time the Louisianan struck, landing an overhand blow to Dempsey's neck. More sparring from a distance occurred followed by a clinch and some infighting. Bixamos began to pound his opponent's ribs repeatedly until Dempsey broke loose and backed away. At the break, Jack landed a jab on Bixamos's face. Again, they clinched and Charley went back to work on Dempsey's ribs. The two men broke and Jack backed away. After a few seconds, he rushed Bixamos while in a low crouching stance and delivered a powerful left on his opponent's stomach. Bixamos recoiled, but quickly caught his breath and pursued Jack, landing a glancing blow on the Nonpareil's nose. The men then fell again into a clinch. When separated, Charley swung at Jack, but came up short and with this, the round ended.

The second round saw many strong exchanges by the pair—Dempsey landing on Bixamos's face and Charley answering with a blow to the head or body. The most significant punch came in the form of a heavy left from Dempsey on Bixamos's right eye, causing some color and swelling, but no cut. As the round ended, Dempsey landed a parting uppercut to the face.

The third round began with some light sparring until the pair fell into a clinch. By mid-round, however, Dempsey broke this rhythm and began to force the fighting, taking charge of the bout. Jack's left began to tap out a beat on his opponent's face and he was able to land and get away with only light retaliation from Bixamos. Jack began to systematically wear down his opponent, pounding him with repeated combinations to the face and landing one particularly devastating uppercut. This was repeated time and again over the third and fourth rounds as Dempsey drove Bixamos all over the ring and against the ropes. Bixamos fought with heart but was powerless to stop the Nonpareil's advances.

By the end of the fifth round, Bixamos was beaten. He had been hammered repeatedly and knocked down three times; with the final time being after a powerful right uppercut that caught Charley on the chin. Bixamos went down on his face and lay panting for several seconds. Bixamos, his face now covered in blood, got to his hands and knees. He struggled to his feet and lumbered back to his corner as the round ended.

When Dunn called for the fighters to come to center ring to begin the sixth round, Charlie, still dazed, with his right eye closed and his face cut up, stayed on his chair in his corner. He had had enough and Dempsey was declared the victor.[17] The time of the match was 18 minutes and 52 seconds.

Despite being twenty pounds heavier, having a greater reach and being in splendid condition the Frenchman was powerless to stop his smaller opponent. "Bixamos met the first real fighter in his life and was whipped by Dempsey in five rounds," reported the *New York Times*. "Bixamos had strength, pluck and endurance, but they proved of no avail before Dempsey's science and matchless generalship. He fought Bixamos on a well-prepared plan. His first design was to induce Bixamos to wind himself by rushing, but the Frenchman saw the snare and acted on the defensive at first."[18] Dempsey then began to work on his opponent's midsection and after two rounds of this punishment, Bixamos was showing the wear. He dropped his guard to defend his ribs and stomach. At that point Dempsey raised his attack and began to launch left- and right-handed missiles—hard and straight—that caught Charley all about his head. When the two drew close, Jack would bomb Bixamos with punishing uppercuts to the chin. At first Bixamos fought back notably, but Dempsey simply wore him down and soon Charley's resistance grew weaker as his strength began to wane.

With a smashing victory under his belt, Jack was beginning to fully enjoy New Orleans with its food, drink, culture and acceptance of the fight game.

A week after the Bixamos bout, Dempsey refereed the Charles Lang versus George Fryer heavyweight bout in the Crescent City. The match was held at Sportsman's Park on March 25, in front of nearly 1,000 fight fans. Lang was reportedly the heavyweight champion of Ohio and Fryer, originally from England, now hailed from Philadelphia. The men weighed in at 194 and 196 pounds, respectively. The bout was a display of power that Fryer won by knockout in the eleventh round with a right-handed missile to the tip of Lang's jaw.

After a few more days in Louisiana, Jack and Jake Stearns decided to travel back to Chicago to try again to set up more bouts. On a side trip to Milwaukee, Jack again was called on to second a local fighter named Frank Ward in his four-round victory over Joe Weidner. Local accounts referred to the fight as brutal and a slugfest, and, true to the times and to Milwaukee's "official" distaste for prizefighting, the bout was actually held in the woods about fourteen miles north of the city.[19]

Not satisfied with their success in arranging bouts in Chicago, Dempsey and Stearns headed west to San Francisco, arriving on April 12. Almost immediately, Jack challenged Charley Mitchell, or any middleweight who would dare, to meet him in the ring. Bay Area sportsman Harry Maynard took Dempsey at his word, offered a large gate for Jack to meet Harry Downie and the fight was set for early May.

It was also during his early days in the Bay Area that Jack met a tall and muscular eighteen-year-old San Francisco bank teller by the name of Jim Corbett. While he was in his late teens Corbett began training and taking boxing lessons from British-born boxing instructor Walter Watson at San Francisco's Olympic Athletic Club.

Watson had been employed by the Olympic in 1884, and he soon brought the club a great deal of fame and good publicity. Watson was "considered to be one of the most professional instructors of 'scientific' boxing."[20] As a fighter first in London and then in New York, Watson displayed exceptional knowledge and skill of the sport. Shortly after losing a heated battle with Mike Donovan he took the position as instructor at the Olympic. Watson's philosophy held that training and boxing both teach the lessons of life, lessons he believed were absolutely essential to success. He believed that as young men became physically fit and learned the sport of boxing, they also learned courage, discipline, caution, forbearance and, if the necessity ever arose, how to defend themselves.

Soon after Watson assumed his role as trainer at the Olympic he met young Jim Corbett. Corbett was tall, handsome,

Dempsey and fellow champion Jim Corbett developed a strong friendship.

fit and he struck quite an image. "What impressed Watson most about Jim was his careful and refined manner of dress, not to mention his pompadour hairstyle."[21]

Under Watson's careful eye, Corbett would become one of the greatest heavyweights of all time, winning the world championship from the great John L. Sullivan by 1892. Corbett was clever, agile and "jack-rabbit" quick. He utilized fast jabs and hooks and possessed excellent footwork along with slippery head and body movements. Corbett was well educated for the time. He was a graduate of San Francisco's Sacred Heart High School and reportedly attended college for a while. An erudite and intelligent man, Corbett continually studied the sport and developed innovations that led to modern boxing techniques and fighting styles.[22]

Dempsey and Mike Cleary had been given guest privileges at the Olympic and in return, the pair would spar periodically, providing entertainment for members. Corbett got to know Cleary and would work with him on occasion. Like Watson, Cleary was keen on Corbett and felt the young man had a bright future in the squared circle. One evening Dempsey was looking for a sparring partner, when Cleary responded, "There's a young fellow over there named Corbett. He'll box with you." Jack was unsure that this young bank teller would provide him much of a workout, but Cleary and Watson responded almost in unison, "Oh, he'll give you a sweat, all right."[23]

In short order, the two had donned gloves and entered in the ring. Corbett recalled later how Dempsey began feinting and weaving as Jim had seen him do while observing Jack spar throughout the summer. Corbett began to move and feint with Dempsey, but he was, by his own admission, too much in awe of Jack to hit him at first. After moving about the ring for a short while, Jack landed a series of body blows, which after a few seconds actually seemed to relax Jim. He responded by becoming more aggressive. Now instead of stepping back the next time Jack feinted, Jim stepped up and assuredly landed a left hook on the side of Dempsey's face. Exhibiting signs of the champion he would become, Corbett confidently followed the hook up with another left to Jack's nose.

Dempsey was impressed with the young man, as were the now many club members who had gathered around the ring. "We slugged with each other all around that place and soon word went through the club that Dempsey and Corbett were hot at it! Billiard cues slammed down on the floors, cards were scattered all over the tables, waiters dropped their steins, and in a moment, the room was crowded."[24] The two continued to match each other and to exchange blows for the next half hour in a furious battle. Finally, after the two men broke from a clinch, Jack caught Corbett across the nose with a sharp right, drawing blood. Corbett said that his temper began to flare until suddenly, the Nonpareil smiled, raised his glove and said, "Boy, that's enough for today." Corbett then relayed, "He put his arm around me and grew quite friendly, even taking me into the washroom, where he examined my nose, finding nothing broken."[25]

The impromptu sparring session gave Corbett a good deal of exposure with the local sporting set and "local newspapers began to mention his name with increasing frequency, extolling the virtues of this clean-cut, 'scientific' boxer."[26] Corbett, considered by many to be the father of the modern fight game, learned well from Watson, but he also learned much from his time with Dempsey. Corbett's encounter with a legend led to a snappy sparring session from which the young fighter learned a great deal about boxing and about himself. The two men would develop a close and lasting friendship over the next ten years and Corbett would often credit his friend Jack Dempsey as one of the most profound influences on his knowledge and skills in the ring.

On May 4, Jack was scheduled to meet San Francisco middleweight Harry Downie in the contest set up upon Dempsey's arrival by Harry Maynard. The match was to be a glove contest at the Bay City's Mechanics' Pavilion, but a last-minute change brought him a different opponent.

While a respectable-sized crowd was gathering at the Pavilion that evening, actual ticket sales were sparse and at 9:30 p.m., as the established time for the show approached, money was still coming in slowly. In an effort to increase ticket sales, show promoters reduced the price of admission to fifty cents, but still the milling throng outside objected and, though still ticketless, they rushed the doors, overwhelming those charged with security. Once inside, the squatters helped themselves to whichever seats were to their liking and continued their raucous display.

The main event was supported by several bouts between local fighters. These were more glorified sparring sessions than serious matches, but they were harbingers of the undercards that would become a staple of boxing events by the turn of the twentieth century. First up that evening were Tom Kelly and a mysterious entry described only as "a stranger from Butchertown." They were followed by George Hamill and Ed McDonald. Next up were Bill Price and June Dennis in a bout that was so violent and the fighters so unruly that the referee, a police captain named Douglas, ordered the bout stopped and the two pugilists out of the ring. The final bout before the main event featured featherweights James Maloney and Joe Brown.

As the early sparring came to a close and the crowd made ready for the main event, it was announced by Edward Willis that Downie had left the arena. Apparently, "Downey, disgusted by the influx of deadbeats, had bundled up his scanty fighting apparel and gone home."[27] Willis stated that Downie refused to enter the ring for fear that due to the high number of unpaid admissions, the promoters would be unwilling or unable to meet the terms of the pre-fight agreement in which the winner would receive seventy percent of the gate to the loser's thirty. "A messenger was dispatched to Downie's retreat, but the derelict pugilist sent back word that he wanted the guarantee of $500 before he would appear in the ring."[28]

The large and unruly crowd greeted the news of Downie's defection with groans and hisses. Promoter Harry Maynard had to do some quick thinking to save the event. He needed a substitute for Downie and he needed one quickly. A young West Coast fighter named Tom Barry volunteered to take Downey's place if guaranteed $250 whether he won or lost. Maynard, who was desperate for a fighter, accepted the proposition. Despite the fact that Barry had not been in training for a fight, he actually put on a good show and the bout turned out to be an exciting contest.

"At 10:40 o'clock, Dempsey and Barry stepped into the ring. Barry was seconded by Maurice Leo and Pete Lawler. Dempsey was seconded by Charles Taylor and Martin Murphy. Mike Cleary was selected to act as referee."[29] Clarence Whistler and John Hart were selected as timekeepers.

As the first round opened the fighters were cautious, each not knowing what to expect from their unanticipated opponent, but Barry, ten pounds heavier than Dempsey, soon began to force the work. After a superficial exchange of blows, Dempsey rushed at Barry, driving him backwards with a clean left-right combination that sent Barry flying through the ropes and clear off the stage. Some at ringside claimed that the fall through the ropes was caused not so much by a blow as by a rush and shove, but regardless of the cause, it was nearly devastating to Barry. "The fall was so severe that it was thought for a moment that the fight was over, but Barry unexpectedly bounded back to the stage smiling, and rushed fiercely at his opponent."[30] Despite his pluck and courage, Barry fared no better this time. Jack caught the enthusiastic Barry with a hard blow on the neck that felled him. Again though, Tom was up in a flash.

"During this first round, Barry very cleverly stopped some hard and well-directed blows. The little work that Dempsey did showed him to be a thorough master in the science of pugilism. He played with Barry as easily and unconcernedly as a cat would with a mouse."[31]

The second and third rounds were much calmer than the first. Although Barry continued to try to get inside and force the battle, he appeared to be in awe of Dempsey's long, left-handed reach. Dempsey worked his way towards his opponent and gave the crowd one or two shows of infighting, landing repeated jabs and uppercuts. Although clearly growing tired, Barry continued to stand up well to his opponent's work.

By the fourth round, Barry was beginning to show the signs of wear and it appeared that Dempsey could take the fight whenever he pleased. Still, Barry hung in and lasted the entire chapter. He was determined to make the champion work for the knockout. Dempsey toyed with his opponent, but never went for the kill. The fifth round, however, would be different.

As soon as the fifth round began, Dempsey came at his opponent and fired a piston-like left that caught Barry flush on the neck. The blow staggered the Californian. Jack followed up with another hard left and down went Barry for what looked like the finish. As the referee began his count, Dempsey was sure that he had won, but much to his shock, Barry made it to his feet before Cleary could reach ten.

While he was on his feet, Barry was so plainly at the mercy of the New Yorker that Dempsey dropped his hands and made no further attempt to strike his helpless opponent. Still, the terribly weakened Barry would not yield. At this point, the Nonpareil simply gave him a shove that overturned Barry. The shock of landing on the floor again "revived Barry and when he rose he rushed determinedly at Dempsey, who met him with a well-directed right-hander that laid the local man on his back and ended the fight."[32]

After seventeen minutes and five rounds, the fight was over. Promoter Harry Maynard may have been even more relieved than Barry. He'd had a difficult evening starting with concerns over slow ticket sales followed by the gate crashing of the unruly crowd and finally the defection of Downie. After the event was over, Maynard told the press—and anyone else who would listen—that he would never again make any match with Harry Downie and he would furthermore use every resource at his disposal to prevent anyone else doing so.

As they left the ring, both fighters were the recipients of cheers and ovations, Dempsey for his superior skills and magnanimity towards his opponent and Barry for his grit and gameness. While he had not trained for this fight, Barry gave it all he had and forced his antagonist to do his best before he could claim victory. As was reported in the local press, "Under the circumstances Barry did very well, although it was evident that he is no match for Dempsey, even at his best."[33]

On May 11, Jack was back at the Mechanics' Pavilion where he squared off with local middleweight champion Tommy Cleary. Located in the San Francisco Civic Center at Grove and Larkin, the Mechanics' Pavilion was built in 1882. It was a large barn-shaped structure that could hold more than 11,000 persons. The building was originally used for musical concerts, political conventions and circuses, but soon became well-known for hosting prizefights. John L. Sullivan was a regular at the Pavilion and it was here that the Boston Strong Boy knocked out Paddy Ryan in three rounds in 1886. Ten years later it was here that legendary western lawman Wyatt Earp declared Tom Sharkey a winner by foul over Bob Fitzsimmons. Fitzsimmons had thoroughly walloped Sharkey throughout the fight and, after dropping Sharkey with a blow to the chest, was called for a low blow by Earp. Needless to say, the outcome remains controversial to this day. In addition, Jim Jeffries defended his world heavyweight title in the Pavilion three times, including a ten-rounder in 1903 over Jim Corbett.

The Pavilion, also known as the Madison Square Garden of the West, played another key role in San Francisco's history. At 5:12 in the morning on April 18, 1906, San Francisco was hit with a strong earthquake. While the Mechanics' Pavilion withstood the earthquake many nearby buildings did not. Central Emergency Hospital was hit hard and much of the building was reduced to rubble:

> By 5:30 am, patients from the hospital, along with people injured in the quake were brought into the arena, whose doors had been forced open. By mid-morning, Mechanics' Pavilion had become both hospital and morgue, as beds from neighboring hotels were being brought in by the hour. Unfortunately, by 1 pm, flames from the Hayes Valley fire reached the roof of Mechanics' Pavilion, and chief surgeon Dr. Charles Miller ordered the building evacuated. Within hours, Mechanics' Pavilion was gone.

The site now hosts the Bill Graham Civic Auditorium, allowing the location to continue to be a major hub of entertainment for over 130 years.[34]

With its important civic work still two decades in the future, the Pavilion was, in 1885, still the scene of various meetings and athletic contests. The main event between Dempsey and Cleary on May 11 was to have been preceded by an advertised series of bouts, but the entire undercard was omitted when the designated fighters decided to strike at the last minute for $7.50 a piece instead of the contracted $2.50. Harry Maynard, still steamed at the way he had been treated a week earlier by Harry Downie, was in no mood to accede to their demands. Instead of giving in, he simply cancelled the undercard portion of the evening's events and the fighters got nothing. The payoff for the match was for all of the gate receipts. This was quite a nice night's work as a nearly sellout crowd had paid $1 apiece for admission.

As the crowd gathered and the fighters and their seconds readied themselves, selections were made for referee and timekeepers. "The selection of a referee consumed a great deal of time. Mike Cleary and Charley Mitchell were called upon but did not respond. Finally, it was decided that Frank Crockett should be chosen and soon after crowded through the ropes."[35]

At 10:30 p.m., the men entered the ring. Referee Crockett called the men to the scratch and the pair advanced to center where they "clasped hands tenderly, as if they were about to part forever." At the call to fight, the men came back together, but this time with fists clinched and with an entirely different mindset.

The bout was a heavily one-sided affair, with Jack in control and Cleary never really in the fight at all. While Cleary was the larger man, Jack knocked him out in five rounds. "The contest consisted in Dempsey's administering heavy punishment smilingly, and Cleary taking it grimly until unable to stand."[36]

Cleary made some fight of it early in the first round, but Dempsey would repeatedly throw a punch then quickly take several steps back, inducing Cleary to rush in. He would then stop, set up and plaster his opponent with a straight right-hander to the face. After falling for this trick several times, Cleary began to stay back and attempt to fight at long range, but this approach did not work either as Dempsey would continue to step in, land and dance back or at other times just fire off and land series of long distance volleys. At one point Cleary rushed Dempsey, but Jack "caught his head in chancery." Crocket separated the fighters before Dempsey could inflict any damage.

Early in the second round, the men exchanged some hard blows, but in short order, Jack's superior ring skills simply overwhelmed Cleary. Dempsey used his left to great effect as he repeatedly jabbed Cleary about the head and received very little return. Cleary's face was beginning to show the wear of the constant punishment.

Dempsey almost finished the bout in the third round when he landed a powerful right-hand blow on the local man's ear that sent him reeling and almost out. But Cleary stayed on his feet and answered the bell for the next chapter.

As the fourth round began, Cleary came out swinging for the fences. At one point he managed to get his entire weight behind a wicked left that landed hard on Dempsey's neck. The blow clearly registered with Dempsey, but only served to strengthen Jack's resolve to pay his opponent back in kind. He opened up a barrage on Cleary who, as a result, suffered severely in the fourth round.

In the fifth round, Dempsey took complete control and determined to end the contest. He connected with one stinging left that found its mark just below Cleary's ear. The powerful impact of that missile spun Cleary around and drove the San Franciscan into his corner. There Dempsey dropped the bruised, bloody and beaten man to the floor. Cleary gathered himself and once more, rose to his feet. Dempsey, sensing a knockout, was on Cleary like a cat. He fired off another stunning blow to his opponent's chin and four more hard shots to the San Franciscan's neck and body, the last of which floored Cleary. The bout appeared to be over. Crockett immediately stepped in, declaring Dempsey the winner, but Cleary's corner and his local fans—who were legion—insisted the fight go on. Within seconds of the continuation, Dempsey laid him out again and, to make sure it was really over this time, San Francisco Police Captain Douglas stepped in and called a halt to the affair. For a second time Crockett raised Dempsey's arm, declared him the winner and the Nonpareil was awarded the sizeable gate receipts.

While no match for Dempsey, Cleary was a respectable fighter. He would continue to climb into the ring periodically throughout the early 1890s, but, like so many pugilists, when his skills waned he had little to fall back on. He drifted for a while, eventually winding up on the street. He fell in with other troubled types and eventually found himself in Montana where he encountered bigger problems.

In late 1894, while in Helena, Cleary became acquainted with a gambler by the name of Frank Dorrity. In addition to his gambling, Dorrity was a known killer. After one long night of carousing, the two had a heated argument during which threats were exchanged. Dorrity ran for his gun, but Cleary was quicker to his pistol and shot the gambler in the back of the neck. Dorrity hit the ground and bled to death on the spot. On February 18, 1895, Cleary was convicted in district court of manslaughter.[37]

Jack decided to stay in San Francisco after his victory over Cleary. On May 22, he seconded Mike Cleary of New York in his bout against Charley Mitchell at the Mechanics' Pavilion. The fight was a brutal affair lasting just four rounds before the police intervened. The bout had two named referees—Tommy Chandler and Billy Jordan. After the police stopped the fight, the pair disagreed on the outcome, "Jordan claiming Cleary had the best of it on account of knocking Mitchell down twice and Chandler claiming the fight for Mitchell. It was finally decided a draw amid the most intense excitement."[38] Many in attendance believed, however, that another round or two would have finished Cleary.

On June 5, Dempsey was scheduled for what many thought would be a very difficult battle for him against noted local pugilist Jim Carr. The pair met each other in front of 2,000 patrons in San Francisco's Wigwam Theatre under Queensberry Rules. Tom Barry was chosen as referee. In Carr's corner was Jack Keenan and in Dempsey's was Martin Murphy. Before the contest began, "Dempsey was presented with an exquisite basket of flowers, surmounted by a white dove, presumably as an emblem of peace."[39]

The first round was fairly even as both men sparred cautiously, looking for an opening. Carr landed several good lefts to Dempsey's chest, and Dempsey responded with some hard blows to Carr's neck and face. While they traded a good many blows, nothing of great note occurred during this round.

In the second, Dempsey pressed the fighting by landing a left uppercut under Carr's chin. When he repeated this several times, Carr grabbed Jack and clinched hard to avoid any more punishment. The two wrestled and pushed for the remaining few seconds until the round ended. While he absorbed a good many of Dempsey's punches, the fact that he knew well how to tie his opponent up and wear him down in the clinches showed that, coupled with his strong showing in the first, Carr appeared to be the best fighter Dempsey had yet met on his western tour.

Carr came out swinging in the third round, using his right to great effect as he landed several stinging blows to his opponent's ribs. Dempsey, however, made a strong statement near the end of the round when he planted a blow "that would have felled an ox" square on Carr's nose and caused a flow of blood that ran down his face and dripped onto his chest.[40]

In the fourth round, Jack was cool and collected as he delivered numerous powerful blows that had a visible effect on Carr. The San Franciscan fell into a clinch three separate times and when the round was over, "Dempsey was still fresh, but Carr appeared pretty well used up."[41]

The fifth round was less eventful, with both men sparring more cautiously, but Jack landed a number of telling left-handed blows on his opponent that served to further weaken the already weary Carr.

In the sixth round, both men rushed at each other as the round began, but Dempsey was clearly the more serious aggressor from the start. He fought Carr all around the ring, eventually getting the Californian into the corner where, after a constant pounding, Jack dropped him to the sawdust. Jack continued to use his lightning left to great effect, very nearly finishing Carr, but the San Franciscan survived the round.

The seventh round started badly for Carr. He was tired and wobbly on his legs. Dempsey kept after him and twice dropped him to his knees. When Carr attempted to rally and struck Dempsey several hard blows to his right side, Jack returned fire and hit Carr so hard that he fell through the ropes and landed in a heap as the round was coming to a close. Had the round not ended, he would have been counted out right then and there.

Dempsey drove Carr into his corner early in the eighth round and pounded on him there until the San Franciscan was able to work his way out and clinch. Jack knocked his opponent to the ground twice and several other times the San Franciscan fell as much from being groggy as from the Nonpareil's punches.

When time was called for the start of the ninth round, Carr could hardly make it to scratch. He was wobbly and could barely stand. Almost as soon as the round began, Dempsey knocked Carr down so hard that he landed under the ropes. Carr was unable to rise in the allotted time, Barry declared Dempsey the victor.[42]

Carr later said that his fight with Dempsey was one of the most important of his career. He stated proudly that "I faced him for thirty-four minutes. In the third round he broke my nose, but I stayed six rounds after that."[43]

On June 17, 1885, a ship arrived in New York Harbor, containing over two hundred packing cases and more than three hundred and fifty individual, formed copper and steel pieces. The cargo, once assembled, would become known to the world as the Statue of Liberty. The monument, designed by French sculptor Frèdèric-Auguste Bartholdi and engineer Gustave Eiffel, was a gift from the people of France to the people of the United States, commemorating a century of friendship between the two nations. The statue was assembled on Bedloe's Island in New York Harbor over the next sixteen months and was officially dedicated by U.S. President Grover Cleveland on October 28, 1886.

The statue, which immediately became known as an enduring symbol of freedom and democracy, was originally scheduled to be delivered in time for the American Centennial celebration in 1876, but fundraising efforts were slow. After initial attempts to raise money for the project fell short, myriad additional avenues for fundraising were tried, including, appropriately enough, boxing matches.

After defeating Carr, Dempsey traveled to Nevada City, Nevada, where he threw down a challenge to fight any man his size in the area. The challenge was accepted by a local fighter of some note by the name of James Rodda. In a great example of the inconsistencies that could accompany fight reports of the time, some articles state that the bout was actually held fifteen miles from Nevada City in Colfax, California. In addition to being called James, one report referred to Rodda as Alexander while another called him Jack. One erroneous account discounted the bout altogether and has Jack attending a wrestling tournament in Grass Valley with Duncan C. Ross and "other men of muscle."[44]

The match between the Nonpareil and Rodda was set for July 4. During the bout, Jack wasted little time in knocking Rodda out at two minutes and thirty-five seconds in the second round.

Next up for Jack was Jack Keenan of Philadelphia, whom he would engage with bare knuckles under Queensberry Rules on July 20, in a quiet spot about a half mile from Barney Farley's roadhouse, near the southwest corner of San Francisco's Golden Gate Park. Some state that there was a $1,000 purse, but it is unsure if any funds changed hands at all—this was a grudge match.

The battle was, in reality, more of a fistfight between the two to assuage Keenan's pride than it was an actual prizefight and in truth it was not much of a fight at all. Dempsey had no desire to do battle with Keenan, but try as he might, Dempsey could not dissuade Keenan from engaging him.

Keenan was once considered a rising lightweight contender and he had become so vocal in his contention that he could best Dempsey that Jack determined to give him the chance to try. There had been bad blood between the two for some time, dating back to a bout in which Dempsey handled Young Mitchell in his victory over Keenan in New York. Things got worse between the two as Keenan continued to rave about how he was a better man than Dempsey. One particular sarcastic comment finally got under the Nonpareil's skin. Dempsey asked Keenan what he meant by it and if he was trying to start a fight. Keenan responded, "That's just what I want, exactly. You meet me in the city tomorrow with two friends, and we'll settle it."[45]

The two met at 2:00 p.m. the next afternoon, in Jack Hallinan's Cremorne Garden Theatre. Once again, Dempsey tried to reason with him. The Nonpareil was taller, heavier, had a longer reach and by virtually all accounts was Keenan's superior in the ring. Dempsey told Keenan that it was not necessary to fight or to prove anything, but the smaller man would not be dissuaded. Dempsey's words only served to make Keenan that much more determined to fight. "I ain't so sure that you can lick me," replied Keenan, "and I want to try you anyway."[46] Eventually, Dempsey agreed to fight and after buckets, towels and sponges were secured, the two pugilists and their backers climbed into carriages and wagons and headed to Golden Gate Park.

"After about thirty minutes, the party reached Barney Farley's. They then climbed over the hill and into the hollow where the ring was blocked out with bits of turf and where the men began to strip."[47] When they were ready to fight Jack made a final plea with Keenan, but the latter replied that Dempsey would have to beat him before they could be friends. Jack laughed and said that in that case, the two would soon be friends.

Jack Hallinan acted as referee and timekeeper while Mike Smith seconded Dempsey and fighter Billy Hamilton seconded Keenan.

Hallinan, a boxer and wrestler from Australia, was "well-known on the Pacific Coast as a promoter of fistic sport." He helped land fighters for the Golden Gate Athletic Club events. "Hallinan is a noted boxer and wrestler, having often figured in the arena."[48] He made the Cremorne a notorious place, popular with a class of patrons whose money flowed freely. "The history of the place is not a pleasant one. It is a record of immorality, thefts, outrages, murders. But it made money for its owner; Hallinan could now indulge his passion for gambling."[49]

When Hallinan called the men to scratch, Keenan wasted little time in lunging at his opponent and firing a hard but errant left at the Nonpareil, who nimbly sidestepped the blow and returned a vicious left that plowed into Keenan's right eye. The force of the blow caused the eye to swell and virtually close within minutes. Almost immediately Dempsey threw his right and caught his opponent on his left eye with the same effect. An angry Keenan then rushed Dempsey and got in several blows on his face, but Dempsey returned fire, landing hard on his opponent's ribs and opening up several cuts on his face. Though now bleeding badly Keenan refused to quit and rushed Dempsey, trying to catch him with a wild blow, but the Nonpareil stopped the punch with his left and threw a right "that would have felled an ox." Keenan took it full on the mouth, and its force cut both lips and sent him sprawling to the ground in a heap.

Keenan, already bleeding, bruised and nearly blind from the swelling around his eyes, got up in an instant and came at Dempsey with both hands flying. He sent a right to Dempsey's stomach and a left to his nose. Dempsey was able to deflect the right, but took the left flush on the nose. The Nonpareil's return was lightning fast and powerful enough to drop Keenan to the turf again, the victim of a howitzer-like right to the side of the head. The powerful punch caused a cut on Dempsey's right hand and it was later revealed that it broke a knuckle as well.

During the break between rounds, Keenan recovered to the point that he proposed that they do away with the three-minute rounds and just let the second round last to the finish. A smiling Dempsey agreed to the terms stating, "All right, Jack, fight as you please and hurry up, too if you want to do battle. Put up your hands and give me something to warm me up. I'm getting cold with this wind whistling through my whiskers."[50]

When the second round began, Dempsey had no appetite to inflict more punishment and only reacted to deflect Keenan's frequent rushes. While sparring, the Nonpareil encouraged Keenan to give up, but the latter responded that he was not licked yet. Once Keenan landed punches to Jack's face and stomach, but again, Dempsey landed a right so hard in retaliation that Keenan went down on the grass. Again, he rose and rushed Dempsey and again a hard smash from the Nonpareil's left—this time to the jaw—put Keenan back down. That was all. Keenan "could not get up for another go, and the seconds peremptorily declared the battle at an end. Keenan held down the turf for about five minutes before regaining sufficient strength to get up, and then had to be assisted on with his clothes."[51] It was a heavily one-sided affair, with Dempsey winning on a decisive two-round knockout in what was reportedly secured in just eleven minutes.

According to Dempsey, the party went to a local house where the woman who lived there took pity on Keenan and washed his face and cleaned his wounds with hot water. After she was through, Keenan went to a mirror and, looking through almost entirely closed eyes, gazed at his damaged face. "He is not an Adonis in looks by any means, and we all had to laugh heartily when he exclaimed, 'Jack Dempsey, you ought to be ashamed of yourself to spoil my beauty this way.'"[52]

After helping Keenan into a carriage, the party returned to Hallinan's, where they assuaged their thirsts with the drinks of their choice and put any bad feelings behind them. Keenan, his face bruised, badly beaten and his eyes almost shut, shook hands with Dempsey and told him that they were now friends. "I tell you he is as game a man as ever lived and as true a friend, when he is your friend, as you will meet in a day's walk."[53] Although he suffered very few cuts, bruises and abrasions, Dempsey did break the middle finger and knuckle of his right hand during the fight and had to take a few weeks off to let them heal.

On July 22, Dempsey seconded Tom Cleary in Cleary's bout with Jim Carr in San Francisco. His participation would cause him some trouble, but it was trouble with which he was all too familiar. In a letter to a friend in New York dated August 1, Jack mentioned, "I have been arrested with Tom Cleary, Charley Taylor and Con McCormack on account of the Cleary-Carr fight. Carr has skipped. We are out on $3,000 bail each."[54]

In that same letter to his friend in New York, Jack mentioned that he would love to meet George La Blanche in San Francisco for an even split of prize money, or a 60–40 or 70–30 split or for all gate receipts, whichever La Blanche preferred. He said that he hoped that La Blanche's backers would put up the money and the fight would come off. "A good many of the sporting fraternity think I am afraid of the Marine, and I only await the opportunity of showing that I am not."[55] Even with this open challenge, some in the sports writing world and particularly at the *Boston Globe* would periodically repeat the same claims time after time that Dempsey was afraid to meet their local man and that Jack was "empty-headed" and "stupid" for thinking that anyone would travel across country to fight him.[56] Jack would not have to wait terribly long to get his chance to prove his mettle, as he would meet La Blanche the following March in New York.

There have long been reports that Dempsey was scheduled to meet Bat Masterson's friend and fighter John P. Clow in Rawlings, Wyoming, sometime in late August or early September. A blurb in the newspapers stated that "John P. Clow, middleweight champion pugilist of Denver, has entered into engagements to meet various Eastern pugilists including Jack Dempsey, Jack Burke, George La Blanche, J. Miller of Nebraska, and others."[57] Dempsey in turn stated in late August that he was anxious to go to Cheyenne and fight Clow for $1,000 a side sometime in the next eight weeks. Jack promised to "make Clow realize next morning that he has been doing some fighting."[58] At this point, however, I have found no evidence that a bout ever came off which is too bad—it might well have been a good one.

Clow led a short but interesting life and he was a man who certainly lived life for all he could get from it. He was a good-sized man who stood just under six feet and bridged the gap between middleweight and heavyweight during his career, but he gladly took on anyone regardless of their size. In the ring Clow was fearless. He was tough, quick with his hands and feet and had a reputation for possessing a left fist packed with dynamite. Although the clarity around titles was less precise at the time, Clow was considered by many authorities to be the middleweight champion of Colorado in 1882. He was also said to have won the heavyweight championship of Colorado and Wyoming in 1885 when he defeated blacksmith and future liquor, gold and petroleum business magnate Harry Hynds in a six-round decision at the Rawlins, Wyoming, Opera House. Clow was also awarded the *Police Gazette* Heavyweight Championship Medal for Colorado during this time. Western legend Bat Masterson became acquainted with the young Pennsylvanian and took him under his wing, acting as his trainer, business manager and promoter.

During his career, Clow defeated such men as "Denver" Ed Smith, Jack Hanley, George Morrison, Dave Campbell, Joe Denning, Mike Boden, Mike Dunn and Denny Killen. He also battled but lost to Dominick McCaffrey, Jake Kilrain, Mike Conley, Jim Fell and Duncan McDonald. He fought Jack Burke to a couple of draws. An impressive resume.

According to family records, John P. Clow was born in Pennsylvania in February 1861. He married Alice Theresa Cole who was seven years his junior and the couple had one child, a daughter named Mabel who was born on May 10, 1890.

Clow made a good name for himself in the ring, but his life outside of the squared circle was apparently as violent and rough and tumble as his life in it. Clow had an affinity for

Bat Masterson's Wildman, John P. Clow.

gravitating towards trouble. It was quite common to find him in saloons; gambling houses and brothels, and he had a voracious appetite for all of the temptations found therein. Clow lived his life fast and on the edge, but in time this reckless and wanton lifestyle began to catch up with him. He seemed to hit the bottom in 1890 when, on May 29, just under three weeks after the birth of his daughter, Clow was reportedly shot in a quarrel over money by Grant Hughes in Denver, Colorado. While he recovered from his injuries, he apparently did not change his ways.

Just six months later, Clow's luck finally ran out. He met a brutal death when he was shot by F.C. Marshall in Denver, Colorado, on December 8, 1890. Always a fighter, Clow hung on through the night, but the damage from the bullet was severe and the profuse internal bleeding could not be stopped. He died the next day. The stories varied somewhat, but it seems that Clow's demise came about in a predictable manner—he was shot while gambling and cavorting in a saloon that was also a "house of ill-repute." He was only twenty-nine and he left behind a young wife and seven-month-old daughter in difficult straights. Her life shattered by her husband's carelessness and negligence, Alice eventually picked up the pieces, resettled with Mabel in Portland, Oregon, and married a man named George Larrabee. Family lore states that Alice grew to be "a harsh, judgmental woman" who refused to ever speak of John Clow again.

In a clear sign that he was quite happy on the West Coast and that he loved San Francisco, Jack began to show his intention of settling in to the local business and social scene. In a letter to a friend in New York dated August 1, Jack stated, "I have taken a saloon here at 17 Powell Street, and am doing very well."[59] On August 22, the *Police Gazette* also reported this and added that Dempsey and fellow pugilist Tom Cleary had opened an establishment called the Nonpareil Saloon located at 17 Powell Street in San Francisco.[60]

Continuing his California tour, Dempsey traveled south to Los Angeles in late August. He arrived in the City of Angels on Thursday, August 26, and was scheduled to meet Young Billy Manning on Saturday, August 29.[61] The bout was delayed for several days, but finally came off on September 2. The contest was held at Turnverein Hall located at 321 South Main Street in Los Angeles. The gloved fight was to the finish for the gate money. Charlie Schroeder was agreed upon as referee by both sides and Joe Manning and J. Mahoney were selected as timekeepers.

Manning was muscular, feisty and tough, but was short of both stature and reach, and was completely outclassed by Dempsey. In the opening round Dempsey wasted no time taking the fight to Manning and driving him to the ropes with a powerful attack to the body. Finding an opening, Dempsey let loose a left that landed square on Manning's nose. The blow caught Manning's attention and made him briefly fight with a renewed purpose. Driving Dempsey back, Manning was able to land a few body blows before Schroeder called time to end the first round.

In the second round, Dempsey quickly reclaimed control of the fighting. He pressed his advantage and forced Manning from the start. Early in the round he landed a hard left on Manning's chest, dropping him to the floor. The Nonpareil dropped Manning for a second time as he continued to land left-handed blows to the chest, nose and face. The crowd was delighted with the action and encouraged both men to keep it up.

By the third round, Manning was already winded and Dempsey took full advantage of his weakened opponent, delivering straight shots with his left on Manning's face and nose, from which blood flowed freely. By the end of the round, both men were covered with it. As hard as he tried, Manning could not gain advantage. His punches seldom found their mark as Dempsey repeatedly knocked them away. Jack reined blows from start to finish on Manning, who was heavily punished and repeatedly knocked down in the fight.

In the fourth round, Dempsey led with his left and battered Manning's nose. Manning was able to get a solid blow in on Jack's chest, but he got worse than he gave as Dempsey returned fire with several missiles to Manning's face. "Manning was knocked down again and again, and when time was called he could scarcely stand, and was covered with blood. He was carried to his corner while Dempsey looked as fresh as when he began."[62]

As the fifth round was about to begin, some in the crowd tried to convince Manning to quit and at that very moment, Police Captain Benedict stepped into the ring and stopped the fight due to the brutal nature of the beating that Manning was taking. After a chorus of boos and catcalls, he held firm, but then agreed that the fight could go on only if larger gloves were used. Both men put on larger gloves and the delay gave Manning time to gather himself, but when time was called, Dempsey immediately set upon his opponent and struck him heavily on the jaw which he followed up with a vicious combination. A solid left uppercut from the Nonpareil landed squarely under Manning's chin, but in return Billy was able to land heavily on Jack's neck. The fighters fell into a clinch and the round ended.

Jack led off the sixth round by firing a sledgehammer-like left that landed on Manning's ear and felled him like a tree. Billy refused to stay down, but after jumping to his feet, he was clearly in trouble and lashed out desperately, apparently unable to see Dempsey clearly. Jack floored Manning twice more before the round ended, but the bloody and beaten fighter refused to quit.

In the seventh round, Dempsey let go a straight left that caught Manning on the right ear once again sending him to the ground. Manning rose quickly and began to swing at Jack wildly, but ineffectually. Again, Dempsey remained composed and fired a return volley that sent Manning down in a heap.

"In the eighth round, Manning staggered to his feet, but was quickly floored by a heavy left hander from Dempsey. When he arose again Dempsey was just letting go another blow when the police ordered the fight stopped."[63] Manning was badly beaten, his face and body bruised and bloody, while Dempsey looked fresh. In the confusion and excitement, referee Charlie Schroeder forgot to declare Jack the winner, but it was clear to all what the outcome was. In reading

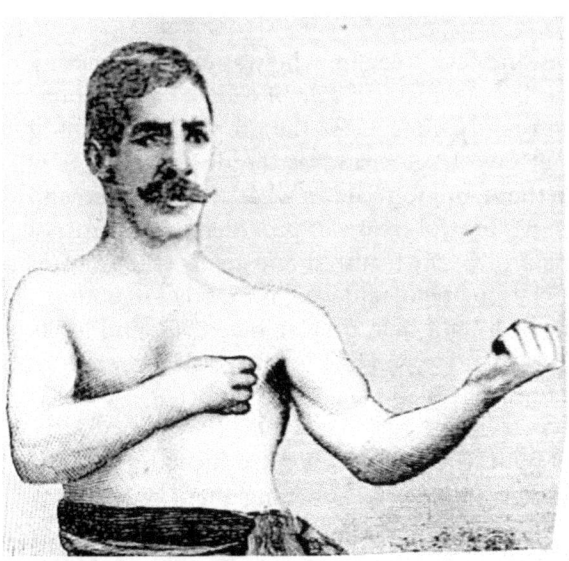

Billy Manning.

descriptions of the fight, it is clear that Dempsey's victory was all the more impressive as he primarily used his left all through the match and was hesitant to use his injured right hand. Jack was cheered and carried off the stage by the happy crowd.

Manning continued to fight through the 1890s and stayed active in the West Coast boxing scene for the remainder of his life. He married and became a well-known and respected physical fitness trainer, "having among his pupils General Leonard Wood, General (Nelson) Miles, and other military men." He died suddenly at home in Los Angeles on November 1, 1918, at age 59.[64]

In late August, it was announced that Dempsey and Tom Norton had signed for a six-round mill to be held on the evening of September 12 in Sacramento's Armory Hall. Each man had deposited a $100 forfeit with A.J. Rhoades.[65] Norton was the middleweight champion of Sacramento. Again, Jack proved himself the Nonpareil as he pounded his opponent for eleven minutes before the referee stopped the fight in the fourth round, giving Dempsey the win by technical knockout.

Norton later claimed that he was not in proper condition for the fight having sprained his ankle several days before the bout, which required him to spend several days in bed with his foot elevated. The Sacramento native claimed that he asked for a postponement, but that Dempsey and his team would not consent. He also commented that Dempsey was not his match and that Jack "acted unfairly" in going for the knockout given Norton's injury. Most reports ignored or mocked Norton's whining and even Norton's hometown newspaper gave the pugilist very little sympathy. They noted that "Norton has a greatly-inflamed leg, but no one who saw him jumping about so spryly in the ring would have thought there was anything wrong with him."[66]

On September 14, Joseph Taylor laid a challenge to have Dempsey meet Oregon heavyweight Dave Campbell for a stake of between $1,000 and $2,000. Dempsey and his team accepted and a bout was set for the Portland area in late October or early November. The fight would ultimately come off on November 2.[67]

On the evening of October 7, Dempsey and Jack Keenan, who was currently acting as Dempsey's trainer, left San Francisco on the steamship, *State of California*, to travel north to Portland where he would tour and ready himself for the proposed upcoming battle with Dave Campbell. They were met by a large crowd at the docks when they arrived in Portland. The men were taken to the Arlington Saloon where they relaxed and met with many of Campbell's supporters. A wonderful treat was provided in the form of a detailed description of Dempsey: "He is a pleasant featured and mannered man of boyish appearance and is about 5 feet 7½ inches in height and weighs exactly 148 pounds. Dempsey has a healthy, florid complexion, with light hair, grayish blue eyes, and looks enough like Campbell to be taken for his brother. He was neatly attired in a check suit with black dicer, neat chain, and carried a gold headed cane." The reporter also commented on Jack's "slight physique."[68]

The pugilists met that evening at 6:00 p.m. when they were introduced by Colonel Joe Taylor. The men shook hands, sat and talked amiably. Basic arrangements were made for the contest.

On October 8, the *Brooklyn Eagle* published a letter from Jack to fight promoter John Courtney of New York. Jack was still on the West Coast but would soon be traveling east. Dempsey told Courtney that he had read of the challenge Courtney had made to Dominick McCaffrey to meet Dempsey for anywhere between a $2,500 and $5,000 purse. Jack's letter said that while he did not have a very high regard for McCaffrey's ring skills, he "would fight him on a week or an hour's notice."[69] Dempsey added that he would be glad to be matched with others, including Pete McCoy.

The Nonpareil met Dave Campbell on November 2, in the Washington Territory just north of Portland, Oregon. The bout had been proposed in mid–September and a letter of agreement signed on October 12. The bout was to be an eight-round glove match for a $2,000 purse under the Queensberry Rules. Side betting ran at a furious pace and it was widely reported that over $20,000 changed hands during this bout.

Dave Campbell was a good fighter who died a great hero.

The extremely popular Campbell was a large man standing almost six feet tall and was described as a clever boxer and a quick, hard hitter. He was described a few years later as follows: "Dave Campbell, the champion heavyweight of Oregon, a fair complexioned, handsome young athlete, whose form is a model of grace and strength."[70] Large, quick, muscular and a heavy favorite of fight fans in the Pacific Northwest, Campbell was expected by the local set to defeat Dempsey.

After Jack arrived in Portland, he set up his training headquarters at Joe Taylor's Willamette Palace, where Jack Keenan acted as his trainer. Jack trained hard during the week and in the evenings, he began to build a local following by putting in appearances at the local theaters and oyster houses.

A contingent of Californians arrived with Dempsey and soon the betting was heavy. The Oregonians had never seen Dempsey fight and, believing that their giant could lick anyone, could not lay down bets to back Campbell fast enough. Jack, who never looked very large or much like a pugilist in street clothes, did little in appearance to dissuade their confidence. "A Portland newspaper candidly acknowledged that when Dempsey paid their office a visit and quietly handed his card, they actually felt sorry that he had to stand before the giant Campbell and be knocked to pieces."[71] Jack reportedly just smiled and stated that he would break their giant's nose in the third round.

The day of the fight arrived and at 2:00 o'clock in the morning, the steamer A.A. *McCully* pulled out of a Portland dock in a cold, steady, drizzling rain. About 200 souls, including Dempsey and his supporters, were onboard. The *McCully*'s departure was the signal for about twenty other crafts to cast off and follow the steamer to the battleground. Campbell followed in the steamer *Fleetwood*. A site had not yet been selected and a number of officials from the Washington Territory attempted to tag along to make certain that no prizefight was held in their jurisdiction. They apparently were unsuccessful.

After a search of several hours, a location was agreed upon and no local authorities could be found. The site stood across the river from the town of Saint Helens, about thirty miles north of Portland. A ring was quickly pitched in a newly mowed field. The weather was still disagreeable as the cold, misty rain continued to fall, but the wet conditions did little to dampen the enthusiasm of the large crowd assembled. A local newspaper described the events as follows: "About 3,000 sports went down the river to a small island about twenty miles from Portland. A ring was pitched and several huge bonfires tempered the chilly night air. Nearly all the money [some $15,000] was upon Campbell, and as the men stripped for battle everyone said, 'poor Jack, poor Jack.' Dempsey looked like a mere pigmy beside his formidable adversary. Before the end of the third round, however, it was 'poor Dave.'"[72]

As the contest was about to begin and the men came to center ring, the Oregonians were confident and anxious to see their man whip this legendary Easterner and Campbell, known as "The Willamette Chief," smiled with confidence as he looked upon his smaller opponent. "Duncan McDonald of Butte seconded Campbell and Jack Keenan seconded Dempsey."[73]

At the call of time, Campbell went right at Dempsey and for a minute the men exchanged blows, but Jack dodged the larger man and kept on the move, avoiding any real damage. Twice Jack used his left to great effect as he drove Campbell against the ropes. The Oregonian then rolled out and gathering himself, rushed at Dempsey. When Jack saw the big man coming, "Dempsey sent in an uppercut which staggered him just as time was called."[74]

After an extended rest period between rounds, Campbell came out in the second looking very confident. He rushed Dempsey and swung his powerful right at Jack. The Nonpareil continued to dodge the larger man. Once, while attempting to avoid a Campbell punch, Jack slipped on the wet grass and, while falling down, was hit with a right-handed blow to the forehead that left a dark red mark. The blow, while only glancing, encouraged Campbell and his supporters that perhaps Dempsey was beginning to wear down. They were very wrong.

At the start of the third round, Campbell again rushed at Dempsey. He landed a couple of quick blows that had little effect. He followed up with a left that landed heavily on Jack's jaw. Campbell then fired twice with his right, missing his target both times. Jack responded with a powerful blow to Campbell's jaw. The men continued to spar and Campbell again rushed his opponent. Then, as the massive Westerner hulked over Dempsey looking for an opening, he let go a dynamite-packed right aimed at Jack's neck. Had it struck its intended target, it might well have knocked him down, but the cat-like Nonpareil quickly stepped out of the way of the blast and returned fire, catching the now off-balance Campbell flush on the nose with a fierce uppercut—there is some disagreement on whether it was a left or right, but either way, the damage was done. Jack stepped away, folded his arms and smiled while waiting for the result. Campbell became wobbly, turned completely around and fell flat on his face like a drunken man. "He arose to his hands and knees in the mud, and as he shook his head, the blood gushed out in torrents. He crawled to the ropes, and, catching the top one, staggered to his feet with his head on his hands."[75] A reporter for the *Daily Morning Astorian* stated that "Campbell lay in the ring with a broken nose, unable to come to the scratch, and Little Jack was declared the victor. Campbell had come in contact with one of the Nonpareil's unexpected left-handers."[76] The knock-down in the third was the only time in the bout that either man went down by contact, but it was final. Time was called and the decision was awarded to Jack. After a few minutes Campbell could stand but required assistance to exit the ring. The battle lasted ten minutes and ten seconds.[77]

Upon being declared the victor, Dempsey immediately left the ring to put on warm clothes. Campbell was led to the steamer by his seconds and friends and taken to a stateroom where his nose was attended to. It had been broken in the third round as promised by the Nonpareil.

Following the Dempsey-Campbell bout came a bare-knuckle, London Rules fight to the finish between Larry Sullivan of Scranton, Pennsylvania, and Tom Ward of Astoria, Oregon. "This was a bloody affray for 72-rounds, when Sullivan threw up the sponge."[78] The bout lasted one hour and forty minutes.[79] The fight was reported to be both dirty and bloody with both men receiving a tremendous amount of punishment. In seven rounds Sullivan was knocked down, and in seventy the combatants clinched and fell, "Ward falling on top forty-one times and Sullivan twenty-nine."[80]

After the steamers reached Portland, Campbell was transported back to his lodgings in a closed coach. He rested for several days. Dempsey and the California contingent took an ocean-going vessel for their return trip to San Francisco.

Campbell would continue to fight and improve in the ring through 1891, when he knocked out Larry Sullivan in January of that year. Campbell came to Oregon from his native Pittsburgh in 1878. The popular and muscular athlete was blessed with a charming personality that helped to make him an extremely popular fighter and ensured his celebrity in the Portland area. Five years after his loss to the Nonpareil, Campbell was described in flattering terms by the *Salt Lake Tribune*. "Campbell is an all-around athlete and is physically a model. He is a clever boxer and a quick, hard-hitter." After describing the Dempsey bout, the article went on to say that "after the battle Campbell traveled with the Nonpareil and learned much regarding the science of boxing and ring tactics. He boxed a ten-round draw with Jim Corbett in Portland a few weeks previous to the meeting in New Orleans when Corbett conquered Kilrain."[81] While no one disagreed that Campbell fought well, the decision was questioned by many who saw the bout and believed that Corbett was holding back and easily handled Campbell.[82]

Campbell, a longtime member of the Portland fire brigade, was named the city's fire chief in May of 1895. He was extremely popular and he helped to modernize his department. Tragically, the former pugilist was killed while fighting a fire at a gasoline storage facility in the early morning of June 26, 1911. Reports state that Chief Campbell was trying to determine the best way to attack the stubborn blaze when tragedy struck. He ordered his men out of the building, then "walked coolly into the burning place in search of a possible solution to the grave problem that confronted him and his men. Warned of the risk, he said simply that it was necessary for him to go inside."[83] While he was at the heart of the inferno, an accumulation of hot gases caused an explosion that brought the building down on him. He had seen to it that his men were safely outside, "but he died as a gasoline tank let go."[84] Chief Campbell was only 47 years old. An estimated 150,000 mourners lined the streets of downtown Portland to view his funeral procession. In 1928, the Campbell Memorial, complete with a brass relief image of the chief, was erected in a downtown park. The memorial is named in his honor but is dedicated to all Portland firemen killed in the line of duty.

Dempsey was in heavy demand now. On November 6, Dempsey's backers sent $1,000 to Richard K. Fox as a forfeit deposit for a proposed bout with either George La Blanche,

Pete McCoy or Dominick McCaffrey for $5,000 a side. They added that if Jack Burke could not secure a bout with Mike Cleary, Dempsey would also be happy to challenge Burke.[85] The *National Police Gazette* noted that Arthur Chambers was ready to match Tommy Stefek against him, that Frank Moran, who managed Sullivan, wanted to set up a bout for Pete McCoy against him and that Tom Henry's managers were trying to arrange a match. Directly below that report was a wire from Jim Fell of Cincinnati who stated that he would meet Jack under any prizefighting rules.[86]

On the evening of November 21, Dempsey appeared along with Tom Cleary, Jack Keenan, Bill Davis, Joe Petty and Spud Murphy at an evening of boxing exhibitions held at Liberty Hall in Astoria, Oregon. Jack and Cleary sparred together for an uneventful four rounds. The evening was touted as "grand athletic entertainment" and "the finest entertainment of the kind ever seen in Oregon."[87]

On the night of Monday, December 14, Jack met Thomas F. Barry, considered by many to be the middleweight champion of the Pacific Slope.[88] It was Tom Barry who had stepped in to fight Dempsey when Harry Downie failed to show up for a bout in San Francisco the previous May. The outcome of this fight would be much the same as it had been in the Mechanics' Pavilion in May, with Dempsey again taking the contest handily. Barry had recently been married and by all accounts he was a popular man of high moral character and quiet, temperate habits.

The men agreed to fight with small gloves under *Police Gazette* Revised Queensberry Rules, for a purse of $500 and two-thirds of all gate receipts. Both men were said to be in splendid condition, with Barry weighing in at 170 pounds while Jack registered 157 pounds.

Due to the Oregon Legislature's recently passed laws against prizefighting, the contest, like the Campbell affair the month before, was originally to be held just north of the Columbia River in the Washington Territory.[89] Some accommodation with authorities was reached, however, and the bout came off on the assigned evening and in Oregon at Portland's Turn Halle. The accommodation was that the event would be fought for "scientific points" under police supervision.

"A tremendous crowd was present, and many had come from San Francisco to witness the mill." The police had gotten wind of the intended bout and planned to stop it, but so much good publicity had been given the event and so many planned to attend that the constabulary reconsidered and after extracting a promise that the men would box "scientifically," they allowed the fight to proceed. "The police had the feather drawn over their eyes by this ruse."[90]

The fight was brief, but full of action. In the first round the fighting was fast-paced, but neither man landed any particularly punishing blows. In the second round, however, Dempsey began to come alive. Landing two hard blows on Barry's stomach, Jack forced the westerner to double up. While he was stepping back after landing the blows, he also delivered a heavy right on Barry's head. After a few seconds Barry recovered and the two exchanged punches evenly for the remainder of the round.

The third round was lively as Barry led the fighting. He followed Dempsey around the ring and landed two solid lefts on Jack's neck, but the Nonpareil moved quickly away, forcing two right-handers to fall harmlessly away from their intended targets. A sharp exchange then followed through the end of the round.

By the fourth round, Barry was beginning to show some signs of wear and Dempsey was anxious to finish him. His corner, however, convinced him to be careful and the round was therefore unexciting as Jack exercised caution and Barry simply sparred for wind and dodged Dempsey's jabs.

Dempsey was growing impatient. He decided that regardless of any advice from his corner or the presence of the police, he was going to take this fight to Barry. As the fifth round started, he tore into Barry and reigned blow after blow on the westerner's jaw and head. Barry began to "reel and totter." He rushed Jack twice and clinched to both keep his footing and to attempt to smother Dempsey's punches, but each time, Dempsey fought his way out of the clinch and drove Barry across the ring.

In the sixth round, "Dempsey paid no attention to the police or his seconds as he went right at the Pacific Coast champion, punished him terribly, and then knocked him down by a terrific blow on the neck. Barry fell like a log and refused to fight any longer, and Dempsey was declared the winner."[91]

While Barry gave it his all, the fight was a fairly tame, one-sided affair as Jack took control of the bout early. Jack had floored Barry twice in the seventeen minutes of fighting, finishing him at two minutes into the sixth round. Many present speculated that the fight would have lasted only half the time had Dempsey not been held back by his promise of a "scientific" bout to the police and his seconds, who were trying to comply with that promise. The *Brooklyn Eagle* correspondent commented, "In the sixth-round Dempsey knocked Barry down and could have knocked him out if necessary, but Barry gave up the fight."[92] Dempsey had shown himself quite well on his first Pacific Slope swing and his fans on the West Coast were becoming legion. After some initial skepticism toward the young easterner, the Portland sporting set was becoming quite enamored with Brooklyn's Nonpareil.

A few days after Jack's defeat of Barry, he left Portland by train, heading east to Brooklyn for the holidays. Jack was traveling with Dave Campbell, Tom Cleary and Jake Stearns, who was referred to as their manager for the trip. Apparently, the journey was interrupted by several evening exhibition sessions along the route. Reference has been made in several local newspapers to an exhibition match in Butte City, Montana, between the Nonpareil and Campbell. The party arrived in St. Paul, Minnesota, on December 20. They spent the day as the guests of John S. Barnes and several local sporting men with whom they toured the city and dined before boarding the 8:15 p.m. train to Chicago for the next leg of their journey. While in town, Dempsey authorized Barnes to make a match for him with Patsy Cardiff. Jack specified that it should be a finish fight for a sum of somewhere between $2,500 and $10,000 and take place at a mutually agreed upon location sometime in the next several months.[93] Cardiff responded the next day, stating that he was very willing to meet Dempsey, but in a show of bravado, said that he doubted the sincerity of the challenge and questioned that Dempsey could win such a contest.[94]

Dempsey determined to stop off in Chicago for a couple of days to see friends and to break up the journey a bit. He arrived in the Windy City on Monday, December 21, and would catch the evening train on Wednesday, but while in town, he became involved in an unexpected brawl. On Monday evening, while Jack was out with friends he was accosted by a burly local slugger named Patsy Duffy. Duffy who weighed roughly 180 pounds, approached the Nonpareil and said, "So you're the notorious Jack Dempsey are you?" Dempsey amused those present when he acknowledged that he was indeed Jack Dempsey, but that he had no claim on notoriety. Duffy, not amused by Jack's retort, responded, "Well, you're a fighter and we smother fighters in this country." Duffy then wound up and took a swing at Dempsey's head. In a split second the Nonpareil blocked the blow and replied with a blistering right that hit with such force that Duffy fell backwards and sprawled on the floor. Friends of both men quickly intervened, but the unpleasantness was far from over. It took ten minutes for Duffy to be revived, but once he was on his feet, he again foolishly went looking for Dempsey. When he found him, the now embarrassed would be pugilist caught Jack off guard and hit Dempsey in the face. "No one interfered this time and Dempsey gave the big man a terrible pummeling."[95] After the fisticuffs, Jack and his friends dined and drank happily.

The remainder of his stay in Chicago was peaceful, with no one challenging the middleweight champion. He continued his journey to Brooklyn by rail, leaving Wednesday evening as scheduled and arriving home in Brooklyn in the wee hours of Christmas Eve. He commented to reporters that he was going to spend the holidays with his mother, look to set some fights, and would seriously consider returning to the West Coast to reside. "I am ready to fight any man in the world," said Dempsey, "barring Sullivan. He is my friend. I do particularly want to stand up before Charley Mitchell."[96]

On December 26, a large crowd of sporting men gathered at the offices of the *Police Gazette* for the announcement of bouts between Dempsey and Jack Fogarty for a $1,000 prize and another between Charley Holmes and Sam Collyer. Charley Mitchell was an early arrival at the event and when informed that Jack would meet Fogarty, he opined—somewhat bitterly—that Dempsey would do better to set a bout with George La Blanche or some other noted pugilist instead, to build his reputation. Mitchell was extremely frustrated at his inability to secure his own match with Dempsey and took all opportunities to impugn his rival's skills and abilities.

Dempsey soon arrived, accompanied by a large delegation including Jere Dunn, Charley Holmes, Professor Mike Donovan, Martin Dempsey and John Reagan, "who had just come from the battlefield, where he conquered Fred English for a purse of $500."[97]

Dempsey posted a $250 forfeit fee with *Gazette* editor Richard K. Fox to prove that he was willing to meet any pugilist in America except John L. Sullivan. "He stated that he was willing to meet Mitchell with or without gloves, prize ring rules or Queensberry rules, to a finish for $2,500 a side, either private or public, and he would allow the members of the New York press to select the referee."[98]

Some disagreement was seen over the size of the prize in the Dempsey-Fogarty match. Gus Tuthill, Dempsey's backer, stated that the stakes were not high enough at $1,000 and claimed that Dempsey would meet Fogarty for no less than $2,500. He also stated that if this amount could not be made, Dempsey would prefer to fight Mitchell, Jack Burke or Dominick McCaffrey. Fogarty compatriot William E. Harding stated that he would carry the request back to Fogarty backer Arthur Chambers. Chambers signed the agreement but left several options open for Dempsey's choice. Those options were "saying whether the fight shall take place in six or eight weeks; whether in private, with twelve persons present on each side or in public; whether six or eight-ounce gloves; Dempsey to name the place of fighting agreeable to Chambers or toss for choice of selection." Chambers stated that if this agreement was not suitable to Dempsey, the Nonpareil could draw up his own articles of agreement and send them to Chambers for approval.[99]

"After Dempsey had transacted his business, Richard K. Fox brought him into his private office and presented him with an elegant gold medal valued at $250. The medal was sent to the jewelers to have the following inscription put on it: 'Presented to Jack Dempsey, the champion middleweight pugilist of the world, by Richard K. Fox, the proprietor of the *Police Gazette*, Jan. 1, 1886.'"[100]

The medal was designed with the American and Irish flags on each side surrounded by a scroll, and in the center was two pugilists in a ring. After the medal was engraved by the jeweler, it was formally presented by Fox to Dempsey on New Year's Eve morning at 11:00 at the *Police Gazette* offices.

During the last weeks of December, it was noted that Charley Mitchell was in Brooklyn and appearing nightly at a local theater. Dempsey's friends and backers, anxious to goad Charley into a contest with Jack, vowed to dog the British pugilist all during his visit to the City of Churches.[101] Mitchell began his years of avoidance of the Nonpareil by criticizing Dempsey and his backers. "When Jack Dempsey has fought a man of repute, I will make a match with him for any good amount, for money is the only thing I am looking for. I can't make any reputation off of him, for people that know his record know full well that he has never met a man of standing as a fighter, and most of his matches have been fixed beforehand." Not content with that, Mitchell then stated that neither Dempsey nor his "loafing comrades" had better try to make any trouble for him during the remainder of his stay in the New York area, for he would be ready for them.[102]

The Mitchell-Dempsey affair dragged on for years and was unfortunate. The Nonpareil was quite willing to meet Mitchell under certain conditions, but Mitchell continually found reasons to oppose any proposal for a fight. While many observers believed that Dempsey would defeat Mitchell, a victory was by no means a certainty. Charley Mitchell was a very talented fighter. One reporter stated that "Mitchell is a good general, cool headed, cunning and aggressive when it is necessary." The reporter went on to say that if Dempsey and Mitchell ever did come together in the ring it would be a great fight. "Both are great men in their line and deserving of all the fame they have got. It isn't very often that a prizefighter is accused of having brains, but here are two men who are so well supplied in that direction that they have made themselves famous even under conditions and circumstances which were not favorable."[103] Proposed bouts would be floated for the next several years, but regrettably the men never faced each other in the squared circle. More than a few boxing historians agree that Mitchell should be considered as an all-time middleweight great.

In late December, it was announced that Jack would appear daily starting on January 4 at the Alexander Museum at 317 Bowery as a human statue. He would earn a salary of $500 a week and would be assisted in entertaining the public by The Madagascar Soldiers—a flock of flamingoes, each standing 6 feet 3 inches tall, who the public was assured were "positively the only ones brought into this country alive."[104] He was also aided by Miss Jennie Quigley, "the royal midget."[105]

It had been a very good year for Jack Dempsey. He had begun to build his name and reputation beyond the northeast. He had taken on not only men in his weight range, but also larger men, and he met them in venues across America from New York to Louisiana to the Pacific Coast. He had traveled the continent and was in great demand for appearances and sparring exhibitions. Like Sullivan, the newly crowned "Nonpareil" was becoming one of America's first sporting heroes.

1886—The Nonpareil Emerges

Eighteen eighty-six had barely begun when the New Year was interrupted with reports from Boston that Thomas Bogue, manager for George La Blanche, was impugning the Nonpareil's character. Bogue reportedly called Jack a coward and questioned whether or not he had the fortitude and ability to defeat La Blanche.

On January 4, it was announced that Dempsey would meet Jack Fogarty of Philadelphia at 150 pounds, Queensberry Rules, for $2,500 a side. A forfeit of $500 was held by Richard K. Fox and the bout was to be fought within six weeks.[1] The battle would indeed take place on February 3 in New York's Clarendon Hall.

Jack also addressed Bogue's comments on that day by telling journalists that all Bogue and La Blanche had to do if they truly desired a bout with Dempsey was to cover his deposit of $250 which lay at the *Police Gazette* offices. He was certain that in that case agreeable terms could be reached.[2]

On a lighter note, Jack appeared all of the week of January 4 as a "classic athletic statue poser" at the Alexander Museum on New York's Bowery. There seemed to be no end to the variety of events that Dempsey was asked to be involved in. Appearing in front of packed houses all week, "Dempsey's performance was as follows. He first took the position of a man about to enter the ring. After extending his right hand to his imaginary opponent he put himself in position ready for battle, with his left hand and foot thrown forward and his right across his chest in guard. Dempsey showed the audience how four of the men he had defeated lay after he had knocked them down. Dempsey then showed the positions a good fighter should take in defense and attack when in battle, and the illustrations were well received."[3]

On January 11, Jack and Tom Cleary headed to Boston for a quick trip to size up and feel out La Blanche. La Blanche, a French Canadian born George Blair in Point Levi, Quebec, on December 19, 1856, was known as the Marine because of a six-month hitch he served in the United States Marine Corps in 1883 and 1884. He began his boxing career in 1882 and continued to fight for nearly two decades. La Blanche, while not a great technical fighter, was tough, quick and agile.

Before leaving for Boston, Jack stated that he was willing to fight La Blanche for fun if necessary. Upon arriving in town, the men registered at the Adams House, where they rested a bit and then took breakfast, after which they headed to Mike Gleason's saloon at 157 Court Street about 9:00 a.m., where they inquired after the Marine. A messenger was sent for La Blanche and shortly thereafter the Marine walked in. The men greeted each other cordially as they eyed each other. They then walked over to the bar where they took a drink and began to chat. "Dempsey immediately confronted La Blanche and said, 'I came here at once to prove to you that I am a game man. I will fight you right away for $1,000 a side.' La Blanche said, 'I have no money, Dempsey,' "Well,' said Dempsey, 'I will fight you for fun, with bare knuckles or gloves, just as you like.' La Blanche still pleaded poverty but said he would fight soon."[4]

Tom Bogue joined the group before beginning a walking tour of the various sporting resorts of the city. They wound up back at the Adams House, where Jack hosted La Blanche, Bogue and Cleary for their early afternoon meal. "During the dinner, which was informal in character, the best of feelings prevailed."[5] After their meal was finished, the party called upon Billy Mahoney, visited with Jack Lynn at the Bijou Club, saw Sullivan's mahogany parlors and the new club room at the corner of Hollis and Washington Streets and dropped by at Patsy Sheppard's. At 4:30 that afternoon, after a whirlwind visit, Dempsey and Cleary boarded their train back to New York.

The day spent between the two pugilists served several purposes. It calmed speculation in some quarters as to why Jack might be avoiding La Blanche as he now quite clearly was not. On the other hand, it also ramped up speculation that the two would soon meet in the squared circle. Dempsey certainly hoped so. Coming off a string of fine victories, Jack was ready to fight all comers, but seemed to always have a special interest in whipping La Blanche.

La Blanche distanced himself from the comments attributed to Bogue, expressing his opinion that Dempsey was game and a fine fighter as well as a gentleman. Bogue for his part denied the slanderous comments. In an open letter to the *Police Gazette* sporting editor dated January 15, Bogue stated, "I certainly never made the remarks nor caused them to be printed. Moreover, I do not believe such slander would impair Mr. Dempsey's standing, backed as he is by a record unsurpassed by any man in his profession."[6]

Jack had to get back from Boston soon for he had obligations awaiting him in New York. On January 13, Jack attended an evening of "scientific boxing" held at the New York Athletic Club. The management of the club had promised the police that there would be no "brutal slugging," but rather an evening of boxing for points and displays of the manly art of self-defense. Many politicians and police officials were on hand. The evening had six bouts on the card, the highlight being a dandy six-rounder between lightweight champion Jack McAuliffe and Jack Hopper, also of Brooklyn. The first three rounds were fairly even as the two men kept up a steady drum on each other, but by the fourth, it was a different matter. McAuliffe maneuvered Hopper against the ropes and landed consistently strong blasts for the final minute of the round. In the fifth, McAuliffe kept up the pressure, charging Hopper "like a buffalo across the prairies" and hammering him until he finally sent his opponent through the ropes. No sooner than Hopper had gotten back to his feet and into the ring, McAuliffe knocked him down again. It was no better for Hopper in the sixth round as twice more McAuliffe sent him through the ropes after a relentless pounding.[7]

After the six scheduled bouts, the crowd received an additional treat. Dempsey, as a special favor to the club's board, climbed into the ring, where the 148-pound Nonpareil sparred three friendly exhibition rounds with a local but little-known fighter named Mike Mulrey. "He made Mulrey very tired before the last one ended, though."[8]

A benefit was held for Jack on January 15, 1886, at the Germania Assembly Rooms in the heavily German Bowery section of Manhattan. The Assembly Rooms were located at 291 & 293 Bowery near the intersection of East Houston Street. "The building was a two-story warehouse that contained a barroom, a restaurant, a billiards room, meeting rooms, and a bowling alley. Beer flowed freely and food was appropriately priced; lunch, the main meal served at the club, could be had for fifteen cents. The Germania was a place where local organizations held their meetings."[9]

The venue was packed that evening with a varied crowd of businessmen, local elected officials and sporting men of all types. "Horse owners, jockeys, pool sellers, pedestrians, fighters, oarsmen, marksmen, ball players, and in fact, all sorts of professional sports were in attendance."[10] During the evening, Dempsey was presented with a gold medal from the *Police Gazette*'s Richard K. Fox to celebrate the Nonpareil's great success during his recent western tour.

In an unusual twist, Dempsey would meet three different fighters that evening. He would meet Jimmy Murray, Tom Henry and Professor Mike Donovan one after the other, each for four rounds. What made this so unusual is that while Dempsey often sparred with multiple opponents during exhibitions, two bouts were not billed as exhibitions, but as actual fights. The night's referees were Billy O'Brien and a gentleman named "Plummer"—most probably Ed, who had refereed Dempsey's bout with Bob Turnbull in 1884.

First up was Murray, whom Dempsey dispatched easily. Murray, who hailed from Providence, Rhode Island, stood just over five and a half feet tall. He was a muscular scrapper who hit hard and had a magnificent right hand. For two rounds Jack took it fairly easy, just tapping Murray gently, but the crowd was anxious for more and vocalized their disapproval with hisses and catcalls. Jack picked up the pace in the third and fourth rounds. "He rained blows fast and furiously on the face and body of his opponent."[11] Murray could do nothing with Jack and spent most of the bout trying to evade the heavy right hand of the champion. "After the fourth-round his face was as red as a beet, and he breathed a sigh of relief when referee Plummer ordered the men to desist."[12]

In the evening's second bout, Jack squared off with his old rival, good friend and sparring partner Tom Henry. This was the pair's third meeting in less than two years, with the first match ending in a draw, and Jack taking victory in the second bout in six rounds. "Dempsey from the start hit hard, but he found Henry's guard a trifle stronger than Murray's, and for that reason he failed to administer any great amount of punishment."[13] Despite his stronger bulwark, Henry too was handily defeated by his antagonist.

Last up was Donovan. This would be the first of two times the legendary pugilists met in the ring. The bout was fought on scientific principles and the two men contented themselves with tapping each other lightly. "Dempsey surprised nearly everybody by his skillful work, and the old sports admitted that if he were a little bigger he would prove a dangerous opponent to the invincible Sullivan."[14] While the bout was declared an exhibition fought for science and officially a draw, many in attendance believed that Dempsey won this bout on points over the four rounds.[15]

Between Dempsey's three bouts, additional sparring sessions were held between Jack McAuliffe and Jimmy Nelson, George Taylor and Billy Dacey and Mike Mulrey and Denny Costigan.

Jack was on top of his game and enjoying himself immensely, but he had met a young lady in Portland the previous summer and for the first time, he had begun to make some noise about returning to Oregon and retiring from the ring. He would struggle for the rest of his life between his sincere desire to settle down and raise a family and his addiction to the ring. An example of his internal struggle came during the very interview in which he first mentioned the possibility of retirement. After mentioning the possibility,

Jack couched the comment with the caveat that until he did retire, he would meet all comers at 154 pounds. Regardless of his future plans, however, the Nonpareil was the man to beat as 1886 got under way. "Dempsey has proved himself a wonder and if he is beaten it will be by over-matching himself."[16]

On January 23, the *Police Gazette* reported that Jack had been matched to fight New York amateur champion Joe Ellingsworth in Hoboken, New Jersey, sometime in late February. This was news to Dempsey and his camp. Ellingsworth had been a good amateur, but with no real professional experience, Dempsey's backers saw no benefit in their man fighting the young man. Ultimately the fight never came off, but this would be the first in a series of attempts by Ellingsworth's people at bringing the two fighters together. More serious attempts at setting contests were made with Charley Mitchell, Pete McCoy and La Blanche.

To that end Dempsey dispatched Gus Tuthill to Philadelphia in late January to meet with Arthur Chambers and arrange a fight with Chambers's protégé Jack Fogarty. Dempsey told Tuthill to agree to the bout for any amount of money and a battle was quickly arranged.

Chambers was a former prizefighter from England who turned professional after leaving the Royal Navy in the 1860s. He fought in the United States and Canada throughout the 1870s, winning the American lightweight championship by defeating Billy Edwards in 1872. Chambers eventually settled in Philadelphia where he opened a bar. After leaving the ring, Chambers remained an active figure in the sport by engaging in exhibition bouts and by advising and supporting numerous fighters, including John L. Sullivan and Jack Fogarty.

Jack Fogarty.

Jack traveled home to New York from Cincinnati on the night before the bout. The Nonpareil had been in the Queen City appearing with a vaudeville company in exhibition matches all week. After the Fogarty bout in Manhattan and a short hop back home to Brooklyn, Dempsey would rejoin the company in Buffalo.[17]

Fogarty was a smart and scrappy fighter who hailed from Philadelphia, where he managed the Ariel Athletic Club. Fogarty was then in the middle of a brief but busy three-year career.

Dempsey met Fogarty over the witching hour on February 2 and 3, in the back room of Clarendon Hall at Thirteenth Street between Third and Fourth avenues in Manhattan. The men fought twenty-seven rounds for a purse of $3,000 a side. Fogarty stood just under 5'8" and weighed 150 pounds. Jack stood as tall but weighed three pounds less.

The police had gotten wind of the bout

and were on the lookout for any gathering of Dempsey, Fogarty and their backers. To keep the police away, the bout was kept very quiet and the appointed hour was revealed only to a select few—maybe forty in all. Each man paid $25 admission to witness the bout, making up a side purse of $1,000 which was added to the $2,000 already offered. "To avoid police interference the ticket holders were divided into squads, who were met at various resorts by guides, who conducted them to a hall up town, where a ring was pitched."[18]

Shortly after 11:00 p.m., Fogarty appeared on the scene. He had quietly slipped through the darkened streets to the rendezvous. Soon thereafter, those in the know drifted in. One by one, they slipped into the unlighted hall and, taking a seat, quietly and anxiously awaited the mill. Finally, with everyone in the hall, "the doors were locked, the windows covered with heavy hangings and the gas lights above the ring turned up."[19]

Jack wore dark trunks with green colors around his waist. He was seconded by Dave Campbell, Alf Powers and his trainer, Tom Cleary of California. Chambers and Billy Edwards, the great bare-knuckles fighter, were in Fogarty's corner. Their man sported white, knee-length knickers, white canvas shoes and blue colors around his waist. Al Smith was selected to serve as referee and two members of the New York Athletic Club served as timekeepers. To further avoid any hint of a prizefight to the police, a muffled bell was used to signal the beginning and end of each round. The men wore skintight, two-ounce kid gloves and agreed to three-minute rounds under the Queensberry Rules.

"At 11:30 o'clock each, with his seconds, stepped into the ring in splendid condition.... The timekeepers' watches marked 11:40 when Referee Smith called time for the contest which required 27 rounds to decide."[20] "The men received their instructions and with all doors locked and a lookout posted, the bell rang and the bout was on."[21]

Fogarty did his best to take the fight to Dempsey, but Jack was cool and confident from the start and toyed with his opponent, using strategy and superior ring knowledge to draw Fogarty out. He was cautious at the outset, avoided leading and stayed on the defensive, feinting and picking off his opponent's punches until Fogarty was tired, discouraged and rattled. Dempsey then went at his opponent, landing well placed and damaging blows, the most notable of which left a red mark on Fogarty's face while another landed on the Philadelphian's stomach.

Periodically, Fogarty would get a punch in as a reminder to Jack that his opponent was certainly a dangerous foe. One in the second round caught Dempsey flush on the chin and staggered him, and another was a lightning bolt to Jack's rib cage, but the Nonpareil responded immediately with a straight left that bloodied Fogarty's nose.

In the third round, Fogarty came out like a man on fire, but again Dempsey confounded him and began to score powerful shots to the Philadelphian's mouth and almost closed Fogarty's left eye. Repeatedly Fogarty's swings landed short or were ineffective while Dempsey made every blow count.

In the fourth round, Dempsey landed a howitzer-like blow straight to the face that split Fogarty's lip almost up to his nostril. Blood spurted from the wound as if the boxer had been knifed. Jack followed up with a hard right to Fogarty's jaw that left the Philadelphian off balance, causing him to collapse to the ground. He got up, but only to receive another blow to the mouth. Once again, before the round was over, "Dempsey almost knocked his antagonist down with a blow to the stomach."[22]

In the fifth round, Dempsey concentrated on his opponent's nose and ribs. By the time Smith ended the round Fogarty was bleeding heavily and was clearly tiring. The sixth and seventh rounds saw Dempsey following Fogarty around the ring during which time the former used his left arm as a shield and his right as a hammer to deliver still more punishment on the Philadelphian.

Dempsey was clearly winning the fight, but in the eighth round, he suddenly began to tire. His hands appeared too heavy to hold up and he spent much of the round on the move, avoiding contact with his opponent. The ninth round continued much the same with Dempsey playing for time and wind and Fogarty chasing him around the ring and trying to press the advantage, but repeatedly missing with his blows as Dempsey danced and weaved just out of reach. Fogarty became a bit winded from chasing Dempsey around the ring for two rounds and in the tenth, the Nonpareil rallied and, having caught his breath, he resumed his offensive from the first seven rounds. Fogarty had lost his best chance at defeating Dempsey. For two rounds he appeared stronger, but he simply could not get close enough to make his blows land and do damage.[23]

"In the eleventh, Fogarty was knocked down by a blow on the jaw, but he got up and fought again though covered with blood."[24] The twelfth round was much the same with Dempsey scoring another clean knock-down.

Fogarty recovered a bit in the fifteenth round and, after receiving a left-hand jab, fired back with a powerful right to Dempsey's rib cage that landed with such effect that it sent the Brooklyn boy on a visit to the mat. Dempsey was up in a second and quickly recovered, but the blow was a reminder that his opponent was dangerous and that any single blow could change the tenor of the bout. He would continue to press the fighting, but he would remain wary of his larger and powerful antagonist.

By the sixteenth round Fogarty was a mess. His cuts were deep, his blood flowed freely and his left eye was nearly closed, but he continued to fight on as Dempsey battered and bruised him round after round. According to Richard Fox, "Fogarty was all the time growing weaker and was a horrible sight to contemplate. His left eye was closed and had to be lanced, while in the eighteenth-round his nose was broken by a quick uppercut with which Dempsey caught him while recovering from an almost knock-down blow."[25]

In the twentieth round, Fogarty was nearly out on his feet—there is no way that the fight would be allowed to continue today. When Jack dropped him again, he lay on the ground for almost ten seconds until Chambers told him to get up. As soon as he did, Fogarty met another salvo, including a terrific right-handed blow from Dempsey that resulted in a broken jaw.[26] The *Police Gazette* disputed that Fogarty's jaw was broken, but reported a badly cut lip, badly swollen eyes and neck and a broken nose. Whatever the total carnage, the massacre continued for the next six rounds, but the Philadelphian refused to stay down.

By the twenty-second-round Fogarty was clearly weakening. In a show of gamesmanship, his seconds, Arthur Chambers and Billy Edwards began trying to rile Dempsey by calling out remarks to their man that were clearly aimed at the Nonpareil. "You can lick the duffer; don't be afraid of the coward." This offended Jack's second, Tom Cleary, who mouthed invective back at Chambers and Edwards, but in typical cool-headed fashion, Dempsey, while pounding his opponent, ordered Cleary back to his corner and to calm down.

After pounding Fogarty unmercifully with lefts and right, Dempsey sent him to the ground again in the twenty-seventh round. Fogarty struggled to get to his feet, but once there, he began wobbling around like a newborn colt. According to Cleary, "Dempsey punched Fogarty all around and forced him to his corner where he gave him a left-hand swing in the nose. Fogarty fell and turned over on his belly and lay there stunned on the ground for fifteen seconds. When he got up the time keeper told him to give up the fight and Dempsey also told him to quit as he could do nothing. Fogarty went to his corner but could not rise from his stool when called to scratch. Chambers came over to Dempsey and threw up the sponge."[27] The bout lasted for a brutal hour and forty-seven minutes.[28]

While the men appeared evenly matched in size and conditioning, Dempsey was by far the superior fighter. "His antagonist was game, strong, wicked, clever, but not Dempsey's equal."[29] Jack used his superior skills and ring generalship to soundly defeat his opponent. Fogarty stood little chance when he climbed into the ring with the Nonpareil that winter's night. He was a good fighter, but Dempsey was at the top of his game. Fogarty continued to box sporadically through the early years of the twentieth century, but he eventually left the ring to participate in another brutal sport—local politics. Fogarty died at the relatively young age of fifty-five in Philadelphia on February 4, 1921.

Dempsey was declared the winner and was awarded half of the $6,000 purse with the other half divided among the various backers. Jack immediately and magnanimously handed Chambers $250 to give to Fogarty. Reportedly, Chambers turned over only $100 and kept $150 for himself which, upon hearing about it later, made Dempsey furious.

Mike Donovan, commenting on fights to a finish in a letter to the editor of the *New York World* in 1896, wrote of the Nonpareil's superiority during even a well-matched bout. "There was Jack Dempsey and Jack Fogarty, who fought to a finish down in Clarendon Hall in Thirteenth Street. Good fight it was, too, although Dempsey cut his man into ribbons."[30]

Dempsey headed to his mother's home in Brooklyn after the bout. Jack had some bruising around his ribs and chest and some damage to two knuckles on his left hand, but otherwise, he barely had a scratch. He was seen the following day out on the town, and later with his friends at his mother's home in the Eastern District of Brooklyn. Both his hands were bandaged, but he promised that they would be fine when he met Peter McCoy in three weeks.

Dempsey was to appear on February 5 in the ring at Harry Hill's with Mike Cleary at a benefit for Cleary and "true to his promise, he was there, but his left hand was bound up and when he was excused by the master of ceremonies he was heartily cheered."[31] Cleary sparred instead for three rounds with John Reilly. It was also announced that Dempsey would travel with Mike Donovan to Binghamton, New York, to appear in a "scientific wind-up" at the City Opera House on February 12.[32]

Dempsey had now entered the high point of his career. He was undefeated and recognized by most as the middleweight champion of North America. He was in great demand and drew crowds wherever he went. Dempsey had now so distinguished himself in the ring that the *Police Gazette* observed after the Fogarty fight, "John L. Sullivan and Jack Dempsey now stand on par as the greatest pugilists of the age at their respective weights." The paper added that those who had doubted Dempsey's dominant position "should now come to the conclusion that Dempsey is not only a two-handed, clever and scientific pugilist, but a man that, when he is in front of his opponent is not only a terrific hitter, but a first-class general."[33]

On February 9, Dempsey looked fit and rested as he refereed the Jack Fallon–John Banks bout in New York. The next day Jack was interviewed by a *New York Sun* reporter upon returning to the Rochester House on Bleecker Street after a long and brisk walk.

During a post-exercise rubdown Jack told the reporter that he was working hard to get in top condition not only for the upcoming McCoy fight, but also for a proposed bout with La Blanche. Dempsey was put out with La Blanche and his supporters who were once again calling Dempsey a coward and making the ridiculous and provocative claims that La Blanche was the true middleweight champion. Dempsey had originally sought to wait six months to fight La Blanche in order to give the broken knuckles on his left hand a chance to heal. He had now had enough of La Blanche and his camp and was ready to go. "I'll fight whether my hand is all right or not," Dempsey said, "and those who back me can count on it that I will be there."[36] Within a couple of days the splints came off his left hand and in short order, he was back in the ring sparring.

The pugilists were anxious to meet. Tom Bogue was however only willing to wager $1,000 on La Blanche and Dempsey would not settle for less than a $2,500 guarantee. The matter remained unsettled, "until a Broadway hotel keeper interested himself in the affair. He consulted with a number of clubmen...and collected a purse of $1,500 to be presented to the winner in addition to the $2,000 stake money already deposited. This satisfied the high-minded New York slugger and arrangements were begun to bring the two men together."[37]

On the evening February 16, Jack was at the Gilsey House in Manhattan where he and his backer Gus Tuthill signed the articles of agreement for a match with La Blanche, to be held in March within fifty miles of New York City. "Articles of agreement in duplicate, signed by La Blanche and Bogue, his backer, were sent on from Boston to Al Smith."[38] The contest was to be a winner take all fight to the finish under Queensberry Rules with the men wearing small gloves. The fight was for $1,000 a side with an additional subscription purse of $1,500. The subscription purse was in essence the gate for the bout. "The purse has been made up by twenty gentlemen interested in the manly art, each of whom pays $75 for the privilege of seeing the contest. Each however, is permitted to bring one friend along."[39] After the papers were signed, Jack stated that he would go into training under Tom Cleary, Dave Campbell and Al Powers in Newburgh, New York. The fight was eventually set to be held on the night of March 12.

In the meantime, Jack had accepted a challenge from notable middleweight Pete McCoy of Boston. Dempsey met McCoy in Jersey City on Wednesday, February 24, at the Oakland Avenue Skating Rink in front of an estimated 4,000 people. The two men fought six rounds lasting twenty-three minutes. The Nonpareil won the fight and claimed the prize, estimated by various sources as having been anywhere from $1,000 and $6,000.

The 29-year-old McCoy was born in County Kerry, Ireland, and had arrived in America when he was seven. The Boston man stood just over five feet and nine inches tall and weighed in at 147 pounds. He had a short, stocky neck, grayish blue eyes and a prominent red moustache. McCoy was a talented fighter who had never lost in the ring. He fought and won the longest Queensberry bout in recorded history to that time—a two-and-a-half-hour, thirty-two-round tilt with the much larger Duncan McDonald in Butte, Montana. He did not care to brag. Of the fight with Dempsey McCoy said, "I do not say that I expect to knock him out, but I certainly think I can best him."[40] McCoy set up his training camp at Long Island's Hawthorne Hotel in Parkville, New York.

According to boxing historian Tracy Callis, "McCoy was quick and agile, had fast hands and carried a good right-hand punch." He also would shift his feet quickly and fight skillfully with either hand. The *Brooklyn Eagle* described McCoy as one of the most scientific and shiftiest pugilists that ever entered the ring in this country. He never cared about how strong his opponent was and was not averse to giving away substantial amounts of weight to his opponents.[41] McCoy fought many ring notables in his time. In addition to Dempsey he met Mike Donovan, Johnny Reagan, Dominick McCaffrey, George La Blanche and Jake Kilrain and for several years in the 1880s, he fought John L. Sullivan regularly in exhibitions around the country.

For this bout, Jack set up his training headquarters at the Merchant's Hotel in Newburgh, New York. Tom Cleary put Dempsey through a normal regimen that included running, long walks, lifting dumbbells, hitting the heavy bag, jumping rope and sparring. He reduced his weight from 160 pounds to 148 pounds by the time of the contest.

On fight night the spacious venue was packed full of fans from all professions and walks of life. There were politicians, military officers, lawyers, merchants, managers from various local athletic clubs and fighters, many of whom had traveled from New England and Chicago. Jersey City's Police Chief Murphy and a force of fifty of his officers were on hand to keep order and to step in should the fight get out of hand. Among those present were George La Blanche and Tom Bogue, who wanted to take advantage of this chance to see Dempsey in action just weeks before the Marine himself would meet the Nonpareil. La Blanche and Bogue sat in the reporters' gallery during the evening.[42]

The first part of the evening held a series of three-round contests between lightweight fighters, as well as several wrestling matches. The four thousand on hand were anxious for the mill to begin. Just before 11:00 p.m., McCoy jumped over the ropes and into the ring. He was followed immediately by Dempsey.

In McCoy's corner were Dan Gill of Boston and his trainer Tom Evans. McCoy stood an inch taller than Dempsey and at 151 pounds was just three pounds heavier. He was attired in white knee-length tights and white knee socks. His boxing shoes were made of canvas with rubber soles. Gus Tuthill and Tom Cleary looked after Dempsey, who wore his famous dark blue trunks. Jimmy Ryan and Mike Cleary were chosen as co-referees and William E. Harding as timekeeper.

The first round began quickly with more than the usual parrying as the two skillful pugilists tried to figure each other out. They smiled at each other as they maneuvered. Suddenly Dempsey fired a left that landed on McCoy's right ear and McCoy with no hesitation countered with a straight left that found Dempsey's neck. Jack countered with several hard lefts that impressed the crowd with their rapidity and accuracy. The two then exchanged punches and landed on each other's eyes and noses. Jack missed with his left and McCoy countered with a left to Dempsey's right eye and another right to the left side of his head. The round went on in this manner with both men showing well. At the end of the three minutes, they returned to their respective corners where their seconds plied them with brandy and water.

Round two began with McCoy breathing heavily and favoring his right hand. Dempsey fired both lefts and rights, but McCoy, showing his characteristic quickness, dodged out of the way. McCoy fired a left that fell short and Jack countered with a powerful left to McCoy's jaw. McCoy countered to the head. The pair continued to exchange blows in a heated exchange, but Dempsey seemed to get the better of the fighting, landing hard punches on the nose, right eye and ribs of his opponent and driving him into the ropes. By its end, this was Jack's round.

Round three saw a rapid exchange in which Dempsey landed on McCoy's nose and the latter returned the favor by dropping a left to Dempsey's cheek just below his right eye. After several exchanges McCoy began to wear down. He became desperate and lunged at Jack who while remaining cool, landed a tremendous blow to McCoy's neck, sending him staggering. McCoy recovered quickly, and the two exchanged a few blows before falling into a clinch, during which Dempsey landed several hard uppercuts on his opponent's chin. He continued landing hard to McCoy's stomach and nose with both hands. The men had another rapid exchange as the round ended. The crowd cheered both men but agreed that this, too, was the Nonpareil's round as he had landed more telling blows and had forced most of the fighting.

The fourth round started quickly, with both men landing head and body blows, but McCoy was showing the damage done by Dempsey's continual blows and was beginning to fight defensively. McCoy continued to throw punches, but with nowhere near the effectiveness of Dempsey's. Late in the round Jack countered his opponent with a left cross that staggered the Boston man and before he could recover, Dempsey landed three more punishing blows to the face and one to the ribs. As the round was ending, Jack landed two more scorching blows to McCoy's body.

Dempsey forced the fighting in round five while McCoy largely fought in reverse. A right cross to the jaw almost ended it, but McCoy kept his footing. Jack got in several more blows before McCoy could recover. Still, the Boston man fought on as best he could by landing several blows to Dempsey's face. The Nonpareil finished the round by firing two cannon-like rights that landed on McCoy's jaw.

Round six may have been the best of the fight as both men showed extremely well. McCoy, knowing that the odds were heavily against him by now, fought desperately looking for a knockout. He landed heavily on Jack's eye, face, chin and chest and got the better of the next several exchanges. McCoy fought hard, "but Dempsey sent in two terrific hits on the face and chin, following them up with a left-hander on the nose and a right-hander on the ear."[43] After a final series of body blows and uppercuts from Dempsey, McCoy was spent. He leaned into his opponent in an attempt to halt the punishment. The men were still in a clinch when time was called.[44] The bout was decided for Dempsey.

The fight was described as "a rattling good mill" between the two unbeaten fighters. While he had won decisively, it was no walk in the park for Dempsey. "He punished McCoy very badly in the fourth round, but the latter showed up in excellent form in the fifth and sixth rounds...."[45] While the fight was clearly Dempsey's, McCoy put up a notable battle. It was estimated that when the receipts were counted up, Dempsey took home around $6,000.[46]

McCoy continued to fight through 1893, the year of his death. He drowned in Long Island Sound on November 8, 1893, near New London, Connecticut, after either falling or having jumped off the ocean tug *Scranton*. The tug's captain, Daniel McNulty, said that the vessel was traveling from Hoboken, New Jersey, to Boston, Massachusetts, and that he did not know whether it was an accident or a possible suicide.

On March 3, Dempsey met Joe Denning in a three-round exhibition match in Newark, New Jersey. Denning was a thirty-seven-year-old Brooklyn native. The large man with an impressive moustache stood just under six feet tall and weighed 190 pounds. In 1884, he was proclaimed by some to be the heavyweight champion of Dempsey's hometown of Williamsburg. Denning was not a polished boxer, but he was big, strong and powerful and therefore always a danger to land a devastating blow. The men traded jabs for the allotted three rounds and gave those assembled a good show for the price of admission.

After the Denning exhibition, which was really more of a tune up for the La Blanche tilt, Dempsey and his entourage returned to Newburgh where Jack was still under the training eyes of Al Power, Tom Cleary and Gus Tuthill. Dave Campbell had arrived from a previous engagement and was also working with Jack in the ring.

There were a number of Boston sporting men who were willing to back La Blanche over Dempsey because they believed that Jack was not quite the fighter he was reported to be and that a number of his victories were flukes. His inability to knock out McCoy further convinced them of their position and thousands of dollars were invested by La Blanche's backers. They believed that Dempsey's supreme self-confidence would eventually cause him difficulties and they believed that La Blanche was the man to exploit Jack's weaknesses. Dempsey's supporters simply laughed at these assertions as they had little respect for La Blanche's ring skills.

One boxing reporter described La Blanche's style in the ring as follows: "The Marine is a very hard man to get on to. He holds his head down on one shoulder and keeps his guard good and high. He is as strong as a bull and is very shifty." The reporter continued by describing La Blanche's manner of attack. "As quick as he delivers a blow he follows it up and hustles his man so that he has little time to recover."[47]

On March 11, the party left Newburgh by train and headed for Manhattan. Dempsey, sporting a moustache, was dressed in an old and battered brown hat and blue pea jacket in an effort to move about in public without raising attention. "Dempsey rode in the smoking car all the way down, sleeping most of the time, but getting out for a moment at Fishkill for a lunch. He ate some roast beef, one potato, dry toast and a farina pudding, and drank a bottle of Bass."[48] The party arrived in New York's Grand Central depot at 2:30 p.m. They proceeded to the Hartman House at Forty-Third Street and Vanderbilt Avenue. After reaching his room, he bathed, received a rub down from his trainers and took a nap. After rising, he went to the barber shop for a shave and a haircut at which time he lost the moustache.

La Blanche, Bogue, Danny Gill and Patsy Shepherd left Boston on Wednesday night and arrived in New York early Thursday morning. They remained in the city until just after noon when they boarded a Boston bound train, but exited the train in Harrison, New York. Harrison is a small town twenty-two-miles northeast of New York City, just north of Long Island Sound. Upon reaching their accommodations, La Blanche rested until evening. Dempsey's party arrived in Harrison at 8:51 p.m. by train and the bulk of the paying sports and their guests got in at a quarter past ten.

The local train station was filled that evening with the pugilists and their backers, reporters and the men who had paid to see the fight. This congregation was described as "some of the richest men in this city in company with ex-bruisers, gamblers, prize fighters, men about town, stock brokers, club men and well-known athletes," who were described as slinking about "in the shadows of the fences and between rows of trees tonight like an army of well-dressed burglars."[49]

For days there had been a great deal of speculation among reporters, the police and the sporting set as to when and where the bout would take place. The police were anxious to squelch the entire affair and sent their spies among the sports, using threats to arrest anyone involved if the fight came off inside city limits. The reporters and others who wished to see the fight also looked for tips as to the time and location of the match. Many of these would-be attendees were given so-called "straight tips" by men paid to provide false information. As a result, they were sent on wild goose chases and "went off to as many different places as there were recipients of the aforesaid tips, where they vainly waited for the fistic champions."[50]

Despite the best attempts to throw the authorities off the scent, Sheriff Duffy of Westchester County received a telegraph that the fight was to take place that night in Harrison, five miles from where he was in White Plains. The sheriff immediately organized a posse and set off to arrest the pugilists and others involved in the match. As the posse fanned out, word of the police dragnet made it to those in Harrison and smaller groups of men began to travel on to Mamaroneck, Rye and New Rochelle to avoid being arrested by the oncoming officials. Dempsey, La Blanche, Tuthill and Bogue, also aware of what was happening, quickly headed off in the darkness through the countryside toward White Plains and somehow avoided Duffy's men. They eventually made it to Mamaroneck in time to catch the 10:55 p.m. train back to New York. The backers regrouped later in Stamford, Connecticut, and around midnight they agreed that because of the police interference, the fight must be postponed for that evening. A new time and place for the encounter would have to be determined in the next few days. All of the backers then returned home. Numerous attempts were made to set battlegrounds in New Jersey as well as in a stable on 54th Street in Manhattan, but in both cases, they were warned off by the local constabularies. La Blanche was also being selective to avoid a location with a heavily pro–Dempsey crowd. Jack told one reporter, "La Blanche and his friends got scared of the crowd. Why I'm willing to meet him in Boston alone, for I'm sure I am a better man than he is."[51]

On the Ides of March in 1886, the *New York Times* reported that after several false starts, the Dempsey–La Blanche encounter finally came off. "While the law-abiding citizens of Larchmont, New York were sleeping quietly yesterday morning, Jack Dempsey, of this city, and George La Blanche of Boston, the two well-known pugilists, met near that place and decided the middleweight championship."[52]

La Blanche and his backers were not eager for this opportunity to meet Dempsey to fall away and talk of a Dempsey–Arthur Chambers contest being staged in its place may have helped spur them to reach a site agreement. Eventually the location was set for the outskirts of Mamaroneck, New York, in Westchester County on Long Island Sound just north of New York City. The bout was rescheduled for the early morning hours of Friday, March 12, but when the men and their backers arrived at the designated location on Thursday evening, they were greeted by scores of sporting types who had heard about the fight but had not contributed to the purse. In this case, the "straight tips" seemed to have failed. After some discussion, it was agreed that the sports who were determined to see the bout would contribute something to the purse and the fight was postponed and moved to the neighboring village of Larchmont. The fight eventually took place in a barn near Rye, New York, on the borderline between New York and Connecticut. There were only forty spectators present, including three reporters.

In the late-night hours of March 13, the pugilists, their backers and the selected sportswriters met at the Atlantic Dock in Brooklyn where they boarded the *Ocean King*, a tug boat that ferried them across Long Island Sound to a landing site near the selected fight location. The *Ocean King* dropped anchor and the men were ferried to shore where carriages were waiting to carry them on the final leg of their clandestine journey.⁵³

Finally, in the early morning hours of Sunday, March 14, 1886, the Nonpareil met the Bostonian to determine the middleweight championship. La Blanche, who weighed in at 155 pounds, came into the contest with a professional record of 14–3–5 after a successful amateur run in the military.

A flurry of excitement greeted the men as they entered the ring. Dempsey was outweighed by his opponent by a full eight pounds. La Blanche wore blue trunks and dark fighting shoes with his socks rolled down below his calves, as was his custom. The Marine was seconded by Tom Bogue and former fighter Patsy Shepherd. Dempsey also wore dark hose and white gaiters and was looked after by Gus Tuthill and his trainer Tom Cleary.

The referee chosen for the bout was James O'Neil of New York and the timekeepers were two well-known members of the New York Raquette Club. O'Neil informed the fighters that they were to do battle according to the Queensberry Rules with gloves and three-minute rounds partitioned by one minute of rest. He also informed the crowd to be quiet lest they become raucous and alarm the neighbors. The men then shook hands and O'Neil began the fight at just past four o'clock in the morning with these words: "Are you ready? Time."⁵⁴

The fighting began cautiously as the two men circled and sparred lightly. While Dempsey was the taller, La Blanche was much stouter with broad shoulders and heavily muscled arms. In time, La Blanche landed a series of three body blows on Dempsey, the third of which landed the Nonpareil against the ropes. Dempsey retaliated with a blow to La Blanche's neck that staggered him. This stopped the sturdy La Blanche for only a few seconds and he retaliated by landing a powerful and damaging right to Dempsey's ribs just as time was called on the round.

In the second round, La Blanche again took the initiative and rushed Dempsey, forcing his opponent against the ropes and delivering a hard left fist to Jack's jaw which was followed by several powerful body blows. La Blanche's followers were heartened by their man's strong showing thus far and offered to bet more money with any or all takers. Dempsey was not cowed by the attack and kept his hands working. Jack connected several hard blows on La Blanche's forehead and jaw that landed with "resounding" smacks. "For every

George La Blanche, or "The Marine," was Dempsey's hated and bitter foe.

blow delivered by the 'Marine,' he received, if anything, a harder and more punishing one in return."[55] Infighting then ensued and the larger man pushed Dempsey into the corner intent on dealing out some punishment, but Jack adroitly ducked and stepped away while landing a driving, churning left into the Marine's belly. The round ended in nobody's favor.

In the third, La Blanche continued to press the fight by rushing Dempsey, but the Nonpareil continually defended himself with grace. "He skillfully avoided the swift rushes made by his antagonist, and, gently stepping aside, he planted several heavy blows on La Blanche's body as he rushed past."[56] At one point during the round, La Blanche caught Dempsey on the ropes and delivered a rapid combination, but Jack recovered quickly and began returning blow after blow. As the round ended, La Blanche dropped his head while attempting to land a right on Jack's neck, but he was short, drawing an uppercut to the face from the Nonpareil. Dempsey's punch caught La Blanche square between the eyes, drawing first blood.

In the fourth round, La Blanche tried again to bring the fight to Dempsey, but he paid for his enthusiasm. He became sloppy and began receiving heavy blows to his head and face, one of which raised a very large knot on the Bostonian's right eye. Jack now began to let loose, forcing the fighting and landing regularly and heavily on his opponent for the remainder of the round.

By the fifth, the Marine was in trouble. When he stood for the opening bell, "he presented a sorrowful spectacle. His eye was discolored and nearly closed, his forehead was cut and bleeding, and his nose was swollen and of a crimson hue."[57] At the bell, "Dempsey and La Blanche came together like two buffaloes. It was give and take to the close."[58] While the round was somewhat even, Dempsey took the offensive and during the action, La Blanche received a cut to the left cheek from which blood flowed freely down his neck and chest.

In the sixth round, Dempsey again forced the fighting, sending La Blanche to the ropes and getting the better part of the exchanges. "From this point it was plain to be seen that Dempsey, bar accident, would win, for any impartial judge would have at a glance seen that the Boston champion was outclassed and has been greatly over-rated by an illustrated paper published in Boston."[59] The final minute of the round was uneventful as the two fighters tried to conserve energy.

La Blanche was a terrible sight when he came to scratch in the seventh round. It was clear that short of a miracle, he was a beaten man with little or no chance of defeating Dempsey. Jack continued to deliver great punishment, but through it, La Blanche fought back, refusing to quit.

Dempsey went on the offensive again in the eighth and ninth rounds. Using his powerful left to inflict further punishment on La Blanche, Jack was able to keep his distance and avoid the worst of the return blows. The Marine tried to rally in the ninth, but Dempsey countered with a series of thunderous uppercuts and powerful left hooks that left his opponent a bloody mess by the time the round ended.

In the tenth round, the fighters came out swinging, each landing some missiles, but they quickly tired and the rest of the round devolved into a wrestling match as the two fighters fell into clinches. Once as the referee shouted for the fighters to break, La Blanche dropped his hands and was hit on the jaw with a stunning blow by Dempsey. As the Marine sprawled to the canvas, Patsy Cleary claimed a foul, but referee O'Neil denied it ruling that Dempsey was already in the act of swinging at the call of break. Several times

La Blanche attempted to rush Dempsey, but each time Jack repelled the invasion with punishing uppercuts. La Blanche was also able to land several combinations to the body, but again Jack would quickly right himself and dodge the next blow. The force of one of the errant blows nearly carried the Marine over the ropes. The remainder of the round was characterized by fierce infighting.

In the eleventh round, Dempsey took the offensive again as "the New Yorker's terrible left kept visiting the Bostonian's visage like a piston-rod, doing awful execution."[60] La Blanche, however, badly beaten and with blood flowing freely from cuts on his face, rose to the occasion once more and delivered wicked blasts to his opponent's face and body with both hands. Jack, too, was beginning to show some abrasions and bruising on his face and body.

In the twelfth round, La Blanche came out fighting, landing two hard shots on Jack's neck and a vicious blow to the nose that badly scraped the skin, but it was too little too late. The Marine was a bruised and bloody mess. He was exhausted and becoming unsteady on his feet and his punches, while still possessing some power, were becoming wilder and less reliable. By this time Dempsey had found his second wind and, unlike his withering opponent, was still sharp. He landed several powerful blows that all but finished the Bostonian.

By the thirteenth round, La Blanche was a defeated man. He was still game and sprang upon Jack early, but he was unsteady and it was clear that he would not last much longer. Dempsey, sizing up the situation, set about the work of finishing off his opponent. When called by O'Neil the men met at center ring and began trading punches, but the Marine quickly faded. Dempsey pressed his advantage and went for the finish. After absorbing several more ferocious shots, La Blanche's hands dropped to his side, his chin fell to his chest, both of his eyes were bruised and swollen shut and his face was a swollen, bruised and bloody mess. He fell at Dempsey's feet. The Marine tried to rise several times, but when he could not, O'Neil declared Dempsey the winner. Richard Fox described the scene in real time, as follows: "La Blanche totters and in a moment, he is flat upon his back. Dempsey draws back and waits for him to rise. But the gory face is only half lifted from the ground before it sinks back again. And then a painful sight is witnessed. La Blanche is fairly knocked out, but the game heart of the plucky fellow struggles to sustain him. Again, and again he tries to rise, sinks back, turns over and wriggles on the ground like a worm."[61] Somehow La Blanche made it to his feet before he was counted out, but as he raised his hands for battle, he merely staggered towards the Nonpareil. As the Marine stumbled forward, Jack, instead of landing an easy coup de grace, reached out and caught his vanquished rival as he was falling. The Nonpareil then magnanimously assisted his pitiable antagonist to the chair that was waiting for him in his corner. There would be no reviving La Blanche for the next round tonight—time had been called and the referee cried out, "I give the fight to Dempsey."

As the men sat in their respective corners, their post-fight comments were telling. "The 'Marine' sat in his chair bleeding, battered and bruised. When asked if he were hurt, said, faintly, 'I am hurt, Dick, badly hurt, but it was a square deal.' Across the ring Dempsey was asked how he felt and if he was hurt. He replied, 'Well, I won, but you can bet I was hit hard.'"[62]

After the men had rested for a few minutes, the principles and the crowd quickly dispersed, "and nothing was left to tell of the great event but a few blood stains on the floor and the strong odor of tobacco fumes which pervaded the atmosphere."[63] La Blanche and his entourage headed east by carriage for Boston and Dempsey and company by tugboat for his home in Williamsburg. The tug landed at noon at Hunter's Point and Jack was met at several saloons in which he stopped by congratulatory crowds. "After a bath he started out for a walk. He was followed by a great crowd and cheered enthusiastically."[64] Jack then headed for his parent's home in the Fourteenth Ward. Upon entering the home Jack reportedly handed his mother "the $1,000 that Gus Tuthill, his backer, gave him."[65] Afterwards Dempsey went to his hotel where he hosted several of his sponsors and his trainer Tom Cleary for dinner.

Jack looked reasonably well given the roughness of the fight, but he did display some facial bruising, a split upper lip and a cut on the bridge of his nose. One story—apocryphal or not—claims that Jack received the severed upper lip when La Blanche head-butted him after the bout as Jack attempted to share $300 with the Marine and his team. If true, it is clear that La Blanche did not get the cash. La Blanche was never known as a gracious loser—or winner for that matter. Even though he was thoroughly and completely whipped by Dempsey, La Blanche had the temerity to tell reporters in Boston that Dempsey only won the contest on a foul and was obligated to give the Marine a rematch.[66] It is even more interesting since while still in the ring and immediately after the fight La Blanche stated openly that he had lost "purely because Dempsey was the better man." Noted boxing writer John B. McCormack who wrote under the pseudonym "Macon" commented several weeks after the contest about La Blanche changing his tune. "Now he claims that he really won the fight in the tenth round on a foul blow which knocked him so abroad that he hardly knew what he was doing during the remaining three rounds."[67]

La Blanche's effort against Dempsey was competitive but unbalanced, sloppy and he seemed unprepared. The Marine was simply overmatched by Dempsey's quickness, ring generalship and terrific left hand. La Blanche might have shown better had he worked harder in training and not simply counted on a knockout punch. To many observers, the long-held belief about the Marine persisted—that he was a naturally gifted fighter who never reached his potential due to his lack of discipline, love of the bottle and unwillingness to put in the hard work required to be his best. According to one reporter, "La Blanche has a great dislike for any occupation that has the semblance of hard work attached to it and he proved this when he was matched to fight Jack Dempsey. He could have then entered the ring as a middleweight if he had not taken matters in that easy negligent style, to which he is so partial at all times."[68]

There were, as always, a few gripers who claimed that Dempsey was lucky and La Blanche the better fighter, but virtually everyone who saw the bout conceded that Jack had clearly whipped the Marine. John L. Sullivan commented in regard to the fight that "La Blanche was the bigger man and he can hit as hard as I can, but the result of this fight proves that he has no science. Although I bet my money on La Blanche, I am not surprised that he was whipped."[69] Even La Blanche's close friend Bill Kenny said that he had sized up both men from their fights with Pete McCoy and from that had advised his friends to put their money on Dempsey. McCoy himself said after the fight that he was not at all surprised by the outcome and that Dempsey was "a good 'un."[70] According to the *National Police Gazette*, "La Blanche was never in the race after the third round and even Al Smith, one of his strongest supporters, admitted Dempsey would win after the fourth round had been fought."[71]

The first of the two Dempsey–La Blanche matches was fought in a barn in a clandestine location in the middle of the night. In an interview conducted more than seven years later Dempsey would comment on his distaste for the middle of the night, cloak and dagger nature of early prizefighting. "It is too bad," said Dempsey, "as boxing is a great sport and is not half so brutal as football. It is a manly exercise and an accomplishment of which any man ought to be proud, even though he does not use it in a professional way. I can see no objection to contests under the eye of the police, but I will not and cannot defend such as are fought between two days in a barn."[72]

After sharing the meal with his backers, Jack left his home in Williamsburg and lay low. In the days following the La Blanche fight, Dempsey was not to be seen. Reportedly a bond had been issued for his arrest, and he went to New Jersey until the post-fight furor had worn down. On March 19, however, Jack was spotted in Brooklyn with Tom Cleary and Gus Tuthill as they occupied a box during a concert at the Lee Avenue Academy of Music.

The next day, a story ran in the *Brooklyn Eagle* in which Dempsey's friend John Shanley attempted to put aside any rumors that Jack would meet local amateur champion and the recently turned professional Joe Ellingsworth. The brash Ellingsworth challenged Jack to fight for the championship on the same terms that Dempsey had met La Blanche—$1,000 a side and a $1,500 purse. He stated boldly that if Dempsey failed to accept the challenge, he would claim the middleweight championship for himself. The young man had absolutely no credentials to meet Jack in a championship contest and was simply looking for a way to make a quick name for himself. According to the *Police Gazette*, "He was brought forward by his backers as a wonder but has never as yet done anything wonderful."[73] He began challenging the Nonpareil to a contest on a regular basis. Shanley responded contemptuously, "Fight Ellingsworth? Dempsey has no time to fool with a small fry like Ellingsworth. Why Joe is only an amateur and his challenge was issued for the purpose of obtaining notoriety." Shanley indicated that Ellingsworth had better stick with the amateurs and not annoy "real" fighters.[74]

After more challenges by Ellingsworth, Gus Tuthill went by the *Police Gazette* offices and "left $1,000 to cover the $250 Ellingsworth posted and agreed to match Dempsey to meet Ellingsworth according to London prize ring rules, at 154 pounds for $5,000 a side and the 'Police Gazette' Diamond Belt." That day Dempsey went to see Ellingsworth. He told him, "I want to stop all this talk about fighting. Ellingsworth, go and cover my $1,000. I want you to understand that I am not afraid to fight. I had to fight my way up from the bottom of the ladder." Ellingsworth responded that he could not raise more than $1,000 to maybe $1,500. Dempsey indicated that if that were the case, there would be no fight and Jack said, "Well, you can raise $4,000 more and you will have to fight as hard for $1,000 as for $5,000."[75]

Dempsey also indicated that upon advice from Tuthill and Richard Fox, he would be taking a short rest after his recent series of taxing ring contests, but if Ellingsworth were really spoiling for a fight, he would be happy to set one up between Joe and his friend Dave Campbell.[76]

At about this same time, Dempsey, during an interview with sportswriter John B. McCormack, stated why he was a pugilist. In recalling the $100 he won in his debut fight with Rug McDonald, Jack stated, "I gave him [McDonald] $25 and kept the remainder. Then I determined to be a fighter, not because I liked the business, but because of the money in it. That's all I have ever fought for and it is for money that I am in the ring now." Then, stating his philosophy towards accepting bouts, the Nonpareil said, "I never intend to fight again unless upon my own terms, which are not less than $5,000 a side and the fight to be in private. People say that these terms are extravagant. They may be for some but they are not for me. I am not going to risk being imprisoned for a term of years merely to oblige some young fellow who wants to make a reputation by fighting me."[77] Dempsey was not specifically speaking of Ellingsworth, but his comments clearly spell out why Jack saw no self-benefit to stepping into the ring with the young, brash amateur and therefore why he had little interest in Ellingsworth's challenge.

In the days and weeks following the bout, La Blanche began claiming that Dempsey got lucky and could not defeat him again. He stated that "before our fight I thought I could whip Dempsey, now I know I can whip him." La Blanche challenged Dempsey to another contest under the same conditions as their first meeting, but near Boston, "instead of at Dempsey's door [New York]."[78] Just about everybody including Dempsey laughed at the Marine's contention that he could beat Jack this time around and Dempsey and his backers saw no profit in a rematch then. "Dempsey is now looked upon as the phenomenon of the prize ring. He can fill any attraction and does not consider La Blanche any attraction therefore he will not agree to make a show of himself for La Blanche's benefit."[79]

After the post-fight furor had calmed, Jack returned to public view and gave a lengthy and reflective interview to a *Brooklyn Eagle* reporter on April 3. During the session he spoke on a range of topics including the difficulties of being a famous person or what he termed "lionizing." Dempsey commented that successful persons were constantly in the public eye and were asked to be present at various functions. This was true of people in all disciplines. He lamented "poor Sullivan," who suffered greatly from this. "Wherever he goes, a crowd follows him and points at him, and men push each other against him and keep him shaking hands. If he stops on the street a crowd surrounds him and stares in his face in gaping curiosity till it's a wonder the man doesn't lose his reason."[80]

Jack expressed that he avoided crowds when possible and that he tired of the same questions being asked again and again. "'Who are you going to fight next?' 'What do you think of this fighter or that?' These men never speak or think of me as anything other than a slugging machine. It never strikes them that I have ideas on any other subject, or that any other subject would interest me."[81]

The Nonpareil then made a startling comment. "Now the truth of the matter is that I am heartily sick of fighting. I would like to stop and go away somewhere for a rest." The article went on to point out that while Dempsey was tired of fighting and was under constant pressure from his mother and his sister to quit the prize ring, he kept himself in good condition and always ready for the next challenger. Jack again admitted that he was in the ring for the money, the sum of which he could not match in any other profession, "and consequently I fight."[82]

On April 10, Jack met both Mike Cleary and Jack Fogarty at New York's Cosmopolitan Hall. The Cosmopolitan, located at Broadway and Forty-First Street, was a popular venue for theatre, concerts, exhibits and meetings as well as for sporting events.

The bouts were the main events of an evening in which Jack was awarded a silver-, gold- and diamond-encrusted middleweight championship belt by W.E. Harding, who was representing the *National Police Gazette*. Prior to presenting Dempsey with the belt, a telegram from *National Gazette* editor-in-chief Richard K. Fox was read. Fox, who was in Jacksonville, Florida, stated that he regretted that he could not be in attendance that evening and authorized Harding to do the honors in his stead. While not a sparse crowd, the event was not as well attended as the organizers had hoped. The *Brooklyn Eagle* speculated, "Perhaps more people would have attended if the admission price had not been so exorbitant, $3 being charged for a reserved seat."[83]

The belt awarded to Dempsey was a beautifully crafted item designed by Robert F. Cooke, of 164 Fulton Street in New York. The belt was made of silver and gold. Six panels and a shield were connected by silver ropes and ring stakes. The shield was 12" by 15" with a golden fighter surrounded by a wreath of laurel. Other golden fighters, horse shoes and diamond-encrusted fox heads adorned the panels. Inscriptions read, "1886," "Police Gazette Middle Weight Champion Prize Ring Belt of the World" and "Presented by Richard K. Fox, of New York." On other panels were portraits of Dempsey and Fox and the coats of arms of England, Ireland, Scotland and the United States.[84]

The *National Police Gazette* Championship belt awarded to the Nonpareil in April 1886.

The event that evening showcased several bouts that were to be "scientific" and the participants "agreed" that no slugging would be allowed. These promises were made to keep the police and the anti-boxing set from interfering with the occasion. In reality, the promises meant nothing for, as was reported, "No police interference took place as it was announced that there would positively be no slugging allowed, and though some of the contestants hit as hard as they knew how, it was not sufficiently hard to call for official rebuke."[85]

At 9:00 p.m., lightweights Frank Sweeney and Lew Clark made their ways to the ring. Steve O'Donnell, the fighter and wrestler, was chosen as the master of ceremonies and before the bouts began, he announced to the crowd (but really for the benefit of the authorities present) that there was to be no slugging or knocking out. Despite the promise to the police, the men slugged it out for three brutal rounds and, while Sweeney delivered the cleanest blows, the bout was ruled even.

The second bout of the evening was another three-round contest between Joe Fowler and George Young. Fowler's commanding advantage in reach allowed him to dominate the contest and earn a clear-cut victory.

Dempsey and Cleary soon entered the hall to thunderous applause. O'Donnell then read another letter from the absent Fox in which he referred to Dempsey as "Middleweight Champion of the World" and congratulated him on his sterling career.

Following the reading of Fox's letter, Edward F. Mallahan gave a short speech and presented Dempsey with a trophy. The Nonpareil then received an immense floral arrangement the length of a man's arm arranged by the Neal Florists in the Bowery. The arrangement was complete with a boxing glove. Jack gave no speech but waved to the adoring crowd and gave his thanks to the presenters and all of those present.

Dempsey and Cleary then sparred for three very light rounds which left the crowd dissatisfied. Both men were in fine form and moved gracefully about the ring merely sparring and tapping each other. The action was, however, too slow for the frustrated crowd as Dempsey was just toying with Cleary. After the previous bouts, the crowd was anxious to see more fast-paced and decisive action.

While Dempsey took a break, Young Madden fought three arduous rounds with either Jack Hopper or Johnny Mack, or possibly Hopper and Mack fought—reports from the time are conflicting. Whomever it was that met in the ring that night, it was reportedly a good three-round fight. By all accounts that I have seen, the pair—whichever pair it was—engaged in a hard-fought battle that kept the audience engaged and ready for more.

After another short break, Dempsey and Fogarty entered the ring. The men having met only two months before in their twenty-seven-round affair were familiar with each other's style and they did not hesitate to mix it up again tonight. While they were cautious as the bout began, Dempsey began peppering his opponent with combinations which the crowd roundly applauded. Fogarty gave as good as he got, however, and the fast-paced action pleased the crowd.

In the second round, both men attempted to force the action. Fogarty worked repeatedly on the Nonpareil's body and landed a stinging blow to Dempsey's nose that caused the Nonpareil to back up into the ropes, but Dempsey, using his powerful left, fought back, continually pounding the Philadelphian about the head and body.

The third round was exciting as each man brought the fight to his opponent and exhibited great boxing skill and science, but the fourth was red hot. "Dempsey forced the fighting, driving Fogarty all around the platform, sending his left with good effect, while his right sought the neck and face of his plucky opponent who fought with all his strength, getting in some good body blows, one which sent Dempsey against the ropes."[86] Following up, Fogarty threw a powerful uppercut which, had it caught Dempsey, might have felled him like a tree. Instead, Dempsey, showing his quickness and skill, sidestepped the rocket and countered with a left hook that staggered Fogarty. The men were still furiously going at each other when time was called. Just after 11:00 p.m., the bout and the nights' entertainment were over and as the crowd dispersed into the late night air, they could be heard discussing their pleasure with the fighting.

Fogarty and Dempsey met in another exhibition on April 20, in the Hudson River town of Newburgh, New York. Master of Ceremonies Ed Dillon secured the Newburgh Opera House for a night of boxing and the house was filled with patrons, many of whom traveled from as far as Philadelphia, Brooklyn and New York City to attend. Dillon also had the Nonpareil's championship belt on display for the crowd to examine. The purse was said to be substantial.[87]

While in Newburgh, Jack engaged himself in another athletic encounter as well as a bit of mischief. Jack and his trainer Tom Cleary made a wager of supper over who could cover the distance of a mile the fastest in a row boat. The men engaged the services of two young crew athletes who provided the boats and teamed up with the pugilists. Dempsey and a young man named Willis were in one vessel while Cleary and a young man named Sherwood manned the other. The race was easily won by Dempsey and his partner, but there was a hitch. "Before starting out, Jack had succeeded in fastening an empty paint pail at the stern of his opponent's boat, which acted somewhat as an anchor. It was not discovered until the champion's craft was so far ahead that it became impossible to make up for the lost time. Cleary and Sherwood knew they had been had and laughed at the prank. Cleary agreed to buy supper but vowed to straighten out accounts with the Nonpareil."[88]

On April 24, short articles ran in a number of newspapers around the country stating that Jack was engaged to be married. In a short blurb found on page one next to an article detailing the rapidly deteriorating health of former President Chester A. Arthur, mention was made of the pending nuptials. "It is rumored in sporting circles here that Jack Dempsey is engaged to be married to a wealthy, highly connected lady of Portland, Oregon."[89] The rumor was true. The young lady was Margaret Brady and the two would be married in Portland in July.

Jack was in Pittsburgh on April 23, 24 and 25, where he and Jack Fogarty would appear in front of crowds of around 2,000 persons in two four-round exhibitions at the Casino Rink. Dempsey and Fogarty were accompanied by Gus Tuthill, Tom Cleary and Denny Costigan. After climbing off the train, "the party immediately repaired to the Monongahela House, where they had breakfast, after which they were taken in charge by some Pittsburghers, who had carriages in readiness and were escorted through the South Side mills and glass houses on a tour of sight-seeing."[90]

On April 24, Jack was tendered an exhibition in the Iron City which was attended by two thousand persons. After several contests between local pugilists, Dempsey and Fogarty appeared and fought four rounds with soft gloves. After the match, Jack attended a banquet given in his honor and hosted by Pittsburgh mayor Thomas F. Hughes and a number of influential business leaders. "Dempsey's unassuming ways made him a host of friends."[91]

A very brief description of the exhibition on April 25 ran as follows: "The fight was a friendly bout and was declared a draw."[92] After the exhibition Dempsey was asked by reporters about his next matches. Jack reiterated that he was happy to meet Charley Mitchell anywhere for $5,000 a side. When asked if he was willing to step into the injured Frank Glover's place and fight Jack Burke in Chicago on May 3, Dempsey responded that it would be impossible as he was scheduled to appear all week in Philadelphia during the last week of April and already had bouts scheduled with Jimmy Ryan on April 30. The Nonpareil added, however, that if the Burke fight could be postponed by a week or so, he would be available and happy to meet "The Irish Lad." The next day Dempsey received a telegram from veteran fight promoter Charles E. "Parson" Davies asking him if he would meet Burke for eight rounds on May 10. Jack was willing, but his manager Tuthill responded to Davies that it would take $5,000 a side in a finish match to get Dempsey in the ring with Burke. Negotiations were in earnest, however, and while the May date was unworkable, the two would meet in San Francisco in November.

According to his biographer Mark Dunn, Charles E. "Parson" Davies was "Chicago's

Greatest Sportsman" and a "maker and shaper" of boxing during the last twenty-five years of the nineteenth century. He was well known as a leading promoter of athletic events all over the country. Davies was instrumental in helping to arrange John L. Sullivan's championship fights with Paddy Ryan and Jake Kilrain. Davies managed Sullivan, James J. Corbett, Joe Choynski, Tommy Ryan and Peter Jackson at different times in their careers.[93] William H. Vanderbilt once mistook Davies for a minister and the nickname "Parson" was born.[94]

On April 26, fresh off the express train from Pittsburgh, Jack met Ned McCann of Chester, Pennsylvania, in a glove contest at the Theatre Comique in Philadelphia. "The theatre was packed as the talent were aware that the Chester representative would do all he knew how to stand up the four three-minute rounds."[95] Dempsey was the larger of the two men, but throughout the first round he continually drew McCann out and enticed him to force the fighting. Dempsey was happy to lay back on the defensive and counter while McCann wore himself out. Dempsey chiefly threw his dangerous left which nearly always found its way through the Philadelphian's defenses. "For nearly two rounds he kept McCann at arm's length, but towards the close of the second round, when the Chester boy showed signs of being blown, Dempsey suddenly brought the fighting to close quarters, using both hands."[96]

The third round opened with the Nonpareil repeatedly landing his left jab on McCann's face. As he continually chopped away, McCann's nose began to bleed profusely. In the final minute of the round, Dempsey again moved in close and began hammering away at his opponent with brutal combinations, dropping his opponent just as the round was ending. McCann had to be helped to his corner.

McCann was patched up just enough to answer the bell for the fourth round, but he lasted only half of the chapter. Dempsey hacked away with his left until he saw the opening he wanted. Jack fired his right and landed hard upon McCann's neck, dropping him to the floor. "He was knocked down three times, and the last time failed to come to time."[97] Thoroughly defeated, McCann lay on the ground, barely able to move while referee Dominick McCaffrey administered the count of ten and then declared Dempsey the victor. McCann was awarded $50 for staying in the ring with Dempsey for as long as he did. All present considered it a commendable effort.[98]

On April 28, Dempsey fought again at the Theatre Comique against local fighter Charles "Bull" McCarthy, who clearly fared better than McCann. "Charley" McCarthy was a pig iron carrier from Port Richmond in the River Wards section of Philadelphia. Pig iron carriers worked in foundries and had the hot and physically demanding job of shaping the cooling but still red-hot iron with crow bars and sledge hammers. Very few men were physically fit enough to be an iron carrier and even the best of them could not stand up for many years under the strain. It was clear that Jack was facing a tough and robust physical specimen in the ring that night.

McCarthy reportedly did not make much of a show in the first couple of rounds but came out swinging in the third and gave the Nonpareil several good licks. Dempsey did what he could to finish the Philadelphian in the final round, but McCarthy moved about the ring quickly and managed to avoid much punishment. The rugged iron worker still looked as fresh as he did at the start. McCarthy lasted the four splendid rounds, "and though Jack had by far the best of the hitting, he could not knock Mac out." Referee James Dawson called the bout a draw as McCarthy ended the contest on his feet. After the conclusion of the fight, "Jack admitted that he was as tough a knot for a green-horn as he had met for a long while."[99] The proud local man received $100 for his efforts.

On April 30, Dempsey met Jimmy Ryan in front of a packed house for the final bout of his engagement at the Theatre Comique. Ryan was a well-respected local fighter who had fought Dempsey twice already, most recently to a four-round draw in Dempsey's saloon just the year before. Ryan's left hand and wrist were tightly bandaged to provide support for a damaged knuckle. After a brief argument over which set of gloves should be used, the men came to center ring and waited for the call of time.

In the first round, both men moved quickly and did very little damage to the other. Jack came up short on several punches when Ryan stepped back and out of range of the Nonpareil's thrust. Both men got in a few light hits, but nothing of note.

In the second round, Dempsey landed twice with force on Ryan's stomach, making the Philadelphian wince, but Ryan came right back and landed a couple on the Nonpareil's body. The remainder of the round was fought at long distance as the men lobbed mortar shots that mostly fell short. The crowd was getting restless and they called for more action. They would soon get it.

The third round opened with Dempsey landing a power shot to Ryan's midsection that stopped Jimmy for a few seconds and caused him to grab Jack and fall into a clinch. When Dempsey emerged from the grappling, he began to look vicious. He landed a left that immediately brought up a knot under Ryan's right eye and though Ryan did his best to fight back and landed a few good blows, Jack continued to land missiles to his opponent's nose, mouth and body.

In the final round, Ryan did his best to evade the Nonpareil, but Dempsey landed time and again on his face and head. Ryan stayed in close to cut off any long-range missiles and as such, Dempsey could not land any debilitating blows. As the round came to an end, the crowd wanted more and Dempsey asked for one more round. Ryan, however, citing his broken knuckle, begged off. "The referee decided that Dempsey had the best of the four rounds and gave him the victory."[100]

On May 5, Jack, Denny Kelliher and Tom Cleary headed west to Oregon, but not before spending the previous evening in Brooklyn dining with old mates from his Fourteenth Ward School. The party crowded into the wine room at Brooklyn's Metropolitan Hotel located at Grand and First streets. The men were all members of a social organization called the Order of the Full Moon. During the evening Jack was presented with a diamond scarf pin. The presentation address was read by Joseph C. Hecker and went as follows: "Brooklyn, ED, May 4, 1886. Friend Jack—Accompanying these few remarks is a slight memento of our regard and friendship. Prize it, not for its pecuniary worth, but accept it as a lasting remembrance of the 'Moons' to whom your memory will ever remain dear. May your fame and glory continue to shine as the radiance of the star emblazoned on this emblem. With God speed and many fond remembrances of...."[101] Each of the attendees' names were then included in the note.

Jack was touched and made a short reply to his friends with whom he had grown up. He mentioned how happy he was to be with them that evening, how proud he was of the stick pin and that he would wear it always with feelings of the highest regard for his friends in the Fourteenth Ward. He then sat down and the men enjoyed themselves far into the night.

The next morning, Jack headed for the West Coast. While heading west, Dempsey, as was his habit, laid over in Chicago for a few days. There he visited with friends, took in a fight and looked after some business. During this time, Chicago was a hot bed of activity following a period of labor unrest highlighted by the May 4 bombing and shootings in that city's Haymarket Square. The violence that occurred on that day had been brewing for the previous year as the city's unions, organized workers and socialists agitated for higher wages and shorter hours while the larger manufacturers—most notably the McCormick Harvesting Machine Company—resisted these demands and continued to attempt to control costs.

Tensions between the unions and management rose and resentment simmered for months. The situation began to boil over on May 3, when an assembled group of unionists attacked a group of non-union McCormick workers as they left the plant after their shift that day—a shift of eight hours. During the attack, one person was killed and several others were injured.

News of the violence quickly spread and by the next morning labor leaders were calling for a rally to be held that evening at Chicago's Haymarket Square. The affair was generally peaceful until the final speaker began agitating for violence, death to industrialists and mob rule. Hearing this, the police decided that it was time to bring the rally to a close. As the speaker climbed off the wagon and the crowd began to peacefully disperse, one of those assembled tossed a small, homemade dynamite bomb at the gathering of policemen. When the bomb exploded, one officer was killed instantly and six more lay mortally wounded along with two protesters. Several officers responded by randomly discharging their weapons at the dispersing crowd. In addition to the seven police officers killed that night, sixty others were wounded in the evening's violence. It was estimated that civilian casualties numbered from four to eight and at least forty more were injured. It is also believed that many more were injured in the event, but they left the scene fearing arrest.

The Haymarket affair caused widespread panic and suspicion by many Americans against organized labor, socialists and many immigrants who were seen as anarchists and revolutionaries. Demands were made for arrests and the Chicago police felt the pressure for swift results. After a highly questionable investigation, nine men were charged with murder, anarchy and conspiracy in the Haymarket affair. One of the accused fled the country before he could be apprehended, but the other eight were arrested and tried. Despite a lack of evidence and the fact that several had not even attended the rally, the eight were each found guilty on all charges. Seven received the death penalty and one a fifteen-year sentence. Two had their sentences commuted to life in prison, one committed suicide in his cell by blowing off half of his face with a dynamite cap held in his teeth like a cigar and on November 11, 1887, the remaining four were hanged.[102]

During his stay in Chicago, Jack declined another offer from Charles E. "Parson" Davies to meet Jack Burke as a stand-in for an eight-round glove contest already scheduled for May 10. Davies asked Dempsey to stand in for Frank Glover who was unable to fight. While Jack declined the eight-rounder, he expressed his willingness to fight either Burke or Charley Mitchell in a finish match for $85,000. There were no takers.[103]

While Dempsey could not be enticed into the ring that night, Mitchell agreed to meet Burke and the two sparred ten rounds on May 10 in front of a crowd of five thousand at Chicago's Battery D. In the tenth round, with both men exhausted and covered with blood, the bout was called a draw. "At the close Jack Dempsey stepped on the stage and challenged Mitchell to a fight to a finish with skin gloves for $5,000. Mitchell did not reply."[104]

After the bout John L. Sullivan, who was one of a good number of other ring celebrities also in attendance, commented that while he had always had a good opinion of Mitchell, he believed there were men who could whip him. When asked if he were one of those men the Strong Boy responded, "Yes, myself for one, and Jack Dempsey for another. If Dempsey and he come together I shall be with Dempsey."[105] There were a great many who agreed with him. His opinion of the Englishman seems to have soured a bit over time. He did not care for Mitchell and was not at all impressed with his braggadocios personality. The next year, Sullivan had this to say about Mitchell: "There is a middleweight named Jack Dempsey, who with $5,000 in hard cash drove Charley Mitchell out of Chicago and Dempsey [unlike Mitchell] never pretended to be able to lick me. Dempsey's money was ready for months to make a match with Mitchell, but he [Mitchell] always found an excuse in backing out."[106]

The next day, Dempsey met with Parson Davies, Jack Burke and Mitchell in a Windy City saloon. Jack reiterated to Mitchell that he was anxious to fight him for between $5,000 and $10,000 a side. Dempsey added that he would meet Mitchell with "knuckles or skin gloves in any state or territory" with the only stipulation being that it must be within the next four weeks.[107] Mitchell—no friend of Dempsey's—took a minute to respond, telling Jack that he would agree to meet him for those stakes but the fight must not be set to occur before eight weeks. Jack, who was becoming highly irritated with Mitchell, told him that due to previous commitments, there was no way he could meet him at that time. Mitchell then refused the offer entirely. Jack now became fully enraged and "he declared he could lick Mitchell, and there would have been a fight in the saloon had not friends interfered."[108] It was thought that a fight would still be arranged in the near future, but clearly no agreement would be made that night.

Fight promoter and manager Charles E. "Parson" Davies.

Dempsey commented to reporters the next day, "My proposed fight with Mitchell is off. We met yesterday in Parson Davies' place. He wanted me to put on a pair of gloves and fight him in a hall. I have no time for these kinds of fights." Dempsey continued, "What I wanted was a fight to the finish, either with bare knuckles or skin gloves." Mitchell showed no interest and the frustration in the room grew. "There was some further talk and I finally offered to fight him then and there as we stood. Burke and Davies interfered and had they not we probably would have had some fun." Dempsey added, "I am confident that I can lick Mitchell, but I will not meet him anywhere nor on any terms unless it be in the squared circle, and we are to fight to a finish."[109]

After a week in Chicago, Dempsey traveled on to St. Paul where during another interview in the lobby of the Merchant's Hotel, he continued to show great frustration with Mitchell and with his own inability to get the Englishman to commit to a bout for a reasonable purse. Speaking about the Burke-Mitchell fight Dempsey commented, "I think Mitchell is greatly overrated. He took an exceedingly unfair advantage of Burke. That fight was a cut and dried affair." Jack continued, commenting that the bout was set to be a draw and the purse divided evenly. Jack commented that Mitchell went for the knockout, but that he "would have probably been knocked out himself had Burke been in the condition he should have been. As the affair was a prearranged thing, Burke did not train for it."[110] True or not, the Nonpareil was clearly frustrated with Mitchell and was not willing to give him any credit for his pugilism.

Jack was certainly not a lone voice in the wilderness when he commented that the British pug was avoiding him. Many reports could be found that echoed this sentiment. Sportswriter John B. McCormack commented, "Mitchell appears afraid of Jack Dempsey. His objecting to Jack's challenging him publicly to a fight to a finish, on the grounds that it was ungentlemanly, is laughable." McCormack went on to say that men like Mitchell and Dominick McCaffrey, who were larger than Dempsey, would agree to meet Jack in a fight limited to a stated number of rounds but hesitated to agree to a finish fight. Dempsey was at a disadvantage when he was limited to six or eight rounds to wear a larger opponent down. "Jack sensibly wouldn't have it that way and when it comes to going to a ring in the morning, dinner kettle in hand and knowing there is no leaving it until one or the other is done up—they hesitate and halt in a manner that was not the wont of the champions of former days."[111]

Sullivan weighed in once again on the matter of Dempsey and Mitchell. The heavyweight found himself musing one day in 1887 while his arm was mending after being broken in his battle with Patsy Cardiff. He expressed his thoughts on a great many other fighters' sincerity when challenging him while he was recovering from his injury. "I won't fight anybody now until my arm gets well, and as soon as it does they'll all stop talking. You watch them." Sullivan continued, "You see fellows like Kilrain, Mitchell, and Cardiff like to shoot off their lip when I'm about a thousand miles away, and as soon as I show up they simmer down and keep quiet." Sullivan called them "sprinters" for their ability to quickly run away from a fight. "Regarding Dempsey, Sullivan said: 'I'll give Dempsey credit, though, for being the only man on the whole lot who talks business. Dempsey'll fight, he will, and you'll notice that none of the foot racers care about meeting him. Now Mitchell is shooting off his mouth about fighting me; why don't he go and shoot off his mouth at Dempsey?'"[112]

Dempsey planned to stay in St. Paul for about two weeks. While there, his *Police Gazette* diamond championship belt was put on display in the windows of the Boston Department Store on Third Street.

Jack had a ring appointment in St. Paul's Exposition Rink with middleweight Jack "Paddy" Norton. The contest was set for five rounds. The *St. Paul Daily Globe* commented that the fight favored Dempsey. "If Norton stands up, he gets $50. If he goes out, he gets $25. The go will be with large gloves as Chief Clark has declared that he will not allow the men to meet with light mitts. Norton would have to no show with Dempsey if light gloves were used, but he may be able to stand up under the pressure of pillows."[113]

Dempsey, Costigan and Tom Cleary went up to White Bear Lake for several days to train prior to the bouts at the Exposition Rink. All three were on the card for the evening of May 20. Cleary was scheduled to meet Chris Murphy over four rounds and Costigan was to meet John S. Barnes.

The evening began with a six-fight undercard which included a hastily arranged exhibition between Cleary and Costigan when Murphy was unable to appear at the last minute. This was followed by a second bout for Costigan in which he met a local fighter by the name of Clung. The main event between Dempsey and Norton was next. After a bit of a wait, the crowd began to grow anxious, but finally, a few minutes past 10:00 p.m., Cleary, Costigan, John Barnes, Tom Jefferson and Ed Kelly all entered the ring with their arms filled with bottles, sponges, towels and boxing gloves. The crowd began to cheer and clap wildly as the men were followed closely by Dempsey and Norton. Dempsey wore his customary dark tights, socks and boxing shoes. "Dempsey appeared to be in fine condition stripped as he was from the waist exhibiting his brawny shoulders and full chest." On the opposite side of the ring sat Paddy Norton who had agreed to stand up with the Nonpareil for five rounds in exchange for $50. "Norton was in bad condition, not having trained a day for his meeting with Dempsey." Norton was reported to be twice Dempsey's age and he had a face "that indicated determination and doggedness." Norton wore black tights, red stockings and dark shoes.[114]

Sets of six- and eight-ounce gloves were brought into the ring and Dempsey insisted on the six-ounce, but Norton refused, insisting on the larger mitts. Dempsey reluctantly conceded and put on the "pillows." Calls were made for various men to be appointed as referee and after several were debated, Patsy Mellen of Minneapolis was chosen. Jerry Murphy and John Barnes were chosen as timekeepers for Norton and Dempsey, respectively.

At eighteen minutes past ten, time was called and Dempsey and Norton walked slowly to center ring. Norton was generally expected to fight a defensive battle and his plan was simply to stand up for the five rounds. Both men appeared to be in good humor as they circled and felt each other out. When Dempsey laid a powerful left on Norton's neck, Paddy's demeanor became a bit more serious. The crowd began to cheer wildly when he responded by landing several sharp blows to Dempsey's neck and ribs. For the remainder of the round, Dempsey followed Norton around the ring landing lefts and rights with terrific force. While Norton made several defensive blocks, he also took quite a number of hard blows, a couple of which staggered the Minnesotan against the ropes. Each time, however, Norton took the punishment and showed considerable grit by staying on his feet. In the closing seconds of the round, Dempsey forced Norton into the corner and landed a hard right to his opponent's jaw.

As round two began, both men looked fine. For a man who had not trained much, Norton's wind and general condition seemed good. Then Dempsey led the attack with a feint with his left that was followed by a vicious right uppercut that caught Norton on the nose and started the blood flowing. Norton rallied with a short-left body blow that caused Dempsey to grunt and the local fans to cheer loudly. Dempsey came back with a powerful left-handed rocket shot to his opponent's ear that sent Norton sprawling into the ropes. Again, Paddy rallied with a right to Dempsey's ribs. Jack followed with a right-left combination to the neck and stomach as the round ended. It was warm and both men were perspiring freely and breathing hard, but the out of shape Norton was beginning to look exhausted.

The minute's break helped both men come to the third round looking fresh, but that ended quickly for Norton. Dempsey opened the round with a powerful swinging right that caught Norton under the ear and dropped the Minnesotan to his knees. Paddy was up in just a few seconds, but he spent the rest of the round on the defensive simply trying to keep away from the Nonpareil. Dempsey landed regular combinations but refused to finish Norton. Instead he played with him "as a cat would toy with a mouse." As the round was ending, Dempsey pounded Norton with a terrible right-hand blow that knocked the Minnesotan into his corner. Norton was helped to his feet but was clearly wobbly.

As Norton came out for the fourth round, he was groggy and showing signs of weakness. At first, he seemed ready to call it an evening, claiming that he had agreed to fight only four rounds, but that argument quickly fell apart and the round began. As the two fighters neared one another, Dempsey fired an uppercut that caught Norton on the nose and again the blood flowed freely. "This was clearly Dempsey's round, and he fought Norton all over the ring, knocking him against the ropes and hammering him at will, but Norton refused to go out, and when time was called he sank into his chair rather bloody, but in fair condition." At that point, he took off his gloves and refused to fight the agreed-upon fifth round. Again, Norton claimed that the agreement had been for only four. He failed to come out when the referee called time for the fifth round and Dempsey was given the decision.[115] The crowd was displeased with the final outcome, but the police who were on hand soon quieted everyone down and the rink was cleared. The general impression was that while Norton fought a fair contest, he should have come out for the fifth round. Also, most everyone agreed that Dempsey could have easily and probably should have knocked his opponent out in the third round.[116] The next day the official articles of agreement were produced. The articles were signed by John S. Barnes and Thomas Jefferson representing Dempsey and Norton, respectively, and the document showed very clearly that Norton had agreed to stand before Dempsey for five consecutive rounds.[117] Jack received the win and Norton received the $25.

On May 26, a battle was announced between Dempsey and Patsy Cardiff. The bout was to be in Minneapolis's Washington Rink for a still undetermined six or eight rounds and held on June 7 so as to not interfere with Dempsey's scheduled exhibition in Chicago with John L. Sullivan. After further discussion, it was decided that the contest would be for seven rounds with the referee given the discretion to add an eighth if the battle was not decided in the allotted seven. "Cardiff's manager got Dempsey to sign articles of agreement giving seventy-five per cent of the gate receipts to the winner with the understanding that private articles were to be drawn up guaranteeing Dempsey $1,000 if he would meet Cardiff." All seemed to be in order, but on May 28 the bout was off again. It was learned later that the Cardiff camp failed to make the $1,000 guarantee by the agreed upon date—May 28—and Dempsey and company had had enough of the games and called the bout off.[118] Apparently Cardiff found out about the guarantee and did not care for the arrangement. "When Dempsey had signed the articles for publication Cardiff told him to whistle for his $1,000 guarantee. Dempsey promptly told him that he would not meet him." As usual, Jack refused to be had.[119]

Jack was also scheduled to meet local middleweight Ed Moehler at Minneapolis's Leland Rink over four rounds on May 25. In a pre-fight interview, it was reported that

Moehler "is willing to admit Dempsey's superiority, he is confident of his ability to stand up for four rounds."[120] On the night of the contest a fair-sized crowd was on hand to see an evening of mixed entertainment from tumbling to juggling to wrestling, all mixed in with a four-contest evening of boxing. After the three fights of the undercard, Dempsey and Moehler entered the ring to close out the evening's entertainment. Moehler had agreed to meet Dempsey over four three-minute rounds and was to receive $50 for his trouble. From the start Moehler's only fight plan seemed to be to stay away from the Nonpareil. Dempsey followed him around the ring throughout the entire contest and landed blows pretty much at will.

In the first round, Jack landed several hard lefts to Moehler's midsection and from that point on the Minnesotan seemed about ready to give in. He was several times urged to stay on by his corner man Jack Caldwell. The remainder of the bout went along the same way. In the fourth and final round Moehler went down several times in an apparent attempt to avoid being hit. He did not know enough about boxing to stay down for the bulk of the allotted ten-second count, however, and received additional punishment as a result. As poor as the contest was from a pugilistic standpoint, the groggy and wobbly Moehler still managed to hang in there for the full four rounds. It may have been the toughest $50 he ever made.[121] Moehler tried to capitalize on his "fame" as the man who stood before Dempsey for four rounds. On June 4—to his credit—he met 39-year-old ring veteran Charles Hadley, an African American. This was at a time when many white fighters refused to meet colored fighters in the ring. Unfortunately for Moehler the outcome of this bout was another loss. While he fought a reasonable battle, Moehler showed a lack of science and the very experienced Hadley outfought him by a good margin, knocking Moehler out in the fifth round. Moehler was full of determination, however. He continued to fight periodically through 1892, though with generally unfavorable results.

In all, Jack's trip to Minneapolis was a profitable one as he cleared around $3,000 for just a few nights' work—the equivalent of roughly $70,000 today. This was money he hoped to use to open a business in Portland and to settle down with Maggie and raise their family.

After his bout with Moehler, Jack traveled back to Chicago where he was slated to meet heavyweight champion John L. Sullivan in a sparring match on May 31. The established legend and the rising legend were to spar at the Le Grande Skating Rink on North Clark Street. The men had met on several occasions and certainly knew of each other's ring reputations. Through this, they had begun to develop a mutual respect and it was agreed that a joint ring exhibition should be in the offing.

The much-ballyhooed match had advance ticket sales in the thousands and enthusiasm for the meeting was running high. Unfortunately, the scheduled bout was cancelled when civic officials intervened. An overly zealous group of do-gooders who called themselves the "Chicago Citizens Committee" put pressure on City Hall and the local constabulary to stop this and other events they felt were of questionable moral nature. News reports from the time stated that "no more sparring exhibitions are to be allowed in Chicago. The Citizens' Committee wrote a letter to the Chief of Police demanding that the law in relation to prize fighting be strictly enforced, and that functionary says he will do it to the letter."[122]

On June 2, 1886, daily journals across the nation carried the news that President Grover Cleveland had married Frances Folsom in a White House ceremony. This was the first presidential marriage in U.S. history and at twenty-one, Frances became the nation's youngest First Lady. Cleveland had known Folsom—the daughter of Oscar Folsom, one of his Buffalo law partners—her entire life. In 1885, Frances, then a student at Wells College, visited the president at the White House. Although Frances was twenty-seven years younger than Cleveland, the couple began a written correspondence and in a short time, they were engaged to be married. The Clevelands had five children. They lived in New York after Cleveland's electoral defeat in 1888, returning to the White House upon his reelection in 1892. They retired to Princeton, New Jersey, upon completion of the president's second term in office in 1897.

In July, the Nonpareil responded to Dominick McCaffrey's comments that he would "attend to Jack Dempsey in the fall." Like Charley Mitchell, McCaffrey only wanted to meet Dempsey in a contest with limited rounds, clearly putting the Nonpareil at a disadvantage against much larger fighters. Jack told reporters on July 9 that he would meet McCaffrey any time McCaffrey pleased and at any weight differential, but it must be a finish fight under London Rules with kid gloves. Like Mitchell in May, McCaffrey refused to agree to these terms.

After Jack arrived in Portland in July, he wrote a letter to the *Brooklyn Eagle* stating that he was very happy in Portland and had so many friends that he thought he would settle down there permanently, get married and leave the prize ring. He stated that he wanted to open a hotel and saloon, but friends in Portland, looking to add to his list of options, made him a deputy coroner. It was reported that Jack took over $10,000 in fight winnings with him to the West Coast to help him settle in Portland.[123]

On July 27, Jack Dempsey married Margaret D. Brady, of Portland, Oregon. The ceremony was held at 10:30 in the morning at St. Francis of Assisi Catholic Church in East Portland, with the Reverend Father Louis Verhaag officiating. The church was packed a full hour before the ceremony with the overflow crowd compelled to stand in the back of the church and along the side aisles. "The chancel was handsomely ornamented with bouquets and the large statues of the Savior and Virgin Mary were also florally decorated."[124] The bride, "dressed in a rich, tan colored satin, trimmed with velvet," was accompanied by groomsman Daniel Mulligan and the groom by bridesmaid Alice Ward. "Upon the conclusion of the impressive rites, St. Peter's Grand Mass was sung and celebrated, after which the reverend father delivered a brief discourse setting forth the beauties of religion and the importance of taking it into all the relations of life. He dwelt especially upon the sacred

Rev. Fr. L. Verhaag.

character of marriage and exhorted the newly-wedded couple to be faithful to the pledges just made." After the ceremony a reception was held at Maggie's parents' home in the Stephens addition of east Portland.

Several boxing people were present at the wedding including lightweight Ed Touhey, Margaret's maternal uncle. Touhey, also from Brooklyn, was a boxer and referee.[125] Jack met Margaret (or Maggie, as she was known to friends) while touring and boxing on the West Coast in 1885. The following morning, the couple left for their honeymoon trip to San Francisco.

Maggie was described as a beautiful girl. One newspaper described Maggie as "a stately, dark haired beauty."[126] A reporter from the *Brooklyn Eagle*, who met with her in January 1887, wrote the following, "I had heard that Dempsey had secured a matrimonial prize, but I was scarcely prepared to meet such an intelligent and well-bred woman. She is about 22, above the average height, and of slender, but shapely figure. She has a fine complexion, regular features, arched eyebrows and large brown eyes."[127] The report stated that while she was a Portlander, she was born in New York and lived there until her parents went west when she was seven. During her interview she said that until she met Jack about a year earlier, she had no acquaintances in the sporting world and even now knew a few of Jack's associates as well as Jack Burke and his wife, whom she declared was a charming young woman. Another report stated that Margaret's "dark brown hair gracefully fell over a high forehead and was caught up in a fashionable coiffure behind."[128] Margaret said she did not like prizefighting and that Jack seldom spoke of it with her. She also expressed her desire that her husband give up the ring and settle into a business.

The couple lived for a time with Margaret's parents, James F. and Ellen T. Brady, in east Portland. Jack's father-in-law was reportedly a master blacksmith and machinist who "by thrift and industry had become one of its [Portland's] solid citizens and a property owner."[129]

Jack and Maggie would settle into a loving marriage and have two daughters—one named Alice and the other Anne, born in 1888 and 1890, respectively. Jack and Maggie eventually bought their own home and made their residence in Portland.

In mid–August, Jack Burke again challenged Dempsey to a bout. It was reported that Burke had "written a letter complaining of 'Jack' Dempsey's failure to arrange a glove contest with him. He now challenges Dempsey to a fight for the gate receipts or otherwise between September 22, and November 1, in either Minneapolis, Omaha, Denver, or San Francisco."[130]

Burke, known as "the Irish Lad" even though he was born and raised in London, was a well-known athlete and popular fighter of the late nineteenth century. In addition to his noteworthy career in the magic circle, Burke was also a successful rowing enthusiast. He began his ring career as a bare-knuckle fighter in London in 1878. He squared off with many notable fighters of the era including Jem Gaiger, Charley Mitchell, Jake Kilrain, John L. Sullivan, James J. Corbett and Peter Jackson. Burke was anxious to gain a victory after coming off an eight-month stretch in which he had registered four straight draws and an eight-round point loss to Peter J. Nolan in Cincinnati on July 5.

On August 23, the Nonpareil was asked by reporters what reply he had made to Burke's challenge. "Dempsey says he will box Burke eight rounds or more, Queensberry rules, the match to take place in San Francisco between now and October 1st next, the winner to take all gate money. He does not want the match to come off later than October 1st, as he expects to engage in business about that time and give up prize fighting."¹³¹ Reports were many that Jack was once again considering giving up the ring at the encouragement of his new bride and her family. Dempsey was serious in his consideration of exiting the ring for good, but he was also terribly conflicted about the decision. It appears that John E. Dempsey, on the one hand, was lured by the quiet and calming appeal of settling down into a job in the business world and quietly raising a family in Portland, but the restless Nonpareil, on the other hand, was not quite ready to give up the ring.

Jack Burke.

On August 24, Burke's backer, Parson Davies, wired Dempsey from Chicago that Burke accepted the offer to box him over eight rounds in San Francisco, Queensberry Rules, with small gloves and the winner to take all gate receipts. Burke and Davies headed for the West Coast on September 16.

After their honeymoon, Jack and Maggie remained in San Francisco where Jack began to train for the Burke fight. He was apparently working very hard and was in great condition. The *Boston Globe* reported, "Jack Dempsey is trying general athletics at San Francisco where he has been for several months. He recently ran 150-yards in seventeen seconds and won a running broad jump competition, clearing seventeen feet, three inches."¹³² While Jack continued his training in San Francisco, Burke set up his training camp to the north in Sausalito.¹³³

The fight did eventually come off, but not by Dempsey's October 1 deadline. A delay was announced on that day as follows: "The glove contest between Jack Burke and Jack Dempsey, which was originally fixed to take place in San Francisco, California, has been postponed on account of the failure to procure the necessary city license. No date will be fixed until a license shall be procured."¹³⁴ The reason the fight was postponed was more than just clerical. The bout was being held up due to local politics and the California gubernatorial election of 1886. San Francisco Mayor Washington M. Bartlett refused to grant a license for the fight until after the impending state election was held. Bartlett was a candidate for governor in that election and would not risk alienating any of the anti-prizefighting voters by granting the license before the votes were counted.¹³⁵

Bartlett was elected governor and on November 16, he approved the license for Davies.¹³⁶ Bartlett had been swayed by a number of points. First, of course, the election was over. He no longer needed to worry about disaffecting the anti-boxing constituency.

In addition, and maybe most significantly, Bartlett received both encouragement and some pressure from local fight promoter Pat Sheedy and San Francisco political boss Christopher A. Buckley.

November 1886 "found [John L.] Sullivan and a whole galaxy of boxers in San Francisco under the management of Pat Sheedy." Sheedy arranged a four-round contest between Sullivan and former bare-knuckle champion Paddy Ryan to be held on November 13 at the Mechanics' Pavilion. The always clever Sheedy had a dual purpose in scheduling this bout. With the campaign now successfully behind Governor-elect Washington, Sheedy sought to break the logjam that was inhibiting prizefights from being approved by taking advantage of the great local interest in pugilism. A full house and an enthusiastic crowd would help his cause. On the night of the contest, the venue was bulging with a crowd of nine thousand ebullient boxing fans cheering on the fighters. Sheedy had invited Buckley to be his guest at the event knowing that a favorable review from the Democratic Party principal would help pave the way for the Dempsey-Burke battle and other bouts in the near future. "At the match Monday night, when the house was packed, Sheedy led in Buckley by the hand and shouted, 'Make way, gentlemen, make way for Mr. Buckley,' and hustled judges, senators and bankers aside to permit the blind Democratic chieftain to take a front seat. A retainer, well posted in ring matters, sat beside Buckley and kept the blind man posted on the progress of the match."[137]

Buckley, referred to as "Blind Boss Buckley," was a saloonkeeper and former railway conductor who, while he never held any elected office, came to rule the San Francisco Democratic Party in the late nineteenth century. His influence in state matters and federal patronage further increased his sway. Buckley, known for his kindly manner and generosity as much as for numerous allegations of corruption and bribery, lost virtually all of his eyesight during the peak of his power, but he never let it slow him down. He would memorize city ordinances and contracts when they were read to him and could often recognize people by their handshakes.[138]

The Sullivan-Ryan event was a huge success in every way. Attendance was high, enthusiasm was high and the fight was a reasonably good one with Ryan putting up a good battle early on. As Ryan began to tire, Sullivan took control and decked him three times in the second round. After this, Ryan had nothing left, but bravely came to scratch for the third session. Sullivan, sensing victory, dropped his opponent twice more in the third round—the final time with a devastating right to the jaw that put Ryan on the canvas for the count. The final point of success for the evening was an act of great magnanimity by Sullivan after the knockout. As Ryan "lay stretched on the floor, Sullivan gathered him up in his arms and carried him to his corner."[139] The pulsing crowd cheered the champion and his actions. The Blind Boss had a great time that evening. The next day, Buckley and Sheedy began to grease the wheels to make certain that Mayor Bartlett would sign the approval license for promoter Parson Davies. Instructed by Mayor Bartlett, the city License Collector—a man named Conroy[140]—issued the license immediately and the bout was arranged for Monday, November 22, at the Mechanics' Pavilion in San Francisco.

At the time of the delay, Burke was reportedly in terrific fighting shape, so to keep him sharp and trim and to earn an income while waiting for a resolution to the political impasse, Parson Davies took Burke and a troupe of pugilists on a tour of California towns, performing in exhibition matches and offering stakes to local men who could last five rounds with him with small, soft gloves under the Queensberry Rules. The tour was reportedly "coining money" at every stop. The report read, "It's a chilly day when the ever genial 'Parson' doesn't turn a mascot dollar or two."[141] During the second week of October, Davies returned to Chicago for a week to take care of another pugilistic project, the Paddy Ryan–Frank Glover bout at Battery D.[142]

As Sheedy correctly predicted, interest in the fight was high. Some believed that following the match between Sullivan and Ryan at the same venue just nine days after would dwarf interest in the Dempsey-Burke contest, but this was not to be the case at all. In fact, many believed that the latter contest was the better event of the two and "if however, public interest in the two contests is to be measured by results, then the Burke-Dempsey affair has proved itself a much more interesting and important event than was the 'great knockout' of Ryan by Sullivan."[143]

On the evening of the bout, fight fans, anxious to see the contest, began to gather early. "A vast crowd of people surged into Larkin Street as early as 4 o'clock in the afternoon, bent on obtaining early admission to the Pavilion and securing good seats."[144] As they waited, people were abuzz over the impending contest, but also about the death of former President Chester A. Arthur as news spread that he had passed away that day at his home in New York after a period of illness. When the doors opened at 8:00 p.m., the massive crowd surged forward, sweeping with them a squad of policemen who had been deployed as security. The venue was filled with an estimated 8,000 patrons, a good thousand past its normal capacity. The gate receipts were estimated to be at least $10,000.

During the evening, Dempsey's elaborate *Police Gazette* gold-, silver- and diamond-encrusted middleweight championship belt was on display and many patrons examined it closely.

With the overflow crowd now in place, all eyes were on the center of the Pavilion. "A large stage was erected in the center of the building and before the main event there were several contests between local boxers."[145]

The gloved bout between Dempsey and Burke was scheduled for ten three-minute rounds and one-minute breaks to be fought under the revised Queensberry Rules. In the days before the fight, Hiram Cook had been chosen to serve as referee, but he failed to appear at the Pavilion at the appointed time. When it became clear that Cook was not going to serve, there was a long wrangle over an alternate choice, with both Burke and Dempsey arguing against several nominees. Calls were made for John L. Sullivan or Paddy Ryan to referee the bout, but both refused. In an unusual twist, Frank Crockett and Jack Hallinan, the proprietor of San Francisco's Cremorne Garden, served as joint referees—one representing each fighter. Steve Taylor of New York was announced as the second for Burke and Denny Costigan for Dempsey. It was agreed that the winner would take seventy-five percent of the gate and the loser twenty-five. At the pre-fight weigh-in, Dempsey registered a solid 157 pounds with Burke tipping the scales at 162 pounds.

During the long discussions over the referee, a loud crash was heard throughout the arena. The thunderous clap was the smashing in of the entrance doors at the Hayes Street side of the Pavilion, through which more than one hundred men flooded and succeeded in witnessing the contest for free.

Both men entered the arena to loud applause. At 10:24 p.m., the overflow crowd cheered loudly as Burke stepped into the ring followed quickly thereafter by Dempsey. "Dempsey, in stripping, looked fully fifteen pounds lighter than Burke who was heavy on muscle, but splendid in wind."[146] The men shook hands and time was called at 11:08

p.m. with the men coming quickly toward the center of the ring. No sooner did the men come together than the action began with Dempsey striking Burke in the ribs with a solid left and a right-hander on the ear. Burke responded quickly by landing his left on Dempsey's cheek. The men continued to circle the ring. In what appeared to be a bit of gamesmanship, Jack then surprised everyone in the place. "After this unexpected performance he coolly turned his back on his formidable looking opponent and walked to his corner to resin the soles of his shoes, leaving Burke looking surprised in the middle of the ring, while the spectators laughed."[147] When Jack returned, the men continued with careful sparring, each landing tepid shots—Dempsey with another left, Burke with a counter that landed on the Nonpareil's cheek. In all, the fighting, which was mostly at close quarters, slightly favored Burke. The men were locked in a clinch as time was called ending the first round.

More cautious sparring marked the second round until Dempsey began forcing, playing at Burke's stomach. He landed twice with his left when Burke clinched. In breaking away, Dempsey swung a heavy right-hander on Burke's stomach."[148] Burke landed two rights to Dempsey's mouth and lefts to his neck and ribs before the round came to an end. Both men scored well and the round was even.

Although both men were still in good condition, the third round was plodding as both fighters clinched, threw rather tame punches and searched for openings that never came. The only noteworthy action came when Dempsey landed a stinging blow to Burke's nose. The fourth round was decidedly more exciting. Dempsey and Burke both landed sharp body blows, Burke following his up with a heavy right to the back of Dempsey's neck. The Nonpareil responded with another hard blow to Burke's midsection. The Irish Lad responded by forcing Dempsey into the ropes, trying to land another heavy blow to his neck, but Dempsey was simply too fast and wiry and he juked and ducked—some say slipped—under the missile. Burke continued to force the fighting for the remainder of the round, with the New Yorker becoming more cautious and acting chiefly on the defensive.

The fifth round began with Dempsey missing on a heavy blow to Burke's stomach and Burke countering with impressive combinations of his own. After those shots landed, a smile came over the Nonpareil's face. This was not at all uncommon for Jack, who frequently responded with a broad smile after receiving hard blows. The smile was generally one-part appreciation for a blow that got past Dempsey's tight and quick defenses and one-part message to an opponent that said, "Okay, you landed, you got me, but I'm fine and is that all you've got?" As the round wore on, Dempsey occasionally fired off big blows, but Burke managed to avoid most of them. Infighting was common as the two pugilists began to wear down a bit from the fast pace and wear and tear. The round ended without clear advantage to either man.

The break seemed to agree with Burke, and he looked fresh as the sixth round opened. Dempsey was clearly still showing some signs of fatigue. Early on, Burke landed a right-handed bomb on the side of Dempsey's head, followed by a left uppercut that registered with the Nonpareil. Dempsey shook it off as best he could and answered with a left-right combination to his opponent's mouth and chest. The round came to an end with Burke landing a powerful right to Dempsey's cheek.

While each man landed some cursory jabs in the seventh round, they traded very few heavy blows. The round was mostly given to sparring as both men were playing for some rest as they again showed signs of being winded.

"In the eighth round, the men appeared to be fresher than in the previous round. Dempsey again led, but was too short, and Burke countered. Jack led again, and Burke met him with a heavy right-hander on the throat. Burke forced the fighting from this point."[149]

As the ninth round progressed, Burke launched several salvos at Dempsey's nose. The Nonpareil fought back, landing a right to the Irish Lad's face. Burke came right back at Dempsey and the two engaged in infighting for the rest of the round. "Towards the end of the ninth-round Burke took the offensive and the fighting became heavy and close, both men receiving some hard knocks."[150]

Dempsey started out fast in the tenth and final round but was short on several swings. Each time Burke countered, one of which caught his opponent flush on the neck. The two continued to trade jabs when someone in the crowd yelled time, but the referees, after realizing what had happened, instructed the men to keep fighting. The two went back at it and tapped each other lightly until time was officially called by the timekeepers.

With the contracted ten rounds finished, Burke took off his gloves, but Dempsey kept his on and wanted to continue. "Burke insisted that ten rounds having been fought that match was finished, but on Dempsey declaring his readiness to go on, Burke put on the gloves again. A consultation was now had between the men and their seconds and the referees. They were unable to agree on anything, however, and the master of ceremonies, stepping forward, announced to the audience that, as the license provided for ten rounds, he was obliged to decide that the fight had been finished...."[151] As such, the co-referees, Crockett and Hallinan, agreed with the master of ceremonies that the bout was over. The debate now centered on who won the contest. After much consideration and arguing about each man's merits, the fight officials could not agree on a clear-cut winner and a draw was called.

When the decision was announced, there was a mix of applause and hissing as the crowd milled about in a state of confusion. Despite the frustration over the outcome, the crowd remained orderly and soon began to disperse.

Despite the usual scrapes, bruises and soreness, both Dempsey and Burke were "fresh and vigorous" after the fight. They were tired but unhurt, and both had been willing to continue had the officials agreed to more rounds. The gate receipts from the bout were a pot of $10,500—much less than expected after the gate-crashers' appearance—which was split between the combatants. Jack wrote in a letter to his brother Martin, "I am sure if it had been to a finish I could have beaten him."[152]

Others agreed with the Nonpareil's assessment. After commenting that the bout was one of the best and most clever that he had witnessed, John L. Sullivan was asked about his opinion of Dempsey. "I think as I always did, that he can lick anything on legs in America that is near his own weight." Pat Sheedy, who had predicted a draw due to the weight disparity and the limited number of rounds, stated that he thought Jack was not as sharp as he sometimes was, but he still got the better punches in overall. He then added that had it been a finish fight, Dempsey would have won. The two referees agreed that it was a close fight, but predictably they disagreed on the outcome. Jack Hallinan thought that Burke got the better of Dempsey overall and would have won had they fought a few more rounds. Frank Crockett agreed with Sheedy that Jack was "way off" in his condition but stated that with hard gloves Dempsey would have broken Burke's nose. "He surprised me by the way he walked up round after round and let Burke have it straight in the mug—with return of course." Crockett added that he knew the contest would be decided as a draw when Hallinan was chosen as the other referee, "for Hallinan always decides the way his money is bet."[153]

Almost immediately, speculation ran high about a rematch between the pugilists, this time the contest to be a finish fight with skin gloves.

Over next few months, Jack and Margaret traveled with several other fighters who participated in sparring exhibitions throughout the West and Midwest. One of the early events was held on December 6 in Portland's Turnhalle. The theatre was a large four-story structure located on First Street between Oak and Pine and was home to the German American Society of Portland. Veteran fight promoter Charles E. "Parson" Davies, who was the manager of the show, had gathered Jack Burke, Dave Campbell, Denny Costigan, Charles Daily, James Bates and Jack Keenan, along with the Nonpareil, to appear nightly in a series of three-round exhibition bouts and other entertainment, all for the admission price of a dollar. Throughout the tour the fighters would meet each other nightly and Jack traded off fighting each man on different nights.

Throughout December, the troupe fought its way from Portland to Chicago, performing in one and two night engagements in cities along the route. After a show at the Walker Opera House in Salt Lake City in which the Nonpareil sparred four rounds with Ohio heavyweight Charley Lange, the group traveled up to Cheyenne, where Dempsey sparred with Jack Keenan on December 20, in front of what was described as a tremendous crowd. The *National Police Gazette* stated that the best bout of the evening was an evenly fought three-rounder between Keenan and Denny Costigan. The *Gazette* reported that "some excellent sparring was done on both sides." The report continued by stating, "Although the combatants were nearly evenly matched, it was evident that Keenan had a little the best of it." They then added, "No bruises on either side."[154] According to Parson Davies, on the troupe's second night at Butte City, Montana, "Dempsey knocked a local fighter named McAuley through the ropes into the wings, knocking him out. [George] Morrison, a pugilist who has twice fought John P. Clow and whipped him once, tackled Burke at Cheyenne. Morrison is a strong young fellow of twenty-three. He stands five feet eleven and weighs 190 pounds. In the second-round Burke used his right so vigorously Morrison almost went under, and in the fourth-round Burke gave him both left and right, cutting his eye open and knocking him into the scenery, putting him to sleep."[155] The men then headed on to Omaha, Council Bluffs and Milwaukee while en route to Chicago where the tour would wind up.[156] Dempsey's championship belt was on display in each city throughout the tour.

While spending the Christmas holidays in Chicago, Jack responded to questions about his earlier statements that he would like to meet heavyweight champion John L. Sullivan. The Nonpareil said that he had great respect for Sullivan and that while he would never make any crack at him, there had now been so much talk about a meeting between the two that Jack would be anxious for a match. "I will bet $1,000 that John L. Sullivan cannot knock me out in six rounds, and if he wants to make the match I can name a man who will bet another $1,000 on me. He can have all the money he wants. Understand me, I'm not getting a swelled head so that I think I would stand any show to whip Sullivan, but I know he can't stop me in six rounds, and I'm willing to back my opinion with hard cash."[157] It was agreed that Dempsey would not risk his reputation as a "game and manly fighter" and simply try to avoid Sullivan for six rounds to gain a win by default—he would actually engage the Boston Strong Boy. Many felt that being game would be his doom in such a bout. While Jack was supremely confident in his chances most other observers thought he was foolish to step into the ring with the heavyweight champion. "Dempsey is a wonderful pugilist—a Sullivan in his class—but he is flying his kite too high when he essays to meet a man over fifty pounds heavier, taller, stronger, and a hard hitter."[158]

On December 27, Jack and Denny Costigan sparred in Milwaukee wrapping up the tour. As the busy and eventful year came to a close, the Dempseys traveled east to New York to spend the New Year's holiday with Jack's family. They arrived on the Pennsylvania Railroad on the evening of December 30 and were met by Jack's friends Ed Plummer and Gus Tuthill. While at the station, Jack responded to reporters' questions by reasserting his willingness to meet Sullivan or anyone else in the ring. He reiterated to reporters and friends that he believed that he could stay six rounds with Sullivan and that Tuthill was willing to back him with additional cash. When asked about his recent fight with Burke in San Francisco, Jack said, "I believe that I honestly won the fight. I closed his eyes and gave him a good many heavy blows." He added that Burke apparently had no taste for meeting Jack again as he refused to make another match with Dempsey. The Nonpareil then responded to inquiries about his trip home and his plans while there. "My principal object in coming east was to make my New Year's calls upon my friends." Dempsey continued, "but I hope to be able to combine business with pleasure. My trip to the west was profitable and pleasant, but there is no place like New York."[159]

The group then went to Jack's mother's home on North Ninth Street in Brooklyn. The elder Mrs. Dempsey greeted Jack and his new bride ebulliently. That evening, Jack was given a reception at the Rochester Hotel on Bleeker Street in Manhattan. During the event Jack spoke again of his contest with Burke in San Francisco and his opinion that he had bested Burke. He also mentioned his recent challenge to Sullivan and declared himself ready to meet anyone in the world in or near his weight class.[160] He added that his sole ambition was to fight Dominick McCaffrey. Asked about her views on all of this, Maggie, who was by his side at the press briefing, stated her displeasure with her husband's present calling.[161] On New Year's Eve, Jack and Maggie dined at the Coleman House, a five-story hotel at the northwest corner of Broadway and 27th Street. The fashionable establishment was the scene of prize fight negotiations for champions like Sullivan, Corbett, Jackson, and the Nonpareil in the late 19th century. Maggie was described as "a pretty woman who has no enthusiasm for anything connected with the prize ring, although it is evident she is devoted to the champion."[162]

1887—Breaks and Gashes, but Still on Top

Jack spent the New Year's holiday showing his new bride the sights and sounds of New York City and specifically his home borough of Brooklyn. While Maggie was originally from New York, she had left as a young girl and Jack no doubt wanted to reacquaint her with the metropolis. During this time, regardless of his indications to the new Mrs. Dempsey, Jack was actively seeking new fights. He indicated that he would fight for another year before retiring, but he wanted to make it a good one.[1] Jack said that another fight with La Blanche could be in the offing and the possibility of a bout with Dominick McCaffrey was real, but both men were more anxious to meet John L. Sullivan than each other. When he was told that Sullivan had responded to his challenge by stating that he would break Dempsey's jaw, Jack responded, "I understand Sullivan said he could break my jaw in such a contest. Well, I am of the opinion that when he or any other man attempts to break my jaw, I shall be actively employed in preventing him. I have faith enough in myself to believe he cannot do it, and I am willing to go with Sullivan where a six-round contest on the level can and must take place."[2] Jack went on to say, "We will fight there and if he stops me inside of the six rounds, he can take all the gate receipts. Neither he nor the spectators will be able to say that I went down before I was knocked down, or that Sullivan did not have a fighter who meant business before him. I am not spoiling for a fight, but I will fight any man to a finish for $5,000 a side or upwards."[3] Later, when asked why he was anxious to fight Sullivan, Dempsey replied, "I never desired to fight Sullivan, but I would sooner be licked than to have it said that I was afraid to meet him or any other man and I feel sure that he can't whip me in six rounds."[4]

On January 8, Dempsey met with Richard K. Fox in the *Police Gazette* offices regarding a bout with British fighter Jem Smith whom Sullivan was heading to England to engage. The two decided that if anything fell through between Sullivan and Smith, Dempsey would sail to England and challenge Smith himself.[5]

"On January 19, Jack Dempsey, the champion middleweight pugilist of America alighted from a train at the Broad Street station, Philadelphia. He was smoothly shaven, wore a tall hat, a close-fitting overcoat and a diamond as large as a pea sparkled in his four-in-hand scarf. He looked more like a theological student than a fighter."[6] Jack came to Philadelphia to meet with Mr. Ryan, the manager of the International Theatre Comique located on Sansom Street above 8th Street in that city. After his arrival he met Dominick McCaffrey for a drink at a bar on Vine Street and then headed on to see Mr. Ryan at the theatre. Jack's previous engagements at the Comique had gone well, and he readily agreed to terms for another appearance during the first week of February, during which he would meet three local fighters. Dempsey addressed local reporters at the station who were curious what he and McCaffrey had spoken of. "Yes, I saw McCaffrey, but we didn't talk fight." Then Dempsey added, "You can say that I am agreeable to anything that McCaffrey may suggest." Having missed the eight o'clock train for New York Jack, like a dutiful husband, sent Maggie a dispatch that he would catch the nine o'clock train and arrive home an hour late.[7]

The Comique Theatre engagement began on Monday evening, January 31, when Jack met local heavyweight Mike Boden, who, according to the *Philadelphia Record*, outweighed Dempsey by a good twenty pounds. The *National Police Gazette* stated that Boden stood just under 5'8" and weighed 175 pounds. Boden was described as "a pocket Hercules—stout, short and chunky. He is a rusher and a very difficult man to do any quick, effectual work with."[8] Boden, who originally hailed from Canada and was nicknamed "The Canuck," was a standard on the Philadelphia fight scene appearing regularly at the Comique, Clark's Club and Arthur Chamber's Saloon. Though popular, he was a mediocre boxer who won about one out of every four to five fights during his career. Still, as a southpaw with some power, he could be dangerous. As such, Dempsey determined to engage him warily throughout the battle.

During the first two rounds Dempsey, who was reportedly not in his usual top condition, had a more difficult time connecting than he normally might. Boden forced the fighting and even landed a solid blow to Dempsey's midsection that momentarily staggered the Nonpareil,[9] but he was awkward enough that he still had trouble connecting with Jack, who dodged or blocked most of his opponent's blows.

During the third round, Boden went down just as Jack hit him with a light blow. Boden recovered quickly and, showing grit, was up in an instant and rushed at Dempsey, again trying to force the fighting. In the fourth and final round, the tough Canadian again took the fight to Dempsey, but as he continually rushed Jack, his porous defense enabled the Nonpareil to pepper Boden with a great many straight blows to the face and body. "Sparrow Golden was referee and gave the fight to Dempsey, a correct decision and one that voiced the opinion of all present."[10]

Shortly after the conclusion of the bout, Boden stated that he had backers who would support him for a rematch with Dempsey at $1,000 a side, but as Jack refused to fight him for less than $5,000 a side, this never came off. Boden continued to fight in Philadelphia for a while longer and eventually branched out to New York, Atlantic City and Pittsburgh, even heading as far west as New Orleans and Chicago, but his fortunes in the ring never improved. He continued to be a tough but plodding street fighter who employed rough and crude tactics that were easily offset by trained pugilists with superior ring skills and knowledge. Boden finished his career in 1896 with a less than spectacular 9–30–8 record.[11]

Next in line was Jack Langdon, who met Dempsey for a mid-week bout at the Comique on February 2. Langdon of Philadelphia's Port Richmond neighborhood was a semi-regular at the Comique. He and Dempsey were of similar size. Mike Cleary was the timekeeper and Langdon, a mediocre fighter with a poor record, was at least partly responsible for breaking Cleary's arm with his hard head when the two met the previous year. Cleary struck Langdon at one point during their May 5, 1886, bout and the impact broke his arm, causing a brief retirement for Cleary. Despite the injury, Cleary defeated Langdon in four rounds.

The bout with Dempsey would not prove much better for Langdon. Dempsey started after his opponent immediately after referee Billy McLean called time and using his left, landed hard on Langdon's stomach. The Philadelphian quickly recovered and rushed Jack. The pair exchanged numerous blows before they broke. Shortly after the break Dempsey landed another hard blast to the stomach which angered Langdon and he rushed Jack again. As Langdon approached his opponent, the Nonpareil swung a lightning left that caught the Philadelphian on the neck and sent him sprawling to the floor on which he sat for several seconds before making it up to his knees. Although the round was not over, one of Langdon's handlers entered the ring and attempted to assist the dazed pugilist back to his corner. Dempsey protested vehemently and referee McLean intervened, ordering Langdon back to scratch immediately. During the remainder of the first and throughout all of the second round Dempsey did as he wished with Langdon.

In the third round, Dempsey smashed his opponent all over the ring. Langdon was able to keep his feet and land a strong counter to Dempsey's chest toward the end of the round, but Jack countered in turn with a heavy blow that sent Langdon sprawling through the ropes and down to the ground. Magnanimously, Jack helped his opponent up, keeping him from rolling off the stage. McLean then instructed the men to resume fighting. "Dempsey again opened up on him with a hard left-hander that cut Langdon's cheek, and followed it up with right and left-hand blows, every one of which nearly carried Langdon off his feet."[12] In the fourth and final scheduled round, Dempsey began battering Langdon again, but he soon lost interest in doing further damage to the helpless man and began to hold off a bit. Once, Langdon came alive and slugged Dempsey in the face, but the round, like the entire fight, was all Dempsey's. Newspaper accounts stated that "during the whole four rounds Langdon was punched and battered" by the Nonpareil. They continued, "His countenance was beautifully painted in crimson when time was called."[13] After four rounds, McLean awarded the bout to Jack.[14]

On February 5, Jack met Denny Killen to close out his weeklong engagement at the Comique. Killen, who was the brother of heavyweight contender Pat Killen, fought respectably for three rounds and held his own against Dempsey. The Nonpareil, however, took control of the contest in the final chapter and won this bout in the allotted four rounds. His week's work netted Jack $1,000, but he did not look as sharp as he would have liked and failed to knock out any of his three opponents. Each man got $25 to step into the ring and would earn another $50 if they were on their feet at the end of the fight. Each man collected the extra $50.

During his stay in the City of Brotherly Love, Jack was hoping to set up a bout with Dominick McCaffrey. He instructed his backers Gus Tuthill and Frank Trainor to approach McCaffrey's backers about a match to the finish for $1,000 a side, but the men were informed that the Philadelphian was out of town.[15]

Shortly before his leaving town, Jack met with McCaffrey, but there was no talk of setting up a fight between the two. McCaffrey had just returned from a brief trip to Florida and the meeting yielded little other than a general agreement that the pair should meet in the ring. Arthur Chambers said of the cordial but meaningless meeting, "It's a funny thing that when Jack Dempsey announced he would meet all comers in Philadelphia, Dominick McCaffrey suddenly left Philadelphia for a trip to Florida for his health."[16] Before climbing aboard his train out of Philadelphia, Jack commented that while he was not really looking for a fight, he would be agreeable to whatever McCaffrey were to suggest.

On February 15, Jack, Billy Madden, Jem Carney, Ned Mallahan and about five hundred other admirers attended an evening salute to Jack McAuliffe at the City Assembly Rooms on Washington Street in Brooklyn. McAuliffe was to be presented with a diamond-studded silver belt emblematic of his lightweight championship. The event had eight boxing and wrestling matches, the highlight of which was a bout between McAuliffe and Billy Frazier of Boston. The police were on hand and aware of some bad blood between the two. Captain Campbell warned the men to keep it scientific. "Nevertheless, the four rounds fought were enlivening, Frazier being at a disadvantage because he was afraid of the police, while McAuliffe was not."[17]

On February 19, John P. Clow issued a challenge in the newspapers, offering to fight to a finish, with or without gloves, any man in America who did not exceed 165 pounds for a purse of between $1,000 and $2,500 a side. Clow said that he was especially interested in meeting Dempsey "because he claims the middleweight championship." Jack stated that he was interested in fighting Clow, but his going price was a good bit higher than the westerner's offer.[18]

Dempsey was set to accept challenges from all comers for a second week at the Comique Theater in Philadelphia on March 21, but this engagement was apparently cancelled by order of the police. With the Philadelphia engagement cancelled, Jack traveled west in mid–March, stopping off in Rochester, New York, where he participated in an exhibition at the Washington Rink on March 15. The event was a resounding success with over 1,800 in attendance. During the event, Jack boxed with both Denny Costigan and Jack Coyle.

Jack and Costigan left Rochester for Detroit, where they put on sparring matches for several days. On March 22, Jack sparred four rounds for points with a local fighter named Tom McMahon in Detroit. While Dempsey took the decision, McMahon proved he was no pushover when he landed a hard left-hander on the Nonpareil's nose that caused considerable bleeding.[19] For the remainder of the week Jack sparred with Denny Costigan.

After completing his engagements in Detroit, Dempsey and his troupe headed back to Western New York State for a week's engagement at the Adelphia Theatre in Buffalo during the first week of April. The advertisement in the Buffalo newspapers trumpeted, "$30 to any boxer, big or little, who will set-to with either Mr. Dempsey or Mr. Costigan."[20] In addition to the sparring, patrons could watch the John Tills Marionettes as well as Professor Paul Welizman, who was reportedly a Russian high-wire walker, all for between 15 and 25 cents admission. According to reports, "Jack Dempsey and Denny Costigan were among the attractions at the Adelphia Theatre, Buffalo, NY last week. On Wednesday evening there was some fun as a result of the attempt of 'Sandy' Banister, a lanky novice, to win $100 by stopping with Jack through four rounds. He was knocked head over heels into the orchestra in the second round and in the next was thoroughly done up."[21]

On April 9, Jack met local welterweight Billy Baker at the Adelphia Theater. The event was billed as a "sparring match" using four-ounce gloves under the Queensberry Rules. Baker stood to gain a $100 purse supplied by theater owner Colonel T.E. Snellbaker if he was still on his feet after the four three-minute rounds. With Baker outweighing Dempsey by thirty-five pounds, the betting odds were favoring Baker to survive. This was an interesting bout in that it was only scheduled for four rounds and the Nonpareil could only win by knockout.

The event was a huge box office success, as fans from all over Erie County and the

Niagara region flocked to attend. "The Dempsey-Baker sparring match at the Adelphia last evening drew the largest crowd that has been seen in the house for years. It was impossible for another man to get within the doors, and several hundred were obliged to turn away. Quite a crowd remained in the hallway until the event was finished."[22] Even the spaces leaning on the bannister of the steps leading to the gallery were selling at a premium.

As was usual, Denny Costigan was on hand to work Jack's corner, while James Wilson and Joe Vanderbusch seconded Baker. Baker wore maroon tights while Dempsey's were black.

When referee Charles Perkins brought the fighters together at mid-ring, the size differential was evident. While their heights were similar, Baker was clearly the much heavier of the two, outweighing the Nonpareil by more than thirty pounds. It was soon also clear, however, that Baker was not in the best of fighting shape. The men sized each other up at the opening, but by the middle of the first round, Jack worked in several heavy lefts to his opponent's jaw and a hard smash to the ribs. Baker was only able to land one strong counter punch in retaliation. Still, as the round came to a close, both men seemed fairly fresh. "Only once did the champion get in an undercut [*sic*] on Baker's well braced jaw, and that had little effect. Baker got numerous side blows on the jaw which, although they must have stung, were not much heeded."[23]

The second round opened with Dempsey landing two straight rights to his opponent's face, causing the color of Baker's nose to match the maroon shade of his tights. Jack followed that with an uppercut that missed when Baker reflexively stepped away. From that point on, the Buffalo man fought strictly on the defensive, making only a few tepid swings at the Brooklyn man.

The third round was clearly Dempsey's as he hammered away at Baker's body with solid lefts and followed those up with several "stingers" to the ears and the mouth. While there were a number of minor exchanges between the two, Baker made little effort to retaliate.

As the fourth and final round began, Dempsey again assumed the offensive. Dempsey danced around his opponent landing punches almost at will, but given the size differential, Baker was able to stay on his feet. Dempsey would move into close range and land punches on Baker's face, but the Buffalo native was often able to step back and juke out of range. "A dig to Baker's ribs and a feint by Dempsey were followed by three hard raps on the Buffalo man's jaw. Another heavy left-hander served as a forcible reminder of the champion's strength."[24]

Baker fell into a clinch after that and as the men were separating, he was able to land a wildly swinging right on Jack's cheek. The blow was solid but put the Nonpareil in absolutely no danger. Still, having had little else to cheer, the heavily pro–Baker crowd rose to their feet and roared wildly. "In the fusillade of blows that followed, Dempsey gave Baker several stingers on the nose, but failed to draw the claret."[25]

As the round and fight drew near an end, encouragement was shouted to both men— to Dempsey to finish Baker and to Baker to stay upright. Jack continued to hammer away at his opponent, and Baker did get a final crack before timekeeper James Conlisk signaled the end of the round. After four rounds, the Buffalo man was still on his feet and much to the overflow crowd's delight, he did manage to land a few blows on Dempsey. He was clearly, however, no match for the Nonpareil in terms of boxing science. While Dempsey undoubtedly outfought his opponent, the bout was ruled a draw as Jack had failed to score a knockout. In some newspapers the fight was recorded as a "No Decision." The Buffalo man won his $100 purse and he was quite satisfied with it. "I didn't come to knock him out," Baker exclaimed afterwards. "All I wanted was to stand up four rounds." For his part Dempsey said that he wished he'd had more than four rounds to score a knockout. He also stated that Baker "was possessed of considerable ability on the defensive, although he hinted that the latter would stand no show in the long run."[26]

On April 19, it was announced that Jack would journey to Cleveland, Ohio, in early May to face 23-year-old Patrick "Reddy" Gallagher.[27] Inside the ring Gallagher was described as being a strong and very hard-hitting brawler who came at his opponents in rushes. He also had a long reach and was quick and elusive.[28] Outside of the ring Gallagher was described as being a polite, quiet and well-behaved gentleman who, while not a complete teetotaler, seldom took a drink.

On Monday, May 2, Jack met Gallagher at the Frankfort Street Gymnasium in Cleveland. "A large number of sporting men were present and the exhibition proved to be first class."[29] The large number was estimated by some sources as being around 300, each of whom paid a $5.00 admission.[30]

The bout was scheduled for six rounds under the Queensberry Rules with four-ounce gloves and it actually went the distance, which is somewhat remarkable given that Jack broke his left arm just below the elbow during the second round.

The bout began around 10:00 p.m. Dempsey, who was seconded by his friend Denny Costigan and Charles Perkins of Rochester, weighed in just over 150 pounds while the 5'8" Gallagher tipped the scales at 156 pounds and had Mervine Thompson and H. Park in his corner. The referee was Mike Ryan, "a local professor of boxing."

The first round was rather tame, as both men sparred lightly, feeling each other out. Gallagher landed a couple of strong blows to the body and one to Dempsey's head, and Jack landed a terrific uppercut to his opponent's jaw, stopping the rushing Gallagher in his tracks at the end of the round. While both men landed several jabs and combinations, nothing remarkable was achieved and the round was considered a draw.

"In the second round, Dempsey drove Gallagher to his corner where they clinched. In breaking away Dempsey got in the only heavy blow of the fight. He made a straight shoulder drive for Gallagher's jaw, which he struck full and square."[31] The force of the blow broke Jack's left arm just below the elbow. No one but Jack knew of the injury until after the fight as he feared that his seconds or referee Mike Ryan might call a halt to the match if they were made aware, but that was it for the really heavy blows. With Dempsey unable to land solid lefts and with the exception of an occasional power right, much of the remaining rounds were full of scientific sparring in which Gallagher showed good form. By the end of the second round, Gallagher was bleeding from his mouth and Dempsey from his nose.

The third round was lively, and both men were punished. Dempsey landed a strong right to the side of Gallagher's head that briefly dazed the Cleveland fighter. According to Jack, he then attempted to follow up with a left, in hopes that his injury was not serious. But when Jack delivered the portside missile he "was surprised at the pain it gave him, suspected the reason, and used it but 'as a bluff' to use his own words, until the end of the fight."[32] The *Morning Oregonian* agreed that it was apparent that something was amiss with Dempsey, commenting in their May 3rd edition that after the second round Jack did not strike a meaningful blow with his left.[33]

In the fourth round, both men circled and jabbed. The only real heavy blows occurred when Gallagher received punches to the body and head, and Dempsey on the nose. Despite his lack of left-side armament, Dempsey managed to keep Gallagher at bay for significant portions of the fight by landing occasional power rights to his opponent's head and rib cage. The fifth round was full of clinches as Gallagher was growing less confident of his chances and more afraid of punishment from the Nonpareil's strong right hand and Dempsey was held somewhat in check by his injury. During the round, Dempsey did land two sharp rights on the side of Gallagher's head, but the slower action did not suit the crowd.

The sixth and final chapter of the bout was wholly uninteresting, bringing periodic hissing from the audience. Each man landed an effective blow—Gallagher a bolt to Jack's chin and Dempsey a right on his opponent's cheek—but that was about it for the heavy action. As the round drew to a close the crowd continued to hiss because of the slow pace. Dempsey stepped forward at the call of time and said, "Gentlemen, my arm has been broken since the second round." The Nonpareil then showed his arm to those in the ring. A local physician, Dr. Gleason, who was in the audience examined the arm and quickly declared it fractured between the wrist and the elbow. Referee Ryan then declared the bout a draw.

Later, Dempsey said, "I knew I had to be careful and so saved myself to make the battle a stand-off." Jack added that he was confident that had he not suffered the injury he would have defeated Gallagher. He then went on to praise his opponent. "He is a good man and one of the improving kind." In summation, Dempsey said that he clearly would not be able to fight in the near term and would have to look at his long-term options as his injury healed. In a comment that was telling of his internal struggle between settling down to a quiet life with Maggie and the lure of the prize ring, Jack commented, "Of course, I cannot say whether I will again enter the ring, for, as you know, a man once in the biz finds it hard to give up."[34]

Dempsey's broken arm was set late that night by the noted Cleveland surgeon Dr. C.C. Arms at St. Alexis Hospital.[35] The physician reported that it was a simple fracture of the radius of the left arm and that a full recovery was expected, with Jack's arm becoming as good as ever. Despite the encouraging initial diagnosis, reports over the next few days grew less optimistic. Dr. Arms and other physicians who continued to examine Dempsey's arm were now of the opinion that the Nonpareil was through in the ring.[36] "I do not think that Mr. Dempsey will ever be able to fight again," said Dr. Arms upon re-examination of the break. "The bone will knit and the arm will be apparently as good as before, but he will find that he cannot depend on it for striking hard blows. Mr. Dempsey, for all that he has a splendid physique, is a small-boned man, and this will be against him."[37]

Jack with his left arm now in a cast and sling, planned to travel back to Brooklyn the next day, but was detained by the police pending the resolution of two legal items. First, he was arrested and tried on May 4 under the Ohio state law prohibiting prize-fighting. If Jack was found guilty, the penalty could bring as much as a $250 fine and up to three months in prison. The law, however, had an exemption for fights held at athletic clubs and in gymnasiums. When this point was made by Dempsey's attorneys the judge threw out the charges and released Jack and his party.

In the other legal wrangling, Dempsey found himself being sued in civil court on charges of a breach of contract. Earlier in April, a man named J. Geary, claiming to be

Jack's agent, had telegraphed Thomas Curry, the owner of a Cleveland sporting hall, to arrange for Dempsey to appear in an exhibition. The arrangements were finalized, but Jack, knowing nothing of the event, failed to appear. When he arrived in town for the Gallagher match at a rival athletic hall, Curry sued for damages. A civil trial was set for Friday, May 4.[38] By Wednesday afternoon, however, the suit and all charges were dropped when it was proved that Geary was acting on his own, and that Dempsey had no knowledge of either Geary or the April exhibition. Jack promptly left for Brooklyn, arriving the next evening by train. With his bandaged left arm in a black silk sling, Dempsey immediately made his way to his hotel in Williamsburg for some rest.

Once back in New York, Dempsey was placed under the care of Dr. A.J. Ward, an orthopedic surgeon recommended by Richard Fox. Dr. Ward had a good reputation and had seen great success over the past several years treating athletes who had suffered various injuries.[39]

Interestingly, John L. Sullivan suffered almost the exact same injury as Dempsey at roughly the same time. Sullivan broke his left arm during a bout with Patsy Cardiff in Minneapolis in mid–January of 1887. Others also commented on the irony. According to the *New York Sun*, "It is rather strange that the two best fighters America has produced should have their fistic careers interrupted by similar injuries inflicted in almost the same manner. Sullivan swung his left arm and it collided with Patsy Cardiff's hard head, breaking the radius. Jack Dempsey swung his left and Ruddigore Gallagher stopped it so suddenly with his right that Jack's radius snapped like a pipe stem."[40] In both cases, their physicians stated that the breaks would heal completely, but also speculated that neither man would be able to fight again. In both cases, however, the physicians were only half right; the bones did heal completely, but Sullivan and Dempsey each continued to enter the ring for a number of years afterward.

For several weeks, multiple news stories continued to speculate on the real fear that the damage to Jack's arm could be permanent, but soon those fears were allayed as reports on the Nonpareil's recovery began to circulate. After visiting with Jack and Denny Costigan a couple of weeks after the Gallagher fight, a reporter who wrote under the pseudonym "The Rambler" in the "Walks About the City" section of the *Brooklyn Eagle*, wrote that he found Dempsey in high spirits and that "the bone is knitting satisfactorily and very little pain or fever is in the process."[41]

During the interview, however, Jack stated once again that regardless of the prognosis for his arm, his intentions were to leave the prize ring and go into business. "I will never fight again unless I am forced to do it to earn a living," he said, "and that is very unlikely. I don't like the business and never did and now is a very good time to drop it." Jack said he would go into some other business, but preferred it not be owning and operating a saloon. He also indicated that his dislike for Charley Mitchell and desire to whip him in the ring would not influence this decision. "Oh, my grudge against Mitchell is not so deep seated as all that." Jack said that the bluster and dislike had mostly passed away.[42]

Dempsey's opponent, Reddy Gallagher, was a fascinating man who continued to fight professionally through the mid–1890s. During his pugilistic career he fought such notable men as Dempsey, Charley Mitchell and Johnny Herget, a.k.a. Young Mitchell. In late October of 1894, Gallagher announced that he had promised his new young wife Mary that he would not fight again. While he would slip a bit from time to time, Gallagher was mostly true to his word, appearing in the ring only a handful more times, with most of those being exhibition bouts or wrestling matches. An avid and skilled athlete, the

153-pound Gallagher also loved football and baseball. He played football for the Denver Athletic Club's semi-professional eleven, for whom he started at right guard and in 1892, became captain of the squad.

After his fighting days ended Gallagher became the boxing instructor at the Denver Athletic Club in Colorado, the owner of the Lewiston Hotel and the wealthy operator of a successful real estate company. Gallagher was also a sportswriter and he became the sports editor of the *Denver Post* from 1929 until the time of his death on November 13, 1937, in Denver.[43]

Gallagher was an active member of Denver's Good Shepherd Roman Catholic Church and the Parrish website still recalls their former member as follows, "Patrick R. 'Reddy' Gallagher was among the most colorful parishioners. He was called 'Reddy' because of his red hair and readiness for fisticuffs. As Denver's prime proponent of the sport of boxing, he was a pugilist himself, coached others, staged many fights, and, in the 1920s, began a long career as a sports writer for *The Denver Post*. Although he supposedly could neither read nor write, Reddy could dictate and knew more about boxing than anyone else around. Shortly after his death, his wife donated the Gallagher Memorial Sanctuary at Mt. Olivet Cemetery, in honor of her late husband. The chapel, with its pink marble walls, also serves as a mausoleum for the bishops and archbishops of Denver."[44]

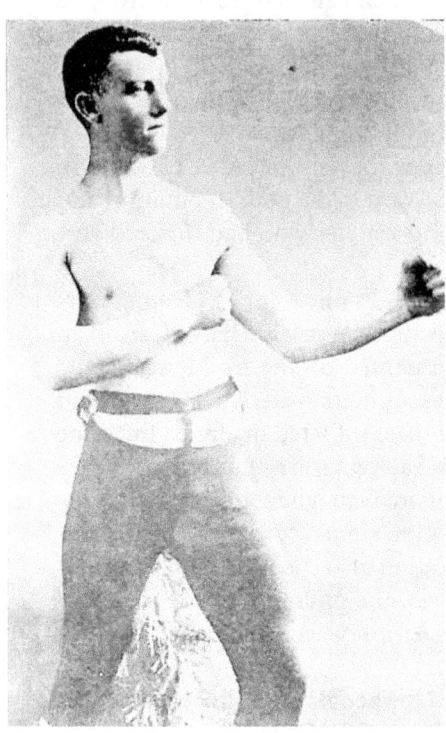

Patrick "Reddy" Gallagher.

Dempsey found plenty to keep him occupied in the weeks following his injury. During the last week of May, it was reported that Jack was a proud father as Maggie gave birth to their first child, a beautiful daughter. The couple named their new little girl Alice.[45] Never able to stay away from the ring for long, Jack and Gus Tuthill found time enough to second Jack Files during his June 2 fight with Johnny Reagan in which Reagan took a forty-four-round London Rules victory.

After the bout, the *Brooklyn Daily Eagle* ran an article about the fight and mentioned Jack questioning Reagan's courage and his ability to stand up to the strain during the latter's contest with Files. "Johnny was told of what Dempsey had said of him, and he at once conceived the idea of wrestling the championship of the middle-weight class from the Nonpareil."[46]

In early June, Reagan began itching for a fight with Dempsey. Jack was clearly unable to step into the ring in the immediate future, but despite his claims that he was through with the prize ring, Dempsey would again climb between the ropes and fight after his arm had fully healed. Instead of retiring Dempsey and Jack McAuliffe went in search of Reagan's backer to attempt to set up a bout between McAuliffe and Reagan. On June 6 they headed to the offices of the *New York Clipper* where they found no one. The pair then continued on to the *Police Gazette* offices where the backer Billy Reed was found.

They offered a bout for $1,000 a side for ten rounds or, if they preferred, to a finish. Reed expressed interest in the proposal and the men then haggled over weight. McAuliffe and Dempsey stipulated that Reagan—naturally a larger man than McAuliffe—weigh no more than 140 pounds at ringside. It was agreed that the two sides would meet in Richard Fox's office again on June 10. The pugilists and their backers continued to haggle but could not agree on terms and the McAuliffe-Reagan contest never came about, but Reagan would get his shot at Dempsey before the year was out.

Dempsey and McAuliffe joined together in mid–June on a tour of exhibition matches. They opened in Newburgh, New York, on June 15, and proceeded from there to Buffalo. On June 28, the Dempsey and McAuliffe were at Cronheim's Theatre in Hoboken, New Jersey, to give a four-round exhibition. The crowd was small—just over three hundred people. The sparring on the tour was rather tame as these were Dempsey's first real ring sessions since he broke his arm in the Gallagher bout. Still, he looked to be in good condition and while he held back the power shots, he was as quick with his feet and hands as usual.[47]

The Nonpareil was in Providence, Rhode Island, on Independence Day, to spar a four-round exhibition at Lowe's Opera House with local heavyweight Jack Ashton. Dempsey looked to be returning to his old form as he feinted and threw punches with authority, moved quickly around the ring and easily dodged his opponent's attacks.

Ashton was a decent fighter who fought some of the more notable men of the era during his career, including George Godfrey, Billy Madden, Jake Kilrain, Joe Lannon and "Brooklyn" Jimmy Carroll. He was probably best known as a favorite sparring partner of John L. Sullivan, Dominick McCaffrey and Peter Jackson, each of whom he squared off with in multiple exhibition contests. Standing just under six feet and weighing in at around 175 pounds, Ashton was a good-sized man. He "was neither a power hitter nor a fancy boxer type but he was a scrappy and game fighter who gave it his all."[48] Ashton was a Sullivan loyalist who revered the champion despite John L.'s penchant for making the Providence man the butt of cruel jokes.[49] Like his hero, Ashton was a lavish spender and a heavy drinker who died in 1893 at age 30 from erysipelas, a bacterial skin infection often caused by a cut characterized by blisters, fever, shaking and chills. Though treatable today with antibiotics, it proved fatal to Ashton in 1893. In the typical fashion of the day, the pugilistic community came together and held a benefit at New York's People's Theatre to raise a purse for Jack's widow Louise Dempsey Ashton in March 1893, two months after her husband's untimely death.

August 20 found Jack in North Adams, Massachusetts, where he sparred four exhibition rounds with Jake Kilrain at an Ancient Order of Hibernian family picnic. The match was fought with soft gloves in front of several thousand people, including men, women and children. J.J. Delanthy of Cohoes, New York, was chosen as referee.[50] "Each round lasted three minutes and a few hard blows were exchanged. During the third-round a large elevated platform holding 200 persons, fell twenty feet to the ground. Many people were bruised, but none seriously."[51]

In late August and early September, rumors began to circulate that rather than retire, Dempsey would fight Johnny Reagan in December within 100 miles of New York City sometime between December 9 and 14. The fight was to be for $2,000 a side and a forfeit was deposited with Richard Fox for Dempsey by his backer Jake Stearns on August 29. The two fighters were to sign letters of agreement within the week.[52]

When asked later why he had agreed to meet the fairly inexperienced Reagan for so small a purse—just $1,000 a side by the time of the actual event—Dempsey stated that it came after the Nonpareil had seconded Jack Files in his forty-four-round knockout loss to Reagan the previous June. Due to harsh words and general baiting, "Reagan's faction wanted to get up a fight between him and me, and as Reagan had talked so much I determined to have satisfaction. I wanted to get at him with bare knuckles and it was not the money consideration that led to the match. I knew I could beat him anyway."[53]

Although fully recovered from the broken arm, Jack's health was not as it should have been. He had recently been confined to bed in his rooms at the Metropolitan Hotel located at the corner of Grand Street and Kent Avenue. The Nonpareil had reportedly become quite ill with a cold after attending a baseball game in late August. The cold developed into pleurisy—an inflammation of the double membrane (pleura) that lines the inside of the chest cavity and surrounds each of the lungs.[54]

Jack's physician, Dr. Peter Hughes, was called in and upon examination, determined that Jack's right lung was highly congested and inflamed. He told Dempsey to stay in bed for the remainder of the week. One has to wonder if this was the first round of Jack's ultimately fatal bout with tuberculosis and consumption.

The physician-induced bed rest forced Jack to miss the initial meeting at the offices of the *Police Gazette* between Reagan, his sponsors and Jack's own sponsors. Jack was well represented, however, and after some negotiation, terms were agreed to and the fight set.

Despite the agreeable negotiations, Dempsey and his backers were a little bit sore about the circumstances that brought the bout to fruition. Little in Reagan's record indicated that he was in Dempsey's class. His "big" fights included a defeat of Jack Files long past his prime and a bout with Tom Henry that Johnny was decisively losing until Reagan's supporters broke through the ropes and demanded a draw be declared for fear that their man would soon lose. Reagan challenged Dempsey to a bout shortly after the Nonpareil broke his arm in the Gallagher fight. This attempt by the comparatively unknown Reagan "to reap pugilistic fame at the expense of an incapacitated champion made Dempsey and his friends naturally a little angry"[55] In short, the terms agreed to for the fight were only barely tolerable to the Dempsey camp and the Nonpareil was ready to whip Reagan.

Of their upcoming bout Jack said, "I do not seek this fight. After my arm was broken Reagan challenged me and I promised to fight him when I was well, and I now propose to make my word good. I conceded almost everything to him, but there are a few points to which I objected." Dempsey really only insisted upon two points. He wanted to wear kid gloves—a somewhat minor point—and he was insistent that the crowd be kept away, with only each fighter's seconds, a few supporters and the referee in attendance. Reagan had wanted it open. "I would not for a moment entertain such a proposition. I want to have no thugs around when I fight, so I sent word that there should be only the seconds and the referee present. I want to have no repetition of the disgraceful scenes at the Reagan-Henry fight. I want to have no drunken roughs around."[56]

A benefit picnic was held on Dempsey's behalf on September 11 at High Ground Park on Myrtle Avenue in Brooklyn. To Jack's delight, among the first arrivals at the event "were Charley Mitchell and his father-in-law Poney Moore, Billy Madden and Jake Kilrain. Also attending was Johnny Reagan." The afternoon was filled with wrestling, dancing exhibitions and one boxing match between Joe Denning and Jack Fallon. Earlier in the month it was said that Dempsey would spar with both Jack Fogarty and Jack McAuliffe. This fell through as his physical condition would not allow for it. McAuliffe commented to one reporter that between his illness and his broken arm, the Nonpareil was not yet his old self. "Jack didn't look well," he said, "but he's got a good recovery and this weather will knock his sickness out of him." The reporter commented that "Dempsey's sickness has told on his looks and sprightly step, but the old fire is in his eye and has not been dimmed."[57]

At one point, Kilrain introduced Dempsey to Mitchell. Mitchell bowed to Dempsey and exuberantly extended his right hand, grasping Jack's. The Nonpareil courteously returned Mitchell's bow. Madden and Kilrain bantered good-naturedly back and forth that Dempsey and Mitchell should step into the ring here and now as a finale to the picnic, but even had Mitchell been willing, Dempsey was in no condition with his illness and not yet fully repaired arm, both of which had caused his doctors to warn him against sparring.

Despite the cool feelings between the Dempsey and Reagan camps, Jack, now on the mend from his bout with pleurisy, attended a benefit for Reagan on September 12 in Brooklyn which netted Reagan around $700.[58] After four preliminaries which included a match between Reagan's younger brother and another local man named Donovan, the elder Reagan engaged in a three-round wind up with Jack Files.[59]

Two days later, Jack appeared rather clandestinely at the City Assembly Rooms in New York where Reagan was set to spar with Paddy Smith. The match was the final event of the evening and Dempsey, wrapped up in a heavy overcoat, slipped in unnoticed about 11:00 p.m. It did not take long for several people to recognize him and gather round to talk and shake his hand. Mostly recovered, but not strong enough to stand for long periods of time, several friends escorted Jack to the press gallery and got him a seat. From there Jack watched Reagan challenge Smith and critiqued his upcoming opponent before leaving for home and his bed.

Jack indulged in one of his great interests when he attended the Brooklyn Jockey Club races on September 21. The Nonpareil was an avid horse racing fan and thoroughly enjoyed spending an afternoon at the track. Reports stated that "he still shows traces of his recent illness, but he says he is rapidly recovering and that he feels as strong and as hearty as ever." When he was asked if he and Charley Mitchell had become friendly since Mitchell had shown up at his benefit at High Ground Park Dempsey said flatly, "No." Jack added, "Kilrain and I are warm friends and so is Billy Madden and myself. They came over to spar for me and Mitchell merely came along as a spectator. I wouldn't have him spar at any benefit of mine."[60] Clearly there was not much of a thaw in the relationship.

During this time, Jack was asked to train his old friend Jack McAuliffe for the latter's October bout with Jem Carney in Boston. Jack was agreeable but said that due to his illness, he could not travel to Boston to do so. At that point, McAuliffe and his tribe immediately packed up and moved their camp to Rockaway Beach on Long Island.

Dempsey and McAuliffe were nearly inseparable as young men when they worked together in the cooper's shop in Williamsburg. McAuliffe was born on March 24 1866 in Cork, Ireland and like Dempsey, emigrated to Brooklyn with his family as a small boy.

It was common to see each man in the other's corner during their respective bouts. "McAuliffe was a most dashing fighter and picturesque character. He was always full of rollicking Irish humor and the possessor of a clever intelligence. Jack [McAuliffe] loved the good things of life and when he started to train for a contest it was nothing unusual for him to show up for the training period weighing as high as 174 pounds."[61] The Carney bout was rescheduled to November 16 and to keep McAuliffe sharp, Dempsey worked him hard in training camp, but also set up several exhibition ring appearances for his friend, some including himself. In mid–October, as Jack was fully recovered and now in training himself for the upcoming Reagan mill, the pair appeared at Bancroft's skating rink in New Bedford, Massachusetts.[62]

The Nonpareil's childhood friend, Jack McAuliffe.

During late September, Jack signed for two tune-up fights to take place prior to his match with Reagan. The first was with Pete McCoy for $1,000 in October, and the second was an eight-rounder with Jack McGee, to be fought for $700 in Boston the following month.

Jake Starnes, in a meeting with reporters, commented that Jack's health was rapidly improving after his bout with pleurisy. Starnes told the reporters, however, that "Dempsey has reason to feel concern for himself as he has had a slight hemorrhage of the lungs. He had a pulmonary trouble two years ago, but it ceased when he went to New Orleans and then to the Pacific coast."[63] Starnes also reiterated that Dempsey and McAuliffe would make a tour of the sporting cities of the East Coast and that Dempsey was still planning to second McAuliffe in his upcoming bout with Jem Carney.

Jack made his first serious appearance in the ring since the Gallagher bout on October 11 at Warren Lewis's Casino in Hoboken, New Jersey, where he squared off against Big Ed Reese of Jersey City in a four-round bout. This was the first of several contests Dempsey scheduled to help assure his preparedness for his December date with Reagan. Dempsey, in his familiar blue tights, was described as being in good trim, but looking like a schoolboy standing beside Reese, "who had a chest like a hogshead and arms like a horse's legs."[64] Reese, who was nicknamed "The Slasher" by his mates in the Scottish-American Club of New Jersey, was described as "a burly, muscular boxer."[65]

The match started just before midnight, when veteran pugilist and referee Tom Barker beckoned the men to center ring and called time. Despite the size differential, Dempsey controlled the action. He moved well and showed his old-time cleverness. Jack Files, who was in Dempsey's corner for that bout, remarked on how well the Nonpareil feinted throughout the bout. "How he can kid a feller!" said Files.

In the opening seconds, Dempsey caught Reese off guard with a blistering left to the jaw that laid the New Jersey man on the stage. Reese was on his feet in no time, but he need not have bothered getting up. Seconds later, he was down again after an almost identical left-handed blow from the Nonpareil. Jack may have felt some discomfort in his left arm after the second blow, for he decided to stop delivering these pile-driving shots. He'd tested his left arm and it had responded as he'd hoped. He simply toyed with Reese from here on out making "a plaything out of his antagonist." Once in the fourth and final round, Reese managed to get Dempsey against the ropes and hammer his ribs a few times, but Jack quickly rolled out and in no time sent the big man through the ropes and onto his head. Referee Barker determined that Dempsey clearly had the best of the match and decided the bout in favor of the Nonpareil.[66] One observer noted, "Judging by the way Jack Dempsey pummeled Ed Reese of Jersey City at the Casino, Hoboken, October 11, he must be getting into pretty good condition for his fight with Johnny Reagan."[67]

Two nights later, Jack was again at the Casino in Hoboken where he squared off against Jim McHugh in a five-round bout. McHugh, a middleweight who hailed from Hoboken, was Jack's physical twin. The men were both 5'8" and weighed 150 pounds, but Dempsey had by far the lead in ring experience.

From the start, Dempsey had control of the fight, continually jabbing McHugh in the face and stomach. McHugh's attempts to defend against Jack's blows were largely unsuccessful. At the opening of the first round, Dempsey began to feint in an effort to size his opponent up. After a few seconds of this, however, Jack let go a lightning fast left that caught McHugh square on the nose. He then followed up with blows to the ribs and face, forcing McHugh back into his corner. McHugh's efforts to return fire were either off target or neatly blocked. Satisfied, Dempsey then turned and walked back to the center of the ring to wait for his opponent to recover. Embarrassed and frustrated, McHugh rushed Dempsey, catching him off guard, and landed a sharp right to the Nonpareil's face shortly before the round ended.

In the second round, McHugh forced the fighting which led to some heated sparring in which the Hoboken man landed repeated shots to Dempsey's body, but by the third and fourth rounds, McHugh was spent and Dempsey toyed with his adversary, hitting him as he pleased. At the end of the fourth, Dempsey was declared the winner, but the crowd wanted more and both fighters were game, so a fifth round was fought. Having already won the fight, Dempsey simply sparred with McHugh and gave the crowd their money's worth.[68] The *Boston Globe* reported that McHugh was knocked out, but that seems unlikely given that he was on his feet at the end of the fourth round and the spur-of-the-moment fifth round was more of a light sparring match.[69]

In an interesting side note, McHugh's second for this fight was Steve Brodie, who became famous the previous July after reportedly jumping from the Brooklyn Bridge and surviving. Brodie apparently jumped to win a $200 bet, but his leap led to much more. The publicity he received led to speaking offers and endorsements which enabled him to purchase a saloon in the Bowery section of Manhattan. The saloon doubled as a museum for his jump and proved to be very successful in its own right. Brodie was also able to parlay his bridge jumping into a successful acting career.

The final bout in this engagement at Lewis's Casino was against former foe Billy Dacey on the evening of October 15. In years past, Dempsey had stated that Dacey had caused him more difficulty than any other opponent that he had faced due to his strong jab and the fact that Jack had not yet mastered the skill of avoiding or blocking it. At this juncture, however, Dempsey had long since developed his skills far beyond those of Dacey. The *New York Evening World* compared the fighters to a greyhound and a bulldog, stating that Dempsey—the greyhound—depended on speed, and Dacey—the bulldog—depended on strength. In describing the fight, the *World* reporter said, "Speed won on the principle that half a dozen mallets are a deal more effective than a cannon shot that doesn't land."[70] While Dacey fought with vigor and gave all he had, Dempsey had little trouble dispatching his opponent in the allotted four chapters, toying with Dacey for three rounds, but cutting loose in the fourth to settle the matter in his own favor.

It had been a successful tune-up week for Dempsey. He had looked good and displayed his conditioning and his old form which was important to prove that he was fully recovered from both his broken arm and his recent bout with pleurisy. Still, as good as he looked, he had to remember that these were only short bouts against less difficult competition. The *New York Sun* stated that "Jack Dempsey was the bright particular fistic star of a Hoboken music hall last week and easily got away with the three opponents pitted against him. In these three encounters he has displayed so much of his old-time skill, vigor, and form that his admirers are in raptures and predict the easiest of victories for him in his contests with Peter McCoy, Johnny McGee, and Johnny Reagan." The writer went on to say that while he was impressed with how good Dempsey looked, "his admirers must remember that the men he is engaged to tackle are far superior in caliber to the lads he met last week and that Jack will want to be as fine as silk to do them in a canter."[71]

Jack went south to Wilmington, Delaware, for a series of four-round, gloved battles at the Grand Central Theater. The Delaware city had been the recipient of a great many fistic encounters thanks to officials in the City of Brotherly Love. "Philadelphia authorities having prohibited boxing exhibitions and glove contests, patrons of the manly art in that city now go over to Wilmington, Delaware, to see the stars of the ring put up their 'dukes.'"[72] The Grand Central announced that Jack would be engaged at the theater during the first week of the month followed by a week's appearance by featherweight Ike Weir, "The Belfast Spider."

Starting on Monday evening, October 31, Jack was scheduled to spar with four men. Originally scheduled for the week's bouts were Ned McCann, Joe Ellingsworth, Frank Bosworth and Mike Boden, who had given Dempsey a tough bout the previous January in Philadelphia.

As is often the case, what was planned and what actually occurred were different. The Ned McCann fight came off as scheduled with Dempsey defeating the Chester, Pennsylvania, man on Monday, and Jack defeated Frank Bosworth of Providence, Rhode Island, on Tuesday. The Mike Boden fight was postponed to be rescheduled at a later date. Instead, Jack met Denny Kelliher of Philadelphia on Thursday, and Bill Gabig. "The Mysterious Fighter" of Pittsburgh, on Saturday. Dempsey defeated each of these fighters in four rounds. Gabig was a heavyweight trial horse who never quite made the grade in the big-time, winning about one in every four fights over the length of his career. Still, Gabig was a tough brawler and was always quick to his feet after being knocked down—which is good, because it happened often. During a bout against Mike Conley, the Ithaca Giant, the previous February, Gabig made ten round trips to the canvas and back. He was, however, still on his feet at the end of the fourth and final round to see referee Ed McGuinn award the bout to Conley.[73]

The contest with Kelliher was looked at as a phenomenal victory as Jack had his way with the much larger man. The bout was very even for the first two rounds with Kelliher showing a great spirit as he endeavored to find Jack's jaw with his dangerous right and drop him early. Despite Denny's science and power, Dempsey's now-mended left appendage began to cut the Philadelphian's face badly by the third round. In the fourth, Jack landed combinations at will on the 220-pound Kelliher causing those present to conclude that he would have no problem vanquishing Johnny Reagan in their upcoming bout. "Bets were freely offered of 100 to 40 on Dempsey against Reagan, with no takers."[74] The Wilmington contests were extremely successful for Dempsey who won all four bouts on points. "Dempsey proved to the satisfaction of those present that he is still the invincible."

It is interesting to note that the brash youngster Joe Ellingsworth, after all of his self-promotion, demands for a fight with Dempsey and claims of ring superiority over Jack, backed out of his Delaware meeting with the Nonpareil, just days prior to the bout. The *Brooklyn Eagle* noted, "It is said that Ellingsworth has secured a position in a prominent athletic club and will not again enter the ring."[75] Which begs the question, if he were really so eager to meet Dempsey in the ring, could the braggadocious young man not have waited a few days to accept the position with the "prominent athletic club"?

After his engagements in Delaware, Jack was planning to head to New England where he would meet Pete McCoy in a glove contest to the finish during the second week of November. The bout was scheduled to take place at the Cribb Club in Boston for a purse of $700 but was declared off on October 30 when McCoy got into a disagreement with several club members. This left just one contest for Dempsey prior to his bout with Reagan, a gloved fight with Jack McGee in the next couple weeks.

With the McCoy fight off, instead of heading to Boston after fulfilling his contract in Wilmington, Dempsey traveled back to Brooklyn in the company of his backer Jake Stearns. The men boarded the train home on Monday, November 7. After a short stay in Williamsburg, Jack returned to Rockaway Beach to finish training his friend Jack McAuliffe for his rescheduled lightweight championship bout with Jem Carney.

On November 11, Richard K. Fox of the *Police Gazette* hosted Starnes, McAuliffe, Jack Fogarty and Dempsey at the *Police Gazette* offices in New York where they met with Reagan, Frank Stevenson, Billy Madden and Billy Reed to witness the deposit of the final $500 a side for the upcoming middleweight championship contest. Fox was confirmed as the stakeholder and the principles agreed that he would name a referee on December 9.

It was also agreed that revised London Rules would be used requiring skin-tight gloves. The men were to be weighed at ringside before they entered the ring. Neither could weigh more than the agreed 154 pounds.

In a turnabout, Dempsey agreed to allow a limited crowd of onlookers to view the contest. "It was supposed at first that tickets were to be sold to witness the fight, but, judging from the conversation of the principals, a well-known athletic club will subscribe a purse larger than the stake money. This will confine the spectators to the members of the club and their friends."[76]

After meeting with Reagan and his advisors, Dempsey headed to Boston for a fight, but not his. Jack was there to second his old pal Jack McAuliffe during his lightweight bout against British champion Jem Carney. Dempsey had been training with McAuliffe at Rockaway Beach and the two had worked each other into marvelous condition. A report from that time stated of the two friends, "Dempsey and McAuliffe are hard at work down at Ruland's Hotel, Rockaway Beach, and both are doing well." The article continued by noting that "Dempsey's seconding will be much more valuable to McAuliffe than it would be to another class of fighter." The reporter pointed out that "a successful pugilist invariably wants his principal to fight as he would himself, and as McAuliffe is a pocket edition of Dempsey and fights the same style, the advice will be better than it would be for a right hand rushing fighter."[77]

The McAuliffe-Carney match was held at one o'clock in the morning near the Atlantic Hotel, in a ring pitched in a stable on Revere Beach in front of roughly fifty spectators. It was a masterful gloved, finish contest under Queensberry Rules in which the two reportedly fought for almost five hours and a seventy-four-round draw, but the scene was a wild one. Both men slugged it out for all they were worth and by the end of the bout both fighters' faces were a mess. McAuliffe was described as having "an ear on him as large as an English walnut, an injured nose, both his eyes nearly closed and lumps and swelling on his forehead and ribs." Later, Dempsey told a *New York Evening World* reporter that Dr. Hughes lanced McAuliffe's swollen ear "and a cupful of blood and water came out."[78]

As the fight wore on, McAuliffe and his corner were appealing to Stevenson to call a foul against the British fighter for continually hitting low, headbutting, gouging and kneeing his opponent. In the final round, Carney allegedly did so again and dropped McAuliffe to the mat. The confusion was described as follows. "In the seventy-fourth and last round, after some heavy exchanges, the men clinched and both fell to the floor, with Carney on top. The friends of both parties rushed into the ring demanding the fight for either man, everybody claiming 'foul.' After a great deal of milling about and noise, referee Frank Stevenson, frustrated that he could not regain order declared that as this was, "a fight to a finish, and as neither man had been knocked out, he should not do otherwise than postpone the fight to some other time."[79] With referee Stevenson still in the middle of the ring calling for a postponement, neither pugilist was ready to call it an evening. There was a great deal of confusion over Stevenson's ruling and many implored the fighters to keep at it.

"Carney, with a blackened left eye, was standing in the center, begging McAuliffe to come on, while Con McAuliffe and Jack Dempsey were holding the American on his chair."[80] Neither man was satisfied with a postponement. Carney's seconds—Arthur Chambers and Nobby Clark—argued for a continuation as did Dempsey and Con McAuliffe. While he took a great deal of visible punishment, many observers felt that McAuliffe had the better of the brutal contest, but it was to be a finish battle and it had not been decisively concluded. "McAuliffe had been advised as he could fairly have done to claim the stakes, but he refused, saying he had been called a coward and preferred to fight and win on his merits. Stevenson did not really think that either man committed a palpable foul."[81] Dempsey claimed that Carney routinely fouled McAuliffe but was such a good ring general that he was able to get away with it. In addition to the low blows, the Nonpareil stated, "You know Carney, every time he struck at Jack, would butt him with his head and give him the knee."[82] Dempsey claimed that after the thirtieth round all of McAuliffe's injuries came from Carney's "gouging tactics." "He would ram his fingers into Jack's eyes and butt him with his head when by a rush he got him over against the ropes."[83]

The bout eventually ended after the owner of the stable in which the contest was held ordered it stopped due to its length and the noise and ruckus. Eventually, the ring was broken down and the pugilists agreed to meet again and settle the question, but just a few weeks later the forty-year-old Carney announced his retirement from the ring and no return bout was ever fought. Almost immediately after the battle, Dempsey and the McAuliffes returned to Brooklyn.

In a November 22nd interview, Carney responded to his being a dirty fighter. Of the McAuliffe fight he stated, "It was the most disgusting piece of business I was ever engaged in." After claiming that he chased McAuliffe for most of the fight, Carney said, "They wouldn't let me fight him close-to, and every time I'd take a step forward to get on to him his gang would yell 'foul' and say I was trying to kick him, till I was really afraid I might foul him accidentally. McAuliffe is the biggest cur I ever saw."[84] Clearly the events of the fight left the two with no love for one another. McAuliffe determined to head to a resort upstate for a period of rest and recovery and declared that he would not fight again for several months. Soon after, Carney traveled to New York, raising speculation that a second bout might be in the works, but he chiefly saw to other business and left for Boston after just a couple of days.

On November 18, Dempsey and trainer Tom Meagher left Jack's home for their training headquarters at Ruland's Hotel at Rockaway Beach. Jack had been working out, but now had to get serious about his training for the upcoming bout with Reagan. Reagan and his trainer Bob Smith were undergoing the same regimen at Nick Thompson's Hotel in Fort Hamilton where they had been encamped since early November. Dempsey held the edge in prefight betting.

A *New York Sun* reporter visited Dempsey's training camp on November 23 and reported that Dempsey put in long miles of roadwork followed by a thorough dousing with cold sea water and a rub-down. Dempsey then swung dumbbells, hit the heavy bag, sparred and then after Maggie and Alice arrived, sat down to dinner. Dinner consisted of roast mutton, seasonal vegetables and some dry toast. Jack then ate some pudding and washed everything down with two bottles of Bass Ale. When asked about the pudding Jack said, "Well, I'm very fond of sweets. My regular trainer Alf Power will be down tomorrow and he will keep his eye on me all the time and I won't get any of them, so I'm making hay while the sun shines."[85]

In late November, Jack gave an interview during which he stated, "I see there has been a great deal of talk between Pete McCoy, Denny Kelliher and George La Blanche about me. Now you can say this for me: I will fight Denny Kelliher, Pete McCoy and George La Blanche eight rounds or to a finish, the first two for a purse of $1,000 and the last $1,500, the fights to be at intervals of two weeks. I mean this whether I win or lose the Reagan fight."[86]

Speculation about the Reagan-Dempsey bout were rampant for the week before the event actually came off. It was widely known that the bout had been agreed to and would be held in early December in the New York Metropolitan area, but exactly where and on what date remained a mystery. Reports that the bout had occurred or that it soon might ran in the newspapers daily. One account read that Springfield, Massachusetts, police were on the lookout for the bout being held in their jurisdiction on December 5.

With speculation about time and location running rampant, an initial attempt to bring the bout off was set for the town of Islip on the southern shore of central Long

Island on December 10, but this attempt failed when police discovered the plans and warned both sides off. Reports state that when the fight party reached the depot at nearby Hunter's Point, they were warned that the police in Islip were waiting to prevent the bout.

The fighters and their parties, attempting to stay one step ahead of the law, agreed not to proceed on to Islip. The fight was postponed and the new time and location were set for Monday morning, December 12, in the vicinity of Flushing, Queens, on Long Island. Once again, however, the fight was prevented, not by the authorities, but by the hand of Mother Nature. The fight was "prevented by fog so dense that the principals could not leave this city on the boat chartered to take them to the battleground."[87]

It had been a long and frustrating night. The fight parties and the several approved spectators had begun arriving at the appointed East River wharf in the wee hours of the morning on December 12. They soon began to board the vessel that would convey them to the appointed battlefield. With the men waiting on deck, the journey was delayed as the tug boat's captain waited for a heavy fog to lift so that they might proceed to Flushing. One New York newspaper described the scene as follows. "So heavy was the fog on the Sound on Sunday night, however, that the captain of the tug which had been chartered for the occasion refused to leave the wharf."[88] The frustrated enthusiasts impatiently waited in the pea-soup fog until daylight when it was reluctantly agreed that the bout would again have to be postponed.

Not to be deterred, the parties disembarked and held an impromptu meeting on the wharf. They agreed that the now twice delayed contest would be held in Huntington, Long Island, at daybreak on Tuesday morning. The group then dispersed and the fighters and their parties again returned to their respective training camps.[89]

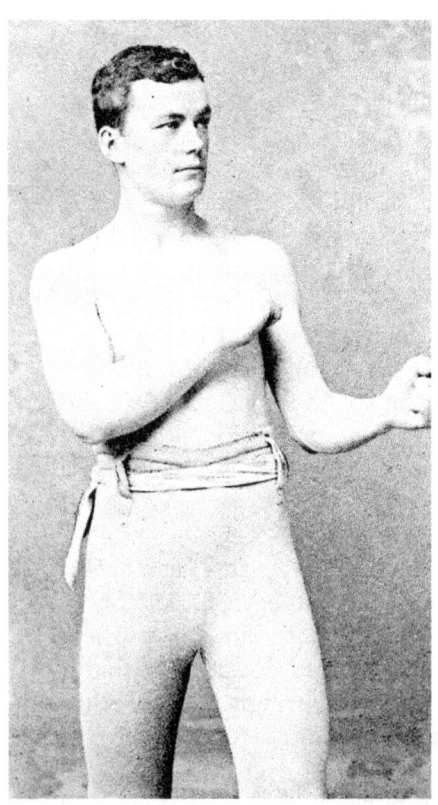

Johnny Reagan.

After the two failed attempts to bring Dempsey and Reagan together in the ring, the third attempt was successful as the pair met on December 13, 1887, on the shore of Long Island Sound.

At 11:00 p.m. on Monday night, twenty-five men and the crew set out on a tug boat and finally reached Lloyd's Dock on Lloyd's Neck, the site chosen as the "battleground," at 6:45 in the morning. By 7:33 a.m., the work on the ring was complete. It was of regulation size, measuring twenty-four feet square, and having eight posts through which two ropes were stretched. The site chosen for the ring was a sandy and marshy patch close to the water which would prove to be problematic as the fight progressed.

Frank Stevenson, a balding, moonfaced man with heavy eyes, was chosen as referee. He reportedly cut a fine figure "in wing collar, bowler hat, and dark suit" as he "eyed a hunting-case watch in his right hand."[90]

The fighters entered the ring at 8:10 a.m., symbolically throwing their hats into the center as they climbed through the ropes. Dempsey came out first, sporting blue tights and blue socks with fighting shoes. Around his waist Jack wore a dark-colored silk handkerchief with checks. Reagan wore white tights and socks. He wore a white silk handkerchief with blue dots for his colors. Both men wore kid gloves, but Jack did not have the fingers of his gloves cut.[91] Both men weighed in at 147 pounds. Reagan was 21 years old and stood five feet, six and a half inches. The 25-year-old Dempsey held a two-inch height advantage. In Dempsey's corner were Denny Costigan, Billy Madden and John Murphy with Reagan seconded by Mike Costello, his trainer Bob Smith and Professor Mike Donovan.

The bout was briefly delayed when Reagan had to send back to the tug for his fighting shoes which had been inadvertently left onboard. The shoes were quickly retrieved and brought into the ring. As Reagan sat in his corner putting them on, Dempsey's corner objected to Reagan's footwear which had a large and very sharp spike under the big toe of each shoe rather than under the ball of the foot where it should have been. After a heated discussion, referee Frank Stevenson allowed the shoes to be worn. Dempsey's manager then protested, "I give notice now that if Reagan spikes Dempsey I shall claim foul at once, as these shoes are unfit to be worn."[92]

After the dispute was discussed, Stevenson called together both sides and ordered the fighters and their seconds to shake hands. They shook with a smiling Dempsey commenting to Reagan, "It seems that we are to meet, after all."[93] Stevenson then proceeded with the coin toss to determine the fighters' corners. "The umpire for Reagan tossed a $20 gold piece for choice of corners. The umpire for Dempsey called 'tails' and won. He chose the corner which gave the sun to Dempsey's back, and left it in Reagan's eyes."[94]

As the fighters and their seconds settled into their respective corners, "Denny Costigan offered to bet $300 to $250 that Dempsey would win but found no takers. At 8:30 o'clock a Maltese cross was formed by the principals and seconds and two minutes later the fight began."[95]

The first two rounds saw some heavy slugging by both fighters. In the first, after a great deal of sparring and feinting, Reagan fired an errant left at Jack's body which Dempsey avoided by stepping aside. Reagan tried once more, but Dempsey again dodged the blow and this time countered with a left-handed missile that found its mark hard upon Reagan's right cheek. Finally, Reagan landed successfully with a left to Dempsey's jaw that Jack responded by stepping in and connecting with two hard blows to the body. Reagan swung in retaliation but missed again and the two men fell into a clinch and infighting ensued. During one rush by Reagan, the spike on his left toe scratched Dempsey just below the left knee. Pulling back in pain, an angry Dempsey told his opponent, "Be a little careful, John."[96] The round continued with each man sparring cautiously. While locked in the clinch, "Reagan made play on Dempsey's kidneys. The latter succeeded in back-heeling his antagonist and fell heavily upon him. This ended the first."[97]

The second round opened with the men quickly clinching and wrestling. When Reagan rushed Dempsey and very nearly caused another cut with his cleat, Dempsey claimed that Reagan was guilty of fouling by jumping in the air and spiking him. The referee cautioned Reagan against the practice. The round ended with Dempsey again back-heeling Reagan and falling upon him heavily.

In the third round, both men were busy and landed many punches, but Dempsey seemed to be in control. Reagan, in one of his frequent rushes toward Dempsey, managed to do what Costigan had feared and spiked Dempsey on his left leg. The spike in the toe of Reagan's shoe caught the Nonpareil between the shin and calf muscle on his left foreleg.

The five-inch gash was very deep and long, exposing the bone. A cry went out from Dempsey's corner with Jack's men demanding that Reagan be disqualified as he had now twice cut the Nonpareil with his cleats. Reagan and his corner argued just as vehemently that the cuts were accidental. "Meantime Reagan got up and walking over to Dempsey's corner, said in tones of great earnestness, 'It was an accident, Jack, upon my word it was. I would not do anything wrong purposely.' Dempsey, who was in great pain, shook his head and then cut short his umpire's protests by saying, 'Never mind, I'll fight on anyway.'" After listening to both sides and reacting to Dempsey's comment, Stevenson chose to overlook the fouls.

At the end of the round, Dempsey's corner tended to the gash which was bleeding profusely. Whiskey was poured on the laceration and a handkerchief was tied around the wound as the champion headed out for the fourth round. Reagan's trainer Mike Donovan claimed that he offered to file the spikes down before the fight began, but he claimed that Dempsey said he did not care one way or the other. According to Donovan, Dempsey blamed him for the wound, even though, "I had urged Reagan to have the spikes filed off, knowing they would do him far more harm than good."[98] Donovan, an honorable man was surely telling the truth. My guess would be that no one from Dempsey's camp really examined the shoes closely until the fight was about the begin.

In the fourth round, Reagan landed heavily to the body before the two started the close infighting that was characterizing the early part of this fight. Reagan was able to throw Dempsey down, but both men landed with a splash in the water that had risen and was now a couple of inches deep over half the ring.

By the fifth round, Dempsey was forced to move partly out of his corner to avoid the water from the rising tide. During the action, both men continued fighting desperately, with Jack once again back-heeling his opponent and falling heavily upon him.

The sixth round saw some of the hardest and most scientific blows delivered during the fight. The water was becoming bothersome, giving both combatants much trouble. An exasperated Reagan rushed at Dempsey and while wrestling in the resulting clinch, picked the Nonpareil up and threw him heavily down to the ground. By this point, the water was high enough that when Jack landed, salt water splashed all around.

In the seventh round, the icy water was getting higher and calls were beginning to come from both corners to halt the match and move the ring to higher ground as well as to award Jack the fight on a foul per the wicked gash on his left foreleg. Dempsey would have none of it and continued to fight on, launching a powerful blow with his left which Reagan barely escaped by ducking cleverly.

By the eighth round, the men were sloshing all over the ring in water that had risen well past their ankles. Despite the water, the men moved quickly and took turns swinging and occasionally landing blows until Reagan slipped and fell into the salty water. Half a minute later, in the midst of a fierce exchange, both men went down in the brine. As Dempsey got up and wiped the water from his face, Reagan's corner saw a trickle of blood coming from his nose. Donovan, Costello and Smith all called "First blood!" and it was awarded even though it was noticed by all in attendance that Reagan too had blood on his lip at the time.

The condition of the ring was becoming untenable. The men looked like drowned rats and as they rose again from the salty brine and fell into a clinch, one of the seconds yelled to the fighters, "Shake hands: we will have no more of this here." Stevenson, however, ordered the fighters to finish the round.[99] Jack threw Reagan down again, and after a few more minutes of wrangling like ducks, time was called ending the eighth round. "The water was two or three inches deep all over the ring and the referee, amid great excitement, ordered the men to shake hands and go back to the boat until another ring could be pitched on dry land."[100] The time for the first eight rounds was eighteen minutes.

The camps discussed where to resume the bout. It was first proposed that the new ring be pitched and the fight finished on a nearby road, but Reagan's seconds were insistent on setting the ring on turf. Stevenson then ordered everyone back onto the tugboat and the search resumed for a new battleground. The fighters removed their wet clothes and attempted to rest. The tug made its slow journey upriver while Dempsey's seconds doctored his wounded leg with whiskey. The proposition was made that the fight should be postponed and resumed in a couple of weeks while the wound healed, but Dempsey was ready to continue and would have none of it. "What," said he, "nurse a sore leg for two weeks and try to train with it? I'd sooner fight with both legs cut off."[101]

After a couple of hours, the tug, which had ambled about ten miles to the west, landed at an abandoned dock set among a beautiful hilly backdrop at Sands Point, New York. A clearing with a large turf area was found on top of one of the lower hills and the ring was pitched for a second time.

The location of the second battlefield was reportedly on the estate of Superior Court Justice Richard O'Gorman who upon receiving word that the fight had taken place on his property summoned his longtime caretaker Jim Hanley. "I am told there was a prize fight on my place yesterday," said the judge sternly to his employee of over twenty years. "There was your Honor," responded a nervous Hanley. The judge then responded, "Well, Jim, I want to say one thing to you. If there ever is another I'll discharge you, unless you let me know in plenty of time so I can see it myself."[102] Justice O'Gorman, a native of Dublin, apparently had a good Irishmen's taste for the prize ring.

Just before noon, Dempsey, wearing the same blue tights which had been dried before the steamboat's boilers, was aided by his friends to the site of the ring, his leg so stiff and sore that it was difficult for him to climb the hill by himself. Reagan, having changed his clothes, was now clad in green tights and stockings and he soon entered the new ring. As the fighters made ready, "there was another squabble over the choice of corners. Reagan's handlers claimed the right to toss for a fresh choice, but Dempsey's would not agree. At last the latter gave way, as they had in every dispute that arose during the day, in order to get a fight."[103] Another coin toss was held to determine the corners and soon after, at precisely 12:10, time was called and the bout resumed.

The ninth round saw a great deal of infighting by Dempsey and Reagan as the two determined to take control of the fight. Dempsey then began to show the fighting skills that had made him a champion. The Nonpareil in true champion's fashion, overcame his considerable discomfort and began to pummel his opponent by firing mortar-like shots to the ribs that landed hard and fast and caused Reagan to grunt with pain. It also was evident that Dempsey was the better wrestler of the two and Reagan may have begun to regret his asking for the fight to be held under the London Rules. "Dempsey went right at Reagan and a clinch ensued during which terrific in-fighting was done. It was ended by Dempsey back-heeling Reagan and going down with him heavily."[104] The firm, frozen turf at the second battlefield made the impact of the landings considerably more jarring. According to Patrick H. "Paddy" Roche, a former New York State Senator and owner of the Rosemore and Brighton Beach Hotels, who was one of the witnesses to the bout,

"The Nonpareil kept tossing Johnny at every opportunity despite Mike Donovan's repeated queries, 'Is this a wrestling match or a fist fight?'"[105] As the fight wore on Reagan battled hard and showed great determination, but Dempsey consistently showed his ring superiority.

By the tenth round, Dempsey landed a hard left to Reagan's ribs and a powerful right to the nose that drew blood, but Reagan fought hard and generally made a good show of himself, landing occasionally and blocking several of Dempsey's missiles. The next nine rounds were much the same with Dempsey in control landing heavy blows and Reagan being thrown and back-heeled by the Nonpareil. The fighting by both men was described by witnesses as "of the most savage character." Through it all, Reagan fought hard and patiently waited for a break which he might play to his advantage. "It was evident that the latter [Reagan] had the worst of the bargain in agreeing to the London Rules. He went on, however, like a Spartan."[106]

Over the next several rounds, the fighting was fast and furious by both men, but was clearly in the Nonpareil's favor. As is often the case with injuries received during sporting events, Jack regained some use of his wounded leg as some of the stiffness lessened through use. Thanks to a combination of adrenaline, sheer toughness and probably a bit of whiskey, Jack ignored his wounded leg and moved in and out quickly, landing powerfully on his opponent with both hands and throwing him down with regularity. According to Roche, "Dempsey hurled Reagan to the frozen ground so violently in the twelfth-round that Johnny had to be carried to his corner."[107]

Dempsey was now clearly in control of the bout and proceeded to put on a clinic of London Rules pugilism for all those present. "Reagan made many falls in order to escape the sledge hammer blows of the Nonpareil, which were given straight from the shoulder."[108]

In the twentieth round, Dempsey kept hammering at Reagan's ribs until the oozing of blood made the body appear raw. "When Reagan took a knee to avoid another fall from either the Nonpareil's constant hammering or another throw down, Dempsey cursed him and told him to get up and fight."[109] Dempsey's corner complained to the referee that Reagan's going down to avoid blows was unfair, but Stevenson saw no reason to caution Reagan as it was evident that in short order, Johnny would be defeated.

The twenty-first through twenty-fifth rounds were brutal with both men fighting furiously. Reagan was thrown to the ground twice during this stage of the fight. Again, Dempsey held the edge in points.

"Rounds twenty-six through thirty-four were remarkable only for the way in which Dempsey hit his man and the frequency with which Reagan went down to save himself."[110] Many in the crowd, including Dempsey's own corner, urged him to hit Reagan while he was down on his knees, due to the earlier spiking foul, but Jack would have none of it.

In the thirty-second round, Jack scored his cleanest knock-down. Dempsey drew Reagan out, coaxing him into opening up with a left. Jack, expecting a punch, deftly avoided the oncoming missile and countered with a powerful right cross to the head that dropped Johnny like a rock. He got up but continued to receive a persistent pounding from Dempsey throughout the thirty-third and thirty-fourth rounds.

Reagan seemed to have regained some energy in rounds thirty-five through thirty-eight. He was more active and frequently rushed and swung at Dempsey, but all with little result for Reagan as Dempsey continued to hammer away at his opponent's rib cage.

"In the thirty-ninth round, Dempsey's right again found Reagan's jaw hard enough to send Johnny crashing to the earth. Jack put everything he had behind the punch in order to end the battle. It would have finished many a heavyweight, but Reagan came back and gamely toed the scratch in the fortieth round."[111] The constant beating Reagan was taking from Dempsey's fists and from landing on the hard ground was clearly taking its toll on Johnny. His body was showing considerable bruising and he was bleeding from several cuts and scrapes.

In the forty-first round, both men landed vicious combinations that registered, but Reagan was beyond tired. He missed with a wicked left to Dempsey's head which Jack countered by sending back a hard blow to his opponent's body. Jack then landed a hard shot to Reagan's chin. When Johnny countered to the body, he slipped and went down again. Despite his gameness, it was clear that Reagan could not last much longer.

The next three rounds practically closed the battle. "In these three rounds Dempsey unmercifully punished Reagan, whose lips were puffed and his left eye closed."[112] Dempsey looked none the worse for wear with the exception of a slightly swollen left eye. Despite his best attempts, Reagan had difficulty landing any damaging blows, while Dempsey continually peppered his opponent with hard and well-placed missiles. During the forty-third round, Reagan made one last effort to win by rushing Dempsey, but Jack lured his battered opponent into the corner where he smashed him with a hard left-right combi-

Dempsey in a bout against Johnny Reagan.

nation. He then grabbed the weakened fighter and threw him violently to the ground. The forty-fourth round was no better for Reagan as he was now completely at Dempsey's mercy. Jack landed three powerful shots right on the face and then threw Johnny to the ground once again.

Badly beaten, Reagan still steadfastly refused to quit, but at the start of the forty-fifth round, seeing that their man had no chance to win, his corner made every attempt to get their man to concede, but again he said no.

In Dempsey's corner, the Nonpareil told his seconds that he was going to finish his opponent in the forty-fifth round, for Reagan's sake if for no other. When the fighters met at center ring, Dempsey lured his wobbly opponent to the corner where he then unloaded on the weakened man with a left-right-left combination to the chest and head that caused Reagan to drop like a log. Once again, Johnny somehow managed to struggle to his feet, but he was terribly unsteady. With Reagan barely able to stand, much less defend himself, his seconds had seen enough. Since their man stubbornly refused to quit, they took matters into their own hands as they "jumped into the ring and threw up the sponge."[113] As they assisted their man and began to help him back to his corner, Mike Donovan told referee Stevenson that it was clear that Reagan could not win and therefore they felt they must give up the fight. Stevenson declared Dempsey the winner. Jack went across the ring and spoke to Reagan, uttering encouraging words to his badly battered and disheartened opponent. After the two shook hands, an ebullient Nonpareil, despite his badly cut leg, jumped over the ropes and ran down the hill to the waiting tug boat. Were it not for the viscous gash on his leg, some swelling under his left eye, and a few barely noticeable scrapes, he had barely a visible mark on him.

The fight was over just past 1:00 p.m., and it had reportedly lasted forty-five rounds and sixty-nine minutes. In the first ring, there were eight rounds and eighteen minutes and in the second, thirty-seven rounds and fifty-one minutes.

It took just a few minutes for the ring to be disassembled and the passengers, buckets, ropes and stakes loaded onto the tug before the ship was off for home. It was agreed by those in attendance that Reagan was as game as they come and no coward, but he was clearly overmatched. The tug arrived at its home dock by mid-afternoon.

Dempsey was up and out early the next morning. He had virtually no visible marks on him but walked with a bit of a limp as he favored his wounded leg.

At 11:00 a.m., accompanied by his backer Jake Stearns, Denny Costigan, Tom Glass of the *Brooklyn Eagle* and a number of other friends, Jack headed to the offices of the *National Police Gazette* to claim his $2,000 stake for the fight. Fox handed him the check and Jack and Stearns signed the receipt. Reagan himself was not in attendance as he was still resting from the punishment he took during the battle. In his stead Reagan sent his backer Billy Reed to represent him, pick up his share of the stakes and shake Dempsey's hand. When Dempsey inquired as to Reagan's condition, Reed responded, "He is all right. There is nothing the matter with him much that shows."[114]

Reed clearly tried to downplay the loss and the severe beating Johnny had taken and later Reagan did the same. While he admitted that he was squarely beaten, Reagan stated that he had frequently been beaten up worse in fights that he had won and that both the use of the London Rules and the transfer of the ring to the harder surface of the second location worked against him. "It was more of a wrestling match than a prize fight, and as Dempsey was the better wrestler, he won." While there was no doubt a good deal of wrestling and throwing down, Reagan seemed to forget that the London Rules called for this. He also conveniently forgot to mention the heavy blows from Dempsey that landed on him regularly throughout the bout—including the left-right-left combination to the chest and head that ended the fight.

Referee Frank Stevenson said, "It was one of the best and fairest fights I ever saw." He went on to say that he believed that Reagan would have done better under Queensberry Rules. "Dempsey is too good a wrestler and he was right at home. He is a wonderful man."[115]

A reporter for the *New York Sun* pointed out that even with Dempsey in agony with his leg badly cut Reagan could not hit him effectively. The reporter also mentioned a comment made during the thirty-fifth round by Reagan's friend Mike Costello who noted, "Dempsey hasn't a mark on him." The reporter then asked, "Now, if Reagan couldn't plant a blow in that number of rounds on Dempsey that would mark his face or body, what chance would he have with him in a Queensbury fight where he could not go down to avoid punishment?"[116]

To put an end to this speculation, Dempsey and his oft-time backer Jake Stearns made a return call on Richard Fox at the *Police Gazette* offices and left a challenge for Reagan that stated that since Reagan was not satisfied with result of the recent contest under London Rules, Stearns offered "to match Dempsey against Reagan to fight with two ounce gloves, under Queensberry rules, for $1,000 a side and all net gate receipts, all to go to the winner."[117] Stearns also stated that he hoped to hear from Reagan very soon and that he was willing to discuss terms if these were not completely acceptable to Reagan or his backers. The challenge went unaccepted.

In an interview with reporters later that day, Dempsey spoke about the gash, saying, "The first time the spikes hit me it felt as if the bone were prodded, but the next time it seemed as if I had received a strong electric shock. The pain was so intense that I fought like thunder to forget it. I am going to lay up for a while now and take things easy."[118] Jere Dunn, the notorious gambler and backer of fighters and racehorses, commented that "Dempsey is a good one. He would not claim the fight on a foul when he had every opportunity to do so." He then added, "and even when his seconds claimed it for him he declaimed against it."[119]

The day after the bout, when Reagan was asked by reporters about the peculiar spiked shoes, he responded, "I did not know that there was anything wrong about them. I gave the order to a shoemaker who said he knew all about making them. The cut in Dempsey's leg was purely an accident, as I stated at the time, and not an attempt to take unfair advantage."[120] In Reagan's defense, it was noted that he had a habit of stepping forward when attempting to deliver a blow that tended to throw his left foot in an outward motion.[121] This could have been a reason for the contact, but there was no excuse for the sharpness or positioning of the spikes on the shoes.

Trouble continued to brew over the spiking incident in the weeks after the fight. Dempsey tended to believe that it was intentional and certainly in violation of the London Rules of the ring. The gash was seen to by Jack's physician, Dr. Peter Hughes, and it took three stitches to close. "I don't blame Reagan for it," said Dempsey, "but there are friends of Reagan's who wanted to injure me for life, and some of them know more than they would care to confess about these shoes."[122]

Jack dined that afternoon with Gus Tuthill and Jere Dunn at the Hoffman House. His leg was still apparently swollen, stiff and quite painful, but overall, he was reportedly in good condition and apart from his limp, it was difficult to tell that he had been in a prizefight just a day earlier.[123]

After lunch, Dempsey decided to cash his check before heading home. He walked to the Franklin Square elevated railroad station and took a train to Fulton Street where he entered a bank and drew his $2,000. "There won't be much for me," he said, "after expenses are paid. There's no money in these fights to a finish. I was browbeaten into this fight by people who never expected to see me well enough to accept the challenge and who expected to call Reagan the champion of the world, but I didn't go into the fight expecting to make money."[124] Dempsey was correct in his assessment of a small payout. For his troubles, Jack is said to have netted exactly $62 in his victory over Reagan.

After concluding his business at the bank, Jack went over to the Lee Avenue Academy to purchase three tickets to a show for his wife and her parents. He then stopped in at a bar across the street from the Roosevelt Street ferry station as he waited for his transport to take him back to Brooklyn. Word soon spread that the Nonpareil was in the saloon and a crowd composed chiefly of longshoremen, gathered. They cheered him and shouted tributes. Before he left the bar, Jack handed the bar keep a $5 bill and with it bought his admirers a round of beer.

That evening, the Full Moons gave a party at the Metropolitan Hotel in honor of Jack's victory. Despite the pain from the gash, Dempsey led the revelry. There was singing by the Full Moon's chorale and sporting men from all around New York and Brooklyn were there. During the event, former Assemblyman P.H. McCarren delivered a tribute after which Jack was presented with, "a handsome diamond scarf pin, a gold watch and chain and a diamond locket as a token of esteem of his many admirers." Overcome, Jack made no speech, but simply mouthed the words, "thank you."

On December 17, Dempsey was visited by a *New York Sun* reporter at his lodgings in the Metropolitan Hotel in Williamsburg. Jack was found sitting in a bootblack's chair and chatting with several friends and supporters. He had a shoe on his right foot, but a slipper on his left, due apparently to continued swelling of his left leg caused by the gash received three days earlier against Reagan.

When asked how he felt, Dempsey responded, "I am well and hearty, but I am troubled a little bit in mind about Reagan's bluffing." Reagan had commented since the bout that Dempsey won only through superior wrestling skills, and that had the bout been fought under Queensberry Rules, Reagan would have far outclassed the Nonpareil. Jack commented that Reagan had a difficult time finding backers to cover the $1,000 for his side of the purse while in Dempsey's words, "I can be backed against any pugilist living anywhere near my weight for $10,000." Dempsey continued that he went to Reagan and his backers a week before the fight and offered to guarantee a purse of $1,500 for a gloved match under the Queensberry Rules, but Reagan would not consent to this, instead saying that they must stick to the original agreement. That was fine with Dempsey for, as mentioned before, "I knew I could beat him anyway."[125] Siding with Dempsey, the *New York Evening World* noted that Reagan's claims that he could best the Nonpareil under Queensberry Rules were simply a ridiculous dodge. "It will be remembered by readers of the *Evening World* sporting column that Reagan said before the fight with Dempsey that he would surprise the Nonpareil when it came to London prize-ring rules, as he could out wrestle him."[126]

The reporter asked about the spiking and whether or not Jack thought it was intentional. Dempsey said that he was now beginning to think so as his agents who had investigated it had reported that Beneke Brothers, who made the shoes, stated that they had been instructed by Reagan and Bob Smith to place the spikes under the toe instead of in the usual position under the ball of the foot. Reagan responded to this by stating in a letter to the newspaper that he and Smith alone were responsible for ordering the shoes and that the manufacturer may have made a simple mistake in the placement of the spikes. "We asked the maker if he understood how to put the spikes in and he said he did. If the shoes were wrong, the fault lies with him." He emphasized that Mike Donovan had absolutely nothing to do with the shoes.[127] Regardless of whose fault it was that the spikes were placed out of position, Reagan, Smith and Donovan—all seasoned pugilists—should have known by looking at the shoes that they were in violation of the London Rules, and dangerously so.

In examining the wound, the reporter stated, "When the bandages were taken off, the leg was nearly twice its original size. A cut on one side was nearly three inches long. This had been sewed up and the stitches were still in it. Another jagged crease showed where the first spiking had been done."[128]

At the conclusion of the interview, Dempsey reiterated that he would be happy to stand again against Reagan under Queensberry Rules for six, eight or ten rounds, but that the winner must take the entire purse. The previous day, Dempsey's backer Jake Stearns had posted $1,000 with Richard Fox to match Dempsey with Reagan under *Police Gazette* Rules and under the stipulation Dempsey mentioned above.[129] No word was received from the Reagan camp. Dempsey added that after the proposed bout, he was likely to return to San Francisco and retire from the ring. Dempsey stated that he had won dozens of ring battles with no defeats and had nothing left to prove. He then added, "I have now got a wife and child and I want to look out for them."[130] Once again, it appears that Dempsey was truly torn between his role as loving husband and father and his alter ego as the Nonpareil. It was an internal battle he would fight for the rest of his life.

Despite the pain from his wound, Jack kept busy over the next few days visiting friends, determining his future and being seen about town. On December 19, he and Jack McAuliffe headed to Saengerbund Hall on Schermerhorn Street in Brooklyn, to attend an evening benefit for trainer Jack McMasters.

On the evening of December 22, a benefit was given in Jack's honor at the Palace Rink on Grand Street in Brooklyn. Dempsey was, of course, in attendance, "and in spite of the slight lameness still existing in the leg which Johnny Reagan ripped open with his spikes, he will box three men, three rounds each and a wind up."[131] Jack was scheduled to meet Jack McAuliffe, Tom Henry and Jack Files, but Joe Denning stood in for Files. "Half the famous boxers of the two cities will take part in the entertainment and there will also be some fine club swinging and wrestling."[132] The event was described as "a corker."

Twenty-five hundred people crowded into the Palace Rink on the evening of the event. A squad of policemen was also on hand, but with the exception of several noisy demonstrations, the crowd was orderly. In attendance that night were noted athletes, sporting men, politicians and businessmen. Trainer Jack McMasters whose benefit Dempsey had attended just three nights earlier was the master of ceremonies.

The evening opened with a three-rounder between Frank Chrysler of Brooklyn and Fred Chandler of Bristol, England. The excitement in the contest came in the second round when Chrysler drove Chandler into the corner with a blistering two-handed attack. This bout was followed by a tame but interesting match between New Yorkers Larry Boylan and Tom Kelly, the "Harlem Spider." The sparring of the pair was greeted with applause. Next up were Tommy Ward and Jimmy Stephenson, both of Brooklyn. New Yorkers Jack Hopper and Jack Boylan then fought for three hard-hitting rounds and finally Jack's brother Martin wrestled Phil Casey. While Casey outweighed Dempsey by fifty pounds, each man won a fall. The boxing then continued with Larry Boylan entering the ring for a second time with Eugene Hornbacker and then Billy Dacey squared off with Jack Long. Hornbacker and Dacey got the best of their respective bouts. The final preliminary was a four-rounder between Tommy McCarthy and Sam Williams, the "Black Diamond." The pair fought a hard-hitting and spirited four-round encounter, but the bout was ruled a draw.

Prior to his exhibition matches, Dempsey was presented with a large floral horseshoe made with the word "Champion" spelled out on it in red roses. Thanking the crowd, Jack stated that he would be appearing in Billy Madden's play *Around New York* at Poole's Theater when it opened on January 2.[133]

As the evening wound down, the crowd was delighted to see the Nonpareil climb into the ring with Jack McAuliffe, Tom Henry and Joe Denning. Dempsey went three rounds with each man and each time put on a show that brought the crowd to their feet repeatedly. The excited crowd was abuzz with chatter as they spilled out of the arena and into the streets after the event was over.

As 1887 drew to a close, the Nonpareil was at the peak of his ring career. Patrick F. Sheedy, a Chicago gambler and a one-time manager of John L. Sullivan's, had this to say about Jack on that Christmas Eve: "You asked me just now if I thought Sullivan to be the greatest fighter in the world. Well, I don't. I think him to be the biggest, but the greatest fighter I ever saw or heard of is Jack Dempsey, and he is the greatest in general, too." After pointing out that Dempsey had fought dozens of bouts against larger men and still triumphed, Sheedy added, "If he weighed ten pounds more—that is, if he scaled 160 pounds—I think he could beat anybody under the London prize ring rules."[134]

On December 27, Jack and Dominick F. McCaffrey met at the Coleman House in New York where they signed articles of agreement to meet on January 31, 1888. The agreed upon purse was to be $2,000 and gate receipts. The men also agreed that "in case of police or other interference" the men would abandon all claims on the other's share of the purse.[135] That afternoon it was announced to the press that "Dominick F. McCaffrey, of Philadelphia and Jack Dempsey of Brooklyn, middleweight champion of America, signed articles of agreement this morning for a ten-round Marquess of Queensberry contest, at catch weights, to take place near this city, for $2,000."[136] McCaffrey stated that he would train near his home in Philadelphia, while Dempsey decided that he would return to his favorite training quarters, Ruland's in Rockaway.

On the same day as the meeting at the Coleman House, Richard Fox received a cable from the Pelican Club in London, stating that they were willing to back British fighter Toff Wall in a bout against Dempsey, if Fox was willing to back the Nonpareil. Fox responded that he was willing to back Dempsey and he would also sponsor the manufacture of a new championship belt for the winner.[137] The existing belt had become

Dempsey's personal property after he had won three defenses of the championship. Fox stated that the new belt would be made of solid gold and "surpass any belt in existence in beauty of design and money value."[138] Fox wired back to the Pelican Club that Dempsey was in New Haven, Connecticut, and that he would consult with the Nonpareil about the offer upon Dempsey's return to New York. When asked about the offer, Dempsey said that after he had finished his engagement with McCaffrey, he would take a trip to England to fight Wall for the middleweight championship of the world.[139] The fight was strongly considered, but terms could not be agreed to and, after a second stab at it in February 1888, the idea was dropped. One year later a final attempt to set a date was reported on February 4, 1889, when the San Francisco Athletic Club tried to match Wall against Dempsey, but Wall refused the offer.

On December 29, Dempsey met old foe Tom Henry in a three-round exhibition in Brooklyn.[140] Earlier that day, he had also received word that William Renaud of Ottawa was anxious to back John Clow in a match with Dempsey for a purse of between $3,000 and $5,000.[141] Jack was in high demand, and the offers for matches kept pouring in. Jack finished out the year getting ready for a week's engagement at Poole's Theater at Fourth Avenue and Eighth Street. Dempsey and Denny Costigan were to appear as pugilists in Billy Madden's play, *Around New York*.

1888—Professor Mike Donovan and a Chink in the Armor

The year 1888 was an extremely busy one in the ring for Jack. In addition to more than a dozen exhibition bouts, Dempsey met several notable fighters including Dominick McCaffrey, Billy Baker, Joe Coburn, James Stevens and Professor Mike Donovan.

Jack, Margaret and their young daughter Alice, along with a few friends, spent the New Year holiday relaxing in Troy, New York, at the home of Jack's friend, former city Alderman John G. Fox. In an interview conducted by the *New York Sun* on New Year's Day, the Nonpareil answered an array of questions ranging from his thoughts on the Reagan fight to his plans for the future.

The *Sun* reporter asked Jack if he'd fully recovered from the effects of the spiking in the Reagan fight, to which Jack responded, "Not quite. I hope it will be all right soon though." Jack then went on to respond to the rumor that he only made $62 in that fight, saying, "The fight was only for $1,000 a side and that $62 was all that remained after the expenses were paid. One of my backers, however, did the handsome thing." As no other explanation was given, we can only assume that a little more cash made its way into Dempsey's pocket.

When asked if he was considering visiting England to fight for the world middleweight championship, Jack responded, "I am as near England now as ever I shall be so far as fighting is concerned. I have no intention of going there to fight. As the challenged person I have the right to name the fighting ground. Toff Wall challenged me. I have not challenged him." Jack went on to say that Wall had not technically challenged him, but rather the challenge was presented by William E. Harding representing the Pelican Club of London and he was not certain that it actually came from Wall. The reporter pointed out that Wall was planning to come to America in February, to which Dempsey stated, "If he wants to fight, I will give him a battle."

Asked what other plans he had for the near future, Jack responded, "I shall remain in Troy until next Tuesday. I am engaged to appear in Billy Madden's new play on Monday. I shall go on Tuesday and spar the balance of the week." The play, *Around New York*, was described as "a sweet and simple love story" told in three acts and was being produced by the lead actor Billy Madden at Poole's Eighth Street Theater. Madden was best known as a former pugilist, club boxing instructor and a trainer for heavyweight champion John L. Sullivan.[1]

Dempsey's sole role in *Around New York* was as a boxer who would spar a few rounds nightly with either Madden or Denny Costigan. "I have no speaking part at all, but just come on the stage and spar with somebody, that's all. Standing in the wings we see plenty of fun, I can tell you."² One Washington newspaper described Dempsey's role as "the pugilist, who will sustain a character demonstrating the manly art of self-defense." The paper went on to state, "The entertainment comes well recommended."³

Dempsey told a New York sportswriter during the run of the play about how he and Costigan would tease Madden about his first leading lady, whose hand he won at the end of the play. The actress portraying Madden's character's true love was elderly and very plump. Jack and Denny would laugh and tease Billy about his "true love"—"Ah, there, Billy. Did you win her again?," "Was it a raffle?," "Where are you going to plant her?" and the like. In short order, Madden found a young starlet to fill the role.

When asked whether he had any bouts in the works beyond his upcoming tilt with Dominick McCaffrey, Jack responded that he did not. Of the McCaffrey bout Dempsey stated, "Where that meeting will occur I don't know, but the date is January 31. I will get $1,000 whether the fight occurs or not. Then too, I am to get a share of the gate receipts."⁴ The reporter asked Jack what he thought of Sullivan. Dempsey smiled and replied, "I am very glad that I am not heavy enough to meet Sullivan because if I were I certainly would endeavor to meet him and then I know that I would be licked." When asked about his willingness to meet Charley Mitchell, Jack responded that while he was not looking for a fight, he would gladly accept one should Mitchell and his backers agree to one for a reasonable purse.⁵

The ten-round battle with McCaffrey was scheduled to take place in Jersey City on the last day of January, but problems arose when the city's mayor Orestes Cleveland objected to the bout taking place in his town. Mayor Cleveland refused to approve a resolution passed by the city council granting a permit for the contest to the Warren Athletic Club.⁶

While his and McCaffrey's backers worked to get around the mayor's intransigence, Jack continued to tour with Madden spending several evenings at Troy in *Around New York*. The show then moved on to Rockaway Township, New Jersey, Baltimore and Washington and Jack began a whirlwind travel schedule up and down the East Coast for the next few weeks.

Before heading to Baltimore, Jack stopped off in Brooklyn for a couple of days to take care of some business. On Sunday, January 15, he was in Baltimore to continue his engagement with Madden in *Around New York*. The three rounds of nightly sparring had its benefits, providing the bulk of Jack's early training for the upcoming bout with McCaffrey.

The following day Dempsey arrived in Boston at 6:30 a.m. by train on the Boston and Albany line. He was met at the depot by Denny and John Kelliher and the party immediately went to the Adams House Hotel where Dempsey checked in and had breakfast. The Nonpareil was scheduled to meet Denny Kelliher that evening in a three-round exhibition bout in the old Music Hall. The event was a benefit for Kelliher during which as many as thirty-four pugilists and wrestlers were scheduled to appear in the ring. The *Boston Globe* predicted a first-class show. "Kelliher is one of the most gentlemanly fellows in the profession and is sure to draw out a big audience."⁷

While waiting for his breakfast Dempsey spoke to a reporter who had spied him as he arrived. The reporter commented that Jack looked to be in terrific condition to which the Nonpareil responded, "My engagement with Billy Madden does not interfere with my training in the least. It only takes a few minutes every night, before and after which, my time is my own. I train regularly and eat just as I always do when I am in training for a big fight. I am now down to about 145 pounds."[8] Dempsey also went on to say that he was willing to meet La Blanche again and was anxious to meet Charley Mitchell, but he was not primarily in the fight game to fight, but rather to make money, and therefore the purses would have to be substantial. Regarding Mitchell, Jack stated, "I should like nothing better than a meeting with him. In fact, I have always been anxious to get a go at him, but handsome Charley has studiously kept out of my way. Why, I had my hands full of money one day while out West and I held it up in his face, but he skipped out."[9]

On Monday evening, January 23, the Music Hall was packed with the largest crowd to ever witness an athletic event in that venue. Three-thousand five-hundred people came out to honor Kelliher, but also to see the great Nonpareil in action in a rare Boston appearance. When Dempsey appeared in the hall, he was greeted with a thunderous applause and calls for a speech. Jack stopped and acknowledged the crowd, but the extent of his address was simply to say, "Gentlemen, I appreciate the honor you do me tonight, but I am not much of a hand at public speaking and do not like to attempt anything that I cannot do well."[10] Even that short comment was enough to gain him more applause.

After eleven three-round preliminary bouts and a wrestling match, the main event was ready to begin, and at 10:30 p.m., Kelliher climbed into the ring along with his brother John and Paddy Kerrigan who were to be in Denny's corner. Moments later, Dempsey emerged from his dressing room and worked his way through the crowd and into the ring. Jack was seconded by James McKeon and Ed McAvoy. As he entered the ring, the master of ceremonies introduced Dempsey as the "champion middleweight of the world" and the hall again erupted with applause. The emcee was a bit generous as Jack had really only been declared the middleweight champion of America.

Time was called and both men sparred cautiously for a long time, causing the crowd to grow impatient. Soon, however, the men began to mix it up, trading left jabs and light blows, many of which were blocked. Suddenly, the Nonpareil showed his stuff as he rushed into an opening and landed four solid blows to Kelliher's head. These were returned with only light taps to Dempsey's neck.

In the second round, Kelliher was bleeding slightly from the nose and mouth, but he picked up the overall pace, landing several blows on Jack's stomach. After the two men each traded several more blows to the stomach, Jack landed a solid punch to Kelliher's head, but only once as Denny had learned from the combination in the first round and quickly stepped back out of range. The round ended with the men fighting in close near the ropes and trading punches. Just before the bell, in an effort to avoid one of Kelliher's blows, Dempsey jumped back and nearly fell off the stage. He would have landed on the floor had he not been caught and righted by several spectators in the front row.

Round three was the best of the fight. Each man began swinging with more gusto than in the previous two staves, with Dempsey forcing the fighting early, but Kelliher's defense was solid and he repelled most of the Nonpareil's attacks. Denny fought back, but Dempsey kept on the move and was a difficult target to reach. After Kelliher missed with an uppercut, Dempsey, spying an opening, swung a hard left and caught his opponent flush on the nose causing it to bleed freely. Kelliher responded, landing a few blows, but Jack pressed the attack for the remaining seconds of the round until time was called. The bout was over and the 3,500 on hand rose to their feet and gave both fighters a generous round of applause.

The local press described the fight and Dempsey's first pugilistic appearance in Boston as the "greatest event in pugilistic circles during the past week." The story continued, "His set to with Denny Kelliher was by no means a brilliant one, as he sparred much too cautiously to satisfy the large crowd assembled in the hall. It could be seen, however, that he is very clever while his position is well-nigh perfect." The paper went on to say that they believed that Kelliher was a tad nervous being in the ring with the champion, but also stated that Dempsey was extremely careful of and stayed away from the "sledge hammer right of the Quincy pugilist which has gained him his reputation of being a very hard hitter."[11]

The next day Jack returned briefly to New York. On Tuesday morning he was off again for Washington where he resumed his place as sparring partner for Madden in *Around New York*. The troupe would perform all week in the nation's capital at Kernan's Theatre.

It had been announced in New York on December 27, 1887, that Dominick McCaffrey and the Nonpareil had agreed to a fight under Queensberry Rules for $2,000.[12]

McCaffrey had developed quite a name in the fistic community. He had boxed John L. Sullivan, knocked out all the trial horses of Philadelphia and was a challenger of Charley Mitchell. "McCaffrey was much heavier than Dempsey, and the fans were generally of the opinion that Dempsey was tackling too big a man."[13] Jack himself stated that while McCaffrey said he would step into the ring ten or twelve pounds heavier than Dempsey, the Nonpareil was of the belief that his antagonist would outweigh him by a good thirty pounds when the two stripped for battle.[14]

McCaffrey began his training in Philadelphia, but in mid–January he transferred his training camp to Atlantic City where he was headquartered in the Sherman House.

Pittsburgh's Dominick McCaffrey.

There he was being trained by Alf Lunt.[15] Lunt, also a Philadelphia pugilist, had a volatile relationship with McCaffrey, but in between disassociations, would train him.

On January 18 came the previously mentioned announcement from Jersey City Mayor Orestes Cleveland that he would not allow the bout to take place in his city. Mayor Cleveland refused to sign a resolution passed by the city common council granting a permit for the exhibition to the Warren Athletic Club. In short, Cleveland, who took a dim view of prizefighting in general, questioned the club's legitimacy. It was now incumbent upon McCaffrey and his backers to secure another location for the bout. Thanks, however, to the intervention of a committee of local sporting men and other notables, a meeting was arranged during which the mayor was assured that no "slugging" would occur, and this would be a "scientific bout." Given the committee's assurances, Cleveland withdrew his opposition and therefore his order forbidding the fight.

With the bout now approved, Dempsey met the Pittsburgh heavyweight at the Pavonia Skating Rink in Jersey City, New Jersey, on January 31, 1888. McCaffrey stood 5'9", and typically weighed in at a sturdy 165 to 170 pounds, all of which he needed as he fought some of the biggest names in the ring during his era. He was the first man to challenge for the world heavyweight championship when he climbed into the ring with a much larger John L. Sullivan on August 29, 1885. McCaffrey had earned a chance to fight Sullivan after he defeated Mitchell the previous October in New York. Although he gave up more than 40 pounds to Sullivan, McCaffrey was well trained and fought with heart, lasting six rounds before referee Billy Tate stopped the fight to save Dominick from any further punishment. Some reports claim that McCaffrey and Sullivan agreed to fight one additional round, but whether six or seven, McCaffrey could always brag that he had lasted twenty minutes in the ring with Sullivan, longer than anyone else had up to that time.

> On the evening of the fight, Dempsey had dinner with a friend at the Astor House, and in the course of the meal made a bet with his friend that McCaffrey would not land one of his famous right-hand blows during the entire bout. In view of McCaffrey's well-known skill with his right hand the bet seemed almost like taking candy from a baby, and Dempsey's friend jumped at it. But Jack that night displayed such wonderful ability at ducking, dodging, side-stepping, and general all-around leg work that not once did McCaffrey's right-hand punch find its mark....[16]

The rink was jammed with 5,600 spectators each of whom paid between $1 and $10 to gain entrance. Another thousand or more milled about outside waiting for any word of the proceedings. "An elevated stage twenty-six feet square had been erected in the center of the floor."[17] In the crowd that night were the usual mix of political figures, businessmen, fighters and sports, including most notably Harry Hill, Billy Madden and Joe Coburn.

Prior to the main event, Master of Ceremonies Steve O'Donnell announced that a number of undercard fights would be held. These included those between lightweight champion Billy Dacey and Jack Long, Jimmy McCormick and Jack Halpin, Tom Allen and Tom Green, Philadelphian Bill Dunn and Jack Fallon of Brooklyn, Jimmy Connors and Fiddler Neary, George Young and Joe Fowler, and Mike Gillespie of New York and Pennsylvania heavyweight champion Denny Kelliher. Needless to say, these bouts took some time to complete and the main event was put off for quite some time. One newspaper reported that "before the big guns came on boxing bouts were had between lesser lights. There was a long and dreary wait for the principal gladiators. The wait lasted from ten minutes after ten to half past eleven." The holdup after the preliminaries was primarily due to a disagreement over who the referee would be. After a half hour the crowd began to grow impatient, jeering and calling for the fighters. Soon Harry Hill addressed the crowd and pleaded with sportsman Jim Wakely to act as referee, but he declined. Finally, after long discussion and several more attempts to secure a referee, Jere Dunn was induced to serve as the third man in the ring. "It was 11:37 p.m. before the men entered the ring. Mr. Dunn announced that 10 rounds, Marquess of Queensbury rules, was to be the battle. Three-ounce gloves were used."[18]

McCaffrey was seconded by Jim Patterson and Alf Lunt and Dempsey had the benefit of the services of Denny Costigan and Gus Tuthill. Finally, at 11:40 p.m., Dunn called the men to approach center ring and the fight began.

The two men came together with McCaffrey towering a full head above Dempsey. McCaffrey stood up very straight, but he carried his hands low. He kept his feet close together while Dempsey's left foot extended far forward. The men circled cautiously feeling each other out, each taut and scuttling backwards at the slightest twitch of the other's arms. McCaffrey was a large, powerful and dangerous man. "Dempsey looked like a child beside him and everybody in the house who knew and favored the Brooklyn boy felt afraid that he had undertaken too big a contract and would get hit once or twice with blows that would knock him through the roof or drive him through the floor."[19] Jack wheeled and moved away very cautiously for much of the first round. McCaffrey looked for an opening, carefully avoiding Dempsey's vicious left. Suddenly, McCaffrey took a sharp swing with his left, but fell short of his mark, leaving himself open. Jack struck quickly, landing hard shots on his opponent's forehead and nose. McCaffrey did place one strong blow on Dempsey's forehead and opened a small cut. The remainder of the round saw light sparring, but few notable moments.

The second round was spirited from the start as a vengeful McCaffrey rushed Dempsey before the Nonpareil could even get out of his corner. Dempsey dodged, ducked and gracefully pirouetted around his much larger opponent and smacked McCaffrey on the chin. McCaffrey fell into a clinch as he regained his stride and then caught Dempsey with a body shot that caused Jack to retreat with the Pittsburgh native in full pursuit. Knowing he had to act quickly, Dempsey turned sharply and countered with his left, stopping McCaffrey in his tracks with a powerful blow to his right eye and gaining a precious few seconds to recover. In just a few seconds, McCaffrey was again in pursuit and the two traded blows. Jack ducked a powerful right and countered with a stinging right of his own which landed just over McCaffrey's left eye. Again, McCaffrey came at Dempsey and again Jack struck, this time landing a blow to his opponent's stomach. After two rounds, Dempsey was moving well, landing often and seemed to have an answer for anything McCaffrey tried.

In the third round, Dempsey took the lead, peppering his opponent with solid shots to the nose, the eye, the chin and the ear. The Nonpareil effectively began enticing McCaffrey to move in close and then fired off howitzer-like blasts at his opponent. One description of this read, "While McCaffrey was admiring the beauty of the slowly receding fist it would suddenly leap at his head like a flash of lightning. McCaffrey got one of these in the mouth that nearly shook his hair loose."[20]

In the fourth and fifth rounds, McCaffrey continued to rush Dempsey in an attempt to force him into a corner, but time and time again, he was repaid for his efforts with sharp blows to the head and body. McCaffrey did land a good left to Dempsey's jaw in the fifth, but for the most part, he threw frequent punches at Dempsey that came up short time and again. Dempsey, with cat-like quickness, avoided most of McCaffrey's missiles and glided away from them, smiling at his opponent. McCaffrey was beginning to become frustrated and he was clearly tiring.

In the fourth round, Dempsey began to dance around his opponent again, but suddenly broke rhythm, stepped in and let loose a powerful blow that landed flush on McCaffrey's eye. The Pittsburgh native was shaken, but returned fire, missing Dempsey, who had already moved away to a far corner of the ring. The frustrated McCaffrey went after him, determined to catch Jack and hammer him, but it was again a fruitless endeavor. "He used both hands with fearful effect on the air immediately above Dempsey's ducked head."[21] Dempsey countered, rising up and landing an uppercut that caught McCaffrey flush on the chin. For the remainder of the round, Dempsey continued to land three or four blows for every one that McCaffrey snuck through. One blow to the side of the head raised an ugly welt on McCaffrey's right temple. Repeatedly he landed combinations to the chin, the eyes and the neck, and Jack played his opponent's midsection like a drum.

In the fifth round McCaffrey showed some signs of success when he tore after Dempsey, cornering him and landing a powerful blow to the forehead and another to the back of Jack's head. Again, Dempsey rolled away and refused to let the blows slow him down as he dodged, weaved and laughed at McCaffrey. Jack then countered, catching his opponent on the nose.

In the sixth round, Dempsey, rather than dance about, made a stand, unleashing a coiled left to McCaffrey's mouth that clearly stung the Pennsylvanian. Jack then followed that up with another left to the mouth, a right to the neck and a sharp right to the stomach. While McCaffrey got in some blows, Dempsey got in far more and clearly controlled the bout. At one point, a frustrated McCaffrey rushed Jack and tried to push him over the ropes, but Dempsey rolled away from the larger man. Jack's face had a few slightly red marks, but McCaffrey's face was showing wear and his right eye was swelling noticeably.

Very little changed in the seventh round. McCaffrey continued charging Dempsey and Dempsey continued sidestepping the rushes. Each time Jack would use the opportunity to land combinations to his opponent's head and body, smashing his fists repeatedly against the Philadelphian's ribs and shoulders.

In the eighth round, McCaffrey let go one terrific right-hand blow that looked like trouble for Dempsey. "It seemed impossible that Dempsey could escape, but he was away so quickly it only brushed the tip of his nose. If a fly had been there the fly would have been killed."[22]

The ninth and tenth rounds saw no change. McCaffrey was simply unable to outfight his opponent. Time and time again, McCaffrey came at Dempsey, landing only glancing blows while Jack rained harsh counter punches on the Pennsylvanian. In one observation from a ringside reporter, McCaffrey threw a powerful right, "but Dempsey kept out of his way, struck his Pittsburgh antagonist a dozen sharp ones on the head and body." The report continued, "McCaffrey's forehead and left eye began to swell and when the tenth round was ended Referee Jere Dunn remarked this is the most scientific fight the people here have seen in years, and Mr. Dempsey is the winner."[23]

By 12:30 in the morning, after forty-five minutes of fighting, the bout was complete. Though McCaffrey outweighed Dempsey by almost two dozen pounds, the Nonpareil was quicker and out boxed his larger opponent throughout the ten-round battle. Dempsey's poise and ring generalship were evident, his defensive skills abundant and his solid, powerful, accurate punches frustrated the Pennsylvanian all evening long, a fact that McCaffrey himself acknowledged after the bout had ended.

According to Richard Fox, "Dempsey had decidedly the advantage in the majority of the ten rounds contested, and he certainly out-generalled his antagonist at every point. He stopped and ducked and hit and got away with marvelous cleverness. McCaffrey, though a good man, was too slow for Jack, both in hitting and avoiding punishment. Dempsey used his left with terrible effect, while McCaffrey tried to get his right in, which is his best hand. Dempsey got in by far the most and the clearest hits."[24]

After McCaffrey retired from the ring in 1895, he was hired as the boxing instructor at the Manhattan Athletic Club in New York City where he remained until 1900 when the then 37-year-old McCaffrey took a job in his native Pittsburgh as a bailiff for the

Allegheny County court system. The popular and very sociable tipstaff remained there for over a quarter of a century until, with his body wracked by lung cancer, he died on December 29, 1926.

As for Dempsey, he came away from the McCaffrey bout with minimal damage. In addition to the usual color and abrasions, the Nonpareil's left hand was damaged. During an interview the day after the bout a reporter asked him, "Is that your terrible left which is swollen?" to which Jack replied, "That is my terrible left. I thought it was broken in the third round, the way that it felt when I struck McCaffrey."[25] During the interview he also complimented McCaffrey as a fine fellow and a good sparrer. He also claimed that McCaffrey was one of the hardest men to hit that he had ever faced. "He stopped a lot of those blows that I am credited with getting in."[26]

In Jack's rooms at the Metropolitan Hotel in Williamsburg, Denny Costigan said, "We are making arrangements for an exhibition in Troy next week. Jack is all right. There is nothing the matter with him but a slight soreness in his left thumb." He added, "In the third round he hit McCaffrey on the forehead and thought he broke his own thumb. He didn't let it bother him, though, in the fight. Today it's a little stiff, that's all. His face is not marked at all."[27]

Professor Mike Donovan commented on the day after the fight, "Jack Dempsey is the most scientific fighter that ever appeared with bare knuckles or gloves."[28] McCaffrey was equally complimentary of the Nonpareil, admitting that Dempsey had beaten him fairly. He went on to say, "He is the cleverest man I ever met. I have only $5,000 in the world and I'll back him for every cent of it against any man of his weight."[29]

A couple of days after the McCaffrey bout, George Godfrey, the recognized colored champion pugilist of America, told a reporter, "I see that Jack Dempsey is willing to meet any man living for a purse of $1,500." Godfrey went on to state that several athletic clubs would be anxious to be his backers and that raising that sum would not be difficult. He then added, "I should like to meet the Nonpareil very much."[30]

On Sunday, February 5, Jack and Costigan headed for Albany and Rochester for a week's engagement in *Around New York*, but as they walked through the crowded lobby of the Metropolitan Hotel, Dempsey was asked by a reporter about McCaffrey's interview in the previous day's papers. McCaffrey claimed two points that irritated the Nonpareil. The first point was that Jack only landed three more blows all night than did McCaffrey. To this, Jack smiled and said, "I was under the impression that he was kept so busy that it was impossible for him to tell how often I hit him."[31] The second point was, to Dempsey, more troubling. Although McCaffrey cried poor to Jack after the bout, that he had lost money on the fight as a result of cost overruns, the Pittsburgh native told the paper that he had made a tidy sum. "Before the contest, he agreed to pay me $2,150, but gave me only $1,900. He made such a poor mouth over the balance, $250, that I told him to let it pass." After a quick review of the gate receipts and other costs, Jack added, "If McCaffrey banked $3,000 as he states, he can well afford to pay me the $250 he still owes me."[32]

After concluding his comments, Jack, Maggie and Denny caught a waiting cab and headed to the station to catch their train for Albany. The group arrived later that day in the New York capitol where "admiring friends met them at the depot in a barouche, and the afternoon was spent in riding about the city." Later in the day, Jack and Maggie took a train for the short trip to Troy where they would be the guests of former Alderman Fox during their stay in the Albany area.

When Dempsey was asked about meeting Toff Wall, he stated that he would meet him on American soil, but only for the largest purse ever fought for.[33]

On Tuesday, Jack and Denny Costigan took a side trip to Rochester where they did their sparring session during *Around New York*. After its run in Rochester, the play would move on to other cities in New York and then travel throughout the Midwest in the spring. Jack's next ring exhibition was during a benefit tendered for him in Troy, New York, on Thursday, February 9. During the evening Mike Lucie took the honors in a bout with Jack Fallon and Bob Haight battered Billy Young of Brooklyn in a three-round battle. The crowd heartily applauded when Jack first sparred with Denny Costigan and then with Tom Henry.

On February 18, Dempsey met Billy Baker at the Adelphia Theatre in Buffalo, New York. Baker was a tough nut for Dempsey to crack the previous April and tonight would be no different. Like before, the bout was only scheduled for four rounds, and the Nonpareil could only win by knockout. The men were introduced to the crowd at the Adelphia at 10:30 p.m., prior to a wild middleweight bout between Buffalo native Benny Strauss and Jack Kehoe of Detroit.

The second Dempsey-Baker bout ran much as the earlier bout had, with Dempsey winning points on style, punches landed, ring generalship, science and technique, but Baker, again outweighing the Nonpareil by over thirty pounds, staying upright for the duration, thus winning another $100 and another no decision.[35]

Immediately upon his return to Brooklyn, Jack went to visit with his old pals Jack and Con McAuliffe, whose father Cornelius had passed away suddenly at his home in Williamsburg on February 10 from Bright's disease. The senior McAuliffe, only 43 when he died, had been a cooper and had gotten both his sons and Dempsey, all great friends from Public School 17, jobs at his cooperage firm.[36]

On the evening of March 1, Dempsey attended a lightweight prizefight between Boston's Jack Havlin and Jack Farrell of Harlem. While Havlin took the brunt of the beating for six rounds, he came alive again in the seventh, dropping Farrell four times before being declared the winner. Dempsey greeted Havlin in the ring after the fight and shook his hand, congratulating him.[37]

It was announced in March that Dempsey had leased a bar and small sporting venue at 203 Front Street in Manhattan. The place was remodeled and a grand opening night was planned. Some were disapproving of this move, noting disappointingly that Jack had "decided to double up with John Barleycorn, the invincible who sooner or later knocks out all who stand up before him."[38] Clearly, the Nonpareil was simply trying to capitalize on his name and popularity and continue to feather the bed for the day he finally left the ring. Temperate beliefs set to the side, it's hard to find fault with a man for planning for his family's financial future.

On March 10, John L. Sullivan met Charley Mitchell in what was called by some a contest for the world heavyweight championship. The two had come together in 1883 when Sullivan whipped Mitchell in a police-interrupted bout, but after being trounced for the entire first round Mitchell mustered all of his strength and let go a powerful and desperate punch that caught John L. on the jaw and floored him for the first time in the champion's career. Sullivan pummeled Mitchell in retribution, but he never forgot it. Mitchell, who was a master at irritating people, made sure of that. In 1884, Mitchell complained, "I've been treated badly by the papers." He went on to state that he was never downed by Sullivan and that he had never fouled him. Worse yet he claimed, "I really won the fight in the first round." Mitchell claimed that the first round was shortened and that had it not been, he would have knocked Sullivan out before it ended.[39] This sort of self-aggrandizing talk was typical of Mitchell. The Englishman's smart mouth and his whole demeanor irritated the champion to no end and helped make Mitchell what Gary Weiand described as "the great hate of Sullivan's life."[40]

The men met at Baron Rothschild's training ground at his estate in Chantilly, France, about twenty miles north of Paris. The contest was held outdoors in a driving rainstorm under London Prize Ring Rules and fought with bare knuckles for stakes of £1000.

While Sullivan was the favorite and outweighed Mitchell by thirty-five pounds, Mitchell was quick, elusive and a very good London Rules fighter. Although he was continually knocked down by the larger man, Mitchell got up each time and kept challenging the champion. Sullivan was clearly not well-trained for this bout and Mitchell took full advantage of this. Sullivan scored the bout's first knock-down, but Mitchell drew first blood. Both men suffered great punishment during the bout—their faces cut, bruised and swollen, their hands swollen and damaged and their bodies marked and scraped.

John L Sullivan (right) and Charlie Mitchell in Chantilly, France, 1888.

When it was apparent that the men could barely raise their arms and both had clearly reached their limit, referee Bernard J. Angle declared the bout a draw following the thirty-ninth round and after more than three hours of fighting.

One cable from Chantilly said, "The Sullivan-Mitchell fight ended in a draw. Mitchell was very cunning and Sullivan was unable to knock him out. Both men were exhausted and their hands were badly hurt. Sullivan's friends are unable to explain why he did not do better." Another cable stated that "the Sullivan-Mitchell fight occupied three hours and eleven minutes and was decided a draw after thirty-nine rounds. Toward the finish of the fight, Mitchell improved and was doing better before the referee declared the contest a draw. Sullivan was cold and much weakened by the pelting rain. Much walking around the ring was indulged in during the fight. Both men have black eyes."[41]

Mitchell, while receiving a great deal of punishment, avoided losing simply by keeping away from Sullivan and making his very large opponent chase him around the ring. Sullivan had trained very little for the contest and was out of shape. By the thirty-ninth round Mitchell was bruised and battered and clearly showing the marks of battle. Sullivan was exhausted from running after his opponent all afternoon and decided to stop doing so and instead draw Mitchell in. Mitchell would not be lured into the trap and just kept running around the ring, while Sullivan kept waiting for him to draw closer. The untimed London Rules rounds dragged on and on. Realizing that this could go on for a very long time and sensing the frustration of Sullivan and the crowd, the referee, Bernard Angle stopped the spectacle and called the contest a draw. Much of the assembled crowd booed the decision as they questioned how a man who did little but run around and then slide into his opponent deserved a draw. They pointed out that Mitchell did not really fight, he simply avoided Sullivan's punishing fists as much as he could. His fight plan was simply to survive. There was agreement that had this bout been fought under Queensberry Rules, Sullivan would have made short work of the Englishman.

During the fifth round, Sullivan injured his right arm, but even then, Mitchell had no real interest in engaging his opponent. Sportswriter Tom Lees told the story that Mitchell denied intentionally spiking Sullivan's legs. When told of this later, Mr. Lumley of the *Illustrated News* smiled and said, "Mitchell is a good talker, but his chat won't go down with the public who are acquainted with the facts." He added, "I see he says that Sullivan never bested him in four rounds. Why, when Mitchell was in New York a short time ago Inspector Williams told him to his face in the Hoffman House that he saved him from a licking in Madison Square Garden on two different occasions and the Inspector knows when a man is getting the worst of it."[42]

In the days following the Sullivan-Mitchell bout, with the news of the contest coming in from France, Jack was quoted as saying that he was anxious to meet Mitchell and believed that his chances of beating him were good. To make his case, Jack pointed out that he had defeated McCaffrey who had bested Mitchell and drawn with Burke who drew with Mitchell. Dempsey, no fan of Mitchell's, was now further aggravated with him over his bad mouthing of and tactics against Jack's friend Sullivan.

About this time, Jere Dunn sent a telegraph to "Pony" Moore, Mitchell's backer. In the cable Dunn extended an offer on behalf of Dempsey, to meet the British pugilist either in Europe or North America. Dempsey was challenging Mitchell to a London Rules finish fight for $10,000 a side and even offered to allow a British referee. Jack's backers also offered Mitchell $500 for travel and training expenses should the bout come off in America, only asking the same for Jack should the contest be held in Europe.[43]

Even with all of these concessions from the Dempsey camp, there was no agreement from Mitchell and it seemed as if there might never be a match between the Englishman and the Nonpareil. The speculation that Mitchell preferred to avoid Dempsey continued to circulate. "Jake Kilrain is credited with saying that Mitchell would rather face any man on earth than Jack Dempsey."[44]

Also getting in on the challenges was Englishman Toff Wall, who was rumored to be coming to America and looking for a fight with Dempsey. There had been talk of a bout between the two for most of the past year and the pot was being stirred on both sides of the Atlantic. This time the contest was being proposed by Jack's friend and backer Pat Sheedy as well as by Dempsey's recent victim, Dominick McCaffrey. It was to be a ten-round, glove contest held in Jersey City. Jack stated that he was more than willing and he looked forward to the fight, but he left it there. Sheedy, however, could not resist taking a verbal poke at the Englishman and commented, "Wall is no cleverer than the Marine" and that "no short-armed, bull-necked, sawed-off has any chance with Master Dempsey, particularly in a 10-round contest."[45]

At 5:30 p.m. on March 11, Jack stood in the lobby of the Metropolitan Hotel in Williamsburg chatting with several friends. He was described as wearing "a stylish suit of black clothes, a fine chinchilla overcoat, and a new silk hat." He looked healthy and had his travel bag in hand. Having said goodbye to Maggie and Alice, he was on his way to the train station.[46] That evening Dempsey boarded the Pennsylvania Railroad's Westbound No. 9 sleeper to Pittsburgh to join his mates for several shows of Billy Madden's *Around New York* in the Iron City. It was a memorable and nearly fatal trip for the Nonpareil and others on board the No. 9. The train was barreling along from New York to western Pennsylvania just as one of the fiercest snow storms ever recorded was bearing down on the region. For several days, meteorological events had been coming together would create a terrific late winter storm that blanketed the Northeast. The result was one of the most severe blizzards in the recorded history of the United States. Snowfalls of up to five feet were noted in parts of Pennsylvania, New Jersey, New York, Rhode Island, Massachusetts and Connecticut. Northern New England and Eastern Canada were blanketed with as much as two to three feet.

The Great Blizzard of '88 began with a sudden shift of the upper-air Jet Stream that brought frigid arctic air into direct contact with the warm, moist air found in the Gulf Stream. This turned an ordinary rainstorm off the Carolina coast and some unseasonably mild temperatures into what became known as the Great White Hurricane. In less than a day, temperatures plummeted from the mid–50s into the single digits. Heavy rain turned to heavy snow overnight and fierce winds reaching as high as eighty miles per hour caused extensive snow drifts. The heavy snow and winds also caused severe traffic disruptions by road and rail and brought down telegraph wires, disrupting communications throughout the region.

The blizzard was felt throughout the northeast, particularly east of the Allegheny Mountains from northern Virginia to central New England. Pennsylvania and the New York Metropolitan area were severely affected. More than thirty inches of snow fell and drifts as high as ten feet were recorded. Parts of New York City were paralyzed for nearly thirty-six hours. The blizzard was more than inconvenient, it was deadly. Over four hundred persons were killed due to the extreme weather. Nearly half of those were in New York City alone. Many died from exposure to the extreme temperatures and sustained winds. Even the famous were not spared the ravages of the storm. Former United States Senator from New York and Republican leader Roscoe Conkling was found suffering from hypothermia in Union Square. He was cared for, but he died of pneumonia a month later on April 18.

The East Coast was paralyzed from Quebec to Washington, with rail travel stalled, telegraph lines down and shipping at a standstill. Over two hundred ships were either grounded or disabled and nearly half of the fatalities brought about by the storm were related to the maritime industry. New York and other cities learned a great deal from the effects of the storm. Paralysis of elevated rail lines paved the way for putting the trains underground, resulting in the subway systems we know today. Downed power and communications lines led to some municipalities placing utility wires underground.

In the wee hours of March 12, 1888, in the midst of this blizzard, the westbound No. 9 train, on which Dempsey was a passenger, was hurtling through the snowy Pennsylvania night. Suddenly, the No. 9 collided at full speed with an eastbound freight train which had derailed and fouled the westbound track near Huntingdon, Pennsylvania, around 3:40 a.m. Shortly before the collision, George Esterline, the conductor on the eastbound freight train, noticed that an axle on a coke car had been broken and caused that car and thirteen others to tumble onto the westbound track. Esterline reportedly said to his brakeman, "My God, boy, there's our cars on the other track and Number 9 is due right here." As the crew of the disabled freight train were swinging their lanterns in warning, the "Western Express, known as No. 9, in the charge of engineer Robert Gardner and fireman Charles F. Moyer, turned the sharp curve at the cut and rushed, shrieking and whistling, into the jaws of death."[47] The train was running at forty miles per hour when Moyer, who had climbed out on the engine with his oil can, saw the oncoming danger. The unfortunate man was on the side of the engine that faced the wreck and he knew his time was up. He yelled out a warning to Gardner that caused the engineer to put on the brakes, but it was too late to avoid the danger. Number 9's engine was badly mangled as it made contact with the cars of the freight train that lay strewn across the tracks. "The freight cars toppled over and came back just as the third sleeper was passing. The side was torn off every passenger car, except the last one. The steps were torn from every car and that their occupants escaped instant death is regarded as wonderful."

When the train finally came to a stop, twisted and torn metal and shattered planks of wood lay on the freshly fallen snow, giving the scene a surreal appearance. With the lights of the trains out, confusion and disorientation reigned in the darkness. Men and women, half-clothed and stunned, tumbled out of their berths and wandered about the terrible scene, waiting for help.

The horribly mangled body of the 26-year-old Moyer was found under the third sleeper car. "Engineer Gardner was found wedged in between the boiler and tender, his hand firmly grasping the throttle. He was caught just across the hips and remained there for over two hours, until the wrecking train came and pulled the engine away." During the wait, Gardner could only sit there in the cold, dark early morning, courageously enduring untold agony from his internal and external wounds and wait for release. The frigid night temperature had fallen below zero and he was mercifully covered with a warm blanket. He spoke rationally with those around him but had to know his time was up and encouraged those about him to help others. When he was finally released he was carried to a bed in an undamaged sleeper car where he lay for a while in a semi-conscious state. The brave engineer fought the spasms of pain as the life ebbed from his broken body. His final words were reported to have been, "None of the passengers killed—that's good. Lay me down—down, boys. Good bye."[48]

The local press interviewed the passengers and train's surviving crew and of course when it was discovered that the Nonpareil was on board, he was asked to comment on the matter. The *Huntingdon Globe* wrote the following, "Jack Dempsey, the pugilist, was on the train, en-route for Pittsburgh. The only thing that troubled him was the death of the engineer and fireman."[49]

Jack and his fellow travelers had dodged a bullet in part due to the quick and courageous actions by Gardner and Moyer. In time, another train arrived to take the passengers on to their destination in Pittsburgh.

After finally arriving in Pittsburgh on March 13, Jack checked into his hotel for some rest and a meal. He would spend the next several days in the Steel City before moving on to Cincinnati where *Around New York* was playing on its Midwestern tour. He would also engage in an evening of sparring with Peter Nolan and Con Riley before returning to Brooklyn in mid–March for exhibition matches with old friend Denny Costigan. He was looking forward to a short rest after his arduous week on the road.

On March 21, however, the Nonpareil suffered a misfortune more disturbing to him than any foe he could ever meet in the ring—his beloved dog "Boy" went missing.[50] Boy, a Newfoundland, apparently followed a lady to New York and back on the Fulton Ferry, but after the ferry docked and the passengers had disembarked, Boy disappeared. Boy was not easy to lose as he was nearly as big as his master, weighing in at 120 pounds. Jack, who had spent much of the day on the 21st searching Brooklyn in a cold March rain, told the local papers that he would pay a liberal reward for Boy's return. Jack's friends and fans kept their eyes open for any signs of the dog and reports of sightings came from the Ferry area and Henry Street. Luckily for Jack, Boy was safe and in the care of a young lady who resided at 45 Henry Street. Jack went immediately to the residence and found Boy. Upon seeing his friend, Dempsey apparently exclaimed, "Well, now, Boy! Ain't you ashamed of yourself? You had me chasing all over the city after you in the rain yesterday."[51]

Apparently, Boy had quite the time during his adventure. He played horse for the young woman's two children and when the other boarders came home that evening, they played with him and fed him well. Once they saw in the paper who the dog was, they contacted Dempsey immediately.

After a bit of a light fight schedule for Dempsey, he began to ponder his next opponents. In late March, George Godfrey, the colored heavyweight champion, told the *Boston Herald* that he had backers willing to put forth $1,500 for a fight between Godfrey and any man in the world. Godfrey told the *Herald* reporters that he believed that he could whip Dempsey, Sullivan and Jake Kilrain. "I don't see what Sullivan ever did to warrant the hullabaloo about him. Kilrain is a good one, but he has done nothing that makes him look very big in my eyes." And then Godfrey threw down the gauntlet to Jack. "When recently a purse of $1,000 was offered for a fight between Dempsey and me, Dempsey held off for $1,500. Well, now's his chance."[52] The fight between Godfrey and Dempsey never occurred although as talented as both men were, it might have been a good one.

Godfrey seemed a bit disingenuous in his comments about his potential rivals, especially Jake Kilrain whom he had already battled twice, once to a draw in 1882 and once to a TKO loss in 1883. He would meet Kilrain once more on March 13, 1893, at the California Athletic Club in San Francisco when Godfrey would lose to Kilrain by way of a forty-four-round knockout. One has to wonder how "big" Kilrain looked to Godfrey as he stared at the ceiling of the California A.C. from his prone position on the canvas.

In addition to Godfrey, there was also the matter of Charley Mitchell. Mitchell had withstood tremendous punishment during the brutal thirty-nine-round bout with Sullivan, but he had avoided losing mainly by running away from and sliding into Sullivan. Most observers agreed that Mitchell would have had no chance against Sullivan under the Queensberry Rules. Many believed that Jack should once again challenge Mitchell and that Dempsey would easily defeat the Englishman. But that was easier said than done as Mitchell had routinely avoided the Nonpareil and refused to accept his challenges.

Jack Ashton, one of the parties that crossed the Atlantic with Sullivan, spoke with a reporter after the Sullivan-Mitchell bout. When asked his opinion of Mitchell, Ashton reponded, "He's only grown stouter," said Ashton, "and I know he will not have anything to do with Jack Dempsey, because he told me that he would have no show with the Nonpareil. Dempsey, I am sure, would kill him."[53] When Sullivan was asked about a contest between Jem Smith and Dempsey, the big man stated about Smith that he would have trouble with Jack because "his arms are not long enough." He continued with a compliment for the Nonpareil, saying, "You can take my word for it, Jack Dempsey can lick them all, one after another."[54]

In the weeks following the Sullivan-Mitchell bout, many in the pugilistic community were anxious to see Mitchell meet Dempsey in the ring. One reporter asked Jack if he was going to challenge him and the Nonpareil responded, "I am not." When asked why not, Dempsey responded, "I will not fight any more unless I am forced to do it." The reporter continued to press, "About how much forcing do you think it will take?" Jack smiled and said nothing. Finally, the reporter asked if he wanted to fight Mitchell, to which Jack responded, "Don't ask me." Dempsey would not say it, but the truth of the matter was that while Jack desperately wanted to fight Mitchell and had no doubt that he could whip him, he was now a married man and had promised Margaret that he would not climb into the ring and fight again unless forced to do so.[55]

The running feud heated up a bit in early April when reporters visiting his Williamsburg residence asked Dempsey what he thought about Mitchell's backer Pony Moore's pronouncement that Jack's challenge to Mitchell had not yet arrived. The Nonpareil, his patience being stretched thin, responded with a disdainful smile, "That's all bosh. I never sent a challenge. If Mitchell wants to fight he knows where to find me. My money is always ready and he need not fear we will not give him a square, stand up fight." Jack added that the sooner the two could meet the better as he looked forward to beating Mitchell.[56]

Jack continued, stating that he would prefer to meet Mitchell in a finish fight under London Prize Ring Rules and would agree to a fight of four, eight or ten rounds. "I have challenged Mitchell often when he was in this country without receiving any reply, excepting that I was not in his class. Now I am making money and doing a good business and would like to be let alone and take care of my mother, wife and child; but Charley Mitchell has aggravated me so much that I would just like to meet him in the ring, even if it is only for fun, and I don't mean to be a blower, but will do as I say."[57] Denny Costigan was present at the interview and chimed in, commenting, "I feel certain that if Mitchell ever wants him in the ring, Dempsey will win." Costigan added that with proper training, Jack would be a dangerous threat to anyone he met in the ring. "Dempsey is big enough to fight any pugilist on the list."[58]

The verbal sparring continued between the two men for quite some time with one calling out the other time and again. In August, Dempsey offered to meet the Englishman at $10,000 a side. Referring to the past slight in San Francisco, the *Brooklyn Eagle* noted that, "Mr. Charley Mitchell is a British pounder of renown and his conquest might well tempt any American hard hitter. But it is not a mere triumph of this sort which now attracts Mr. Dempsey. It appears that upon a certain occasion Mr. Mitchell refused to speak to him upon the public street. In Mr. Dempsey's own words, 'He cut me dead.' Later he further and deliberately violated the courtesies common to gentlemen, rudely tearing up instead of kindly answering a respectful letter of invitation to combat, and refusing to throw off his stolid indifferences even when called 'a cur.'"[59] Needless to say, Dempsey and the sporting public were ready for the meet—only one question remained, was Mitchell?

Other fighters were interested in setting matches with the Nonpareil. Middleweight Pete McCoy and his backers proposed a return bout with Dempsey in Providence, Rhode Island. The fight was to be at $1,500 a side, light gloves, under Queensberry Rules and witnessed in private by only prominent club men of Boston and Providence. As Dempsey had already defeated McCoy in six rounds at the Oakland Avenue Rink in Jersey City two years before and was not very interested in a rematch.

Johnny Reagan resurfaced from his "retirement" over the summer when Jack McAuliffe challenged him to a glove contest of up to ten rounds to be held in Jersey City, New Jersey. Reagan refused the offer, stating that he was instead looking for a rematch with Dempsey. Reagan said, "I am anxious to get on another match with Dempsey and I will fight him according to Queensberry Rules, either for a limited number of rounds or to a finish." The bout never came about as Dempsey saw little to gain from fighting Reagan again after having already decisively defeating him. Additionally, Reagan had only a half-hearted interest in fighting Dempsey again. He saw it as more of a good pay day than anything else. Reagan would continue to fight for several more years including a strong showing when he fought Pete McCoy at the Puritan Athletic Club in Long Island City, New York, on May 1, 1890. McCoy gained a 10-round points decision in that contest.

On April 3, Jack sparred with popular Eastern District heavyweight Joe Denning at a benefit at the Grand Street Palace Rink near Wythe Avenue. The men met in the windup of an evening of entertainment that included an eight-fight undercard and a brass band that played between bouts. Steve O'Donnell was the master of ceremonies and police Captain George W. Bunce was the referee. Bunce's officers were on hand but were undisturbed by the contests and with their captain heavily involved in the proceedings, no interference with the evening's events occurred.

After the eighth bout, the brass band played and soon, the Nonpareil appeared on stage, greeted by a thunderous ovation. He sparred four lively rounds with Denning, "during which he gave evidence of his proficiency and tact. In the last round he sparred lively and punched his opponent seven or eight times in the stomach, nearly knocking the wind out of him. Denning too, got in a few good knocks."[60]

A few days after the Denning exhibition, Jack headed north to Boston where he sparred with 52-year-old Joe Coburn on April 9. A benefit had been arranged for the ring veteran to be held that night at Boston's Parepa Hall. A fight card had been set to showcase lightweights Billy Edwards and Arthur Chambers, middleweights Jack Fallon and Mike Cleary, Mike Boden and Captain Daly and finally, the mill between Coburn and Dempsey. Jack received compensation for his appearance that night and some, including Mike Donovan, questioned this. In an open letter to the *New York World* Dempsey stated that Coburn had offered him $200 for the fight of which he received but $150. "If Mr. Coburn did not think my services worth that amount he would not have offered it."[61] As noted earlier, Dempsey never made any bones about the fact that he was in the fight business for money. Dempsey commented, "I would not take up so much of your valuable space were it not for the fact that I wish to set myself right in the eyes of the public, as Mr. Donovan has been circulating stories trying to prove me an ingrate."[62] It is fair to say that relations between Dempsey and Donovan were strained dating back to the spiking of Jack's leg during the Reagan bout.

Joseph Henry Coburn began his ring career on May 1, 1856, when he fought Edmund "Ned" Price to a draw in Spy Pond, Massachusetts, just outside of Boston. In his prime he was known as an intelligent, crafty battler who was quick and agile. His footwork was good, and he hit with two fast hands.[63] Another description noted that Coburn "delivers a blow like a pistol shot, and jumps back in an instant, and is on his guard before his opponent can return the compliment, inflicting punishment without receiving any in return."[64] Coburn was an interesting sort. He was born in County Armagh, Ireland, in 1835. He immigrated to the United States in 1850 and became a brick layer. He fought either in matches or exhibitions, against some of the greats of his day. In addition to Dempsey, he was matched against John L. Sullivan, Charley Mitchell, Dominick McCaffrey and Jem Mace. He continued with exhibition matches into his 50s.

He also climbed into the ring to compete in at least one Greco Roman wrestling match. About five hundred persons filled the Central Park Garden on August 9, 1876, to watch Coburn wrestle local boxer John Dwyer. Dwyer was a skillful heavyweight who packed a punch. He was also a man of very decent character, not like that of many others in the fighting profession during his time. His physique was magnificent, his view of life was mature and, to him, pugilism was something that he pursued because he excelled at it. His brother was Alderman William Dwyer.[65] Dwyer defeated Coburn in a hard-fought contest for $250 per side. The pair soon returned to more familiar pursuits when they met in the boxing ring for a glove contest at Mallahan's Saloon on West Thirtieth Street—again for $250 aside.[66] After eleven rounds, this fight ended in a draw.

Coburn frequently found himself in trouble with the law. In March 1877, Coburn was sentenced to ten years in prison for felonious assault with intent to kill New York City police officer William Tobias the previous month. He served only five years of his sentence before being released in December 1882.

In May 1885, Coburn was arrested on charges of robbery after allegedly stealing $950 from Charles Carter at Coburn's Saloon. The charges were later dropped and Coburn was released. In August, Coburn got into a skirmish with a police officer and an onlooker, but ultimately, no charges were pressed. In November 1887, Coburn was again arrested, this time for being under the influence and for wrangling with a man on the street in New York. Again, he was released and no charges preferred.

Coburn died of pneumonia at 242 West Thirty-Fifth Street in Manhattan on December 6, 1890, at the age of 55. He was buried at Calvary Cemetery in New York on December 9.

Jack and Denny Costigan were engaged to spar at Harry Miner's Eighth Avenue Theatre in Manhattan during the week of April 16 and the following week Jack was on the bill for the Great Silbon Specialty and Burlesque Company at Brooklyn's Grand Theatre. The event was a part of an evening of diversified entertainment that included comedy, music, burlesque and a trapeze act. Jack was to meet different men for three rounds each during each evening's show.[67]

On April 23, Jack met James "Billy" Stevens in four rounds at the Grand. Stevens was a local truck driver who answered the call when it was announced that "Dempsey would spar with any man willing to stand a pounding at his hands."[68] While Stevens was certainly game, it was not much of a match.

From the start, the lithe and muscular Stevens showed his quickness in the ring—not in the rapidity of his punches, but in the speed with which he danced around Dempsey and attempted to keep Jack from getting close to him. Jack eventually caught up with his elusive opponent and from then on, Dempsey toyed with him, landing powerful punches almost at will.

In the final round, Jack hit Stevens on the side of the head near his ear and rattled him. "Stevens staggered and whirled around as if he had been shot and would have fallen had not Dempsey held him up until he recovered."[69] As the round ended, Stevens had recuperated enough from his dizziness to stand on his own, but on legs as wobbly as a newborn colt he attempted to make his way to his corner. Dempsey, always the gentleman, put his arm around his opponent, helped Stevens to his stool and apologized to Stevens, stating that he had forgotten himself in the excitement of the moment. Stevens accepted the Nonpareil's plea for forgiveness then sat down in his corner.

Jack's celebrity around New York had grown to the point that he was constantly in demand to appear at events or to endorse something or someone. On May 6, he stood in for John L. Sullivan as the official starter for a world championship, long-distance walking race at Madison Square Garden. The forty-five participants apparently had to cover five hundred and twenty-five miles in six days,[70] one hundred in the first twenty-four hours.[71] The walkers made their tramp on the sawdust-covered oval. When Sullivan failed to put in an appearance at the Garden, Dempsey agreed to start the men. At midnight, "when all was in readiness, Manager O'Brien said, 'Ladies and gentlemen, John L. Sullivan promised me that he would start this race. If he had not, I would not have announced it in the papers. As he has disappointed us, I have Jack Dempsey, who will start the men.'" On cue, Jack vaulted over the railing from his seat next to the scorer's table and stepped forward to start the race. The always popular Nonpareil then bowed to a loud applause from the five thousand spectators. "Referee Kennedy then said, 'They are all ready, Jack,' and Dempsey, in a low tone said, 'Go!'" And with that, the forty-five men started their long trek with a rush.[72]

The reason for Sullivan's absence was later explained by a reporter for the *Boston Globe*. Apparently, Sullivan was fully intending to attend the race and collect a $500 fee for his time until he was apprised that a judgment for $1,800 had been given against him in New York. The judgment "had been put in the hands of a sheriff for collection" and if Sullivan kept his appointment at the Garden, "he would be lodged in Ludlow Street jail until the debt was satisfied."[73] Deciding that he would be $1,300 to the good if he avoided the sheriff, Sullivan decided to maintain his freedom and not to travel to New York at that time.

Jack and Denny Costigan journeyed to Providence, Rhode Island, for the May 23 bout between Jim Fell and "Sparrow" Golden. In addition to working his corner with Costigan during the fight, Dempsey was one of the principle backers for Fell. Between two and three hundred spectators attended the contest at Providence's Racquet Club that evening. Fell had the better of Golden, who was out of condition, throughout the fight. After being punished badly for five rounds, the exhausted Golden sank to the floor and was unable to rise for several minutes.[74]

Dempsey had developed a wide range of interests. In addition to pugilistic events, Jack attended myriad other social functions. He loved a wide variety of sports, from foot races to horse races to baseball. He loved the theater and the fine arts and he had grown fond of hunting and fishing as well. In mid–June, he was sighted at the Suburban Handicap thoroughbred race at Belmont Park and by June 26, Dempsey was back in Brooklyn and attending the horse races at Gravesend Race Track, where he watched a six-race match in the mist and rain.[75] It was noted in the *Police Gazette* that Jack "is now one of the heavy betters on turf events and his efforts to select and back the winning horses are crowned with just as much success as his battles in the prize ring have been."[76] Two nights after his day at Gravesend, the Dempseys attended a reception and evening of musical entertainment at Clarendon Hall in honor of the New York Philo-Celtic Society.[77]

Dominick McCaffrey paid a visit to Dempsey on June 27, in an attempt to schedule another bout with the Nonpareil. McCaffrey talked of arranging a glove contest under Queensberry Rules of ten or twelve rounds for gate receipts with the winner taking the larger share. Dempsey insisted on a guarantee to be certain that his share of the receipts did not fall below a certain amount. His fear was that the gate might be somewhat light for a contest with a man whom he had already beaten. McCaffrey was unwilling to do this and no bout was arranged.[78] One sportswriter applauded Dempsey for standing firm. "A very cunning chap is Dempsey and when I recall how little money he got out of his early battles I cannot but admire him for insisting in getting a shade the best of his matches at present." The reporter continued, "Jack fought many times for the price of a suit of clothes and fought hard, too. He was gaining fame then and now that he has it, will make it pay. He demands that McCaffrey give a certainty as an inducement to box...."[79]

Jack had an interesting evening on July 5, while staying in Rockaway Beach for a few days of rest. A band of fifteen to twenty toughs from the Bowery section of south central Manhattan had been drinking at Ruland's Hotel that evening. At about 9:00 p.m. one of their crew decided to "clean out the place." A large-scale fight broke out between police officer Peter Geiss, who tried to intervene, and several of the gang. More policemen were quickly summoned. Several officers arrived soon thereafter and while outnumbered, began to go about restoring order, but the ruffians would have none of it and began pummeling the bluecoats. Hearing the commotion, Dempsey, who was staying nearby with his family, appeared on the scene accompanied by Joe Denning, Denny Costigan and several other associates. It was a good thing for Brooklyn's finest and a bad ending to the evening for the Bowery toughs.

The tide in the battle began to turn as soon as Dempsey and company waded into the thick of the brawl. The *New York Sun* reported that "his 'terrible right' had its usual vanquishing effect."[80] In the very dramatic style of the day, one reporter who was on the scene described the affair as follows. "Springing into the thick of the melee the shoulder hitters unmasked their batteries with telling effect. For the space of ten minutes the bar room was a pandemonium with curses, blows, flying glasses and bottles and the smashing of chairs. The Bowery boys quickly recognized the nature of the foes they were pitted against and began to beat a retreat betaking themselves to the train to the city." Order was restored and no charges filed as the men dematerialized into the sea of people in the streets. None of those restoring order were seriously hurt. Jack was hit on the neck with a broken chair but was fine. "A number of the New York toughs will bear evidences of the efficiency of his 'terrible right' for some days."[81]

By mid-summer, much was being made of a proposed bout between Jack and middleweight legend Professor Mike Donovan. The champion and the former champion had been on unfriendly terms since the Reagan fight after which Jack accused Donovan of having Reagan intentionally try to maim him with his spikes, thus causing the bad gash on Jack's leg. Donovan denied it completely and openly resented Dempsey's accusation. A war of words ensued. Asked if Dempsey were a great middleweight, Donovan, changing his earlier tune, responded, "No, he is not. I can name a dozen who could best him and I know he could not stand an hour before such men as Patsey Reardon, Rocky Moore, Dan Kerrigan or George Rooke."[82]

The fight community was divided as to whether or not Donovan could stand with Dempsey, but the professor stated his belief that he would win. "Nothing would give me greater pleasure than to meet Mr. Jack Dempsey in a public ten-round contest, with gloves, and decide who is the better man. I feel I can best him; in fact, I know I can. He has said some disagreeable things about me which he never ought to have said."[83] Donovan continued in his denunciation of the Nonpareil, saying that "the men whom Dempsey has whipped were mere boys in comparison with the men whom I have whipped."[84]

Responding to Donovan's comments in an interview in his saloon on Front Street, Jack said, "Why I can lick him in one punch. He is an old man, a retired champion, and it would be a shame to take his laurels from him. What credit would it be to me to defeat him?"[85] Donovan, who was just forty years old, took exception to Dempsey's comments and called him out again.

Dempsey's friend and colleague Jack McAuliffe had this to say when asked about the Nonpareil's imbroglio with Donovan, "Donovan is losing his head. He is now over 40 years old. He belongs to a class of fighters who think they are able to whip every man when they have a few glasses of beer. Billy Edwards was very popular until he got filled with the same idea and he had it knocked out of him. Age is against a fighter, although he may not realize that such is the case."[86]

On August 1, tragedy came to the Dempsey family when Jack's mother Alicia Lennon Kelly Dempsey died at her home on North Tenth Street in Williamsburg. Mrs. Dempsey was just fifty-two years old. It was a difficult time for Jack as he had always been very close to his mother. "The pugilist has always been very tender in his treatment of his mother, and she has not lacked for attention in the two weeks of her illness."[87]

A week later a *New York Evening World* reporter met with Dempsey and Denny

Costigan and asked about the proposed match between the Nonpareil and Mike Donovan. Jack said he was tired of hearing a lot of "nonsense" about the older and long retired Donovan being able to whip him. He also thought that the bout would be a financial bust. "I don't see where there is a cent of money in it," said Jack. "I don't believe anybody would come to see me whip a man so completely 'off' as Donovan, but if he can raise that $2,000 he talks about I'll meet him six rounds or sixty."[88]

Another lingering fight proposal that stuck under Dempsey's craw was addressed the next day by Jack McAuliffe who called Johnny Reagan out on his claims that he could best Dempsey under Queensberry Rules. McAuliffe in an open letter to the *Evening World* personally challenged Reagan to a Queensberry bout of four to ten rounds. "I'll bet him $1,000 and all the receipts of the house that he won't defeat me." McAuliffe added that "in order to give him a chance to show his skill I will agree to box at catch weights, which will be from fifteen to twenty pounds in his favor." To show that he was not bluffing, McAuliffe deposited $250 as forfeit and proposed that the principles meet at 10:00 a.m. on August 10 at the *Police Gazette* offices to sign articles of agreement.[89]

I have uncovered an event that is difficult to explain in Dempsey's movements in mid–August. On August 15 it was reported by the *Omaha Daily Bee* that Jack was briefly in town the previous evening. According to the short article, Dempsey was heading west to Denver for a couple of weeks. While on a brief stopover in Omaha, Jack was reportedly wined and dined in sumptuous style by a group of noteworthy locals whom they list by name. While in town, he also granted an interview to a local reporter during which Dempsey said that "he was going to Denver for a few weeks' pleasure and recuperation." He noted that he had no planned bouts but hoped to arrange something with Toff Wall soon.[90]

The conundrum is that Dempsey was apparently in New York on August 13, where he gave an interview and was not traveling west. There is also no question that the Nonpareil was in New York—not Denver—on August 18. The assuredness comes from the fact that Dempsey was arrested on that date for attending the George La Blanche–Jack Varley prizefight in Yonkers held earlier in the day. The bout was held on the deck of the Hudson River tug boat *Egbert Myer*. The Nonpareil and a number of other sports were arrested after the bout had ended and the police river patrol boat pulled up alongside the tug. The officers quickly got the fighters, their parties and most of the spectators on board the police boat and then went looking for others. Each time one of the resisters was caught he was greeted with derisive cheers and laughter by those already in police custody. First, pugilist Ed Plummer was caught, then Mike Costello and then Denny Costigan. Finally, Dempsey was discovered wearing blue work coveralls, his face and hair blackened and pretending he was hard at work oiling the engines.[91] Apparently Jack was betrayed to the officers by his own gold pocket watch and chain and the expensive clothes they caught glimpses of under his coveralls. The prisoners were all taken for arraignment at the Manhattan Detention Complex, known to New Yorkers as "the Tombs." The arrests were all for show, however, as Justice Powers dismissed the disorderly conduct charges against all the spectators and levied small fines on the fighters. It is well documented by several newspapers and by the City of New York that Jack Dempsey, the Nonpareil, was in Manhattan on that day.

There is no doubt about whom the *Bee* meant, though, referring to Jack as "the redoubtable Nonpareil, and the champion middleweight of the world."[92] Dozens of newspapers, however, carried the La Blanche–Varley fight story and placed Dempsey at the bout, on the tug and in front of Justice Powers just three and a half days later. Unless Dempsey changed his mind about his Denver trip and headed back to New York shortly after leaving Omaha, the *Bee*'s report is in error. There is also the chance that someone was impersonating Dempsey and managed to fool the locals who wined and dined him.

In the early hours of a cold, rain-soaked August 31, a brutal murder was committed in Buck's Row, a quiet back street in the Whitechapel section of London. The horribly mutilated body of Mary Ann Nichols was discovered around quarter of four that morning by Charles Cross and Robert Paul, local cart drivers who were on their way to work. Unknown to anyone at that time, the men's gruesome discovery was the first act in a macabre mystery that would play out in the streets and back alleys of London's East End for the next ten weeks in what were to become known as the Jack the Ripper murders. Officially, the police lump the murders of eleven women in Whitechapel—running from April 3, 1888, to February 13, 1891—as the Whitechapel Murders, but of those eleven only five are fully attributed to the notorious and still unnamed killer.

The similarities in the eleven murders were location—the Whitechapel section of east London—and the fact that each of the victims was a known prostitute. But aside from that the similarities begin to break down. While some researchers attribute a possible sixth murder—that of Martha Tabram on August 7 as Jack's first, the first two killings and the last four were very different in style from the five "canonical murders" committed from late August to early November 1888, and thus not included in the Ripper's horrific annals. Before he was finished, Jack the Ripper would butcher four more women—Annie Chapman on September 8, Elizabeth Stride and Catherine Eddowes within an hour of each other on September 30 and, his final victim, Mary Kelly on November 9. What caused him to kill and then abruptly stop, no one knows for certain. To this day, none of the Whitechapel Murders have ever been solved.

If there can be any silver lining to this series of ghastly murders it would be that they brought a spotlight on the meager living conditions in the slums of London's East End. There was a loud public outcry against the high crime rate and the overcrowded and unsanitary living conditions in the East End. By 1890, several Acts of Parliament were passed setting new codes for housing in an effort to address these scourges. In the following years the worst of the slums were demolished and new housing built.

In early September, Dempsey became involved in a heated argument with Jake Kilrain at the Nonpareil's saloon and hotel on Front Street, opposite the Fulton Market in New York. During Kilrain's visit the topic of a Dempsey-Mitchell tilt came up. Kilrain expressed his opinion that in such a contest, the Englishman would be victorious. The conversation became heated when Dempsey construed Kilrain's comments to be a slight, and for a while it appeared as if the two would square off themselves. "The affair, however, wound up amicably. Stevenson one of Kilrain's companions, declining to hold a check with which the Nonpareil offered to bind himself to fight Mitchell."[93] Jack appeared ready to fight Mitchell, regardless of his promise to Maggie to stay out of the ring. In his view, Mitchell's slights toward him and the constant speculation about a contest between the two antagonists was justification that he was being "forced" to fight. The bad feelings between Dempsey and Kilrain continued to fester for some time. There was also serious speculation that Dempsey would be the "unknown" fighter paired with Kilrain in a battle being scheduled by a syndicate headed by Arthur Lumley.

After their meeting at Dempsey's, Jack commented about Kilrain, "I never saw so changed a man in my life as Kilrain is. Before he went across the water he was as modest a fellow as you would want to meet, but now he is the biggest braggart I know of. A dozen times while we were talking I wished we were somewhere else than in my house, for I wanted to roast him, and twice I told him so. In my own house I didn't want to talk fight with him or any of his friends, but he kept poking 'Chawley' Mitchell at me so persistently that I had to." Before the meeting ended, Jack offered to fight both Mitchell and Kilrain. The two continued to jaw back and forth for some time, but no fight between the two ever materialized.

About that same time, Richard Fox reported that he was in receipt of a dispatch from the California Athletic Club of San Francisco offering a $5,000 purse for a contest in their facilities between Dempsey and Mitchell. Commenting on the possibilities of either a Mitchell or Kilrain fight being made, a prominent New York sporting man remarked, "I look upon Dempsey as a great general and notwithstanding Kilrain's advantage in height, reach, weight and strength, Jack would be able to hold his own. But I am in hopes that Jack is not the unknown. I want to see him fight Charley Mitchell when he arrives in this country, and you will find me ready to put up $5,000 that he can whip him. But you mark my words: Mitchell will not make a match to fight Jack Dempsey."[94]

At one point Mitchell claimed that he was in no hurry to fight Dempsey, but he would do so if he found there to be no money in giving sparring exhibitions around the country. To this Jack responded, "I never challenged anybody except Mitchell, and I've challenged him till I'm tired. If he wants to fight he'll have to challenge me."[95]

There must have been some brave but foolhardy, petty thieves in Brooklyn in the Nonpareil's day for it was reported in mid–September that Jack was the victim of a theft. "Jack Dempsey's valuable gold hunting case watch, made by Benedict Brothers and numbered 14,560, was stolen from him a few days ago by some pickpocket. He promised to reward anyone returning it to him."[96] The idea of bumping up against the Nonpareil and reaching into his pocket to steal anything was clearly not a smart one. Dempsey was anxious enough to recover the watch that he offered a $75 reward for its return with no questions asked.[97]

In late September, it was announced that arrangements had been agreed upon by Donovan and Dempsey for a six-round glove contest fought under the Queensberry Rules to be held in the coming weeks. Further negotiations set the fight at Brooklyn's Palace Rink on Clermont Avenue on November 15. Dempsey was reportedly to receive two-thirds of the gate with Donovan settling for what remained.[98]

That Donovan was willing to come out of retirement to meet the Nonpareil is a testament to how angry he was over being accused of encouraging Reagan to spike Dempsey in their fight the previous year. Jack made Donovan even angrier when he refused to take seriously the veteran's challenge to fight and reportedly remarked, "What, that old-timer? I'll lick him with one punch."[99] Donovan vowed to make Jack regret saying that for the rest of his life. Many would argue that he did.

Donovan, the boxing instructor at the New York Athletic Club, was the former middleweight champion and had fought many a great battle in his time. One of the most legendary was with William McClellan. The men met several times over their ring careers, but on August 18, 1879, they met at Platt's Hall in San Francisco in a firecracker of a bout that lasted ninety-four or ninety-six rounds—varying sources report each. The affair was a seesaw battle in which each man took and relinquished control during the nearly four-hour contest. Much to the dissatisfaction of the large assemblage, referee William Barnes declared the bout a draw just past 1:00 a.m.[100] "These two men battled at the middleweight limit in California for ninety-six rounds, at the end of which time the affair was declared a draw."[101]

In the weeks before the Dempsey-Donovan encounter anticipation grew among fight fans as rumors of bad feelings between the combatants continued to surface. "Donovan, once the champion middleweight of America, felt aggrieved, it is said, because of the rapidly growing popularity of Dempsey, added to which the story runs that the latter on one or two occasions treated the former in a very indifferent, if not supercilious, way. The blood of Donovan's couldn't stand that...."[102]

There was a wide variety of opinion over the contest. Referring to this bout, the *Brooklyn Eagle* commented that Donovan "ought to go down easily, for he is old and slow and short of wind and has no reason at all for challenging such a man as Dempsey, except spite, which he ought to suppress, as he gave the middleweight champion serious provocation during the Dempsey-Reagan fight."[103]

Donovan began his training in earnest in October with his sessions being supervised by Denny Butler. Butler was a talented athlete who was famous as a boxer, world-class swimmer and fight manager.[104]

Jack trained in Rockaway Beach where his preparation consisted chiefly of ten-mile runs, work on the heavy bag and swims in the ocean. The regimen was consistent, but only halfhearted. Dempsey was only going through the motions and he erred significantly by not taking Donovan seriously.

During his time training for the Donovan contest much continued to be said about matching Jack with both Jake Kilrain and Charley Mitchell. Dempsey reiterated on more than one occasion that he was willing to meet either or both. In October it was rumored that Dempsey was the "unknown" fighter who would meet Kilrain in the coming months.[105] In early November an offer was reportedly extended by a prominent New York sport to provide a $5,000 purse for a finish fight between Dempsey and Mitchell. Mitchell had arrived in New York in late October but was insistent that he was only in the States to see to some real estate, not to fight. Kilrain supported Mitchell's statement as he told the press that while Mitchell would be in New York for some time and was in terrific condition, "Charley is not here for any fistic honors this time. He has come here to look after some property and will not enter the ring."[106]

Dempsey told the *New York World* that he was willing to take on Mitchell on any terms and was more than happy to fight him for the proposed $5,000 purse in either New York or San Francisco.[107] In mid–November Mitchell stated that he had no plans or interest in fighting Dempsey or anyone else. "I don't want to fight just now," said Mitchell, "as I am rather tired of that kind of business. Fighting has no particular charm for me were it not for the money that is made out of it." Mitchell added, "To get a reputation is what I have been after and that I have got. I can make more money in one month traveling through the country than my 'bit' of a $5,000 stake fight amounts to and not get a scratch on my face. Let those fight that want to and I will look on."[108] Despite the offers by Dempsey and calls to the ring made by multiple newspapers and most of the fight fraternity, it seems that Mitchell was not interested in entering the ring with the Nonpareil.

On November 6, former U.S. Senator Benjamin Harrison was elected to the presidency. Harrison, the grandson of former President William Henry Harrison, defeated the incumbent President Grover Cleveland. While carrying almost 100,000 fewer popular votes than Cleveland, Harrison carried the Electoral College 233 to 168, thus unseating his opponent. The major issue in the campaign had been the tariff, with Harrison championing the side of the high tariff and protectionism and Cleveland squarely in the free trade camp.

The night of the Dempsey-Donovan fight finally came and speculation about the contest ran high. The Palace Rink was located near the Grand Street Ferry in the Williamsburg section of Brooklyn. "The Palace Rink is an ancient skating hall. The stage is at the upper end, and the ring was fully twenty-eight feet square—large enough for any pugilists."[109] "The hall was gaily decorated with red, white and blue streamers, but many of them were pulled down by adventurous spectators who climbed out on the chords of the rafters the better to view the contest."[110] The Rink was filled to capacity with over 2,500 patrons each of whom had paid between $1 and $5 per ticket. It was agreed that win, lose or draw, Dempsey would receive sixty-five percent of the gate to Donovan's thirty-five. It was also agreed that the men would wear four-ounce gloves.

Many notable sporting men and fighters were present as well as numerous businessmen and local officials. Perhaps the most noteworthy was the Marquess of Queensberry himself. He had arrived from San Francisco a week before and had paid his respects to Richard Fox. He was anxious to see Dempsey before sailing back to England. The master of ceremonies, Steve O'Donnell, soon got things going as he introduced the first bout of the evening.

Four preliminaries preceded the main event. Billy Hart and Jack (Frank?) Boyd were up first followed by Frank Chrysler and Jack Shanley, Brooklyn Jimmy Carroll and Ed Connors and finally Jack Shea and Dempsey's old antagonist Jack Boylan.

Boyd and Hart, both lightweights, were evenly matched and all business. The men mixed it up from the start, both landing heavily with their punches and each giving as good as they got. The final round saw the crowd on their feet as the two pugilists stood toe to toe trading blows. Boyd did all of the leading, but Hart landed more often, including several hard-cross counters that gave him the nod. The crowd was no less pleased with the Chrysler-Shanley bout, in which both men fought furiously, but Shanley landed the heavier blows and took the bout.

Connors and Carroll, middleweights, fought three rounds of solid action. "[They] went at each other like wild bulls and hit the very hardest they knew how from the call of time." "They came out like lions, and their arms flew till the air seemed to be filled with revolving wheel spokes." "They showed up magnificently and made a hurricane finish."[111] The fight was appropriately judged a draw.

The final preliminary included Shea and Boylan. Shea was young and enthusiastic, throwing hard and frequent punches, but with little effect. Boylan, who had given Dempsey a run for his money twice in 1883, was simply too ring savvy for the young man. Boylan took some pity and pulled his punches, mostly boxing his opponent about the ears and doing just enough to get the win and leave an impression on young Shea.

The main bout of the evening was scheduled to start around 10:00 p.m., but the men waited for close to an hour to enable actor and comedian Nat Goodwin and his party of friends to make their way over to Brooklyn from Manhattan where Goodwin was playing in a vaudeville act.[112] During the wait, Denny Butler addressed the crowd and asked them on behalf of Donovan and Dempsey to refrain from smoking during the rest of the evening. Jack DeMott of the New York Athletic Club gave a lecture on athletics and its benefits. He then described how Donovan and Dempsey would use only defensive tactics and bore no ill will towards one another. This drew waves of laughter from the assembled. Finally, Dempsey's brother Martin and a young volunteer wrestled.

At 10:50 p.m., with Goodwin and his friends settled in their seats, the fighters made their way into the ring. Much uncertainty surrounded the choice of a referee as one nominee after another declined to serve. Dempsey and Donovan had agreed that they wanted and trusted "Handsome" Pat Sheedy, but when asked by O'Donnell to serve, Sheedy refused. "Not for the world," Sheedy replied. "They are both friends of mine and I want to keep them so." He also indicated that he and Dempsey had recently had words and he would not want Jack or anyone else to think him biased towards Donovan. When told that it was Dempsey who had suggested his name, Sheedy still replied firmly, "I can't help it, I won't act."[113] Finally, at the request of both fighters, well known sporting manager Billy O'Brien consented to serve as the third man in the ring. Ed Plummer was named timekeeper. Dempsey also consented to the use of four-ounce gloves.

With the spectators now in-house and the referee chosen, it was now time for the main event. Donovan was the first to jump over the ropes. His lean muscles, smooth, unwrinkled face and graceful visage made him look younger than his forty-one years. Only a gleam of gray in his carefully brushed hair betrayed his age. The professor stood 5'8" and weighed in at 149 pounds. He wore a moustache and looked natty in white knee breeches, red knee stockings and black fighting shoes. As he sat in his chair in his corner being rubbed down by Denny Butler and Tom Lees, he told his seconds that he was fighting for the old timers that night. In addition to Lees and Butler, Donovan had his brother Jerry, the former 140-pound champion of America, in his corner.

Dempsey then came in to the arena to the great cheers of the crowd. At 5'8" Jack weighed in at 147 pounds. His pale, thin face always drew a sharp contrast to his finely muscled body. He wore his famous blue trunks and the kerchief around his waist that he had worn in all his fights. Jack was seconded by Gus Tuthill and Denny Costigan.

Ring legend and boxing instructor "Professor" Mike Donovan.

Dempsey was quiet in his corner while Donovan smiled and joked in his. A reporter at ringside commented, "Donovan was the embodiment of fire and high spirit and aggressiveness and Dempsey of quietness, modesty and invincible courage."[114]

At eleven o'clock, the fighters met at the center of the twenty-four-foot ring (although Donovan remembered it at twenty-eight feet) and shook hands to a standing ovation from the crowd. The men returned to their corners and time was called as the fight began.

Donovan started things quickly, launching a blow at Jack's stomach that the Nonpareil avoided by hopping back. Undeterred, Donovan shot a left at Dempsey's head that Jack blocked, but he followed this up with another that found its mark. The stiff punch caught Jack off guard, but he was even more shocked when the Professor landed a combination to the head and face. Dempsey quickly righted himself and fired back with a strong right to Donovan's stomach, much to his supporters' delight. He then continued his two-fisted attack, landing again and again on Donovan's ear, nose and jaw. Donovan withstood the onslaught like a stone wall against the wind. According to noted referee Charley White, "The first round brought forth the most beautiful exhibition of feinting, sidestepping and ducking that I have ever looked upon."[115] Dempsey landed two heavy shots to the professor's mouth, and an angry Donovan responded with a solid shot, square on Dempsey's nose. The remainder of the round was full of heavy action with both men landing and blocking punches, but the old veteran Donovan landed more heavy blows and exhibited greater defensive skills, thus gaining a slight nod for the round.

In the second round, Donovan again pressed his opponent. He fired a missile at Jack but missed and Dempsey countered with another sharp pop on his opponent's mouth and another on the neck. Donovan seethed with anger and planted a heavy right-hand blow to Dempsey's neck. When he swung again, Jack ducked, spun and retreated. Donovan was on him like a cat, and when he caught Dempsey, he showered the Nonpareil with punches to the head and body. In defense, Jack swung at the professor, landing a left on Donovan's head, but missing on other attempts. Undeterred, Donovan pursued Dempsey with vigor. He landed a direct shot on the Nonpareil's face, causing Jack to retreat to avoid further punishment. Dempsey turned to cough and Donovan pounced, landing hard on both Jack's mouth and neck. This infuriated Dempsey who lit into Donovan, landing crushing lefts to his mouth and eye with no return. The men then fought at close quarters for the remainder of the round. While Dempsey landed many good shots, the Professor did as well and in the opinion of many in the arena, Donovan was winning the fight.

As the third round commenced, Jack knew that he had to take charge or risk losing the bout. He came out of the blocks quickly, shooting a powerful left that Donovan turned away. Both men fired off volleys of vicious lefts and rights, but most were deftly blocked. Each landed blows to the neck and stomach. Dempsey then "gave Donovan a pile driving smash on the nose, another behind the ear and another on the mouth, three beauties, with no return."[116] By the middle of the round, both men were landing punches at a rapid rate, but Dempsey was a shade busier and took the round.

In the fourth round, Donovan came out of his corner looking fresh. He energetically fired an opening volley but failed to land. Jack then rushed him and landed a left and a right. Donovan retreated with Dempsey in full pursuit and landing multiple blows. Donovan steeled himself to the onslaught, stood his ground and managed to turn the tide, fighting Jack into the corner where he fired several volleys, one of which caught Dempsey hard in the midsection. When Jack countered, the professor deftly moved his head and the missile glanced off the back of his skull, registering no discernable effect. Dempsey landed hard on Donovan's ribs, but Mike returned fire, landing twice on the side of Jack's head. When the two fell together in a clinch, Dempsey tried a right uppercut, but the crafty Donovan sensed it coming and backed away, letting the blow fall harmlessly in the air. The men continued to trade blows and wrestle for the remainder of the chapter, each displaying strong punching and defensive skills. The New York Herald described the action this way: "To the end of this round there was much science shown and the stopping was of the most scientific order."[117]

The furious action and the closeness of the contest had the crowd "intensely excited" during the intermission between the fourth and fifth rounds. Both fighters leaped up and met at mid-ring as the fifth began. Donovan soon connected with a solid left to Jack's body and Dempsey returned fire with a combination to the professor's head. Dempsey attempted to score a knockout blow with two straight rights to his opponent's face that were described as "regular pile drivers' so clean and sharp that the crowd gasped almost in unison. Donovan rallied splendidly, and to the end of the round delivered effective blows and had a decided lead on points on Jack."[118] The round ended with Donovan landing a sharp body blow on Dempsey.

As the sixth and final round began, both fighters knew it was still anyone's contest. This round would decide everything. Donovan took a swing at Jack but was short of his mark and Dempsey countered with a wicked left that the professor blocked. Jack then followed up with a smashing left to his opponent's mouth. He then struck Mike on the jaw and a fierce exchange followed, with Donovan catching blows on his neck, eye and mouth and Jack on the stomach and ear. During the round, blood was seen on the Nonpareil's mouth. Donovan then sought to land a combination to Jack's head catching him first with a left in the face and then on the neck. Jack responded with a terrific shot to the eye that staggered Donovan, but the professor was not weakening a bit. Dempsey kept up the pace and despite the age differential, Donovan stayed with him all the way. The professor and the Nonpareil stood toe to toe in the middle of the ring and traded shots to the head and body in terrific exchanges as the spectators grew wild with excitement. At the end of three minutes, time was called and the battle done.

Referee O'Brien judged the bout a draw, calling it one of the greatest fights he had ever witnessed. According to Richard Fox, O'Brien's decision, when "taking everything into consideration was the only decision he could give, for neither was defeated. Both could have fought on indefinitely."[119]

An ebullient Donovan, obviously well pleased with his performance, went over to mingle with the crowd where he shook hundreds of hands. Dempsey was a bit disappointed with the draw. He fought reasonably well, but had not bested his opponent in any way, and there were a good many in the crowd who felt that Donovan should have gotten the nod. By many accounts, the professor surprised and, some would argue, defeated the "out of shape" Dempsey, who most likely did not take Donovan seriously. The New York Herald stated flatly the fight "was declared a draw, but the thousands who witnessed it know that however the affair goes upon record and whatever the younger man's lack of condition, he was emphatically bested by a man who was fifteen years older."[120] The New York World supported the draw, but praised Donovan's work, "Never before did Dempsey meet so great a general or so skillful a boxer as Donovan, and that Mike did not secure the decision was entirely due to a strong rally by Dempsey in the last round. From the start Donovan did all the leading."[121] The 2,500 enthusiasts piled out into the cold night air, well pleased with what they had just witnessed.

Dempsey believed that he could defeat the talented but much older man without a great deal of difficulty. Unfortunately for Dempsey this was not the case. Instead of taking Donovan seriously and training hard, Jack "tried to play with him and got a terrible pounding. He had found a man who could hit him at last. Still he could not believe that Donovan was his equal, and it was not till the fourth round that he began to fight his hardest. By that time, he was convinced that he was facing a man who was his equal in science and skill and cunning. Donovan had given him some powerful surprises."[122]

There was, of course, immediate speculation around a rematch. Jack said he would be open to a second fight with Donovan, but he doubted it would occur. Donovan, in an interview from his home at 1101 Tenth Avenue, said that he would love the chance to meet Dempsey again and prove that he was Jack's master. "On the night of the match Dempsey was licked before he came on the stage and Dempsey knew it. He was afraid of me. I hit him whenever I liked and I can do it again." Donovan added, however, that he might not be able to meet Dempsey again due to constraints from his employer. He relayed that "the day after the last match the president of the Athletic Club came to me and said. 'Now, Mike, we want you to stop. We need all your time at the club and cannot permit you to box in public again.'"[123] Dempsey hearing this simply laughed at Donovan's claims and commented on the convenience of the excuse provided by the club president.

Regardless of the level of truth or confidence Donovan had in his winning a rematch, his job at the club was of primary concern to him, and understandably so. He was 41 years old, the sole provider for his wife and six young children and he obviously enjoyed his job, for he would hold the position until he retired in 1914 and would remain with the club in an emeritus status until his death in 1918. After his engagement with Dempsey, many of Donovan's backers at the New York Athletic Club "are in such ecstasy over the great showing he made that they are booming him for an increase in his salary of 50 per cent." Donovan received much glory for his performance against Dempsey, but after all expenses were paid, he made just $16.25 for his trouble. He did, however, gain a good measure of satisfaction with his terrific showing against the Nonpareil, which in the end may have been more important than a big payday. He believed that he had bested Dempsey and many in the arena also saw it that way. According to the *New York Herald*, "The referee called it a draw, claiming it was one of the grandest battles he ever saw—and he's an old-timer—but two-thirds of the audience and many of the fighters present claimed Donovan was the winner."[124] Many of those who gave Dempsey the edge did so only by a slight margin and some on the fact that Dempsey's blows were the heaviest of the bout.[125]

After the bout with Donovan, Jack entertained a number of friends at Frey's Hotel in Rockaway Beach. Dempsey and his family then traveled north to the Finger Lakes region and spent some time at Raquette Lake in the Adirondack Mountains of upstate New York. Jack wanted to relax and spend several weeks in the mountains fishing and shooting. Before leaving for his trip Dempsey added that he intended to work hard during his time at the lake and return to New York in top condition. "I was in poor fix when I met Donovan, but I have no one to blame for that." Jack gave the professor full credit. "Donovan was in excellent order and he deserves all credit for it."[126] Dempsey hinted that after he regained his form and conditioning he would welcome a second match with Donovan.

During this time, the Athletic Club of San Francisco again offered a purse of $5,000 for Dempsey and Mitchell to fight a finish bout at their club. Once again, Dempsey was ready and willing, but Mitchell made no commitment.

In a letter to the *Philadelphia Press* on November 23, Charley Mitchell, who was touring with Jake Kilrain in a theatrical engagement, called Jack out once again, saying that Dempsey was not in his class in the prize ring and that he could knock him out within eight Queensberry rounds or he would give Jack $1,000. Speaking with reporters in the lobby of Philadelphia's Continental Hotel, Mitchell contended that "Dempsey is doing his talking now, but if he ever raises sufficient courage to quit his gang and agree to a fight where the best man will win, this country will be without a middleweight champion." Mitchell continued his rant against Jack by saying, "Those who cry cur the longest and loudest are generally the ones to first display the streak of yellow dog when put to the test. They can bark much louder than they can bite." Mitchell then told a wholly fanciful story about how he had soundly defeated Sullivan in their recent battle in France. He spun a ridiculous tale of how he defeated Sullivan and inflicted the greater of the fight's punishment on the Boston Strong Boy. Mitchell stated that Sullivan had one black and closed eye, the other badly swollen, his lower lip and left ear both badly cut and bleeding. Press reports from the time indicate that both men had facial swelling and bruising but agree that the Briton had done all he could to avoid the champion. They also state that while Mitchell did draw first blood in the eighth round, it was only after Sullivan had already laid him on the ground. Mitchell then claimed that the only reason the bout ended in a draw was that his second, a man called Baldock, was bribed by Sullivan's desperate friends to enter the ring and call for a draw. He claimed that there were several Bostonians who would verify this, but when pressed, Mitchell refused to call on them to testify or even reveal their identities, because he claimed, "I think it's well enough to let the dead rest."[127]

There is little if any truth in Mitchell's contentions that his second was paid off to throw in the sponge, that he won the bout or that he avoided punishment while administering a severe beating on his opponent. While Sullivan was exhausted from chasing the Briton around the ring and did have some facial bruising, the only real damage he suffered came from Mitchell's sliding into Sullivan's legs with cleats high. Most of those who attended the contest severely condemned Mitchell both for his running away from and for his sliding into Sullivan. Most agreed that Mitchell deserved a draw at best and that he did not so much fight as survive. His best showing was an example of how not to lose a fight. There was also general agreement that Mitchell would have had no chance against Sullivan under the Queensberry Rules. To Mitchell's remarks, Sullivan smiled and responded that he would meet Mitchell again at any time over the next five weeks the Briton preferred and in any city in the country that Mitchell chose. Asked if he thought that Charley would accept his challenge Sullivan smiled and responded that he could not see why he would. "He has shown himself to be afraid of Dempsey...."[128]

The *Brooklyn Eagle* made clear their opinion of Mitchell's rebuke of Dempsey. "The patronizing tone Mitchell adopts is regarded as amusing. Outside of his drawn battle with a dilapidated Sullivan and his drawn sparring contest with Dominick McCaffrey, whom Dempsey worsted in the same kind of contest, Mitchell has no record, while the man whom he affects to despise is recognized all over the world as a wonder." The paper went on to say that Mitchell's claims that he was superior to Dempsey were absurd, and that his offer was widely seen as a ploy to offset the prevalent belief that he was afraid to meet Jack in a fight to the finish. "He was chased out of San Francisco by Dempsey, and in Chicago and St. Paul and New York a year and a half ago Dempsey publicly shook money under Mitchell's nose and plainly challenged him to make a match."[129] When asked about the efforts of Mr. W. R. Vice of the San Francisco Athletic Club to bring about a fight between Mitchell and Dempsey, Sullivan added, "Yes, and Mitchell's attitude shows that he is a big blow!" Sullivan continued, "Jack Dempsey is ready to fight him, but he will not fight." In conclusion, Sullivan said, "You will find that I am right when I say Mitchell will not fight anybody."[130] Given the copious fistic talents of Mitchell it really makes very little sense that he so steadfastly refused to fight Dempsey, but at every turn, he seemed to come up with an excuse to avoid him.

Many were anxious to make the fight, including the San Francisco A.C.'s Vice and well-known horse racing owner Phillip Dwyer. It was also reported that Dempsey sent a wire to Mitchell, now in Baltimore, asking him to agree to a fight for $5,000 a side. Once again, no reply was received. Vice was authorized by the San Francisco A.C. to offer the men a purse of between $5,000 and $7,000 with the only stipulations being that the fight be to a finish and held in their club's rooms. "The sporting people of the Pacific coast are anxious to have the superiority of one of these men established."[131] Vice said that he had received a letter from Mitchell before he sailed from England stating that he would meet Dempsey after his arrival in America, but after the Englishman arrived in New York, he wrote to Vice stating that the fight would have to wait as his "affairs" were in an unsettled state and he could give no definite answer regarding a bout. Vice said, "California people feel kindly toward Dempsey and will bet that he is an easy winner." Vice added that he was determined to arrange the bout. "I will meet with Jack the night of November 26 in New York and together we will see Mitchell. I am confident that I can offer them inducements that will cause them to sign the articles of agreement."[132] Dempsey might have agreed, but Mitchell remained non-committal. As one sportswriter put it, "Dempsey accepted the offer of the club when it was $2,000 less than it is now and unless Mitchell follows his example, but one conclusion can be drawn from his refusal, and that is that he feels in his bones that Dempsey is his master."[133]

In a published article from November 25, Jack responded to an offer of a bout with Charley Mitchell and even came off his demand for a finish fight. "I read the notice and feel quite thankful to Charley Mitchell for his magnanimous offer. I will bet him $5,000 that he can't stop me in eight rounds. He has made a proposition and he has an unlimited amount of cash, he can well afford to stand the racket. He had better consider the proposition of the California Athletic Club. If he is so confident why does he not accept that offer of $5,000 and I think they will give more than that." Dempsey added, "I have said that I would fight him and am willing to do so and will do my best to win."[134]

Upon his return from the Adirondacks on December 8, Jack addressed a crowd in front of his saloon on Front Street. He looked to be rested and in good health after his time away. As had been the case throughout the year, the subject of Charley Mitchell came up. When asked about Mitchell's offer to fight, Dempsey responded, "I don't think it's worth talking about. Mitchell must be either an ass or a fool to offer me $1,000 to meet him in a house that would net him perhaps $10,000." When asked if he would meet Mitchell to a finish, Dempsey replied wearily, "Yes, if I ever get the chance. The offer of the California Athletic Club is satisfactory to me, except that I think all championship matches should be fought under London prize ring rules. They always have been. I don't know that the California Athletic Club wants to have us meet under Queensberry rules. I hope not. But anyhow, I am ready to meet Mitchell. The Golden Gate Athletic Club of San Francisco has also offered to put up a purse, so Mitchell has more than one opportunity to meet me."[135]

The running feud between the two men seemed to have no end. Dempsey continued to lay out challenge after challenge, each for $5,000 a side or more, to which Mitchell responded with offensively unreasonable counter proposals. A reporter for the *Chicago Herald*, pointing to Mitchell's clearly financially unacceptable challenges, commented that "it is plainly evident that Charley Mitchell is not nearly so anxious to engage in a game of fisticuffs with Jack Dempsey as he would like to have the public believe."[136] Sullivan, in an outpouring of his own powerful dislike of Mitchell, commented, "There is a middleweight named Jack Dempsey, who, with $5,000 in hard cash, drove Charley Mitchell out of Chicago, and Dempsey never pretended to be able to whip me. Dempsey's money was ready for months to make a match with Mitchell, but he always found an excuse to back out. Mitchell would not fight a man who was his equal, but always wanted to fight the man on top, whom I claim was myself. By so doing he had nothing to lose, but, on the other hand, had lots to gain by defeating me."[137]

Mitchell soon went to New York to promote the proposed bout between Sullivan and Kilrain, and he promised to put up a large part of that gate, but in a lengthy press conference at the *Police Gazette* offices, he managed to say little of substance and he produced no financial backing for that fight or his proposed bout with Dempsey. "Another act of the pugilistic farce was seen today, when Charles Mitchell did four hours talking and kept locked the combination safe in which he has his money."[138] Mitchell talked about the fight and how he would provide the purse, but when it was pointed out that Sullivan had already put up $5,000 for a bout with either Mitchell or Kilrain and the funds were being held at the *New York Clipper* offices, the Briton began backpedaling. Mitchell commented that if he went to the *Clipper* offices and put down his $5,000 he would be arrested for accepting the fight, but if they could meet in say, Canada, a fight could be arranged. All many saw was simply another excuse and another dodge.

When the subject turned to Dempsey, Mitchell started in with his "I didn't come here to fight" and "I have enough money" lines. He stated that he was tired of hearing about the California Club's offer and would have nothing more to say about it. Representatives of the *Police Gazette* then produced a just-received telegram from Secretary Jameson of the Golden Gate Athletic Club of San Francisco that read, "Dempsey and Mitchell can fight here. Will give $5,250 for them." Asked for his response to the latest offer, Mitchell responded noncommittally, "I'll fight him ten rounds, but I didn't come here to fight." He then abruptly left the office without putting up the money to back Kilrain.[139] Jack commented that he was ready to fight Mitchell to a finish and was ready to accept the offer from San Francisco.[140] The next day Mitchell was asked by a reporter about both fights and he responded, "You know I would rather spar Jack Dempsey with gloves in Chicago than meet him in any other way or place." Now, with a concrete offer and agreement from Dempsey, Mitchell suddenly claimed that Chicago was the place. Regarding the proposed Sullivan-Kilrain bout, he again hid behind a Canadian meeting with Sullivan and his backers and not a quick, in town trip to the *New York Clipper* offices.[141] This was typical of Mitchell's responses. Try as he might, Dempsey could neither quiet Mitchell nor get him to agree to a reasonable fight offer. Clearly, Mitchell was more interested in jawing than fighting.

Jack hit the stage once again in December as one of the main draws in a variety show at Hyde & Behman's Theatre. The theater was a large brick building that stood on the west side of Adams Street, between Fulton Street and Myrtle Avenue in Brooklyn. In addition to serving twice as a theater, it had been used as a market and a temporary morgue at the time of the 1876 Brooklyn Theater fire in which more than one hundred and fifty lives were lost. Hyde & Behman's Theatre itself was lost to a fire in the early morning hours of June 10, 1890, when a fast-burning conflagration reduced the place to rubble.

Appearing with Rice's Vaudeville Syndicate of Popular Artists, Dempsey's role once again was to spar several gloved rounds with Denny Costigan at each show. The two were to give an exhibition of the "manly art." After an evening of singing, juggling, comedy routines and acrobatics, Jack and Denny took to the stage.

Of the first performance it was reported that "Jack Dempsey, the distinguished pugilist, was greeted at Hyde & Behman's Theater last night by an immense audience that sat patiently, even gleefully, through two and a half hours of miscellaneous entertainment in order to see him punch the head of one Dennis Costigan."[142] The bouts were tame but active as the men would wallop each other, then acknowledge each blow with a laugh. Costigan, Jack's trainer and close friend, was overweight and out of shape, but he could still fight and he gave as good as he got. "Their set-tos were loudly applauded."[143]

In a chorus that was getting monotonous, on the evening of December 12, Billy O'Brien representing Charley Mitchell called on Dempsey. He stated that his purpose was to make a match between Mitchell and the Nonpareil for ten rounds in either Brooklyn or Jersey City. The two spoke for over an hour, but Jack was firm that before an East Coast bout could be arranged the pair must accept the California Athletic Club's offer of $10,000 for a finish fight in their auditorium. Dempsey stated, "I guarantee Mr. Mitchell that I will meet him in Brooklyn or Jersey City in a ten-round contest after our battle has been decided in San Francisco." The sum offered by the California Club was an enormous amount for the time—the largest ever offered up to that time and Dempsey refused to risk it by meeting Mitchell for a pittance prior to securing that payday.[144]

On December 15, Jack celebrated his twenty-sixth birthday, and his friends packed the theater that evening. After his sparring match with Costigan at Hyde & Behman's Theatre, Jack was presented with a floral arrangement with a banner that read, "To Our Champion, Jack Dempsey, December 15, 1888." After the show, the company returned to the Metropolitan Hotel for dinner and a long evening of drinks, songs and stories. The hotel was decorated with flowers, flags and streamers and an orchestra played throughout the evening, with the party not breaking up until the wee hours of Sunday morning.

Jack went back upstate to Raquette Lake in the Adirondacks for a few days around Christmas to relax and enjoy the tranquility and the mountain air. Upon his return, he was met by friends at his saloon on Front Street. He was asked what the New Year would bring for his fistic career. Dempsey again reiterated that he was anxious to meet British middleweight champion Charley Mitchell. Jack stated that he would prefer to engage Mitchell at the California Athletic Club because he had promised the management of the club that he would do so when he fought again on the Pacific Slope.

Dempsey was selected as timekeeper for Jack McAuliffe during the latter's December 26 bout with Jake Hyams of London in a ten-round glove contest at the Palace Rink in Brooklyn's Williamsburg section. After gaining control of the bout fairly early on, McAuliffe spun Hyams around with a flurry of murderous lefts and rights to the head and body and knocked him out in the ninth round in front of 8,000 enthusiastic fight fans.

Eighteen eighty-eight had been a busy time for the Nonpareil both in and out of the ring. Despite a mediocre showing against Donovan, Jack met with great success in the ring and his reputation continued to grow. Dempsey was in heavy demand on the touring, stage and exhibition circuits and seemed to be constantly on the road. On the downside, he had lost his dearly beloved mother over the summer. Despite that difficult loss, it is fair to say that 1888 was a pinnacle year for the Nonpareil.

1889—The Nonpareil Is Brought to Earth

The year 1889 began just as 1888 had ended—on a contentious note for Dempsey and English boxer Charley Mitchell. On January 3, Jack received a dispatch from Gus Tuthill that Mitchell was leaving the United States very soon and there was no prospect of a fight being arranged.

Jack who had to be exhausted with Mitchell, repeated to a reporter from the *Baltimore American* that he believed that Mitchell was afraid to meet him. He complained bitterly about what he felt were Mitchell's now yearlong series of cowardly excuses and clearly unacceptable counter offers. "His excuse this time is a disabled hand. That is a good one. Two years ago, however, in Chicago, when he was in the peak of condition, and doing sparring matches with Burke at the Battery D Hall, I met him in his dressing room one night, and even went so far as to slap him across the face with $2,500 in bills and dared him to cover it to a finish." Jack continued, "The California Athletic Club offered a big purse some few weeks ago if Mitchell and I would agree to meet in their rooms. It was a big bait, and I would have loved dearly to have gotten possession of a greater portion of it. You all know Mitchell's excuse."[1]

Elaborating, Jack reiterated that his main interest in pugilism was not his love of the sport, but rather that it was a lucrative business. He added that he had fought enough battles in his life and was only anxious to fight one more—against Mitchell.

Mitchell for his part responded during a visit to the New York offices of the *Police Gazette*. He complained about unfair press coverage and called Dempsey a "rat" who was simply trying to gain fame on the strength of the Englishman's name. Given the fact that Dempsey was—save for John L. Sullivan—already the most well-known and respected prize fighter in the world, this was a foolish, even ridiculous, claim. Mitchell completely disavowed the story of the slap in the face in Chicago and claimed that Dempsey actually ran to get a revolver from a desk drawer to protect himself when Mitchell threatened to punch him that night. This is also a scurrilous claim on Mitchell's part. In the first place, Jack never feared a fight with any man and second, how would he possibly have known the location of a hidden and loaded revolver in Charley Mitchell's Chicago dressing room?

Dempsey was in good company that day, however, as Mitchell also cursed and condemned Sullivan to the *Police Gazette* representatives. The Englishman hurled ridiculous epithets, calling John L. a "big bluffer" who dodged fights by having fits of drunkenness and illness. He added that the Boston Strong Boy was "a 'loafer' and a 'first class good for nothing'" who could no longer get a drink in Boston unless he bought it himself.[2] Sullivan was indeed given to fits of drunkenness, but he never dodged a fight in his life—drunk or sober.

When news came in mid–January that Mitchell was on the verge of sailing back to England, Dempsey was incredulous. He wrote a letter authorizing his backer Jimmy Wakely to go to any lengths to make a match with Mitchell. Wakely made it known that he was putting up a $1,000 forfeit for a $5,000 a side match to be held on the same card as the proposed Sullivan-Kilrain battle. Mitchell was apprised of the challenge and responded during a conference at New York's Hoffman House that he was not afraid to meet Dempsey and proof of that fact was that he had outfought Sullivan in France and did so with a broken hand. He then trotted out the old story that he was duped by one of his seconds into settling for a draw and that the public knew this to be true. It would appear that Mitchell thought that if he repeated this story often enough that people might start to believe it as fact. The broken hand element was a new wrinkle in the story, and it became a convenient excuse for not fighting. "I will state that I have been endeavoring to take such care of my hand as would enable it to get strong, so that I could risk it in a fight to a finish, but I regret that after consulting with one of the foremost surgeons in the United States I cannot make a fight to a finish."[3] Mitchell continued, saying that his match with Sullivan should be proof of his fearlessness and that if he had "the tools" to do so, he would indeed do so.

On January 2, Jack sparred four rounds with James McNamee of the Hornbacher Athletic Club. In describing McNamee, it was said that the Brooklyn man was "a handsome young fellow and knows a lot about boxing. He has sparred frequently with Jack Dempsey and has proved himself worthy of meeting good men."[4] In addition to the Hornbacher, McNamee often fought out of the New York and Manhattan Athletic Clubs.

McNamee continued to fight for a number of years and gained some local fame. He was nearly killed by a powerful right-hand blow to the back of the head thrown not by a pugilist in the ring, but by Herman Lyons, a lodging house watchman who had gotten into a scuffle with an inebriated McNamee in the wee hours of August 15, 1896. Lyons was arrested and McNamee was taken to the Hudson Street hospital.

From New Year's through mid–January, Jack and Denny Costigan traveled with Rice's vaudevillians around the East and Midwest. On December 31, the troupe began a week-long engagement at Kernan's Theatre in Washington, D.C. His opponent on that first night was not Denny Costigan, but a large local man named George Northridge who was in reality more of a wrestler than a pugilist. The papers reported that "a local heavyweight boxer named Northridge stood up for three rounds before Jack Dempsey last night at Kernan's Theatre." The match was a decidedly one-sided affair with Dempsey hitting his opponent pretty much as he wished and avoiding most of the local man's punches, but "Northridge evidenced considerable skill for a novice."[5] Northridge would capitalize on his newfound fame by fighting for a $200 purse just three weeks later when he met a gentleman by the name of Childs for the Maryland and District of Columbia heavyweight championship. Northridge apparently got the better of Childs during the fight, which was more of a wrestling match than a true prizefight, but he lost by disqualification on a foul during the twenty-second round.[6] "There was more wrestling than actual fighting and Childs was by far the more used up at the finish. The fight lasted 26-minutes." Childs won the championship in the twenty-second round by way of foul.[7] The troupe moved on to Baltimore for another engagement before heading west to Pittsburgh.

On January 14, Rice's vaudevillians were at Harry Williams's Academy in Pittsburgh where the crew spent the balance of the week appearing that Monday followed by shows on Wednesday, Thursday, Friday, twice on Saturday and matinees on Tuesday and Thursday. After the engagement, press reports commented that "Jack Dempsey, the Nonpareil, and Denny Costigan did a big business last week at Pittsburgh. Manager Rice says Dempsey is a great drawing card and very popular."[8]

The show was not all that was on Jack's mind during his first day in the Steel City. Several newspapers carried a letter from Mitchell in which the British pugilist insulted both Dempsey and Sullivan, stating that both men's reputations were overblown and that "there will come a day of reckoning between Jack Dempsey and several others and myself someday, and I will be there, as sure as you are living."[9] By this point, Dempsey had put up with about enough out of the brash Briton. He both telegraphed and posted a letter to one of his backers, James Wakely in New York, once again encouraging him to do all in his power to provoke Charley Mitchell into meeting the Nonpareil in the ring before he left for England. Jack started the letter as follows, "Friend Wakely: I see that Charley Mitchell is going away to England. Now you can do me a great favor by going to him and doing your best to get him to make a match. If necessary, taunt him or blackguard him into making one. I am afraid that the contemptible cur will never come back." He continued by asking Wakely to be certain that Mitchell saw the letter and then respond quickly, for if there was any chance of meeting Mitchell before he left for England, Dempsey would come to New York immediately, even risking "being sued for breach of contract by my manager, Peter Rice."[10] Upon receipt of the messages, Wakely went in search of Mitchell. The Englishman responded that he was sailing that day for England on the *Britannia* and that he was still nursing a damaged left hand, broken in the third round of his fight with Sullivan. Mitchell set sail to England from New York City on January 16.

After Mitchell had returned to England and almost immediately challenged Jem Smith to a bout, the *New York Sun* commented, "Charley Mitchell has, unintentionally perhaps, paid Jack Dempsey the highest compliment one pugilist can pay another short of acknowledging him his superior, by refusing to fight him even a limited number of rounds before spring and then challenging Jem Smith to a twelve-round contest before he was a week in England." This was outstandingly poor of Mitchell, because he and his doctor—E.L. Keys—had claimed in a letter to the editor of the *New York World* on January 15 that his hand was so badly off that surgery would do no good and Mitchell might never enter the ring again.[11] The *Sun* then mused upon the wonderful recuperative powers of the broad Atlantic Ocean.[12]

The *Sun* had also commented earlier in January that Mitchell had no one to blame but himself for his bad press in the United States. He had come to America with the prestige of giving Sullivan a very difficult fight and earning a draw, but upon his arrival, he did nothing but complain about that decision and attempt to belittle Dempsey. After attacking these two popular fistic idols and endlessly talking about how he far outclassed both men, Mitchell "then evaded in every way possible a fight with [Dempsey]."[13] The *Police Gazette* observed that "it always takes two to make a bargain and as Dempsey was willing and Mitchell was not willing, the proposed battle between Dempsey and Mitchell will not be consummated."[14] That seems to have summed the monotonous Mitchell affair up very nicely.

Jack was back at home in Williamsburg for a few days in late January to rest and see to his saloon on Front Street. While there he and Costigan attended the Varunas' amateur boxing tournament in the Clermont Avenue Rink on January 23. On January 24 Jack and Costigan traveled to Cleveland and then Cincinnati to continue their engagement with the Rice theatrical company. "Dempsey's tour has been a great success and in every town and city he and Costigan have appeared he has met with tremendous receptions."[15] When questioned about Charley Mitchell by a *New York Sun* reporter, the Nonpareil, certain that there was little left to add, simply smiled and said, "I don't think I could make my position in the Mitchell matter any plainer than I did in my letter to Wakely and which Jimmy made him read." Still smiling, Dempsey quickly changed the subject to the tour. "How about my trip? We are having a good time and showing to big houses. Any eggs? No, nary an egg yet, and I don't expect any," said Jack with a wink.[16]

On January 26, it was reported by *Police Gazette* sporting editor William E. Harding that a biography had been written on Dempsey's life story and would be published later that year. The book was ultimately co-written by Harding and *Police Gazette* publisher Richard K. Fox and was titled *Life and Battles of Jack Dempsey: A Complete History of All the Battles Fought by the Nonpareil.* The biography was an eighty-two-page work with descriptions on Jack's life and fights through that time.

Fox, born in Belfast, Ireland, in 1846, had a lifelong love of journalism. When he was twelve he became an office boy for a religious publication called the *Banner of Ulster*. Several years later Fox joined the staff at the *Belfast News Letter* where he worked in the business office for a dozen years. Fox left Ireland in 1874 with dreams of purchasing and running a newspaper. He landed in New York and three days later, he took a job at the *Wall Street Journal* where he remained for a year. In 1875, he joined the *National Police Gazette* as business manager. By 1876, Fox had saved up enough money that he was able to buy the *Gazette*. He immediately changed the magazine's format and image from that of a scandal sheet into a weekly sports publication that featured boxing. Fox helped popularize boxing in the late nine-

Richard K. Fox wrote the first biography of the Nonpareil, *Life and Battles of Jack Dempsey*, in 1888.

teenth century through his *Police Gazette* coverage of the fight game and through several books written on popular fighters. He is also considered the father of the championship belt after creating and handing out a number of silver, gold and diamond belts to pugilistic champions. While the *Police Gazette* covered many sports and Fox was known as a strong supporter of a wide variety of sporting events, "his intimate friends said that he knew nothing of any game or sport, except boxing."[17] It was said that journalism and boxing were his passions and for all he did for it, boxing never had a better friend.

While the Rice-Star Specialty Company was in Cincinnati, it was reported that on February 1, 1889, Jack had requested of Harry Weldon, sports editor of the *Cincinnati Enquirer*, "a telegram be sent to the California Athletic Club, asking if they would guarantee a purse of $5,000 for a fight with Dominick McCaffrey, at San Francisco."[18] Jack intimated in the telegram that he would agree to almost any terms for a return bout and stated in the telegram, "I would be only too pleased to accept such an offer to fight McCaffrey."[19] The proposed contest was to be a gloved fight to the finish and McCaffrey expressed his willingness to wager large sums in addition to the gate. The club's secretary responded that the board would take up the matter and present their response soon.

By early February, the show was in Buffalo, where Jack and Denny Costigan sparred a three-round exhibition during the first week of that month. During the week, the pair made plans to go to San Francisco with another variety show and give sparring exhibitions. About this time, reports began to circulate that Dempsey would accompany Sullivan and his trainer Jack Hayes to New Orleans in early April to help the Boston Strong Boy ready himself for the upcoming heavyweight championship bout with Jake Kilrain. Hayes commented that Sullivan and he would go to New Orleans around April 1 to begin training for the fight and several publications indicated that the Nonpareil would go with them.[20] However, no immediate comment came from Dempsey, who had not yet been persuaded.

Dempsey and Costigan intended to continue on to Chicago for a few days and then attend the world lightweight championship between old friend Jack McAuliffe and Billy Myer on February 13, at Burche's Opera House in North Judson, Indiana. The McAuliffe-Myer fight lasted sixty-four rounds over four hours and twenty-seven minutes, ending in a draw. The two would meet twice again in 1892. McAuliffe would knock Myer out in fifteen rounds in New Orleans in the first contest and then, three months later in Chicago, the men would fight to a six-round draw.

Jack returned to Brooklyn on February 15, after touring with the Rice vaudeville troupe throughout several upstate cities. He was determined to spend several weeks in town seeing to his saloon as his partner had been ill and needed Jack's assistance. While there, he commented that he had again heard from Mr. Lamartine R. Fulda, the president of the California Athletic Club, who was asking about convenient times to arrange the proposed bout with Dominick McCaffrey. Jack said that he told Fulda, "Any time that could be agreed on between the club and McCaffrey would suit me. So, you see the fight may be considered definitely on. The only trouble previously lay in the fact that we would not fight for a smaller purse than $5,000."[21] Dempsey stated that the dates of a proposed western tour were not solid at that time and that his saloon business should likewise not interfere with his preparations for the proposed bout. Jack added that he had advised McCaffrey against buying a saloon in San Francisco. "He will make more at fighting," said Jack.[22]

On February 25, Jake Kilrain announced in Baltimore that he "positively refused to listen to any proposition looking to a glove contest for scientific points with Jack Dempsey." Kilrain said that he would meet Dempsey in private where police interference would be minimal, or he would fight him over twelve rounds for a purse, but that he feared that a public finish fight would, due to interference, finish in a draw. Kilrain opined that he had "everything to lose and little to gain by such a fight even if the bout were decided in his favor, while Dempsey could lose nothing in defeat and would add to his laurels in case of a draw." Instead, Kilrain was seriously considering an offer to go to England and fight Charley Mitchell.[23]

Talk turned to another Englishman in March when Jem (Ted) Pritchard challenged Jack by cablegram to meet for somewhere between $1,000 and $5,000 a side. Jack was willing and stated so, commenting that he preferred to meet at the Pelican Club, but he also said that he was willing to go to England if necessary to meet Pritchard. "All I want is fair play, and I have confidence enough in the people over there to believe that I will get it."[24] Not everyone agreed. "It appears to me absurd for Dempsey to think of receiving fair play in England when two pugilists bred and born in that country cannot mill for any large sum and receive fair play. Smith was not allowed to defeat Greenfield, neither was Pritchard allowed to conquer Hayes and how can any American who is to battle for a large stake against an Englishman expect to receive fair play?"[25]

Jack stated that if Pritchard was not interested, the offer stood as well for Mitchell, Jem Goode, Toff Wall or any other middleweight in England. Dempsey told a reporter that he feared that the British sportsmen might think poorly of him because of recent comments made by Charley Mitchell. Several British newspapers including the *Licensed Victuallers' Gazette*,[26] had made the assertion that Jack, along with Dominick McCaffrey and John L. Sullivan, was cowardly, out of shape or both, and that a gang of ruffians followed behind Dempsey and caused disruption before, during and after his bouts. This irritated the Nonpareil, of whom the *Pittsburgh Dispatch* commented, "He blames that whelp Mitchell for this assertion."[27]

About this time, Johnny Reagan began challenging for another bout as well. Reports of a $2,000 purse from the Southern California Athletic Club in Los Angeles surfaced and the usual newspaper speculation began to circulate. Dempsey indicated that he was very interested in fighting Reagan again, but not for so low a purse.

Another article that ran about that time was a humorous one about the Nonpareil, his friend and fellow pugilist Mike Cushing and Jack's horse Dan, whom the *New York World* described as "not pretty to look at, but a terror on the road." A further description painted Dan as "a snorting, tail-switching, raw-boned animal and is a perfect terror to all Jack's friends; but, nevertheless, it is a trotter possessed of remarkable speed, and Jack prizes it highly." Managing Dan was a good workout and Dempsey loved to take him for long, brisk drives. He claimed it was as good as hitting the bag for several hours.[28]

Apparently, Dempsey convinced Cushing to join him on a carriage ride through southern Brooklyn. Cushing was wiry, quick and carried a stinging punch. "He looked more like a school-teacher than a fighter but he could handle himself well."[29] When the carriage got out onto a long stretch of open road, Jack gave Mike the left line and kept the right for himself and then, with several whoops, Dan was off. The harder the two athletes pulled on the reigns, the faster the horse went. At one point the carriage apparently sidewiped another and the encounter was described as follows, "Suddenly, there was a smash and the men glanced backward in time to see a stray wheel they had taken off a man's buggy." After an extended time, the carriage came to a stop and the two men, disoriented from the great pace and tired from pulling the reigns and from laughing agreed that it had been a great ride.[30]

Jack accompanied Denny Costigan and Tom Henry to Clifton, New Jersey, where the two were to second Brooklyn pugilist Mike Cushing in his match against British lightweight Harry Bartlett. Jack was cheered and applauded as he entered the arena and was later called upon to flip the gold coin before the bout, allowing the winner of the toss to choose their corner of the ring. Cushing won the toss and later the match when Bartlett withdrew in the fourteenth round.[31]

In mid–March, Dempsey headed to Pennsylvania for several fistic engagements. On March 18, Jack was scheduled to fight Jim Daly, a local fighter in the small, mid–Pennsylvania town of Houtzdale just north of Altoona. I have found absolutely no news of this bout, but it is certain that Dempsey was in the area on that day. On the morning of March 18, Jack refereed a bout near Altoona between Jim Murray of Philadelphia and local fighter James Christian. About two hundred people attended the lightweight match held in the basement of a brewery near the Fountain Inn in Cresson Springs about nine miles west of Altoona. The terms of the fight were Queensberry Rules with skintight gloves, to a finish for $200 and gate receipts. Christian was introduced as the lightweight champion of central Pennsylvania. Both men weighed in at 115 pounds. Christian had the better of the action throughout and Dempsey declared him the winner when the Altoona boy broke Murray's jaw in the fifth round.[32]

A few days later, Jack was back in New York. He had been called as a witness in a lawsuit by attorney David A. Sullivan against Mike Donovan for $122.76 in legal services which Sullivan was claiming were owed to him by Donovan in relation to the previous November's match with Dempsey. Testifying in City Court in Manhattan, Jack stated that Donovan's share of $576 was handed to one of the professor's team members and that there had been no attempt to avoid Sullivan by either Dempsey's camp or Donovan's. Jack also commented that in his six years in boxing, he had never seen a time when it would take $122.76 in legal services to prepare a fighter for a bout.

On March 27, Dempsey and McAuliffe spent the afternoon at the track. The pair attended the card of five thoroughbred races at Clifton Racetrack in New Jersey. By report, "They found it more difficult to hit winners than to make effective upper cuts in a sparring match," but apparently, they saw some terrific racing, including "a splendid finish in the second race."[33]

On March 30, Dempsey and Denny Costigan joined John L. Sullivan, Billy Mahoney and about four hundred other attendees at the Jack Ashton–Joe Lannon prizefight held in Burrillville, an agricultural and mill town in the northwest corner of Rhode Island. The actual location of the fight had been kept secret right up to just before fight time. The venue was ultimately revealed to be the town hall. The closest train stop was a little over a mile away from the fight venue. Coaches were promised to transport the throng but when they were nowhere to be found, the crowd was faced with making a mile-long slog through the dark Rhode Island countryside, still muddy from winter's melting snows. Some of the crowd got lost temporarily, including Joe Lannon, who showed up an hour late to his own bout. Newspaper reporters who were along for the slog described the scene as follows, "The ring was located over a mile away and a bountiful supply of swamp, fences and hills intervened. There was considerable growling at the prospect of a long, dreary walk, but the crowd finally tackled it. The night was calm overhead, but underfoot it was quite muddy." Those who made the mile-long trek witnessed a brutal battle in which both men fought fiercely, but in the nineteenth round, Ashton dropped Lannon with a powerful blow from which Lannon was unable to recover. Ashton was declared the winner by knockout.[34] Dempsey and Costigan paid visits to Brockton and Boston, Massachusetts, after the fight. While there, Jack considered fight options, but also relaxed and "spent the greater part of his short stay in playing billiards with his friends in the Adams House."[35]

On April 11, Dempsey saw a story that the Southern California Athletic Club was offering a purse of $3,000 for a bout between Dempsey and Johnny Reagan. He immediately headed to the *Police Gazette* offices accompanied by Denny Costigan, Tom Evans and Professor Healy. "A messenger was dispatched to find Reagan or his backer Billy Reid, but neither could be found, and after waiting two hours the Nonpareil went to his hotel opposite Fulton Street." He told a reporter that in order to secure a bout with Reagan, he would agree to Queensberry Rules and would concede $1,000 to Reagan, win or lose. Jack added, "There certainly could be nothing fairer than that." Reagan eventually passed on the match, stating that he did not care to meet Dempsey until after he had fought Charley Mitchell in October.[36] Dempsey was disappointed in this response as he was genuinely anxious to meet Reagan again. He told a journalist in March that he would love another match with Reagan. "There is nothing I would like better. My opinion of Johnny Reagan is that he is the best man of his weight there is. Besides being a clever fighter, he is the gamest and pluckiest man I ever fought."[37] Ultimately no rematch with Reagan occurred and some faulted Dempsey for not accepting the terms, but Jack had other plans for larger stakes in mind.

In mid–April, the subject of Charley Mitchell arose again when a dispatch came from well-known New Orleans sporting figure Bud Renaud, who was offering $5,000 for a match between the Englishman and Dempsey in the Crescent City. The fight was to be held under London Rules sometime between January 1 and March 1, 1890. Renaud set the following conditions for the bout: He would choose the venue and keep all gate receipts, Dempsey and Mitchell would train within ten miles of New Orleans and the proposed bout would be to a finish and under the London Prize Ring Rules.[38] Renaud stated that as soon as the match was agreed to and signed by both parties he would deposit the amount of the purse in the bank. "He also guarantees all possible protection and promises to use every effort to secure fair play for both parties."[39] On the night of April 18, Jack received written confirmation of Renaud's offer. When asked about the dispatch, Jack indicated that he was highly interested in Renaud's proposition, but that he seriously doubted Mitchell would agree to the conditions proposed by Renaud. He was correct as, once again, Dempsey was ready to sign articles, but Mitchell backed away from the bout.

During the week of April 15, Jack and Denny Costigan were scheduled to spar at the Grand Theatre in Brooklyn. In addition to his bouts with Costigan, it was advertised that Dempsey would meet all comers.[40]

The day after the final show at the Grand, Jack, his family and Denny left Brooklyn and traveled west to Portland, Oregon, to visit Maggie's family. After a few days in Portland,

Dempsey and Costigan would head to San Francisco where they would join the Williams Specialty Combination troupe and tour the West Coast for seven weeks. While heading to the Western Slope, the party briefly stopped over in several cities including Pittsburgh, Chicago and St. Paul. After checking in at St. Paul's Merchants Hotel, Jack gave an impromptu news conference in the lobby, where he explained that after visiting family in Portland he and Costigan would head south to San Francisco to see about arranging a fight—perhaps with Joe Ellingsworth. From there, said Jack, "Costigan and I go down to Los Angeles, where we join a theatrical combination, giving sparring exhibitions all through the Pacific coast country."[41]

On April 22, 1889, the Oklahoma Land Rush began at noon when an estimated fifty thousand homesteaders staked claims to parcels in the Unassigned Lands—considered to be some of the best unoccupied public land in the United States. These settlers could claim up to one hundred and sixty acres of land and receive the title provided that they lived on and improved the property. The town of Guthrie offers an example of the drastic changes brought to Oklahoma that day. *Harper's Weekly* reported, "Unlike Rome, the city of Guthrie was built in a day. To be strictly accurate in the matter, it might be said that it was built in an afternoon." The report continued, "At twelve o'clock on Monday, April 22, the resident population of Guthrie was nothing, before sundown it was at least ten thousand. In that time streets had been laid out, town lots staked off, and steps taken toward the formation of a municipal government."[42]

The party arrived in Portland on the morning of April 26. Upon their arrival in the Rose City, Jack told reporters that he was game for another fight against a quality fighter if a big enough purse could be arranged. According to Dempsey, "The larger the man, the larger the purse."[43]

After a few days in Portland, the men headed as planned for San Francisco for what they described as pure pleasure. Jack did, however, indicate that before leaving he would be in touch with the boards of several West Coast athletic clubs to schedule fights. Several theater engagements were also planned, beginning with San Jose on April 29. Appearing in the shows with Jack and Denny were to be Brooklyn Jimmy Carroll and his trainer Dick Toner, Johnny Reagan and the Japanese wrestler Soramichi.[44]

The Southern California Athletic Club of Los Angeles was still proposing a rematch for Jack with Johnny Reagan, but Reagan was nursing an illness and stated that he could not accept. New York fighter Joe Ellingsworth, who grew up in a family of boxers and who had been trying to arrange a fight with Dempsey since at least 1885 when he won an amateur middleweight title,[45] volunteered to take Reagan's place on the card. When asked about the proposal Jack replied, "If the Southern California Athletic Club will give a purse of $3,000 for a fight between Ellingsworth and myself I will, of course, agree to fight him. He says he wants to take Reagan's place without receiving the $1,000, win or lose. Well, that suits me better and as soon as he is ready to make arrangements, I am."[46] The arrangements for this bout would cause Dempsey more grief and questionable press than he could have guessed.

After the early speculation that a bout would be set up between Ellingsworth and Dempsey, the Southern California Athletic Club determined to have Ellingsworth meet La Blanche instead. On May 7, however, Joe received a telegram from the management at the Southern California Athletic Club that read, "Come as agreed. Wire us the day you start. The match is between Joe Ellingsworth and Jack Dempsey, not the Marine." Ellingsworth told reporters in New York that he received word from Los Angeles that "La Blanche had broken his contract with the Southern California Athletic Club and engaged with the California Athletic Club of San Francisco to fight Mike Lucie." The club then told Ellingsworth that they would honor their end of the commitment and find a new opponent to meet him. Ellingsworth intimated that it would be Dempsey and said that he would leave for Los Angeles immediately.[47] All very well and good, but Dempsey himself had not been consulted and had not agreed to the meeting.

In an action that further fueled the rumors of a bout between the two New Yorkers, Jack himself traveled to Los Angeles to appear in a show for the Harry Williams Specialty Company at the Los Angeles Theatre during the week of May 13.[48] The trip, however, had been previously announced and had nothing whatsoever to do with Ellingsworth. When Dempsey passed through the city on May 3 and continued on to a quiet, out-of-town location, many speculated that he was off to a nearby spot to complete his pre-fight training. In truth, Dempsey was merely headed for a few days' rest at the shore in Santa Monica.

Dempsey's pugilistic opinion was highly valued and often sought after by others in the fight game. An example of this would be a hastily called meeting in the Los Angeles train depot. As he returned from his brief trip to the shore, Dempsey was given a telegram sent by Mike Lucie, the Troy, New York, fighter with whom he was well acquainted. Lucie was scheduled to meet George La Blanche later that month in San Francisco and he was requesting a meeting with the Nonpareil at the depot. Lucie seemed a bit nervous and sought Dempsey's consult regarding staying in Los Angeles for several days instead of proceeding to San Francisco for the scheduled bout. In a response that highlights his belief in upholding agreed upon commitments, Jack responded emphatically, "Don't you do it, my boy. Just go on and have it out with La Blanche as you have agreed to. We will treat you good when you come back."[49]

Heading Dempsey's counsel, Lucie continued north to San Francisco where he met La Blanche on May 28, in the rooms of the California Athletic Club. Through six rounds, Lucie showed better than the Marine. Rounds seven and eight were fairly even as Lucie began to tire. By the thirteenth round, La Blanche landed a heavy right-hander on the worn-out Lucie's jaw and knocked him out, winning the match. Lucie had fought a three-round exhibition against Dempsey the previous summer in Troy when the Nonpareil had offered to meet anybody in that town and Lucie accepted the challenge. During the match Jack, using larger, padded gloves, "smothered" Lucie over three rounds. The challenger commented after the bout that the Nonpareil was "far above him." Following the La Blanche-Lucie bout, many pointed out that Dempsey easily stopped Lucie with soft gloves in three rounds while "it took La Blanche thirteen rounds to defeat Lucie, and with small gloves, too."[50]

Following his meeting at the train depot with Lucie, Jack headed downtown and checked into the Nadeau Hotel on Spring Street and First Street in Los Angeles, where he would lodge for the week. On May 11, Jack, who loved the shore as much as anything in the world, traveled back to Santa Monica to spend the day enjoying the ocean and the sights. He apparently dined sumptuously just prior to his scheduled departure that evening and while he leisurely enjoyed a splendid meal washed down by a good claret, he tarried too long and missed his train back to Los Angeles, forcing the Nonpareil to stay overnight in Santa Monica.[51]

During an exhibition on May 16, Dempsey soundly defeated Professor Murray, the trainer at the Los Angeles Athletic Club. The *Los Angeles Daily Herald* reported, "Mr. Murray has a local reputation for being very quick and active, with good use of his hands. It was most painfully evident last night that he was at a terrible disadvantage in the matter of skill." The newspaper added that "Dempsey did some very pretty work and scored many nice points over his antagonist." The *Herald* also pointed out that with Ellingsworth in the front row there was little doubt that Dempsey held back some of his more "clever" moves.[52]

While in Los Angeles, the pressure for a bout with Ellingsworth only increased as the latter decided to follow the Nonpareil to the City of Angels. In mid–May, it was reported in the Los Angeles press that the directors of the Southern California Athletic Club had deposited a $3,000 purse for a match between the two men and that both fighters were in that city and training for the bout which was to be scheduled for July 4.[53] Dempsey told a *Los Angeles Herald* reporter that while he had not been consulted about the bout, he would gladly meet Ellingsworth for the purse offered by the Southern California Athletic Club if President L.R. Fulda and the board of San Francisco's California Athletic Club, who had right of refusal, would agree to "hold him clear of his engagement to them for that reason."[54]

On May 20, however, it was reported that Jack seemed to be avoiding signing the final agreement for the Independence Day bout. The question of why arose. To Ellingsworth, who always had an unrealistically high opinion of his own talents, it was obvious that Dempsey quaked at the very thought of facing him in the ring. He wrote in an open letter to a Los Angeles newspaper that Jack had not signed for the bout, was afraid to do so and should therefore give up his claim to the middleweight championship. Upon reading the article, Jack approached Ellingsworth and confronted him. "Did you write this?" asked Dempsey. "Yes, I wrote it and I stand by it. What have you got to say about it?" replied Ellingsworth. According to the Los Angeles press, Dempsey could only respond by saying that he wanted more money to fight. Many wondered why Dempsey wouldn't fight and defeat this brash young man.

Obviously, as seasoned and talented a pugilist as Dempsey, who was not afraid to fight the biggest names in the ring of his day, was not afraid to meet the largely unknown and untested Joe Ellingsworth. The more informed answer as to why Jack was hesitant to sign is two-pronged. The first issue is that he was in hot pursuit of a position as head trainer at the California Athletic Club of San Francisco. In addition, he was close to agreeing to a match with George La Blanche and would soon be under contract to meet the Marine later that summer. As such, he was in no position to irritate the administrators of the California A.C.

The second and more important reason is that Jack had been around the fight game long enough to know how to bargain. Per his earlier stated view, that his main interest in pugilism was not his love of the sport, but rather that it was a lucrative business, Jack was simply trying to make the best deal for his side that he could. The *Brooklyn Eagle* noted, "Ellingsworth takes a good deal of stock in himself, but there are few others who do." The paper continued, pointing out that "if Dempsey met him half way, the betting on him would be at odds of 3 to 1 at least. Dempsey has about $3,000 that he can bet, so he could not make more than $1,000 that way."[55] In short, by not fighting Ellingsworth, Dempsey was looking to improve Ellingsworth's betting odds and therefore increase his own payoff when he finally defeated the braggadocios young New Yorker. Plain and simply put, Dempsey had reached a point in his life where professional boxing—with the possible exception of a chance to meet Charley Mitchell—was more about money than it was about ego or pride. Jack had nothing more to prove. He was growing tired of fighting and longed more and more for the solitude of life with his pretty young wife and growing family. If the money wasn't right, he chose not to fight.

One place the money always seemed right for Jack was on the stage and, as noted, by the middle of May, he and Denny Costigan were back with the Harry Williams Specialty Company sparring to packed theatres. The pair appeared in what was described as a "programme of rare excellence" along with noted vaudevillians King Kalkasa, "The Japanese Wizard" and the usual collection of comedians, actors, singers and musicians at Sacramento's Clunie Opera House on May 22 and 23.[56] The troupe then traveled west, appearing at the Oakland Theatre on the 24 and 25.[57]

During the late afternoon of May 31, 1889, the nation suffered a devastating tragedy in the form of the Johnstown, Pennsylvania, Flood. Johnstown, which took the brunt of the devastation from the torrent of raging water from the flood, is an industrial town located in the Laurel Mountains about seventy miles east of Pittsburgh. The flood was precipitated by the catastrophic failure of the South Fork Dam which was situated on the Little Conemaugh River, fourteen miles upstream from Johnstown. Two days of the heaviest rainfall on record had already swelled the local rivers over their banks, but when the man-made reservoir known as Lake Conemaugh, which was held back by the South Fork Dam, began to rise to dangerous levels, trouble was on the horizon. A frantic wire was sent to the towns downstream that read, "The dam is becoming dangerous and may possibly go!" The earthen dam and its spillway could not handle the pressure of the rising water in the two-mile long lake and, despite frantic efforts to strengthen the dam and divert the water, the over-burdened barrier finally broke. The dam's failure unleashed a torrent of twenty million tons of water. As the enormous displaced lake began to pour into the river below, the devilish waves it created set their sights on the towns of South Fork, Mineral Point, Woodvale and East Conemaugh.

As the water roared through the valley, the torrent swept up everything in its path—homes, shops, trees, animals and people both alive and dead. The tremendous wall of water and debris that hit Johnstown was estimated to be between thirty-five and forty feet tall and traveling at forty miles an hour. Two thousand two hundred and nine souls, including ninety-nine entire families and three hundred and ninety-six children were lost in Johnstown and the many smaller towns along the Little Conemaugh. The raging waters carried the bodies of some of the victims hundreds of miles downstream and some were not found until years later. Thousands who escaped the flood's initial fury lost everything they owned as the raging torrent leveled anything in its path. Four square miles of Johnstown's downtown were destroyed. In addition to the thousands of broken and devastated lives, the flood caused $17 million in damage, the equivalent of nearly a half billion dollars in today's currency. The Johnstown tragedy was referred to as "the greatest horror that the present world has known."[58] The aftermath saw over $3.7 million in relief funds raised from nations all over the world. Also, Clara Barton, a nurse and founder of the Red Cross, arrived on-site with her team on June 5 in what was the first major relief effort ministered to by that storied organization.

By the first week of June, the California Athletic Club of San Francisco ended any further speculation about a Dempsey-Ellingsworth bout by announcing that Jack would instead be busy preparing for a contest for the middleweight championship that would be held in their auditorium between Dempsey and George La Blanche. The fight was to be held at the athletic club on August 27 with the winner of the bout receiving $5,000 and the loser $1,000. A *Police Gazette* article pointed out that this would not be a championship contest because "in the first place they are not limited to the championship scale of weights which is 154 pounds. Then again, they are to use gloves which are barred in all battles for either the feather, light, middle or heavyweight championship."[59] While change was coming, London Rules and bare-knuckles were still considered the standard for championship contests.

It was also announced that Jack would begin his duties as the club's fitness instructor on July 1. Later that year one San Francisco newspaper described Dempsey's work as follows, "Jack Dempsey is now giving boxing lessons to the members of the California Athletic Club." The report continued, announcing that Dempsey was instructing the heavy and middle weight classes, and Jack's friend Jimmy Carroll of Brooklyn was teaching the light, feather, and bantam weight classes. "Dempsey and Allen are with their pupils on Monday, Wednesday and Friday evenings, Carroll and McCarty on the alternate nights. With such teachers the club should have pupils who will cut a hot pace for the boxers of any athletic organization in America."[60] The source gives no other identification on "Allen" and "McCarty," but one can assume they were local fighters and boxing instructors—very possibly Frank Allen and Billy McCarthy.

The Dempsey–La Blanche fight was an enormously popular news event all around the country and great crowds of people began reading the plentiful stories about the fighters and even attending the men's Sunday training sessions. Dempsey trained at the beautiful Neptune Gardens in Alameda near Oakland, just across the bay from San Francisco. Neptune Gardens was a lovely gazebo-filled park containing, among other attractions, an animal menagerie of monkeys, eagles, raccoons, badgers, foxes and bears. In addition, and for no logical reason, it was also becoming well known as a training camp for prize fighters. "Those who have seen Dempsey say he was never in finer trim and though he would make a better showing with skin gloves, they expect an easy victory for him."[61]

Some were not so convinced of an easy victory for the Nonpareil. The specter of Dempsey's hard-fought draw with Mike Donovan was still on many minds. Although referee Billy O'Brien had ruled that bout a draw, many questioned the decision and the first real chink in the Nonpareil's armor was exposed. Regardless of O'Brien's ruling in the ring the previous November, the difficulty that Jack had with Donovan "to a pugilist of Dempsey's position, was equivalent to defeat."[62]

During his training at Neptune Gardens, Jack seldom missed an opportunity in his leisure hours to shoot fowl from the old Alameda Bridge. Dempsey had become quite an avid hunter while living in Portland and was a notable shot. It became common for boys to line up under the bridge in boats and watch while Jack downed passing ducks. "Jack did not want the birds he shot but took much delight in watching the boys fight like wharf rats for the game which they secured by means of boats they had anchored under the bridge." Jack commented that "it was too much fun to watch the urchins skim out from under the wharf in their frail craft the moment they heard the bird strike the water, and race for it."[63]

La Blanche set up camp north of the city and across the Golden Gate on the Marin Peninsula side in Sausalito. He was headquartered at the Dexter Cottage where he was being trained by John Donaldson. In addition to getting into fighting condition, his goal was to shed enough pounds to come in at fight time as a middleweight. He reportedly entered training camp at 170 pounds but worked himself down to 158—the middleweight limit for gloved fights under the Queensberry Rules—by fight time. The Marine stated in a letter to friends in Philadelphia, "I will fight lighter this time than ever before and I will fight harder." La Blanche continued, "At all events, if he does me again I cannot plead lack of condition for I am very fine. I am very confident of victory."[64] Reports from La Blanche's camp, however, could sometimes tell a different story. They spoke of his "erratic methods of training and of his indulgence in liquor."[65]

On June 5, Dempsey took a break from his training regimen and seconded Joe Choynski as he fought Jim Corbett in one of that pair's four battles. The fight was a resumption of a bout fought a week earlier in a barn in Marin County that had been stopped by the police in the fourth round. This time the battle occurred on a barge that was moored in Benicia Harbor on the Sacramento River near the town of Fairfax.

Corbett was surprised to learn that his friend Dempsey was to be in Choynski's corner. Corbett tells the story of how on May 30, the date of the initial battle, he ran into Jack as the two headed for the arena. "As I left the house I ran into Jack Dempsey headed the same way. We shook hands and he said to me, 'Jim, I'm going to second this fellow, but I'm only doing it because I am getting $1,000. I don't know him at all, and it's not because I want him to win.'" Corbett smiled and responded, confidently, "That's all right, Jack. You can't make him whip me."[66] The two walked the remaining distance to the battleground laughing, still close friends full of admiration for one another.

The fight—after it was resumed on the barge—was a savage affair in which both Choynski and Corbett took great punishment. Several times, referee Patsy Hogan tried to stop the fight and rule it a draw, but neither man would have it. By the final round both men were bruised, battered and bleeding heavily from cuts on their faces and Corbett's hands were damaged. By the twenty-seventh and final round neither man had much left, but Corbett managed to put everything into one last blow that connected with Choynski's jaw and dropped him like a rock. Hogan counted "Chrysanthemum Joe" out, but he need not have bothered as the sponge that Dempsey threw from his corner landed on the floor almost as quickly as Choynski. Corbett, who himself could barely stand, was declared the winner.[67] The *Washington Star* noted, "Corbett broke both of his hands and at the end of the twenty-seventh round Jack Dempsey, who was behind Choynski, threw up the sponge."[68]

On the morning of June 10, Jack reportedly got into a brawl with a very large, rough-and-tumble San Franciscan welterweight named Dan Egan who inexplicably went by the moniker the "Montana Kid." Dempsey was strolling around the city with some friends when they were approached by a clearly inebriated Egan, who challenged Dempsey to a battle then and there. The Nonpareil demurred and, according to a report in the *Police Gazette*, maligned Egan's pugilistic ability in a recent bout with Billy Hennessey. When Dempsey began to turn and walk away, an extremely furious Egan got the drop on Jack, grabbing him and throwing him roughly to the ground. Egan immediately jumped on top of Dempsey and began kicking Jack and hitting him with both fists. Jack tried to fight back but was still groggy from his head hitting the floor. When Dempsey's companions tried to assist, Egan's entourage stood in the way. In short order the police arrived and pulled the stubborn Egan off.

When Jack finally got to his feet, his eye was blackened and his face swollen and cut. "A short time afterwards the Kid again attacked Dempsey and attempted to renew the fight, but a policeman arrested the Kid." At the police station Egan boasted of how he would whip Dempsey when he saw him again.[69] While Jack found an open bar, had a drink and then went home to rest, the Montana Kid hit the town, believing in his mind that he was a victor over the middleweight champion and not simply a big, tough thug who got the drop on Dempsey in a street brawl.

Actually, a number of newspapers ran a story contradicting parts of the earlier reports. James Thornton, who was traveling with the variety troupe, was with Dempsey that day and witnessed the encounter. He agreed that Dempsey had tried to avoid a fight but commented that Dempsey had actually landed a few good shots on the Montana Kid.[70]

After a short rest, Jack went back to the California Athletic Club where he climbed into the ring to meet Mike Lucie that evening in a scheduled three-round exhibition. The state of his face and eye were no doubt the subject of much conversation by the patrons of that evening's event. Other than the facial marks, Dempsey looked none the worse for his earlier altercation with Egan as he sparred easily with Lucie for the three rounds much as he had during their exhibition in Troy, New York, the previous summer.[71] Those in attendance cheered the pair as Lucie gave it his best, but was unable to match the Nonpareil's speed, quickness and science. At the conclusion of the bout Jack put his arm around his friend and commented on his improvement over the previous twelve months.

After his exhibition with Lucie, Jack returned for a short visit to see his family in Oregon. He arrived in Portland on June 13 and planned a weeklong rest before returning to California to resume training for his return match with La Blanche. While at home in mid–June, Dempsey received a telegraph from James Wakely, a backer of John L. Sullivan, asking Jack to second Sullivan in his upcoming fight with Jake Kilrain in Richburg, Mississippi. Jack responded that he was flattered by the offer but would pass for fear that the long travel and the humid southern summer air would interfere with his training for the La Blanche battle.

While not attending the fight, Jack had weighed in with his opinion of who would win. In April, he stated that he had recently seen Sullivan, who was in very good condition, and while he felt it would be close, Sullivan was gamer than Kilrain and would take the day. He commented, "I firmly believe that Sullivan wants to fight."[72] As it turned out, Jack was correct, and Sullivan had the fight well in hand regardless of Dempsey's presence or lack thereof.

This historic battle was the last bare-knuckle heavyweight championship fight. The London Rules fight went seventy-five rounds in the blistering sun and oppressive temperature of 104 degrees, with Sullivan taking control of the fight early. He was determined to press his advantage over Kilrain and show that while his opponent was beginning to wilt in the heat, he was not. Sullivan even refused to sit down in his corner between rounds. When asked about it he responded, "Why should I? I only have to stand back up again." At the end of the seventy-fifth round Kilrain was virtually out on his feet. His face was badly cut and swollen and his head was wobbly. He could barely stand, much less throw a punch. A physician took Kilrain's second Mike Donovan aside during the break and advised, "Kilrain will die if you keep sending him in there." As Jake stumbled to his feet and into the next round, Donovan heeded the physician's advice and threw the sponge into the ring, thus ending the bout.[73]

In late July, Jack took another week off from his training camp and returned to Portland to see his family. He spent about a week visiting at home, seeing friends and tending to business. Dempsey, accompanied by Denny Costigan and Dave Campbell, left Portland for San Francisco by steamer on August 3 and arrived in the City by the Bay on the sixth. Sad news came from New York later that night. Jack's stepfather Patrick Dempsey had passed away at his home at 93 Wythe Avenue in Brooklyn. Jack, who had just arrived in San Francisco from Portland earlier that day, was notified by telegraph by his brother Tom. It had been just a year since his mother had passed.[74]

Jack met another Dempsey—former opponent Mike Dempsey—on August 22, in a scheduled eight-rounder at the California A.C. According to the *National Police Gazette*, Mike, "who has not engaged in any matches of late, is once more desirous of trying his fortune within the squared circle."[75] Happy to help out a friend and fellow New Yorker, the Nonpareil viewed the fight as a good live action tune up for the upcoming La Blanche tilt. In what amounted to little more than an extended sparring session for the Nonpareil, Jack got in a good ring workout and then dispatched the unrelated Dempsey with a hard right to the jaw in the seventh round.

On August 27, 1889, Dempsey and La Blanche squared off in their rematch at the California Athletic Club in San Francisco in what was questionably billed as a bout for the middleweight championship of the world. At the weigh-in, La Blanche, despite his boast to his friends about being lighter, not only missed the 154-pound middleweight championship qualification mark, he missed his stated 158-pound goal. When he tipped the scales at 161 pounds, all debate about the championship ceased and the fight was immediately declared a non-title bout.

Dempsey's *National Police Gazette* championship belt had been on display at a tailoring establishment on Grant Avenue for the previous week and it had added to the excitement about the contest. In anticipation of a large crowd—over two thousand viewers showed up—the fight was held in the recently acquired drill hall, formerly used by the National Guard.

In describing the facility, one journalist reported, "The new exhibition hall of the California Athletic Club (formerly Armory Hall) located directly opposite the gymnasium of the club, was crowded to its utmost seating capacity last evening." He continued, "The phenomenal success of the California Athletic Club and its increase in membership, compelled the Directors to seek larger quarters for their monthly exhibitions, and in securing Armory Hall the club adds another peg in the ladder of success, the seats being well arranged and built on the incline running from the north and south sides of the ring, which is thirty-two feet square and elevated from the floor about four feet. There is a gallery in the north end capable of seating about 300 persons, and in the south end private boxes, which will hold several hundred. The reporters' stand is located in a gallery on the east side of the ring, and was built expressly for members of the press, and to the credit of the Directors none others were admitted. Directly opposite, and on the west side of the ring, an elevated gallery has been erected for the time-keepers, and directly over their heads, and in full view of every person, is the dial which points to the expiration of the three minutes fighting time and the one-minute rest, according to the Marquess of Queensberry rules."[76] In the middle of the hall sat a simple, rough-hewn ring constructed with wooden posts and casually strung ropes.

Dempsey was the odds-on favorite to defeat La Blanche, but it was widely agreed that the Marine was a better fighter than he had been when the two met in 1886. Bob Turnbull, Jack's former ring opponent and now a sports reporter for the *New York World*, commented, "I was the only sporting writer who gave the correct tip when these men met at Larchmont three years ago. Since then I have had many chances of watching the work of both. With the men in equally good condition, and barring accidents, I cannot see where La Blanche should give Dempsey much trouble." Turnbull went on to say that Dempsey was well aware that La Blanche was an improved boxer. No longer the "hot headed, impetuous fighter of three years ago," the Marine avoided the immediate rush and spent more time feeling out his opponents before assuming an aggressive style.[77]

Just before eight o'clock, the crowds outside the club began to move toward the doors of the hall. They soon found seats and, once settled in, were ready for the evening's events to begin.[78] Billy Jordan, the master of ceremonies for the evening, announced the undercard. Jordan introduced former Dempsey opponent Billy Dacey, who boxed four lively rounds with Jack Delancey. Billy McCarthy and Joe Choynski followed with Choynski going down in the second round and sliding on the side of his face under the ropes, filling his ear with resin. Choynski came back, however, and the pair fought four rounds to a no decision. "Gus Brown and Young Frenchy came next and gave a very amusing set-to of four rounds, Brown holding his own with Frenchy."[79] The preliminary bouts between the local fighters lasted for over an hour.

At 9:25 p.m. the two fighters of the main event entered the arena at virtually the same time, jumping over the ropes and into the ring to an enthusiastic reception. After several minutes of raucous cheering for the principles, the master of ceremonies announced that due to La Blanche's weight of 161 pounds, the fight would not be for the middleweight championship. The two camps then debated whether to wear four- or six-ounce gloves. The Nonpareil, with his small hands, always preferred the lighter option. "After some talk about the gloves, the dispute was settled by a toss-up, Dempsey winning." It was then agreed that the men would wear the four-ounce gloves. La Blanche was seconded by Professor John Donaldson, who fought out of Minneapolis and Cleveland, and by Paddy Gorman of Australia. Also in his corner was his trainer, pugilist Jimmy Carroll of England, who had been working with La Blanche over the previous several months. No friend of Dempsey's, Carroll was anxious to see La Blanche defeat the Nonpareil at any price. Denny Costigan and Dave Campbell looked after Dempsey. "C. C. Coleman acted as timekeeper for the club, while Ed Graney looked after La Blanche's interests and Mr. Luxe, Dempsey's. H. B. Cook acted as referee and veteran timekeeper George Harting held the watch. At 9:36 the men shook hands and time was called."[80]

The men sparred cautiously for a few moments. Shortly thereafter, La Blanche went on the offensive, rushing Dempsey and clearly playing the aggressor. He led with his right, but the always quick and agile Dempsey jumped back effortlessly and avoided the blows. Undeterred, La Blanche kept up his assault, but time and again, Jack easily avoided or deflected La Blanche's attacks and landed heavy counter punches during the Marine's rushes.

The second and third rounds were much the same. Dempsey was able to land heavily on the Marine's jaw several times and in the third, he landed a heavy blow that caused La Blanche to stagger briefly. Beyond that, clinching and light sparring was the norm. As the third stave ended, neither fighter could be said to have built up a significant advantage and little harm had been done to either man.

While Jack landed a number of light blows in the fourth round, La Blanche controlled that chapter by landing several unanswered punches on the Nonpareil and repeatedly forcing him back and putting him against the ropes.

The fifth round devolved into a wrestling match, as the pair continually swung at each other and then fell into the clinches. There, La Blanche made good use of his natural strength and the ten-pound weight advantage by leaning on Dempsey and shoving him about. At one point, the Marine threw Jack to the floor and then landed a sharp blow to his forehead as the round was called.

La Blanche was booed lustily by the pulsing crowd when early in the sixth round he "lifted Dempsey on his hip and tried to throw him to the floor. La Blanche followed this with several rushes but accomplished very little."[81] Cries of "foul" could be heard throughout the crowd but Cook ignored the claims.

The seventh and eighth rounds were full of spirited, give-and-take action as the two pugilists landed repeated heavy blows on each other. The pattern seemed to be that La Blanche would fire off a right to Dempsey's ear and Dempsey would counter with a hard shot to his opponent's jaw, then La Blanche, then Dempsey, and on it went. At one point in the eighth round, La Blanche staggered Dempsey after landing an illegal but stinging blow on the Nonpareil's jaw during the break from a clinch. Again, cries of foul filled the air, but none was awarded. The eighth ended with spirited fighting from both men.

In the ninth round, La Blanche again drew the ire of the crowd as he rushed Dempsey at the opening bell, wrapped his arms around the Nonpareil and threw him heavily to the ground. Once more, the crowd demanded a foul be called but again, Cook refused to comply. Jack quickly rose and soon rallied, catching La Blanche on the chin with a sharp uppercut. The torrid action continued through the end of the round much as it had in the previous two chapters. Still, however, through nine rounds, little serious damage was done by or to either fighter.

"In the tenth round, Dempsey landed heavily on the Marine's nose and mouth without return. After a call of time La Blanche rushed at Dempsey and caught him on the mouth, drawing first blood. Dempsey's seconds claimed a foul, but it was not allowed."[82] Several times La Blanche rushed Dempsey only to have the Nonpareil step to the side and hammer the Bostonian on the jaw. By the end of the round, however, the continual pounding by Dempsey began to take its toll and La Blanche appeared to be groggy.

The eleventh and twelfth rounds were slow as the two men clinched and grappled more than they threw punches, but in the thirteenth and fourteenth rounds, Dempsey came alive again and rocked his opponent several times with multiple strikes to the jaw, ribs and neck.

The fifteenth and sixteenth rounds saw each man take the lead in rushing the other, but regardless of who the aggressor was, both were tired and the action quickly devolved into a series of clinches. Dempsey scored heavily at the close of the sixteenth by landing a powerful and stinging blow to La Blanche's nose.

The seventeenth round saw a return to fast action as the two traded blows, each giving as good as he got. Dempsey opened again on the Marine's jaw and received a blow on the ear in return. The Marine then lunged at Jack, but the Nonpareil took advantage of an opening and landed a combination to his opponent's neck and windpipe.

In the eighteenth round, La Blanche opened by landing blows to the side of Dempsey's face and neck, but Jack responded with four hard rights to La Blanche's jaw and neck. These blows rattled the Marine who was clearly beginning to wear down. The Nonpareil was now beginning to take control of the fight.

In the nineteenth round, Dempsey worked his opponent hard by landing seven powerful blows to the ribs. The Nonpareil then dropped La Blanche with a resounding punch to the mouth that brought about the first knock-down of the evening. The crowd applauded and cheered wildly.

The twentieth through twenty-fourth rounds were slow, with the men circling and landing lighter blows while each looked for an opening. La Blanche was fighting valiantly but was clearly showing the effects of the cumulative punishment he was taking. Dempsey knew he was in control and seemed content to wear his opponent down gradually.

"Little or nothing was done in the twenty-fifth round, but in the twenty-sixth Dempsey forced the Marine into the corner and pounded him on the neck until the latter staggered like a drunken man, and a knock-out seemed to be approaching."[83] Further descriptions of the action in the twenty-sixth state that "this was a hot one, both men fighting all the while. It was give and take throughout, without any advantage to either."[84]

"From the twenty-sixth to the thirty-first-round Dempsey worked on the Marine's ribs."[85] During those last six rounds Dempsey landed several sharp blows to the body, concentrating effectively on La Blanche's rib cage and the collective effects of the pounding were beginning to tell. The Marine at times was seen to be staggering around the ring on wobbly legs and looking unsteady on his feet. Dempsey was by far the fresher of the two men at this point and he was building a seemingly insurmountable lead.

In the thirty-second round Dempsey began to press La Blanche. Clearly in control of the bout, the Nonpareil forced the Marine into a corner and mercilessly pounded him against the ropes. La Blanche was continuing to weaken under the heavy pummeling. He knew the fight was Dempsey's unless he did something now. For thirty-one rounds over an hour and thirty-six minutes, Dempsey had outclassed and outpointed his larger rival. Over that time, he had "gradually jabbed the Marine to a condition of 'grogginess,'"[86] but was himself still fresh. Dempsey, overconfident and looking to finish the Marine, was, however, getting a bit sloppy. Jim Corbett, sitting at ringside, saw it and commented to friends, "Jack is getting careless."[87] La Blanche saw it too. He continued to hold on, to clinch and buy time, waiting for an opening. It was clinch, break, clinch, break as the crowd grew frustrated with the lack of action, but eventually it happened. Dempsey stepped away from one break with his hands too low. La Blanche saw his opening. He thought of a punch that his trainer British lightweight Jimmy Carroll recently taught him, a punch that if delivered correctly could yield devastating results, but a punch that was looked on by many as a dirty tactic and even tacitly illegal.

Knowing that he would lose without a miracle, La Blanche determined to use the punch and it was now or never. The Marine somehow managed to muster up what remained of his strength, leap up, whirl around and catch Dempsey with a terrific backhanded blow to the jaw. Jack never saw the illegal strike coming and he went down like a shot, falling heavily on his face and breaking his nose. With blood spurting from Dempsey's nose and the timekeeper reaching the count of seven, an awestruck Denny

Costigan shouted, "Get up Jack!" Dempsey raised himself to his knees and looked around the ring with a dazed looked on his face. He was about to struggle to his feet, but time ran out and Cook declared La Blanche the winner by knockout. Seconds after the call, Jack finally got to his feet. He staggered to the side of the ring and clutched the ropes for support. He looked at La Blanche through groggy but contemptuous eyes and told the Canadian to fight on, but La Blanche, knowing that he had just gotten lucky to a degree he never in a thousand years could have imagined, refused to tempt fate. He quickly took his $5,500 and left the arena.

The following day's newspapers reported the unbelievable news. There was some discrepancy as to where exactly La Blanche's punch had caught Dempsey—the jaw, the chin, the temple, the nose, but there was no uncertainty as to the result. One report read, "…in the thirty-second round after a breakaway from a clinch, the Marine suddenly pivoted and got in a terrific swing on Jack's nose, which it is reported is broken. Dempsey went down and failed to respond at the call of time and the fight was awarded to La Blanche."[88] Another report stated, "This was the blow which won the fight. Dempsey came up groggy and stood up before La Blanche who had pluckily taken a vast amount of punishment until the thirty-second round was reached, when a terrific swinging blow from the Marine's right landed on his jugular and knocked him out."[89] This blow, known among other names as the "Pivot Punch" and later, the "La Blanche Swing," was barred by the New York State Athletic Commission and most of its sister bodies, "partly out of respect to the memory of the Nonpareil," according to the *Tacoma News Tribune* while revisiting the issue thirty years after the fight.[90]

The *Syracuse Daily Standard* reported of Dempsey, "He rose twice to his hands and knees and the blood poured upon the floor. He went down helpless and then rose again, dazed and bewildered. One hand went up as if appealing to the crowd or referee and he then staggered to his feet with a game effort but had to seek the ropes to keep his feet and hang there. It took Jack more than a minute to be able to stand on his own power. La Blanche stood in his corner, smiling. Dempsey was furious and tried to bate the Marine to keep fighting. When it was clear that La Blanche would not fight on and that Dempsey had lost the bout, Jack staggered over to the Marine, shook hands and asked imploringly, 'You'll give me another fight won't you?'"[91]

As soon as the cloud of disbelief of what had just happened began to clear, Dempsey's corner and many in the crowd began calling for La Blanche to be disqualified for the blow. The pivot punch was not considered fair, but it had never been officially outlawed in California. Cook listened to the arguments, but in the end, he declared La Blanche the winner as the crowd sat in a shocked silence.

Cook might not have been the most sympathetic ear for the disqualification argument given his reputation for allowing pugilists to get away with fouls in the ring. Cook believed in letting pugilists fight with little interference from officials. The *Police Gazette* stated, "It appears that Referee Cook takes it upon himself to let men fight as they please." In fairness, it is noted that both men committed fouls that were ignored, but it appeared to assist La Blanche most greatly. "If the reports of that battle are correct, and there is no reason to believe that they are not, the club's official referee, Mr. Cook, permitted deliberate fouls on the part of both men, and allowed Le Blanche to clinch and throw Dempsey on three different occasions, which is in direct violation of the Queensberry rules." The article continued by stating that the California Club itself was not the best venue to seek a draw or a disqualification. "The club is known to be opposed to draws and decisions on fouls, and its course in that respect has led to injustice to some men who have fought fair and square under the rules, while others have taken undue and mean advantages by striking foul blows and wrestling. The three falls which La Blanche gave Dempsey after a wrestling bout must have tended greatly to weaken the Nonpareil."[92]

La Blanche attained his goal of defeating the Nonpareil that night, but because he was over the weight limit he did not win the middleweight title. While he won the fight that evening, the Marine's roughhouse tactics throughout the bout caused his reputation to suffer greatly and, largely due to the questionable blow, his status as a fighter was ebbing. Soon thereafter and as a direct result of La Blanche's action that evening, the pivot punch was officially outlawed.

Even before he left the ring, La Blanche found himself having to answer questions about the punch that ended the bout. Unbelievably La Blanche stated, "They call it a chance blow, but I had things all right anyhow."[93] What a simply amazing comment—and totally detached from any reality. I suppose he thought if he said it enough, people might start believing it. He might even start believing it himself. La Blanche also refused to answer any questions about the fairness of his actions.

Recalling the bout thirty-eight years later, Jack McAuliffe described the fight and the punch this way, "It was a punch used with a swing starting from a left-hand lead. The body would be swung clear around as on the heel as a pivot with the right arm up and the elbow stuck out shoulder high horizontal to the body. It was the theory that if the elbow did not strike the opponent on the jaw, the fist was sure to land with terrific force and momentum."[94] After recounting how Carroll taught La Blanche the pivot punch and how the Marine used it in desperation after receiving from the Nonpareil "an unmerciful beating and staggering along the ropes," McAuliffe discussed his frustration with the maneuver. "I was angry at the illegal tactics used and determined to seek revenge for my good friend Dempsey. I determined to go out to San Francisco and paste this guy Carroll who taught La Blanche the pivot punch."[95] He did go and the two would meet the following March when McAuliffe battered the Briton for a forty-seven-round knockout.

An explanation of the pivot punch used by La Blanche to knock Dempsey out.

Opinions varied only

slightly on who was actually the better man that night. La Blanche's supporters of course claimed that their man had won by waiting for an opening and then finishing Dempsey. Many in his camp also claimed that he could do it again, but those who sided with La Blanche were in the minority. Just about everyone else in the boxing community disagreed. Even six years later, in Jack's obituary, the *Yakima Herald* of Washington commented that La Blanche defeated Dempsey "on what was universally considered a 'fluke.'"[96]

Most believed that a rematch was almost impossible because La Blanche knew he was completely outclassed in the ring by the Nonpareil that night in San Francisco and he won a disputed victory on a fluke punch that he could never repeat. Perhaps Jack's brother Tommy Dempsey said it best. "Jack can whip La Blanche every time," claimed Tommy. "The blow was a chance one. La Blanche would be afraid to face Jack tomorrow. A team and four could not drag him into the ring to face Jack again."[97] Jack clearly agreed with his brother and with the multitude of fight fans who knew he stood head and shoulders above La Blanche in the ring. One of Dempsey's friends also added that the padded gloves had hindered the Nonpareil. "It was the five-ounce gloves that played hob with Jack when he last fought the Marine. Had they worn skin tights Dempsey would have cut him into ribbons and you would never have heard of any pivot blow." The friend then added, "but I don't like these mufflers."[98]

A year after the bout, Dempsey said of the outcome, "It was the referee's fault that I did not win. He should have given the fight to me on a foul. La Blanche struck me the most cowardly blow I ever saw delivered in the prize ring."[99] Jack would never forgive La Blanche for either the cheap blow or the lack of a rematch, and clearly the Marine's unwillingness to climb back into the ring with Dempsey when virtually everyone knew that the Nonpareil was the better man was a point of bitterness and frustration for Jack. Numerous athletic clubs and backers made inducements to get the two back together, but La Blanche refused all of them. Over a decade later Denny Costigan remembered that "a club offered to give them a purse of $8,000 and Dempsey offered to present La Blanche with $2,500 just to get in the ring, but he wouldn't. Ever since that time Dempsey held La Blanche in supreme contempt." Costigan continued by recalling one night at the California Club when the pair were attending an evening of fights. That night, the referee gave some bad decisions and after one bout ended, La Blanche "came over to where Dempsey and I were standing and said to us, 'What do you think of the decision?' Dempsey replied curtly, 'It was as crooked as you are.' La Blanche turned and went away without saying a word."[100] The *Brooklyn Eagle*, in describing the outcome, stated, "The defeat was a mere accident, however, and was won by the Marine on a terrific chance blow after he had been staggering around the ring for some time under the severe punishment he had been subjected to by Dempsey."[101]

The timekeeper in San Francisco that night was George Harting, a fight veteran who held the watch at countless fistic battles in the Bay Area during his lengthy career. In an interview Harting gave in 1913, he remembered the outcome this way, "The defeat of gallant Jack Dempsey was one of those unexpected accidents that are bound to happen. La Blanche was practically beaten when it happened." After describing the blow that sent Dempsey to the ground Harting continued, "To show how strong the fight instinct was in Dempsey, while unable to arise he crawled along the ropes, pulled himself up and called upon La Blanche to fight." Harting then added, "La Blanche's victory was in the shape of a fluke."[102]

But for all that was said and written after the bout, the reality was that Dempsey had been defeated. Had Dempsey soundly beaten La Blanche for all but the final seconds of the fight's thirty-two rounds? Yes. Had La Blanche employed illegal grabbing and throwing tactics throughout the fight? Yes. Was the coup de grace a fluke punch thrown in desperation by a beaten fighter on the verge of losing the bout? Absolutely. Should the Marine have been disqualified by Cook on the spot for delivering the Pivot punch? Very arguably, yes. But while all of this is true Cook chose not to disqualify La Blanche and no matter how one-sided a fight may be, any bout can be decided on a single blow, which spells out the truth in the old saying that a fighter must protect himself at all times. The reality is that Dempsey lost. He was cold-cocked and unable to regain his feet within the allotted ten seconds. Dempsey not only lost the bout and his undefeated record, but many contend that the defeat also cost the Nonpareil his absolute self-confidence in the ring and maybe outside of it as well. While Jack would continue to enter the ring for five and a half more years and still had some highlights ahead, his pugilistic career was never the same. He was no longer "nonpareil." His reputation began to wane and his health to slip. Many would argue that his mental health also began to suffer. Dempsey's fluke loss to George La Blanche cost him dearly. The *National Police Gazette* ran a headline that read simply, "The Nonpareil Vanquished."[103] Never were truer words written. In many respects, the Nonpareil was sent to the floor that night, but only a mere mortal arose.

Jack took the defeat very badly. After the battle he sat in his dressing room gazing at the floor. His nose was badly swollen and discolored. As the reality of the loss set in, Dempsey shook his head sadly and said, "He will never give me another show. I asked him if he would and he said 'Yes,' but I am afraid he will never let me have another go." When told that he was still the middleweight champion and that many pugilists still wanted bouts with him, Jack said dejectedly, "Get me another fight. Bother the championship. Any weight at all, only give me another. I had the fight in hand and was making it a waiting one. When we got together I saw the blow coming but could not get away from it. I suppose I was careless."[104] And he was. With the fight well in hand, Jack should never have gotten close enough to La Blanche for the Marine to land that shot. Sheer carelessness presented Dempsey his first loss. After changing back into street clothes, a dejected Jack Dempsey returned to Neptune Gardens for a rest.

In some ways, the chance blow that ended the fight reminded some in the boxing community of the first Sullivan-Mitchell bout in May 1883 during which John L. was drubbing the Englishman throughout the first round. After Sullivan had dropped Mitchell for the third time in the round, Mitchell suddenly landed a desperate right-handed blow square and with full force on the champion's granite-like jaw that, according to the *New York Sun*, "capsized him," sending the champion to the floor for the first time in his career.[105] Unlike Dempsey, however, Sullivan was back on his feet immediately as if to show that he was unfazed. He then angrily tore into Mitchell and exacted a brutal revenge over the remaining two rounds. Jack would unfortunately never get the chance to exact his revenge on La Blanche.

Years later Denny Costigan remarked, "Jack never forgot that swing as long as he lived. In his subsequent fights, when his opponent made a motion to deliver the La Blanche swing, it nearly scared him to death."[106]

Eminently respected fight referee George Siler was giving an interview before the Corbett-Fitzsimmons bout in 1897 and, when asked about the use of the pivot blow, commented, "Oh, you mean that old trick that La Blanche successfully played on poor Jack Dempsey. Well, that went out of existence with that fight. I don't think that either Corbett or Fitzsimmons would entertain the idea of resorting to such a blow. It is dead and should remain so."[107]

The pivot punch and his defeat of Dempsey was absolutely the pinnacle of George La Blanche's career. He fought the virtually unknown "Texas" Jack Burke to a nine-round draw in September. Several months later La Blanche was found to be involved in a plot to throw a bout against Young Mitchell. On February 20, 1891, La Blanche and Mitchell were scheduled to meet at San Francisco's California Athletic Club with the Marine the heavy favorite to win. Mitchell, whose given name was Johnny Herget, won the bout by knockout in the twelfth round, but it was later discovered that the Marine took a dive. "Herget was not a party to the throw down, and after he learned that he had been made a stool pigeon of, he threatened to kill La Blanche on sight. The affair created a great sensation in sporting circles, though no money was lost by the intended victims, owing to the fact that the fake was exposed before the bets were paid. La Blanche realized that his ring career was ended there, and he made the best of a bad bargain by engaging in any number of questionable boxing bouts."[108] La Blanche's luck seemed to have run out, and he eventually found himself fighting for small purses in the Midwest, the Northeast, and in his native Quebec through 1899. In fairness, La Blanche fought quite a number of contests over the next dozen years and some against good fighters, but he seldom won. He would win only a small handful of his remaining contests—each victory coming against virtual unknowns, and one by disqualification. The following news report from March of 1892 is a case in point. "George La Blanche, the Marine, was whipped again by Frank Childs, a colored middleweight of Los Angeles, Thursday night. La Blanche fouled and kicked his antagonist."[109] The Marine was through and he knew it. He was using his name and notoriety and simply fighting for a paycheck.

La Blanche was a free spender and a hard drinker who, when drunk, became an uncontrollable ruffian. He was forced to sell his San Francisco saloon due to poor management, legal issues stemming from unpaid taxes and the fact that he started drinking more of his own liquor than he sold to his customers. In 1894 La Blanche was arrested in Chicago and arraigned on charges of assault and battery, carrying concealed weapons and disorderly conduct. "He was arrested on a warrant which was sworn out by his wife, who alleges that the Marine exercised his pugilistic propensity with her as the victim."[110]

In late September 1898, La Blanche was seriously injured when he fell off a moving freight train in the Hoosac Tunnel in Franklin, Massachusetts. He suffered a head injury and was knocked unconscious. La Blanche was thought to be a vagrant when he was picked up and taken to Franklin County Hospital. After regaining consciousness, La Blanche, his head still cloudy from concussion, stated that he wanted to get back "from" California to see his mother and sister.[111] The following bleak description of La Blanche was carried by several news services. "Penniless, practically friendless, sorely stricken and a miserable object, George La Blanche, once champion middleweight boxer of the world, lies in a public hospital, the result of a spree."[112] The clear tragedy in that description is only compounded by the fact that even that pitiful vignette gives La Blanche too much credit—he was never the middleweight champion of the world. His drinking got worse, his saloon and money were gone and his ring opportunities were quickly drying up. From there, his already ruinous life went into a freefall.

Nearly destitute, La Blanche hooked up with ex-lightweight Mike Daly and the pair found themselves destitute and desperate in Bangor, Maine. On February 16, 1903, the men were each found guilty of larceny after robbing a drunken man in a Bangor hotel. They were sentenced to two years each. La Blanche blamed his downfall on alcoholism. In 1908, he was arrested for vagrancy in Fitchburg, Massachusetts. La Blanche remained in the area due to the fact that his sister Adeline Gagnon and her husband Esdras made their home in Lawrence. He would die in a Lawrence, Massachusetts, hospital on May 3, 1918.[113] An appeal was made for funds to help bury the indigent former pugilist and $177 was raised. A funeral Mass was held at St. Anne's Church, after which La Blanche was buried at Sacred Heart Cemetery in Lawrence.[114]

As anxious as Dempsey was to get a return match with La Blanche, he predictably had a difficult time in doing so. "The new conditions existing in the California Athletic Club leave little hope for an encounter between the two men. Five-ounce gloves, which will hereafter be used in all club matches, are too big for a man of Dempsey's build to use against a man like the Marine and Dempsey will in all likelihood return to his home in [Brooklyn], where he has been promised a great benefit. It is reported that the Nonpareil has become disgusted with his position as boxing instructor of the California club and that he has tendered his resignation, but that the directors refused to accept it."[115]

On September 5, Dempsey returned overland from San Francisco to Portland. He spent a few days visiting friends and making some plans. He tried to stay busy and was seen in town shaking hands with those he met. After a few days, Dempsey continued on to the spa and resort at Wilhoit Springs in the foothills of the Cascade Mountains just south of Portland, where Margaret was visiting. During the late nineteenth and early twentieth centuries, Wilhoit Springs was operated as a popular health and pleasure resort. In 1899, an analysis of the healing waters of the spa was described in the book, *The Mineral Waters of the United States and Their Therapeutic Uses*.

Jack was happy to be back in Oregon with his family, but was, as usual, anxious to plot his next move. Maggie commented during their stay at the resort that she was encouraging her husband "to retire from the slugging business and go on a farm near Mt. Angel. Up to the present time, it is not known whether he will accede to his wife's wishes or not."[116] As little as a week later, however, Dempsey showed that while Maggie wanted him to retire from the ring, he was less than anxious to quit and certainly not now, with the bitter taste of the La Blanche affair still fresh in his mouth. In mid–September, Jack told reporters that he was ready to meet any man approaching his weight with gloves of any size and that he was ready with the money at any time for another chance at La Blanche.[117]

After the stay at Wilhoit Springs, instead of traveling east to Brooklyn, Dempsey returned to San Francisco, thereby squashing newspaper rumors that he would be going home. "There is no truth in the statement that Jack Dempsey is coming east for the present. He is engaged as instructor at the California Athletic Club with a handsome salary."[118]

It was reported that Jack had laid out a challenge to La Blanche to meet him anywhere, anytime, "to fight to a finish with skin tight gloves or bare fists, for $10,000 or $20,000 a side, and that he has deposited $1,000 as an evidence of good faith."[119] Adjusted for inflation, that sum would represent between a quarter and a half million dollars today—no small sum, but the Marine, who was always in difficult financial straits, refused to consider the offer. It seems clear that Tommy Dempsey was correct in his earlier assessment of the Marine.

On the evening of Saturday, October 5, Jack got a bit of a smile while attending a series of exhibition matches at the Olympic Club in Portland. During one event in which

La Blanche was on the card and matched against Dempsey's old friend and backer Brooklyn Jimmy Carroll, Jack was introduced—rightfully—as the middleweight champion of the world. The several thousand in attendance gave the Nonpareil a long and raucous standing ovation. All of this was too much for the Marine to take, so he retreated to the bar and took several glasses of beer. Between gulps, La Blanche commented to a friend, "So he's the middleweight champion, is he? Well, we'll see about that!" Again, La Blanche had no title claim. He failed to make either the agreed upon 158-pound fight limit or the 154-pound middleweight championship bout limit prior to his bout with Dempsey and the match was fought with gloves under Queensberry Rules. It was clearly announced before the contest that the championship was not being fought for. Dempsey was still the legitimate titleholder, but nonetheless it grated on the Marine's nerves.

When La Blanche's actions and words were mentioned to Dempsey, a smile came to Jack's face and he commented, "All he has to do is accept my offer and we'll see who is the better man." By that, Jack was referring to his challenge and the $1,000 he had deposited to bind another bout with La Blanche as well as the offer of the California Athletic Club to host the battle and to guarantee a large purse for the bout. The money had not been covered by the Marine, nor had La Blanche commented on Dempsey's or the club's offers. Jack realized that he might not be able to get La Blanche to agree to meet him again in the ring, but short of that, he was absolutely going to make him uncomfortable and watch him squirm. Within the month, Jack would quadruple his $1,000 offer.[120]

Jack was not quite through fighting that year. On October 8, Dempsey met featherweight boxer Tommy Warren in Mike Smith's saloon on Market Street in San Francisco. Warren asked Jack if it were true that the he had called him a liar and a faker for his part in the recent Warren-Murphy "fiasco" at the California Athletic Club. When Dempsey replied that it was true, Warren launched a right at Jack's face that Dempsey dodged. When the blow fell short, Jack sprang up and fired half a dozen blows that dropped Warren onto the barroom floor in a heap. After a few minutes, a demoralized and thoroughly beaten Warren was assisted from the saloon by his backers.[121] "Warren was taken to a neighboring drug store for repairs."[122]

Also, that evening, the board of directors of the California Athletic Club met and decided to match La Blanche against an unknown fighter for a large purse in a January contest. Many believed that the unknown pugilist would be Dempsey.[123] Jack was reportedly so disgusted that the California A.C. had not yet named him as the unknown pugilist to face La Blanche that he resigned his position as trainer for the club. The club directors refused to accept Dempsey's resignation.

While he had no fight of his own on the horizon, Jack was actively training Young Mitchell for his upcoming bout with Johnny Reagan in San Francisco on October 29. Jack was also to be in Mitchell's corner for the bout.[124]

On November 5, Dempsey and several friends paid a late-night visit to La Blanche's saloon in San Francisco. After a few drinks Dempsey told the Marine that he wanted to fight him again and was calling in La Blanche's promise of a rematch proffered while the pair were still in the ring the previous August. "La Blanche hemmed and hawed and finally said he didn't propose to take chances with anybody." Dempsey offered $500 to La Blanche if he would consent to a match, but again, the Marine declined. Dempsey countered that he was certain that the California Athletic Club could be induced to put up a purse of $5,000 for such a bout and Dempsey added that win or lose, he would give La Blanche $3,500 of that purse. The Marine remained noncommittal, saying only that he would consider the proposal and give an answer in a week.[125]

In early November, it was reported that La Blanche admitted to Dempsey that he would not fight him again because he was afraid. In one report, the *St. Paul Globe* titled the article relaying the story, "La Blanche is a Coward." The report went on to quote the Marine as stating to Dempsey in a meeting at the California Athletic Club, "I'll not fight you. I have got to the height of my ambition and I will not meet you any more, I am afraid of you."[126] La Blanche was so frustrated with that report that he wrote a letter to the editors of several papers and commented that he was no coward, but still refused to meet Jack again. Clearly, La Blanche was anything but a coward, but just as clearly, he had no desire to meet Dempsey again. The Marine did not necessarily fear the man, but he clearly feared losing to him again.[127]

Much was made of a proposed bout between Jack and Young Mitchell that was announced as pending in mid–November. The directors of the California Athletic Club proposed the match and Mitchell was excited to accept. Jack was, on the other hand, a bit leery about meeting his friend and pupil.[128] The club offered $3,000 to the winner and $500 to the runner up, but the money was not the issue for Jack. He simply did not wish to see his friend and pupil across the ring from him at this time. While the proposed bout with Mitchell was still up in the air, the club announced concrete plans for Dempsey to meet Australian middleweight Billy McCarthy for a $1,800 purse in January in San Francisco.[129] While it wound up being in February, this fight did come off. The men signed the fight contract on December 3 in the offices of the California Athletic Club.

Many were unsure that Dempsey could defeat McCarthy. For one of the first times in history, a large portion of the sporting world had doubts about the Nonpareil's ring prowess. "Some were of the opinion that Dempsey would have a walkover, while others were not so certain of it."[130] Repeated concerns about his increasingly unclear health condition and the questions raised by his defeat by La Blanche in August suddenly made Jack's ability to win a question rather than a sure thing. It did not matter that he was still the middleweight champion, nor did the poor quality of La Blanche's win matter—it was still a defeat for Dempsey. One observer noted, "Dempsey is a clever man and a game fighter, but he is not strong enough to knock out McCarthy with five-ounce gloves. He might do it with bare knuckles. Dempsey is scientific, but McCarthy is too rugged to be put to sleep by frail Jack, unless it happens to be with a terrific swing."[131] The mention of "frail Jack" was an indication of how much opinions had changed in just a few months.

Others were not in agreement and questioned McCarthy's ring ability. Writing his weekly column in the *National Police Gazette*, the "Referee" said that he could not understand why the directors of the California A.C. would make "such an unequal match" and that "against Dempsey, I fail to see how he will have a ghost of a show." After comparing the men's style in the ring and concluding that Dempsey was clearly the superior fighter, the "Referee" stated, "The only hypothesis upon which I can account for the directors of the club making such an unequal match is that they want to give Jack a lift up the ladder of fame again, as well as to replenish his depleted exchequer."[132]

Jack was readying himself to train for the McCarthy bout, but also working to help train and second Jack McAuliffe, who would be arriving in San Francisco just after New Year's to make ready for his aforementioned grudge match with British Jimmy Carroll. McAuliffe would return the favor and second Dempsey in his match with McCarthy.

In mid–December, Jack also found time to go duck hunting with noted baseball professional Mike "King" Kelly. Kelly was wintering in California before heading back to Boston for the baseball season. The pair stood in Jack's favorite spot on the Alameda Bridge and took target practice. It was reported that each had a clear eye and provided duck for the evening's supper.[133]

In late December, Jack decided to pay another of his periodic visits to George La Blanche at his saloon on San Francisco's Stockton Street, and press for a rematch. Jack demanded an answer to his challenge from La Blanche. When the Marine responded that he would not fight Dempsey because he could get an easier fight, Jack responded, "Oh, you flatter me. But I'm here to talk business. You know I was ready any time in three years to meet you if you could get the money to make a match, and when you got a purse in the California Club I fought you. Now it's one victory for each, and I want to have the question settled between us by another fight." Again, the Marine refused and Jack responded, "Then to put it plainly, you are afraid to fight?" La Blanche responded that he was not afraid and would consider fighting Jack again when he was ready to. Dempsey continued to increase his offer to La Blanche of more and more of the gate. It was obvious that this was not about money to Jack, but about pride. He guaranteed La Blanche two thirds of the purse regardless of outcome and frankly, he probably would have fought him for free. He continued to goad La Blanche until the Marine finally responded, "Well, yes, all right, if you want to put it that way; I am afraid of you. I can get easier game than you, Jack." Satisfied for the moment with a public confession of fear from La Blanche, Jack stated that he would return in a week to hear the Marine's response to his offer of a fight.[134]

1890—In Search of the Marine

Dempsey was extremely anxious to expunge the stain of his knockout at the hands of La Blanche as soon as possible. Regardless of the quality of La Blanche's victory, the fact remained that he had lost. Although it was a fight he controlled throughout, he had still been defeated, knocked out cold in the ring. His pride was hurting and his ego was bruised—he felt embarrassed. Like most people, La Blanche was aware that his win over Dempsey was a fluke he could likely never repeat, so he steadfastly refused to meet Jack in the ring again. Still Dempsey and much of the boxing world were anxious to see a rubber match between the two. One of Dempsey's friends commented, "Dempsey once defeated La Blanche and La Blanche defeated Dempsey. The deciding bout is now overdue. The best two out of three should decide the matter."[1]

If La Blanche refused to fight him, Dempsey would regain victory and positive press by defeating other opponents. "La Blanche would not consent to a return match, so, for the present, the most available man, therefore, to match against Dempsey was the Australian middleweight champion McCarthy, who had recently arrived in [San Francisco], and where he had gained some prominence by his easy best of Denny Kelliher."[2] In December Dempsey signed an agreement to meet the Australian middleweight champion in late January.

Once again, Jack's health became an issue. While he and his inner circle tried hard to keep news of Jack's periodic physical maladies under wraps, inevitably, news would leak out. In early January while in San Francisco, he began to weaken again while training for his upcoming bout with McCarthy. The official line from the Dempsey camp and from W.R. Vice, the chairman of the California A.C.'s boxing committee, was that Jack had a bad chest cold.[3] "He says that he has been suffering from a severe cold, which settled on his lungs and completely stopped his training. He is under the care of a competent physician and is now convalescent, and expects to be all right next week and able to resume work."[4] Dempsey's backers, the directors of the California A.C. and various news reports tried to put a good spin on the story, stating that Dempsey "chose" not to attend the Billy Murphy–Ike Weir bout in San Francisco in January as a precaution against worsening his condition. In actuality, it was an attempt not to reveal that he was actually so ill that he could barely rise from his bed. In time, Jack's condition did improve dramatically and he worked himself into good condition. Still, repeated bouts with chest colds, other similar maladies and long periods of isolation caused concern. With this most recent illness, Dempsey wasn't seen for over a week and only communicated through his trainers, which only acted as an accelerant to heightening speculation about his condition.

Regardless of the claims, many people were seriously concerned about Dempsey's overall health. His illness was serious enough that the McCarthy fight had to be postponed from its original January date. Again, the rumors that Jack might be in the early stages of consumption began to circulate.[5] His weight was reported to be down to 134 pounds, a full twenty off his normal fighting weight of the time. Two years before, Jack had battled pleurisy and pneumonia that had laid him low for more than four weeks and also dropped his weight below 140 pounds. Periodic statements such as, "It is reported that Jack Dempsey, the pugilist, is a victim of consumption and will never fight again,"[6] began to circulate in the dailies. He regained his strength, but he then fought Reagan soaking wet in the cold December air for more than forty-two rounds. While many impressive ring performances were still to come, Dempsey's weakened lungs were cause for concern.

Predictably, Jack set up his training camp at the beautiful Neptune Gardens across the Bay from San Francisco in Alameda. He had grown fond of training there. Lightweight champion Jack McAuliffe and Billy Madden arrived in San Francisco from Portland on board the steamer *Santa Rosa* two weeks before the fight. McAuliffe was preparing for his upcoming bout with British Jimmy Carroll and was anxious to get into a rigorous training schedule and lose some weight. He was also anxious to support his old friend Dempsey and help prepare him to meet the Australian champion. Coming off the loss to La Blanche and battling concerns about his health, Dempsey could use the support of his friends. Reports had it, however, that Denny Costigan and Dempsey had words, and that Costigan and Pete McCoy left San Francisco on an eastbound Northern Pacific train a couple of days before the fight due to a spat.[7] The two had reportedly been arguing for weeks and finally, Costigan decided to go.[8] If indeed there was any truth to the story, the falling out did not amount to much and was put quickly behind them as Dempsey and Costigan and, for that matter, McCoy, remained close friends. There was some bad blood between McCoy and Denny Kelliher that might explain McCoy's leaving and Costigan might have gotten caught up in that spat. At any rate, Denny Kelliher would take over Dempsey's training for the few days remaining before the fight.

In the weeks before the bout, reports from Dempsey's camp were that he was in fine condition, but some fans were unsure and began wagering that Dempsey was not his old self and that McCarthy would find him an easy mark. Lingering doubts persisted in some quarters that the Nonpareil was still too weak from his recent health issues and lacked the stamina and strength to defeat the larger and very durable Australian. Jack did not share their concerns. He was anxious to regain the victor's laurels and put the La Blanche debacle behind him. In the last few days before the fight, the odds moved heavily back to Jack's favor at 100 to 60.

On February 18, 1890, Dempsey met McCarthy at the California Athletic Club gymnasium in San Francisco. Both Dempsey and McCarthy, along with Australian heavyweight legend Peter Jackson, were employed as boxing instructors at the club which had recently been described by *Harper's Weekly* as "a Remarkable Athletic Organization." Describing the facility and its state of the art gym and event facilities, *Harper's* went on to say that the club "is conceded to be the richest athletic club in the world. It has a membership of about 1,700, comprising the cream of the clubbable men on the Pacific slope."[9] The auditorium was well lit with large electric lights hanging from the ceiling. In addition to the floor seating, the venue was equipped with balconies, each with twenty rows of seats all providing unobstructed views of the ring.

The purse for this fight was reportedly $1,800, with $1,500 going to the winner. It was agreed that while it was a middleweight championship contest, the men would fight according to Queensberry Rules and wear four-ounce gloves. As reported earlier, the fight had received a certain level of skepticism since it had been announced several months earlier. In addition to the "Referee" writing in the *Police Gazette*, an article reporting on McCarthy having gone into training for the bout stated that "the match has occasioned much controversy, and it is the general opinion in San Francisco that Dempsey will have an easy thing of it."[10] But in truth, the Australian was a clever fighter with a lot of skill.

McCarthy, who was born in 1860 in London, England, had ultimately settled in Sydney, Australia, where he fought exclusively for three years until sailing with his Australian middleweight championship belt for America in the summer of 1889. After tuning up with several young Bay Area fighters—including a young Joe Choynski—McCarthy set a November date in San Francisco with New Englander Denny Kelliher, whom he defeated by TKO in twenty-three rounds. He now challenged the Nonpareil and the date was originally set for January.

McCarthy was described as being indebted to nature for his good physical makeup. "His countenance is manly and open, possessing a sharp and penetrating eye that almost looks through the object in front of him, which gives animation to his face. His form is athletic and commanding and denotes uncommon strength and courage."[11] He is also described as kind, generous, intelligent, witty and mannerly.

Both men were ready, having overcome illness and injury. Jack had chiefly put his battle with what was described as "the grip" behind him and looked fit by fight night. McCarthy had sprained his hand a few weeks before while wrestling and friends at his camp had expressed fears that the injury might either postpone the bout or limit their man's ability to fight. By the evening of the contest, however, McCarthy's hand had recovered sufficiently and by all estimates, he seemed fit.

McCarthy's greatest concern going into the fight seemed to be making weight. The middleweight championship was to be on the line during the bout and therefore he needed to weigh in at no more than 154 pounds. He had had trouble making weight for his recent bout with Denny Kelliher when he came in at 157. He claimed to be weak in the days before that fight due to the weight loss. McCarthy took steps to avoid that scenario again. "He tried to induce Dempsey to have the weighing take place several hours before they entered the ring. Dempsey refused, stating that he had to quit making concessions to his opponents. 'If I get licked this time Mac, I'll be in the soup,' added Dempsey, 'and I can't afford to take any chances.'" McCarthy shrugged his shoulders and replied to Jack, "Well, you'll have a bloomin' fine feed before you fight, while I'll be bloody well starved, you know."[12]

Over two thousand spectators were in attendance at the gymnasium for the highly-anticipated bout. The excitement level ran high. "The sporting community had looked forward to this contest with the greatest interest for the past two months, and as the time for the event approached, other pugilistic occurrences in the city were overshadowed. Nearly every man who saw Dempsey go down before La Blanche last August was anxious that the Nonpareil should be given an opportunity to retrieve his lost honors...."[13]

Several preliminary bouts were fought early in the evening. It was just past 9:00

p.m. when Dempsey and McCarthy stepped into the arena to rousing applause. A condition of the bout was that both men were to come in at no more than 156 pounds and both made it. At ringside, McCarthy weighed in at 151¾ pounds to Dempsey's 147½. McCarthy was heavier, but Dempsey had a great advantage in height and reach.

There was a coin flip for choice of corners which McCarthy won. He intentionally chose La Blanche's "lucky corner," thus relegating Dempsey to the same corner that he occupied during his loss to La Blanche the previous August. McCarthy was in hopes that the ghosts of that night would still haunt Jack.

Jack McAuliffe and Denny Kelliher seconded Jack, while British Jimmy Carroll and Paddy Gorman were in McCarthy's corner. After the men entered the ring, it was announced by club President Lamartine R. Fulda that the four-ounce gloves to be used had been tampered with and would have to be repaired. According to Fulda, the gloves "had been ripped and considerable padding removed." Fulda oversaw the repair and "the gloves were fixed in order that the rules of the police department would not be infringed."[14] This repair took almost thirty minutes.

The fight finally commenced after 9:30 p.m., when Hiram Cook of San Francisco, who had been named referee, called the fighters to center ring. Sitting in the same corner as the previous August, staring across the ring at British Jimmy Carroll, and with Cook as referee, Dempsey could not have helped but to see some ghosts. His goal was to vanquish them.

The first round began quickly as the two men moved rapidly to the center of the ring. Dempsey caught McCarthy with a sharp left to the chin, but that was the only real contact of note. McCarthy had limited success in attempting to force the fight by driving Dempsey into the corners. He did land sharply to Jack's midsection and again on his neck, but he could accomplish little more as Dempsey dodged virtually all of the Australian's leads.

There was quick action in the second round as "McCarthy walked up like a locomotive with a clear track."[15] Jack backed away extending his left, but McCarthy ducked under it and came up with an uppercut that only missed doing serious damage as Jack, still showing his characteristic quickness, leaned in, fell forward and into a clinch. After the break, McCarthy continued his attack, firing punches as fast as he could move. Dempsey then moved his head with cat-like quickness, deftly avoiding three vicious left-right combinations. McCarthy was marvelously quick, but he was also wild. After another miss, Dempsey buried a hard left jab into his opponent's stomach, "provoking a grunt that could be heard all over the hall."[16] The Nonpareil then began pounding away at his opponent, landing several hard blows each to the face and body. At one point, "Dempsey caught McCarthy savagely in the face twice and then gave him a terrific right hander on the body."[17] As McCarthy attempted to retaliate, Jack would slip away. A frustrated McCarthy was only able to land glancing blows as Dempsey took another round.

In the third chapter, McCarthy came out fast, "but was met with a right hander on the mouth. He did not flinch, however, and a moment later got in a hot uppercut on Jack's mouth."[18] Dempsey returned fire, landing several left-right combinations to his opponent's chin and rib cage and then fluidly slipped back out of range to avoid a fearful swing from his opponent. McCarthy showed his skills as well. "The Australian ducked well and saved himself from a fierce blow aimed at his neck. Just as the round closed he struck Dempsey hard in the wind and received a hot one on the forehead in return."[19]

As McCarthy circled in the fourth round, Dempsey patiently watched for an opportunity. Again, McCarthy seemed anxious to work Jack into the corners, but Jack's quick feet and ability to dodge enabled him to move away and avoid many of his opponent's blows and enabled him to avoid getting trapped against the ropes. Jack, with his left arm extended, held McCarthy at bay. Jack waited patiently and when his opportunity finally came, it came in spades as the Nonpareil's left repeatedly found the Australian's nose, head and neck. When Dempsey missed on another blow, McCarthy took advantage of the misfire and countered heavily on Jack's jaw. The remainder of the round saw McCarthy attempt to catch Dempsey as the Nonpareil danced about the ring and avoided the Australian's jabs and heavy punches. Dempsey got in two solid uppercuts once when McCarthy finally managed to back him into the ropes. After landing these shots, Dempsey rolled off the ropes and let go a heavy left which McCarthy ducked, but in so doing, he fell and landed heavily. The Australian was up in a flash and continued pursuing Dempsey but had little fortune in inflicting any damage.

When the fifth round opened, the Australian made an attempt to rush Dempsey, but had little luck as he was forced to dodge a hard left. While avoiding the left, however, McCarthy got tagged by a clean, hard drive to the ribs from Dempsey's right. The men then traded punches at mid-ring for a good half minute, but McCarthy was clearly getting the worst of the blows and was getting frustrated. Pulling a page out of the La Blanche playbook, McCarthy lunged at Dempsey. He then pivoted and swung a sledgehammer-like blow at Jack's head that the Nonpareil nimbly dodged, causing it to glance off the side of his head and fly harmlessly over his shoulder. Jack returned fire, smacking McCarthy with a hard right on the jaw that turned the Australian around. After sustaining a sharp attack to the head and body, McCarthy showed some spirit and responded by rushing his opponent and landing numerous well-placed shots around Dempsey's ears.

McCarthy, anxious to capitalize on his momentum from late in the previous round, was the first to scratch when Cook called the men to center ring to start the sixth session. The men traded blows, Dempsey landing on the Australian's midsection and McCarthy on Jack's jaw. McCarthy, using his left, then let go "with a vicious uppercut which failed of its mark, and then inexplicably walked to his corner, closely followed by a shocked Dempsey. The men rested a moment, and then Dempsey repeated his attack on his opponent's body, landing heavily three times. [McCarthy] seemed a trifle flurried as the round closed amid applause for Dempsey."[20] McCarthy had continually led with his left hoping for a chance to land a hard right but, repeatedly denied by Dempsey's quickness, that chance never came. "A close rally occurred on the ropes and Dempsey, after missing two leads, planted a heavy blow over the Australian's heart."[21] Despite the Australian's best efforts, this was again the Nonpareil's round and McCarthy seemed a bit frustrated as the session ended with a heavy round of applause for Dempsey.

It was Dempsey who began the action in the seventh round, firing repeated shots at the Australian, but McCarthy showed great quickness in dodging and blocking the Nonpareil's missiles. McCarthy let go one bomb, "the force of which brought the giver to his knees."[22] Those of Dempsey's volleys that landed struck McCarthy on the jaw, but just before the round ended, McCarthy landed the most impressive punch of the round — a solid right to Dempsey's chest.

In the eighth round, McCarthy landed another hard blow to Dempsey's ear, but when he tried to follow up with another, Jack sidestepped the powerful punch causing the Australian to miss so badly that the momentum of the swing almost carried McCarthy to the floor. Dempsey then countered and doubled McCarthy up with a solid right to the stomach. McCarthy recovered and landed on Jack's ear and then tried another backhand blow that Jack dodged and fired back with a straight left to the Australian's mouth.

The ninth was an active round in which both fighters scored points—Dempsey with sustained attacks to the neck and body, McCarthy with a hard left to the Nonpareil's stomach and still another questionable, turning, backhand blow to the nose. Cook clearly was not going to call a foul for hitting with the back of his hand, so McCarthy decided to take advantage. He also landed a heavy shot to Jack's chin. This round was full of action and those on hand cheered both fighters as the gong ended the skirmish. Most at ringside called this round a draw.

In the tenth round, Dempsey continued to hammer away at his opponent's body, wrenching out several clear and audible grunts from McCarthy. Still showing a great deal of fight, the Australian responded with vicious attacks landing frequent uppercuts, but the Nonpareil was too quick for him and avoided much heavy punishment until late in the round when McCarthy planted a hard left to the champion's stomach. While the round might have been Jack's, the Australian's determined nature kept it close.

Both men looked strong as the eleventh round began. Dempsey let McCarthy move freely around the ring at first, but soon began lobbing bombs that caught his opponent on the jaw, ribs and chest. Jack continued throughout the round landing hard, clean blows and beginning to wear the Australian down. Jack then landed several clean blows, two of which virtually knocked McCarthy's head around sideways. As the round was ending Dempsey's right fist landed hard against McCarthy's throat and again against his stomach.

In the twelfth round, McCarthy repeated his turning blow, again catching Dempsey on the nose, but Dempsey, barely fazed, fired a short right that smashed the Australian on the chin as McCarthy lunged after the champion. Again, McCarthy was frustrated by his inability to keep up any sustained pressure on Dempsey.

As the thirteenth round began, "Dempsey aimed a wicked blow for McCarthy's neck, but the latter saved himself by a neat duck."[23] The fighters then exchanged a series of inconsequential blows and repeatedly fell into the clinches. The round ended with Dempsey landing several hard shots to his opponent's jaw and chin.

The fourteenth round was clearly Dempsey's as the Nonpareil landed multiple hard punches to McCarthy's stomach and neck. After dropping a stinging left on the Australian's jaw, a second blow to the stomach doubled McCarthy over. He recovered and took a huge swing at Jack's head, but Dempsey again sidestepped the blow, the force of which threw McCarthy off balance. "Jack, like a shot, swung in right on his neck, which was decidedly the best blow of the fight."[24] Billy hung on to the end of the round, but was clearly tiring and beginning to show the effects of Dempsey's persistent battering.

In the fifteenth and sixteenth rounds, Dempsey began to toy with his opponent, landing numerous punches designed to continue to wear down McCarthy. He also continued to move quickly, making the Australian wear himself out throwing many punches that struck nothing but the air, each of which aimed at the spot where Jack had been just a split second earlier. Dempsey "landed on the Australian's body and jaw about as he pleased. The latter's eyes and cheeks began to show signs of severe punishment, and when the round closed, he was evidently very groggy."[25] Dempsey began landing his jabs at will as the round ended, and the Nonpareil fired off two mortar shots—a left and a right—that exploded on the Australian's jaw. As he walked back to his corner after the bell, McCarthy was spitting blood.

Dempsey continued his onslaught in the seventeenth round, reigning blows upon his opponent from start to finish. "The fighting was sharp throughout, but it was evident from the first that Dempsey was determined to retrieve his fame lost in the fight with La Blanche. McCarthy did some very clever fighting both offensive and defensive, but in the 17th round he began to grow groggy, and from then on it was evident that Dempsey had him whipped."[26] During much of the round the Australian was not in it at all. Jack clearly had McCarthy beat, but he was still unable to floor his sturdy opponent.

The eighteenth round mirrored the previous chapter, with the Australian fighting hard—perhaps emboldened and fortified by the whiskey his seconds supplied him during the break—and Dempsey moving about the ring quickly and avoiding most of McCarthy's blows. Jack would often back away or duck a punch, but quickly come inside and land hard counters to his opponent's head and body. The men declared a cessation of hostilities long enough to blow their noses, but with nasal passages cleared, quickly went back at it. The round soon ended with blood trickling from McCarthy's mouth and Dempsey's nose.

The nineteenth through twenty-first rounds were highly uneventful as McCarthy was showing the signs of exhaustion and Jack, tiring a bit from many rounds of constant action, was happy to slow the pace somewhat and catch his breath. McCarthy was too tired to throw the heavy bombs that he had attempted throughout the contest and instead came inside and attempted to engage the Nonpareil with hooks and uppercuts. That was fine with Dempsey who knew that he could block or avoid the short blows, but still feared the powerful desperation blow such as La Blanche had employed. Dempsey heeded his corner man Jack McAuliffe's advice and kept up a steady drum beat on McCarthy's face, but was still unable to finish off the stubborn Australian. Some observers opined that "the Nonpareil evidently fear[ed] an ambuscade to an extent that caused him to forgo several apparently tempting openings for a knockout blow."[27] These rounds were light on action as the men circled and engaged in light sparring. Both fighters welcomed the break and the only real action came when McCarthy dropped a blow on the top of Dempsey's head and received a return punch in the nose for his efforts.

The twenty-second round saw a return to the frenzied pace of the earlier staves. After waiting for an opening, Dempsey fired a volley of lefts and rights that landed hard on the Australian's neck and ribs and turned McCarthy completely around. When Billy returned fire and landed heavily on his opponent's stomach, Dempsey reactively shot back a powerful left-handed jab that landed like a lightning strike on McCarthy's chin and nearly dropped the Australian. Billy's knees buckled and it looked like he was on his way down, but through sheer persistence, he managed to stay on his feet.

The twenty-third through twenty-fifth rounds followed a familiar pattern with McCarthy giving it all the fight he had, but the bout clearly staying in Dempsey's hands. Dempsey would move in and jab, then retreat when McCarthy looked like he was ready to strike back. Even the retreats seemed to work in Dempsey's favor as he landed several blows to his opponent's jaw while stepping back. Little was decided in these rounds. Jack was still clearly in command of the fight but could not for the life of him put an end to the contest by finishing his opponent. He knew the fight was his, but he was being cautious. Even though McCarthy looked unsteady and ready to drop, Jack was extremely wary about being lured in too close. The specter of the George La Blanche fiasco was still on his mind.

In the twenty-sixth round, Dempsey came close to finishing his opponent. Several strong combinations to McCarthy's head left the Australian dazed and Dempsey in complete control. Finally, fully satisfied that his opponent was finished, Jack became a bit bolder. He began to crowd McCarthy hard and to hit his opponent when and where he pleased. After a clean, hard crack to the jaw, the Australian grew so tired and woozy that his hands dropped, leaving him practically defenseless. "McCarthy staggered around the ring like a drunken man, but although Dempsey continued to rain blows on his neck he still kept his feet until the Nonpareil, in pity for his victim, asked him to give up. McCarthy refused, and as the round was about to close Dempsey would not punish him anymore but took him by the arm and led him to his corner amid cheers from the spectators."[28]

McCarthy answered the bell for the twenty-seventh round, but he was still unsteady on his feet and Dempsey determined to end it there. The Nonpareil struck a powerful blow to his opponent's face that dropped McCarthy and bloodied his nose and mouth, but again, the Australian rose. Dempsey dropped him again moments later with a straight smash to the face that widened the cut on McCarthy's mouth, but again the Australian rose. And so it went for the remainder of the round. Again, Dempsey implored his opponent to quit, but to no avail. As the round ended, Jack dropped McCarthy again. McCarthy slowly managed to get to his knees and, struggling, rose to his feet once more just in time to avoid a knockout. At this point, the crowd joined the chorus and began to plead for the Australian to stop. McCarthy, now covered in blood, was led to his corner.

As the bell tolled the start of the twenty-eighth round, all present knew that the affair could not continue for long. From the crowd could be heard mingled cries of "Knock him out, Jack!" and "Give it up, McCarthy!" "McCarthy staggered to the center of the ring and Dempsey implored him to give up."[29] Despite Jack's pleas, the Australian still refused to admit defeat. Dempsey then beat McCarthy back into the corner where several strong shots, most notably a blow to the face, dropped the Australian. Again, McCarthy arose, waiting until the count of seven and refusing to admit defeat. The weakened fighter was forced to lean against the ropes for support and Jack walked over to finish him, but when he saw McCarthy's horrible state, the Nonpareil instead looked at the referee and said that he had no stomach to continue beating the pitiable Australian. At that moment, Paddy Gorman, McCarthy's second, jumped into the ring, stopped the fight and dragged McCarthy back to his corner. The time was 1:52 of the twenty-eighth round. At that point, Dempsey was finally declared the winner by Cook and the crowd cheered him wildly in admiration of both his ring skills and the concern and compassion he showed for his badly beaten opponent.[30]

The official time for the bout was one hour and fifty minutes, but the fight in reality ended much earlier. That McCarthy continued to rise to his feet and take the tremendous punishment handed to him by the Nonpareil is a testament to his courage and toughness, but why the bout was allowed to continue when it was clear that he was thoroughly beaten and had no chance of winning can only be explained by the more relaxed concerns for the fighters' safety at the time.

As Dempsey left the ring and made his way back to his dressing room, he was mobbed by the crowd, many deliriously happy that the Nonpareil appeared to be back on the winning track. It took the combined efforts of three police officers to spirit Jack through the crowd and to the safety of his dressing room. Once there, Jack stretched and jumped about trying to loosen up. He then sat back to get a leg rub from his seconds. Jack showed very few cuts or bruises and when asked how he felt, Dempsey replied that he was fine, except for his left arm which he sprained in the fifth round. When asked for his thoughts on McCarthy, Jack replied, "He made a game, hard fight and the only thing I regret is that he was not allowed to go out when I begged him to, as he was at my mercy and I didn't want to hurt him."[31]

The scene in McCarthy's dressing room was wholly different. The Australian was in bad shape, stretched out on his dressing table, his lips and nose terribly swollen and his chest bruised and marked from Dempsey's volleys. "He had scarcely touched his bed before he became nauseated and he threw off much blood." When he was able to talk, he commented, "I don't know what happened. I went queer in the eighth round and was alone blind for a few moments. I wonder if anything could have been done with those gloves."[32] McCarthy was still dazed from the pounding he took during the bout and no one took this comment seriously. In a press conference on February 20, the Australian "expressed his entire confidence in Dempsey and said that he always looked upon the Nonpareil as a square, fair fighter and not one who would take an unfair advantage of his opponent." McCarthy added that he completely dismissed "the idea of Jack having anything to do with tampering with the gloves."[33] The fairy tale of the supposed poisonous solution on Dempsey's gloves gained very little traction in the days after the fight. The *Police Gazette* reported that "the Australian states that it was the pernicious drugs placed on the gloves that stupefied and partially blinded him early in the fight." Richard Fox rejected this claim out of hand, stating that it was a common ruse among the defeated. "Every pugilist, oarsman and wrestler and trap shooter and athlete generally makes an excuse when he is beaten, and it has been the case during the past thirty years and will continue to be the case."[34] The directors of the California Athletic Club looked into the matter and as Fox predicted, it was much ado about nothing. More than likely this was, as Fox stated, an attempt to provide an excuse and nurse a bruised ego for, as the *New York World* reported the day after the bout, "at the end of the twenty-eighth-round McCarthy's prestige was a thing of the past and Dempsey was once more lifted to the high pinnacle he occupied so long and bravely."[35]

After being examined and pronounced fit by a physician, McCarthy was taken from the Club to the Hammam baths where he would clean up and begin his healing.

Regardless of the questionable back-hand blows and claims of glove tampering, McCarthy and Dempsey became friendly after the bout. While speaking with a reporter a month later, the Australian showed the unique character of pugilistic friendships when he said, "Jack is an exceptionally good man and a friend of mine, but I wish I had broken his jaw two weeks ago because it's business."[36]

Dempsey now looked forward to a rematch with La Blanche. The Marine had stated that he would fight the winner of the Dempsey-McCarthy contest and the Nonpareil was ready. Former lightweight champion Billy Edwards was present at the fight and said that Dempsey's victory convinced him that Dempsey was as good a man in the ring as he ever was. "Dempsey's defeat by La Blanche doesn't prove anything further than a chance blow can prove a very lucky thing for the man who inflicts it." Edwards continued in expressing his view, "I believe that Dempsey can whip La Blanche under almost any conditions and with any kind of gloves."[37] While Dempsey saw his victory as a step toward a rematch with La Blanche, he was also just glad to be on the winning side again and take some of the sting away from his defeat the previous August. It was also good for his wallet. "Since Dempsey's victory, the champion has been flooded with offers from all parts of the country to give exhibitions and engage in glove contests."[38] In the days following the Dempsey-McCarthy fight it was reported that George La Blanche was angry with officials at the California Athletic Club for allowing Dempsey and his friends to shower La Blanche with "taunts and denunciations" in order to goad him back into the ring.

While the rematch never occurred, La Blanche offered to stake his profitable San Francisco saloon as a prize to the winner of the bout.[39] At first, Jack was hesitant, stating that he was not interested in half of La Blanche's saloon, but soon he decided that this was fine as he was anxious to exact retribution from the Marine for almost any stakes.

At a press conference at the California Athletic Club on February 21, Jack told club president Fulda and the assembled reporters, "I don't want to fight Young Mitchell [John Herget]. I look upon him as my boy and think him wrong in challenging me, but I shall teach him a lesson when we meet in April." Dempsey continued in saying that it was La Blanche he was after. "I will meet La Blanche in the ring before a club or on the green with bare knuckles, skin gloves, or five-ounce gloves, London Rules or Queensberry Rules, and bet him $10,000 to $2,500—that is giving him four to one—and if he don't accept this proposition he declares his actions plainer than words that he is afraid to meet me again. I have offered him every dollar of a $3,500 purse to meet, win or lose. He would not do that and I have made a number of liberal offers to him, but this last one is best. If he can whip me he can win anywhere from $50,000 to $100,000. Now let's see what he will do."[40] It was reported by numerous newspapers that La Blanche refused to fight Dempsey under any circumstances and that "much indignation was expressed at the Marine's refusal to give Dempsey a chance to win back lost laurels."[41]

Under the headline, "La Blanche Afraid," and the subheading of "Dempsey Makes Him Quail Before an Open Challenge," the *Daily Morning Astorian* reported that on February 25 both Dempsey and La Blanche attended a meeting at the California Athletic Club during which the club directors attempted to schedule a third bout between the Nonpareil and the Marine. When club president Fulda asked the men if they would fight, Dempsey immediately responded that he was willing, but La Blanche "turned quite pale" and responded, "I decline." Dempsey was incredulous. "Why, you said you would fight the winner of the McCarthy-Dempsey contest and I should think you would be ashamed to decline after your rash promise. What are your objections to fighting me?" La Blanche replied, "I can afford to do without fighting as now things are coming pretty easy with me." Fulda then asked La Blanche if any price would tempt him, to which the Marine responded, "Not at present."

Dempsey, rising from his chair in anger, interrupted, asking, "What is at present, La Blanche? Are you afraid of me? Why don't you fight? Confess that you are afraid." La Blanche murmured that he was not afraid. "Well," cried Dempsey, "you are afraid and I'll bet you $10,000 in coin that you are. You won a battle from me on a fluke and you know it. You are afraid to fight me and you know it, way down in your heart. I'd be ashamed to show my face if I were you, after all the roasting you have had from the papers and people."

La Blanche sat quietly and gazed at the ceiling while listening to Dempsey's tirade. Finally, Dempsey calmed down and, compelled by club director Fish, Jack apologized for his outburst if not for his righteous indignation. La Blanche was encouraged to consider the offer as well as another for $1,000 purse for an East Coast bout that was read out loud in a telegram from New York. Still La Blanche refused as the meeting concluded.[42]

On February 26, La Blanche again offered to put up his saloon as his share of the purse. In a letter he stated, "My business I estimate to be worth $10,000, but in order to prove to Dempsey that I am not afraid of him I will sacrifice it for half that sum. Let Dempsey or his backers put up $5,000 in some secure hands pending the fight and if he defeats me I take down the $5,000 and Dempsey walks into my saloon as sole proprietor. Should I prove the victor, Dempsey takes back the $5,000 and I return to the saloon."[43] The Marine added that these were the only conditions under which he would meet Dempsey.

After his victory over McCarthy, Jack, with his old spring back, was in high demand once again. Clubs from New Orleans to New York to England were proposing fights with the Nonpareil matched against various fighters, including Mike Donovan and Toff Wall. Still Dempsey preferred to stay on the West Coast and challenge La Blanche. Still bucking for a rematch, Johnny Reagan stated that he was also interested in meeting Dempsey again "for a limited number of rounds."

A week after the confrontation with La Blanche, at the February 25 club meeting, Jack was given permission by the board to pursue fights in Portland and points north. He wasted little time in doing so. Three days later Dempsey announced that he had accepted a $500 guarantee to travel to Tacoma, Washington, and meet Tom Cleary in a four-rounder followed by a six-round bout with soft gloves versus Chicago's Jack Burke.[44]

Jack and Maggie arrived in Portland on the steamer *State of California* on the evening of February 27. Jack was met by a score of reporters and admirers. When asked how he felt, the Nonpareil responded, "Never better, I am feeling splendidly, but came here to see my folks and rest for ten days."[45] Escorted by a crowd of friends, they arrived at their East Portland home later that night.

The next day, the Dempseys held a reception for friends and the press corps. When a journalist for the *San Francisco Examiner* asked him about La Blanche's offer to surrender his saloon should Dempsey best him, Jack was incredulous. After again denouncing the Marine as a coward, Jack said, "Bah, that saloon is a great big bluff. He says it's worth $10,000, does he? Well it's not worth a hundred dollars to me. In fact, I wouldn't take it as a gift." Jack continued, "It is a low-down groggery and a resort for the vicious and depraved of both sexes. Gentlemen don't go there nor ever will no matter who owns it…. I might allow him $500 on it and then close it up for the good of the city." Dempsey then closed his comments on the subject by stating, "La Blanche can get $5,000 and a good deal more out of me if he knocks me out again, but he can't get it as a sure thing for getting knocked out. Why don't he come up like a man and try for the purse offered by the California Athletic Club? Then he can put up as many thousands as he wants to on the side and he will find the money ready to cover it."[46]

La Blanche was asked the next day about Dempsey's comments and the Marine responded to the *Examiner* reporter that Jack was bluffing. "If he wants to fight let him, as I said before, accept my terms. If he don't, let him shut up. That's all I've got to say about Mr. Dempsey and his propositions to make a match with me."[47]

Many agreed with Jack that La Blanche's proposition was ridiculous. One news article stated that the proposition "is regarded by a majority of the sporting men of the country as a remarkable piece of gall. La Blanche says that his saloon business, just started in San Francisco, is worth at least $10,000 in his mind. He will not put up any cash but proposes to put half the value of his saloon up against $5,000 of Dempsey's money. Then, if [La

Blanche] loses the fight, he is to take down $5,000 and hand over the saloon to Dempsey. If he wins, again he takes the $5,000 cash and keeps his saloon. It is a sort of proposition whereby he offers to fight for $5,000 certainly. His estimate of $10,000 as a value for his business may be correct, but it is dollars to doughnuts he could not sell it tomorrow for $2,500."[48] La Blanche would not own the saloon for much longer at any rate. The property would be seized by the sheriff of San Francisco in July over non-payment of taxes and fees to the city.[49] Things did not get any better for the Marine after that. He was arrested on July 24 on a warrant charging him with grand larceny for misappropriating $500 during a competitive footrace. He was bailed out.[50]

As was stated above, Jack was not interested in the saloon, but soon he decided that he was so anxious to exact retribution from the Marine that he would go ahead and agree to the terms for the chance to get La Blanche back in the ring with him. In this one case, he didn't care about the money or the terms, Jack just wanted to whip the Marine. As Dempsey began to warm to the idea however, La Blanche once again began to retreat from his offer.

A year after his loss to the Marine, Dempsey summed up his frustration with the bout and La Blanche's refusal to give Jack a rematch. "I had the fight well in hand, when in running after La Blanche, who was running away from me, he turned and hit me a fearful swinging blow on the left temple with his elbow. The force of the blow knocked me down and my head striking the floor, I laid there." Dempsey then continued, saying that he had tried repeatedly to entice the Marine back into the ring with varying offers of $1,000 to $5,000, with no acceptance from La Blanche. Finally, he relayed that several friends had offered several thousand each to La Blanche to make the fight. "There was $6,000 for him, win or lose, but he still refused to meet me. Then I said, 'George, I would meet Sullivan on these terms. You must be afraid of me.' He replied, 'I am afraid. I think I can get easier game than you.' Dempsey continued, 'It is for this reason that I have given up hope of ever again getting on a match with La Blanche.'"[51]

The war of words would continue between the two with Jack laying out generous offers and La Blanche making unattractive counters until eventually, things quieted down. Sadly, the rematch never occurred. It would have been a good one.

On March 13, Dempsey met 40-year-old ring veteran John Clark in Seattle for a four-round exhibition bout. Clark was born in County Galway, Ireland, in 1849, but he grew up in England. He was the lightweight champion of America twice. "He was a bouncy, feisty competitor who ran a boxing school and owned a billiard hall in Philadelphia, traveled the country giving exhibitions, and competed in the ring with many all-time great fighters. During his career, Clark defeated such men as Billy Payne, George Travers, Edward Toohey, Mike Haley and John Tully."[52] He did not defeat Dempsey, but neither did he lose. The contest was ruled a no decision after four rounds.

After a successful trip to Seattle and Tacoma, Jack headed home to Portland for a St. Patrick's Day exhibition in the Rose City. On the morning of March 14, Jack boarded a ferry to take him from Seattle to Tacoma where he intended to catch a train to Portland. Once in Tacoma, Jack boarded the wrong train and was several miles down the track before he realized his error. He got off the train with his luggage at the next town. "He hired a handcar to take him back to Tacoma, only to find the Portland train gone, and he was obliged to hire a special train to take him to that city."[53] The special train reportedly cost the Nonpareil $175. After a couple of days in Portland, Jack was on board a steamer heading for San Francisco passing through the Golden Gate in the early morning hours of March 18.

Jack McAuliffe gained a measure of revenge for his close friend Dempsey when he met British Jimmy Carroll on March 21 in San Francisco. McAuliffe was in the middle of his reign as the lightweight champion of the world, which ran from 1886 to 1893.

Carroll, the British lightweight and not Dempsey's friend and colleague from Brooklyn, was George La Blanche's trainer before the second Dempsey–La Blanche bout the previous August. It was Carroll who taught La Blanche the reverse pivot punch that the Marine used to defeat the Nonpareil. For whatever reason, Carroll hated Dempsey and encouraged the Marine to use the questionable pivot punch to defeat him. Neither Dempsey nor McAuliffe would ever forget that fact and nursed almost as big a grudge against Carroll as they did against La Blanche. When McAuliffe came to know this, he immediately challenged Carroll to a bout to be held in San Francisco. That night, Dempsey worked the corner—along with Billy Madden—in a bloody, forty-seven-round bout. As always, Jack was delighted to second his old friend from the cooperage.

When McAuliffe announced that his old friend Dempsey would be in his corner, Carroll immediately raised a vociferous protest. Carroll argued to the California Club's officers that as an employee of that institution, Dempsey should be ineligible to participate as a second. "The directors pointed out that Carroll himself, who is also an employee of the club, had acted as a second for McCarthy in the latter's fight with Dempsey last month. They therefore suspended the rule and allowed Dempsey to go behind McAuliffe tonight."[54]

The fight was billed as being for the lightweight championship of the world and the gymnasium was full by the time the contest began, just past 9:00 p.m. McAuliffe used his superior hand and foot speed to take the lead early in the bout, but Carroll hung in through tenacity and will power, even knocking McAuliffe off his feet in the twelfth round. Both men were tired and bloody by the forty-seventh round, but McAuliffe had a bit more gas left in his tank than had his opponent. He dropped Carroll twice in that round, the first time with a powerful right-hander for the count of four and the second with a powerful blast to the mouth that leveled Carroll for the count of ten and the victory. Fueled by the lingering outrage over the mistreatment of his old friend Dempsey by the Carroll-backed George La Blanche, McAuliffe was determined to take a measure of justice out on Carroll. "Jack punished Carroll for 47 rounds before knocking him cold. At the end of the fight, as he looked down at Jim Carroll's prostrate body, Jack sneered, 'That's for my pal, y'bum!'"[55]

Jack Dempsey left San Francisco on March 29, returning to Portland by sea on the steamship *Columbia* with the Vice Director of the California Athletic Club. The ship arrived in Portland on March 31. Jack was anxious to get home as Maggie had just given birth to the couple's second child, Anne Margaret Dempsey, who was born on March 29, 1890.

In April, multiple rumors began to circulate that Dempsey would be matched with a British middleweight, either Alf Mitchell or Toff Wall. Challenges to match Jack with these fighters came from San Francisco's California Athletic Club, the Arlington Athletic Club of Buffalo and then, over the next week, the Puritan Athletic Club of New York, who would offer a $1,800 purse for the same. In responding to the challenges, Dempsey said, "Toff Wall is the English middleweight fighter I want to meet. If he will not fight I want to meet any other first-class man weighing 154 pounds in England for any amount from $5,000 to $10,000 and will flip a penny to see on which side of the Atlantic we meet."[56]

There was also the news that Dempsey's nemesis George La Blanche had signed to fight Young Mitchell. For various reasons, the two would not actually meet until February 20, 1891, but the Marine's willingness to meet Mitchell and not Dempsey, raised more than a few eyebrows. In an article titled "La Blanche, the Dodger," the *Pittsburgh Dispatch* commented that La Blanche's agreeing to fight Mitchell and consistently refusing to set a rematch with Dempsey showed that the Marine "has some dread of the Nonpareil." The writer continued, "In other words, La Blanche is a veritable dodger and has dodged Dempsey so long that the sporting public must now be convinced that the very last man he desires to meet is Jack Dempsey."[57] Although Dempsey would rather have met and defeated La Blanche in the ring, there certainly must have been some solace in knowing that much of the public opinion held that Dempsey soundly whipped the Marine in both of their matches, and La Blanche only won the second by a fluke and questionably legal punch and that La Blanche was now running scared, fully realizing that the Nonpareil would easily win the rubber match.

After spending several weeks at home in Portland, Jack began touring with Joe McAuliffe's troupe of fighters and appearing in exhibitions throughout the Northwest where there was apparently good money to be made. McAuliffe was a notable heavyweight based out of San Francisco who met many of the top fighters of his era. While not a great boxer, the "Frisco Giant" who stood 6'3" and at more than two hundred pounds was a powerful man who had size on his side.

As the tour progressed and proved extremely popular in city after city, reports on Jack's future became common. According to news reports, the combination of sound money from the McAuliffe tour and his frustration over La Blanche's refusal to fight caused Jack to abruptly leave his employment at the California A.C. and to consider retirement from the ring. "Jack Dempsey is making so much money with a troupe of heavy and light weights that he will give up prize fighting for a living."[58] These rumors of Dempsey's retirement were common and sometimes fueled by Jack himself. Maggie was certainly anxious for him to exit the ring and part of Jack was ready to as well, but another side of the Nonpareil could never walk away.

Starting in Portland in late April, the long tour wound its way north to The Dalles and to Seattle. It would then progress eastward through several western states and on to St. Louis, Ohio, Pennsylvania and New York. Dempsey was joined on the tour by Paddy Gorman of Australia, former ring opponent and now friend Dave Campbell, Mike Flaherty and Mike Brennan, the Port Costa Giant. The quintet typically sparred in front of large crowds with large gates.

In Seattle, on May 2, Jack and Gorman fought a four-round exhibition at the Seattle Athletic Club. The *San Francisco Call* reported that "the Seattle papers state that Gorman made it very lively for the champion, notwithstanding Dempsey's cleverness."[59]

While touring, Dempsey would help whip up interest in the exhibitions by displaying his *National Police Gazette* championship belt in the windows of hotels and prominent stores of the towns in which they fought. While in The Dalles the belt was in the window of the jewelry store of Mr. S. Young, where, given the sash's gold, silver and jewel makeup, it was right at home. From Washington the group headed east to Montana.

The combination appeared for a two-night engagement at Maguire's Opera House, the Lyceum Theater in Butte, Montana, and one night at the Evans Opera House in Anaconda, Montana, on June 11–13 and Monday, June 16, respectively.[60] During the Butte engagement, Dave Campbell met Montana middleweight champion George Kessler in a four-round battle, which became infamous more for the events after the fight than for the actual bout. In what was to be a low-key, "scientific" affair, emotions became heated after each man felt the other was a bit overzealous in his aggressiveness. After the pair had been slugging it out for three and a half rounds, Butte Sheriff John E. Lloyd jumped into the ring and demanded an end to the fight. When they ignored him, a constable by the name of Waters aided Lloyd in separating the two and dragging Campbell back to his dressing room. Minutes later Campbell appeared back on the stage yelling to the crowd, "Gentlemen, I can whip George Kessler in a square fight for $1,000 to $2,000." His rant went on for another minute or two and he then returned to his dressing room. In a moment there was a loud crash in the dressing room—the sound of falling stove pipes and furniture—as the battle resumed out of sight of the crowd. With Kessler and Campbell back at it, the police rushed in to break the men apart. The men were both placed under arrest. The next morning, appearing before Judge Newkirk's court, cooler heads prevailed—they both plead guilty for disturbing the peace and paid a fine of $50.

The troupe moved on to Utah for shows in Salt Lake City's Golden Gate Club on June 20 and 21. Great crowds descended upon the Clift Hotel "to gaze upon the manly form of Jack Dempsey."[61] The Dempsey combination attracted large crowds during both appearances at the newly opened venue.[62] One report stated that the events were a great success, especially the Dempsey-Gorman tilts.

The June 20 bout between Dempsey and Gorman was described as a rousing affair in front of a packed house at the Golden Gate Athletic Club. The event featured three bouts between local fighters. Steve Davis and Oscar Black opened the evening with a bout that featured three rounds of hard and rapid hitting. The contest drew loud applause from the crowd. Master of Ceremonies Edward Kelly then introduced Frank Fitzgerald and a local man named Purcell, who provided four entertaining rounds. After this bout, Dave Campbell gave an exhibition with Indian clubs. Extremely popular during the late nineteenth and early twentieth centuries, Indian clubs are bowling-pin shaped clubs made of wood. Like hand weights, they are lifted and swung in certain patterns as part of exercise routines. They typically range from a few pounds each to as much as fifty pounds or more.

Following Campbell's exhibition, another bout featured Davis and Wiley, followed by another between Campbell and Mike Brennan. Brennan was a slugger from California who fought many noteworthy fighters of the era. The bout was lively as the men exhibited their quickness, science and power over four exciting rounds. As the pair left the ring, the crowd rose to their feet and sounded a loud applause that continued for several minutes.

As the crowd talked about the Campbell-Brennan match, Dempsey and Gorman approached the ring for the highlight of the evening. Jack weighed in at 159 pounds to Gorman's 175. The two sparred neatly for three rounds, "entertaining the audience with an exhibition far in excess of general expectation."[63]

Another report of the June 20 exhibition stated that Dempsey looked fit and as able as ever. The story ran as follows, "The wind-up was between Jack Dempsey, the middleweight champion of the world, and Paddy Gorman, the Australian pugilist. Dempsey's appearance was the signal for enthusiastic applause from the sports. The Nonpareil is in very good condition and he is as quick and as strong as when last seen here. His bout with Gorman was a very lively one and was characterized by some hard fighting. Dempsey of course had the best of the contest, but Gorman made it interesting for him."[64] During his stay in Salt Lake City, as was the case throughout the tour, Dempsey's championship belt from the *Police Gazette* was exhibited in a storefront window, this time at Hollander's Department Store.

It was reported that on June 21, Dempsey and several friends were shooting pool in the Whitehouse billiard room. When a crook "rolled" a drunken Irishman and took his money, "Dempsey made the fellow return his plunder and called him a thief." At that point a man named Willard who was apparently with the crook, stood up for his friend and slapped the Nonpareil in the face. "Quick as a flash the prizefighter landed squarely in Willard's face and dropped him under a billiard table." Willard quickly realized that he was "monkeying with the wrong man and got away as quickly as possible."[65]

The *Salt Lake Tribune* chronicled the troupe's itinerary as follows, "Manager Charley Dexter and the Jack Dempsey combination are at the Clift House. After this evening's exhibition at Independence Hall they go to Park City for a Saturday night spar and then go straight to Denver. From thence they give exhibitions in Colorado Springs, Pueblo and Dodge City. Paddy Gorman, champion of Australia, is standing up against Dempsey in a four-round contest of three minutes each. Dave Campbell, the Oregon champion, and Mike Brennan, the Fort Custer giant, make up the second team."[66] The report also added that four- and six-ounce gloves were being used in all bouts on the tour.

From Salt Lake City, the crew moved on to Colorado where they appeared in Colorado Springs, Aspen and Denver before heading to Hutchinson, Kansas, and then to Missouri for an Independence Day match in St. Louis. The exhibition in the Gateway City was held at Brotherhood Park and about two thousand spectators showed up. The program was a varied one that began with a bicycle race, a footrace and a wrestling match before Dempsey and Australian middleweight Paddy Gorman were introduced for their bout. Dempsey and Gorman were greeted with cheers and then quickly opened up on each other for two rounds until a St. Louis police sergeant named Hall and his men rushed onto the field forcing the pair to stop. Dave Campbell then gave a demonstration with Indian clubs and soon after a baseball game was played, ending the day's activities. Jack was scheduled to meet Charley Daly in an exhibition the next day.[67]

An interesting point about Dempsey's health was noticed during his stay in St. Louis but was not reported until the following January—just before his contest with Bob Fitzsimmons in New Orleans. A reporter for the *St. Louis Post-Dispatch* commented in an article previewing the bout that Dempsey looked to be in good condition but noted that this was contrary to his appearance just six months before. "Dempsey when in St. Louis last summer looked very thin and had a short, hacking cough, which many held was a sure indication of consumption. He was also drinking very hard and has been ever since La Blanche broke the great middleweight's long list of victories by knocking him out with a chance blow when the Nonpareil had all but won the fight."[68] Again, Dempsey's precarious health and increasingly heavy drinking were a topic of note.

While in St. Louis, Jack was asked by a reporter if he was willing to meet John L. Sullivan. With a smirk, the Nonpareil responded, "The big fellow would pick me up, turn me over his knee and spank me. There is only one Sullivan."[69] Jack also indicated that he hoped to either stay in Portland or settle in California after he officially retired from the ring. He said that he hoped to live there the balance of his life, as he liked both the climate and the Western people. From St. Louis, the crew would make their way east to Pennsylvania and upstate New York, where they would spend the rest of July and August.

On July 22, the members of the troupe, including Dempsey, were in attendance at a glove contest between Billy Baker of Buffalo and Thomas McCarthy of nearby Olean, New York. The bout was held in the amphitheater at Buffalo's Arlington Club. Paddy Gorman seconded McCarthy and Dave Campbell was appointed as referee. In the fight, McCarthy clearly outclassed Baker over six rounds.[70]

On July 28, the troupe gave an exhibition in front of a good-sized crowd at the Gaiety Theatre in Buffalo, with Dempsey meeting Mike Brennan. After five four-round bouts Dempsey was introduced, reportedly met with a great ovation and "displayed his ability to advantage" in defeating Brennan. The fight of the evening, however, involved Dave Campbell and Paddy Brennan. Brennan was anxious to get the cash award being offered to any man who was still on his feet at the end of four rounds with Campbell and reportedly suffered great punishment to do so. "Paddy was punched all over the stage and bled like a stuck pig but managed to stay four rounds."[71]

The next stop was the Wagner Opera House in Bradford, Pennsylvania, on Thursday evening, July 31.[72] During this event, the Nonpareil fought twice with exhibitions against both Gorman and Brennan. The very warm evening began at 8:40 p.m., when Master of Ceremonies John McNerney introduced Reddy Knerr and John Crooker, two lightweights who sparred a lively three rounds and ended with a draw. Next up were two men described only as "two colored men representing Bradford and Olean." The Bradford man won. This contest was followed by matches between Tom McCarty and Paddy Gorman, McCarty and Mike Brennan and finally, Dempsey and Gorman. Reports the following day described the exhibition as follows, "Jack Dempsey and Gorman put on the 'mitts' and gave a very clever exhibition of their skill and after Gorman had been disposed of, Dempsey had a 'go' with Brennan."[73] By all reports, Dempsey's sparring was very effective.

Throughout the summer, rumors of possible fights and a variety of opponents for Dempsey continued to swirl. Various reports had him considering bouts with Jack Burke, Alf Mitchell or Toff Wall in England, George La Blanche in San Francisco, Reddy Gallagher in Fort Worth and Pete McCoy and Mike Donovan in New York, but the most persistent rumor had Jack meeting Bob Fitzsimmons in either San Francisco, New York or New Orleans.

On August 4, the group, now known as Jack Dempsey's All Star Athletic Combination, appeared for what proprietor Frederick Bastable and his business manager George Wright billed as "The Sporting Event of the Season." The evening of exhibitions was held at the Standard Theater in Syracuse. The weather was again quite warm and, while this may well have kept the crowd down a bit, those who braved the summer heat were well entertained. The card began with a match between Syracuse residents Boss Peters and Eddie Murray in which Murray won easily in a three-round match. Next up were Mike Brennan and Joe Dunfee of Syracuse. Dunfee handled himself very well against the larger and more experienced Brennan, but after receiving several hard shots from the Syracuse man, Brennan woke up and began to work harder. The three-round contest ended with Brennan landing several sharp blows to Dunfee's ribs. The third bout featured Murray again, this time breaking in an 18-year-old lightweight by the name of Danny Callihan who was making his professional ring debut. While Murray toyed with him for the most part, Callihan comported himself well throughout much of the fight. He defended himself well, blocking or avoiding most of Murray's punches. The next two bouts featured Gorman and Campbell then McCarthy and Brennan. The final bout of the evening featured Gorman and Dempsey in a three-rounder. Jack landed more heavy blows throughout the match, but Gorman rebounded and looked sharp at the end of the third round. Ed Degan of Syracuse refereed the bouts.

Jack returned home to Brooklyn on August 24 to attend a benefit in his honor the next day at the Grand Street Palace Hall near Wythe Avenue. He was scheduled to spar four rounds with his friend Brooklyn Jimmy Carroll. "Jack McAuliffe and others will also spar at the benefit, which sports say will be a big event."[74]

Jack arrived in town on the morning of August 24, per the Albany day-line boat. That afternoon, he made his way to the offices of the *New York Illustrated News*, where he and his manager Charles Dexter met with friends and reporters. Among those present were Jack McAuliffe, Gus Tuthill, Harry Hill, Jimmy Wakely, Jack Cusack, Charley Johnston, Jimmy Carroll of Brooklyn and amateur middleweight champion Pat Cahill. During the session, Jack was asked what he planned to do with an offer from Australian middleweight champion Bob Fitzsimmons. Dempsey responded, "I have yet received no challenge from him. I have seen several alleged challenges published in the newspapers but have not been communicated with directly." He was also asked about his multiple attempts to schedule a rematch with La Blanche and whether he thought the Marine would finally agree to meet him again. "I can't tell. I've tried pretty hard to bring him to the scratch but could never get him there. I think I have one or two efforts left, however. I think he will have to fight when he gets hard up for money."[75]

The Palace Theater held a full house of roughly four thousand people and every seat seemed to be taken at the benefit for Jack the next evening. "The little building was packed to suffocation with people who cheered themselves hoarse when they saw the Nonpareil come on the stage in the old blue tights which he has worn in half a hundred hard won victories. He looked as strong and well as ever his friends had seen him looking."[76] The *Trenton Times* described the gathering as "the largest and most enthusiastic gathering that ever welcomed a prizefighter home."[77]

The evening's entertainment began at 8:00 p.m. with a mixed division bout between Little Joe Fowler of Bristol, England, who weighed 135 pounds, and New Yorker Johnny Banks, who weighed a good twenty-five pounds more. Given the weight disparity, Banks looked like a sure winner, but he joked and toyed with the Englishman in the first round. As Banks clowned, Fowler, described as a "fat little white man," saw his opening and hammered away at his opponent who made little effort in return. Fowler's tenacity and high level of activity paid off and the bout was judged a draw. Dave Campbell was up next and he gave his usual exhibition of Indian club swinging that was enjoyed and loudly applauded.

The next bout featured Dave Benjamin and Eddie Avery, the 105-pound champion of Long Island. Benjamin, who weighed 103 pounds, had gained a solid reputation two years earlier when he fought in the Varuna championship at the Varuna Boat Club in Brooklyn. Most in attendance thought that he defeated his opponent Cal McCarthy, but McCarthy got the nod. Benjamin's style was described as cool, clean and scientific two-handed fighting. Benjamin started fast and kept the pressure on Avery by landing staggering blows to his opponent's neck, face and torso, but Avery was able to right his ship and fight his way back into the contest. By the second round he was taking control. "Benjamin went down in the second and Avery's seconds claimed a clean knockdown."[78]

Next up, local Greenpoint native Bob Dunlap met lightweight Jack Quinn. "Quinn, who was fit to fight for his life, dealt easily with his antagonist until the last round, when he uppercut Dunlap heavily several times and had him bleeding and dazed. Dunlap clinched and wrestled attempting to regain his form, but he had been hit so hard that Police Captain Short stopped the bout."[79]

Campbell then reappeared to box with Tom McCarthy, champion heavyweight of Western New York. McCarthy tipped the scales at 195 pounds. This bout was followed by Professor Healy of New York and Frank Conley of Brooklyn. Both men gave what was described as a good exhibition and received loud applause.

Jack McAuliffe and an overweight Denny Costigan met next. After a loud and long applause, the two friends of Dempsey participated in a hard-hitting fight. The bout was lively and both men displayed what was called clever fighting by the local papers.

The crowd came to their feet for the next two fighters, Harry Pickford and William McDermott—both eight years old. The pair were the mascots of the Manhattan Athletic Club and they sparred three lively rounds.

In the next bout, Tommy Kelly, the 105-pound champion of the world, met Englishman Benny Murphy. Kelly had the advantage in reach, landing several hard blows on Murphy and bloodying his nose in the first round. They sparred lightly after that, as Kelly took it easy on his ineffective foe.

After a short musical interlude from Patsy Doody, two Brooklyn men, Johnny Ward and Johnny Murphy, sparred three rounds.

Finally, with the crowd calling for the Nonpareil, Master of Ceremonies Harry Hill called on Dempsey and Carroll who weighed 150 and 160 pounds, respectively. The applause for Dempsey was deafening and lasted for several minutes. "He was in fine condition and looked every inch a fighter as he stepped forward to box three rounds with Jimmy Carroll. Jack sparred with his old-time lightness and grace of action, and his friends cheered lustily every point that he made."[80] Carroll also fought well, stopping many a well-aimed punch from the Nonpareil. "They sparred lightly, but cleverly, but without any intention of showing supremacy."[81] Both men were cheered throughout the three-round exhibition. At the conclusion of the bout, Jack was presented a floral horseshoe bouquet by his friends in Williamsburg.

After the main event, the festivities continued at the Metropolitan Hotel where Dempsey's friends attended a banquet in Jack's honor. As usual, Dempsey's event had an impressive style. The food, the drink, the decorations and the floral designs were on the grandest scale. During the evening, the Nonpareil was presented with a very fine intaglio emerald ring by a gentleman from Atlantic City named John Dempsey.[82]

Shortly after his return to Brooklyn Jack met his old pal Jack McAuliffe for a night on the town and wound up stopping in around midnight for a drink at Jimmy Wakely's saloon at Forty-Second Street and Sixth Avenue. During the course of the evening the conversation turned to their old profession of barrel making. At some point a reporter from the *Brooklyn Eagle* asked Dempsey what kind of cooper he used to be. "I was way up," replied Jack. "There wasn't a better cooper in the city of Brooklyn." To which McAuliffe replied, "You never was a mechanic at all. You was only a common laborer, and all you did was to set up barrels." Dempsey responded that McAuliffe was full of it and asked his friend, "And what were you?" McAuliffe responded, "I was a mechanic," to which the Nonpareil responded, "Ho, ho! You were a daisy mechanic. The most you could earn was $12.50 a week while I used to earn $18.00 a week." McAuliffe laughed and stated, "Never in your life!" Dempsey told his pal to check the books of the shop to prove his claim. After some more good-natured ribbing Dempsey challenged his friend to a $100 wager that he could make two barrels to McAuliffe's one. Dempsey also claimed that his barrels would be of superior quality. McAuliffe at first demurred, claiming that he did not want to take his friend's money, but after a bit more goading, the two agreed to the contest to be held within a week at their former employer, Lorin M. Palmer's Cooperage. Each man backed his ability with a stake of $100 which was held by Jimmy Wakely.[83] When the event finally occurred, the men cut it short, determining that they were both rusty at their old trade and a round of drinks at the local pub was a better use of their time.

On Sunday, August 31, Jack left for Pittsburgh to meet Jimmy Carroll of Brooklyn, with whom he was to spar throughout the week at Harry Williams's Academy Theater. Dempsey and Carroll would appear twice on Monday, September 1, and then in matinees throughout the week. The Labor Day crowds were heavy, and the theater had to turn away patrons at both shows. The successful event was reported by the local press as follows, "The Henry Burlesque Company presented a variety of attractive features. The mystifying Crowley, McIntyre and Heath, black face comedians; Helen Courtland, the singer were all good, and the company shone as a whole in a travesty of Gilbert and Sullivan's 'Gondoliers.' But the sparring of Jack Dempsey and Jimmy Carroll was naturally the strongest point in the show for a holiday audience."[84]

The weeklong appearances provided very good and comparatively easy money, but the wear and tear of the ring and the constant travel were beginning to grow a bit old to Jack. Maggie had not traveled with Jack for much of the past year because of the birth of the couple's second child, Anne. According to his manager Charley Dexter, Jack was missing his family. "I think Jack has become a trifle homesick already and will return as soon as possible" to Portland.[85] While he was anxious to see Maggie and the children, instead of heading west, Jack headed east to Brooklyn with Dexter, arriving on the evening of September 8. He was met at the station by a number of journalists who wanted to know which of the numerous fight offers received the Nonpareil would accept. Jack said little on the subject and quickly climbed into a coach in which he was whisked away to his lodgings at the St. James Hotel.

Dexter ran into the reporters later in the evening and stated that Dempsey planned to stay in New York for several days, and then travel to Atlantic City for a couple of weeks for some rest. After that he planned to head back to New York to discuss and consider his fight options and settle his affairs before heading to his home in Portland to see his family and tend to his West Coast businesses.

On September 11, news out of New York stated that Dick Roche and Jimmy Makelee, who ran affairs at the Puritan Athletic Club in Long Island City, New York, had decided to offer a purse of somewhere between $5,000 and $7,000 for a glove contest over twenty-five rounds between Jack and the New Zealander Bob Fitzsimmons. "Ruby Robert," as

Fitzsimmons was known, was coming off a notable knockout victory over Billy McCarthy in May in San Francisco, shortly after his arrival in the United States.

When asked about the offer Jack responded, "I have not made up my mind just what to do, but I am open to box any man in the world at 145 pounds, for a suitable purse and as much money on the side as my opponent may desire to wager." It was noted that Dempsey had wealthy Brooklyn supporters who would back him for any amount up to $25,000.[86]

Fitzsimmons was roughly Jack's age, having been born on May 26, 1863, in the Cornish town of Helston on the extreme southwest tip of England. He was the youngest of twelve children. His Irish father and Cornish mother moved the large family to New Zealand when Bob was nine. The Fitzsimmonses settled in a Cornish community in Timaru, located on New Zealand's South Island about one hundred miles south of Christchurch. Here Bob became a blacksmith in his brother's smithy and began to develop an interest in pugilism. The constant hammering motion necessary to the blacksmith's trade helped Bob develop the strong back, shoulders, arms and hands that would aid in making him a great fighter and one of the era's hardest hitters.

In 1880 and 1881, Fitzsimmons was an amateur champion in New Zealand and turned professional shortly thereafter. After establishing himself in Australia throughout the 1880s, Bob sailed for America. He arrived in San Francisco in the spring of 1890 and by May had defeated both Frank Allen and McCarthy. After his subsequent knockout of Arthur Upham in New Orleans in July, talk turned to the Nonpareil. The interest was high among fans and the various clubs were anxious to host a battle between the two men.

Shortly after the Puritan A.C.'s offer, another offer arrived from Galveston, Texas, for $11,000. The offers kept getting sweeter, but not everyone was pleased by this. Sheriff M. J. Goldner of Queens County, New York, made the following comment. "I see that the Puritans have gone ahead and offered to have the fight in their club house at Long Island City. They reckon without their host. They can't have the fight there because I will stop it."[87] Suddenly, for both financial and logistical reasons, other cities including Galveston, New Orleans and San Francisco all began to sound like better options. Regardless of the sheriff's comments, the Puritan was still in the picture and countered purse offers from other clubs for the honor of hosting the contest.

Bob Fitzsimmons, a legendary all-time ring great.

Fitzsimmons was a good bit more decided about where the bout should be held when he stated in early October, "We don't know when we will leave for Frisco as the Olympic club has notified me that Jack Dempsey has accepted a $12,000 offer to fight me in New Orleans. I telegraphed him and told him that I would not fight anywhere but in the Olympic Club of New Orleans or the California club. The Puritan club would give $15,000 to get the fight in its club, but I would not fight there for $50,000, and I told them so and that settles it."[88] The Olympic Club offer came to both men by wire from club officer R.M. Frank.

Jack responded that he might prefer the Puritan, whose offer was now $10,000. "I have not given my friends here an opportunity to see me perform for a long time, and great numbers of them desire that my next match should come off within easy distance of the city of Brooklyn." Dempsey added that the idea that Fitzsimmons would be at a disadvantage by fighting on the Nonpareil's home turf was nonsense. "Everybody who knows the men at the head of the organization, Messrs. Wakely, Stephenson and Dick Roche, knows that they are as honorable as any men in the sporting world."[89]

In late August, news came that Jack Burke of England wanted to meet Dempsey. The Ormonde Club of London was offering a 500-pound purse. Jack was miffed, however, that no challenge from Burke had arrived. "Burke is one of the many men who have been talking at me instead of to me. I tried every way to get a fight with Burke when he was in San Francisco, but he would not face me. It is strange if he is now anxious to fight."[90]

Soon thereafter, Jack, who was relaxing by the sea at Rockaway Beach, received a note from Richard K. Fox that relayed an official offer of a bout with Burke from the Ormonde Club. Jack responded that he was willing if terms could be reached, but he would not concede to Burke an ounce over the 154-pound middleweight limit. Many in the fight community encouraged Dempsey to accept a challenge from Burke. One reporter stated that "Dempsey clearly demonstrated his superiority over Burke when they fought on the Pacific Slope and when he could hold his own with the alleged Irishman at that time, he should be able to tie if not conquer him. Dempsey would be received like a hero in England." The article continued, stating, "The champion's name and fame have preceded him and he would find that by the trip he could combine pleasure with great profit. He would land in England as the recognized middleweight champion of America and he owns the 'Police Gazette' championship belt which he fairly won, to prove his right to the pugilistic premiership." The article closed by calling Dempsey "one of the pugilistic wonders of the century" and "a veritable prize ring hero." Needless to say, a year after his loss to La Blanche, Jack Dempsey still had a legion of believers and his convincing victory over Billy McCarthy in February only strengthened their conviction that Dempsey was still the best middleweight in the world.

Another rumor was that Dempsey and Mike Donovan would meet once again. Donovan was agreeable if the purse and the gate were split evenly and he could get his club's permission. Jack responded, "If proper arrangements can be made nothing would suit me better. I shall want a guarantee. I don't wish to contend for nothing. If that point and the point of police protection is settled I will face him in six, eight, ten or twenty rounds."[91]

On the night of September 18, Messrs. Wakely and Roche of the Puritan A.C. sent another note to Fitzsimmons in New Orleans asking if "Ruby Robert" would meet Dempsey at the Puritan for a $10,000 purse if fair play were guaranteed.

Almost a week later, the Galveston Athletic Association sweetened the pot again. In a telegram to Dempsey—now on his way west to Portland—association president William Reppen and committee chairman E.T. Dopps offered $11,000 to the pair to meet in the coastal Texas city.

Dempsey and his manager Charley Dexter left Brooklyn on the morning of September 23 heading west for San Francisco, Portland and Seattle, where Jack would spend some time with friends and family and see to affairs before heading to New Orleans. They spent the evening of September 24 in Chicago, where he received another telegram, this one from Fitzsimmons, in which the challenger reiterated that he would fight nowhere but the Olympic Club in New Orleans or San Francisco's California A.C. Dempsey responded to the offers by saying that he was not in this business for glory, but rather cash, and that regardless of where the bout was held, he would accept no less a purse than the amount offered by the Puritan. He also stated that even though he was the reigning champion and should have the choice of meeting place, he was so anxious to meet Fitzsimmons that he would waive that unwritten rule and agree to a bout if the other clubs would offer the $11,500 purse held out by the Puritan and if Fitzsimmons would guarantee Jack $1,000 in case the contest were put off for any reason. "If Fitzsimmons will guarantee me $1,000 in case of such stoppage, I'll go on, or I'll toss up with him as to whether it's Puritan, or I'll meet him half way. Anything so as we can get together and stop the newspaper talk."[92]

On October 10, Dempsey told reporters in Seattle that he had written to President Peterson of the Olympic Club in New Orleans accepting the purse and asked that Peterson send the articles of agreement to sign. Dempsey commented, "I would prefer to fight in the Galveston Club, for it offered more money, and I informed the officials of that organization to that effect, and told them, furthermore, to secure Fitzsimmons. The Australian, however, seems to be afraid to meet me outside of New Orleans."[93] Dempsey said that he was unsure of why Fitzsimmons insisted on New Orleans as all of the serious offers from reputable clubs offered large purses.

After all of the wrangling, it was confirmed on October 30 that Jack would meet the New Zealander at the Olympic Club of New Orleans. It was agreed that the bout would be held the following January, with a purse that was reported to be a cool $12,000, only a thousand of which would go to the loser.[94] This was reportedly the largest purse ever offered for a prizefight up to that time. Dempsey was keenly interested in the large purse—as anyone would be—but in Jack's case he had an additional reason. Dempsey was beginning to look to his future after boxing and was considering business opportunities in Portland and Seattle. Dempsey's partner in the Portland saloon was his sometimes manager Charley Dexter. The watering hole was a popular resort for the sporting set and Jack was hoping to replicate that success in Seattle where he had become part owner of another saloon.

On November 11, Dempsey signed articles of agreement for the bout with Fitzsimmons. Jack had agreed in principle to the terms of the fight three weeks earlier but asked that a final weigh-in occur at ringside just five or ten minutes before the bout. Fitzsimmons and his backers agreed to this change and the contract was drawn up. Dempsey sent a dispatch to the president of the Olympic A.C. stating, "Have signed articles and mailed them to you. Any fair man that your club may select for referee will suit me."[95] It was agreed that the men would meet in the ring for the middleweight championship of the world on January 24 and the purse would be a whopping $12,000.

Dempsey told a Brooklyn friend in a letter that he had signed for the contest and was glad to do so "because people who said I was afraid to meet him will now know different." Jack stated that he did not see the size differential as a handicap. "He is taller, bigger and heavier than I, but his being confined to 154 pounds, which I think is six or seven pounds below his fighting weight, is an advantage in my favor. I can fight at 150, but at 154 I shall be stronger, while I think he will have none too much strength for a bruising, protracted fight at middleweight." He was still wary of Fitzsimmons's height, long reach and reputation as a great pugilist. "I have made up my mind that Fitzsimmons must be a first-class man." Dempsey closed on an optimistic and gracious note, commenting that he expected a fair fight. "The Olympic A.C., in fact all the Southern sporting men, are fair-dealing people. I ask no favors and all I want is fair play, and I am certain the New Orleans sporting fraternity will see that I receive it."[96]

While Dempsey saw an advantage in the size differential, many others did not. While conceding that Jack would have plenty of supporters, one reporter stated his belief that the smart money would be on Fitzsimmons. "Sporting men on the Pacific Slope and in New Orleans who have seen both the New Zealander and the champion fight will undoubtedly back Fitzsimmons, owing to the fact that he is bigger than Dempsey, equally scientific, and has a longer reach and possesses the endurance and hard-hitting qualities."[97]

The day after he agreed to terms for the Fitzsimmons contest, Dempsey left for Seattle to see to his new saloon. He would remain there for almost three weeks seeing to his business.[98] Maggie and the girls traveled from Portland to be with Jack during his stay and on November 30 the Dempsey's left Seattle to begin their journey to New Orleans for the fight. They left the Emerald City for San Francisco in the morning traveling by the steamer *California*, which arrived in the City by the Bay on December 3. They relaxed for a long weekend.

In a tragic note, Peter Dempsey, a cousin of Jack's, was fatally stabbed on December 7 by two young Polish men in Brooklyn when he heroically came to the aid of Mary Allen, a local sixteen-year-old who was being harassed by the pair. The men reportedly grabbed the young woman from the door of her home and attempted to drag her into one of their rooms. Dempsey heard her screams as he was passing by, ran into the building and confronted the two men. During the struggle, Mary escaped and ran into the street where her screams attracted two police officers who entered the building and found Dempsey lying in the hallway with three stab wounds. The men were immediately arrested and charged with murder, kidnapping and criminal assault. Dempsey was taken to his home where he was treated by physicians, but despite heroic measures he died a short time later.[99] Bravery and action clearly ran in the Dempsey family.

The Dempseys departed San Francisco on the evening of December 8, winding their way by rail south to Los Angeles. After a couple of days of relaxation in Los Angeles the party again embarked by rail on the next leg of their journey. In Denver they transferred to a sleeper car attached to a Texas and Gulf train bound for Fort Worth.[100]

On December 12, the Dempsey family made a brief stop to change trains in Fort Worth. Professor John Clark had attempted to have Dempsey stopover in that city and participate in a boxing exhibition, but his telegraph arrived too late for Jack to arrange to do so. Instead he arranged for a crowd to meet Dempsey's train. "Quite a crowd of local sports were at the Union depot when the Fort Worth and Denver City passenger train pulled in last night and Dempsey was given a right royal reception." Jack addressed the crowd, stating that he was in excellent health and confident about his chances of defeating Fitzsimmons. After adding that he would soon return to Fort Worth and arrange an exhibition through Clark, the Nonpareil and his entourage were transferred to the Houston and Texas Central Depot where they boarded a train for Galveston.[101]

The stopover in Galveston was brief—just a few hours on December 13. Jack was simply there to secure a training base and was soon on the three o'clock train for New Orleans. He was to be in New Orleans for but a few days, beginning his preparations for the Fitzsimmons bout. Jack, Maggie and three-and-a-half-year-old Alice arrived in the Crescent City on the evening of December 13. Younger daughter Anne was still just eight months old and remained with Maggie's family in Portland. The president of the Olympic A.C. made plans to slip the family through the train station quietly and then spirit them away by coach to their lodgings at the St. Charles Hotel.

On Monday, December 15, detailed plans for the bout with Fitzsimmons were finalized in New Orleans. Dempsey and his managers met with British Jimmy Carroll, who was representing Fitzsimmons. Carroll claimed that Fitzsimmons was under the weather and could not attend, but many suspected that Bob's team was simply trying to keep Dempsey from seeing his large rival before the fight. This disgusted Jack, as he wanted to lay an eye on Fitzsimmons before the bout to size up his opponent. It did not help that Carroll showed up as the Australian's representative, for "if there are two men on the face of this broad earth who despise each other with all that the word despise means, they are Jack Dempsey and Jimmy Carroll."[102] The bad blood between the two pugilists dated back to at least the second Dempsey–La Blanche fight when Carroll trained the Marine and was reportedly behind La Blanche's controversial use of the pivot punch. Carroll was especially mouthy during this meeting in New Orleans and it would not have taken much more encouragement for Dempsey to have gone after him, but cooler heads prevailed and the meeting was concluded peacefully, if not amicably.

It was agreed that the men would be weighed at ringside and that neither could exceed 154 pounds. At this point, Jack tipped the scales at a solid 150. It was also agreed that the referee for the match would be selected on the night before the fight.

Also, on Monday, December 15, Jack celebrated his twenty-eighth birthday with a dinner party at the St. Charles. Jack "telegraphed Fitzsimmons to run over and assist in the celebration." The Fitzsimmons camp once again responded that Bob was ailing from a very severe cold, but the following day Carroll told a *New York Sun* reporter that the cold was not necessarily the reason for his absence. Jack took that as yet another dig at him by Carroll.[103] Many also believed that "the cold" was not real and was simply a ploy to keep Jack from seeing Fitzsimmons before the men stepped into the ring.

Dempsey and his entourage left the Crescent City on December 17 to head for Galveston, Texas, where he was to train. During his training, Dempsey also planned to travel to Dallas at some point to participate in an exhibition match. Some felt that Jack was not taking his training seriously enough and he was either over confident in himself or was taking his very talented opponent much too lightly. Just before Christmas, Jack's friend Tom Maher received a telegram from the Nonpareil asking Maher to join him and Denny Costigan in Galveston to help Dempsey train. Maher wasted no time heading south, catching a 4:00 p.m. train on December 22.[104]

While on the Texas coast, Dempsey trained as the guest of the Galveston Athletic

Club. The club's president, E.T. Dodd, had "taken a great interest in Dempsey" and was doing all he could for the champion. Sporting men in Galveston were "all worked up over the contest and it is expected the majority of the club members will accompany Dempsey to New Orleans and back him to defeat the New Zealander."[105]

On December 18, Jack McAuliffe, in a broad-ranging interview with a reporter from the *Brooklyn Eagle*, addressed the upcoming contest between his old friend Dempsey and Fitzsimmons. The lightweight champion was planning to head south to be with Dempsey and work his corner during the bout, but currently he was busy in the Eastern District giving boxing exhibitions with Jimmy Nelson, another old barrel-hammering mate of his and Dempsey's from their days at the cooper shop on North Third Street. Nelson too had followed the path to pugilism and was currently the boxing and training instructor at the Brooklyn Athletic Club.

Asked about Dempsey's chances against the New Zealand man, McAuliffe responded, "Fitzsimmons is a very good man, but all this newspaper talk about his wonderful ability as a fighter is a gag to affect the betting. He has a long reach, is a hard hitter and I believe dead game. I think he will give Dempsey a good battle, but I don't imagine the middleweight champion's friends need have any fear about the result."[106]

McAuliffe had stepped away from the ring for a while after the sudden death of his wife, actress Katie Hart, the previous February. He was using the extended sparring tour with Jimmy Nelson to get back in fighting shape and was beginning to entertain possible bouts. McAuliffe was considering bouts in New Orleans with either Andy Bowen of that city or Billy Myers, the "Streator Cyclone."

After receiving a telegram from Dempsey urging him to come to Galveston without delay and train him for the Fitzsimmons contest, McAuliffe decided to shut down his show and head south. McAuliffe finished out the week for shows that were already sold out, but then packed up and left Brooklyn for Texas on January 2, 1891.

1891—At the Hands of Ruby Robert

With the announcement that Jack would meet Fitzsimmons at the Olympic Club of New Orleans, the fighters and their supporters began to scurry to get ready for the contest. The purse for the January bout was to be $12,000 and was reportedly the largest ever offered up to that time for a prizefight. It would be the equivalent of more than $300,000 today.

After signing for the fight in the Crescent City, Dempsey rented a cottage near the beach in Galveston, Texas, where he set up his pre-fight training camp. Maggie prepared his meals and saw to his welfare. Although Dempsey's health had been on the decline over the past year Jack was anxious to put on a good show for the public and, unlike Fitzsimmons, he was constantly in front of his fans. He would give boxing exhibitions, and strolled and played baseball publicly on the Galveston beach.

Helping Jack get in shape for the bout were Denny Costigan, "Mike Conley, the Ithaca giant, and Jack [Tom] Maher, while he picked up a suitable sparring partner wherever he could find one. Gus Tuthill was still his manager."[1] While not much on finesse, Conley, like Fitzsimmons, was a large, muscular heavyweight who packed a powerful punch. Ultimately, Dempsey also sought the help of boyhood pal Jack McAuliffe, who agreed to come to Galveston to aid his friend. Tuthill and Jere Dunn were also on hand to keep an eye on British Jimmy Carroll who was training and backing Fitzsimmons and whom none in Dempsey's camp trusted. "Jack's friends fear some trickery on the part of Jimmy Carroll and to frustrate it they intend to see that he and his principal, Fitzsimmons, live up to the strict letter of the articles of agreement."

In many ways it appears that Carroll's intense dislike of the Nonpareil was a major impetus behind the fight—that and the bad blood between Carroll and Dempsey. Jack's friend and backer M.A. Gunst of San Francisco, who was also a friend of Fitzsimmons, determined after speaking with the Australian that "Fitzsimmons never wanted to fight Dempsey, but was hurried into a match by Carroll who despises the Nonpareil and wants to see him whipped."[2]

On January 5, Dempsey and Conley were in Dallas for an exhibition match. Conley stood six feet tall and weighed roughly 190 well-proportioned pounds, but the quicker Dempsey had no real problem handling him. At 9:20 p.m., the Nonpareil was introduced as the middleweight champion of the world and was met with roaring cheers from the large Texas crowd. "For three rounds they gave their enthusiastic audience an exhibition of the most scientific boxing ever seen in Dallas. When Conley struck out, Dempsey was always out of the way, but ready with a return blow that sounded through the theater and brought cheer after cheer."[3] McAuliffe arrived in New Orleans on January 5 and proceeded to Galveston the next day in time to meet Dempsey on the Nonpareil's return from Dallas.

The contest with Fitzsimmons was ultimately set for the evening of January 14, 1891, with the middleweight championship on the line. Interest among the sporting public was high as the bout drew near. The betting public lay their money down on their favorites—both sides sure that their man would prevail. It was announced that special trains were being arranged to bring the throngs of fans to New Orleans from Chicago, Boston, Philadelphia, Louisville, Cincinnati, Buffalo and other points. A series of special trains from the West were also scheduled to bring delegations of Dempsey's admirers from San Francisco and Portland.

In the week before the fight, New Orleans was abuzz with preparations for the contest. An advertisement from the *New Orleans Item* promoted the bout as follows: "Grand International Glove Contest, for the Middleweight Championship of the World and a Purse of $12,000 between Jack Dempsey, The Nonpareil, and Bob Fitzsimmons, The New Zealand Wonder.... General Admission $10.00."

On the afternoon of January 12, Dempsey, McAuliffe, Gus Tuthill, Mike Conley, Thomas Maher and others from the Dempsey camp caught the 3:00 p.m. Southern Pacific train to New Orleans where they planned to lay low until the evening of the bout.

When the train arrived in the Crescent City in the early morning of January 13, the crowd of reporters and fans who were at the depot began looking for Dempsey. Instead of Dempsey, they saw Maggie with young daughter Alice and McAuliffe who explained that his friend would not arrive until the next morning. The crowd then followed McAuliffe to the St. Charles Hotel where he checked in. Soon after McAuliffe had left the depot, three men, Dempsey, Mike Conley and Tom Maher, emerged. Dempsey "was bundled up in warm clothing with a soft gray hat pulled over his face...." It was reported that he was suffering from "a touch of malaria" but stated that it did not amount to anything and had not interfered with his training.[4] The men "jumped into a cab and were driven rapidly to the South Side where they put up at a private residence."[5] After enjoying some breakfast and a rest at the St. Charles, McAuliffe, Maggie and Alice joined Jack on the South Side. The Dempseys checked into a rented home where they intended to stay and where they continued to keep a low profile.

Dempsey's secret arrival in New Orleans begs the question—why did he avoid the press and the crowds gathered to greet him? He had always enjoyed mingling with the crowds that greeted him. Malaria is a mosquito-borne disease and mosquitoes are not a big problem in Galveston in December and early January, which makes Dempsey's claims at least curious. The symptons of malaria are similar to those of tuberculosis. Most likely Jack's "touch of malaria" was another flare up of his consumption. It couldn't have come at a worse time for the Nonpareil.

Fitzsimmons and Jimmy Carroll were finishing their fight preparations at their training grounds in Bay St. Louis, Mississippi, just northeast of New Orleans. Fitzsimmons, Carroll and their wives stayed in a small cottage. Fitzsimmons had a good training camp and those who saw him in the ring were impressed with his conditioning and with the way he easily dodged and deflected the punches of his sparring partners. It was said by observers that Fitzsimmons was "quick as lightning and dodges every blow. His long arms reach over and strike his antagonist at apparently impossible distances."[6]

Fitzsimmons and Carroll kept a low profile throughout their training, working quietly and arduously. The Australian put a great deal of emphasis on building his endurance. Reports stated that Fitzsimmons "has been seen training largely for wind, evidently feeling the necessity for it, running eight and ten miles a day, doing a great deal of walking, practicing at his former trade, horseshoeing, hitting the bag and sparring with his trainer, Jimmy Carroll, and such other persons as come along."[7]

At one point, Fitzsimmons left his camp, traveled to New Orleans for a day and then continued on to Galveston completely incognito to attend the January 2 fight between Arthur Upham of New Orleans and Paul Pitzlin of Houston. Fitzsimmons attended the bout in secret to observe Upham's trainer and chief second—Jack Dempsey. Fitzsimmons also knew Upham, having knocked him out in five rounds in New Orleans the previous July. Watching the bout gave Fitzsimmons a wonderful opportunity to witness Dempsey during the contest and observe how he thought during a bout. The match was fought for an $800 purse before the Galveston Athletic Club. Upham won in the twenty-third round.[8]

In the final days before the bout, Fitz continued to do some light training, but in general began to rest and reserve his energy. While he was comfortable with his conditioning and with his chances, he knew that any fighter who entered the ring with Dempsey—albeit a shadow of the former Nonpareil—was up against a formidable foe and one that could still pull off a masterful performance on any given night. Fitzsimmons was an intelligent and thoughtful man whose respect for Jack was enormous.

At the Olympic Club, officials oversaw preparations for the fight. The facility was ready to accommodate as many as six thousand fans. "The amphitheater in which the fight takes place will seat 240 persons in the reserved seats and 4,250 in the ordinary ones."[9] While general admission was $10, a box with up to six seats could be had for $100. Individual seats in these boxes ran $16. The prices were high for the time, but the club officials stated that it was necessary to cover the $12,000 purse for which they were solely responsible. The prices did not, however, negatively affect the turnout. The club was certain they could sell out as they recently had for the Andy Bowen–British Jimmy Carroll fight. A sellout would yield roughly $40,000 and assure a tidy profit even after prize money and expenses were paid. By January 5 tickets sales were brisk and forty boxes had already been sold.

On January 13, the day before the bout was scheduled, a rumor was started by a local newspaper that Louisiana Governor Francis T. Nicholls had changed his mind and decided not to allow the fight to go on as planned. The paper went on to say that Governor Nicholls would call out the state militia to suppress the contest if needed. A *New York Sun* reporter engaged Louisiana Attorney General Walter Henry Rogers on the street that afternoon and asked him about the story. Rogers confirmed it, stating that should they fight, he would prosecute the offenders vigorously, and in addition, he would move to have the Olympic Athletic Club's charter revoked. By that evening, however, word came from␣icholls himself that he would allow the contest to proceed. The rumor had apparently been manufactured by those in the community who hoped to persuade the governor to stop the bout. It would appear that Attorney General Rogers was among their number. The *New York Sun* commented, "There is no doubt that the fights which have recently been decided in the Crescent City are distasteful to the better class of people living here [New Orleans]."[10] A great sigh of relief was breathed by most of the city—apparently those not counted among the "better class"—who either supported the bout or were benefiting from the tourism and business it brought in.

It is an interesting point that at least on a regional level—and perhaps reluctantly in many quarters—boxing was finally starting to become an accepted and mainstream entertainment event. Prizefighting was beginning to be seen as sport and skill rather than strictly as two Neanderthal brutes hammering each other in front of their bloodthirsty and greedy fans. The following paragraph from the *Brooklyn Eagle*—which had so clearly opined against the evils of the sport as recently as 1883—sums up boxing's newfound acceptance perfectly. "The fight attracted attention throughout the country as an attempt to elevate the prize ring. The money put up is a small fortune, $12,000, and, as it is understood that there is to be a big bet at the ring side, the winner will pocket the net sum of $15,000 to $16,000. Such rewards, undreamt of in the days of old, ought certainly to encourage pugilism and bring out the best men. The prize fight as conducted before the Olympic club does away with all the old-time secrecy. The pugilists are not compelled to hide away, to train in secret, to slip off to the appointed meeting place before daybreak. The crowd present is not the audience to be seen about the ring in old days of toughs, roughs, and criminals. There is no danger of police interference or that partisans of the defeated man will clamber over the ropes to interfere in the fight—this is no longer possible."[11] Jack Dempsey with his superlative ring skills and his positive image outside the squared circle had a great deal to do with the sport's steadily increasing acceptance and success. Boxing was clearly gaining a grudging tolerance, if not respectability, in mainstream America and with that acceptance came the larger purses. Twelve thousand dollars was a respectable sum of money in 1891—a small fortune in those days.

The $12,000 purse was not all that was at stake during the pending contest. "In addition to the purse there was an outside wager between the men of $2,500 a side. Furthermore, it was to be for the middle-weight championship and for the new *Police Gazette* middle-weight belt, to be presented by Richard K. Fox."[12] Dempsey had held the *Police Gazette* belt for almost five years and held it against all comers for the specified time. As such, the original belt was Dempsey's personal property and Richard K. Fox was now offering as a replacement a new and more elegant and costly trophy as the emblem of the championship.

Jim Corbett arrived in town several days before the date of the match in order to spend time taking in the sights of the Crescent City. Corbett was probably the most prominent, but absolutely not the only pugilist attending the bout. "A large number of them have wintered down here, finding that the Gulf States, in most of which there are no laws against prize fighting, or at least against glove contests, offer them the largest purses."[13]

A dozen trains full of Dempsey's supporters from San Francisco, Portland, and the New York metropolitan area were among the first to arrive. Soon New Orleans was brimming with boxing enthusiasts many of whom had fat wallets and were adding plentifully to the city's coffers.

On the evening of January 13, approximately five hundred persons filled the rooms of the Audubon Athletic Club to attend a benefit in honor of the Nonpareil. Many who attended no doubt wanted to see Dempsey in the ring before laying final bets on the upcoming bout. Dempsey would spar four rounds with Jack McAuliffe, but nothing terribly strenuous, as he would meet Fitzsimmons the following evening.

In an early match, Denny Costigan and Mike Leary apparently whipped up such bad blood that they had to be separated at the final bell. Still angry with one another after they left the ring, they had to be separated once again outside their dressing rooms and the police had to be called in to keep them apart until they were dressed and had been led away from the arena.

Prior to the main event, referee Patsy Doody of New York's Fourth Ward won the hearts of the crowd when he sang them two heartfelt songs. "The crowds cheered him to the echo and a shower of silver coins and bank notes was thrown into the ring. It took the Fourth Warder several minutes to pick up the money and when it was safe in his pocket he tapped his leg significantly and remarked in his rich Irish brogue, 'Well, boys, I don't walk home anyhow.'"[14]

Dempsey's boyhood friend Jack Skelly told a reporter from the *Yonkers Daily News* once "one of the most comic fistic fellows I ever knew was Patsy Doody." Skelly continued, saying, "Patsy lived in the old fourth ward, New York, where he was well known for his wit and humor. He could dance a jig and sing a comic song as well as any man on the vaudeville stage."[15] Doody had some fun with Fitzsimmons, saying that he too would challenge Fitzsimmons as long as the Australian would agree to Doody's terms. "You lower yourself to the bottom of a well," he told Fitzsimmons, "and let me throw stones at you."[16] Doody would die from consumption at his home in New York only a year later. A news story at the time of his death stated, "Patsy Doody, the well-known New York sporting character, died last week. Doody had no particular calling. He was a manager, handler, and educator of fighters and could use the gloves pretty well himself. When fighting was dull, Patsy always turned his attention to the concert halls and made a good living by giving entertainments. His boast was that he never had to 'work.'"[17]

After Doody finished his entertainment, Dempsey was introduced and received a thunderous round of applause. "His face was ruddy and the skin was tightly drawn over it, while the muscles of his arms showed prominently."[18] McAuliffe was then introduced and received a similarly raucous ovation. During the bout Jack sparred cautiously and McAuliffe seemed as if he was able to hit his old friend at will. This may have been the first public inkling that something was amiss with Dempsey. Although it was just a friendly sparring match, Dempsey did not leave those present at the Audubon that evening with a very positive impression of his current skills. He was slower than usual and unable to block or avoid the bulk of McAuliffe's punches. As the crowd began to file out, a number of persons were heard saying "That little fellow will never lick Fitzsimmons" and "My money goes on Fitz." The concern of those present was not unfounded. The *St. Paul Globe* noted several days before the fight that while Jack looked physically fit, he was lighter than usual and also a bit slow. "What makes Dempsey's friends afraid, however, is a belief that the Nonpareil is not the man he once was. His defeat by La Blanche, while undoubtedly an accident, has nevertheless shaken confidence in Dempsey a little, as it proved that there was a possibility of his defeat, despite his phenomenal career in the ring."[19]

On the morning of the bout, Jack, Maggie and Alice took a carriage ride around the city. The Nonpareil seemed relaxed and was said to be in good humor. The crowd that night in the great amphitheater at the Olympic Club was estimated at five thousand enthusiastic, but orderly, spectators. "The crowds in the street were enormous, but the police had roped the block, and this proved a wise precaution. Overcoats were very comfortable."[20] The doors were opened for admission at 6:00 p.m., but a crowd began to gather an hour earlier with many among the throng vociferously demanding admission. "When the doors were opened, there was a grand rush, which for a few moments threatened to swamp police officers, ticket takers and ushers before it. Into the amphitheater the waiting multitude poured like a raging torrent amid shouts, howls and cheers which speedily made the place a veritable bedlam."[21] The police contingent was quite large, however, and the crowd seemed to take notice as they remained boisterous but orderly throughout the contest. Among the notables present were Jim Corbett, Jake Kilrain, Andy Bowen, Brooklyn Jimmy Carroll, Patsy Doody, noted wrestler William Muldoon and Parson Davies, among others.

The wagering money had continued to pour in, but by now had swung so much in favor of the New Zealand blacksmith that one newspaper reported, "If the Brooklyn pugilist is successful, the city will be in sack cloth and ashes."[22] For much of the past week opinion had been trending away from Dempsey and toward the New Zealander. The day before the bout Muldoon stated, "I have my money on the one that my judgment tells me is the better man—that is, on Fitzsimmons." Muldoon added, "My sympathy is all with Dempsey."[23] The smart money was on Fitzsimmons, but Dempsey still retained the public's heart, if not its confidence.

Though their number was dwindling, some fight analysts were still of the opinion that Dempsey had the wherewithal to win, but only if he got inside and worked on Fitz' midsection. "If Jack can get within Fitzsimmons' guard and keep up a tattoo on the latter's stomach and ribs he will win, otherwise the battle will in all probability go to the Australian."[24]

The Olympic Club was ready for the fight. "Electric lights re-enforced large astral oil lamps and made the place as bright as day."[25] The ring was set in the center of the 150-by 120-foot amphitheater and was outfitted with thick wooden posts and hemp ropes surrounding a hard-packed sand-and-turf fighting surface. "The ropes and stakes were padded. Four feet from the ring was another enclosure with barbed wire instead of ropes. Between the two rings were chairs for the seconds and the wire fence insured the pugilistic parties from outside interference. Between the ring and the stands was a sort of excavation, in which the press stands were placed."[26] Behind the tables for the press were the fifty reserved boxes. Behind those, rising from the ground level to the rafters, were the general admission pine bleachers. One interesting note is that the arena had a retractable roof. The amphitheater was built with high walls that were able to hold up a truss roof, "so constructed that it can be removed in case of warm and dry weather or used as a protection from cold and rain. The somewhat chilly weather of late led to the place being well roofed tonight."[27] While retractable roofs in sporting venues date back to at least the Roman Colosseum, they were still rather unique at this time.

Colonel Alexander Brewster was selected as the referee for the bout and Professor John Duffy, boxing trainer of the Southern Athletic Club, was the timekeeper for Fitzsimmons, with Jimmy Colville of Boston acting in that capacity for Dempsey. The master of ceremonies for the evening was former New Orleans mayor J. Valsin Guillotte.

Just before 9:00 p.m. Guillotte stepped through the ropes and addressed the crowd. He called for order and then introduced Brewster. Guillotte then called forth the pugilists and the men entered the ring promptly at 9:00 p.m. Fitzsimmons, wearing a brown overcoat, was the first through the ropes, followed by his seconds Doc O'Connell and Jimmy Connelly and his bottle-holder Jimmy Robison. "He walked knock-kneed with a cat-like movement, and his red hair was bristling and there was a sarcastic turning of the lips at the small amount of applause with which he was welcomed."[28]

As soon as Fitzsimmons sat down in his corner on the southwest side of the amphitheater, Dempsey entered the ring by vaulting lightly over the ropes. Following Jack were his seconds Jack McAuliffe and Gus Tuthill and Mike Conley as his bottle-holder. Jack was wearing neat, rubber-soled canvas boxing shoes and his familiar blue boxing tights that he had worn in so many victories over the previous eight years. "He sat in his chair and scanned Fitzsimmons with a cool, cynical smile. An admirer of Dempsey's threw an old shoe in the ring as an omen of good luck."[29]

Fitzsimmons then stripped off his overcoat. He was wearing silk boxing shorts of crimson red with a band of white at the waist and leather boxing shoes. "An involuntary burst of applause came from the audience when his form was exposed to view. He was a perfect specimen of manhood six feet in height, with arms as long as a yard stick, thin legs, but powerful shoulders and chest, upon which the muscles stood out solid and firm like a whalebone."[30] Fitzsimmons, it was said, had an abnormal wealth of muscle about his arms, shoulders and back and his extremely long arms gave him a tremendous advantage in reach over most of his opponents. Dempsey, though four inches shorter than Fitzsimmons, was also described as presenting a favorable impression. "The muscles of his arms, shoulders and legs, while not prominent, appeared to be in condition of perfect development, and his broad, strong calves showed up well. His flesh had a healthy glow."[31]

"The men weighed in the presence of the audience, Fitzsimmons marking 150½ and Dempsey 147½."[32] It was noted that Fitzsimmons had weighed a pound over the middleweight limit at 6:00 p.m. that evening and was sent out in the company of British Jimmy Carroll, his lead trainer, to work down a bit. During the weigh-in, the police examined the fight gloves for several minutes before declaring them legal. As the men and their seconds walked about the ring readying themselves for the battle, much of the conversation was congenial, but when Carroll came across Dempsey and McAuliffe, he refused to shake either man's hand. At 9:25 p.m., Dempsey walked across the ring and extended his hand to his opponent. Fitzsimmons took Jack's hand and shook it cordially. At 9:30 the gong sounded and both men approached center ring where Brewster instructed them to shake hands again and then fight.

The first round was fairly even, with both men leading and connecting several times. Carroll, Fitzsimmons's lead trainer, drawing on his substantive knowledge of Dempsey's fighting style, called out to his man, "Don't box this fellow. Put him out quick."[33] Fitzsimmons listened and continually rushed Dempsey, chasing all around the ring, but Jack was generally able to keep him off and land some good shots in retaliation. Homer Davenport, who in time would become a noted political cartoonist, was a young man on his first newspaper assignment during the contest. Davenport was sitting at ringside near Fitzsimmons's corner and noted that "Fitzsimmons' rushes in the first round were so fierce that Dempsey never had time to put up his hand, so busy was he in keeping away from the blacksmith."[34]

At one point in the first round, Fitzsimmons did land a hard left to the jaw and crowded Jack into the corner. After a clinch, the men broke and continued the chase. After the break, Dempsey caught Fitzsimmons with a straight right to the mouth followed by a hard body blow. Jack was then able to land several good blows to his opponent's rib cage and stomach but was typically paid back in kind. The round was scored by most to be a draw.

In the second round, Fitz came out cautiously, but soon began crowding Dempsey and doing most of the leading. Early on he landed a right-right-left combination to Jack's head that registered with Dempsey. Jack then danced and avoided his opponent, but Fitzsimmons was relentless, continuing the assault, crowding, pushing and landing powerful combinations to Jack's head and chest. While Jack was able to get in several good blows on Fitzsimmons's nose, ear and head, the round was clearly the Antipodean's. The Nonpareil's weakened lungs were already beginning to wear down, causing him to be winded and grow concerned. Dempsey knew he was not his old self and he clearly saw that in Fitzsimmons he was battling a man worthy of his reputation.

At the start of the third round, Fitzsimmons took the initiative by rushing Dempsey, landing a hard blow on Jack's ribs and stepping quickly aside to avoid the counter. Fitzsimmons then wound up and fired a vicious right that Jack ducked, but the sound of the missile whistling past his ear warmed the Nonpareil up again. For most of the remainder of the third round, Dempsey moved in and out, pursuing and retreating and staying active. When his opponent cornered him, Jack would fire back and send Fitzsimmons in retreat. For the first half of this round, Dempsey looked as if he had a chance, but things

A fight sketch from the Bob Fitzsimmons–Nonpareil Jack Dempsey (left) bout on January 14, 1891.

soon changed. About midway through the round, Fitzsimmons got through Jack's defense in one of his bull rushes. He landed a hard left just above Dempsey's nose, opening a gash on Jack's forehead. Towards the end of the third round, Fitzsimmons crowded Jack into a corner and opened up on the Nonpareil. Moments later, a smashing right to the chest from the Australian knocked Jack down. Dempsey was up at once but appeared groggy and unsteady on his feet. One reporter commented, "Jack was weak and again ran away from the lanky fighter. This was Bob's round."[35]

In the fourth round, Jack once again showed some life, connecting with a vicious combination to the New Zealander's face and midsection. He then clinched to avoid the return. Upon separating, Dempsey caught Fitzsimmons with a left uppercut and followed that with a cannonball to the ribs. Jack kept up the volley by landing a hard blow to Fitzsimmons's neck, but Bob soon righted himself and quickly returned fire, landing four body blows in rapid succession. The two then came together at center ring, each landing strong blows, but the Nonpareil's lungs weren't fit for this pace. During the exchange, Dempsey visibly began to tire and from that point on, it was all Fitzsimmons. Bob took advantage, landing three times on Dempsey's mouth with straight rights and a left to the nose. At this point, Dempsey's mouth was cut and swollen and his nose began to bleed. Beyond tired, "Dempsey almost fell, but caught the ropes and recovered, giving his opponent a heavy clip on the chest."[36] Once again Fitzsimmons rushed Dempsey and landed three hard blows on his opponent. These rushes continued and frequent combinations to the head and body by the New Zealander easily made this Fitzsimmons's round. It was in this round that Dempsey said his nose was broken. This turned out to be false, but it says something about the power of the punches delivered by Fitzsimmons.

The remaining nine rounds were a series of victories for the New Zealander, each paving the way for Fitzsimmons to win the fight in the thirteenth round by way of knockout. Jack would start each round rested and showing some fight, but after a minute or two, his energy began to wane, exposing him to more damage from the heavy hands of his rival. After receiving steady punishment from the powerful blows of Fitzsimmons, Dempsey was fatigued and his legs grew wobbly. While he was still effective in short bursts, he no longer had the stamina to fight full-on for an entire three-minute round.

The fifth round opened with both men again rested and looking fresh. As in the previous round, the Nonpareil of old was back, but just for a couple of minutes. He knew he had to strike quickly in each round before he began to tire. Once more, Jack showed his old agility, moving well and landing several hard blows to Fitzsimmons's neck and midsection. The Nonpareil moved quickly and fleetly in and out, landing and avoiding the Australian's counters. Once when Fitzsimmons landed clean blows to Jack's chin and nose, Dempsey quickly gathered himself and just laughed. "The Nonpareil braced up and fought hard, landing two heavy drives on Fitzsimmons' ribs which made that worthy grunt."[37] Suddenly though, Fitzsimmons connected with two blows to Dempsey's chest and a couple more to the neck that shook Jack and left him unable to respond. The pair fell into a clinch from which Jack slipped and fell to his knees. He scrambled to his feet but was caught again with a deep blow to his chest.

In the sixth round, the men exchanged blows in rapid fashion, but again Fitzsimmons got the better of the exchanges, once landing a powerful left to Dempsey's jaw that brought out a chorus of "Oh's" from the crowd. Dempsey clinched to catch his wind and avoid falling, but another right to his neck drove him to his knees. It was becoming glaringly apparent to all on hand that Dempsey was in trouble. Toward the end of the round,

Fitzsimmons landed a vicious blow on Dempsey's chest that staggered the Nonpareil. Jack made it to the end of the round, but only just.

The seventh round was an active one that opened with both men sparring. Jack came out fast and landed a hard blow on his opponent's neck, but Fitzsimmons responded, catching Jack with a sharp uppercut to the chin. This and several heavy blows to the ribs once again sent Dempsey to the ground. Jack got up and answered back with an uppercut to the Antipodean's chin. Taking his turn, Fitzsimmons returned fire, sending his weakened opponent into the ropes. Again, Jack came at Fitzsimmons and hammered through the New Zealander's defenses, landing a powerful blow to the stomach. Tiring, the men fell into a clinch along the ropes. While the pair wrestled, Fitzsimmons managed to get in a blow to Dempsey's ribs that sent Jack sprawling back and falling between the ropes. His seconds rushed to his assistance, but Jack jumped up on his own and called on Fitzsimmons to square up again. Dempsey's body was scraped and bruised and his face and lower lip were cut and bleeding.

In the eighth round, Dempsey looked tired and battered, but managed to land several light blows. Fitzsimmons, on the other hand, looked fresh and tried to finish his exhausted opponent by hammering away at Dempsey's face, neck and body, but Jack fought back and showed a little life. Unfortunately for Jack, it had little effect. Bob began crowding Jack to wear him down further and landed a left on the nose. Dempsey swung lightly, but his blows were now slow and weak. Fitz landed repeatedly, raining blows to the head and body. Exhausted, "Jack fell on the ropes and the tall 'pug' landed his right on the famous fighter's nose. Jack hugged Fitz, who struck him body blows again and again. Another right swing demoralized Dempsey and he was punched all over the ring."[38]

The ninth round saw an early exchange of body blows, but that was really all of the action from Dempsey. After the initial exchange between the two men, Fitzsimmons took complete control, landing virtually at will. Now tiring earlier and earlier in each round, Jack clinched repeatedly, simply trying to last to the next bell, but at each break, he received withering punishment from Fitzsimmons. After one exchange, Jack landed a few light blows, but in return "Fitzsimmons hit Dempsey several raps in the ribs and he fell heavily. He rose and was knocked down twice again. He could hardly stand, and when Fitzsimmons knocked him down again, he couldn't get up."[39] Despite his severely battered and exhausted condition, the fight continued because the round ended before Dempsey could be counted out.

By the tenth round, Fitzsimmons was completely in command of the fight and landed his punches regularly on the sluggish Dempsey. Jack's only real defense was to clinch Fitzsimmons to limit the punishment and avoid visiting the canvas, but it was of little use. Despite his efforts, Dempsey went down three times and was nearly out, but all three times he rose, determined not to quit. The few blows that Jack managed to land did little damage and were repeatedly countered with powerful blasts from the blacksmith's fists. At one point, "Fitzsimmons picked him up, having knocked him down, and said, 'Jack, you are whipped; I can't hit you.'"[40] Despite Fitz's urging, Dempsey refused to stop. After receiving another severe blow to the stomach Jack was wobbling around the ring with unsteady legs. He was close to going down a fourth time but was saved by the bell ending the round.

Fitzsimmons completely controlled the eleventh chapter, repeatedly landing savage combinations that drove Jack into the ropes. After two ferocious lefts, Dempsey staggered and went down. Still, Jack managed to climb to his feet, but only to walk into the meat grinder again. After he went down a second time in the round, Dempsey's corner threw a white towel into the ring, but it went unnoticed by the referee and Jack rose, barely able to stand, but still unwilling to quit.

The twelfth round was simply pitiful. Jack, unable to win, but unwilling to concede, barely able to land a meaningful blow and unable to defend himself, staggered around the ring on quivering legs. Dempsey continued to absorb tremendous blows from Fitzsimmons, who at this point really only wanted to lay Dempsey out to end the slaughter. "Bob led right and left on Jack's head. Bob punched Jack all over the ring. Jack countered and attempted to drive Fitzsimmons to the center of the ring, but in his exhaustion, he nearly fell down from that effort." Jack fired an uppercut but missed. He gathered himself and fired again. "Dempsey made a swing at Bob and missing, turned half around and began staggering across the ring. Fitzsimmons was after him like a cat. He almost tip-toed after the staggering fighter, and when he got close enough, he landed a blow near the base of Dempsey's brain that sent him forward."[41] Dempsey landed on the ground with a terrific force and lay there, with his chin buried in the soft clay surface for several seconds. The *Montreal Herald* described it as follows, "Bob fought fair and landed left on stomach and face and knocked Jack down. Again, Bob swung right, and again the Nonpareil went down."[42] After a few seconds, Jack rose slowly, unsteadily, his mind in a fog. He stumbled for a few seconds trying to regain his balance. He was tottering and groggy. Had it been anyone but the Nonpareil, the fight might have been stopped right there. He clearly could not win, but no one had the heart to actually stop it and tell Jack he was through. Once, near the end of the round, after laying the Nonpareil down again, Fitzsimmons lifted Jack in his arms and helped him to his feet. Sure the fight was over, Fitzsimmons walked back to his corner and began removing his gloves. Somehow, and incredibly, Dempsey staggered to his feet, stumbled over to the blacksmith and repeated his declaration that he would not quit as long as he could stand. He then lurched forward and fell against Fitzsimmons as time was called on the round.

By the thirteenth round, it was truly over. At the bell, Jack rose and headed to the center of the ring. Upon reaching his opponent, he swung heavily at Fitzsimmons's head. He missed badly and staggered forward. Fitzsimmons, ready to put an end to the carnage, went after him. As Jack began to right himself, he was met by a terrific combination from Fitzsimmons's flashing fists. These were the final blows of the match. "Fitzsimmons' long right landed heavily on Jack's left ear. Dempsey staggered around the ring and fell in a heap."[43] Dempsey tried twice to rise, but this time his efforts were in vain and referee Alexander Brewster finally awarded the fight to Fitzsimmons. The total time of the bout was forty-nine minutes.

Dempsey was lifted by Fitzsimmons, Tuthill and McAuliffe and carried to his corner. Jack's head began to clear and he sat on his stool, badly beaten, heartbroken and weeping. In the opposite corner, Carroll was wild with joy and shook the New Zealander with both hands. Fitzsimmons, however, was less joyful. Showing a great deal of class and compassion, he walked back across the ring to his now vanquished opponent and knelt down. Leaning in close and holding Dempsey's limp hand, Bob spoke words of praise and encouragement into Jack's ear. Though happy with his victory, it was difficult for Fitzsimmons to see the former Nonpareil in such dire straits, for he admired, respected and genuinely liked Dempsey. "To my dying day," said Fitzsimmons, describing the fight, "I will see Dempsey lying there with the little red bubbles bursting as he breathed heavily into the red earth. I picked him up and helped carry him to his corner. I never lifted a braver man to his feet."[44]

The crowd saw a desperate fight and a struggle for survival, "which proved a game and bloody one. Dempsey fought long and well, but he was outclassed. He was a defeated man before the fight was half through and acknowledged the fact in the tenth round. Nevertheless, he continued to defend his fast slipping honors until he could no longer stand."[45]

Describing Dempsey's pluck, a ringside reporter wrote that "throughout, he displayed all his old skill, and perhaps more than his usual intelligence, but the gods were not on his side. Instead of using his powers on the offensive and exercising his judgment to select the proper moment to lay his enemy low, he was engaged in preserving his defeat from the appearance of an utter collapse."[46] Another report stated that Dempsey was "scarcely in it" but pointed out that the New Zealander "had a longer reach, was more sinewy, weighed more, and was taller." The report added that, of Dempsey, "it must be said to his credit that he was overmatched."[47]

While he was thoroughly beaten, Dempsey showed the heart of a lion and that he had no quit. Political cartoonist Homer Davenport, who witnessed the bout at ringside, noted in his post-fight assessment, "Dempsey simply would not be whipped, that was all, and the punishment he took was terrible. Fitzsimmons dropped him time and time again in his tracks, but he always managed to get to his feet and seemed determined not to be whipped."[48]

As the fighters left the ring, Fitzsimmons was barely bruised or scratched while Dempsey looked like he'd been through a war. "Dempsey was badly punished; swollen face, cut lips and nose, and a bad mark or two on his body were plainly visible."[49] After being helped to his dressing room by McAuliffe and others, Jack was attended by a physician. "He was a sorry spectacle as he lay back with closed eyes. His nose is broken, and his eyes will both be very black. The Nonpareil is heart-broken and would say nothing."[50]

Jack was carried back to his boarding house by carriage where his wounds were more thoroughly treated by physicians. It is claimed by some that "after the referee had counted the fatal ten seconds Dempsey cried as if his heart would break, and his closest friends could not console him."[51] There were even some reports that claimed that Dempsey had died either from his battle wounds or from a self-inflicted gunshot wound. The unfounded rumors were quickly dispelled. Newspapers throughout the land reported, "Jack Dempsey slept under the influence of opiates last night. The bridge of his nose is broken and his ribs were so sore after he was driven home from the ring that he continuously groaned and tossed until the physician that accompanied him from the club administered a strong narcotic. This morning he looked badly bruised and swollen about the face and mouth, his skin is reddened and sore and a piece the size of a man's hand is scraped from the back of his neck on his left side."[52] Jack lay in bed surrounded by Maggie, McAuliffe and several other friends.

"When Fitzsimmons left the rooms of the Olympic club to meet his wife, who was awaiting him in his apartments on Royal Street, a certified check for $11,000 was presented to him. Today his backers received another check for $5,000 additional, making a total of $16,000 for his night's work. Dempsey has received his coup. He did his best, but he was not in it with the Australian. It was the best fight of its class and of the weight that the world has ever seen."[53]

Immediately after the bout, Fitzsimmons told reporters that while Dempsey battled hard, the fight had not been difficult. He likened the contest to a workout on the heavy bag, though a heavy bag does not fire back. He also claimed that he had picked off most of Dempsey's blows before they reached their mark. Asked what he thought of Dempsey, the New Zealander remarked, "I think he is the gamest and best man I ever met. He can whip any other man of his weight in the country." Fitzsimmons pointed out that Jack's gameness had cost the New Zealander $5,000 from those who promised that amount as a bonus should Fitzsimmons finish Dempsey in ten or fewer rounds. He then continued his praise for Jack by stating, "Dempsey discounts anybody I have ever seen on earth. He certainly won my admiration."[54]

Fourteen years after the fight and ten after the Nonpareil's death, Fitzsimmons kept up the same line. He was quoted as saying that while Dempsey showed a great spirit and bravery, he had no trouble with Jack. Fitzsimmons stated that after the second round, "I knew I could put Jack to sleep any time I felt like it, but I jogged along with him, closing an eye here and putting a mouse on his lip there."[55] Clearly, Fitzsimmons did know he had Jack who was ill and not the fighter he had once been. With Jack in a greatly weakened state, the size differential was just too much to overcome. "He never ought to have been permitted to go up against such a freak of nature," said Mr. Reynolds, a backer. "Jack isn't even a middleweight, properly speaking, and there are only three heavyweights in America Fitzsimmons couldn't whip. They are Corbett, Sullivan, and Jackson. It was like pitting a man against a boy."[56] The *Brooklyn Eagle* commented that while Fitzsimmons fought a clean and honorable contest, he was really just "a heavyweight sweated out and trained down to a requisite figure. He is as tall as Sullivan and with a longer reach."[57]

Even Fitzsimmons's manager indirectly admitted that the size disparity was a problem for Dempsey. When asked after the bout if there was any truth to rumors that his man would square off with Jim Corbett, Jimmy Carroll responded that there was no use in Fitzsimmons going after heavyweights. "I believe he could whip some of the heavyweights, but he might make the same mistake as Dempsey and be sorry."[58]

In earlier days, Jack might have easily defeated a man the size of Fitzsimmons. He might also have bested a man with Fitzsimmons's skills. But a clearly weakened Dempsey could not handle such a combination. Ruby Robert was quick with his hands and very sturdy. He had a powerful punch and could absorb punishment. Jack was a half step slower and, while he was willing, Jack was less able to absorb and weather punishment from a hard blow. Fighting Fitzsimmons at this stage of his career was clearly a tactical mistake for Dempsey, but his pride and his supreme self-confidence would not allow him to avoid the New Zealander.

People struggled with the simple fact that Dempsey had been soundly beaten. That had never happened before. La Blanche's win had been a fluke after Jack had beaten the Marine senseless for over thirty rounds. This was different. It was no fluke. Speculation ran wild. Was it really true that Dempsey was dying? Had the years in the ring finally taken their toll on his body? Was it simply the great size disparity? Was Jack an alcoholic? The *Milwaukee Journal* pointed out, "It is an interesting fact that Fitzsimmons did not taste intoxicating liquors while Dempsey took brandy between each round."[59] The truth was a combination of all of these factors—Jack was sick and dying; his body was badly weakened both from his years in the ring and his illness; the size disparity was too great, especially for a man in his weakened condition and Jack was almost certainly an alcoholic at this point.

In an editorial comment, the *National Police Gazette* commented that Dempsey was "ignominiously licked—beaten is not the word for it. From the first round, when he stood up bold, smiling, confident, until the thirteenth, when he tottered forward, scarcely able to hold up his hands, he was never, in the opinion of spectators, a possible victor."[60]

John L. Sullivan was in Chicago when he received word of Dempsey's defeat. He was astonished and asked the bearer of the news if he was shooting straight with him. When asked by the reporter if he had lost much money on the fight Sullivan responded, "Oh, a few hundred or so ... but it ain't that what breaks me up. I'd bet the same amount on a dead certainty. It's the fact that Jack was done up, see? I admired Dempsey as a fighter and a gentleman. I always regarded him as one of my best friends. Then, I considered him the best middleweight on earth." Sullivan went on to say that while he certainly understood that at some point Dempsey might lose, he did not think it would be now and he did not think it would be to Fitzsimmons. "Well, I guess it is all up with Dempsey now," continued Sullivan with a heavy sigh. "He will never recover from this licking. The poor fellow's heart must be broken."[61]

The Fitzsimmons fight really was the beginning of the end for Dempsey's ring career. He was growing weaker as the consumption that would eventually kill him was beginning to wear him down. Speculation that he was finished in the ring began to circulate. Richard Fox expressed sorrow that Dempsey had lost as he had always had the greatest of admiration for Jack, but he added that it was a mistake to pit the Nonpareil against so much heavier a man. Another spectator commented that he believed that Dempsey had gone stale. "I feel sorry for Jack," he said, "but there is no doubt that he was outclassed. I am very much afraid that Jack is not the man he used to be."[62]

While Jack's career was clearly winding down, Fitzsimmons's was on the rise. Before the year was out, he and Carroll had a major falling out over Carroll's actions and his avarice. In short order the two dissolved their partnership and went their separate ways. Fitzsimmons stated that he was tired of doing all of the fighting yet sharing half of all receipts with Carroll.[63] Fitzsimmons would fight another two decades and, in addition to the middleweight title that he had just wrested from Dempsey; he would capture the world heavyweight title by knocking out Jim Corbett on St. Patrick's Day of 1897. Fitz held the crown for an inactive two years before losing it by knockout in his first title defense to Jim Jeffries in June 1899 at the Coney Island Athletic Club in Brooklyn. Outweighed by almost forty pounds, Fitzsimmons still fought a bruising battle in which both men suffered terrific punishment. Fitzsimmons put up a valiant battle but began to wane in the tenth round when he paid two visits to the canvas. Fitz got cold-cocked by a sharp left hook to the jaw in the eleventh round and was unconscious before he hit the mat. There was no reason for referee George Siler to even start the count and he immediately declared Jeffries the winner and new heavyweight champion.

Bob failed in his attempt to regain the title in 1902, when, after battering Jeffries for seven rounds, he was knocked out in the eighth, but he was hardly through. Fitzsimmons defeated George Gardner for the world light heavyweight championship in 1903, making him the first man ever to capture three world belts in three different divisions. He fought on through 1909, when he decided to hang up his gloves, but like so many fighters, he thought that he had a little more in the tank.

After a four-year layoff, Bob contracted to fight in New York in 1913, but was denied a license by the New York State Athletic Commission. He sued the commission but lost when the New York State Supreme Court upheld the decision. Not to be denied, Bob went to neighboring Pennsylvania where he fought twice in early 1914, winning the first contest in a six-round newspaper decision and battling to a no decision ruling the following month. Despite the indecisive outcome in that second contest, the *Reading Eagle* reported that Fitzsimmons knocked his opponent, Jersey Bellew, down in the second round. Other than a few more exhibitions, however, the now 52-year-old Ruby Robert knew he was finally through. He would die of pneumonia in Chicago just three years later on October 22, 1917.

After Fitzsimmons received his $11,000 cut of the purse and Dempsey his $1,000 it was reported that the club made a whopping $20,000 on the match. This would be roughly $500,000 in today's currency—a phenomenal amount for any sporting event at that time.

On the Thursday after the Dempsey-Fitzsimmons match, Dr. Borde, Jack's personal physician in New Orleans, visited Dempsey and upon further examination reported that Jack's nose was not broken after all and his bruises and cuts were not terribly serious. He left without prescribing any additional medicines. Dempsey convalesced for several days. By Saturday, Jack was out of bed and by Tuesday he was fully dressed and out for a walk. One report stated that a black eye and bruised nose were the only visible marks on him, but when asked how he felt Dempsey laughed and responded, "It's been almost a week now and I still feel the effects of the fight and if you saw my body you would think so."[64] Nonetheless, Jack was on the mend. He was also eating well and entertaining friends. Jack planned to return with his family to the West Coast after a few more days of rest.

In the days and weeks following the fight, there was much speculation about Dempsey's future. Would he retire from the ring? If so, what would he do? Jack McAuliffe told reporters that Dempsey would not accept any job offers as a boxing trainer at athletic clubs nor was he ready to entertain other fight offers yet. The loss did not hurt his drawing power. Within a couple of months after the Fitzsimmons match, Dempsey had received any number of offers to engage in, second, or referee bouts. "Tom Maher, Dempsey's trainer, says that at least fifty telegrams have been received by Jack from theatrical managers offering him advantageous terms if he will travel with them." Soon, Jack would join his friends at Hyde & Behman's Theatre in Brooklyn, where he would spar with Young Mitchell during daily matinees.

While the Nonpareil was still in demand at the box office, the loss was personally devastating to him. His already heavy drinking got worse and his personal demons sent him spiraling deeper into his emotional decline.

Two decades after the bout, Jack Skelly recalled, "In his earlier career he was a lighthearted, playful companion, always ready for a lark and a joke and never aggressive or moody. After his unfortunate defeat by Bob Fitzsimmons, he changed greatly. He grew sad and melancholy and was never the same cheerful fellow. That defeat broke poor Dempsey's heart and sent him in sorrow to an early grave."[65]

The Fitzsimmons bout was to be Dempsey's last official fight until 1893. While he would fight a number of exhibitions with Young Mitchell and "Mysterious" Billy Smith throughout 1891 and 1892, Jack was mostly inactive in the ring. Rumors that he was gravely ill began to surface once again.

After several days' rest, Jack and Maggie left New Orleans for Portland. The couple stopped in Galveston, Texas, and stayed for several days. They then traveled to Phoenix and on to Los Angeles, where they arrived on January 25.

On February 7, Jack and Maggie checked into the Windsor Hotel in San Francisco while changing trains en route home to Portland. They were met by friends and reporters who pressed Jack for information on the Fitzsimmons fight and on his future plans. Dempsey was vague when asked about his future and did his best to steer the conversation away from the still painful Fitzsimmons affair. When he was asked when he knew that he was defeated in that contest, Dempsey responded, "I knew it before the first minute had passed but made up my mind to fight as long as I could stand." Regarding his future Jack said, "I may fight again, possibly the winner of the Mitchell–La Blanche contest, but I can't say just when at present." Dempsey indicated that he was returning to Portland to look into business opportunities and his schedule would be dictated by those opportunities. It is hard to know if he meant his next comment or simply said it for Maggie's sake, but Jack stated, "My hopes are that I can quietly settle down and attend to any business I may go into."[66] After boarding a train later that day, the exhausted couple arrived at home in Portland on February 8.

Jack traveled to Seattle on February 21. Upon his arrival, he showed some good humor regarding his recent loss when he commented to the press, "Were it not for the fact that I would be charged with bluffing, I should certainly challenge Fitzsimmons for another fight under the London prize-ring rules."[67] While Dempsey was not engaging in bouts, he was still interested in keeping his hand in the fighting world with sparring exhibitions and periodic referee duties.

In late February, Gus Tuthill announced that he would back Dempsey against Dominick McCaffrey for a purse of between $5,000 and $10,000 for a finish fight at catch weights. The proposed match may have been more of a way to clip McCaffrey's ears a bit for comments he had been making about Jack. It was stated that "the proposed match grows out of a dispute with McCaffrey respecting the merits of Dempsey as a fighter."[68]

The row apparently began when Tuthill and McCaffrey both attended a party held by friends at a New York sporting club. The two became involved in a discussion on the merits of several prominent fighters. McCaffrey commented that he thought Dempsey was overrated and that he would love to have another chance with him in the ring. That barb was enough for Tuthill, who produced a large roll of bills from his pocket and, snapping off $2,500 on the spot, offered it as a down payment for the match. McCaffrey asked Tuthill if he was sure that Jack would fight to which Tuthill responded that Dempsey would stand by any match that he arranged. Unable to call Tuthill's bluff, McCaffrey began to back down a bit, stating that he would have to check with his backers and with the Manhattan Athletic Club with whom he was employed and whose permission he would have to seek to engage in a bout. When Tuthill said that he would speak to the officials at the club and arrange it, McCaffrey, now feeling the heat from his own boasting, abruptly excused himself. "As the matter now stands, Tuthill is waiting to hear back from McCaffrey or his backers. He is anxious to back Dempsey because he is confident that he can beat McCaffrey."[69]

In March, the London Pelican Club sent a cablegram to the *Police Gazette* offices offering $3,000 for a bout between Dempsey and British middleweight Ted Pritchard. They also offered Jack $500 for training expenses. Pritchard had defeated Jack Burke and his stock was currently high. A number of factors worked against this bout. Jack's health was certainly paramount, but the facts that Pritchard was a heavy middleweight and that the purse was rather small for a trip all the way across the Atlantic made this offer less than enticing. "Jack is well known as a good figurer, and without anything more than previous experience as a guide it is pretty safe to say he will wait until something larger and more tempting in the way of bait is hung up."[70] He did.

Even in decline, the tributes continued to come in. In March, Tom Maher, one of Jack's former trainers, opened a hotel on Grand Street in Dempsey's old Williamsburg neighborhood. In honor of Dempsey, he named it "The Nonpareil."[71]

In late June, reports began to circulate that Dempsey would second Australian Jim Hall in his upcoming bout against Fitzsimmons. The bout was to be held in St. Paul, Minnesota, on July 22. Dempsey was seen as a valuable asset in a fighter's corner. The former Nonpareil, Billy Madden, British Jimmy Carroll and Jack McAuliffe were, "in the opinion of many experts, about the best men in the country to act in the capacity of seconds at the ring side. They are credited with possessing that coolness, excellent judgment, and the discernment of an opponent's weak points so necessary to the success in a prolonged battle."[72]

Dempsey agreed to work Hall's corner and in mid–July he traveled to St. Paul in time for the bout. While there, he caught up with old friend Jim Corbett. Before the bout could be held, however, local authorities intervened and prevented it from taking place. After the bout was cancelled Dempsey, Corbett and several friends decided not to let the trip be a complete bust and wandered east to White Bear Lake where they each registered for rooms at the Leip House.[73] The Leip House was one of the town of White Bear's grand resorts during the Victorian era. It was a complex of hotel buildings and villa cottages with a total one hundred and twenty-five rooms accommodating up to three hundred guests.

The owner of the resort was Colonel William Leip, "who had immigrated to the United States from Germany in 1846 and settled first in St. Paul, where he prospered in the cigar and liquor trade. By 1861, he had taken up brewing ale, and by 1865, he had purchased White Bear's first resort, the Barnum House, located on the strip of land between White Bear and Goose lakes. With his background in the cigar and liquor industries, Leip knew how to entertain the crowds who flocked to the lake by the thousands during the warm months. Through the years, guests could enjoy a large fleet of rowboats and avail themselves of fishing tackle and bait, as well as try out the on-site bowling alleys, a billiard room and a sample room—another name for a saloon. Orchestras often performed at a pavilion along the lakeshore."[74] After several days enjoying the resort with Corbett and other friends, Dempsey returned home to Portland to rest and be with his family.

The rumors of Dempsey's ill health persisted throughout that spring and summer and by July, George La Blanche apparently decided that it might be safe to once again challenge Jack to a rematch. The *San Francisco Call* reported that La Blanche was looking for a return fight and that Jack, who had failed by every effort to coax La Blanche back into the ring in 1889 and 1890, might consent to meet the Marine under the Queensberry Rules. "La Blanche believes that Dempsey has lost all heart since his defeat at the hands of Fitzsimmons, and that his chances of whipping him again are very promising."[75]

In an effort to keep the health rumors at bay, Dempsey continued to make every attempt to stay busy and in front of the public. Jack returned to San Francisco on September 20. On the following evening, he refereed a heavyweight contest at the Pacific Athletic Club between Billy Woods of Denver and Jack Davis of Omaha.[76] Bob Fitzsimmons was on hand, seconding Davis. Master of Ceremonies M.J. Sullivan introduced Jack as the referee to the four thousand in attendance and the Nonpareil was met with great applause.

The bout was an entertaining but cautious affair, with both men mostly sparring, though landing an occasional hard wrap. The pace of the fight picked up in the eighth round, with both men landing hard flurries. In the eleventh round, Davis dropped to the floor in his corner from the effects of Woods's furious combination. Davis "was dazed and bleeding freely from the left eye and mouth. He appeared blinded with blood."[77]

The bout ended late in the thirteenth round when Woods got the better of Davis with a smashing right-hand blow to the head that dropped Davis to his knees. As he got up, Woods again blasted his woozy opponent with a blistering right to the head that sent Davis sprawling against the ropes. With Davis helpless, hanging on the ropes for support and unable to defend himself, Fitzsimmons rushed into the ring to stop Woods from further injuring his man. As Fitzsimmons grabbed Davis, Woods took exception with Bob's interference and the two exchanged invective laced words that almost resulted in a fight between Woods and Ruby Robert.

Fitzsimmons, more worried about his fighter than about Woods, cooled off a bit and began to help Davis to his stool. Fitzsimmons had helped Davis to his feet and the two were making their way to the corner when suddenly and out of nowhere he received a blow to the back of the neck from Woods. Setting his fighter down, the now furious Fitzsimmons turned and went after Woods. A quick-thinking Dempsey saw what was happening and intervened, grabbing Fitzsimmons around the neck stopping him from pounding the waiting Woods.[78] The ring was soon filled with supporters of each fighter with both sides claiming foul. Davis's corner claimed that Woods struck their man a full five seconds after the bell that ended the thirteenth round and Woods claimed that Fitzsimmons's entry into the ring constituted a foul and a forfeit. Dempsey did his best to restore order, but bedlam ensued until Captain Douglass and the San Francisco police entered the ring. In a short time, the constabulary restored order. Dempsey, once again in control in the ring, allowed neither foul claim and awarded the bout to Woods.[79]

Johnny Herget, a.k.a. Young Mitchell.

On September 23, Jack joined Sam Fitzpatrick and Billy Akers in seconding rising middleweight Young Mitchell in his bout with former Dempsey opponent Reddy Gallagher. The contest was held at San Francisco's Occidental Club. Gallagher's seconds in the contest were British Jimmy Carroll as well as his backer, Western legend Bat Masterson.

The bout was full of action as the fighters traded blows for thirteen rounds. While the men fought somewhat evenly throughout, Gallagher seemed to be tiring more rapidly and lacked steam as the seventh round ended. After that, the men continued to exchange sharp blows, but Mitchell seemed more confident and in charge. "In the thirteenth, Gallagher came up a trifle dazed, but he landed two straight lefts under Mitchell's chin. Mitchell suddenly came back at him with a right-hand blow on the neck and a left on the chin. Gallagher reeled and fell on his side, made a slight effort to rise, but fell back and was counted out" by referee Peter Jackson.[80]

In early October, Jack met Mysterious Billy Smith in a three-round exhibition bout in San Francisco for his first public ring action since his loss to Fitzsimmons. It was a fairly informal affair, but it was good seeing Dempsey back in the squared circle as a pugilist for the first time since January.

On October 16, Dempsey met his friend Young Mitchell in a three-round exhibition in the City by the Bay. The exhibition was part of a benefit for Jack sponsored by his friends and backers and held in the Wigwam Building on Eddy Street, which housed the offices of the Pacific Athletic Club. In addition to the gate, donations were made by Jack's supporters from all around the country. By all accounts the fundraising went extremely well, but just how well is still a matter of debate. The single largest donation was said to have been $1,000, tendered by New York turf man Phil Dwyer. Promoter Mose Gunst gave $500 and multiple checks of $100 or greater were given by bookmakers and other sporting men from around the country. In addition, more than four thousand admission tickets were sold at $1 each. There was considerable rumor that Dempsey made between $25,000 and $38,000 from his benefit,[81] but Jack denied this. When asked by a reporter how much he did clear, Jack stated, "I don't know exactly, but it is likely to net me altogether considerably more than $5,000." When the reporter commented that many newspapers put the take at anywhere between $35,000 and $43,000, Jack laughed and responded, "Yes, I know they did and I'll tell you how the mistake happened." Jack stated that a newspaper reporter had mistakenly added "a cipher to the $3,800" when he telegraphed his story to a number of newspapers across the country.[82]

Billy Jordan was the master of ceremonies for the evening in which eighteen bouts—both boxing and wrestling—preceded the main event between Dempsey and Mitchell. After the final preliminary contest five floral arrangements were brought into the ring, "including one that was a huge five-pointed star with vari-colored electric lights." Dempsey, through Jordan, expressed his thanks to his friends, supporters and fans for the wonderful tribute they had given to him.[83]

The match then began with Mitchell landing a left to Dempsey's jaw. After this, the two men traded blows, but each blocked the other several times. "An exchange of left hand blows in the face followed, and Mitchell landed on Dempsey's head with both hands."[84] The first chapter ended with most observers agreeing that the fighting was brisk and fairly even.

The second round commenced with Mitchell leading with a short left that missed its mark and Dempsey countering with a stiff straight left to the face. Despite this strong counter Mitchell had the upper hand during the round. "Mitchell several times landed good lefts on Dempsey's nose, and once sent him sideways to the ropes. Mitchell plainly had the best of the round."[85]

The third and final round was more even than the second. Early on, Mitchell received several straight lefts to his chest, but countered well. Throughout the round Dempsey moved well and showed flashes of his old quickness, on several occasions landing punches and stepping back to avoid Mitchell's counters. The contest ended with a rapid exchange of combination punches by both fighters, all landing on or about the other's head.[86] The capacity crowd rose to their feet and cheered mightily as the action piqued and each man was applauded as the referee called time.

After the benefit, Jack spent a few more days in San Francisco before he and Mitchell traveled north to Portland on the steamer *Columbia*. Dempsey enjoyed some time at home with his family and friends and settled some affairs as he began to ready himself for his upcoming Eastern sojourn. In early November, Dempsey and Mitchell appeared in a series of exhibitions, including an uncharacteristically long six-rounder on November 9. Soon thereafter, Jack, Maggie and Mitchell would leave Portland by train and head east to New York for another series of engagements.

Mitchell had generated a great deal of attention over the past year by knocking out both George La Blanche and Reddy Gallagher. In December, he would make short work of Bill Dacey, knocking the Greenpoint man out in the second round in Brooklyn. It was rumored that Mitchell was a logical candidate to meet the undefeated and rising star Tommy Ryan, who had registered an impressive string of knockout victories since his 1887 professional debut. While on a stop in Chicago as the two were heading east in November, Dempsey and Mitchell met with Ryan and his managers to discuss a possible bout. Dempsey said that he was not willing to fight at 150 pounds anymore and would prefer to stay around 145. Mitchell also offered to meet the Chicagoan at 148 pounds. Ryan—who weighed a solid 140 pounds—and his camp were unwilling to concede either eight or five pounds respectively and no bouts were scheduled at that time.[87]

On November 13, Dempsey returned to New York, arriving by train at Pennsylvania Station at 7:00 p.m. Jack's train was met by several prominent sportsmen from the New York area who greeted him enthusiastically. "Mrs. Dempsey also received a warm welcome and then there was a general introduction to Peter F. Herget [sic] and his wife, the former being known to the pugilistic world as 'Young Mitchell.'"[88] The two pugilists had signed for a ten-week engagement with the Henry W. Williams Company to spar nightly at Brooklyn's Hyde & Behman's Theatre. The men would each be paid $1,000 a week for their services. The party was driven to the Boswyck Hotel in Brooklyn where they would stay during the sparring sessions. Jack said that he was happy to have the work and would not return to the ring until the theater run was complete. He explained to one reporter, "This engagement will pay me more than I could make in the ring. It's easier work and why shouldn't I take advantage of it?"[89]

Reports were that Dempsey looked fit and in good spirits but would not discuss his ring future beyond the contract with Williams. Jack indicated that he might talk about his career at the end of his exhibition run with Mitchell, but his future became the topic of conversation much sooner than he might have imagined.

Jack was met with a great deal of enthusiasm by waiting crowds at the theater. During his first appearance, a crowd "thirty or forty feet" deep was clustered around the stage door and chocked with well-wishers.[90] For the first few days, Jack looked fit and sparred well, even meeting Mitchell twice on November 16, but soon, he began to wear down. He was tiring easily and appeared to be under the weather. A report out of New York in late November stated that Jack had been forced to cancel his afternoon sparring engagements with Mitchell due to an unnamed malady. "Whether he has an intention of cancelling his present contract with the Harry Williams Company could not be learned definitively. He told Larry Killian that he feared he would have to."[91]

Exhibition bouts on November 18 and 19 had to be cancelled. Dempsey was sent home to his rooms in the Hotel Boswyck and to bed by his long-time physician Dr. Peter Hughes of 275 Berry Street in Williamsburg. The seriousness of the illness became evident when Dr. Hughes ordered that no visitors would be allowed. It was reported that Dempsey had taken on a chill earlier in the week and the cold had settled in his chest. "Sleeping potions were administered to the great boxer by Dr. Hughes, and Dempsey's condition was considered serious."[92] Maggie, Mrs. Herget and Mrs. Flaherty attended to Jack through the evening. Young Mitchell told reporters that Dempsey was on the mend and that while he had run a very high fever, he had merely taken a chill, but nothing more serious than that. "It's merely a temporary trouble," said Mitchell. "If Jack knew that any fuss was being made over him he'd be out of bed and down at the theater to spar with me in fewer minutes than you would count without a watch."[93]

After sleeping quietly through the night, Dempsey appeared somewhat better. Despite the improvement, Dr. Hughes, who had been Jack's physician for years, was beginning to understand the seriousness of the Nonpareil's illness. It was becoming clear that he was suffering from tuberculosis.

Dempsey refused, however, to stay down for long. By all accounts, his conscientious nature would not allow him to miss agreed upon appearances and he hated to disappoint those who wanted to see him perform. By November 23, Dempsey was well enough to travel to Philadelphia and spar at the Central Theatre with Mitchell. The two were greeted warmly by the crowd and sparred several rounds. Those on hand reported that "Dempsey looked a little thin, but does not bear any trace of his recent illness. The pair made a pretty scientific set-to."[94]

Still, many reports persisted to run stating that despite putting up a good front, Jack was in seriously poor health. The *San Francisco Call* ran a short article indicating that Jack was extremely ill and the "chest colds" and "chills" that his doctors and associates continually referred to were in reality tuberculosis. "He is guarded with the utmost vigilance, and none but the doctors and kinfolk are permitted to see him. Those who have seen him in his bed sickness say he is suffering from incipient consumption, and that this is but the beginning of the end."[95] The New York *Evening World* claimed that Jack was suffering from a bout of malaria,[96] and this seemed to be confirmed by Maggie Dempsey who said, "Jack seems to be suffering from an attack of malaria, which has left him very weak. Dr. Peter Hughes has been attending him and thinks if he remains perfectly quiet he may be able to go on with his engagement tonight or tomorrow night."[97] Despite these assurances, by early December it was becoming clear that Jack was a dying man. The *Pullman Herald* hit the nail on the head on December 4 when it echoed earlier reports and printed that Jack's condition was worse than his family, friends and doctors were willing to admit: "He is suffering from incipient consumption."[98] The *St. Louis Post-Dispatch* commented the next day, "It appears that poor Jack Dempsey has for the last time jumped into a 24-foot ring...." After stating that he was suffering from consumption that had been evident when he fought Fitzsimmons, the newspaper praised the Nonpareil by stating, "With the exception, perhaps, of John L. Sullivan's, the career of Jack Dempsey has been the most wonderful known in the annals of pugilism."[99]

Still, many refused to admit the truth. A December 9, 1891, article in the *Montreal Herald* was titled, "Dempsey Not in Consumption and Will be in Montreal with Lucie." The paper assured their readers that Jack and Mike Lucie would be in Montreal in three months to attend and spar at a benefit slated in their honor. "Dempsey has been ill of late, but his recovery is almost certain. However, many believe he has gone into consumption and say he is done." The paper called this inaccurate, describing it as "an old 'chestnut'" and referred to a *New York Herald* article that said, "A great many kindly people have been worried during the week by the reports that Jack Dempsey had broken down. It has been gravely announced that the 'Nonpareil' is dying with consumption. This is all moonshine." The *Herald* reported that Jack was staying in Brooklyn and resting and visiting many of his old friends. The paper conceded that Dempsey had indeed been quite ill, but that malaria was the culprit, not consumption. "Malaria has claimed him for its own, it is true, but there is nothing to be dreaded in that. The worst symptoms have been slight headaches, which come on chiefly in the morning, accompanied by disinclination to violent exercise and the unpleasant form of relaxation known as 'that tired feeling.'" They pointed to his active schedule, constant travel and poor sleep habits as he stayed up late visiting with old friends and numerous acquaintances. They also pointed to his hard and frequent drinking.

His malaria has been brought on largely by the libations they poured out and poured down in his honor. When this flow of moisture has been exhausted the air around Jack will become dryer and his malaria will leave him altogether. The reports that Dempsey is dying of consumption are started once in six months. They annoy him a great deal. He has never had consumption nor anything like it. When he was training to fight Johnny Reagan, the same story was started. "I'll show them the queerest consumption they ever looked at," said Jack, "when they see me in the ring." People who were present on that noted occasion remember that he kept his word.[100]

Just before Christmas, Jack was reported as being fully recovered from his recent illness and was seen about Brooklyn looking up old friends. He was spotted on a rainy Christmas Eve out and about visiting friends and doing errands. He told reporters that the reports of consumption were a "clear case of fake" and that while he had been pretty "shaken up" by chills and fever, he was now feeling great.[101] He commented that he was again anxious to do battle with any leading middleweight.[102] That battle looked as if it might come against Irish middleweight Peter Maher and plans were proceeding nicely between Gus Tuthill and Billy Madden, who was acting as Maher's manager.

A bout with Maher was being scheduled for Madison Square Garden for some time in early to mid-January. In late December, however, problems began to arise, not between the fighters or their camps as is so often the case, but rather with the local constabulary. Despite Dempsey and Maher's sincere desire to meet each other and Tuthill and Madden's best efforts to arrange the bout, both sides were being deterred by New York Police Inspector Murray's recent order forbidding prize fights in the city.

On the day after Christmas, Murray called a press conference in which he told those present that what he called "knocking out" matches would not be permitted. He specifically mentioned the Dempsey-Maher bout and attempts to bring Jim Corbett and Charley Mitchell together in Madison Square Garden in February. Murray defended his position by stating, "Now I am determined that these 'knocking out' contests shall not be revived. There will be no prize fighting in this city. If these men get together and violate the law it is my duty to arrest them, and I will do so. Of course, I cannot and do not desire to prohibit sparring exhibitions, but the law does not permit prize fighting."[103]

While local fight bans were nothing new, Murray's recent prohibition was popular with the local anti-prizefighting crowd and other civic do-gooders and was being met— at least openly—with some enthusiasm by local officials. If they could not find a way around the ban they would simply have to wait it out a bit until after the initial frenzy died down a little and prizefighting could resume, as it always had. Gus Tuthill told one reporter that after Superintendent Murray announced that he would allow no hard hitting, he was struck with what seemed to be an easy target for public criticism. "No doubt many persons would go to see Peter Maher and another great many would go to see Jack Dempsey, who is today, after John L. Sullivan, the most popular boxer in America. But that was not enough. We have been informed that in case one man hit the other a little harder than the rules of polite society allow, an arrest would follow. We want no arrests or law entanglements, and we have called this off."[104]

Superintendent Murray's intransigence was especially frustrating for Billy Madden, whose plan was to tour the popular Irish champion around the country while interest in him was still high. He hoped to schedule the Dempsey bout for mid–January, follow that up with a match between Maher and Peter Jackson on January 28 and then schedule Jim Corbett for the Olympic Club in New Orleans in March. Maher and Madden's willingness to meet Jackson was commendable for both men as many fighters and managers of the era avoided colored fighters in general, but especially those of the high caliber of Peter Jackson. Whether it was the fact that the color of Jackson's skin really did not bother them or a big payday trumped their concern about fighting a black man, it is hard to know. Regardless of their reasons, however, it was significant simply that they agreed to a bout with an African American at that time. It was an especially big deal in a time in which many of the greatest white fighters refused to meet black fighters either on principle or, in many cases, simply due to fear of losing.

1892—Convalescence

Dempsey began the year in Brooklyn and despite his weakened condition he endeavored to be as visible and seemingly vibrant in the boxing world as possible. As usual, Jack feared admitting to anyone—perhaps even himself—that he was seriously ill. On January 13 and 16, Jack was present at bouts at New York's Pastime Athletic Club for which he was named referee.[1]

On January 2, 1892, a number of newspapers across the country ran a short paragraph stating that Jack looked well. The piece ran as follows, "Jack Dempsey is out among his friends again, looking to be in fairly good health. He laughs at the idea that he has consumption of anything other than food and he regards that as an indication that he is in good health."[2] Despite the good tidings of this favorable and optimistic report, Jack was actually quite ill for the vast majority of 1892, and spent much of the time convalescing at his home in Portland, Oregon. During the late winter and spring, less positive stories about his declining health countered the good news from January. Clearly, something was not right with Dempsey, but what it was exactly and how serious the ramifications were, no one seemed to know. By mid-summer, however, he was on the rise and beginning to regain some of his old strength and stamina. Anxious to climb back into the ring and resume his career, he began a light training routine and started looking for opponents to engage in some exhibition matches in the Portland area.

Fully expecting to recover, Jack did make a consolation to his wife and friends regarding his future in the squared circle. Dempsey agreed that when he was well enough to enter the ring again, he would endeavor to meet only men closer to his own size. It had been rumored that Jack was considering taking on either Paddy Slavin or Peter Jackson who outweighed him forty and fifty pounds, respectively. It was believed by many that his recent contests with much larger men had exposed Dempsey to unnecessary punishment and thus contributed to his weakened condition, periodic states of exhaustion and ultimately hastened his current illness.

Many newspapers carried reports that Jack might meet Irish champion Peter Maher over four rounds or more at Madison Square Garden on January 14.[3] Maher and his backers were trying to get a bout with Bob Fitzsimmons and thought a preliminary bout with Dempsey would help showcase the Galway man. Maher had extremely quick hands and feet and was a dangerous hitter who moved quickly in the ring and struck his opponents with vicious, paralyzing blows.[4] The men were reportedly ready to sign articles for the fight in early January but try as they might to set up a contest, scheduling the bout in New York proved problematic. The men and their managers were deterred by New York

Police Inspector Murray's recent order forbidding prize fights in the city.[5] As a result of the order, the local constabulary would be cracking down. Eventually, after exhausting all efforts to bring the fight off, Gus Tuthill and Billy Madden met and decided that the proposed bout should be postponed for the time being.[6] Eventually, however, a solution was agreed upon to allow the men to face each other in the ring.

In an interview from February 20, 1892, Arthur Lumley, editor of the *New York Illustrated News*, described how Jack consented to a secret exhibition with Maher. The contest was an exhibition to be held in an undisclosed location and only five persons witnessed the bout. Maher's backers were anxious to get a feel for how their man would look against tougher competition, but they may have been disappointed in the competition as Dempsey was still in no condition to fight. "He put up the best game he could against the Irishman, but Maher finished him in two rounds."[7] Maher looked so good that his backers immediately set up a bout with Fitzsimmons for March 2. After the bout Jack praised Maher's ring abilities and noted that he was a solid fighter.

In truth, given Dempsey's ill health, he probably had no business meeting the Galway native at that time. While he was a powerful puncher, Maher was not a skilled boxer. A healthy Dempsey would certainly have outboxed him, but in Jack's greatly weakened condition, Dempsey clearly had a tough time avoiding Maher's lightning fast, sledge-hammer blows.

After fighting Dempsey, Maher went to Philadelphia and knocked out Joe Godfrey in one round on January 16 at the Fairmont Athletic Club and then traveled to New Orleans where he squared off with Fitzsimmons on March 2. After a wild first round in which each man was floored, Fitzsimmons came around and took control of the fight. Ruby Robert wore the Irishman down over twelve rounds at which point Maher told referee John Duffy that he had had enough.[8] Maher would continue to fight through 1913, and amazingly, he was engaged in over two hundred bouts. He would retire to Philadelphia after ending his ring career and live in that city until 1940, when he died at age seventy-one.

On January 21, California middleweight Alexander Gregganis accepted Dempsey's challenge to fight the Nonpareil for a $6,000 purse at the Olympic Club of New Orleans.[9] This was a significant bout for Jack as Gregganis, also known as Greggains, had recently defeated George La Blanche by TKO in eighteen rounds at the Occidental Athletic Club in San Francisco. If Jack could not get La Blanche to meet him in the ring, the next best thing was to meet those who had defeated the Marine.

Describing the Gregganis–La Blanche bout, the *Los Angeles Times* stated, "At stake was a purse of $2,000. La Blanche was down in the seventh round. The police stopped this bout. Referee Danny Needham gave Greggains the decision despite the fact the Occidental Club president said that the rendering of the said decision would be postponed. But the president said that the club would abide by the decision."[10] Prior to finishing off La Blanche, Gregganis had registered a TKO over Billy McCarthy when the Australian was forced to retire in the twenty-sixth round after breaking his arm. After leaving the ring at the turn of the century, Gregganis went on to become a fight manager and promoter in his hometown of San Francisco.

Although I have found no reason why, this bout between Dempsey and Gregganis never came off. The logical answer may well lie with Dempsey's health, which was certainly precarious and forced him into periods of convalescence. We do know that Jack was weak and his weight was down. Dempsey later denied reports that he had ever agreed to meet Gregganis, citing his health. In late January, it was reported that "Jack Dempsey the prizefighter, was in Chicago, on his way from New York to his home in Portland, Oregon, accompanied by his wife and [children]. He is in very poor health."[11] When speaking to reporters, Jack made it clear that he was not retiring, but simply returning to Portland to rest and regain his strength. "I will fight again if I can get strong and you can rest assured that it will not be before I do." Jack went on to say that if he fought again it would have to be for a large purse and against men of his size. "I have been giving away weight all my life, in fact I was compelled to do so to get on matches." After stating that he won the middleweight championship at 138 pounds, and that most pugilists that size fought as lightweights, Jack concluded, "I have never been anything more than a welterweight, and hereafter will travel in that class."[12]

Jack was named the manager and boxing instructor at the new and very large Pastime Athletic Club in Portland and let it be known that he was still interested in future bouts, with future being the key word.[13] All year he was busily applying himself to his duties at the club and trying to stay fit. On March 22, the Pastime sponsored its first evening of boxing exhibitions. Roughly five hundred members were in attendance in the club rooms, located in Portland's Cyclorama building. The reasonably sized crowd, however, barely made a dent in the room that held five thousand at capacity. Dempsey acted as the referee for the two-fight card. In the first bout, local middleweight Tommy West whipped Chicago heavyweight Charles Hall in one round. In the second contest two local middleweights met and Charles Gleason defeated Ed Burke in just two minutes in the first round.[14]

"Jack Dempsey is placing the Pastime Club of Portland, Oregon in the front very fast. Dempsey is now trying to arrange a fight between Charley Gleason and the Black Pearl."[15] "The Black Pearl" was the nickname of Harris Martin, the one-time "Colored Heavyweight Champion." Martin was a very strong and durable fighter who could both dish out and take a wallop. Dempsey was also instrumental in setting up a bout between Australian welterweight Billy "Shadow" Maber and Billy Smith in June. Things at the club began very well for Jack.

By early July, however, affairs at the club began to become a bit strained. Dempsey got into an argument with a club vice president named Smith who put up the funds for a new saloon in the club and was thus named president. According to Dempsey, Smith wanted to arrange crooked fights to benefit his friends. Jack refused to participate and said the he would not allow it. In May, Dempsey caught his old friend and newly named Portland Fire Chief Dave Campbell shortening a round during a fight between Kid Lavigne and Harry Jones in which Campbell was acting as timekeeper and Jones, a friend of Smith's, was getting trounced. Dempsey told Campbell that he would be unable to act in any official capacity at the club any longer, but in July, with Smith's approval, Campbell was seconding various fighters. An angry Dempsey confronted Smith and when no agreement could be reached on the issues that separated them, it was determined that due to disagreements and financial concerns, the club might be closed and put into receivership.[16]

Attempts were made by Gus Tuthill and the California Athletic Club to induce Jack to climb back in the ring against Johnny Reagan and Australian lightweight Billy Maber, respectively. In July, the California A.C. reportedly tried to match Dempsey with Maber.

Maber reportedly said that he would accept a bout with Dempsey at 140 pounds but would allow Jack "a few pounds." When asked about it, however, Jack responded, "I have received no such offer from the California Club or anyone else. The report probably grew out of the fact that negotiations are being carried on with the view of making a match in this city between Maber and Billy Smith of Boston." Jack went on to say, "I would not fight lightweights, but am ready to try any middleweight who would best Fitzsimmons."[17] In truth, Jack's weight was down a bit and he might not have been terribly out of place fighting Maber if indeed he should have entered the ring as a fighter at all. While Jack did not meet the Australian as a combatant, he did play a role in the Maber-Smith bout in Portland that September when he was named referee for the match.

Even in his weakened condition, Dempsey was able to create news. Throughout 1892 and over the next several years, however, Jack did have one serious rival for headlines. The competition came from a young Bay Area athlete—strong, swift, determined, and with lightning speed—who came roaring onto the scene. His name was also Jack Dempsey and his popularity took off like a rocket, but this was no pugilist. Rather he was a racing, or coursing, dog owned by T.J. Cronin. He was very active and quite successful at Bay Area racetracks such as Ocean View Park and several others and would continue to race for years to come, making a tidy sum for Cronin during that time.

On August 16, Jack met "Mysterious" Billy Smith in Portland for a four-round exhibition. The bout was part of a benefit in the Nonpareil's honor held at and sponsored by the Pastime Athletic Club. A full card of fights awaited the packed house that came to cheer the still wildly popular Dempsey. Other fighters who appeared in the ring that evening were middleweights Billy Hennessey, Jack Magee, Billy Maber of Australia, Tom Kendell of Boston and a number of local pugilists. In the surprise of the evening, Kendall was knocked out in four rounds by local Portland fighter Jack O'Day. The event culminated when Jack climbed into the ring with Smith. The *San Francisco Call* reported, "Dempsey appeared in a bout with Billy Smith of Boston [sic] and, though not in fighting condition, he was greeted with loud applause."[18] The men fought to a draw in an uninspiring exhibition. Regardless, the crowd loved it and cheered throughout. The evening realized a purse of about $1,200.

Jack was always happy to spar with Smith, whom he considered a good fighter and a good drawing card. Jack first met Billy in New Orleans in December 1890 when he was looking for sparring partners as he readied himself for the Bob Fitzsimmons fight. The story goes that the 19-year-old Smith was visiting the Crescent City and wandered into a boxing gym one day. After watching a very talented middleweight shadowbox in one of the rings, he apparently recognized him as the Nonpareil. Upon hearing that Dempsey was looking for sparring partners, the tenacious young man approached Dempsey's manager and volunteered his services. Skeptical that the young man would return, he told Smith to just come back the following day.

The next day, Smith did return. He refused the offer of headgear, but brashly indicated that Dempsey might do well to wear some. Over the next hour those at the gym watched the two men mix it up at a torrid pace, neither fighter willing to give an inch. Billy was a tough and tenacious street fighter who gave Jack a work out. Dempsey got in the ring work he needed and Smith began to make a name for himself in fistic circles. After the session, Dempsey praised Smith's ability and told Billy that he had a bright future in the ring if he wanted to pursue it. During his long career, Smith fought for championships, but he also became well known as one of the dirtiest fighters in ring history.

The Nonpareil reportedly headed by train for New Orleans in late August. He traveled with a party of twenty-five and was in Jack McAuliffe's corner for his friend's second fight with Billy Myer, also known as the Streator Cyclone. Myer got his nickname from his home, the growing coal town of Streator, Illinois.

Some reports speculated that Jack might miss his appointment in McAuliffe's corner. One newspaper declared that Dempsey's life had spiraled so badly out of control that he could not be counted on to be anywhere he was expected. Stating that the Nonpareil's life had degenerated into "a sad state of affairs," the *Chicago Tribune* stated regarding Dempsey, "It seems that since his defeat by Fitzsimmons he has been drinking so steadily that his reason is in a measure dethroned and at his present rate of going his last days will be spent in a mad house." They continued by stating that "he is a wreck physically and mentally and is totally incapable of making another fight. It is doubtful whether he will be here at all."[19] While the *Tribune*'s comments were a bit strong, they were by no means completely off base. Jack's drinking was on the rise. He was a physical wreck and his mental state appeared to be weak due to both his drinking and his bouts of delirium. The newspaper was also correct in the prediction that Jack would not be in New Orleans at the appointed time. Dempsey was indeed a no-show with some reports stating that he telegraphed that he was too ill to attend.

Regardless of the Nonpareil's absence, the battle went on as planned. The bout was held in the Crescent City on the evening of September 5, the result being a knockout by McAuliffe over Myer in the fifteenth round. McAuliffe floored the hard-hitting Myer five times in the fight, with three of those knock-downs coming in the final frame. The third time, Myer could not get to his feet in time as Professor John Duffy, the referee, counted him out.[20]

On September 20, Dempsey was well enough to referee the "Mysterious" Billy Smith versus Billy "Shadow" Maber bout at the Pastime Athletic Club in Portland. While Smith had the edge all night, the fight lasted twenty-five rounds before Maber began to look weak and Smith went in for the kill. Smith dropped Maber four times in the last chapter, the last time coming on a hard right to Maber's jaw. Maber was slow getting up and got to his feet just after the count of nine, at which time Dempsey declared Smith the winner. Maber said he agreed with the decision as his legs were gone.[21]

The fighters, their managers and Dempsey were all arrested after the bout on charges of engaging in a prizefight. The men were indicted on September 22 and arraigned in state circuit court six days later. During the arraignment, each entered a plea of not guilty. The trial date for Smith and Maber was set for November 3. It was determined that the charges against the other men would not be tried until after those of the principals.[22]

On November 4, the defense attorneys interposed "a demurrer on the ground of insufficiency of facts, and that the contest was in no way a prize fight, but simply a scientific exhibition."[23] After hearing the facts in the case and deliberating briefly, the jury for the state circuit court brought back a not guilty decision against Smith and Maber and a recommendation that the charges against the other defendants should be dismissed. The judge immediately dropped all charges.[24]

During the late summer and fall of 1892, the country was caught up in the presidential campaign in which former President Grover Cleveland was attempting to regain the White House from incumbent President Benjamin Harrison, who had defeated Cleveland during the New Yorker's bid for re-election in 1888. It was a particularly bitter defeat for Cleveland, who had won the popular vote but lost the presidency to Harrison in the electoral college. Understanding and accepting the wisdom of the framers of the Constitution, Cleveland graciously accepted his defeat and set his sites on 1892.

By normal standards, the election of 1892 was tame. Harrison, a reluctant politician who really did not enjoy being president, was not anxious to serve another four years in the White House. In addition to the fact that he would rather go home to Indiana and practice law, Harrison had another understandable reason for this. The health of his wife, First Lady Caroline Harrison, was poor and growing progressively worse. Mrs. Harrison, who had suffered from ill health for a number of years, had contracted tuberculosis the previous year. Various treatments and time spent in the country had failed to offer much relief. Mrs. Harrison returned to the White House in late August where her health continued to decline. The campaign took on a somber tone in the final weeks when the First Lady died of tuberculosis on October 25 at the White House.

In November, Cleveland won re-election by a fairly decisive margin in a race dominated by the tariff issue. Harrison vigorously defended the high rates of the McKinley Tariff passed during his term and Cleveland argued strongly for a lowering of rates. The Democrats also called for the repeal of the Sherman Act of 1890, instead calling for the equal intrinsic and exchangeable value of both gold and silver. Cleveland's re-election is the only time that a defeated former president has made good his quest for a return to the White House, thus making Cleveland the only president to serve two nonconsecutive terms.

In early December, the possibility was raised that Dempsey might meet old foe Reddy Gallagher in a finish fight at the Olympic Athletic Club in New Orleans for a purse of $3,000.[25] Gallagher, now twenty-seven years old, had been a boxing instructor at the Denver Athletic Club for some time and was reportedly ready to reenter the ring.[26] Charles Dickson, president of the Olympic A.C., announced that he would offer the purse and Gallagher seemed ready to fight. Dempsey was interested and thought highly of Gallagher, but he was non-committal for a number of legitimate reasons—the money was not phenomenal, he was rusty after not having fought in anything except exhibitions since the Fitzsimmons loss in early 1891, and he was being a bit choosy given his precarious health.

In mid–November, La Blanche, fully aware that Dempsey had been extremely ill for much of the past two years, crawled out of the woodwork and boldly said that he would now be willing to offer Dempsey a rematch at catch-weights for $1,000—terms certainly advantageous to La Blanche since he would not have to work off any weight to come down to Dempsey's level.[27] Rumors were that a match was set for the Olympic Club in New Orleans for some time in late February, but still nothing was arranged.

At that time, La Blanche also wrote to Warren Lewis, the proprietor of New York's Alhambra, "to try and arrange a match for him to fight Jack Dempsey or some other middleweight, the contest to take place in the Coney Island Athletic Club."[28] Lewis attempted to negotiate a $3,000 purse, but terms could not be agreed to by all backers and La Blanche insisted upon fighting at catch-weights. That Jack was not immediately jumping at the chance to meet La Blanche is telling. Dempsey, already not his old self, would not agree to make a contest with this weight disparity. The two sides were just too much in disagreement on terms and the proposed contest simply faded away. Had La Blanche's offer come in 1889 or 1890, the Nonpareil probably would not have objected to the weight differential. He had a history of fighting up in weight, but Jack was beginning to accept that his health was in decline and that he needed to be at least somewhat mindful of fighting larger opponents. The *National Police Gazette*, citing Dempsey's precarious and declining health, commented that "Jack Dempsey has declined the challenge of George La Blanche for another fistic encounter. The ex-middleweight champion says he has retired from the ring forever."[29]

Regardless of reports on his heath and retirement, it appeared that Jack was again becoming a popular opponent and his dance card was once again about to get full. In an interview on December 23, Dempsey defended his hesitance to sign for either fight, exclaiming, "There is no truth in the rumor that I have refused to meet La Blanche or Reddy Gallagher. On the contrary, if any responsible club offers reasonable inducements, I will re-enter the ring."[30] Still, Jack was understandably hesitant. He had been quite ill and coupled with his long period of inactivity in the ring, he wanted to be certain he was ready to fight again. Dempsey also knew that with his declining health, there would not be endless paydays in the future. The training for the contests as well as the bout itself took a lot more out of him than it used to and if he fought again, he wanted the guarantee of a large payday. And, while Dempsey had often teetered back and forth on the subject of retiring from the ring, it seems that this time he was seriously considering hanging up his gloves. Writing to a friend in Brooklyn in December, Jack stated flatly, "I do not want to fight any more for I do not believe I could stand the training. I am doing well and will let fighting alone as far as participating as a principle."[31] Dempsey was serious about retiring, but under the right conditions he would consider a bout.

While there is no doubt that Dempsey wanted to meet La Blanche again—he had actively pushed for a third bout for three years—he would not meet him at anything less than full strength and would not risk losing in a legitimate fashion to a man whom he had thrashed twice before. That said, under the right terms of agreement, he would get himself ready for the Marine. In response to a reporter's question regarding La Blanche's challenge, the former Nonpareil stated, "If any athletic club will put up a $5,000 purse and La Blanche will agree to weigh 154 pounds and be at that weight at the ring side, I will meet him either in the Coney Island or the Pacific Club. I intended not to fight again, but I will accommodate La Blanche, for I am certain I can defeat him easily."[32] From deep inside his soul, Jack Dempsey wanted to avenge the fluke knockout by the Marine in San Francisco, but of all opponents, he did not want to step into the ring with La Blanche until he knew he was ready.

1893—The Road Back

The year 1893 opened with some promise for Jack as his hopes of returning to the squared circle were being realized. After almost two years of limited activity in the ring, his health seemed to be improving and he had a bout scheduled with Billy Keogh in Portland in late February.

Things for the nation, however, were not looking up. As recently as December President Harrison had reported in a national address that "there has never been a time in our history when work was so abundant, or when wages were so high."[1] Unbeknownst to the president, even as he spoke, trouble with the economy was brewing. In fact, it had been brewing for months across many sectors of the economy.

Railroads all across America had been expanding at a feverish pace for decades, thus creating great demand for steel and wood for engines, cars and tracks. Inevitably, the expansion of rail lines began to slow, negatively affecting their suppliers, including the timber and steel industries. In addition, general investment, public consumption and building construction all fell. Agriculture had long been in trouble as well. While the number of farms had increased by nearly eighty percent to four and a half million between 1870 and 1890, almost a third of these farms were encumbered by mortgages. According to Douglas Steeples and David O. Whitten of Auburn University, "The advancing checkerboard of tilled fields in the nation's heartland represented a vast indebtedness." Alternating periods of drought in some sectors and overproduction in others also negatively affected supply and drove down prices, leaving many farmers strapped for cash. Steeples and Whitten observe that "under favorable conditions the millions of dollars of annual charges on farm mortgages could be borne, but a declining economy brought foreclosures and tax sales."[2]

By February 1893, the first outward sign of financial panic began to rear its head when agricultural failures in the United States and Argentina caused a great number of international investors to begin redeeming U.S. currency for the gold it was backed by. As a result, the United States' gold supplies began to dwindle and investors began to call in loans. Highly leveraged from its appetite for acquisition, the Philadelphia and Reading Railroad could not meet its onerous obligations and failed suddenly. Within months, other important firms had closed their doors for similar reasons, and by early April it became abundantly clear that former President Harrison's robust economy was in trouble and Grover Cleveland, who returned to the presidency on March 4, was dealing with a serious financial crisis. "In the middle of April, a precipitous drop in the stock market underscored the seriousness of the situation, and by summer the reversal in the state of the economy from the previous winter was complete."[3]

Before the year was out some five hundred banks and nearly sixteen thousand businesses had fallen into bankruptcy, helping to drive the unemployment rate to nearly twenty percent of the nation's workforce. The nation was fully engulfed in what came to be known as the "Panic of 1893":

> Thus, the recession that began in 1893 had deep roots. The slowdown in railroad expansion, decline in building construction, and foreign depression had reduced investment opportunities, and, following the brief upturn affected by the bumper wheat crop of 1891, agricultural prices fell as did exports and commerce in general. By the end of 1893, business failures numbering 15,242 averaging $22,751 in liabilities, had been reported. Plagued by successive contractions of credit, many essentially sound firms failed which would have survived under ordinary circumstances. Liabilities totaled a staggering $357 million. This was the crisis of 1893.[4]

It was against this difficult national backdrop that Dempsey returned to the ring and to an anxious nation looking for relief and a hero to take their minds off their present troubles. Jack dreamed of stepping in and being that hero, but the reality of such a dream was to be only fleeting. Dempsey's old friend Jim Corbett commented that while Jack "was the greatest fighter that ever lived—head and shoulders over either Sullivan or McAuliffe," the former Nonpareil was in bad straits. Corbett opined that Dempsey should never have been badgered into his second fight with La Blanche "after he had once before proved that he was the latter's superior. The result was he was whipped by a chance blow." Corbett also said that Dempsey should never have agreed to meet Fitzsimmons, whom he described as a "middleweight freak." Corbett added that "poor Dempsey now lives in Portland, Oregon, forgotten, unspoken of, and from all accounts in needy circumstances. He was the good fellow you read about."[5]

On January 17, 1893, Hawaii's monarchy was overthrown as a group of businessmen and sugar planters forced Queen Liliuokalani to abdicate. The group, known as the Committee of Safety and made up of chiefly American and European businessmen, sought to have the island kingdom annexed by the United States. After a bloodless coup, supported somewhat unwittingly by a company of U.S. Marines, the members of the committee got their wish. The queen was overthrown, the monarchy ended and within five years, the islands became United States territory.

On the evening of February 18, Jack was still in Brooklyn and attended the Tub Club Ball at Turn Hall on Meserole Street in Brooklyn. The club was composed of "more or less prominent residents of the upper wards of the eastern district."[6] The Saturday evening ball was the fourth annual masquerade event for the club and ran well into the early morning hours, not breaking up until nearly daybreak. The attendees were described as "leading lights" of the community and their behavior as "frisky, but not indecorous." In addition to Dempsey, Jack McAuliffe was there along with numerous city councilmen and supervisors, businessmen, sporting types and a bevy of beautiful women. Apparently, a Miss Louisa Nudwig made quite the impression. "Louisa Nudwig, a tall and shapely dark-haired girl, proved once or twice that she could do more than talk about that interesting topic [dancing]. Miss Nudwig was not hampered by skirts, either long or short, for she was arrayed in a dazzling silken jockey suit of black and scarlet, and before 4 o'clock in the morning she was the most eagerly sought after young woman at the ball."[7]

In the days following the ball, Dempsey headed west, making his way back to Portland to prepare for his match with Billy Keogh. On February 28, 1893, Jack climbed back into the ring with Keogh at the Pastime Athletic Club in the Exposition Building in Portland. Dempsey, desperate for a bout, broke his own new pledge regarding only fighting men of his size. Keogh was a heavyweight who outweighed Dempsey by nearly fifty pounds and Dempsey had barely been in the ring in two years, having only participated in exhibitions. Many were skeptical that Jack could win and many more questioned if he should even be in the ring at all. The *National Police Gazette* posited, "It seems strange that Dempsey should try to once more gain the fistic fame he lost by his defeats by George La Blanche and Bob Fitzsimmons by meeting a boxer who if he succeeds in defeating, will not materially increase his fistic standing."[8] But Dempsey was never one to pay much attention to what others thought about his pugilistic affairs and so insisted on meeting Keogh. The competitive spirit was still in him and the opportunity to lessen the bitter taste of defeat that he had known since the Fitzsimmons bout was clearly part of his decision.

There was very little betting on the fight as people really did not know the odds. It was hard to admit, but Dempsey was an unknown quantity. He was clearly not the Nonpareil of old—the Fitzsimmons fight proved that—but he was still Jack Dempsey. Keogh was much larger than Dempsey, but Jack had often defeated larger opponents. If his ring generalship and science were still what they were and if he was having one of his "good" days, Jack had a real chance. At the same time, Dempsey had not been in a competitive fight in over two years and who knew what condition he would be in or how his body would react to the layoff. The fight was a large uncertainty.

"The purse was understood to be the gate receipts, with a side bet of $500 each."[9] There were four preliminaries between local light and featherweight fighters before the main event, with the last wrapping up just before 11:00 p.m. Keogh entered the ring at 11:15 p.m. Dempsey arrived just moments later. "Both men appeared in good condition, but Dempsey looked like a pigmy by the side of his opponent."[10]

When time was called for the first round by referee Jack Robertson, both men sprang towards the center of the ring. Dempsey led with his left and worked to the body early on. Keogh worked to the head, catching Jack once cleanly on the jaw. The round saw good action, was fought fairly evenly and ended with the fighters clinching.

In the second round, Jack clearly became the early aggressor. As the round began, Keogh fired a left that barely grazed Dempsey's neck; Jack shot back a right to the midsection, but the blow was deflected by Keogh's right. Dempsey's next punch, however, got in, smashing Keogh in the stomach with his right. After Keogh rushed Dempsey into the corner, the men fell into a clinch and they wrestled and pushed until Jack pulled away and landed a right to his opponent's jaw.

In round three, Dempsey landed on Keogh's stomach early, but Keogh responded by rushing Jack and again fighting him into the corner and attempting to lay him low with several hard blows. Jack slipped out, swinging and missing as he went. After righting himself on firm legs, Dempsey began using his left jab effectively and powdering Keogh on the mouth repeatedly. Keogh, clearly becoming frustrated, rushed Dempsey again, forcing him towards his corner. Once again, Jack evaded his opponent and as he escaped, he landed a solid blow to Keogh's nose. Keogh continued his mad rushes, but Dempsey easily dodged them and led Keogh around the ring."[11]

In the fourth and final round, a thoroughly frustrated Keogh, not knowing what else to do, continued to employ the same tactics. Dempsey continued to dance around his opponent finding openings and landing at will to the head and body, but when Keogh returned fire, Jack, wisely avoiding his opponent's powerful right hand, was nowhere to be found. When the two men did come together and fall into a clinch, the referee called for a break. While breaking away, Keogh struck Dempsey on the jaw and cries of foul were heard throughout the auditorium. "At the end of the fourth-round the referee awarded the contest to Dempsey, who proved that he is still a fighter after two years of inactivity."[12]

The *New York Times* reported under the headline, "Dempsey Still a Fighter," that "Jack Dempsey, middleweight, defeated William Keogh, a heavyweight, last night at the Pastime Club in four rounds. It was his first fight since he was defeated by Fitzsimmons in New Orleans two years ago. Keogh tipped the scales at 190 and Dempsey at 148. Keogh was unable to find Dempsey, who landed at will on Keogh's face and stomach."[13] The *Los Angeles Herald* stated that Dempsey had lost none of his old science. The paper added, "Dempsey showed that he had lost none of his former cleverness and successfully avoided the big fellow's mad rushes and hit him when and where he willed."[14]

Dempsey took on a talented, dangerous and much larger opponent after a two-year layoff and decisively defeated him—so much for Jack's 1892 promise to seek opponents closer to his size. Due to his recent illnesses and his long layoff, many were still skeptical about the reality of Dempsey's return, but for at least this one evening, the Nonpareil was back.

There was a palpable sense of excitement in the air that after a long period of inactivity, Jack Dempsey appeared to be ready to reclaim the mantle of middleweight legend once again. "There is no doubt that Jack Dempsey, the 'Nonpareil,' who has the reputation of being the bravest man who ever entered the prize ring, intends to take up the business once more. Recently he was matched to fight a Western heavyweight of the name of Keogh, who was to finish Dempsey in four rounds."[15] Reports stated that he would fight again against Billy "Shadow" Maber. It was noted that "'the Nonpareil' has wired $1,000 from Portland, Oregon, as a forfeit to fight Maber for $5,000 a side and a $5,000 purse. Maber will cover the money tomorrow, so he says. Dempsey is coming east."[16] Unfortunately, the Maber fight never came off. Jack did, however, continue his return to the pugilistic world by refereeing a bout in Portland between Maber and "Mysterious" Billy Smith in September.

Despite the fact that Jack was a sick man, overly optimistic reports claimed that he was "now in good health." Persistent rumors about his "next opponent" again began filling the sports pages. His win over Keogh was encouraging to his friends and admirers and many believed or were merely hoping against hope, that he had returned to his old fighting form. In late March Gus Tuthill "posted $500 with a challenge to the effect that Jack Dempsey having regained his health and being willing to re-enter the arena, he will back Dempsey to meet any man in the world at 140 for $2,500 a side, the fight to be decided in the club offering the largest purse."[17]

In April, rumors began to circulate that the winner of the bout between Boston's "Mysterious" Billy Smith and Tom Williams, welterweight champion of Australia, would meet Dempsey. Jack had made it clear to friends that he wanted to fight again and it was reported that "Dempsey has recovered from his old pulmonary complaint, and is reputed to be strong. He believes that he can whip any man of his weight breathing."[18] With

Tuthill's $500 forfeit deposited with the *Police Gazette* and Dempsey's issued challenge to any man in the world at 140 pounds, things did indeed seem to be returning to normal.

Prior to their match for the welterweight championship at the Coney Island Athletic Club, both Smith and Williams trained hard knowing that winning this contest could mean the fame and money that would come with a bout against Dempsey. Both men were clearly anxious to meet the former Nonpareil. "It's money man," said the Australian, "to beat Jack Dempsey, and this mysterious chap is the only one as wot stands in my way. Not only is it money in America, but in England and Australia, too, where even the women and children talk of Jack Dempsey."[19] On April 17, a crowd of one thousand five hundred saw Smith land a vicious right to Williams's head and referee John P. Eckhardt count the Australian out at two minutes and thirty-five seconds of the second round, as Smith collected the bulk of the $5,000 purse and a shot at Dempsey.

On May 2, it was announced by Eckhardt, the official referee for the Coney Island Athletic Club, that Jack and "Mysterious" Billy Smith would meet at Coney Island for a $6,000 purse at some point yet to be determined. Judge Newton of the club soon announced the date as June 30 and said that the Nonpareil was once again in good health and had regained much of his old form in the ring. Dempsey, who was with his family in Portland, began to make plans for a trip home to Brooklyn.[20] There was a great buzz of excitement about Dempsey's recent victory over Keogh and his impending return to the East Coast. "Jack Dempsey will try to rebuild the reputation which tumbled when he went out of his class and fell before the blows of lanky Fitzsimmons. The Nonpareil will come back to New York and amid the same surroundings in which he proved himself to be the greatest fighter of his weight in the world he will endeavor to regain his lost laurels." The report continued with the hopeful but guarded statement, "If Dempsey is in good health and strong, he should certainly be able to avoid Smith's rushes and inflict punishment at will."[21] Jack had signed to fight "Mysterious" Billy Smith, but due to his declining physical, mental, and emotional health, his greatest ring opponent was now a multitude of "ifs."

By May 6, it appeared that trouble was brewing on the fight's horizon. Newspaper reports began to circulate stating that Jack had "accepted the Coney Island club offer supposing Smith had signed. He received a telegram from the Crescent City club of New Orleans today stating that Smith had signed with them for a purse of a thousand dollars more than the Coney Island offer. Dempsey is undecided as he accepted the other club's offer."[22] Shortly after this the fight seemed to be back on and set for Long Island. It was reported that Dempsey had received $500 in training funds and would be heading east soon. For a short while, though, it appeared that Jack was nowhere to be found. The *Brooklyn Eagle* ran an article with a headline asking, "Where's Jack Dempsey?" They commented that he had left Portland and had not been heard from since. Another article ran an amusing piece that began, "Lost, strayed or stolen—one middleweight pugilist of blond complexion, with mild blue eyes. Answers to the name of Jack Dempsey. Any information regarding the above, cheerfully received by the Coney Island Athletic Club."[23]

Jack's brother Martin, while being interviewed at his home at 107 North Ninth Street in Brooklyn, was asked by a reporter if he knew where Jack was and if he was concerned that his brother might have accepted the $500 and then refused to fight. Martin was indignant that Jack's honesty and fairness would be questioned and responded, "I cannot for the life of me understand why any fuss is being made over this case. Suppose Jack did receive $500 for expenses? What of it? He is well fixed and will come East with a good many five hundred-dollar bills in his pocket. Jack would not run away with money." Martin continued, "And you can say for me that he will be in town tomorrow or the next day, anyhow. Jack is well fixed, I can tell you and re-enters the ring only for glory. He is in the wholesale grocery business with his brothers-in-law and makes good money at it. Besides, he is the manager of the Pastime A.C. My brother is matched to fight Billy Smith, but from what I hear it looks as if Smith will not be on hand on June 30."[24]

Despite Martin's comments, it was reported the following day that Dempsey was nowhere near Brooklyn, but rather in Seattle. After hearing reports that he was "missing," Jack wired Justice Newton of the Coney Island Athletic Club that he was enjoying a leisurely journey across country and spending a few days in Seattle before moving on. He announced that he would be in Brooklyn long before the scheduled bout—a bout he thought would now be with twenty-four-year-old Austin Gibbons of Patterson, New Jersey.

Tragedy struck on May 11 when Smith's young wife Minnie died unexpectedly of blood poisoning in Lynn, Massachusetts. Before leaving Boston for Portland with his wife's remains, Smith understandably requested a postponement of the contest for sixty days and said that if the Coney Island Club would not agree to his request, he would surrender his forfeit deposit of $500. There was rumor that the fight would be cancelled or that another fighter—possibly Gibbons—would replace Smith, but the on-again, off-again bout had been rescheduled for July 24.[25] Justice Newton in his comments to reporters said that Dempsey's plans fit Smith's fight requests perfectly and that he would now notify Smith of Dempsey's plans to be in Brooklyn for a late July bout. "I have no doubt that the fight will come off now and everything will go on smoothly from this out. The misfortune that came to Smith was one that could not be foreseen and it was natural that it should have interfered with Smith's plans. I shall notify Gibbons also that the original fight has been rearranged, and it is likely that the Jersey boxer will soon meet somebody else before our club."[26]

Dempsey was making his way east and he was expected to arrive in St. Paul on June 29. The local press commented that Jack would meet John Barnes in a boxing exhibition at the Phoenix Athletic Club that evening and was the choice of the club to referee several bouts that evening as well.[27]

Jack's long, winding journey, coupled with his lack of communication on the terms of the fight and concerning his whereabouts, was not setting well with Judge Newton, and the fact that Smith was still not on hand was making him downright nervous. By July 9, the Coney Island A.C. announced that the fight was off for now. At a meeting, the Board of Directors of the club decided that "in the absence of fighters, they have no tangible proof that the men are in proper condition." They hoped to reschedule the contest for some time in September.[28]

Some talk was made of a bout at 142 pounds, arranged by Dempsey's backer Gus Tuthill between Jack and Dick Burge of Newcastle, England, for $5,000 a side, but there were few parties interested in sponsoring such an event. "Referee John Eckhardt said this morning, 'It is a scheme to get the clubs to bid for a fight, but the Coney Island organization will not give three cents for it.'" Eckhardt went on to explain that the bout was being proposed not because it was the best fight, but because Tuthill saw Burge as an easier opponent than Smith for a now weakened Dempsey. He also pointed out that

"Dempsey still has the $500 forwarded by the club for traveling expenses to come on for this fight with Smith. The mysterious man was ready to cover any forfeit Dempsey's backers might put up yesterday, but they did not appear."[29] Despite Eckhardt's negative comments, the fight still seemed a possibility. Reports from London stated that on August 11 "Dick Burge deposited £500 with the *Sporting Life* to bind a match with Jack Dempsey. The fight is to be for $10,000 a side and the championship of the world, the place to be in the United States early in December. The match will be under the Marquess of Queensberry rules."[30] As to Dempsey's erratic behavior, most of the New York sporting set were willing to look beyond it and give Jack the benefit of the doubt.

As he made his way east, Dempsey reportedly fought an impromptu three-round exhibition on July 31, at the Phoenix Athletic Club in St. Paul. According to the *St. Paul Daily Globe*, just prior to a bout between local fighters Tommy Dixon and "a youth passing under the appellation of 'The Omaha Kid,'" the manager of the club announced to the crowd that the former Nonpareil was unexpectedly in the city while traveling east and had consented to spar three rounds that evening. Clearly the crowd was delighted as they applauded wildly. The report stated that "the Golden State sport—a handsome young fellow, looking anything rather than a prize fighter—filled his part of the programme gracefully."[31] Given that Jack was leisurely traveling east and was in the Minneapolis–St. Paul area at that time, this seems to be the Nonpareil and not the Western Jack Dempsey. No mention is made of who Jack sparred with that evening.

Jack was not the only prominent person who was seriously ill during the summer of 1893. Shortly after being sworn in for his second term in early March, President Grover Cleveland felt a smallish bump on the left side of the roof of his mouth near his molars. He gave it very little thought and assumed that whatever it was, it would heal and go away on its own, but by June he noticed that it had grown larger. On June 18, Cleveland was seen by Dr. Robert M. O'Reilly, the official medical attendant for government officers in Washington. Upon examination, Dr. O'Reilly was concerned that the ulcerous growth was cancerous. He removed a small piece of tissue from the ulcer and sent it to a local pathologist at the Army Medical Museum without revealing the identity of the patient. The pathologist confirmed that the tumor was indeed malignant. Upon hearing the diagnosis, the President's personal physician, Dr. Joseph Bryant, advised that the growth should be removed immediately.

Cleveland agreed to the surgery but placed conditions on it, foremost that the procedure must be kept a total secret from the nation. The president was afraid that news of his having oral cancer might cause further panic and worsen the nation's already difficult financial situation. A pro-gold standard, pro-sound money advocate, Cleveland was also determined to have Congress repeal the Sherman Silver Purchase Act of 1890 and feared that any word of his illness would play into the hands of the pro-silver advocates who opposed repeal. This included his Vice President Adlai Stevenson. Cleveland himself came up with the plan: The surgery would be performed on July 1, by a team of surgeons, dental experts and anesthetists on board the yacht *Oneida*. They would sail from New York to the president's summer home in Cape Cod where he would then spend several weeks "vacationing." Congress was in their summer recess and many people, including members of Congress, the Supreme Court and the Executive Departments, left Washington in mid-summer to escape the city's stifling heat.

The President, his entourage and the team of medical experts—all sworn to complete secrecy—boarded the *Oneida* on the afternoon of June 30. To those not in the know, all appeared relaxed and normal. The next morning the yacht weighed anchor and headed up the East River and into Long Island Sound. Just past noon, the President entered the room and sat in the dental chair where he was anesthetized and the procedure begun. The operation lasted approximately ninety minutes, during which time the doctors removed the tumor, five teeth and much of the President's upper left palate and jawbone. The surgery was performed entirely within the President's mouth using a cheek retractor to help ensure that the President wouldn't have external scars. In another nod to "normalcy," Cleveland's mustache was not shaved off.

The *Oneida* sailed for four more days before arriving in Buzzard's Bay on July 5. Cleveland disembarked when the yacht reached his dock at Gray Gables, his summer home. Cleveland's medical team continued to monitor his recovery. A second procedure was performed two weeks after the first, again on the *Oneida*. The remainder of the time in Cape Cod was spent with Cleveland convalescing. In late July, at Gray Gables, Dr. Kasson C. Gibson, a New York prosthodontist, fit the President with a vulcanized rubber prosthesis designed to fill the hollow in his jaw, return the normal shape to the left side of Cleveland's face and restore normal speech. The plan went well and just a few weeks after these major medical procedures, Cleveland appeared to friends and reporters, acting as if nothing had occurred. He talked and fished in Buzzard's Bay like he had never endured an operation. By the end of the first week of August, Cleveland was back in Washington in time for the special session of Congress he had called and by later that month, he had convinced that body to repeal the Sherman Act. A cover story was concocted stating that the president had two bad teeth removed and had suffered from a bout of rheumatism, which seemed to satisfy the curiosity of the reporters and, despite a few stories in the press, the cover plan worked and was not revealed until 1917, twenty years after Cleveland left office and eleven years after his death.

While Cleveland was on the mend, periodic stories that Dempsey was gravely ill continued to surface. On August 12, 1893, newspapers across the nation ran an article declaring that "Jack Dempsey, the Nonpareil, is in St. Joseph's Hospital in St. Paul, where he has been since last Monday. He is suffering from a severe strain."[32] Some articles reported that Jack had simply developed a bad chest cold that he had picked up while visiting Minnesota's White Bear Lake.[33] Other reports stated that Jack was being treated for emotional distress, some even describing it as insanity. They claimed that Dempsey would periodically state that he believed that gamblers were plotting to kill him. "As near as can be learned the doctors attribute the condition of mental unsoundness to excessive drinking and they believe that he will recover from the attack."[34] Some blamed his depression over the loss to Bob Fitzsimmons in 1891 while some blamed his heavy drinking and others said Jack's curious behavior was no different than his usual eccentricities. Maggie and Tuthill actually did admit Jack to St. Joseph's Hospital in St. Paul where he spent several days. He was treated by physicians and it was determined that he was a physical and emotional wreck. He was diagnosed as having a high fever and being delirious, but not insane. Dempsey was discharged from St. Joseph's on August 17. Upon his discharge, Dempsey proceeded to the Merchant's Hotel for a few more days of rest.

Judge Newton, who had been dealing with Dempsey all summer regarding the on-again, off-again Billy Smith fight, believed that there was indeed something wrong with Jack. Smith commented that he had met with Jack twice in Portland, but that he could not get him to sign a provisional agreement with the Coney Island Athletic Club. Smith was of the opinion that Dempsey had no more fight left in him. Smith was also sure to mention the matter of the Club's $500 training advance to Dempsey for the fight that never came off. Smith was no doubt miffed about the lack of a bout with Dempsey but was said to be equally incredulous that Jack was instead now on track to fight Dick Burge in December for $10,000 a side. Burge had deposited $2,500 with the London *Sporting Life* for the fight and Smith was openly furious that with his meeting with Dempsey now off, he was left out in the cold with no bout at all. Smith, however, would not have to wait long for an opponent. A bout was soon arranged with Tommy Ryan at the Coney Island A.C. for August 29.

Rumors about Dempsey's health continued to run rampant. Some press reports stated that Jack was violent and had become a dangerous lunatic. They began to speculate that if Dempsey was truly suffering from a brain weakened by alcohol, that even if his condition improved, it would be irresponsible for any club to sign him to fight due to the chance of a blow to the head being fatal. "This insanity means that alcohol has weakened the brain and a subject of this kind, no matter how much mended, is likely to be fatally injured by a blow on the head such as would be the natural outcome of a ring fight."[35]

Jack's maladies were of course a mix of severe emotional distress and depression, plus his generally weakened physical condition, pulmonary troubles and fever from the deepening signs of the consumption that would kill him. Dempsey's erratic behavior may also have signaled some sort of anxiety or panic disorder. As if these symptoms alone were not enough, they were exacerbated by his heavy use of alcohol. Jack's severe emotional distress and depression were described as "severe mental strain" and the physicians who were treating him at St. Joseph's believed that "the brooding over past defeats has caused his mind to become temporarily unhinged."[36] In short, Dempsey was a physical and emotional wreck. Jack's erratic behavior was linked to a mix of his depressive state, worsening lung damage, fever, deliriousness and agitation due to his illness and heavy alcohol use. Denying reports that Dempsey was mad, his doctors made clear that "he is suffering with fever, which accounts for the report that he was insane."[37]

After Jack's discharge from the hospital, the Dempseys and Tuthill left Minneapolis for Chicago on August 18. After arriving in the Windy City, Jack and Maggie stayed in a quiet, out-of-the-way location for a few days, so Jack could relax and get his wits about him. Gus Tuthill stated to a reporter from the *New York Sun*, "Jack is at present in Chicago with his wife. They are recuperating in a small cottage on the banks of Lake Michigan which I secured solely for their comfort." Tuthill continued, "I can frankly state that Jack is as sound as a new dollar. Furthermore, he was not as sick as generally thought."[38] After a few days of rest, Dempsey appeared somewhat better and his retinue continued to deny any serious illness. Whether or not Jack or any of them believed that he could recover from the tuberculosis that was consuming him or whether Dempsey just wanted to continue boxing for as long as he possibly could, we will never know, but the erraticism continued. He could look fine and seem healthy one day, then have a spell the next. This was difficult to manage, but Dempsey knew he must try. One thing was certain, though, Jack knew that revealing his tubercular state would finish his pugilistic career immediately.

In mid–August, Gus Tuthill was finally forced to acknowledge that Dempsey was not in his right mind. Jack was ill and clearly could not be ready for a prizefight against Smith, Burge or anyone else in the near term. On August 19, Tuthill stated that the fight with Burge was off and that he would forfeit the $4,000 already committed to the fight. On August 21, a telegram arrived from Richard Fox, who was touring the British Isles with his family at the time. Fox, the principal stakeholder for the Burge-Dempsey bout, acknowledged that the contest would not go on and that Burge had agreed to meet Billy Smith in Boston instead.[39]

While Jack was recuperating by Lake Michigan, stories ran in several newspapers that Dempsey was in Racine, Wisconsin. Reports out of Racine in late August stated that Dempsey was in that city and imbibing heavily in liquor and acting erratically. Thinking the man to be either insane or a drunken vagrant, the police decided to detain him after he solicited $20 from a local woman. Trying to avoid apprehension, the man then jumped from a carriage and escaped into the local countryside. The police finally caught up with him after a farmer gave the man a ride back into town. The story states that the man's wife was also looking for her husband and apparently smoothed things over with the local constabulary, taking her husband on to Chicago. The man reportedly told various townspeople and the police that he was in Racine to begin training for a fight, but when pressed, could not say with whom.[40] Other reports called this story rubbish and declared that some faker must have been in Racine impersonating Dempsey. According to Dominick O'Malley, fight promoter and president of Chicago's Columbian A.C., Dempsey had spent the entire day in question with him. He further declared that Jack been under the watchful supervision of his wife and friends and that Dempsey had not left Chicago since his arrival there on August 19.[41] Based on O'Malley's comments there is good reason to question the reports that Dempsey and Maggie were in Racine on August 23 but given that Racine is only about seventy-five miles north of Chicago it is entirely possible that he could have been there. Perhaps the biggest question is why they would have gone to that Wisconsin city. I tend to discount the story, but I cannot completely dismiss it.

Jack's condition was bemoaned by many. Cries of "Poor Jack Dempsey!" rang out in newspapers across the land. The *National Police Gazette* lamented that "in all the history of fistiana the life of no pugilist has been so filled with misfortune as that of Jack Dempsey's since he was defeated by the middleweight champion Bob Fitzsimmons."[42] The *New York Daily News* commented on August 20,

> No men are more subject to the caprice or change of fortune than pugilists. Victory brings them riches, fame and patrons. Their bruises are not heeded in their smiles of success and basking in the sunshine of prosperity their lives pass on pleasantly until defeat comes and reverses the scene. Covered with aches and pains, distressed in mind and body, assailed by poverty, wretchedness and misery, friends forsake them, their fame expires, their characters suspected by losing, and no longer the plaything of fashion, they fly to inebriation for relief and in many instances, a premature end puts a period to their misfortunes. How true of Jack Dempsey.[43]

Jack was luckier than most—he still had an adoring wife, a loving family and many caring friends who stood by him—but the *News* was not far off in their assessment of Dempsey's situation. It was becoming abundantly clear that the Nonpareil's best days were behind him.

On the evening of August 28, Jack and Maggie finally returned home to Brooklyn on the Pennsylvania Express from Chicago. It had been a long, troubling and difficult journey for the Dempseys. Despite the health concerns and wild stories of the previous few weeks, the throng of supporters who greeted Jack at the Pennsylvania Railroad terminal saw a man who looked to be in good health. As he stepped from the platform,

Dempsey was cheered and immediately surrounded by hundreds of friends and fans. New York's Columbia Athletic Club had engaged a brass band who began playing "Home Once More" as he made his way through the crowd. Jack seemed genuinely moved by the greeting as he bowed and tipped his hat repeatedly. He then made his way to Tuthill's waiting carriage that would take Margaret to visit friends in Williamsburg.

Dempsey, Tuthill and company then climbed into another carriage, one in a long line of conveyances that was to carry them from the terminal on Cortlandt Street to the Columbia A.C. "The ex-champion was heartily cheered all along the Bowery and Third Avenue to the club house of the [Columbia Athletic Club] where a social time was enjoyed."[44] The route was lined with bonfires, fireworks and cheering crowds. "It was close on to nine o'clock before the procession reached the clubhouse, and when Dempsey alighted from his coach he was again loudly cheered."[45] Dempsey met with club president Robert Conn and then addressed reporters.

Jack said that he was glad to get back to the east among old friends and he warmly thanked them for the hospitality. Dempsey continued, "I want to say something about those reports from the West regarding my health. How they ever came to be circulated I cannot imagine." He went on to thank Tuthill for getting him back to Brooklyn alive. The general consensus by those who spent the evening with Jack was that he looked fit and "he showed no signs of the mental trouble that he was alleged to have suffered from while in St. Paul."[46]

Asked about his future plans, Dempsey responded that Tuthill would be seeing to future bouts, but that he would stay within the middleweight ranks. "I have decided not to go out of my class anymore. I will neither give nor take a pound."[47] A reporter with the *Brooklyn Eagle* noted that "Dempsey certainly looked in the best of health. He did not show the signs which would be recognized on a man who had been trying to drink everything in sight, as the Western dispatches would have it."[48]

Tuthill reiterated to the press that Dempsey's next bout would indeed be with Dick Burge and that they had not yet decided if Jack would challenge the winner of the next evening's match between Tommy Ryan and Billy Smith to a bout to be set sometime after Jack met Burge in December. Tuthill seemed anxious to get Dempsey back in the ring, but Jack did not seem as excited about the prospect. After Ryan defeated Smith, Billy Madden representing Ryan would visit the *Police Gazette* offices and accept this challenge.

After the meeting at the Columbia A.C., Jack met up with Margaret and dined with friends.

On August 29, Jack sat ringside at the bout between Tommy Ryan of Chicago and Boston's "Mysterious" Billy Smith at the Coney Island Athletic Club. The bout was ruled a draw, but those present believed that Ryan was the faster and more clever of the two. The *New York Times* commented, "Jack Dempsey sat close to the ring and smiled at Smith's inability to land. He will be Smith's next opponent."[49] Despite Jack's clearly deteriorating health, a number of fight people also saw a bout between the rising young Ryan and Dempsey as a real possibility in the near future. At one point after the preliminaries and just prior to the main event, the crowd started calling Jack's name and refused to stop until he was introduced to the crowd, at which time the local patrons gave him a long and boisterous welcome home.[50] The Brooklyn crowd still loved Jack.

Dempsey was undeniably still extremely popular, but had numerous detractors who questioned him for his recent lack of activity and for his seemingly odd behavior. The

Hamilton Daily Democrat of Ohio stated that "the Nonpareil, another pugilistic idol has fallen. Jack Dempsey, once the pride and delight of ring circles, has fallen away from his high place and is now wandering among the horde of nondescript fighters, with which the ring is overburdened."[51] The article continued to take Dempsey to task for his erratic behavior in the weeks leading up to the proposed Billy Smith bout, and for his proposing a bout with Dick Burge, whose character they questioned. The newspaper likened the attempt to fight Burge to "endeavoring to crawl back into the ring over the body of some pugilist who is willing to suffer defeat for the money in the losing end."[52]

The *Daily Democrat*'s comments were mild compared to those recorded by a reporter who wrote under the pen name "Pendragon" in the Buffalo newspapers. In a monument to understatement Pendragon wrote in August 1893 that "Jack Dempsey has never been a favorite of mine." He went on to call Dempsey a "fake" and question his ability in the ring and the legitimacy of his reputation. He also questioned that anything was wrong with Dempsey at all beyond alcohol consumption. After dismissing "the press" as being far too generous and forgiving to Dempsey, Pendragon, who apparently fancied himself a physician and psychiatrist, wrote, "Insanity, as the dictionary is understood, is a terrible thing. Dempsey has not been insane. His trouble is whiskey and whiskey led to the 'D.T.s.' When Dempsey is put right on to the copper bottom, whether he is drunk or sober, he will come down to this—that he can't fight."[53] Soon after writing this piece Pendragon was excoriated by a number of newspapers, including the *National Police Gazette*. Writing in his weekly column, "the Referee" commented that if Pendragon had read Richard K. Fox's biography of Dempsey he "might have discovered that the winner of the 'Police Gazette' middleweight belt had a better record than he claims." After recounting the Nonpareil's long list of victories, the Referee added, "Perhaps, now that Pendragon's memory has been refreshed, he will regret his scurrility and the meanness of his attack on a man once great but who is now in unfortunate circumstances."[54]

After the Ryan-Smith battle, Jack traveled to Asbury Park, New Jersey, to spend a few days relaxing at the home of his friend Walter De Baum. While there, Jack paid a visit to heavyweight champion Jim Corbett. The two friends had a long and cordial talk. The men had been acquainted since their days sparring in San Francisco. The Nonpareil had shared his boxing knowledge with the young Corbett and several years earlier Dempsey had given the Californian a few valuable tips on Jake Kilrain's style prior to Corbett's fight with the Baltimore man in New Orleans. Corbett never forgot this and regarded Dempsey as a friend and ally. Corbett commented that Jack looked fit and could meet virtually any man in any weight class in the world—including and maybe especially, the elusive "Mysterious" Billy Smith. Before Jack left to return to Brooklyn, Corbett insisted that Dempsey and his entourage stay an additional few days as Corbett's guest at his rented cottage near a lake at "The Farm," a seven-acre parcel of land thick with pine trees on Deal Lake just a half-mile from the ocean.

Corbett had set up a training camp nearby and the prospect of having Dempsey join him at his camp pleased Gentleman Jim. Several other fighters were also encamped in the resort area that was known up to that time as a world-famous retreat area for "Prohibitionists and morally inclined health seekers." Far from being counted among the teetotalers, the pugilists added a new element to The Farm's clientele. "Three noted pugilists have selected the town for their training quarters and are hard at work preparing themselves for coming fights. The trio includes Champion James J. Corbett, Jack Dempsey, who is soon to have a 'go' at Dick Burge, and Solly Smith, the featherweight Californian, who is to meet George Dixon on September 25. Corbett and Dempsey are training at The Farm, a romantic spot on Deal Lake, and Smith has taken up quarters within a stone's throw of the champion."[55] One hundred feet west of the cottage was a two-story building that had been fully outfitted as a gymnasium for the champion. The grounds also included roads for running, a handball court, croquet grounds, a tennis court and a shooting range. The lake afforded boating and swimming.

While at the Jersey Shore, Dempsey engaged in some light workouts—chiefly running, hitting the heavy bag, lifting dumbbells and playing handball with Corbett. Jack noted when he returned to Brooklyn from Chicago on August 28 that he weighed 168 pounds and would need to shed twenty pounds before entering the ring again. By mid–October, he was down to 158. He would head back to Brooklyn early the next week and go into heavy training for his bout with Burge.

One interesting story that must attest to Dempsey's recovery has to do with an eight-mile foot race held on September 22. The race took place at the running track at the Asbury Park Athletic Grounds and among the participants were Dempsey, Corbett, Solly Smith, Seward Smith, Jack Oliver and Billy Delaney. The race was open to the public and "was witnessed by the greater part of the population." Delaney retired after running twenty laps, but the other pugilists powered on to the finish. "Corbett and Solly Smith, who hold the ten-mile record in San Francisco, finished close together, the latter winning by forty yards and about a mile ahead of the third man, Dempsey. The time was not taken."[56] The fact that Dempsey, a man recovering from numerous and recent serious health issues, including severe lung dissipation, could run eight miles at all, and apparently at a reasonable pace, clearly speaks to the level of (albeit temporary) recovery he had achieved. While his health would slip again over the next couple of years, he seemed to be in good condition at this point in the autumn of 1893. This said, his health, both mental and physical continued to be unpredictable from day to day.

In late August, it was announced that a benefit would be held in New York in Jack's honor at the Industrial Palace Hall on Lexington Avenue and Forty-Third Street. Jack was going through a time of financial difficulty and his many friends and admirers, led by Gus Tuthill and Richard Fox, were determined to help him out of these straits. The event was scheduled for September 4 and sporting men and others of note were expected to be on hand from as far away as Boston and Philadelphia. "Friends of Dempsey have sent circulars to sporting men in different parts of the country, appealing to them for contributions to a fund which is being raised for the purpose of relieving Jack from his present financial embarrassment." Admirers of Dempsey from all parts of the country reportedly sent in contributions from $5 to $250 in support of the Nonpareil.[57] Not surprisingly, the large hall was expected to be filled to capacity for the event.

The evening was filled with a dozen sparring matches fought by numerous pugilists from around New York. The bouts were, however, fairly calm and friendly in nature as Inspector Williams of the New York City Police Department was on hand to make certain that the exhibitions were scientific and that the pugilists did not hit each other too hard. A dozen exhibitions were held, but the affair was described as "spiritless and tame."[58]

Jim Corbett was on hand and was warmly welcomed as he readied himself to spar several rounds with his sparring partner John Donaldson. When Corbett finished his exhibition, he made a few comments to the crowd. After again inviting Jack to train as his guest at his camp in Asbury Park, New Jersey, he commented "that he thought Dempsey was one of the cleverest fighters of his time and admitted that he learned many points from the Brooklyn fighter."[59] In closing his speech, Corbett stated, "I consider Dempsey the greatest boxer of his weight who ever lived and I tell the truth when I say I copy his style in boxing and fighting."[60] Corbett also wowed the crowd when he handed manager Gus Tuthill $100 to go for the benefit fund for Jack.

It was all great fun, but the highlight of the evening was when the Nonpareil climbed into the ring to box four rounds with his conqueror Bob Fitzsimmons. Jack reportedly looked to be in good condition and strong, "but there is an unhealthy tinge in his flushed face which his friends did not like."[61] The sparring was described as friendly. It was clear during the brief exhibition that he and Fitzsimmons were on very different planes now and while it was a tame exhibition, Dempsey was clearly outclassed. While Dempsey still had plenty of his old tricks, he was unable to move with his old fluidity nor could he hit with his old speed and power. Writing in the *National Police Gazette* a few weeks after the benefit the "Referee" stated that he and "a good many wise people" shared the opinion that Dempsey should never fight professionally again. "He is not the man he was before he went away. His health has been undermined by dissipation and even with the utmost care and training he would never again be able to fight such battles as those which made him famous in days gone by. In sparring with Fitz, he was as slow as a prize hog...." Regardless of the quality of the exhibition, the crowd cheered the local favorite at every opportunity and they were clearly glad to see Dempsey back in the ring.

At one point, a telegram from John L. Sullivan was read. Sullivan praised Dempsey for his poise and skill both inside and outside the ring. The crowd cheered wildly when Sullivan announced that he was putting $50 into the benefit fund. The message closed warmly with Sullivan stating, "Good luck, from your friend."[62]

The show was a splendid one for those who wished to see the stars in the ring. In addition to Corbett, bantam weight champion Bill Plimmer and Australian middleweight champion Dan Creedon both appeared in exhibitions. At the end of the night, $3,682 in gate money and donations was collected against $1,212.43 in expenses. Dempsey was awarded $2,469.57.[63]

After the benefit, Jack returned with Corbett to the latter's training camp in New Jersey. He continued to train there until he and Denny Costigan went over to Philadelphia in mid–September for a week to give three-round sparring exhibitions. From there the pair, accompanied by Corbett, traveled back to New York on September 25 to attend a tribute to Jack McAuliffe later in the week.

Costigan and Dempsey crossed the East River to Brooklyn on October 1. Dempsey was scheduled to meet with Judge Newton of the Coney Island A.C. and Dick Burge, who had arrived in New York on the steamship *Umbria* the day before. Burge was several days later in arriving in America than he expected because he was arrested in Liverpool as he was about to board a ship for New York. The charge was that he seconded a fighter in a bout in Manchester, England, in which a fighter named Flood was seriously injured. After he arranged bail, he boarded the *Umbria* and proceeded on his journey.[64] Speaking with reporters on the docks as he disembarked in New York, Burge expressed surprise that the club was ready with a final offer to host the bout and said that negotiations had better be fruitful for he would not fight for stakes money alone.[65] Burge set up his training camp in the Fort Hamilton section of southwest Brooklyn at Nolan's.

The meeting with Judge Newton did not happen that day as Newton failed to show up. Another meeting was set for Tuesday, October 3, but Dempsey and Tuthill had business out of town and soon boarded a train for Philadelphia. Jack was engaged to spar a few rounds with Denny Costigan and hit the heavy and speed bags for the remainder of the week in a vaudeville show. He would make $500 for the engagement.[66] Tuthill arranged for others to represent Dempsey on Tuesday, but no progress was made at that meeting and the talks seemed to be at a standstill. News reports indicated, "It is intimated that the Coney Island Club will not make a bid for the fight until the Corbett-Mitchell affair is settled."[67]

After Dempsey's multiple sparring sessions in September and October, the press, seemingly in agreement with Jim Corbett's observation, reported that Jack "looked much better than when he first arrived from the West. His stay at Asbury Park, where he has been the guest of champion Corbett, evidently did him a world of good."[68] Dempsey looked good enough that Gus Tuthill set a match with John Clark during his stay in Philadelphia, but the scheduled October 7 contest fell through, reportedly because of a small crowd. "Jack Dempsey was to have boxed with Johnny Clark in the Academy of Music, Philadelphia, on October 7. The affair was well advertised but only sixty people paid and Gus Tuthill, Dempsey's manager, refunded the money."[69] This may have been a first for Dempsey.

On October 10, Burge and his trainer Sam Blakelock were guests of the New Utrecht Athletic Club at an evening of boxing matches being held at the Bay View Park Amphitheater on Sixtieth Street and Third Avenue in Brooklyn. Burge and Blakelock were joined by undefeated former British featherweight champion William Nobby Clark, who was also acting as Burge's manager. The three were chosen to act as fight judges for the evening's bouts. The card held four six-rounders and a wind-up match scheduled for ten.

The on-again, off-again fight fell off one more time in mid–October, but apparently, this had nothing to do with Jack or his health. It was Judge Newton who controlled the bout's fate. The *New York Times* and some of the local clergy had begun a campaign to prevent the proposed bout between Corbett and Charley Mitchell, causing concern among the boxing community and its followers. Looking to stop the newspaper's meddling, a number of the sport's local leading backers sought assistance from the state capitol in Albany. Police Justice Newton, "Boss" McLaughlin of the Coney Island A.C. and Police Justice Tighe of the Varuna Boat Club approached New York Governor Roswell P. Flower asking him not to intervene against their interests. The newspaper reported that since the *Times* and the group of clergymen had begun their efforts to prevent the bout, "officials of the Coney Island Club have been quietly bragging among their set and to the fighters who have appeared in their ring that Governor Flower would not interfere with the Corbett-Mitchell prizefight for the reason that he signed the charter of the club through John Y. McKane's influence."[70] In connection to the Dempsey-Burge fight, the *Times* further reported that Judge Newton had met with Burge and his managers on October 16 and impressed on them the fact that Newton "controlled a monopoly of prize fighting" in America and would dictate his own terms to fighters. This was a bit strongly worded and over the top, but the general facts remain true.

From Dempsey's camp came only news of Jack's health. On October 17, the *Brooklyn Eagle* noted that "Jack Dempsey's health is improving. He is taking good care of himself and now weighs about 158 pounds."[71] Corbett told the press that he believed Jack to be fully recovered from his recent illnesses. "He has worked with me, walked and boxed with me for the last month and with eight weeks training will be fit to give any 142-pound man in the world a very stiff argument." Corbett went on to say, "I consider him the greatest of all the present-day fighters."[72]

Burge and William Nobby Clark met with a *Times* reporter at their lodgings at the Gilsey House and said this of their meeting with Judge Newton: "Mr. Clark and I came to the United States two weeks ago last Saturday in response to an agreement by Gus Tuthill, Dempsey's manager, to back Dempsey against me for $5,000 a side at the Coney Island Athletic Club. I supposed that everything had been arranged between Tuthill and Newton, and that all I had to do was to come here, sign articles, and go into training."[73] Burge stated that he met with Newton and Johnny Eckhardt at the club several times formally and informally and that they continually found excuses for putting off the signing of any fight contract.

Burge continued, "I went to Fort Hamilton and began to train. Hearing nothing from [Newton], I came to New York last week and tried to find him." Burge said that he and Clark ran across Newton at Broadway and Twenty-Eighth Street and asked him for definite assurances that the fight with Dempsey was on. Newton reportedly responded, "The best thing you can do is to pack up and go back to England." The Englishmen went on to protest that they had come to America in good faith and had incurred over $1,000 in expenses in doing so. They demanded an answer as to why the fight was off and why they had been treated so shabbily. Newton replied, "Well, Gus Tuthill has insulted me by trying to dictate terms to me."[74] Newton apparently told them that only he and the Coney Island A.C. could arrange the fight at this time and that he would not have terms dictated to him. Burge added that it was his belief that the *Times*'s stance and a public agitation had also added pressure on Newton, helped to stall his match with Dempsey and possibly would affect the Corbett-Mitchell bout being held on Coney Island. "Oh, it will take place, sure," said Burge, but he predicted that it would change venue to New Orleans.

Burge stated that he was still willing to meet Dempsey in England for £1,000 a side with Richard K. Fox as the purse holder. Dempsey said he was game and willing to meet Burge anywhere, even on Burge's home turf, the National Sporting Club in London. Speculation immediately started that Jack might accompany Corbett on a trip to England in April and negotiate a bout at that time.[75]

Ultimately, the fight never came off. One thing or another—money, disagreements, social and magisterial pressure, or Jack's precarious health—continually got in the way and eventually, Dempsey grew too ill to seriously contemplate a bout. Some even blamed Dempsey's health for the fight falling through at the time. On November 11, the *Washington Bee* reported that Dempsey "has been confined in a private insane asylum at Chicago and his match with Dick Burge, the English champion, is off."[76] In and of itself, that was an amazing revelation since Jack was in Buffalo at that time appearing nightly on stage with Denny Costigan and had not been near Chicago since August.

Burge was born in Cheltenham, England, in 1865. He began fighting professionally in 1887 and was the British lightweight champion from 1891 to 1897. Burge squared off with such notables as Jem Carney, Kid Lavigne and Bobby Dobbs. He fought his last contest on January 28, 1901, in a bout versus Jerry Driscoll that was ruled by the referee as no contest.

In November 1901, Burge ran afoul of the law. It was reported that police in London arrested Burge "on a charge of complicity in the recent Bank of Liverpool frauds." The scheme apparently involved the writing of bad checks and then money laundering to hide the funds. The police had recovered over £100,000 in missing money that had been hidden in plain sight in various banks around London and other cities throughout England. Quite a number of arrests were made in connection with the case, Burge among them. On November 25, 1901, "Burge was brought up in the Bow Street police court and charged with uttering checks aggregating £86,000, knowing them to be forged. He was reprimanded."[77] He was tried, found guilty of fraud in 1902 and sentenced to ten years in prison. Burge was released in the summer of 1909 after serving seven years.

Upon his release from prison, Burge sought to re-establish his reputation by becoming a boxing promoter. With the support of his wife Bella, he succeeded and became a well-known and respected promoter in London. Burge died in London on March 15, 1918, of pneumonia, while serving in the British Army with the First Surrey Rifles during World War I at the age of 52.

While the Burge fight fell through, Jack remained active by returning to touring and giving exhibition matches. In November, he went up to Buffalo where he sparred with Denny Costigan from November 9 to 11. The pair then returned to New York City, where they had an engagement at the H.R. Jacobs Theater to spar during the week of November 13. The men were scheduled to spar for three rounds during the production of *The Bottom of the Sea*, a French play about divers at work on a sunken shipwreck. They then traveled to Boston in December, where Jack sparred with Costigan and fellow Irish native Dick Moore, and finished out the year in Washington, D.C., where Jack put on an exhibition with British lightweight Joe Fielden.

One evening, while the pair was in Buffalo, Costigan met two young ladies upon whom he wished to make a good impression. He invited them to the theater to see that evening's performance, purchased a box in which he placed them and boasted that he would give Dempsey a friendly beating. When that evening's bout began, Jack was surprised at his friend's unusual vigor and harder-than-usual punches. After the first round, Jack commented to his seconds that "Costigan's very strong tonight." The bottle holder smiled and responded, "Yes, he told those young ladies in the box he would make a show of you." Dempsey smiled and responded, "He did, did he?" Pleased by the prospect of a better-than-usual workout, Jack met Costigan at center ring and after Denny landed a hard punch, Jack responded by landing several blows that made Costigan recoil. Denny responded to Jack, saying, "Go easy, go easy. This ain't a fight." Jack responded with another sharp blow to his friend's ribs and whispered, "Let's give them their money's worth." When Costigan protested again, the Nonpareil just smiled and landed his fist on Denny's nose. The two then mixed it up for a couple of more rounds with Denny more than game, but Jack driving him around the ring with lefts and rights. When the bout ended, a smiling Dempsey walked over to Costigan and, putting an arm around his friend's shoulders, whispered, "Say, Costigan, always consult me when you want to make a star play. I deserve your confidence."[78]

Rumors were persistent that Tommy Ryan and Jack would meet sometime in 1894. On October 24, Ryan received a telegram from an athletic club in Chicago offering a $1,500 purse for a six-round gloved contest between him and Dempsey. Ryan, who was in Bridgeport, Connecticut, training for a November 2 match, said that he would be willing to accept pending the outcome of his upcoming bout at the Naugatuck Athletic Club with Harry Jameson.

On December 30, Jack was in Washington, D.C., where he met twenty-five-year-old British fighter Joe Fielden in a four-round sparring match at Albaugh's Theater. Fielden, a native of Manchester, England, had come to the United States to test his skills versus American fighters and while very little has been precisely documented, published reports indicate that he met quite a number of notable opponents during his time in America, including men such as Dempsey, Bob Fitzsimmons, Mike Cleary, George La Blanche, Andy Bowen, Paddy McGuigan, Billy Young and Bobby Dobbs.[79]

1894—The Slowing Champion

At the dawn of 1894, Jack may have been ill and slowing down inside the ring, but he still remained active in both show business and boxing. He wanted to stay active to dispel the rumors surrounding his health, but as usual, he needed the money he could make trading on his name and reputation both inside and outside of the ring.

Beginning in the first week of January, and running throughout the month, Jack was appearing on stage regularly and sparring in three-round gloved exhibitions with Denny Costigan at the new Bijou Theatre at Smith and Livingston Streets in Brooklyn. Mr. H. C. Kennedy had just opened his brand new theater in November and it would go on to become one of the most profitable venues in America in the 1890s. Costigan and Dempsey would spar for several rounds two or three times a week during performances of *The Bottom of the Sea*. One report stated, "In the last act Dempsey will spar three rounds. This will give admirers of boxing a chance to see how quick the hero of fifty-one battles still is, and how he takes the slightest advantage of an opening and displays some clever science in ducking."[1] The pair would also spar with other local boxers for points. The Nonpareil's presence helped keep the seats full as his popularity had not waned in his native Brooklyn and fans were delighted to see him back and in the ring. "The two pugilists were given a warm welcome and in return they entertained their auditors with a rattling 'go.'"[2]

It was reported that Dempsey was considering matches with several strong opponents. Rumor had it that following the Corbett-Mitchell bout, "Dempsey will go to England to try and arrange a match with Dick Burge. Dempsey, it is said, has been taken the best of care, and hopes to prove to his many admirers that he is still able to give a good account of himself."[3] Burge and his backers, hearing nothing back from Dempsey and his camp, moved on and set a contest with Harry Nickless for the 140-pound championship of England. The men met the following May at London's Bolingbroke Club where Burge knocked Nickless out in the twenty-eighth round.

Jack was continually in high demand for his opinion on pugilistic matters. In an interview with a *Police Gazette* correspondent, Dempsey was asked who would win the upcoming battle between Jim Corbett and Charley Mitchell. Jack responded firmly, "I know Corbett is going to win." By way of explanation Dempsey added, "Corbett has everything in his favor. He is taller, younger, more experienced and hits a harder blow." When pressed on the matter of the men's relative experience, Jack said that he believed that Corbett's experience was more practical than Mitchell's. When the reporter pointed out that Sullivan did not believe that height counted for much in a fight Dempsey countered, "I can't agree with John. I know Fitzsimmons' five inches probably won for him his fight with me."[4] While height was only part of Fitzsimmons's lopsided victory, the Nonpareil was absolutely correct that a height advantage can make a difference.

When Gentleman Jim Corbett finally met Charley Mitchell at the Duvall Athletic Club in Jacksonville, Florida, Jack was in Corbett's corner. Corbett was making his first title defense since knocking out John L. Sullivan in September 1892. During the first week of January, Dempsey had repeatedly told reporters that he was certain that Corbett would defeat Mitchell. "To be frank, I think Corbett a cleverer boxer than Mitchell."[5]

After describing Dempsey's run at the Bijou, the *Brooklyn Eagle* reported that "it was from [Dempsey] that Champion Corbett took many points, and after his engagement here he will leave direct for Jacksonville, Florida, to join Corbett, and in all probability will second Corbett in his coming match with Mitchell."[6] Corbett confirmed this when he told reporters that he had written to Jack several days earlier asking him if he would come down to Jacksonville and be in his corner. Corbett continued, "I was very pleased to receive a telegram from him today in which he said that he would be very glad to come. I consider that Dempsey has as thorough a knowledge of boxing as any man in the business and I know very well I couldn't get a better man to advise me. A good second can see the signs of distress in a man quicker than can his opponent, and I think that Jack will be of great service to me."[7]

On January 22, the ten-car Richmond and Danville Special headed south out of New York carrying, among others, Dempsey, Gus Tuthill, Joe Choynski, Parson Davies, Denny Costigan, Brooklyn Jimmy Carroll, Mitchell's father-in-law, and British fight manager George "Pony" Moore from the fight fraternity. The train arrived in Jacksonville on the late evening of January 23. Dempsey then proceeded on to Corbett's training camp in Mayport, a small coastal fishing village a few miles east of Jacksonville. Once there, Jack settled in and he took a workout with Corbett the next day.

The fight was scheduled for January 25, 1894, and was to be fought under the Queensberry Rules, with five-ounce gloves, with a referee selected by the club—Honest John Kelly was chosen. It was also decided that there would be no limit to the number of rounds. In addition to Dempsey, Corbett would have William A. Brady, John McVey, John Donaldson and Billy Delaney in his corner during the bout. At Corbett's demand the seconds were all Americans. He believed that since this was a championship fight that would determine on which side of the Atlantic the heavyweight crown would reside he should be seconded by Americans. Mitchell had only fellow Britons in his corner with the exception of the legendary western lawman Bat Masterson.

The morning of the fight, Dempsey went to the arena to see if everything was in shape for the contest. As one might expect the Duvall Club claimed that everything was all right. Upon inspection, however, Dempsey found several issues with the ring set up and declared that if improvements were not made to the ring immediately, Corbett would not appear at the fight that afternoon. "The club had agreed to pad the posts around the ring and had not done so. Dempsey declared the platform shaky, and consequently it would not be safe when two heavyweights like Mitchell and Corbett were rushing around upon it. He demanded that it be made more solid at once and also that the ropes around the ring be drawn taut."[8] When the club administrators objected to Dempsey's requests, the Nonpareil erupted, declaring, "Fix these things at once or Corbett will never step into the ring."[9] Jim Hall, one of Mitchell's seconds, agreed with Dempsey's assessment and fully endorsed Jack's suggestions. The club soon relented and made the improvements per Dempsey's demands.

The battle over the ring may have been more interesting and taken longer than the main event as Corbett dispatched Mitchell, already woozy by the third round, with a series of head shots culminating in a solid right to the nose that floored the Englishman for the count. Corbett was declared the winner by knockout in his first title defense after just nine minutes of fighting.

In addition to his pre-fight ring inspection and his sage advice between rounds, there was another good reason for Corbett that Dempsey was present in his corner that day against Mitchell. Corbett, like Dempsey and a good many other North American fighters, had very little respect for Mitchell and had grown tired of his endless boasts of ring superiority. For this reason, and to vanquish the Englishman and his self-aggrandizing stories once and for all, Corbett was not just ready to defeat his opponent, he was ready to punish him.

Corbett was uncharacteristically full of rage on the night of the contest. After the first knock-down, Corbett stood over his fallen opponent and glared menacingly at him. "His eyes blazed with anger and his usually pale, sallow face was livid." Referee Honest John Kelly saw this and intervened to make certain that Corbett did not commit a foul. After the second knock-down, Corbett again lurked nearby and when Mitchell finally raised himself to one knee, the uncontrollable Corbett struck his opponent on the head. Immediately Dempsey and Billy Delaney jumped into the ring and grabbed Corbett, restraining him from further battering his helpless antagonist and to keep Kelly from disqualifying Corbett.[10] One report described the scene as follows, "So alarmed were Corbett's seconds with his insane actions that Dempsey fairly leaped upon his back and clutching him around the neck with one arm, slapped him several times in the face with his bare hand, and then with the assistance of big Donaldson and Delaney pushed him into the corner."[11] Despite the brouhaha, Jack calmed Corbett and helped him regain some measure of composure as Jim went on to deliver the third round knockout. "Mitchell's face was covered with blood. He was carried to his corner in helpless condition."[12] That quick action on Dempsey's part might well have saved the fight for Corbett that day. Corbett was clearly right earlier in the month when he stated, "I think that Jack will be of great service to me."[13]

Both fighters were arrested after the fight on the charge of breaching the peace by Sheriff Napoleon Bonaparte Broward. After their arrests, Corbett and Mitchell each posted immediate bonds and were expected in court the next morning.[14] In usual fashion and in short order, the charges were dropped, a small fine paid and each man left town, only mildly irritated with the legal dance that they knew so well.

In an interesting aside, Sheriff Broward was a local steamboat pilot who later became Florida's governor. While in office Broward worked to improve the state's system of higher education, but he may best be known for his plans to drain the Everglades and reclaim the land for agriculture and development. Many people at the time considered the Everglades useless swampland and the drive to drain it and make the land "useful" gained a great deal of support from many citizens of Florida and beyond, including President Theodore Roosevelt. During his race for the governorship in 1904 Broward pledged to build an "Empire of the Everglades." To fulfill this promise, the state would have to destroy the swamp's intricate ecological systems by dredging, creating canals and altering the flow of water in these magnificent wetlands. Alarmed at the potential loss of the Everglades several early conservationists began pushing for their preservation as a direct result of Broward's proposals. Large portions of the swamp were drained before these environmentalists were able to convince society of the swamp's critical role in preserving the ecological system. Despite his ecologically unsound plan and the loss of a percentage of the swamp, Sheriff Broward did the world an unwitting favor by drawing attention to the dangers of the loss of this vital cog in Florida's environment.

After dealing with the requisite, but mostly irrelevant, police warrants for prizefighting, Corbett's party left Jacksonville by train at 11:00 a.m. on January 26.[15] The train headed up the East Coast, stopping for brunch in Washington at 10:00 a.m. the following day. Following a good meal, they were back on the tracks within thirty minutes. The special four-car train sped northward arriving at the Pennsylvania Railroad station in Jersey City at half past three that afternoon. After a ferry boat ride across the Hudson River, they were back in New York where Dempsey was scheduled to appear on the undercard of an exhibition bout between Corbett and Australian middleweight champion Dan Creedon at Madison Square Garden. The event was a benefit in Corbett's honor during which the heavyweight champion would spar three rounds with the Australian. Eight thousand spectators were in attendance for a full night of boxing.

In one of the preliminary bouts, Jack and Denny Costigan met in a three-round exhibition. When Dempsey was introduced by William A. Brady, the crowd cheered wildly and demanded a speech. Dempsey bowed and politely declined, insisting to the crowd that he was no public speaker and soon the bout began. "Thereupon Dempsey went at his old pal and sparring partner Denny Costigan and punched him all around the ring. Denny panted and sweated and the audience exhorted Jack to knock him out, but the courtly Nonpareil simply punched and jabbed poor Denny until there was very little fight left in him."[16] Jack was noted to be fairly spry and in quite good condition, but his weight was noticeably down. "Dempsey has grown very thin of late, but his popularity has by no means been lessened."[17]

No sooner had the Dempsey-Costigan match ended than a roar went up from the crowd—Corbett had left his dressing room and was heading for the ring. For a full five minutes the arena was a cacophony of cheers, clapping, foot stomping, shouts and whistles. In the main event, Corbett outboxed Creedon over three rounds even though he was troubled by his left hand, which he had injured several days earlier while beating on Charley Mitchell in Jacksonville.

In February, Dempsey indicated that he would still welcome a bout with Dick Burge. He stated that he was positive he could win and would welcome any reasonable offer for a purse and side wager. There was speculation that Jack would accompany Corbett to England in April and attempt to set a contest with Burge for that timeframe.[18]

On the evenings of February 8 and 10, Jack refereed amateur bouts sponsored by the Columbia Athletic Club at Grand Central Palace on Lexington Avenue and Forty-Third Street in Manhattan. Shortly afterwards Jack and Denny Costigan hit the road again, this time appearing in a revival of William A. Brady's play *After Dark*. As usual, the pair sparred four rounds during each show of the production. On Tuesday, February 13, they performed in the Academy of Music in Roanoke, Virginia.[19] The *Roanoke Times* reported the next day that the performance "scarcely aroused the enthusiasm of those present."[20]

During this time persistent rumors of a fight to be held in Chicago swirled around Dempsey and either Tommy Ryan or "Mysterious" Billy Smith. While both bouts would occur, neither came about immediately and Jack continued to spar in shows, but mostly he stayed out of the ring and rested for the remainder of the spring and summer.

The *Omaha Daily Bee* stated, "On April 7, Jack Dempsey will essay to knock out Harry Wyatt in eight rounds at Buffalo." Referring to his recent illnesses and ring troubles, the paper went on to say, "Jack had better give up fighting and get into the stable. He couldn't knock out anybody in eight rounds."[21] The gloved bout was scheduled as the marquee event in a night of boxing to be held at the theater at the Star Athletic Club. On the whole, the evening's eight bouts were described by local newspapers as having "little science and less slugging."

Harry Wyatt, an employee at Buffalo's Star Theater, was a popular pugilist in the Niagara-Erie region during the 1880s and 1890s. While not well known outside of that area he had gained a local reputation as a capable boxer who could stand his ground against any competition. His presence at pugilistic events helped to drive up attendance. One report of an exhibition from March 31, 1892, noted that Wyatt was detained at his job and unable to get away for a scheduled bout with another local fighter named Mike Glavine. The *Buffalo Express* noted that "the unavoidable absence of Harry Wyatt from the boxing and wrestling entertainment of the 74th Regiment A.A. at the Armory last night detracted considerably from the interest of the affair."[22] The 74th Regiment decided to remedy what was termed "the unfortunate incident" by scheduling an additional evening of boxing the following Friday night featuring Wyatt and Glavine with the prize to the winner being a gold watch.

The 1894 match between Dempsey and Wyatt was scheduled as an eight-round glove contest. Reports about the agreed upon terms of this bout are a little cloudy with some claiming that to win, Dempsey had to knock Wyatt out or force a withdrawal. Other reports stated that a points win was enough. Either way, it was a battle that Wyatt took very seriously. Many believed that the *Omaha Daily Bee* was correct in their assessment that Jack might have a challenge on his hands. Contests under ten rounds had never been his forte, and with Wyatt's size and the fact that it was a gloved contest, all of these factors were working against Dempsey as he entered the ring that night.

Referee William Welch called the pugilists to center ring and began the fight. The men danced around each other for most of the first round, barely throwing a punch, much less connecting. Wyatt was respecting the legend of the Nonpareil, but not yet realizing that the man in front of him was more of a shadow of that great fighter. Over the next three rounds, Wyatt jabbed with his left repeatedly, landing several times on Dempsey's face. He got in several good rights as well, while Jack barely landed a hard shot. Dempsey looked sluggish and out of condition. In the fifth, sixth and seventh rounds, both men fought cautiously, but Wyatt continued to be the more consistent aggressor. "The eighth was a little more-lively but Wyatt, having much the better of the contest in points, received the decision."[23] This was merely an exhibition and simply by avoiding getting knocked out, Wyatt won the bout, but once again it was clear that Dempsey was no longer the legendary Nonpareil who just a few years before would have quite probably made short work of Wyatt—gloves or not. Taking nothing away from the Buffalo man who was, by all accounts that I've seen, a creditable fighter, Dempsey was clearly no longer on his game—or at least not consistently. His health was up and down from day to day and with it, his ability to train and fully utilize his once formidable skills in the ring. Jack would take some more time off to rest after this Buffalo engagement.

After several months of inactivity and rest, Jack was feeling much better and determined to enter the ring again. Dempsey's backers got to work and he was soon scheduled to meet Billy McCarthy over twenty rounds on September 5 for what was billed as a rematch of their 1890 hook up in San Francisco. This time the pair would meet for a $2,000 purse with the winner to take $1,500. The men agreed to the 154-pound weight limit. The bout was scheduled for 9:00 p.m. in New Orleans at the Auditorium Athletic Club. In early August, it was reported that "Jack Dempsey is in training at Tybee Beach, Savannah, Georgia, with Denny Costigan for his fight with Billy McCarthy, the Australian, which is to take place August 25th before the Auditorium club of New Orleans." The report went on to say, "The Nonpareil is working earnestly as he realizes that McCarthy is a stout, hard fighter. Dempsey needs to pay more attention to preparatory work now than when he was a young champion. The Australian is very big and will have to toil like a coal heaver to get down to 154-pounds, the weight the articles of agreement call for."[24] The article while spot on in its analysis, cites an earlier proposed date for the bout.

Dempsey did the bulk of his training at Tybee Island near Savannah on the coast of Georgia and finished up in the gymnasium of the Young Men's Gymnastic Club of New Orleans. McCarthy trained earnestly and aggressively for over two months at Captain Smith's quarters in the upper district of New Orleans. While in training the Dempsey and Fitzsimmons camps toyed with the idea of a sparring exhibition in New Orleans the day before the McCarthy bout. Both camps and the promoters of their bouts soon thought better of this idea and the exhibition never came off.

As the much-anticipated fight drew near, many felt it would be close. "The contest at the Olympic club on September 5, between Jack Dempsey and Australian Billy McCarthy is coming to be recognized as a very even affair. There is no doubt but what both men have retrograded in the past few years, but it is the general opinion that both have gone back in the same degree. Dempsey is working at Savannah, while his coming antagonist is doing his training at New Orleans."[25]

On the night of the Dempsey-McCarthy bout, the Auditorium A.C. was full and the capacity crowd was anxious to see if Dempsey could again exhibit his old form or whether McCarthy would gain his revenge for his loss four years earlier. "The vast Auditorium was well crowded when John Duffy, as referee, and Johnny Dunn, as master of ceremonies, entered the ring."[26] Sam Stern was named as the timekeeper. McCarthy was seconded by Tom Green, Arthur Walker and Harry Black while Dempsey had Andy Bowen, James Dwyer and Billy Brown in his corner. Bob Fitzsimmons was expected to attend and was anxious to serve in the Nonpareil's corner but was asked not to by the president of the Olympic Club who feared that Ruby Robert would get chilled and not be at his best for his fight with Tom Creedon at the club on September 26.

Dempsey arrived at the arena just after 8:00 p.m. and went directly to his dressing room where he climbed into his familiar blue tights, warmed up and received a rub down from his trainer. At 9:05 p.m., McCarthy entered the ring with his seconds with Jack following shortly afterward. Johnny Dunn introduced the fighters and referee Duffy then called them forward. Time was called for the first round at 9:15 p.m.

Both men appeared to be in good condition and early on Dempsey showed the vigor that he was once known for. Jack's weight, however, was still down considerably and while he looked sharp, he was handicapped by his size and he failed to land many powerful blows. According to the *Baltimore Sun*, "Dempsey weighed at the ring 146-pounds and McCarthy 165."[27] The *National Police Gazette*, however, listed the weights at 140 pounds for Dempsey and 154 pounds for McCarthy. Either way, McCarthy outweighed the Nonpareil by somewhere between fifteen and twenty pounds. Despite saying he would not do so, here Dempsey fought a heavier man again.

The two men fought fiercely throughout the first round, but neither could open much of a lead. McCarthy was on the offensive early, but Dempsey scored the first noteworthy strike when he landed a body blow followed by a heavy left-right combination to the eye and jaw of his opponent. Both men then landed heavily. At one point McCarthy forced Jack into the corner where he landed a sharp left to the stomach. Jack returned fire catching his opponent on the nose and jaw. The round closed with Dempsey's fist landing hard on McCarthy's face. The scoring moderately favored Dempsey.

In the second round, Dempsey landed two left jabs on McCarthy's jaw. After another exchange in which Jack dropped a bomb on McCarthy's nose, the Australian clinched. McCarthy came out swinging and scored a right to the chest that backed Dempsey against the ropes, but Dempsey responded by opening an attack on Billy's head landing heavily to the Australian's nose, neck, body and jaw. The stave ended with the men sparring. This round too closed in Dempsey's favor.

"In the third round, the men clinched and then Jack landed a right on the jaw which nearly knocked Mac down. In the fourth Jack landed a heavy blow on the stomach, another on the nose and got away. In the fifth Jack was the aggressor and scored a right on the body."[28] The *National Police Gazette* noted that Dempsey's work "was done principally with his right after the third round as he sustained rather a painful injury to his left arm above the wrist at the same place where it had been broken in his fight with Reddy Gallagher."[29]

The sixth round saw McCarthy score big with a heavy blow to the body that nearly lifted Dempsey off the ground. Dempsey was forced to clinch to brace himself and recover. After the break, Jack connected with a bullet-like left to McCarthy's jaw. Both men continued to land heavily for the remainder of the session. The seventh was much the same as the previous round, with both fighters landing heavy blows, but the round ending in Dempsey's favor.

In the eighth round, Dempsey started fast, pummeling the Australian with a series of rapid strikes. "Mac clinched to avoid punishment. He missed a right on the jaw and nearly fell through the ropes. Dempsey continued his terrific rights on the body; both landed their lefts on the head and fell on the ropes. There were several clinches in the round mainly due to Dempsey's ring generalship. Jack landed two rights on the jaw just as time was called."[30]

From the eighth to the twentieth rounds, Dempsey controlled the fight, but he could not knock the larger man out. At the start of the twentieth and final round, the two fighters met at center ring and Jack with a broad smile on his face extended his hand to McCarthy. The men shook hands as the referee called "fight." Both men started out cautiously at first, but suddenly, McCarthy began swinging his right wildly. Jack, showing his old form, avoided most of the blows and any real damage. After the flurry from McCarthy, the men began to spar cautiously again. Dempsey landed a hard right on McCarthy's jaw that clearly slowed the Australian, causing Mac to clinch in order to regain his bearing. As the men wrestled, Dempsey, anxious to get the heavier man off him, threw McCarthy to the ground. The Australian was up in an instant. The rest of the round saw the two men spar cautiously as they both continued to look for the opening that never came. Dempsey landed on McCarthy's jaw just as time was called. When the gong sounded ending the fight, a smiling Dempsey extended his hand to McCarthy in a friendly greeting and McCarthy responded. Each man had earned the other's respect. According to the articles of agreement, since both men were still on their feet, the referee declared the bout a draw.

While both men fought fiercely, it was evident that Dempsey got the better of the fight. The *National Police Gazette* reported that, "had the contest been awarded on points scored, Dempsey would have won in a walk, as he walked around the Australian like a cooper around a barrel and planted his gloves whenever and wherever he willed." While noting that McCarthy fought a game bout and "was by no means a whipped man at the end of the contest," the report added, "McCarthy overtowered Dempsey in height and had nine pounds [sic] the advantage in weight, but he was completely out-generaled and never had a chance from the start to the finish."[31] The *San Francisco Call* claimed that Dempsey was once again close to his old form.[32] Others stated that "Dempsey displayed much of his old time cleverness and made the better fight all the way, but McCarthy stood the punishment gamely and the Nonpareil lacked the force to put him out. The fight was declared a draw at the end of twenty rounds. On points Dempsey should have had the decision."[33] The *New York Sun* reported, "The match was interesting, as showing whether the Nonpareil had retained anything of his famous skill. McCarthy put up a very clever bout but was clearly outpointed by Dempsey all the way through. He out-generaled the Australian and could have put him out."[34] The paper contended that Jack, based on the strength of this bout, would gain strong backing for future ring appearances. Due to the lack of a knockout, however, the fight was declared a draw at the end of the twentieth round, "in accordance with articles of agreement, which stipulated that if both men were on their feet at the close of the twentieth round, the contest was to be declared a draw."[35] The purse of $2,000 was then divided evenly. The *Chicago Tribune* stated in their article sub-heading, "Early in the fight Dempsey shows the vim that once made him a champion but handicapped by a big difference in weight fails to land a decisive blow."[36]

The subject of the Nonpareil's health came up yet again in the days after the fight. The *Pittsburgh Press* reported that "Australian 'Billy' McCarthy, who secured a draw with Jack Dempsey last week, passed through Pittsburgh yesterday on his way east. McCarthy says that while Dempsey still retains his wonderful science, he no longer has the power to deliver a blow in which there is the slightest harm. While he could not get near Dempsey and the Nonpareil had pretty much his own way with him, McCarthy says Dempsey could not knock him out in a year."[37] McCarthy's comment was not delivered with any bitterness or malice—it was simply a practical observation that helped spell out the decline in Dempsey's strength and health in general.

Dempsey had fought very well and the crowd and assembled reporters agreed that with the exception of the absent power, he looked much like the fighter of old. It was comforting, like seeing an old friend, but it would be a brief reunion. On this evening in New Orleans, Dempsey was on his game again. Jack's stamina and health held up that night. He worked hard, dug deep and made a terrific showing, but as time would reveal, an era was ending. While Jack Dempsey would enter the ring again, this was the last time an assembled crowd would see the Nonpareil dance in the squared circle.

After his bout with McCarthy, Dempsey remained in the Crescent City and was a part of Fitzsimmons's training team for Ruby Robert's upcoming battle with fellow New Zealander Dan Creedon. Fitzsimmons asked Jack to be in his corner on September 26 along with James Dwyer, Kid McCoy and Sam H. Stern, and of course the Nonpareil was happy to oblige. The bout was held at the New Orleans Olympic Club. The battle ended in the middle of the second round when Fitzsimmons landed a terrific left-hand blow to Creedon's jaw that dropped Creedon for the count.

As was predicted, based on the strength of his performance against McCarthy, Dempsey was in demand again. While many believed he should, he simply could not walk away. On October 4, it was announced that Jack would meet welterweight champion Tommy Ryan in a twenty-five-round contest or a finish fight, at the option of the Auditorium Club of New Orleans. Dempsey was represented at a meeting in Chicago by Dominick O'Malley and Ryan by Parson Davies. The bout was originally proposed to be held on November 7, but it was decided that the contest could not be arranged that quickly nor could the fighters be ready. Instead, the fight was scheduled for December 12 for a $5,000 purse with $4,500 going to the winner and $500 to the runner up. The men were to weigh in at 144 pounds. Professor John Duffy was named as the referee.[38]

The 24-year-old Ryan began his ring career in 1887 by knocking out John Case in five rounds. He then continued his successes, knocking out sixteen of his next seventeen opponents, with only one no contest to mar a string of victories which ran through December of 1891. He first entered the ring while working in a railroad construction camp in Michigan. Boxing historian Tracy Callis describes Ryan as an innovative, smart and scrappy fighter. He was quick, elusive, tough and powerful. Ryan would be ranked by *The Ring* magazine founder Nat Fleischer as the number two all-time middleweight and by a good many others as number one.

Ryan won the championship from "Mysterious" Billy Smith in July when the Chicagoan was granted a points decision by referee Joe Choynski after twenty rounds at the Twin Cities Athletic Club in Minneapolis. Smith stated that he would be in New Orleans for the Dempsey-Ryan bout and he would challenge the winner to fight for $5,000.

In preparing for Ryan, Dempsey initially set up his training camp at Tybee Island, Georgia, and remained there through October and much of November. By December, he traveled to New Orleans where he continued his training. He worked out daily with several fighters, including local favorite Andy Bowen. Bowen and Dempsey were sparring partners and the two were to be in the other's corners in their respective upcoming bouts. On December 6, Bowen and Dempsey put on a four-round sparring exhibition in Savannah, Georgia, just before they broke camp and boarded a train west for New Orleans, arriving there on December 13.

Dempsey and Bowen were each scheduled to fight in a series of contests which were to take place in the Crescent City as part of a three-bout showcase pitting James Barry and Kid Madden on December 13, followed by a December 14 engagement between George "Kid" Lavigne and Andy Bowen and the final bout between Dempsey and Ryan on the following evening. What actually occurred was a tragic ending for one fighter in particular and for boxing in New Orleans in general.

The Barry-Madden fight never came off, as Madden backed out just before the event. In the second of the scheduled bouts, lightweight champion Lavigne knocked Bowen down in the eighteenth round, resulting in Bowen hitting his head awkwardly on the hard, canvas-covered, wooden floor and being knocked unconscious. The knockout blow was described as follows, "Lavigne feinted with his left, and as Bowen ducked, Lavigne's elbow caught Bowen's chin. As the latter straightened up, Lavigne caught Bowen on the point of the jaw with his right and he went down and out."[39]

The fallen fighter was carried from the ring to his dressing room and treated by doctors at the scene. Soon, he was removed from the Club and carried to his home, a pretty little cottage on Thalia Street, separated from the road by beautiful gardens. Bowen and his doctors were met at the door by the fighter's wife and mother. "The physicians who had been called into Bowen's room at the club, accompanied him home and reinforced by the family physician, remained with him to the end."[40] For a while, the Bowen's family physician Dr. Finney and the two other attending physicians, doctors Schubert and Hannan, believed Andy to be rallying, but it was only temporary. In the early morning, Dr. Ed Martin was asked to examine Bowen, but pronounced that there was very little to be done. Around 7:00 a.m., Mrs. Bowen, who had been by her husband's side all night, held his hand and said, "Oh, Andy, say something to me." Bowen seemed to react but could not respond. Despite the attending physicians' best efforts, the young pugilist died of brain injuries at 7:15 on the morning after the fight. He died while receiving last rites by his priest, Father Delaney. He never regained consciousness after hitting his head on the floor. "Bowen's death unleashed a torrent of criticism that forced the cancellation of the third fight, a welterweight championship match featuring Tommy Ryan and Jack Dempsey."[41]

While it was universally conceded that Lavigne's blow to his opponent's jaw had sent Bowen down, it was also agreed that the concussion produced by Bowen's head crashing against the hardwood floor was what killed the New Orleans pugilist. Regardless, Lavigne, his seconds and timekeeper, as well as the referee John Duffy, were all placed under arrest by the New Orleans police. An autopsy would be required to determine the cause of Bowen's death.

New Orleans Mayor John Fitzpatrick had been a witness to the fight and was at Bowen's side as he was carried from the ring. The series of fights had been scheduled under a permit signed by the mayor, and when the stricken fighter was taken to his home, Fitzpatrick was under the impression that Bowen was on the mend. He was shocked the next morning when he learned that Bowen had died. Shortly after the mayor reached his office that morning, he revoked the license for the Dempsey-Ryan match scheduled for later that evening. Mayor Fitzpatrick said of the affair, "I do not know what effect the death of Bowen will have on pugilism in the future." Like many others, he speculated that the unpadded floor and not the punch itself was the culprit. Fitzpatrick, recalling what he had seen, reiterated that the blow from Lavigne was not particularly powerful. "If death was caused by the blow which Lavigne struck, then the sport is dead, but if death resulted from Bowen's head striking the floor, then the death was attributable to a circumstance which can be avoided in the future."[42]

Dempsey was said to be greatly distraught over the death of his good friend Bowen. Jack could hardly talk about the event without tears welling up in his eyes. "Dempsey was found last night on Rampart Street where he said he was vainly trying to drown his sorrow." Dempsey spoke of his distaste for those who called prizefighters heartless brutes. "I'm not a brute. I have a heart," declared Jack. He denounced the carpenters for not placing padding under the canvas in the ring and he stated firmly, "I had rather have lost 100 fights than to have seen Bowen killed."[43] Jack also got wind of a comment, reportedly made by Ryan, that it was a good thing for Dempsey that Bowen had died and the bout had been called off. Jack was furious and went looking for Ryan, who he called a cur for making such a comment. By all accounts he was ready to call the Chicagoan out and challenge him to a bare-knuckle fight to the finish then and there. Upon hearing that Dempsey was on the warpath, Ryan declined the challenge and he and his backers boarded a train for Chicago determined not to meet an enraged Dempsey that day. Though he was the larger man and the favorite going into the now postponed fight, Ryan knew this was not the time to engage the Nonpareil. Ryan, Parson Davies and Joe Choynski headed north to the Windy City where Ryan began nightly sparring exhibitions in that city with Choynski as his partner. The sparring would help keep Ryan sharp while he waited for his contest with Dempsey to be rescheduled.

At nine o'clock on the morning after the fight, Lavigne and his party were taken to the Third Precinct station where charges of murder and accessory to murder were made against them. The men appeared in a crowded courtroom in front of Judge Aucoin. After arraignment, bail was set at $10,000 for Lavigne and $5,000 for each of the others. The hearing date for the case was set by Judge Aucoin for January 2.

At 1:00 p.m. that afternoon, New Orleans coroner Laurensen, assisted by doctors John Lawrens and E. Denegre Martin, performed an autopsy. Also present was a five-man jury to observe and make notes to be used in the inquest. The verdict reached after the inquest was "that the death of Bowen was probably caused by his head's striking the hard floor, for if it had been caused by the blow, his neck would have been broken."[44]

George "Kid" Lavigne.

Jack determined to remain in New Orleans for now to assist Bowen's family as they began to cope with the sudden and difficult realities of Andy's unexpected death.

At Bowen's home, his wife and mother were beside themselves with grief, so Dempsey took an active role in funeral and burial planning. A visitation was arranged at the fighter's Thalia Street home for Sunday. The funeral was held on the morning of Monday, December 17, and was attended by hundreds of Bowen's friends and admirers. Lavigne, his manager Sam Fitzpatrick, referee John Duffy, Billy McCarthy and of course Dempsey, were among the notables present. "Conspicuous among the floral offerings was a large white cross erected upon a bed of white roses and having upon the cross bar the simple word 'Andy.'" At the base of the cross were delicate pink roses and a card that read, "With the sympathy of George Lavigne and Sam Fitzpatrick."[45] Upon entering the room in which Bowen lay, Lavigne knelt by the casket and was so affected that he had to be assisted before he could leave.

The city Attorney General notified the Auditorium and the Olympic clubs that no more fights would be permitted until the Bowen case was settled. Ultimately, Bowen's death was ruled an accident due to his banging his head on the wooden floor. The club was censured for not padding the floor, but nothing more came of it. Cleared of the murder charges on December 27, Lavigne and his staff wasted no time in leaving town.

In late December, it was announced that a new date and venue had been selected for the Ryan-Dempsey bout. On the evening of December 28, Parson Davies received a telegram from the Atlantic Athletic Club's matchmaker, E.J. "Eddie" Stoddard, stating that Dempsey had agreed to the terms of a fight with Ryan at catch weights and a $3,000 purse over fifteen rounds. Upon receipt of Stoddard's message, Davies made travel plans to go to New York where he would "personally settle the details of the match, which may now be regarded as a fixture." Davies left Chicago almost immediately, boarding a 10:30 train to New York that evening.[46]

The contest was set for the evening of January 14, 1895, and was to be held at the Atlantic A.C. at Coney Island. Jack would return home to Brooklyn to fight for the first time in several years. The terms that were finally worked out called for a twenty-five-round contest at catch weights, with the winner to take half of the net receipts. Davies and Stoddard met in New York several times to work out the final points of the contract. Stoddard, Davies, Dempsey and his backers then met to sign the agreement in the athletic club's offices on New Year's Day.

In addition to his negotiations with Davies, Stoddard was also working on setting up a two-fight undercard. With the fight just over two weeks away, his task was to find fighters who were both still available on that night and already in some semblance of fighting condition. Stoddard was very successful in his task. The hastily scheduled preliminary bouts were set to include Sammy Campbell and Frank Patterson followed by a matching of Charley McKeever and Mike Leonard.

The odds makers in New Orleans had set the fight at 100 to 60 in Ryan's favor in mid–December. The odds makers in New York were being no more charitable to Dempsey in setting the early odds. It was estimated that "fully 80 per cent" of the sports in Gotham believed that Ryan would defeat the former Nonpareil. "There has been no betting aside from a few small wagers and Ryan in these had first choice."[47] Many felt that the outlook for Dempsey's career was bleak and would probably not get better. Others without so fatalistic an outlook for Dempsey's career still believed that Ryan was too large an opponent for Jack. "Dempsey's friends in this part of the country are all hopeful, but many of them fear he has made a mistake."[48]

1895—Tommy Ryan and the End

As reported in the *Brooklyn Eagle* on December 31, 1894, Parson Davies, Tommy Ryan's manager, was to meet with officials of the Atlantic Athletic Club at the Grand Union Hotel on New Year's Day, 1895, to sign the agreement for the rescheduled Ryan-Dempsey affair. The Atlantic A.C. officials included Eddie Stoddard, who was also serving in the capacity as Dempsey's representative. The articles were drawn up and the match was proposed for January 14 at the Sea Beach Palace in Coney Island.

Davies was quite ready to sign, his only stipulation being that the bout be held before January 20. The officials of the Atlantic A.C. however were insisting on a later date because it would be impossible to get a steam heating plant installed in the Sea Beach Palace by that time and they did not wish to risk losing attendance due to a frigid arena. The matter was settled when "Jimmie Kennedy, the hustling matchmaker of the Seaside A.C., was called into consultation and it was finally arranged that the Seaside A.C. should take the three bouts arranged for by Mr. Stoddard off the hands of the Atlantic A.C. and run them on January 18, the night before the Dixon-Griffo contest."[1] With all arrangements consented to, the satisfied parties signed the articles of agreement and Davies boarded a train back to Chicago. Davies was scheduled to make a quick turnaround as he and Ryan would head east for Ryan's training camp at Coney Island within the week.

In an interview, Brooklyn Mayor Charles A. Schieren stated that while he was personally against prizefights, he would accept a bout of scientific boxing. Schieren continued his remarks to the reporter by placing the responsibility for keeping order at the match on the local constabulary. The mayor stated that "it now remains with the police department to determine where scientific boxing ends and prize fighting begins."[2]

With agreements signed, the fighters in training and officialdom—while not quite supportive, but at least accepting—the bout looked like a sure thing, but legal maneuverings eventually reared their ugly head and for a while it looked like they might derail the contest. Several members of the Atlantic A.C. were less than pleased with the fact that while their membership had collectively put up the greatest amount of money in support of the contest, the fight card was now being held at the rival Seaside A.C. There was some speculation that the bouts might be delayed if the club members who were dissatisfied with the arrangements invoked the aid of the courts to nullify the transferring of the bouts. The concern, while real, was easily handled and the whole issue was quickly put to bed when Eddie Stoddard made it clear that had the Seaside not been able to accept the bouts, there would have been no agreement with Ryan and Dempsey due to the lack of a properly heated arena at the Atlantic A.C., and the fact that the Atlantic could not pay the required travel and training expenses for the fighters. When asked about the rumor of a shady deal to transfer the bouts, Mr. Williamson, secretary of the Seaside club, stated without hesitation that "there was no necessity for a deal, the Atlantics could not hold it, and the Seaside was the only other bidder."[3]

For several days in early January there was speculation about Dempsey's whereabouts. He had reportedly left New Orleans but had not yet arrived at his training camp in Brooklyn. Some claimed that he had taken ill again and others that he was on a drinking binge. Some said he was in Chicago, still others said he had gone home to Portland. In short, no one seemed to know where Jack was. When Gus Tuthill, who had recently returned to New York himself, was asked about Dempsey's whereabouts, he replied, "I haven't seen Jack for some time. I have been away on a shooting trip and just got back to town. I don't know whether he has been drinking, but from what I hear, this must be the case."[4] This was a rare admission from Tuthill, that Dempsey had any problems at all. Reminders of his disappearance in Minneapolis before his scheduled bout with "Mysterious" Billy Smith were bandied about in several newspaper stories. In truth, Jack, while most certainly drinking, was on board a steamer and making his way to the city.

At 10:30 p.m. on January 9, Jack arrived in New York from New Orleans on the Cromwell Line steamship *Hudson*. The steamer had been expected that morning but had been delayed by fog. Dempsey was reported to be in splendid condition and would immediately resume serious training for the bout with Ryan. The steamer was met by Seaside A.C. matchmaker Jimmy Kennedy, some fans and the press. At an impromptu press conference on the pier, "Dempsey laughed when told of published reports that he had been drinking heavily of late. He said: 'I have not been drinking, and I don't intend to. I am in splendid health but must get rid of some fat. I weigh about 153 pounds but will enter the ring at about 140.'"[5] He told the crowd that he had been training hard in New Orleans and was in good fighting trim before the bout with Ryan had been called off by the civic ban in December. He had continued doing some light exercising on board the *Hudson* during the voyage and felt that he was in fair condition. With eight days remaining until the fight, Jack told those gathered at the pier that he had plenty of time to complete his training.

After spending the night at a Manhattan hotel, Jack continued the next day by carriage to Brooklyn accompanied by Stoddard and Jimmy Allers. They traveled to his friend Jimmy Carroll's Brooklyn House on Coney Island Boulevard where he would be quartered for the next week while he trained. Upon his arrival, he was greeted by Carroll and other friends who joined him in a light lunch.

After lunch, Dempsey traveled to the Seaside Club where he was to select a locker room, check out the training facilities and schedule a meeting with Ryan. The meeting was seen as a goodwill session to smooth things over after Jack had cursed Ryan and sought him out in New Orleans following Ryan's declarations to reporters that it was a lucky thing for Dempsey that Andy Bowen was dead. Jack tried in vain to find Ryan before the latter left for Chicago to challenge him to a fight with bare knuckles in private and to the finish. After their meeting at the Seaside, Jack told reporters that Ryan explained that he had only meant that the postponement had saved Dempsey from a beating, and he apologized for his poor choice of words. Accepting the apology, but not entirely satisfied, Jack still chastised Ryan stating, "He might have had the decency to wait until poor Bowen was buried before making such a declaration."[6]

Jack had a full day of training on Saturday, January 12. He reportedly walked, ran and sprinted a total of sixteen miles in the morning. This was followed by a steam bath and a vigorous rub down followed by a quick plunge in the ocean. The wisdom of diving into the frigid Atlantic in January can be debated, but Jack always did so when in training near the sea. After lunch, Jack hit the heavy bag for forty-five minutes, exercised with weights, jumped rope and swung the Indian clubs. He ended up his busy day of training by sparring "a rattling" six rounds with Jack McAuliffe. The days of heavy training continued this way for the next week.

Several days later, as Dempsey finished what was reported to be a vigorous day that included a ten-mile run, forty-five minutes on the heavy bag and a long session jumping rope and lifting dumbbells, he was asked if he felt ready and if he thought that that he could defeat Ryan. Jack just smiled and said, "Ryan never saw the day and never will that he can best me."[7]

Ryan continued to train in Chicago until January 12, when he, Joe Choynski and twenty-five friends boarded a train bound for New York. They arrived on the evening of January 13 and proceeded to Stubenbord's Hotel where they met Parson Davies and set up camp. Upon his arrival in New York, Ryan told the waiting press, "Dempsey will find out that I am a fighter." He added, "I think I will have a very easy time."[8]

It was arranged for Ryan to do his New York–based training at the gymnasium of the Manhattan Athletic Club on Madison Avenue and Forty-Fifth Street. At times, when he held open workouts, as many as two-hundred spectators were said to be on hand.[9] Like the Nonpareil, Ryan also got in some roadwork, time with the dumbbells, bag work and rope jumping. He worked hard and appeared to be in good condition. Joe Choynski, acting as Ryan's trainer, commented, "Ryan will require very little exercise. He will punch the bag, spar with me and do some light all-around work, including running on the track in the club-house. He will not do anything outdoors." Choynski added that he considered Ryan to be in excellent shape for the fight. Ryan noted that he always took good care of himself through exercise and diet and he pointed out that he neither drank nor smoked.[10]

The great Tommy Ryan was known for his quickness, science and power in the ring.

The Nonpareil's last bout was held on January 18, 1895, at the Seaside Athletic Club in Coney Island, not but a few miles from where he grew up, had worked as a barrel maker and where his pugilistic career had begun in 1883. The *Philadelphia Record* commented in the days prior to the bout that "It has been some years since a prize fight in this vicinity has attracted such a widespread interest as the proposed 15-round contest between Jack Dempsey, the once famous Nonpareil and the middleweight champion of America; and Tommy Ryan of Chicago, who is now regarded as the cleverest welterweight in the United States."[11] While many felt that Dempsey was washed up and that Ryan would emerge victorious, both men had certain advantages going into the bout. Jack was clearly one of the all-time great ring generals. He was also clever and knew no fear. These were traits that would never fail him. Also in his favor was that he was fighting in front of a supportive, hometown crowd who by and large thought the world of him. "Ryan has youth and strength in his favor. He is as quick as a cat and in order to win must force the fighting from the very start. Dempsey on the contrary, will be more than apt to fight on the defensive and in case he finds that he cannot win, will fight for a draw if possible."[12]

The three-bout event on January 18 was the first of a two-night boxing show being promoted at the club. Following the three-bout card on Friday night, the Seaside A.C. would host three more fights the following evening featuring George Dixon of Boston and Australian fighter Young Griffo and an undercard showcasing another Australian, Mick Dunn, and Fred Woods of Philadelphia as well as a six-rounder between Brooklyn's Jack Madden and England's 105-pound champion Eddie Vaughn. The boxing card that Kennedy had put together was being touted as one of the most interesting ever. "At no time in the history of Long Island has there been such an aggregation of pugilistic talent brought together as James Kennedy, the matchmaker of the Seaside Athletic Club, has succeeded in signing for the coming carnival to be held by the club he represents this week."[13] Best estimates state that between four thousand five hundred and five thousand fans paid between one dollar and ten for a seat in the club to see the full card headed by Dempsey and Ryan. Clearly, however, the main story was Dempsey. The local Brooklyn crowd was anxious to watch Jack to see if the Nonpareil had finally returned to form or, if not, if this might just be his final bout in the prize ring. Given the large number of patrons heading to the Seaside Athletic Club's Coney Island amphitheater for the two nights of boxing, special arrangements had been made with the railroad companies to run additional trains before and after the matches so that the patrons would not be subjected to the inconvenience of waiting for undue amounts of time in the cold January air.

The first evening's event began at 8:45 p.m., when ring announcer Fred Burns informed the crowd that baseball umpire Tim Hurst would referee all fights on the card. That night's first match began at 9:00 p.m., with a bout that featured an eight-round match at 122 pounds between Frank Patterson of New York and Sammy Campbell of Brooklyn. In the heated contest Patterson took an eight-round decision. Despite Campbell's advantage in reach, Patterson was the stronger and more scientific boxer of the two. The fight was described as clean, fast-paced and rattling. While Campbell was game and fought well, Patterson took the first round and he never let up. Patterson drew first blood in the third round and throughout the contest out punched and showed better defense than Campbell.

Next up was the ten-rounder between Jimmy Dime of Amsterdam, New York, and Australian Jerry Marshall. Both fighters were in good shape with Dime outweighing his opponent 130 pounds to 126. The first round was scored even with both fighters landing several good blows upon their opponent. In the second round, Marshall landed a hard blow to Dime's nose, but Dime countered with a powerful uppercut that found the Australian's chin. Marshall tried roughhouse and rushing tactics, but Dime's defense held. The crowd began to stir by the fifth round, looking for more clear-cut action and Dime did not disappoint, landing several strong shots to his opponent's rib cage and forcing him to clinch to avoid further punishment.

The next three rounds saw a great deal of action as the two pugilists traded heavy blows. Marshall landed stinging combinations to Dime's body and jaw, but Dime stood steady and returned the blows. Both men were quick on defense and thereby avoided serious punishment. This pattern continued in the ninth and tenth rounds, with both men ducking to avoid blows and countering with hard smashes. Dime again caught Marshall over his heart and heavily on the jaw and Marshall landed a left just as the bell rang ending the ninth. In the tenth, Dime ducked away from several punches and then caught Marshall on the mouth, jaw and stomach. While Marshall was game and continued to fight and land punches, he was clearly beginning to show fatigue. When the bell rang, Hurst declared Dime the victor.

After the two preliminaries were over, the crowd settled in for the main event, but they would have to cool their heels as Dempsey was not yet in the arena. There had been rumors about Dempsey's condition in the days before the fight and his tardy appearance did nothing to quiet concern among the crowd.

Ryan was the first to enter the ring. The crowd was hushed as they sized up the Chicagoan. "He looked splendid. His complexion was clear as a bell and his pompadour hair erect as a lightning rod. He stripped in magnificent shape, his muscles standing out like whip cords."[14] He weighed 145 pounds. Ryan looked supremely confident as he immediately headed for the "lucky" corner—that which had been previously occupied by the victors, Patterson and Dime. In Ryan's corner that night was an impressive assemblage of pugilistic knowledge. His seconds for the evening were "Chrysanthemum Joe" Choynski, heavyweight of San Francisco, Canadian lightweight Harry Pigeon, Australian welterweight Mick Dunn of Sydney and featherweight George Siddons of New York. Ryan smiled and bowed to the crowd as he took his seat in his corner.

About this time, a cheer went up as Dempsey entered the building. He waved and acknowledged the crowd as he made his way to the dressing room. Jack looked terrible. He had been rumored to have been on a bender the evening before that did not end until the sun began to rise. The *New York Evening World* reported that the fight's promoter Parson Davies was aghast when he saw the horrific condition Dempsey was in as he entered the arena. He approached Jack and "argued with him in his dressing room before he showed himself to the crowd, urging him to let it go by default, but no, he would go and went to his ruin."[15]

Dempsey entered the ring at 10:55 p.m. to tumultuous applause and shouts that raised the rafters of the Seaside Club. There was a buzz among the crowd as Jack clearly did not appear to be himself. One report noted, "His face appeared to be drawn and he wore a mustache that made him look unnatural."[16] Jack was accompanied by Brooklyn middleweight Jimmy Carroll, local featherweight Frank Patterson and Jack's brother, Martin Dempsey.

Regardless of his appearance, when Jack was introduced, the crowd cheered wildly. He took a reserved bow and sat down in his corner, but something seemed off. The Nonpareil did not just look bad, he appeared weak and even a bit off balance. Dempsey "fidgeted nervously as he took the loser's corner, and took a long pull at a bottle."[17] When he took off his sweater Jack appeared to be in adequate, but not particularly good, shape. By most accounts he was a bit light. His weight was down slightly as he weighed in at 142 pounds and what was there was not as lean as usual.

Just after 11:00 p.m., the men approached center ring along with referee Tim Hurst. Ryan wore a breach clout and Dempsey his customary long blue trunks. The men shook hands at 11:05 p.m. Hurst instructed the pair to box. The men circled for a minute, each sparring lightly to size one another up and look for an opening. Ryan then struck, hitting Dempsey twice on the side of Jack's head and once on his nose. Dempsey tried to land with two swings, but both missed. Ryan struck again, this time landing on Dempsey's neck. The Nonpareil missed again with a left. His punches were weak and listless, there was no snap and most fell short of their mark. Jack was slow and appeared helpless to get out of the way of or even block his opponent's punches. It was clear from the outset that something was seriously wrong and that Jack was in trouble. This was not the Nonpareil of old. The *New York Times* reported, "He acted like a man in a trance, and the round consisted of little else than a series of pushes."[18]

In the second round, the crowd began to get restless. Ryan struck a light blow to Dempsey's face. Jack countered and landed but did little damage with his blow as the Chicagoan clinched and smiled. On the break, Ryan hit Dempsey hard on the neck and Jack became wobbly. He was as unsteady on his feet as a newborn colt. Tommy stepped back out of what appeared to be a blend of shock and mercy for his once unstoppable opponent. The crowd hissed their disapproval and Ryan resumed his attack. Ryan landed several shots to Dempsey's midsection and then landed to the jaw—all unanswered. After another blow to the mouth and one to the body, Ryan hit Jack on the jaw and sent him to the canvas. The bell tolled as Jack staggered to his feet. From the crowd came shouts of "Take him off!" and "Dempsey's drunk!"[19]

During the third round, Dempsey tried desperately to rally. He was mad and clearly frustrated as he searched for skills that were once so natural, but that had now clearly abandoned him. Jack rushed his opponent, but Ryan fended him off and forced the Nonpareil to the ropes, where he continued to land combinations at will with only modest resistance from the former champion. No matter what Dempsey tried, Ryan stopped it as he simply controlled the fight. "Ryan hit Dempsey whenever he wished on the mouth and in the face, and, in response to frequent yells of the spectators, the gong sounded out, and the fight was stopped."[20]

Announcer Fred Burns said that against Jack's wishes, Dempsey's friends requested that the bout be stopped. Jack argued vehemently with Hurst for the fight to go on, but it was evident to all that he was in no condition to fight. According to the *Baltimore American*, "Ryan could have knocked Dempsey out in the first round, but he let up on the once famous Nonpareil."[21]

Clearly, stopping the fight was the correct decision. As one reporter at ringside observed, "Ryan played with Dempsey as a cat would toy with a mouse."[22] What few in the arena realized was that Jack had no business being in the ring that night. He was badly weakened by tuberculosis, his body showing the signs of the consumption that would take his life. He was mortally ill and had less than ten months to live. He had also been drinking heavily before and during the fight. In a note that clearly explains much about Dempsey's uncharacteristically weak and lackluster performance, the *Brooklyn Eagle* reported that "just before the fight Dempsey was drinking hot whiskey, which may have accounted in some measure for his condition. Dr. Ward has been treating him for a week past for lung and bronchial troubles."[23] Commenting the day after the fight, the *New York Sun* stated, "A ghost of the Nonpareil faced Ryan last night."[24] Ryan commented in later years that Dempsey could not have gone fifteen rounds in the ring by himself that night. He was "beaten from exhaustion of his own efforts."[25] The *Sun* also reported that Dempsey had in his corner "a little black bottle" full of whiskey.[26] True or not, it's hard to know for certain, but given Dempsey's condition and the stories of his recent heavy binges, it seems a reasonable assertion.

It is also hard to know whether Dempsey received more scorn or pity that night. His apparently inebriated condition certainly cost him the admiration of many who could not believe that the one-time Nonpareil would appear in the ring in such a state. Many others were struck in the face with a fact that landed like a straight overhand right—that the stories they had been hearing all summer about the dissipation and tortured mental health of Dempsey were accurate. It was also now brutally obvious that their hero was terribly ill and a complete physical wreck. This was a horrible nightmare that did not end when they opened their eyes.

After the fight, Jack was in bad condition and appeared to some to be acting irrationally, leading to talk that he had gone insane. Dempsey was taken to Rockaway Beach where he was cared for while he rested. He was clearly not in his right mind. In addition to his mental unrest, he was going through bouts of fever and deliriousness brought on by the pulmonary tuberculosis that would kill him within the year. It was reported that during this time he was found brooding over the fight and had actually talked of killing himself. During some spells he even became somewhat uncontrollable. "On Monday night at a Coney Island road house, he became violent, and had it not been for interference of friends, might have ended his existence then and there. As it was, he stabbed himself in the wrist with a table fork."[27]

Dr. John E. Ward was summoned and after he examined Dempsey, recommended that he was suffering from melancholia influenced by worry and drink. Dr. Ward suggested that Jack be sent to an asylum for his own safety. Dr. Ward commented that Dempsey's mind was unbalanced "and he can only hope to revive his shattered faculties by good medical treatment and careful nursing."[28] For a while, Jack was sent to his brother Martin's home in Williamsburg and no visitors were allowed. He was said to be suffering from hallucinations that he was being hounded and persecuted by the police whom he feared would incarcerate him.[29] After additional wild spells, Jack's priest Father Collins from Brooklyn and his former backer Charley Allers were called in to help calm the fighter. It was agreed that a period of treatment was necessary. Allers saw to the arrangements and Dempsey was sent to "the Retreat," a hospital for the mentally unsound.[30]

Dempsey's grave condition was becoming clear and continued to be a hot topic in the press. The *New York Sun* ran an article on February 1 discussing the fighter's maladies.[31] They followed it up the next day with a short piece titled "Sympathy for Jack Dempsey."[32] He was clearly not himself and was even reported to have had words with his lifelong friend Jack McAuliffe just before the Ryan bout. After a few weeks when he had recovered sufficiently, Jack was able to return to his brother's home for a period of additional convalescence. Jack was not sure of his next move, but he was sure of one thing—he wanted to see Maggie and his daughters.[33]

During this time, the talk began of staging a benefit in Dempsey's honor to help him out of his present financial straits and to help expunge the stain of the Ryan debacle. "An effort is being made to get up a testimonial for him and nearly every boxer of note in the East has offered to assist without remuneration." Jack's legion of friends and admirers, realizing the depth of his health and financial difficulties, were ready to step forward and raise the funds to help defray his medical costs and to get him home to Portland, where Maggie and his family could care for him. Despite their cross words in January, McAuliffe was especially anxious to help orchestrate a tribute for his old friend. "McAuliffe quite understands Dempsey's condition and generously believes he is not responsible for his words, so therefore, is anxious to do something to repair the fortunes of his erstwhile friend."[34]

Speaking to the press in early February, Gus Tuthill said that the wear and tear of more than fifty fights had taken its toll on Dempsey. He also believed that the emotional toll of the losses to La Blanche, Fitzsimmons and now Ryan were causing Jack to drink more heavily and act irrationally. Prior to the Ryan bout, Tuthill, alarmed by Jack's appearance, said that he warned Dempsey not to go through with the fight. "He simply smiled and waved me off. You know the whole story now. He was game enough to face Ryan, although he knew the odds were 100 to 1 against him."[35] Tuthill was distraught at seeing his old colleague in such a sad condition.

Dempsey's period of treatment and convalescence helped to curb his drinking and stabilize his troubled mind, but little could be done to curb the tide of the consumption that was now wracking his body. He remained at his brother Martin's home until he was strong enough to travel west. He was well enough to get out occasionally for walks and to spend time with friends. In late April it was noted that "Jack Dempsey was one of the spectators at the Bridge Athletic Club boxing tournament recently in Brooklyn." The report went on to say, "Jack is looking hale, hearty and prosperous."[36]

It was reported in late May that the well-known horse racing man Philip J. Dwyer was the driving force behind plans for Dempsey's benefit at Madison Square Garden in early June. Dwyer, a longtime fan of the former Nonpareil, donated $500 to get the pot going and then stated that he would take the proceeds from the benefit, draw a check with Jack's share of the benefit and send it to Maggie back in Portland. It is reported that Dwyer sent Maggie a check for $3,500 collected from the gate.[37]

The *National Police Gazette* ran a piece on the benefit in early June. Attesting to Dempsey's still considerable popularity the newspaper commented that dozens of fighters including Corbett, Fitzsimmons, Tommy Ryan and others were anxious to help this man who once garnered so much respect in the ring. "It is asserted that greater fighters will appear at this testimonial than have ever before been gathered together under one roof." Demonstrating their backing for the event and encouraging additional support from the sporting community the newspaper added, "The object is a deserving one, and any of Dempsey's friends throughout the country who are desirous of lending a helping hand, may direct their favors to the Police Gazette office, receiving the assurance that the money thus forwarded will reach Dempsey through the medium of the committee in charge of the affair."[38]

A few days later it was noted that "Jack Dempsey's friends are responding nobly to the appeal for aid from the committee having in charge the testimonial which is being arranged for him. The generous proposition of John L. Sullivan to sacrifice a night's engagement to appear at the big benefit at the Madison Square Garden next Saturday night is being discussed by sporting men everywhere."[39] Sullivan initially intended to box with Joe Lannon of Boston, who had been his sparring partner for some time, but ultimately it was agreed that if Dempsey were up for it on the night of the benefit, the Boston Strong Boy would do some light sparring with the Nonpareil instead. What a wonderful treat for the crowd and a touching and fitting tribute to Jack.

On June 8, 1895, less than six months after his loss to Tommy Ryan, a benefit was given for the sick and financially challenged fighter. The amphitheater of the Garden building was filled with thousands of friends and supporters that evening. Among the noted guests from the boxing community were Jim Corbett, Bob Fitzsimmons, John L. Sullivan, Peter Maher, George Dixon, Joe Choynski, Joe O'Donnell, Tommy Ryan, Joe Lannon, Jimmy Barry, Jimmy Handler, Mick Dunn, Jack McAuliffe, Jack Skelly, Kid Lavigne and Young Corbett.

The evening was a mix of boxing, singing and an assortment of "feats of strength" by an eighteen-year-old German named Jarrow. "After juggling with a barrel of water weighing 125 pounds, he lifted a man weighing 250 pounds seated on a chair and then tore two packs of cards in half."[40] The boxing for the evening included George Dixon of Boston facing Jack Lynch of Philadelphia. Dixon apparently gave Lynch all he could handle for three rounds. Joe Choynski then met Bob Armstrong of Washington, Iowa, followed by a three-rounder between Australians Jim Hall and Mick Dunn. Kid McCoy and Harry Pidgeon were next up followed by Peter Maher and Harlem's Pete Burns. Then after John Young of Brooklyn sparred a few rounds with Denver's Jack Keefe, strong men August Johnson of Brooklyn and Halmer Lundin of Chicago lifted dumbbells and heavy barrels for ten minutes.

After the early bouts, the biggest names took to the ring. James J. Corbett was greeted with a long and thunderous applause as he strode to the ring to spar three rounds with John McVey of Philadelphia. "The clever maneuvers of the champion during the three rounds made the crowd howl with admiration."[41] Bob Fitzsimmons then went three rounds with Frank Bosworth, "and he left no doubt in the minds of those who saw his quick work tonight that he had not gone back any and will render a good account of himself when he meets the champion."[42] Sporting men watched the exhibitions closely as Corbett and Fitzsimmons were scheduled to meet in Dallas, Texas, in October. "Those who went to the Garden for the purpose of getting a look at Corbett and Fitz for their coming battle must have gone home disappointed. Each man had such an easy partner that he did not have to extend himself."[43] The fact that the scheduled October bout did not occur until 1897 was probably even more disappointing.

The last bout of the evening was very special. In what was his final ring appearance, Dempsey sparred several rounds with the equally legendary John L. Sullivan. When the men appeared in the ring, they were cheered for several minutes and after many calls for the former champions to speak, John L. gave a short address in which he expressed his thanks to those assembled for supporting his old friend, Dempsey. "Gentlemen, I thank you, one and all, for your kind applause and appreciation. For my old pal, Dempsey's, sake, I would like to see the building filled with money. We are two good old has-beens, but we're made of the right stuff."[44] After a few more words Sullivan concluded by saying, "Mr. Dempsey and myself will now give an exhibition and will do the best we can, although we are two 'has beens.'"[45]

The three-round sparring session was largely uneventful as the men boxed scientifically and no truly heavy blows were landed, much less thrown. Regardless of the modest style of the fighting, the crowd was still delirious with excitement as they watched these two ring legends battle toe to toe. While the exhibition was no doubt tame compared to what it might have been some half dozen years earlier, it was still described—somewhat generously I believe—as "a wild three-round bout."[46] During the exhibition Jack fought at a somewhat reserved pace. His illness was advancing and his strength and stamina were waning. The slower pace helped Jack mask the fact that he was physically tired, but while he was a bit thinner than usual, Dempsey looked all right to the casual observer. But whether apparent or not, Jack Dempsey was dying and this would be his last appearance in the squared circle.

After the benefit, Jack returned to the Bay Side Hotel in Rockaway Beach where he was now staying. Reports circulated throughout the summer on Dempsey's health. One mentioned that he was dangerously ill, his condition precarious, and that "death may come at any moment." The report continued that at noon on June 27 Jack was having heart spasms and fainting spells and that it took some time to revive him. The situation was serious enough that a priest, Father Hornan, was called to his bedside. By that evening, however, he was resting comfortably under the influence of medicines.[47]

On a visit to the hotel in late June, Jack's sister-in-law was so alarmed by his appearance that she immediately called for her husband Tom and brother-in-law Martin to come see Jack. She also sent a telegram to Maggie telling her of Jack's grave condition.[48] When news spread that he was nearing death, a reporter called on Jack at the Bay Side to see for himself. The reporter stated that he "learned that Dempsey's condition was not as alarming as published. True it is that Dempsey had been indisposed and a physician was called in to prescribe, who readily discovered that Jack's condition was due to a heavy cold. His illness was not of a serious nature and he never was in a precarious condition."[49] It's fascinating to read that interview given Dempsey's grave health. By this time, his tuberculosis had advanced into consumption and he had only four months to live, but even now, he was either denying the realities or hiding them from the public.

When Dempsey was asked of his intentions for the future, he responded as if all was well. "I am going up to Brooklyn this afternoon to see my friend Phil Dwyer and settle up the finances in connection with my recent benefit and prepare for my trip to Portland to join my wife and family. I will probably engage in business there. One thing is certain, I fought my last and hardest battle this week when I knocked out my desire for strong drink forever, and I hope to build myself anew and become as big and strong as I ever was."[50] Jack didn't mention, of course, that he was attempting to give up drink on the doctor's express orders, and only to extend his life.

The reporter also claimed that Dempsey looked better than he had in months and that Dr. O.L. Lusk, the Sanitary Superintendent of the Board of Health in Queens, who had been called in to examine the former champion, had pronounced Dempsey fit and physically sound with the exception of the "heavy cold." Conflicting reports, including one in the *New York Herald*, claimed that Dr. Lusk admitted that the pugilist's condition was very serious and that he was suffering from heart trouble.[51] In truth, he had good and bad days, but the Nonpareil was clearly dying.

Jack left his much beloved hometown of Brooklyn for the last time in early July. He traveled a circuitous route cross-country, eventually returning to his adopted home in Portland.

On his way west, Dempsey had stopped over in Montreal for a few days. While there, it was noted that "Dempsey is scarcely able to speak for the gathering in his throat and is wasted to a shadow. He says it is doubtful if he will ever come east again." Jack still commented on the upcoming Corbett-Fitzsimmons bout on which he opined that each man had an equal chance to win.[52]

By July 12, Jack had traversed Canada and was in Vancouver, British Columbia, but the rail travel had been difficult on him. "Dempsey is a physical wreck and looks as though he had but a short time to live. During the journey he fainted more than once, and but for the presence of a woman doctor traveling on the same train it is doubtful if he would have arrived alive."[53] The once indefatigable Nonpareil was so weak upon reaching Vancouver that he had to be carried as he transferred to the train on which he would complete his journey back to Portland. His weakened body and haggard appearance caused a general stir among those who saw him.[54]

A couple of weeks later, Dr. Nathalie A. Snelling, the young San Francisco physician who attended Dempsey on the train to the West Coast, spoke to reporters and confirmed that Jack was dying of consumption and was only keeping himself alive by the use of stimulants.[55] On July 24, Dr. Snelling said that Dempsey was taken sick on the westbound Canadian Pacific train near Vancouver. "I was called in to attend him and found him suffering greatly. When the train reached Portland, Dempsey's destination, he asked me to continue my duties as medical advisor and attend him at his home near Portland. I did so and administered to him for some days after which I left for San Francisco." She added, "Dempsey is dying of consumption and also suffers considerably from heart failure. In my opinion, he is in a very dangerous condition."[56]

Where and how Dempsey contracted the disease is not certain, but in that period, its spread was not uncommon and among pugilists it may have been even more prominent. In a letter I received from boxing historian Mark Dunn, he commented,

> I once asked a doctor about the prevalence of TB among fighters. He said to consider the towels, i.e. the towels used in the bars and the towels used in the fights and at gyms where the fighters trained. He said a bartender would clean a bar with a towel and then dry the glasses with the same towel after wiping off his face. He said it was worse in the fights where the same towel might be kept in the corner through an entire night and have fresh blood and spit on it from a half dozen people. He also said that the bar spittoon was a swirling infection. Guys with TB would spit in the spittoon and it would sit there for a week or more spreading germs all over. It's kind of a sickening thought, but probably true. He thought the guys who did not have TB were the lucky ones.[57]

Jack had felt great sadness leaving Brooklyn and his many friends and fans there. Since he was a small boy, Jack had called the Williamsburg section of Brooklyn his home, but he had also grown to love Portland. The city had become his adopted home. Portland was where he had fallen in love and married, settled down—to the degree that Jack ever really settled down—and he had begun raising his family there. He made the conscious decision to reside on the western slope. "East Portland it must be remembered is the home of Jack Dempsey. He owns a cozy little cottage here, and when not training for a fight or giving exhibition contests, he enjoys home life with his devoted wife and two lovely children as much as anyone can."[58] Jack immediately settled back into his home with his wife and daughters. He also spent a good deal of time at his in-laws' where Maggie could have help with Jack and the girls and he could be cared for as he convalesced. Jack hoped that the change in climate might help him rest, but the moist and cool Oregon air certainly did not help his lungs recover. His health continued to decline throughout the summer and fall and his once virile body continued to waste away.

Soon after his arrival in Portland, Dempsey was examined by his personal physician and close friend Dr. Harry Lane. Dr. Lane pronounced the Nonpareil's case hopeless. "Other physicians of note were consulted, but all agreed with Dr. Lane that the noted ring general might live a few months, but his case must terminate fatally."[59] Dr. Lane, who had been close with Jack since Dempsey had first arrived in Portland ten years before, said that while Maggie was well aware of the terminal nature of her husband's illness, they never spoke of it to Jack. "I never had the heart to tell poor Jack," said the doctor. "He would not have believed me had I told him for he never did take much stock in the opinions of medical men." Dr. Lane said that instead of medical matters they spoke of future plans and the upcoming prizefight between Jim Corbett and Bob Fitzsimmons which Jack hoped to attend. Dempsey opined that it would be a fierce battle, but that he believed Corbett would win if he kept his head.[60]

In early August, the Dempseys traveled east up to the scenic town of Hood River on the banks of the Columbia River for a few weeks in hopes that the rest and fresh air might do Jack's lungs some good, but the illness was too far gone. They returned home on August 30 and Jack's strength continued to wane.

While Jack had been rapidly growing weaker since his return to Portland over the summer, up until a few days before his death the gallant fighter insisted that he would defeat this opponent as he had so many in the ring and make a full recovery. For weeks since his return from Hood River, Dempsey had been convalescing at his home at 389 Grand Avenue in Portland, with Maggie caring for her stricken husband and her parents and siblings providing moral support and helping out the young couple by cooking, cleaning and looking after the Dempseys' two young daughters, Alice and Anne. The Dempsey home was a "neat little cottage" in East Portland. "From the back can be seen Mt. Hood, the timber covered hills and a stretch of country which is pleasing and restful to the eye of one who no longer cares for the turmoil of the busy life of man. Within the cottage is cozily furnished and made as comfortable as loving hands can make it."[61]

The disease had not only severely weakened Dempsey; it had begun to make him appear haggard as well. A reporter commented, "One who had known him in his palmy days would not recognize him now," and went on to state that "he has aged rapidly under the heavy strain," adding that Jack now looked ten years older than his almost thirty-four years.[62] Still, Jack refused to admit that he was dying. Right up until the end, Dempsey kept himself well informed on the upcoming Corbett-Fitzsimmons mill by reading the Portland, San Francisco and East Coast newspapers when he could get hold of them.

On Sunday, October 20, Jack insisted on getting out of bed and getting dressed. "After a romp with his children and a peep into the outer world, he lay down on a lounge in the sitting room and took a nap. When he awoke, he was changed."[63] The energy it took to dress, play with Alice and Annie and to take a short stroll, completely wore him out. He soon returned to his bed and barely stirred again.

On October 23, Maggie Dempsey very cordially accepted a visiting reporter into her home and into the room where her beloved husband lay dying. "Johnnie," she said, "is always pleased to see visitors, and his many friends have been very kind since his sickness. I hope he will recognize you." At first, he seemed to recognize the visitor as he smiled and slowly and gently raised the right hand that had empowered the Nonpareil to so forcefully dominate more than seventy opponents in the squared circle. In short order, however, Dempsey began to slip back into a sort of semi-conscious trance, staring at the ceiling but not really seeing anything. Jack was awake, but not really even hearing the reporter's questions. Maggie tried to get his attention, but he gave no response.

The reporter commented that Dempsey was "but a mere skeleton of his former self." He continued, "The big bunches of steel-like muscle that once covered his limbs and body are all gone, and the bones protrude through the almost transparent skin in a way that is distressing. It is but a shadow of the brawny athlete of former days." Adding that Jack had grown a drooping moustache that hid the firm lines of his mouth, the dying man lying in the bed before him was almost unrecognizable as boxing's formerly invincible Nonpareil. Seeing that it was of no use pressing, Maggie Dempsey led her guest back into the sitting room of her home, saying that "John is not himself today." When the two had sat down, she continued, stating that this was a new and different stage of the disease that would kill her husband. "His cough seems to have left him entirely and he does not suffer so much as he did." She recounted how just a few days before, Jack had been so lively, romping with the children and keeping her on her toes. "Yesterday and today he has been lying there gazing at the ceiling and paying no attention to his surroundings."[64]

Responding to a noise from the sick room, Maggie responded that Jack was looking at his watch and that he knew it was time for Dr. Lane to pay a visit. "He knows when the hour arrives to take his medicine, counts his own pulse and calls for nourishment when he knows he ought to have it." He was barely eating anymore. Maggie would prepare a light meal with some milk and fruit, but that was all.[65]

Another correspondent from the *Chicago Tribune* paid a visit to the Dempsey household on October 24. The reporter was met at the door by Maggie and her daughters. After a brief chat in which Maggie prepared the reporter as to Jack's condition, she ushered the man into the sick room. He described the scene he found at the home as follows. "In a back room upstairs, darkened by heavy curtains lies a man well-known throughout the land who is almost in the last throes of consumption. The dying man, for indeed his days are numbered, is Jack Dempsey, the famous 'Nonpareil,' he who for so long defended his right to the middleweight championship of the world."[66] The reporter noted that Dempsey's darkened room was "filled with the fragrance of sweet smelling roses, Dempsey's favorite flowers."[67] When he met with Jack he sadly discovered a wilted soul with a withered handshake and restless, vacant, unrecognizing eyes. Maggie Dempsey told the reporter that her husband was worse than he had been. "He has never been this way before. He frightens me. Up to Sunday last he was so bright and cheerful that I had partially made up my mind he would soon be himself again. He was continually planning what he would do when well." The reporter wrote that "none of Dempsey's Chicago friends would know him now. He is terribly emaciated even his facial features are changed, for a recently grown mustache hides from view his thin and bloodless lips."[68]

Maggie told the *Tribune* reporter that one bright spot for her husband was the Corbett-Fitzsimmons contest in which he held a special interest. Jack knew both men and considered them his friends. "He knows all about the fight for he has read all the local papers have had to say of it."[69] She pointed out that when the fight was set for Hot Springs, he was pleased with the choice and he told his doctor that he had to hurry up and get well so he could not only attend the fight, but spend time in the popular health resort building himself back up. Because of her distaste for fighting, Jack would rarely speak about it with Maggie, but she reported that he was following the upcoming match quite closely. "John has taken lots of interest in the fight. He reads all the papers and talks about it with the doctor and all others who come to see him, but he won't talk about it with me." Maggie added, "He never did talk about his fights to me." Maggie of course disliked prizefighting and had long encouraged Jack to give it up, so it was rarely a topic of conversation between them. She told the reporter that she overheard Jack saying that the bout would be a long and difficult one between two skilled fighters. "He is a great admirer of Corbett and thinks he will win it if he keeps his head. It will be the fight of his life, Jack said, as Fitzsimmons is strong and brave and a very clever fighter." She smiled as she then recounted a very happy meeting with Corbett in Asbury Park the previous year when her husband and Corbett were training together there.[70]

In an interview with Dr. Lane, the physician stated that he had chiefly been trying to keep his old friend comfortable since his return to Portland and that he held out no hope of recovery. "Poor old Jack's days are numbered, but I have not the heart to tell him so. He is such a noble fellow and so dearly loves his wife and babies." Dr. Lane continued by stating that Maggie was prepared for Jack's passing and that it could come at any time. "Jack may linger along for weeks or even months, and he may die tomorrow—but he cannot escape the inevitable." Dr. Lane praised Jack's courage and tenacity in his fight against his most deadly opponent. "His nerve, force and will power are wonderful. I have seen him lie for hours in a stupor, from which I thought he could never awake, when his heart was merely fluttering; and then, suddenly, he would shake off the lethargy, sit up in bed and discuss ordinary topics with amazing animation and interest." Dr. Lane added that it was one of Jack's dearest ambitions to be present for the upcoming Corbett-Fitzsimmons bout. Sadly, however, the physician lamented that "poor old Jack will never witness the fight and I doubt very much if he will live long enough to hear the result."[71]

By the last week of October, Maggie, her mother and several close friends took turns remaining by Jack's bedside day and night attending to his needs. The once mighty Nonpareil was now growing as weak as a baby. Newspapers around the country began reporting that Jack was dying and that the end might come at any time. "Within the past few days he has been rapidly sinking and it is announced that his hours are numbered."[72] Throughout his final weeks, Jack would have bad days and nights in which he was feverish, restless and hallucinating. These would be followed by periodic rallies where he was more comfortable and alert. A typical report would state, "He had rallied in the morning and chatted in a sprightly fashion for one so weak." Towards the end Jack commented to his wife, "I'm sinking fast, Maggie. I'm about done up." He had soon weakened so badly that he needed Maggie's assistance to take a sip of milk. It was reported that while consumption often renders patients particularly irritable and often hard to manage, "Dempsey has maintained the unfailing good temper and thoughtfulness for others that have always been among his most pronounced characteristics."[73]

By the evening of October 30, Jack's condition was considered so critical that rumors began to spread that he had already died. Contrary to the reports, the Nonpareil was still fighting, but he was sinking rapidly. On the afternoon of October 31, the former champion woke from a troubled rest and spoke weakly to those gathered at his bedside. Finally acknowledging that his end was near, he said, "This is my last day in this world."[74] He was no longer eating and only taking occasional sips of water. Late that evening he said his goodbyes to his daughters and a number of friends who had gathered at the house.

At around 11:00 p.m., the bedridden pugilist's condition began to worsen noticeably. Father Heinrich, Jack's priest at St. Francis of Assisi Church in Portland, administered the last rites of the Roman Catholic Church. As that dark night continued, Dempsey "grew delirious and in his delirium fought over some of his battles, frequently mentioning the name of Jimmy Carroll."[75] In the final hours before he died, it seemed as if the Nonpareil was reliving his battles and ring glories of the past. Drifting in and out of his hallucinations, Jack was seeing the faces of his old friends, associates, opponents and other

THE LATE JACK DEMPSEY AND HIS CHILDREN.
[Reproduced from the latest photograph of the Nonpareil and his daughters, as published in the Oregonian.]

A proud Jack Dempsey with his girls, Alice (left) and Anne.

boxing figures and was periodically even calling out their names. While many of his mutterings were unintelligible, those present said they could make out occasional references to "Costigan," "Conley" and others and at various times, while showing signs of agitation; he called out the name of his old antagonist British Jimmy Carroll. At one point his nurse, Mrs. Armstrong, heard him calling the name of Jim Corbett. She said that after murmuring the name "Corbett," the Nonpareil stirred and said, "I'm at your back, Jim!"

Shortly after 4:00 a.m., he rallied and regained both consciousness and clarity. Jack seemed to know that the end was near. "Dempsey's last act was to kiss the crucifix just before he breathed his last. His last utterance was his wife's name."[76] At 6:35 a.m. Jack slipped back into unconsciousness and ten minutes later, the Nonpareil was gone. Although he had fought as fiercely and as valiantly as he had in the ring, Jack died in the early morning hours of Friday, November 1, 1895. He was just over a month short of his thirty-third birthday. Maggie was still at Jack's side when he passed, as were his nurse Mrs. Armstrong, his mother-in-law Ellen Brady and two friends.

People across the nation picked up their daily newspapers on November 1 and, between stories of two earthquakes—a powerful Italian quake and, closer to home, two distinct shocks that rattled Chicago—they read the terrible news of the Nonpareil's death. Upon hearing the news of his death, many of Dempsey's friends shared their grief and their thoughts about the Nonpareil.

Portland Police Commissioner Mose Gunst, a longtime friend and backer of Dempsey, commented on his old pal, "there was the best man of his weight who ever stepped into a ring." Gunst said, "He was beaten but twice [sic], one of those defeats being by a fluke, and the other administered by a man whom he should never have fought."[77] The fluke was clearly La Blanche, but the man he never should have fought could be Fitzsimmons or Ryan. For some reason Gunst was forgetting one of Dempsey's one-sided losses. Whether referring to Fitzsimmons or Ryan, it is true that Jack was in no condition to fight either man.

Young Mitchell, one of Dempsey's close friends in Portland, said that he knew it was coming, but he was terribly saddened by the loss. "Jack was a true friend and as brave a man as ever put up his hands."[78] In eulogizing the former champion, the *San Francisco Call* stated, "The Nonpareil's fighting qualities were never called into question. Whenever he entered the ring a high classed exhibition was insured. Cleverness and gameness, two of the essential attributes of a champion, he abundantly possessed." The *Call* added, "His popularity was of a National character. Excepting John L. Sullivan, perhaps, no man ever commanded such a following. Particularly was this true of him in and around New York. His manly conduct, together with his staying powers, made for him a legion of admirers."[79] The *New York Times* ran a much shorter article covering just a paragraph, but the newspaper paid Jack a handsome tribute when they stated that prior to his ill-fated bout with Bob Fitzsimmons, "he had carried everything before him in the prize ring, and was as much of an idol almost, as the great John L. Sullivan. His career as a pugilist was remarkable."[80]

The Nonpareil's funeral was held on Monday, November 4. Following a private service at his residence, public services were held at St. Francis Church in Portland. "Requiem mass was sung under the direction of Father Heinrich. Fully 2,000 attended the services. The floral offerings were beautiful."[81] Another report describing the flowers that adorned the casket stated that "the floral offerings were gorgeous and numerous and filled a hack. They were from friends far and near."[82] Only about half of those who attended the service at St. Francis's could get into the church. The remainder stood on the street and strained to hear Father Heinrich. Following the Mass, a procession traveled to Portland's Mount Calvary Cemetery, where Jack was laid to rest in a nondescript grave.

While Jack died of consumption, many still believed that his spirit was never the same after his fluke defeat by La Blanche and, while there may not be a direct medical answer for it, his mental and emotional state certainly suffered. The second La Blanche fight always seemed to haunt him. The *San Francisco Call* reported in the days following his death that "ever since the time Dempsey was defeated by La Blanche by one of the foulest blows a man can give another when contesting for supremacy, and at a time when [Dempsey] had the 'Marine' under his thumb so to speak, the ex-champion middleweight lost courage and hope. In fact, Dempsey grew reckless and seemed to care little for his future. He continuously spoke of that cowardly blow which originated in the mind of [British] Jimmy Carroll as a last resort to win coin less the honor of a victory."[83] His loss to La Blanche broke not only Dempsey's string of over fifty ring victories, it also broke his heart. La Blanche's refusal to give Jack a return bout made the heartbreak worse. The Marine knew that Dempsey—even in a broken state—was his master in the ring. La Blanche refused to seriously consider a rubber match that he knew he would lose as badly as he had their first match in New York and as badly as he was losing the second fight before he threw the pivot punch. But even the facts that he had soundly whipped La Blanche in both encounters and that the Marine was now afraid to enter the ring with him a third time, did not assuage Dempsey's frustration. It gnawed at him for the rest of his life and it may indeed be true that the constant gnawing was another factor in hastening Jack's death.

A photograph of Dempsey in his prime.

Other factors in Jack's long illness and early death have long been argued, but none as strongly as his love of alcohol. At times, the alcohol clearly affected his training and to some minimal degree, his later ring appearances. As mentioned in the introduction to this book, noted boxing historian Tracy Callis states that while he usually overcame his "inclination to consume too much alcohol" it was indeed a serious and growing challenge for Dempsey.[84]

In the days following his death, many newspapers continued to speculate on the role that alcohol may have played. The *San Francisco Call* stated, "The almost universal verdict was that had Dempsey never met John Barleycorn he might still be alive and still be at the head of the list of men in his class."[85] Dempsey's hard drinking certainly bore no unique qualities. While frowned upon by much of upper crust society, drinking was a common event in most of North America, including in the European immigrant social structure, and was certainly a staple of the Irish American community. Michael T. Eisenberg made the following point about John L. Sullivan, but it most certainly applies to Dempsey and many others as well. "Sullivan probably never made a conscious decision to drink. The drinking man's environment was all around him, and he entered into it, with his peers, as naturally as slipping on an old pair of shoes."[86] Sullivan learned to drink as a rite of passage and Dempsey's case was certainly no different.

Jack's illness and heavy use of alcohol undoubtedly accounted for his health issues in St. Paul, Minnesota, in the summer of 1893. Doctors at St. Joseph's Hospital where the Nonpareil was being treated cited extensive alcohol use as a factor in his illness as well as his erraticism. His lungs had been damaged from his undisclosed bouts with pneumonia and he was beginning to show signs of the tubercular condition that would kill him within a couple of years. Jack's erratic behavior was linked to a mix of fever, deliriousness and agitation due to his illness and heavy alcohol use. His doctors at the St. Paul hospital, "to which Jack Dempsey was taken, say he is suffering with fever, which accounts for the report that he was insane."[87]

An article written by Jack's friend and fellow pugilist Solly Smith in 1893 proved to be both appropriate in its tribute and chilling in its foresight. Smith wrote in a column prior to his featherweight championship bout with George Dixon that should he win the fight, he would not make the mistake of "the gallant" Jack Dempsey by meeting opponents of significantly greater weight. Smith said, "I fully realize the force of the old aphorism, 'A good big man can always whip a good little man.'" Smith went on to express his belief that Dempsey's loss to the much larger Fitzsimmons "broke his proud heart, drove him to drink and finally upset his mental equilibrium." Smith continued by acknowledging the rumors that Dempsey was in poor health and probably "not long for this world." He also acknowledged, however, that the Jack Dempsey he knew would gallantly fight for his life against the bitterest foe he had yet faced. As he had in all his ring battles Jack would give it all he had, "but should he die no better epitaph of him could be written than a paraphrase of Byron's immortal lines:

> He left a fighter's name to other times
> Linked with a thousand virtues and but a single crime.[88]

Immortal Nonpareil

Even in death, Jack Dempsey remained a much beloved and revered figure. His friends and fans continued to search for ways to honor him and help and support his widow and children—this despite the fact that they really did not need the help. Several benefits were held in Jack's honor with the goal of raising money for his family. In early December, the *San Francisco Call* reported, "The widow and family of the late Jack Dempsey arrived from Portland, Oregon, yesterday and are domiciled at the Windsor Hotel."[1] Maggie was there as a guest of several prominent citizens who were organizing a committee to hold a tribute night in honor of the Nonpareil later that month. That benefit was held in San Francisco on December 27. Owner Cliff Phillips donated the use of his People's Palace located at the corner of Eddy and Mason streets. Music was provided by the Letter Carrier's Band, which was followed by some vaudeville acts, wrestling matches and a series of four- and six-round ring battles. The matches featured such notables as Tom Sharkey, Joe Choynski, Young Mitchell and Alex Greggains.[2] Another benefit in December raised $800 in honor of Jack,[3] and yet another was held for Maggie Dempsey on Friday, January 17, again at the People's Palace.[4] All seats were sold on a cash basis at the door and a packed house realized a purse of $2,600 for Jack's family.[5] Estimates are that Maggie received between seven and eight thousand dollars in total from the various benefits.

Beginning in early 1896, two efforts were begun regarding the Nonpareil's final resting place. In the months following his death there was a strong effort made to bring Dempsey's body back east for reburial in Brooklyn. This initial effort was spearheaded by Jack's former manager Gus Tuthill and Jack's brother Martin. It was reported that Maggie had already given the group her consent for her husband's remains to be moved to Calvary Cemetery in Long Island City.[6] Had she lived, the reburial might indeed have taken place, but soon Maggie fell ill. Tragically, like her husband before her, Maggie was stricken with tuberculosis and, like Jack, she also died much too young from the wasting effects of consumption. Maggie passed away on the evening of March 1, 1898, just two years and four months to the day after Jack. Maggie had been ailing for some time and had sought a number of cures during her illness. "Last June she went to California in hopes that the change would improve her health, but returned a couple of months ago, little improved, and since that time she has failed rapidly until her death last night."[7] The local press reported that she was survived by her daughters, parents, one brother and two sisters. Per the *Brooklyn Eagle*, she died surrounded by family and friends at her parents' home on Grand Avenue in Portland. "Her physicians state that she contracted the disease from her husband while nursing him in his last illness."[8] Maggie was laid to rest next to her beloved husband at Mount Calvary Cemetery in East Portland.

In addition to those who endeavored to send Jack's remains back to Brooklyn, a large number of friends and admirers believed that regardless of location, a fighter of Jack's renown should have a more noteworthy monument marking his gravesite. The idea was struck down by the cemetery authority at Calvary in Newtown, Long Island, and once again by Dempsey's father-in-law James F. Brady in 1898 after Maggie's death. One idea—true or not—was to have a bronze, life-sized figure of a pugilist in fighting pose standing over Jack's grave. On the pedestal was to have been inscribed Jack's ring record. The cemetery authorities steadfastly refused to permit any such monument to be erected on the grounds over which they had full control. Mr. T.J. McMahon, the office manager at Calvary and clearly no fight fan, stated that the erection of such a monument would be "scandalous" and "vigorously opposed."[9] McMahon stated, "The bronze symbol of a slugger in a home of peace is not to be tolerated."[10] Brady refused to support the efforts of a group led by former champion John L. Sullivan to raise funds and erect such a monument, insisting that the nondescript, four-foot headstone was sufficient. The matter was dropped—for a while.

In 1899, M.J. McMahon of Portland—no relation to the cemetery office manager—who had been Dempsey's lawyer and a good friend became greatly disturbed by the condition of the Nonpareil's final resting place. After a visit to the grave that year, he was so upset by its lack of both care and noteworthiness that when he returned to his office that day, he wrote a poem entitled "The Nonpareil's Grave." He anonymously distributed thousands of copies of the poem, one of which was printed by Portland's *Oregonian* newspaper on December 10, 1899. Three days later the poem ran in Brooklyn accompanied by a brief letter from McMahon to the editor of the *Eagle* describing a movement to have a monument erected over the Nonpareil's grave or possibly to have his body disinterred and reburied in Brooklyn with the consent of the Brady family. McMahon wrote, "I have been asked to call the attention of his friends in the East to the condition and location of his grave, which I have done in the following verses."[11]

In 1901, a new committee was organized with the purpose of raising funds to erect a monument over Dempsey's grave and to give any additional funds to Jack and Maggie's orphaned daughters. A letter was written by the committee's secretary Timothy M. McGrath and placed in the *National Police Gazette*. McGrath stated that the Nonpareil's last resting place was "in an obscure corner of a lonely cemetery" and that the grave was overgrown with weeds and unmarked by any stone. He continued by stating that the committee's intention was to raise enough funds to erect a monument and beautify the area in honor of "poor Jack, who's beautiful character and upright life did much to raise pugilism to a higher plane."[12] The Jack Dempsey Memorial Fund Association was sponsored by the Twentieth Century Athletic Club and located in an office set up in the Columbia Building at 916 Market Street in San Francisco.

Jack's close, longtime friend and former featherweight fighter Jack Skelly, who became a respected fight referee, traveled to Portland in 1910, after officiating a bout in Reno, Nevada. Skelly determined that he would visit the last resting place of his old friend, but he, like McMahon eleven years earlier, was taken aback by what he found. According to Skelly, it was only with some difficulty that he located Dempsey's grave, "unmarked, without a stone to tell of the brave man who lay beneath the green sod." Skelly was quoted in a letter to the sporting editor of the *New York Times* as follows: "Jack

Dempsey, Jack McAuliffe, and myself worked together in the same cooper shop in old Williamsburg, Brooklyn, and we grew and fought our way up to the front ranks of pugilism as lifelong pals, and when I viewed poor Dempsey's weed covered grave it struck me that I should make an appeal to all the followers of the old game and with your kind assistance to try and raise a fund for the erection of a worthy monument over the Nonpareil."[13] Skelly recommended the establishment of a committee of noted men to raise funds for the erection of a headstone to note the accomplishments of the Nonpareil. Eventually, a group of Dempsey's friends and admirers erected a monument on which McMahon's poem is inscribed.

Not everyone was in agreement with the call for a monument. An editorial in the *Morning Oregonian* referred to the effort to erect the monument and then raise funds for the education of Dempsey's two daughters and called for a reordering of priorities. "How would it be to provide for the education of the daughters first, and let the monument come afterwards?"[14] The paper went on to comment that Dempsey was a loving and affectionate husband and father who sought a good life for his family. They argued that Jack would have cared nothing for a stone monument to himself, but rather, he had built an enduring one with his fists during "the palmy days" of his superb physical strength. "Reverse your plans, good friends of Dempsey. See that the daughters are educated if you really want to honor his memory."[15]

The immortal Nonpareil.

It was pointed out nine days later, however, that the Dempsey girls' education and general needs were already being well taken care of by the Brady family. In a letter to the editor, the writer took some exception at the suggestion that the girls were wanting. The earlier report "would seem to imply that they are growing up in ignorance and neglect. Such is not the case, on the contrary, they are living in a comfortable home, surrounded by all the loving care an affectionate grandfather and devoted aunts and uncles can bestow. They are attending one of the largest East Side schools, distant but a few blocks from their home, are well advanced and progressing favorably in their studies."[16] The writer goes on to point out that James Brady, the girls' grandfather, had recently bought a new piano and was providing for a teacher to come in and work with the girls.

Regardless of the assurances of the Brady family and friends, much continued to be made of the circumstances of Dempsey's daughters Alice and Anne. The girls, who were, respectively, eight and five years old at the time of their father's death and a little more than two years older when their mother passed, were never in danger of being uncared for or destitute. Maggie's family immediately took them in and they were raised in a comfortable and nurturing environment at their grandparents' home in Portland.

As noted, a larger headstone was eventually installed for the couple. It stands about four feet tall and lists Jack and Maggie's names, birth and death dates and the inscription, "May Their Souls Rest in Peace." Cemetery management also began taking greater care of the grounds.

It was fairly common for friends and admirers, both famous and unknown, to visit Portland's Mount Calvary Cemetery to see the Nonpareil's grave. As mentioned, Skelly was there in 1910, Jack McAuliffe, Jim Corbett and John L. Sullivan all came by at various times and Bob Fitzsimmons visited regularly when in Portland. On a snowy February 26, 1917, Fitzsimmons, his wife and several friends wrapped in top hats and heavy overcoats, paid a visit to the cemetery. Lanky Bob had just finished a weeklong engagement on the vaudeville stage at the Pantages Theater in Portland, but before he boarded his train, he wanted, as was his custom, to pay tribute to his old nemesis and friend. As Bob and his wife placed bouquets of lilies and carnations on Dempsey's grave, the former middleweight and heavyweight champion paid the Nonpareil this tribute, "Jack Dempsey was the gamest and most gentlemanly fighter who ever breathed. At the time I boxed him every good Irishman was proud of him because he was known the world over as a man whose word was his bond, who always knew how to conduct himself and a square shooter. If I were boxing today I would not regret losing to a man like Jack Dempsey."[17] After Fitzsimmons lay the flowers on the grave and made his tribute to the late Nonpareil, an elderly gentleman who was in attendance read McMahon's 1899 poem, "The Nonpareil's Grave." As the group began to turn and head back to their waiting automobiles, Mrs. Fitzsimmons, a vivacious French woman, commented that she was much impressed with the grave and that despite its meager beginnings, the Dempsey's grave now appeared to be showing signs of loving care. As an *Oregonian* newspaper reporter who was present commented, the grave surely looked peaceful that day tucked in a blanket of white snow.

On October 31, 1900, it was announced that Jack and Maggie's legal affairs had finally been settled. *The Oregonian* noted, "The final report of James F. Brady, administrator of the estate of Margaret Dempsey, deceased, who was the wife of Jack Dempsey, deceased, was approved. The estate, consisting of a house and lot in Stephens' Addition, goes to the children, Alice and Annie Dempsey, aged 13 and 10 years, respectively."[18]

In another interesting note, Jack was still at the center of legal wrangling as late as February 1902, more than six years after his death. *The Oregonian* reported that in court proceedings, "L.L. Hawkins has filed suit against James F. Brady, Ellen T. Brady, and John O'Donnell to set aside certain deeds and mortgages. Hawkins is seeking to collect a judgment for $2,618 recovered July 5, 1894, by the Portland Cyclorama Company against Jack Dempsey, M.E. Freeman, John Elston, and John Robertson. The amount was due for rent for the Cyclorama building, which was occupied by Dempsey. The others were his sureties."[19]

At the Jim Jeffries–Bob Fitzsimmons championship fight in San Francisco in 1902, another effort was made to raise funds for Jack's "struggling" family. Fred T. Merrill of Portland had possession of the *National Police Gazette* belt given to Jack by Richard Fox, and Merrill was endeavoring to sell the belt. "The late Jack Dempsey's belt, which was brought here from Portland, was brought to the ring and exhibited for the purpose of selling tickets for the benefit of Dempsey's widow and children. Volunteers were called for among those active in the ring today to act as solicitors. Among those volunteering were Joe Gans, Jimmy Britt and Young Peter Jackson."[20] Another nice gesture it would seem, but an uninformed one as Margaret had passed four years earlier and as noted above, Alice and Anne were quite comfortable and well taken care of by their grandparents and extended family.

Alice and Anne grew up in comfort and lived full and productive lives. Both girls attended good schools, graduating from St. Mary's Academy in Portland and, as noted earlier, took piano lessons provided by their grandfather. One report from the *Oregonian* in 1905 commented on a recital during which Alice played "Under the Linden Tree" by Gunther.[21] Alice, born in May 1887, married Anthony Joseph Weber in 1910, at St. Francis of Assisi Catholic Church, the same parish in which her parents were married.[22] Weber was the son of a successful Portland businessman. The Weber family built and ran the largest tannery on the West Coast. The couple had two children. Alice passed away on June 22, 1942.

Anne Margaret Dempsey was born on March 29, 1890. After graduating from St. Mary's Academy, Anne attended the St. Vincent Hospital School of Nursing in Portland. She graduated on June 9, 1914, and gave the address for her class of sixteen.[23] Following graduation, she entered the Army Nurse Corps, serving during World War I in France. After the Armistice, Anne and her mates from Base Hospital 46 returned from Europe in April 1919.[24] She then worked as a registered nurse for the Union Pacific Railroad Company and continued her studies, eventually becoming a licensed Anesthesiologist. She was one of the first women to scale Mt. Hood, doing so in the early 1910s. She lived for ninety-nine years, but never married. Anne passed away on May 1, 1989, in Portland and, like her parents, was buried at Mount Calvary Cemetery.

Old friend Denny Costigan died at age fifty-one, on November 18, 1907, at Metropolitan Hospital on Blackwell's Island—now called Roosevelt Island—in New York's East River. Like his friend Dempsey, Costigan died of consumption. Denny's brother John J. Costigan, a contractor in Providence, Rhode Island, instructed that the body be sent to Providence for burial. The newspapers reported, "Dennis Costigan was probably best known as the friend, advisor and perpetual second of Jack Dempsey and was behind that famous fighter in every fight he engaged in, from the early nineties, when he was defeated by Bob Fitzsimmons, up to Dempsey's last fight with Tommy Ryan at Sea Beach Pavilion, Coney Island. For several years past Costigan had acted as a chore man around the Fulton fish market for George Monahan, an old friend."[25]

Jack McAuliffe continued to compete in the ring through 1897, when he fought a ten-round draw with Tommy Ryan in Scranton, Pennsylvania. Some papers recorded this as a ten-round win for McAuliffe and other reports indicate that a draw was agreed upon in advance. An indecisive referee, who changed his mind about the outcome at least twice, made this a contest not worthy of either fighter. Jack continued to participate in sparring exhibitions through at least 1920. "The Napoleon of the Ring" died at his home at 73-20 Austin Street in the Forest Hills section of Queens on November 4, 1937, at age seventy-one. McAuliffe was posthumously inducted into *The Ring*'s Boxing Hall of Fame in 1954 and into the International Boxing Hall of Fame in 1995.

Jack Skelly also continued to fight through 1897. Skelly lived on for many years and remained active in boxing. Jack became a well-known and well-respected boxing referee being the third man in the ring for such fighters as Benny Leonard and Abe Goldstein. In 1922, he was named as a member of the New York State Athletic Commission (NYSAC). He continued to make his home in Brooklyn and lived a long life, passing away on May 24, 1953, at the age of eighty-three.

Richard K. Fox's reputation and influence continued to grow. He became internationally known as editor and publisher of the *National Police Gazette* and continued to publish and promote the weekly journal for the rest of his life. Fox arguably helped change American culture. The *Police Gazette*'s dogged reporting on and backing of athletic events and boxing in particular helped increase the popularity of sports in American society. Newspapers throughout the country, noting the popularity of Fox's publication, began to routinely assign reporters to cover sporting events and in short order started to dedicate whole pages and later, entire sections, of their newspapers to sports. Always a terrific marketer, Fox knew that keeping his publication's name in front of the public was a key to keeping people buying issues each week. In addition to boxing Fox "also gave medals for sculling, football, shooting, running, wrestling and every other branch of sport."[26] It is estimated that he gave away over one million dollars in prizes, championship belts and trophies during his time at the helm of the *Police Gazette*, each with the publication's name on them. After a year-long illness, Fox died at his home in Red Bank, New Jersey, on November 14, 1922, surrounded by his wife and three children.

Harry Hill, one of the Nonpareil's early supporters, would pass away less than a year after Jack. In the 1890s, Hill's fortunes took a turn for the worse. In addition to Harry Hill's Place, Harry had built up a large financial and real estate portfolio. Hill "owned two hotels in Flushing, and had fine Durham and Alderney cattle, fancy dogs, and horses. He built several steamboats to carry passengers and freight between Flushing and [New York]."[27] At one point, Hill was reported to be worth up to one million dollars. Hill's portfolio was, however, not as solid as it appeared on paper. His troubles began when the steamboat business failed and he lost a good bit of his investment in it. Hill also ran into problems with the police when he began objecting to what had become inordinate weekly payoffs reportedly exceeding $300. The payments were protection money to keep the New York police from interfering with the daily operations at Harry Hill's Place. When Hill tried to fight the police and made claims of blackmail against several officers, his troubles worsened. While the offending officers were transferred to other precincts, orders were issued that Hill's Place was not to be allowed to be open after 1:00 a.m. "That was tantamount to closing it altogether as his most profitable business was done between midnight and daylight."[28] In addition, a series of real estate failures, calling of notes that he had cosigned for friends and the failures of his steamship company and hotels all led to tremendous financial losses for Hill. He closed his famous place at Houston and Crosby streets and set up a series of other ventures—one in Harlem where the police continued to harass him and caused him to relocate across the East River, a small hotel in Corona on Long Island that burned to the ground in 1893 and finally a small bar and stable that he ran until his death. Hill came down with a fever and chills and died a week later at his home in Flushing, New York, on August 27, 1896. Hill was sixty-nine years old.

In an article in the *Saint Paul Globe* several years after Dempsey died, he was remembered by the author as "the greatest of his class in the ring." The author continued by saying, "His name thrilled the world—for all the world admires a fighter as it loves a lover. Thousands struggled for a place in the vast concourse that hurried to the arena when Jack Dempsey was to face some other formidable gladiator in a battle to the finish. Men shouted themselves hoarse as he was triumphantly borne from the scene of conquest on the shoulders of his worshippers after he had added another victory to his long list. Columns descriptive of his prowess appeared in public print. Wherever Dempsey went crowds followed that they might get a glimpse of the hero of more than half a hundred battles."[29] Decades after his premature death, the accolades continued. The Nonpareil was inducted into *The Ring*'s Boxing Hall of Fame in 1954 and the International Boxing Hall of Fame in 1992.

When the name Jack Dempsey is mentioned these days most people immediately think of the "Manassa Mauler." To all but the most ardent boxing fans and historians the Nonpareil has been forgotten. His place in the annals of the ring is secure. His record is as solid as granite and his legend firm, but the original Jack Dempsey has all but vanished. Heavyweight Jack Dempsey, through a magnificent and lengthy career and aided by continued press throughout his long life, unwittingly helped to hide the Nonpareil behind the cobwebs of time. Even so, when the records are examined and great fighters are remembered, the Nonpareil's name will always be mentioned with the greatest of all time.

Forgotten by ten thousand throats,
That thundered his acclaim,
Forgotten by his friends and foes,
Who cheered his very name.
Oblivion wraps his faded form,
But ages hence shall save
The memory of that Irish lad
That fills poor Dempsey's grave.[30]

"Jack Dempsey's Grave"
M.J. McMahon
1899

Far out in the wilds of Oregon,
On a lonely mountainside,
Where Columbia's mighty waters,
Roll down to the ocean side;
Where the giant fir and cedar,
Are imaged in the wave,
Overgrown with ferns and lichens,
I found Jack Dempsey's grave.

I found no marble monolith,
No broken shaft or stone,
Recording sixty victories,
This vanquished victor won;
No rose, no shamrock, could I,
Find, no mortal here to tell,
Where sleeps in this forsaken spot,
The immortal Nonpareil.

A winding wooded canyon road,
That mortals seldom tread,
Leads up this lonely mountain,
To the desert of the dead;
And the Western sun was sinking,
In Pacific's golden wave;
And the solemn pines kept watching,
Over poor Jack Dempsey's grave.

That man of honor and of iron,
That man of heart and steel,
That man who far out-classed his class,
And made mankind to feel,
That Dempsey's name and Dempsey's fame,
Should live in serried stone,
Is now at rest far in the West,
In the wilds of Oregon.

Forgotten by ten thousand throats,
That thundered his acclaim,
Forgotten by his friends and foes,
Who cheered his very name;
Oblivion wraps his faded form,
But ages hence shall save,
The memory of that Irish lad,
That fills poor Dempsey's grave.

Oh, Fame, why sleeps thy favored son,
In wilds, in woods, in weeds?
And shall he ever thus sleep on,
Interred his valiant deeds?
'Tis strange New York should thus forget,
Its "bravest of the brave"
And in the fields of Oregon,
Unmarked, leave Dempsey's grave.

Appendix: Dempsey's Professional Bouts, 1883–1895

Abbreviations: W—Win; L—Loss; KO—Knock Out; TKO—Technical Knock Out; D—Draw; EX—Exhibition

Date	NJD's Weight	Opponent	Opponent's Weight	Location	Result	Comments	Referee	Attendance
1883								
7-Apr	130	Ed "Rug" McDonald		Staten Island, NY	W-KO 21		Bob Smith	
14-Aug		Jack Boylan	160	Harry Hill's Pavilion, Flushing, NY	W-KO 23		William O'Brien	40
3-Sep		Harry Force		Outside Elliot's Hotel, Coney Island, Brooklyn, NY	D 11	Magisterial Interference	William E. Harding	
17-Sep		Thomas "Soap" McAlpine		Harry Hill's, New York, NY	D 4		Harry Hill	
15-Oct		Jack Boylan		Harry Hill's Pavilion in Flushing, NY	W 6			
10-Nov		Billy Frazier		New York, NY	W 6			
25-Nov		Robert "Cocky" Turnbull		Clarendon Hall, New York, NY	D 8		Billy Edwards	
1884								
7-Jan		J.J. Bagley		Revere Hall, Boston, MA	D 3	Collar and Elbow	Billy Mahoney	1,000
7-Jan		John McMahon's Unknown/Young Meehan		Revere Hall, Boston, MA	EX 3			1,000
15-Jan		William Mahoney		New York, NY	W-KO 3			
26-Jan		Joe Hennessey		New York, NY	W-TKO 4			
10-Feb		Joe Heiser		Williamsburg A.C., Brooklyn, NY	W 8			
14-Feb		Jim Fell		Billy Madden's Athletic Hall, New York, NY	W-KO 2			
28-Feb		Jim Barry		Billy Madden's Athletic Hall, New York, NY	W-KO 3		Bob Smith	
2-Mar		Joe Hennessey		New York, NY	W-KO 4			
4-Mar		Tom Sullivan		Billy Madden's Athletic Hall, New York, NY	W-KO 2			
6-Mar	148	Billy Dacey		Campbell's Hotel, Coney Island, Brooklyn, NY	W-KO 9		George Giddings/ James Glidden	500
2-Apr		Mike Mallory		Brooklyn, NY	EX 3			
14-Apr		Jim Sweeney		Tom Kearns' Champion's Rest, New York, NY	EX 4			
25-Apr		Joe Heiser		New York, NY	D 6			
1-May	133	Jack Bowles		Clarendon Hall, New York, NY	W-KO 6		George Taylor	
12-May		Mike Mallory		Madison Square Garden, New York, NY	EX 3			8,000

Dempsey's Professional Bouts

Date	NJD's Weight	Opponent	Opponent's Weight	Location	Result	Comments	Referee	Attendance
9-Jul		Tom Henry		Hammel's Hotel, Far Rockaway, NY	D 4	Magisterial Interference	Ned Mallahan	400
30-Jul	137	George Fulljames (For World Middleweight Championship)	130	Crooke's Point at Great Kills Staten Island, NY	W-KO 22			
2-Aug		Professor Walter Watson		Champion's Rest, Philadelphia, PA	EX 4			
4-Sep		Mike Dempsey		Rockaway Beach, NY	W-KO 7		Jack Welch and Tommy Ray	
15-Sep		Jimmy Ryan		Club Theater/Clark's Theatre, Philadelphia, PA	D 7			
6-Oct		Tommy Ferguson		Turn Halle, New York, NY	EX 3		Ed Plummer	
8-Oct		Robert "Cocky" Turnbull		Billy Madden's Athletic Hall, New York, NY	W 8			
21-Oct		Tommy Ferguson		Germania Assembly Rooms, New York, NY	EX			2,500
24-Oct		Tom Henry		Jack Thompson's Eighth-Street Theatre, New York, NY	W 6		Al Smith	Overflow
6-Nov		Tommy Ferguson		Harry Hill's, New York, NY	W 4		Harry Hill	
10-Nov		Tommy Ferguson		Madison Square Garden, New York, NY	EX 4			8,000
20-Nov		Billy Frazier		Alhambra Theatre, New York, NY	W-TK 5		Ed Plummer	80 to 100
30-Nov		Mike Mallon		Philadelphia, PA	W-TKO 3		Henry Rice	
9-Dec		Denny Costigan		Alhambra Theatre, New York, NY	EX 4			
15-Dec		George Wilson		Arthur Chambers' Champion's Rest, Philadelphia, PA	D 4			
19-Dec		Tommy Ferguson		Harry Hill's, New York, NY	EX 3			
1885								
12-Jan		Billy Frazier		Dempsey's Athletic Hall, New York, NY	D 4		Billy Madden	
13-Jan		Jimmy Ryan		Dempsey's Athletic Hall, New York, NY	D 4		Billy Madden	
21-Jan		Johnny Banks		New York, NY	W			
22-Jan		Jim Fell	180	Dempsey's Saloon, New York, NY	W 4		Billy Madden	

352 Appendix

Date	NJD's Weight	Opponent	Opponent's Weight	Location	Result	Comments	Referee	Attendance
26-Jan		Jack Fay		New York, NY	W 3		Billy Madden	
10-Feb		Joe Heiser		Brooklyn, NY	W 8			
19-Mar	142	Charles Bixamos	153	Sportsmen's Park, New Orleans, LA	W-KO 5		Jere Dunn	1,000
Apr	144	Jim Corbett		Olympic Athletic Club, San Francisco, CA	EX	Sparring Session		
4-May		Tom Barry		Mechanic's Pavilion, San Francisco, CA	W-KO 5		Mike Cleary	
11-May		Tom Cleary		Mechanic's Pavilion, San Francisco, CA	W-KO 5		Frank Crockett	
5-Jun		Jim Carr		Wigwam Theatre, San Francisco, CA	W-KO 9		Tom Barry	2,000
4-Jul		James Rodda		Nevada City, Nevada	W-KO 2			
20-Jul		Jack Keenan		Golden Gate Park, San Francisco, CA	W-KO 2		Jack Hallinan	
2-Sep		Billy Manning		Turnverein Hall, Los Angeles, CA	W-KO 8		Charlie Schroeder	
12-Sep		Tom Norton		Armory Hall, Sacramento, CA	W-TKO 4			
2-Nov		Dave Campbell		Columbia and Lewis Rivers, Washington Terr.	W-KO 3			3,000
21-Nov	157	Tom Cleary		Liberty Hall in Astoria, OR	EX 4			
14-Dec		Tom Barry	170	Turnhalle, Portland, OR	W-KO 6		Jack Keenan	
1886								
13-Jan	143	Mike Mallory		New York Athletic Club, New York, NY	EX 3		William O. Mort	1,500
15-Jan		Jimmy Murray		Germania Assembly Rooms, New York, NY	W 4		Plummer	
15-Jan		Tom Henry		Germania Assembly Rooms, New York, NY	W 4		Plummer	
15-Jan		Mike Donovan		Germania Assembly Rooms, New York, NY	EX 4		Billy O'Brien	
3-Feb	147	Jack Fogarty (For World Middleweight Championship)	150	Clarendon Hall, New York, NY	W-KO 27		Al Smith	
24-Feb	148	Pete McCoy	151	Oakland Avenue Rink, Jersey City, NJ	W 6		Mike Cleary and Jimmy Ryan	4,000

Dempsey's Professional Bouts 353

Date	NJD's Weight	Opponent	Opponent's Weight	Location	Result	Comments	Referee	Attendance
3-Mar		Joe Denning		Newark, NJ	EX 3			
14-Mar	147	George LaBlanche (For World Middleweight Championship)	155	Larchmont, NY	W-KO 13		James O'Neil	
10-Apr	147	Mile Cleary	150	Cosmopolitan Hotel, New York, NY	EX 3		Al Smith	
10-Apr	147	Jack Fogarty	150	Cosmopolitan Hotel, New York, NY	EX 4		Al Smith	
20-Apr	148	Jack Fogarty	150	Newburgh Opera House, Newburgh, NY	EX 3			2,000
24-Apr	148	Jack Fogarty	150	Casino Rink, Pittsburgh, PA	EX 4			2,000
25-Apr	148	Jack Fogarty	150	Casino Rink, Pittsburgh, PA	EX 4			2,000
26-Apr	148	Ned McCann	150	Theatre Comique, Philadelphia, PA	W-KO 4		Dominick McCaffrey	
28-Apr		Charles "Bull" McCarthy	150	Theatre Comique, Philadelphia, PA	D 4		James Dawson	
30-Apr		Jimmy Ryan	150	Theatre Comique, Philadelphia, PA	W 4			
20-May	146	Paddy Norton	143	Exposition Rink, St. Paul, MN	W 4		Patsy Mellen	1,200
25-May		Ed Moehler		Leland Rink, Minneapolis, MN	W 4			
22-Nov	157	Jack Burke	162	Mechanic's Pavilion, San Francisco, CA	D 10		Frank Crockett and Jack Hallinan	8,000
6-Dec		Denny Costigan		Turnhalle, Portland, OR	EX 3			
13-Dec		Jack Keenan		Ming Opera House, Helena, MT	EX 3			
15-Dec		McAuley		Butte City, MT	EX 3			
18-Dec		Charley Lange		Walker Opera House, Salt Lake City, UT	EX 4			
20-Dec		Jack Keenan		Cheyenne, WY	EX 3			
23-Dec		McAuley		Butte City, Montana	EX 3			
27-Dec		Denny Costigan		Milwaukee, WI	EX 3			
1887								
31-Jan	150	Mike Boden	175	Theatre Comique, Philadelphia, PA	W 4		Sparrow Golden	
2-Feb	150	Jack Langdon	146	Theatre Comique, Philadelphia, PA	W 4		Billy McLean	
5-Feb		Denny Killen		Theatre Comique, Philadelphia, PA	W 4			

354 Appendix

Date	NJD's Weight	Opponent	Opponent's Weight	Location	Result	Comments	Referee	Attendance
15-Mar		Denny Costigan		Washington Rink, Rochester, NY	EX 4			1,800
15-Mar		Jack Coyle		Washington Rink, Rochester, NY	EX 4			1,800
21-Mar		Tom McMahon		Detroit, MI	EX 4			
22-Mar		Denny Costigan		Detroit, MI	EX 4			
6-Apr		Sandy Banister		Adelphia Theatre, Buffalo, NY	EX3			
9-Apr	148	Billy Baker	183	Adelphia Theatre, Buffalo, NY	ND 4		Charles Perkins	Capacity 300
2-May	150	Patrick "Reddy" Gallagher	156	Frankfort St. Gym, Cleveland, OH	D 6		Mike Ryan	
15-Jun		Jack McAuliffe		Newburgh, NY	EX 4			
18-Jun		Jack McAuliffe		Adelphia Theatre, Buffalo, NY	EX 4			300
28-Jun		Jack McAuliffe		Cronheim's Theatre, Hoboken, NJ	EX 4			
4-Jul		Jack Ashton		Lowe's Opera House, Providence, RI	EX 4			
20-Aug		Jake Kilrain		North Adams, MA	EX 4		J.J. Delanthy	3,000
11-Oct	150	Ed Reese		Warren Lewis' Hoboken Casino, Hoboken, NJ	W 4		Tom Barker	
13-Oct	150	Jim McHugh	150	Warren Lewis' Hoboken Casino, Hoboken, NJ	W 4	Rd5 Added as EX		
15-Oct	150	Billy Dacey		Warren Lewis' Hoboken Casino, Hoboken, NJ	W 4			
Oct		Jack McAuliffe		Bancroft's Skating Rink, New Bedford, MA	EX 4			
31-Oct		Ned McCann		Grand Central Theater, Wilmington, DE	W 4			
1-Nov		Frank Bosworth		Grand Central Theater, Wilmington, DE	W 4			
3-Nov		Denny Kelliher	220	Grand Central Theater, Wilmington, DE	W 4			
5-Nov		Bill Gabig		Grand Central Theater, Wilmington, DE	W 4			
6-Nov		Mike Boden		Variety Theater, Wilmington, DE				
13-Dec	147	Johnny Reagan (For World Middleweight Championship)	147	Lloyd's Neck, NY, and Sands Point, NY	W-TK 45		Frank Stevenson	

Date	NJD's Weight	Opponent	Opponent's Weight	Location	Result	Comments	Referee	Attendance
22-Dec		Joe Denning		Palace Rink, Brooklyn, NY	EX 3			2,500
22-Dec		Tom Henry		Palace Rink, Brooklyn, NY	EX 3			2,500
22-Dec		Jack McAuliffe		Palace Rink, Brooklyn, NY	EX 3			2,500
28-Dec		Opponent Unknown		New Haven, CT	EX			
29-Dec		Tom Henry		Brooklyn, NY	EX 3			
1888								
3-Jan		Billy Madden		Poole's Theater, New York, NY	EX 3			
5-Jan		Billy Madden		Baltimore, MD	EX 3			
15-Jan		Denny Costigan		Baltimore, MD	EX 3			
16-Jan		Denny Kelliher		Music Hall, Boston, MA	EX 3			
23-Jan		Denny Kelliher		Music Hall, Boston, MA	EX 3			3,500
24-Jan		Billy Madden		Kernan's Theatre, Washington, DC	EX 3			
31-Jan		Dominick McCaffrey	152	Pavonia Rink, Jersey City, NJ	W 10		Jere Dunn	
7-Feb		Denny Costigan		Troy, NY	EX 4			
9-Feb		Denny Costigan		Troy, NY	EX 3			5,600
9-Feb		Tom Henry		Troy, NY	EX 3			
18-Feb		Billy Baker	185	Adelphia Theatre, Buffalo, NY	ND 4			
13-Mar		Peter Nolan		Pittsburgh, PA	EX 4			
15-Mar		Con Riley		Cincinnati, OH	EX 4			
26-Mar		Denny Costigan		Brooklyn, NY	EX 4			
3-Apr		Joe Denning		Grand Street Palace Rink, Brooklyn, NY	EX 4		George W. Bunce	
9-Apr		Joe Coburn		Parepa Hall, Boston, MA	EX			
16-Apr		Denny Costigan		Harry Miner's Eighth Ave. Theatre	EX4	Weeklong Engagement		
23-Apr		James "Billy" Stevens		Grand Theater, Brooklyn, NY	W 4			
4-Jun		John L. Sullivan		New York Academy of Music, New York, NY	EX	Postponed		
Summer		Mike Lucie		Troy, NY	EX			
15-Nov	147	Mike Donovan	149	Palace Rink, Brooklyn, NY	D 6		Billy O'Brien	2,500
9-Dec		Denny Costigan		Hyde & Behman's Theater, Brooklyn, NY	EX 4			
15-Dec		Denny Costigan		Hyde & Behman's Theater, Brooklyn, NY	EX 4			
31-Dec		George Northridge		Kernan's Theatre in Washington, DC.	EX 3			

Date	NJD's Weight	Opponent	Opponent's Weight	Location	Result	Comments	Referee	Attendance
1889								
2-Jan		Jim McNamee		Brooklyn, NY	EX			
4-Jan		George Northridge		Kernan's Theatre, Washington, DC	EX			
Jan		Denny Costigan		Baltimore, MD	EX			
14-Jan		Denny Costigan		Pittsburgh Academy of Music, Pittsburgh, PA	EX 3			
18-Jan		Denny Costigan		Pittsburgh Academy of Music, Pittsburgh, PA	EX 3			
4-Feb		Denny Costigan		Buffalo, NY	EX 3			
18-Mar		Jim Daly—Rumored—No Verification		Houtzdale, PA	?			
15-Apr		Denny Costigan		Grand Theatre, Brooklyn, NY	EX			
24-Apr		Denny Costigan		Grand Theatre, Brooklyn, NY	EX			
29-Apr		Denny Costigan		San Jose, California	EX			
16-May		Professor Murray		Los Angeles Theater, Los Angeles, CA	EX 4			
22-May		Denny Costigan		Clunie Opera House, Sacramento, CA	EX 4			
23-May		Denny Costigan		Clunie Opera House, Sacramento, CA	EX 4			
24-May		Denny Costigan		Oakland Theatre, Oakland, CA	EX			4
25-May		Denny Costigan		Oakland Theatre, Oakland, CA	EX 4			
10-Jun		Mike Lucie		California A.C., San Francisco, CA	EX 3			
22-Aug	150	Mike Dempsey		California A.C., San Francisco, CA	W-KO 7			
27-Aug	150	George LaBlanche	161	California A.C., San Francisco, CA	L-KO 32		Hiram Cook	2,000
1890								
18-Feb	147¼	"Australian" Billy McCarthy (For World Middleweight Championship)	151.5	California A.C.—Armory Hall, San Francisco, CA	W-TK 28		Hiram Cook	2,000
11-Mar		Tom Cleary		Tacoma, WA	EX 4			
11-Mar		Jack Burke		Tacoma, WA	EX 6			

Dempsey's Professional Bouts 357

Date	NJD's Weight	Opponent	Opponent's Weight	Location	Result	Comments	Referee	Attendance
13-Mar		John Clark		Seattle, WA	ND 4			
2-May		Paddy Gorman		Seattle Athletic Club, Seattle, WA	EX 4			
16-May		Dave Campbell		Seattle, WA	EX			
27-May		Paddy Gorman		Vogt Grand, Dalles, OR	EX 3			
11-Jun		Paddy Gorman		Maguire's Opera House, Butte, MT	EX 3			
13-Jun		Paddy Gorman		Lyceum Theater, Butte, MT	EX 3			
16-Jun		Paddy Gorman		Evans Opera House, Anaconda, MT	EX 3			
20-Jun		Paddy Gorman		Golden Gate Athletic Club, Salt Lake City, UT	EX 4			
21-Jun		Paddy Gorman		Golden Gate Athletic Club, Salt Lake City, UT	EX 4			
Jun		Paddy Gorman		Park City, UT	EX 4			
Jun		Paddy Gorman		Denver, CO	EX 4			
27-Jun		Paddy Gorman		Aspen, CO	EX 4			
Jun		Paddy Gorman		Colorado Springs, CO	EX 4			
Jun		Paddy Gorman		Pueblo, CO	EX 4			
Jun		Paddy Gorman		Dodge City, KS	EX 4			
Jun		Paddy Gorman		Hutchinson, KS	EX 4			
4-Jul		Paddy Gorman		Brotherhood Park, St. Louis, MO	EX 2	Magisterial Interference		2,000
5-Jul		Charley Daly		Brotherhood Park, St. Louis, MO	EX 4			
28-Jul		Mike Brennan		Gaiety Theatre, Buffalo, NY	EX 4			
31-Jul		Paddy Gorman		Wagner Opera House, Bradford, PA	EX 4			
31-Jul		Mike Brennan		Wagner Opera House, Bradford, PA	EX 4			
4-Aug		Paddy Gorman		Standard Theater, Syracuse, NY	EX 3		Ed Degan	
25-Aug	150	"Brooklyn" Jimmy Carroll	160	Palace Theater, Brooklyn, NY	EX			4,000
1-Sep	150	"Brooklyn" Jimmy Carroll	160	Harry Williams' Academy Theater, Pittsburgh, PA	EX 4			
1-Sep	150	"Brooklyn" Jimmy Carroll	160	Harry Williams' Academy Theater, Pittsburgh, PA	EX 4			
2-Sep	150	"Brooklyn" Jimmy Carroll	160	Harry Williams' Academy Theater, Pittsburgh, PA	EX 4			

358 Appendix

Date	NJD's Weight	Opponent	Opponent's Weight	Location	Result	Comments	Referee	Attendance
4-Sep	150	"Brooklyn" Jimmy Carroll	160	Harry Williams' Academy Theater, Pittsburgh, PA	EX 4			
6-Sep	150	"Brooklyn" Jimmy Carroll	160	Harry Williams' Academy Theater, Pittsburgh, PA	EX 4			
1891								
5-Jan	148	Mike Conley	190	Theater, Dallas, TX	EX 3			
12-Jan	148	Jack McAuliffe	131	Audubon Athletic Club, New Orleans, LA	EX 4		Patsy Doody	500
14-Jan	148	Bob Fitzsimmons (For World Middleweight Championship)	151	Olympic Club, New Orleans, LA	L-KO 13		Col. A. Brewster	4,000
5-Oct		"Mysterious" Billy Smith		San Francisco, CA	EX			
16-Oct		Young Mitchell		Pacific Athletic Club, San Francisco, CA	EX 4			
9-Nov		Young Mitchell		Pastime Athletic Club, Portland, OR	EX 6			
16-Nov		Young Mitchell		Hyde and Behman's Theatre, Brooklyn, NY	EX			
16-Nov		Young Mitchell		Hyde and Behman's Theatre, Brooklyn, NY	EX			
23-Nov		Young Mitchell		Central Theatre, Philadelphia, PA	EX			
1892								
Jan		Peter Maher		New York, NY	EX 2			
16-Aug		"Mysterious" Billy Smith		Pastime Athletic Club, Portland, OR	EX 4			
1893								
28-Feb	148	Billy Keough	190	Pastime Athletic Club, Portland, OR	W 4		Jack Robertson	
31-Jul		Unknown (John Barnes?)		Phoenix Athletic Club, St. Paul, MN	EX 3			
4-Sep		Bob Fitzsimmons		New York, NY	EX 3			
25-Sep		Denny Costigan		Philadelphia, PA	EX 3			
2-Oct		Denny Costigan		Philadelphia, PA	EX 3			
9-Nov		Denny Costigan		Buffalo, NY	EX			

Date	NJD's Weight	Opponent	Opponent's Weight	Location	Result	Comments	Referee	Attendance
10-Nov		Denny Costigan		Buffalo, NY	EX			
11-Nov		Denny Costigan		Buffalo, NY	EX			
13-Nov		Denny Costigan		H.R. Jacobs' Theater, New York, NY	EX			
Dec		Denny Costigan		Boston, MA	EX 3			
14-Dec		Dick Moore		Boston, MA	EX 3			
30-Dec		Joe Fielden		Albaugh's Theater, Washington, DC	EX 4			
1894								
8-Jan		Denny Costigan		Bijou Theatre, Brooklyn, NY	EX 3			
27-Jan		Denny Costigan		Madison Square Garden, New York, NY	EX 3			8,000
13-Feb		Denny Costigan		Academy of Music, Roanoke, VA	EX 4			
20-Feb		Denny Costigan		Grand Theater, Atlanta, GA	EX 4			
21-Feb		Denny Costigan		Grand Theater, Atlanta, GA	EX 4			
7-Apr		Harry Wyatt		Star Athletic Club, Buffalo, NY	EX 8			
4-Sep		Bob Fitzsimmons		New Orleans, LA	EX	postponed	William Welch	
5-Sep	140/146	"Australian" Billy McCarthy	154/165	Auditorium AC, New Orleans, LA	D 20		John Duffy	
6-Dec		Andy Bowen		Savannah, GA	EX 4			
1895								
18-Jan		Tommy Ryan (For World Welterweight Championship)		Sea Side A.C., Coney Island, Brooklyn, NY	L-KO 3		Tim Hurst	5,000
8-Jun		John L. Sullivan		Madison Square Garden, New York, NY	EX 3			

NOTES

Introduction

1. McMahon, M.J., *The Nonpareil's Grave*, 1899.
2. *Webster's New Collegiate Dictionary*, G.C. Merriam Co., Springfield, MA, 1977.
3. Callis, Tracy, "'Nonpareil' Jack Dempsey ... Slick and Quick," http://www.cyberboxingzone.com.
4. *Los Angeles Times*, April 22, 1992, Sports Section C, pg. 13.
5. Brady, William A., *The Fighting Man*, pg. 86.
6. *San Francisco Call*, November 2, 1895, pg. 1.
7. *National Police Gazette*, November 23, 1895, pg. 11.
8. Callis, Tracy, "'Nonpareil' Jack Dempsey ... Slick and Quick," http://www.cyberboxingzone.com.
9. *Brooklyn Eagle*, January 13, 1895, pg. 11.
10. *Brooklyn Eagle*, April 7, 1883, pg. 4.
11. *Ibid*.
12. Reference to Irish boxing legend Dan Donnelly.
13. *Brooklyn Eagle*, September 3, 1883, pg. 4.
14. Fox, Richard K., *The Life and Battles of Jack Dempsey*, pg. 29.
15. *National Police Gazette*, April 10, 1886, pg. 7.
16. *Brooklyn Eagle*, November 23, 1884, pg. 2.
17. Callis, Tracy, "'Nonpareil' Jack Dempsey ... Slick and Quick," http://www.cyberboxingzone.com.
18. *National Police Gazette*, April 3, 1886, pg. 10.
19. *Fort Wayne Daily Gazette*, April 16, 1886, pg. 3.
20. White, Charley, *Syracuse Herald*, "Inside the Ring with the Great Fighters," May 24, 1911, pg. 13.
21. *New York Evening World*, January 15, 1891, pg. 1.
22. *Ibid*.
23. *Ibid*.
24. *Brooklyn Eagle*, May 15, 1887, pg. 15.
25. *Brooklyn Eagle*, April 7, 1883, pg. 4.
26. *New York Sun*, February 2, 1888, pg. 3.
27. *St. Louis Post-Dispatch*, December 15, 1887, pg. 8.
28. *National Police Gazette*, April 3, 1886, pg. 10.
29. *Daily Alta California*, August 26, 1889, pg. 8.
30. *Buffalo Express*, December 7, 1911, pg. 19.
31. Callis, Tracy, "'Nonpareil' Jack Dempsey ... Slick and Quick," http://www.cyberboxingzone.com.
32. McCallum, John, *The World Heavyweight Boxing Championship*, pg. 125.
33. *Brooklyn Eagle*, November 23, 1884, pg. 2.
34. *Boston Globe*, October 25, 1895, pg. 8.
35. *Brooklyn Eagle*, December 24, 1887, pg. 4.
36. *New York World*, March 14, 1900, pg. 10.
37. *St. Louis Post-Dispatch*, March 18, 1886, pg. 8.
38. *Chicago Herald*, November 11, 1888, pg. 18.
39. *San Francisco Call*, June 22, 1913, pg. 45.
40. *Logansport Journal*, December 14, 1888, pg. 5.
41. *Ibid*.
42. *St. Louis Post-Dispatch*, March 27, 1886, pg. 9.
43. *Brooklyn Eagle*, January 8, 1888, pg. 1.
44. *St. Louis Post-Dispatch*, February 4, 1887, pg. 5.
45. *Brooklyn Eagle*, April 4, 1886, pg. 16
46. Callis, Tracy, "'Nonpareil' Jack Dempsey ... Slick and Quick," http://www.cyberboxingzone.com.
47. Blinn, William, *Brian's Song*, pg. 1.

The Evolution of Rules and Equipment

1. *Cambridge City Tribune*, August 25, 1898, pg. 13.
2. Allen, Arly, "The First Boxing Match in England," *IBRO Journal* 90 (June 20, 2006), pgs. 17–18.
3. de Saussure, Cesar, *A Foreign View of England in the Reigns of George I and George II*, pg. 181.
4. Gee, Tony, *Up to Scratch: Bareknuckle Fighting and the Champions of the Prize-ring*, pg. 13.
5. Burgh, James, *Political Disquisitions*, p. 211.
6. http://www.cyberboxingzone.com/boxing/law.htm.
7. British Boxing Hall of Fame website,
8. Corbett, *Scientific Boxing*, pg. 90.
9. *Ibid*., pg. 94.
10. *Ibid*., pg. 80.
11. *National Police Gazette*, April 5, 1884, pg. 10.
12. *Ibid*., December 31, 1887, pg. 10.
13. *Ibid*., November 26, 1892, pg. 11.
14. *Arizona Weekly Citizen*, February 26, 1887, pg. 1.
15. *Cincinnati Commercial Tribune-Gazette*, "What a Knock-out Blow Is," November 1, 1890, p. 10.
16. *Wichita Eagle*, November 30, 1888, pg. 6.
17. *Sacramento Record-Union*, December 20, 1896, pg. 9.
18. *Ibid*.
19. *New York Sun*, November 21, 1884, pg. 3.
20. Fox, Richard K., *The Life and Battles of Jack Dempsey*, pg. 27.
21. Misson, Henri de Valbourg, *M. Misson's Mem-*

oirs and Observations in His Travels Over England, pg. 304.
22. Quoted in Richard Carew of Antony, *The Survey of Cornwall*, p. 44.
23. de Saussure, Cesar, *A Foreign View of England in the Reigns of George I and George II*, pg. 180.
24. cyberboxingzone.com/boxing/london-rules-1838.htm.
25. *National Police Gazette*, February 16, 1889, pg. 7.
26. Letter to the Author from Arly Allen, April 28, 2015.
27. Broughton, John, *Proposals for Erecting an Amphitheatre for the Manly Exercise of Boxing*, pg. 4.
28. *National Police Gazette*, February 16, 1889, pg. 7.
29. *Syracuse Herald*, 1911.
30. *National Police Gazette*, February 16, 1889, pg. 7.

1862 to 1882—From Athgarvan to Brooklyn

1. *Dan Donnelly & Donnelly's Hollow*, http://www.curraghcamp.com/dan.html.
2. White, Charley, *Syracuse Herald*, "Inside the Ring with the Great Fighters," May 24, 1911, pg. 13.
3. *Boston Globe*, October 25, 1895, pg. 8.
4. *Brooklyn Eagle*, December 25, 1887, pg. 11.
5. County Kildare Online Electronic History Journal, Kildare County Library & Arts Services.
6. *Pearson's Magazine*, Vol. 29, April 1913, pg. 469.
7. White, Charley, *Syracuse Herald*, May 24, 1911, pg. 13.
8. *St. Louis Post-Dispatch*, March 27, 1886, pg. 9.
9. *National Police Gazette*, March 22, 1884, pg. 10.
10. *Anaconda Standard*, November 4, 1895, pg. 5.
11. *St. Louis Post-Dispatch*, March 27, 1886, pg. 9.
12. *National Police Gazette*, April 10, 1886, pg. 7.
13. White, Charley, *Syracuse Herald*, May 24, 1911, pg. 13.
14. *Brooklyn Eagle*, December 13, 1887, pg. 4.

1883—The Cooper Enters the Ring

1. *National Police Gazette*, March 22, 1884, pg. 10.
2. Buchstein, Fred, *New York History Review*, "Harry Hill—Saloon Fighting's P.T. Barnum," July 16, 2012.
3. Harry Hill's Infamous Dance Hall, http://www.ashlandelks.org/html/history/corks/environs/harry_hills.html.
4. *New York Times*, August 28, 1896, pg.
5. *New York Times*, August 28, 1896, pg.
6. Fox, Richard K., *The Life and Battles of Jack Dempsey*, pgs. 3–4.
7. *Pearson's Magazine*, April 1913, pg. 471.
8. Ibid.
9. Ibid.
10. *National Police Gazette*, March 22, 1884, pg. 10.
11. Ibid., April 28, 1883, pg. 14.
12. *Brooklyn Eagle*, April 7, 1883, pg. 4.
13. Ibid.
14. Ibid.
15. *Milwaukee Sentinel*, June 14, 1882, pg. 4.
16. *National Police Gazette*, June 9, 1883, pg. 10.
17. Ibid., August 25, 1883, pg. 10.
18. *New York Sun*, August 15, 1883, pg. 3.
19. Ibid.
20. Ibid., pg. 8.
21. *New York Times*, August 15, 1883, pg. 8.
22. *National Police Gazette*, September 1, 1883, pg. 14.
23. Fox, Richard K., *The Life and Battles of Jack Dempsey*, pg. 13.
24. *National Police Gazette*, March 22, 1884, pg. 10.
25. *Newburgh Daily News*, February 13, 1888, pg. 3.
26. *Brooklyn Eagle*, September 3, 1883, pg. 4.
27. Fox, Richard K., *The Life and Battles of Jack Dempsey*, pg. 14.
28. *National Police Gazette*, September 15, 1883, pg. 10.
29. *New York Times*, September 4, 1883, pg. 5.
30. Ibid.
31. Ibid.
32. *New York Sun*, September 4, 1883, pg. 3.
33. Ibid.
34. *New York Tribune*, September 4, 1883, pg. 5.
35. *New York Sun*, September 4, 1883, pg. 3.
36. *New York Tribune*, September 4, 1883, pg. 5.
37. *New York Sun*, September 4, 1883, pg. 3.
38. *National Police Gazette*, September 22, 1883, pg. 10.
39. Fox, Richard K., *The Life and Battles of Jack Dempsey*, pg. 16.
40. *National Police Gazette*, September 29, 1883, pg. 10.
41. Ibid., October 18, 1883, pg. 14.
42. *Brooklyn Eagle*, September 12, 1883, pg. 2.
43. Ibid., September 4, 1883, pg. 2.
44. Ibid.
45. *New York Sun*, September 18, 1883, pg. 3.
46. *National Police Gazette*, March 22, 1884, pg. 10.
47. *New York Tribune*, September 18, 1883, pg. 2.
48. *New York Herald*, September 18, 1883, pg. 5.
49. *New York Sun*, September 18, 1883, pg. 3.
50. *National Police Gazette*, March 22, 1884, pg. 10.
51. Ibid., October 13, 1883, pg. 10.
52. *New York Tribune*, September 21, 1883, pg. 8.
53. *National Police Gazette*, October 13, 1883, pg. 14.
54. Ibid., December 22, 1883, pg. 14.
55. Ibid., October 20, 1883, pg. 14.
56. *Sacramento Daily Record-Union*, February 22, 1889, pg. 1.
57. *St. Louis Post-Dispatch*, March 20, 1892, pg. 24.
58. *National Police Gazette*, March 22, 1884, pg. 10.
59. Ibid., December 15, 1883, pg. 10.

1884—On the Rise

1. Callis, Tracy, "Denny Costigan," http://www.cyberboxingzone.com.
2. *Boston Globe*, January 8, 1884, pg. 4.
3. *National Police Gazette*, January 26, 1894, pg. 14.
4. Fox, Richard K., *The Life and Battles of Jack Dempsey*, pg. 19.
5. *Brooklyn Eagle*, April 21, 1886, pg. 6.
6. Callis, Tracy, "Jim Fell," http://www.cyberboxingzone.com.
7. *New York Sun*, February 29, 1884, pg. 1.

8. *National Police Gazette*, March 15, 1894, pg. 14.
9. *New York Sun*, February 29, 1884, pg. 1.
10. *National Police Gazette*, March 27, 1886, pg. 3.
11. *Ibid.*, April 26, 1884, pg. 10.
12. *Ibid.*, February 23, 1884, pg. 14.
13. *Ibid.*, March 22, 1884, pg. 10.
14. *New York Herald*, March 7, 1884, pg. 9.
15. *Ibid.*
16. *Brooklyn Eagle*, March 6, 1884, pg. 4.
17. *Ibid.*
18. *Galveston Daily News*, March 7, 1884, pg. 7.
19. *New York Herald*, March 7, 1884, pg. 9.
20. *National Police Gazette*, March 22, 1884, pg. 10.
21. *Galveston Daily News*, March 7, 1884, pg. 7.
22. *National Police Gazette*, March 22, 1884, pg. 10.
23. *Ibid.*, May 17, 1884, pg. 10.
24. *Ibid.*
25. Fox, Richard K., *The Life and Battles of Jack Dempsey*, pg. 25.
26. *New York Sun*, May 13, 1884, pg. 1.
27. *New York Tribune*, May 13, 1884, pg. 5.
28. *New York Times*, July 10, 1884.
29. *Brooklyn Eagle*, July 9, 1884, pg. 4.
30. *New York Times*, July 10, 1884.
31. *Brooklyn Eagle*, July 14, 1884, pg. 3.
32. *Ibid.*, pg. 2.
33. *New York Times*, July 27, 1884, pg. 12.
34. *National Police Gazette*, August 16, 1884, pg. 7.
35. *New York Times*, July 31, 1884, pg. 3.
36. *Ibid.*
37. *Ibid.*
38. Fox, Richard K., *The Life and Battles of Jack Dempsey*, pg. 28.
39. *New York Times*, July 31, 1884, pg. 3.
40. *Brooklyn Eagle*, July 30, 1884, pg. 4.
41. *New York Times*, July 31, 1884, pg. 3.
42. Fox, Richard K., *The Life and Battles of Jack Dempsey*, pg. 29.
43. *Brooklyn Eagle*, July 30, 1884, pg. 4.
44. *National Police Gazette*, August 16, 1884, pg. 7.
45. *New York Times*, August 22, 1884.
46. *New York Sun*, August 22, 1884, pg. 3.
47. *New York Times*, August 28, 1888, pg. 8.
48. *National Police Gazette*, August 23, 1884, pg. 10.
49. *New York Times*, September 24, 1888.
50. *Warsaw Daily Times*, September 24, 1888, pg. 1.
51. *Ibid.*
52. *Brooklyn Eagle*, April 20, 1889, pg. 2.
53. *National Police Gazette*, August 23, 1884, pg. 10.
54. Fields, Armond, *Eddie Foy: A Biography of the Early Popular Stage Comedian*, pg. 16.
55. *National Police Gazette*, September 13, 1884, pg. 10.
56. *New York Times*, July 28, 1894, pg. 14.
57. *National Police Gazette*, September 20, 1884, pg. 10.
58. *Ibid.*, September 27, 1884, pg. 14.
59. *Daily Gazette and News Bulletin*, September 5, 1884, pg. 1.
60. *National Police Gazette*, October 11, 1884, pg. 10.
61. *New York Sun*, September 24, 1884, pg. 4.
62. *National Police Gazette*, October 18, 1884, pg. 10.
63. *New York Sun*, October 7, 1884, pg. 3.

64. Fox, Richard K., *The Life and Battles of Jack Dempsey*, pg. 30.
65. *Ibid.*, pg. 31.
66. *New York Sun*, October 9, 1884, pg. 1.
67. *Boston Globe*, May 3, 1887, pg.
68. *New York Sun*, May 6, 1887, pg. 1.
69. *New York Times*, August 7, 1908.
70. *Ibid.*
71. *Boston Globe*, October 22, 1884, pg. 11.
72. *New York Times*, October 25, 1884, pg. 2.
73. *Ibid.*
74. *Daily Cosmopolitan*, November 15, 1884, pg. 4.
75. *New York Times*, October 25, 1884, pg. 2.
76. *Lowell Daily Courier*, October 25, 1884, pg. 4.
77. *National Police Gazette*, November 15, 1884, pg. 10.
78. *New York Sun*, November 7, 1884, pg.
79. *National Police Gazette*, November 29, 1884, pg. 10.
80. *New York Sun*, November 21, 1884, pg. 3.
81. *Ibid.*
82. *New York Times*, November 21, 1884, pg. 5.
83. *New York Sun*, November 21, 1884, pg. 3.
84. *Ibid.*
85. Fox, Richard K., *The Life and Battles of Jack Dempsey*, pg. 35.
86. *New York Times*, November 21, 1884, pg. 5.
87. *New York Sun*, November 21, 1884, pg. 3.
88. *National Police Gazette*, December 6, 1884, pg. 14.
89. *New York Times*, November 21, 1884, pg. 5.
90. *New York Sun*, November 21, 1884, pg. 3.
91. *Ibid.*
92. *National Republican*, December 1, 1884, pg. 1.
93. *Boston Globe*, December 1, 1884, pg. 1.
94. *Reno Evening Gazette*, December 1, 1884, pg. 2.
95. *National Republican*, December 1, 1884, pg. 1.
96. *New York Sun*, December 1, 1884, pg. 3.
97. *Reno Evening Gazette*, December 1, 1884, pg. 2.
98. Fox, Richard K., *The Life and Battles of Jack Dempsey*, pg. 38.
99. *Biddeford Journal*, November 26, 1884, pg. 1.
100. *National Police Gazette*, December 27, 1884, pg. 10.
101. *National Police Gazette*, January 3, 1885, pg. 10.
102. *Amsterdam Daily Democrat*, December 16, 1884, pg. 2.
103. *Daily Cairo Bulletin*, December 17, 1884, pg. 4.
104. *New York Sun*, December 17, 1884, pg. 1.
105. *Boston Globe*, December 18, 1884, pg. 4.
106. *National Police Gazette*, January 10, 1885, pg. 10.
107. *Ibid.*, December 20, 1884, pg. 10.
108. *Ibid.*, January 10, 1885, pg. 11.

1885—A Full Dance Card

1. *National Police Gazette*, January 31, 1885, pg. 10.
2. *Western Appeal*, July 4, 1885, pg. 3.
3. *National Police Gazette*, January 31, 1885, pg. 10.
4. *New York Sun*, January 13, 1885, pg. 1.
5. *Ibid.*
6. *Wheeling Intelligencer*, January 20, 1885, pg. 1.
7. *Omaha Daily Bee*, January 24, 1885, pg. 2.

8. *Boston Globe*, January 23, 1885, pg. 7.
9. *National Police Gazette*, February 14, 1885, pg. 10.
10. *New York Sun*, January 31, 1885, pg. 3.
11. *Boston Globe*, February 12, 1885, pg. 4.
12. *New York Sun*, February, 21, 1885, pg. 1.
13. *Chicago Tribune*, March 3, 1885, pg. 6.
14. Dunn, Mark, Letter to the Author, June 3, 2014.
15. *Chicago Tribune*, March 3, 1885, pg. 6.
16. *Chicago Herald*, March 17, 1885, pg. 3.
17. *Brooklyn Eagle*, March 20, 1885, pg. 4.
18. Fox, Richard K., *The Life and Battles of Jack Dempsey*, pg. 39.
19. *Chicago Tribune*, April 6, 1885, pg. 2.
20. Fields, Armond, *Eddie Foy: A Biography of the Early Popular Stage Comedian*, pg. 16.
21. *Ibid.*, pg. 18
22. Callis, Tracy, "Jim Corbett," http://www.cyberboxingzone.com.
23. Corbett, Jim, "My Life Story," *National Police Gazette*, November 8, 1924, pg.
24. *Ibid.*, pg.
25. *Ibid.*, pg.
26. Fields, Armond, *Eddie Foy: A Biography of the Early Popular Stage Comedian*, pg. 19.
27. *National Police Gazette*, May 30, 1885, pg. 10.
28. *San Francisco Daily Alta California*, May 5, 1885, pg. 1.
29. *Ibid.*
30. *San Francisco Daily Evening Bulletin*, May 5, 1885, pg. 1.
31. *San Francisco Daily Alta California*, May 5, 1885, pg. 1.
32. *San Francisco Daily Evening Bulletin*, May 5, 1885, pg. 1.
33. *San Francisco Daily Alta California*, May 5, 1885, pg. 1.
34. http://www.examiner.com/article/remembering-mechanics-pavilion.
35. *National Police Gazette*, May 30, 1885, pg. 10.
36. Fox, Richard K., *The Life and Battles of Jack Dempsey*, pg. 42.
37. *Morning Oregonian*, February 19, 1895, pg. 9.
38. *Brooklyn Eagle*, May 23, 1885, pg. 4.
39. *San Francisco Chronicle*, June 6, 1885, pg. 1.
40. *Ibid.*
41. Fox, Richard K., *The Life and Battles of Jack Dempsey*, pg. 44.
42. *New York Sun*, June 14, 1885, pg.1; *San Francisco Chronicle*, June 6, 1885, pg. 1.
43. *Los Angeles Daily Herald*, October 6, 1886, pg. 5.
44. *Sacramento Daily Record-Union*, July 6, 1885, pg. 3.
45. *National Police Gazette*, July 1, 1922, pg. 3.
46. *Ibid.*
47. *Ibid.*
48. *Ibid.*, December, 1888, pg. 10.
49. *McKenney's Pacific Coast Directory for Businesses* (Vol. 1886–87).
50. *National Police Gazette*, July 1, 1922, pg. 3.
51. Fox, Richard K., *The Life and Battles of Jack Dempsey*, pg. 48.
52. *New York Sun*, February 6, 1887, pg. 10.
53. *Ibid.*
54. *Boston Globe*, August 11, 1885, pg. 2.
55. *Ibid.*
56. *Ibid.*, November 22, 1885, pg. 3.
57. *Logansport Chronicle*, September 5, 1885, pg. 8.
58. *Salt Lake Evening Democrat*, August 24, 1885, pg. 3.
59. *Boston Globe*, August 11, 1885, pg. 2.
60. *National Police Gazette*, August 22, 1885, pg. 10.
61. *Sacramento Daily Record-Union*, August 27, 1885, pg. 1.
62. *New York Sun*, September 13, 1885, pg. 7.
63. *Ibid.*
64. *Los Angeles Herald*, November 2, 1918, pg. 38.
65. *Sacramento Daily Record-Union*, August 20, 1885, pg. 3.
66. *Ibid.*, September 15, 1885, pg. 3.
67. *Daily Morning Astorian*, September 17, 1885, pg. 3.
68. *Salt Lake Evening Democrat*, October 13, 1885, pg. 1.
69. *Brooklyn Eagle*, October 8, 1885, pg. 1.
70. *Ibid.*, August 26, 1890, pg. 1.
71. Fox, Richard K., *The Life and Battles of Jack Dempsey*, pg. 51.
72. *Daily Morning Astorian*, December 28, 1890, pg. 4.
73. *Sacramento Daily Record-Union*, November 3, 1885, pg. 2.
74. *New York Sun*, November 8, 1885, pg. 7.
75. Fox, Richard K., *The Life and Battles of Jack Dempsey*, pg. 53.
76. *Daily Morning Astorian*, December 28, 1890, pg. 4.
77. *National Police Gazette*, November 14, 1885, pg. 10.
78. *New York Times*, November 3, 1885.
79. *Wellsville Daily Reporter*, November 3, 1885, pg. 1.
80. *Sacramento Daily Record-Union*, November 3, 1885, pg. 2.
81. *Salt Lake Tribune*, June 21, 1890, pg. 5.
82. *Anaconda Standard*, May 27, 1895, pg. 7.
83. *Morning Oregonian*, June 27, 1911, pg. 1.
84. *Daily Capital Journal*, July 21, 1948, pg. 8.
85. *Daily Morning Astorian*, November 10, 1885, pg. 3.
86. *National Police Gazette*, November 14, 1885, pg. 10.
87. *Daily Morning Astorian*, November 21, 1885, pgs. 2–3.
88. *Reno Evening Gazette*, December 16, 1885, pg. 3.
89. *New York Sun*, December 5, 1885, pg. 3.
90. *National Police Gazette*, January 2, 1886, pg. 10.
91. *Ibid.*
92. *Brooklyn Eagle*, December 17, 1885, pg. 2.
93. *St. Paul Daily Globe*, December 21, 1885, pg. 5.
94. *Ibid.*, December 23, 1885, pg. 3.
95. *Democrat Chronicle*, December 24, 1885, pg. 1.
96. *Sacramento Daily Record-Union*, December 24, 1885, pg. 1.
97. *National Police Gazette*, January 9, 1886, pg. 10.

98. *Ibid.*
99. *Chicago Tribune*, December 30, 1885, pg. 2.
100. *National Police Gazette*, January 9, 1886, pg. 10.
101. *Sacramento Daily Record-Union*, December 28, 1885, pg. 1.
102. *St. Paul Daily Globe*, January 4, 1886, pg. 8.
103. *Chicago Herald*, November 11, 1888, pg. 18.
104. *New York World*, December 30, 1885, pg. 5.
105. *Brooklyn Eagle*, December 31, 1885, pg. 4.

1886—The Nonpareil Emerges

1. *Fort Wayne Sentinel*, January 4, 1886, pg. 9.
2. *National Police Gazette*, January 16, 1886, pg. 10.
3. *Ibid.*, January 23, 1886, pg. 10
4. *Boston Globe*, January 13, 1886, pg. 2.
5. *National Police Gazette*, February 6, 1886, pg. 10.
6. *New York Sun*, January 14, 1886, pg. 1.
7. *Ibid.*
8. http://www.opengreenmap.org/greenmap/east-village-eco-culture-map/germania-assembly-rooms-25554.
9. *New York Times*, January 16, 1886, pg. 5.
10. *Ibid.*
11. *Ibid.*
12. *Ibid.*
13. *Ibid.*
14. *Brooklyn Eagle*, January 16, 1886, pg. 4.
15. *National Police Gazette*, January 9, 1886, pg. 11.
16. *Daily Morning Astorian*, January 17, 1886, pg. 3.
17. *St. Louis Post-Dispatch*, February 3, 1886, pg. 11.
18. *Los Angeles Daily Herald*, February 4, 1886, pg. 1.
19. *New York Evening Telegram*, February 14, 1921, pg. 6.
20. *National Police Gazette*, February 13, 1886, pg. 2.
21. Gilliam, A.M., *Philadelphia Record*, February 4, 1886.
22. *Galveston Daily News*, February 4, 1886, pg. 10.
23. *New York Evening Telegram*, February 14, 1921, pg. 6.
24. *Brooklyn Eagle*, February 3, 1886, pg. 4.
25. Fox, Richard K., *The Life and Battles of Jack Dempsey*, pg. 55.
26. *Syracuse Herald*, May 26, 1911, pg. 22.
27. *Brooklyn Eagle*, February 3, 1886, pg. 4.
28. *Galveston Daily News*, February 4, 1886, pg. 10.
29. *Brooklyn Eagle*, February 3, 1886, pg. 4.
30. *New York World*, February 18, 1896, pg. 9.
31. *Cincinnati Enquirer*, February 5, 1886, pg. 2.
32. *Ibid.*
33. *National Police Gazette*, February 20, 1886, pg. 10.
34. *Los Angeles Herald*, February 5, 1886, pg. 1.
35. *Lancaster Daily Intelligencer*, March 5, 1886, pg. 1.
36. *New York Sun*, February 11, 1886, pg. 1.
37. *Boston Globe*, February 16, 1886, pg. 2.
38. *Ibid.*
39. *Brooklyn Eagle*, February 21, 1886, pg. 16.
40. Callis, Tracy, "Pete McCoy," http://www.cyberboxingzone.com/boxing/mccoy-pete.htm.
41. *Salt Lake Herald*, February 25, 1886, pg. 1.
42. Fox, Richard K., *The Life and Battles of Jack Dempsey*, pg. 59.
43. *St. Paul Daily Globe*, February 25, 1886, pg. 1.
44. *Brooklyn Eagle*, February 28, 1886, pg. 2.
45. *Sacramento Daily Record-Union*, February 25, 1886, pg. 1.
46. *St. Louis Post-Dispatch*, February 20, 1886, pg. 12.
47. *Boston Globe*, March 12, 1886, pg. 8.
48. *Ibid.*
49. *Ibid.*
50. *New York Times*, March 15, 1886.
51. *Reading Eagle* (PA), March 13, 1886, pg. 5.
52. *New York Times*, March 15, 1886.
53. *Reading Eagle*, March 13, 1886, pg. 5.
54. *National Police Gazette*, March 27, 1886, pg. 3.
55. *Manufacturers and Farmers Journal*, March 15, 1886, pg. 1.
56. *New York Times*, March 15, 1886.
57. *Ibid.*
58. *Ibid.*
59. *The Daily True American*, March 15, 1886, pg. 2.
60. *National Police Gazette*, March 27, 1886, pg. 3.
61. *The Daily True American*, March 15, 1886, pg. 2.
62. Fox, Richard K., *The Life and Battles of Jack Dempsey*, pg. 65.
63. *The Daily True American*, March 15, 1886, pg. 2.
64. *St. Paul Daily Globe*, March 15, 1886, pg. 1.
65. *Philadelphia Record*, March 15, 1886, pg. 1.
66. *National Police Gazette*, April 3, 1886, pg. 10.
67. *Galveston Daily News*, April 1, 1886, pg. 4.
68. *St. Louis Post-Dispatch*, April 3, 1886, pg. 12.
69. *San Francisco Morning Call*, January 20, 1891, pg. 2.
70. *Boston Globe*, March 18, 1886, pg. 2.
71. *National Police Gazette*, March 27, 1886, pg. 3.
72. *Ibid.*, April 17, 1886, pg. 11.
73. *Ibid.*, December 9, 1893, pg. 10.
74. *Ibid.*, November 13, 1886, pg. 11.
75. *Brooklyn Eagle*, March 20, 1886, pg. 1.
76. *National Police Gazette*, April 10, 1886, pg. 10.
77. *Ibid.*, April 3, 1886, pg. 10.
78. *St. Louis Post-Dispatch*, March 27, 1886, pg. 9.
79. *National Police Gazette*, April 17, 1886, pg. 11.
80. *Ibid.*
81. *Brooklyn Eagle*, April 4, 1886, pg. 16.
82. *Ibid.*
83. *Ibid.*
84. *Ibid.*, April 11, 1886, pg. 1.
85. *National Police Gazette*, April 24, 1886, pg. 10.
86. *Brooklyn Eagle*, April 11, 1886, pg. 1.
87. *Ibid.*, May 5, 1886, pg.
88. *New York Times*, April 24, 1886, pg. 5.
89. *Newark Daily Advocate*, pg. 1.
90. *Salt Lake Daily Tribune*, April 25, 1886, pg. 1.
91. *National Police Gazette*, May 8, 1886, pg. 10.
92. *Ibid.*
93. *New York Sun*, April 26, 1886, pg. 3.

94. Dunn, Mark, *Chicago's Greatest Sportsman*.
95. *National Police Gazette*, April 12, 1884, pg. 10.
96. *Ibid.*, May 8, 1886, pg. 10.
97. *Reading Eagle*, April 26, 1886, pg. 5.
98. *Ibid.*
99. *Chester Times*, April 27, 1886, pg. 3.
100. *St. Louis Post-Dispatch*, May 1, 1886, pg. 11.
101. *New York Sun*, May 1, 1886, pg. 1.
102. *Brooklyn Eagle*, May 5, 1886, pg. 1.
103. *Reading Eagle*, April 26, 1886, pg. 5.
104. *Wellsville Daily Reporter*, May 11, 1886, pg. 1.
105. *New York Sun*, May 16, 1886, pg. 5.
106. *Wichita Eagle*, October 7, 1887, pg. 5.
107. *Chicago Herald*, May 13, 1886, pg. 2.
108. *Brooklyn Eagle*, May 15, 1886, pg. 1.
109. *New York Sun*, May 14, 1886, pg. 3.
110. *Boston Globe*, May 15, 1886, pg. 5.
111. *St. Louis Post-Dispatch*, May 15, 1886, pg. 9.
112. *Chicago Tribune*, April 28, 1887, pg. 3.
113. *St. Paul Daily Globe*, May 17, 1886, pg. 1.
114. *Ibid.*, May 21, 1886, pg. 4.
115. *Ibid.*
116. *Ibid.*
117. *Ibid.*, May 22, 1886, pg. 1.
118. *New York Sun*, May 31, 1886, pg. 3.
119. *Oshkosh Daily Northwestern*, June 1, 1886, pg. 1.
120. *St. Paul Daily Globe*, May 15, 1886, pg. 1.
121. *Ibid.*, May 26, 1886, pg. 6.
122. *Brooklyn Eagle*, May 31, 1886, pg. 2.
123. *Boston Globe*, July 22, 1886, pg. 2.
124. *Morning Oregonian*, July 28, 1886, pg. 3.
125. *Brooklyn Standard Union*, January 10, 1920, pg. 8.
126. *Arizona Champion*, August 7, 1886, pg. 2.
127. *Brooklyn Eagle*, January 16, 1887, pg. 6.
128. *St. Louis Post-Dispatch*, July 29, 1886, pg. 7.
129. *Ibid.*
130. *Newburgh Daily News*, August 21, 1886, pg. 1.
131. *The Morning Review*, August 25, 1886, pg. 1.
132. *Boston Globe*, October 26, 1886, pg. 3.
133. *Goshen Daily News*, October 23, 1886, pg. 7.
134. *Williamette Farmer*, October 1, 1886.
135. *Davenport Gazette*, October 1, 1886, pg. 2.
136. Bartlett was sworn in as governor on January 8, 1887, but he died of Bright's Disease less than a year into his term.
137. *Chicago Tribune*, November 16, 1886, pg. 2.
138. Bullough, William A., *The Blind Boss and His City*, pgs. 138–141.
139. Naughton, W.W., *Kings of the Queensbury Realm*, pg. 78.
140. *Sacramento Daily Record-Union*, November 18, 1886, pg. 4.
141. *Chicago Herald*, October 3, 1886, pg. 2.
142. *Ibid.*, October 10, 1886, pg. 8.
143. *Richmond Daily Times*, November 24, 1886, pg. 3.
144. *Warsaw Daily Times*, November 23, 1886, pg. 4.
145. *National Police Gazette*, December 4, 1886, pg. 2.
146. *Chicago Tribune*, November 24, 1886, pg. 2.
147. *Ibid.*
148. *Warsaw Daily Times*, November 23, 1886, pg. 4.
149. *Ibid.*
150. *Dubuque Daily Herald*, November 23, 1886, pg. 1.
151. *Chicago Herald*, November 23, 1886, pg. 1.
152. *New York Sun*, December 11, 1886, pg. 3.
153. *Chicago Tribune*, November 24, 1886, pg. 2.
154. *National Police Gazette*, January 8, 1887, pg. 10.
155. *Chicago Herald*, December 26, 1886, pg. 2.
156. *Salt Lake Tribune*, December 16, 1886, pg. 4.
157. *Brooklyn Eagle*, December 27, 1886, pg. 4.
158. *National Police Gazette*, December 4, 1886, pg. 10.
159. *St. Louis Post-Dispatch*, January 1, 1887, pg. 8.
160. *Brooklyn Eagle*, December 31, 1886, pg. 4.
161. *New York Sun*, January 1, 1887, pg. 1.
162. *Boston Globe*, December 31, 1886, pg. 10.

1887—Breaks and Gashes, but Still on Top

1. *St. Louis Post-Dispatch*, January 8, 1887, pg. 8.
2. *Brooklyn Eagle*, January 9, 1887, pg. 16.
3. *Goshen Daily News*, January 10, 1887, pg. 4.
4. *New York Sun*, February 6, 1887, pg. 10.
5. *Ibid.*, January 9, 1887, pg. 7.
6. *National Police Gazette*, February 5, 1887, pg. 10.
7. *Ibid.*
8. *Ibid.*, November 26, 1887, pg. 7.
9. *St. Louis Post-Dispatch*, February 1, 1887, pg. 8.
10. *National Police Gazette*, February 5, 1887, pg. 10.
11. *Boston Globe*, February 1, 1887, pg. 11.
12. *National Police Gazette*, February 19, 1887, pg. 11.
13. *St. Louis Post-Dispatch*, February 3, 1887, pg. 8.
14. *New York Sun*, February 3, 1887, pg. 1.
15. *Newark Daily Advocate*, February 10, 1887, pg. 1.
16. *Boston Globe*, February 5, 1887, pg. 8.
17. *Ibid.*, February 16, 1887, pg. 1.
18. *New York Sun*, February 24, 1887, pg. 1.
19. *Ibid.*, March 26, 1887, pg. 3.
20. *Buffalo Daily Courier*, April 6, 1887, pg. 1.
21. *New York Clipper*, April 16, 1887, pg. 75.
22. *Buffalo Daily Courier*, April 10, 1887, pg. 4.
23. *Ibid.*
24. *Buffalo Express*, April 10, 1887.
25. *Ibid.*
26. *Ibid.*
27. *Boston Globe*, April 22, 1887, pg. 10.
28. Callis, Tracy, "Patrick 'Reddy' Gallagher," http://www.cyberboxingzone.com/boxing/gallagher-reddy.htm.
29. *Goshen Daily News*, May 3, 1887, pg. 3.
30. *Boston Globe*, May 3, 1887, pg. 16.
31. *Goshen Daily News*, May 3, 1887, pg. 3.
32. *Boston Globe*, May 3, 1887, pg. 16.
33. *Morning Oregonian*, May 3, 1887, pg. 2.

34. *National Police Gazette*, May 21, 1887, pg. 10.
35. *An Historical Sketch of St. Alexis Hospital*, pg. 50.
36. *Boston Globe*, May 3, 1887, pg. 16.
37. *Washington Evening Star*, May 4, 1887, pg. 3.
38. *Titusville Herald*, May 4, 1887, pg.1.
39. *National Police Gazette*, May 21, 1887, pg. 10.
40. *New York Sun*, May 8, 1887, pg. 11.
41. *Brooklyn Eagle*, May 22, 1887, pg. 10.
42. *Ibid.*, July 14, 1887, pg. 4.
43. Dunn, Mark T., *The Only Thing I Can Do Is to Fight*, pgs. 163–224.
44. Good Shepherd Church website, http://www.goodshepherdchurchdenver.org/about-us/history.
45. *Logansport Chronicle*, June 18, 1887, pg. 8.
46. *New York Sun*, June 29, 1887, pg. 1.
47. Dunn, Mark, "John 'Jack' Ashton," http://www.cyberboxingzone.com/boxing/ashton-jack.htm.
48. Smith, Kevin, *Boston's Boxing Heritage*, pg. 15.
49. *St. Paul Daily Globe*, August 21, 1887, pg. 5.
50. *The World*, August 21, 1887, pg. 3.
51. *St. Paul Daily Globe*, August 30, 1887, pg. 5.
52. *New York Sun*, December 18, 1887, pg. 15.
53. "Pleurisy," http://www.mayoclinic.com/health/pleurisy/DS00244.
54. *Brooklyn Eagle*, September 7, 1887, pg. 4.
55. *Ibid.*, September 3, 1887, pg. 4.
56. *New York Sun*, September 11, 1887, pg. 7.
57. *Boston Globe*, September 15, 1887, pg. 11.
58. *New York Sun*, September 13, 1887, pg. 3.
59. *National Police Gazette*, October 8, 1887, pg. 10.
60. *The Freeman*, September 13, 1913, pg. 7.
61. *St. Louis Post-Dispatch*, September 26, 1887, pg. 10.
62. *Danville-Hendricks County Republican*, October 6, 1887, pg. 7.
63. *New York Sun*, October 12, 1887, pg. 2.
64. *National Police Gazette*, October 29, 1887, pg. 10.
65. *New York Sun*, October 12, 1887, pg. 2.
66. *National Police Gazette*, October 29, 1887, pg. 10.
67. *Brooklyn Eagle*, October 15, 1887, pg. 1.
68. *Boston Globe*, October 17, 1887, pg. 3.
69. *New York Evening World*, October 17, 1887, pg. 3.
70. *New York Sun*, October 16, 1887, pg. 7.
71. *Chicago Tribune*, October 26, 1887, pg. 6.
72. *National Police Gazette*, February 19, 1887, pg. 10.
73. *Brooklyn Eagle*, November 6, 1887, pg. 16.
74. *Ibid.*, November 4, 1887, pg. 1.
75. *Ibid.*, November 12, 1887, pg. 4.
76. *National Police Gazette*, November 26, 1887, pg. 10.
77. *New York Evening World*, November 17, 1887, pg. 1.
78. *The Sporting Life*, November 23, 1887, pg. 7.
79. *Bridgeport Morning News*, November 17, 1887, pg. 1.
80. *The Sporting Life*, November 23, 1887, pg. 7.
81. *Great Falls Tribune*, November 23, 1887, pg. 1.
82. *St Louis Post-Dispatch*, November 17, 1887, pg. 8.
83. *Chicago Herald*, November 23, 1887, pg. 7.
84. *New York Sun*, November 24, 1887, pg. 5.
85. *Logansport Chronicle*, December 3, 1887, pg. 7.
86. *Baltimore Sunday Herald*, January 1, 1888, pg. 6.
87. *Meriden Daily Journal*, December 14, 1887, pg. 1.
88. *New York Evening Telegram*, December 18, 1921, pg. 13.
89. *Washington Evening Star*, December 12, 1887, pg. 5.
90. Gibbs, Alonzo, *Long Island Forum*, August 28, 1965, pg. 151.
91. *Chicago Herald*, December 14, 1887, pg. 1.
92. *Baltimore Morning Herald*, December 14, 1887, pg. 1.
93. *Rochester Daily Republican*, December 14, 1887, pg. 1.
94. *Daily True American*, December 14, 1887, pg. 1.
95. *Ibid.*
96. Fox, Richard K., *The Life and Battles of Jack Dempsey*, pg. 73.
97. *Daily True American*, December 14, 1887, pg. 1.
98. Donovan, Michael J., *The Roosevelt That I Know*, pg. 208.
99. *National Police Gazette*, December 24, 1887, pg. 7.
100. *Meriden Daily Journal*, December 14, 1887, pg. 1.
101. Fox, Richard K., *The Life and Battles of Jack Dempsey*, pg. 75.
102. *New York Evening Telegram*, December 18, 1921, pg. 13.
103. *National Police Gazette*, December 24, 1887, pg. 7.
104. *Dubuque Daily Herald*, December 14, 1887, pg. 1.
105. *New York Evening Telegram*, December 18, 1921, pg. 13.
106. *Dubuque Daily Herald*, December 14, 1887, pg. 1.
107. *New York Evening Telegram*, December 18, 1921, pg. 13.
108. *Daily True American*, December 14, 1887, pg. 1.
109. *Dubuque Daily Herald*, December 14, 1887, pg. 1.
110. *Ibid.*
111. *New York Evening Telegram*, December 18, 1921, pg. 13.
112. *Dubuque Daily Herald*, December 14, 1887, pg. 1.
113. *Meriden Daily Journal*, December 14, 1887, pg. 1.
114. *National Police Gazette*, December 31, 1887, pg. 10.
115. *Ibid.*
116. *New York Sun*, December 18, 1887, pg. 7.
117. *National Police Gazette*, December 31, 1887, pg. 10.
118. *National Police Gazette*, December 31, 1887, pg. 10.
119. *St. Louis Post-Dispatch*, December 15, 1887, pg. 8.

120. *National Police Gazette*, December 31, 1887, pg. 10.
121. *Great Falls Tribune*, December 22, 1887, pg. 3.
122. *Brooklyn Eagle*, December 14, 1887, pg. 6.
123. *New York Evening World*, December 15, 1887, pg. 3.
124. *Brooklyn Eagle*, December 14, 1887, pg. 6.
125. *New York Sun*, December 18, 1887, pg. 15.
126. *New York Evening World*, May 21, 1888, pg. 3.
127. *Ibid.*, April 30, 1888, pg. 1.
128. *New York Sun*, December 18, 1887, pg. 15.
129. *Ibid.*, pg. 14.
130. *Ibid.*, pg. 15.
131. *Brooklyn Eagle*, December 21, 1887, pg. 4.
132. *Ibid.*
133. *New York Sun*, December 23, 1887, pg. 3.
134. *Brooklyn Eagle*, December 24, 1887, pg. 4.
135. *Boston Globe*, January 4, 1888, pg. 8.
136. *St. Paul Daily Globe*, December 28, 1887, pg. 5.
137. *Boston Globe*, December 28, 1887, pg. 5.
138. *Washington Evening Star*, December 28, 1887, pg. 6.
139. *St. Louis Post-Dispatch*, December 29, 1887, pg. 8.
140. *Newark Daily Advocate*, December 23, 1887, pg. 1.
141. *Bismarck Daily Tribune*, December 30, 1887, pg. 1.

1888—Professor Mike Donovan and a Chink in the Armor

1. *New York World*, January 3, 1888, pg. 7.
2. *Brooklyn Eagle*, February 5, 1888, pg. 1.
3. *Washington National Republican*, January 23, 1888, pg. 2.
4. *Toronto Daily Mail*, January 4, 1888, pg. 2.
5. *Boston Globe*, January 5, 1888, pg. 16.
6. *Brooklyn Eagle*, January 19, 1888, pg. 3.
7. *Boston Globe*, January 18, 1888, pg. 2.
8. *Ibid.*, January 23, 1888, pg. 13.
9. *Ibid.*
10. *Ibid.*, January 24, 1888, pg. 3.
11. *Ibid.*, January 30, 1888, pg. 3.
12. *St. Paul Daily Globe*, December 28, 1887, pg. 5.
13. *Milwaukee Sentinel*, September 30, 1911, pg. 22.
14. *Daily Northwestern*, January 13, 1888, pg. 1.
15. *National Police Gazette*, January 21, 1888, pg. 11.
16. *Milwaukee Sentinel*, September 30, 1911, pg. 22.
17. *Fort Worth Daily Gazette*, February 2, 1888, pg. 2.
18. *The Day*, February 1, 1888, pg. 1.
19. *Brooklyn Eagle*, February 1, 1888, pg. 2.
20. *Ibid.*
21. *Ibid.*
22. *Ibid.*
23. *The Day*, February 1, 1888, pg. 1.
24. Fox, Richard K., *The Life and Battles of Jack Dempsey*, pg. 78.
25. *Brooklyn Eagle*, February 3, 1888, pg. 4.
26. *Ibid.*, February 5, 1888, pg. 1.
27. *New York Sun*, February 2, 1888, pg. 3.
28. *Ibid.*
29. *Chicago Tribune*, February 5, 1888, pg. 14.
30. *Boston Globe*, February 3, 1888, pg. 11.
31. *National Police Gazette*, March 3, 1888, pg. 11.
32. *Brooklyn Eagle*, February 6, 1888, pg. 4.
33. *New Ulm Weekly Review*, February 8, 1888, pg. 3.
34. *Buffalo Daily Courier*, February 18, 1888.
35. *Ibid.*
36. *New York Sun*, February 11, 1888, pg. 3.
37. *Ibid.*, March 2, 1888, pg. 1.
38. *National Police Gazette*, March 24, 1884, pg. 11.
39. *Ibid.*, May 31, 1884, pg. 14.
40. Weiand, Gary K., *The First Superstar*, pg. 49.
41. *Brooklyn Eagle*, March 10, 1888, pg. 6.
42. *St. Louis Post-Dispatch*, December 5, 1888, pg. 8.
43. *Nevada State Journal*, March 14, 1888, pg. 3.
44. *Daily Northwestern*, March 28, 1888, pg. 2.
45. *Boston Globe*, March 15, 1888, pg. 11.
46. *New York Sun*, March 12, 1888, pg. 1.
47. *Huntingdon Globe*, March 15, 1888, pg. 2.
48. *Ibid.*
49. *Ibid.*
50. *Brooklyn Eagle*, March 22, 1888, pg. 4.
51. *Ibid.*, March 23, 1888, pg. 4.
52. *Boston Herald*, March 27, 1888; *Brooklyn Eagle*, March 27, 1888, pg. 3.
53. *Boston Globe*, April 9, 1888, pg. 9.
54. *Atlantic Daily Telegraph*, May 11, 1888, pg. 4.
55. *Brooklyn Eagle*, April 1, 1888, pg. 1.
56. *New York Sun*, April 7, 1888, pg. 1.
57. *St. Louis Post-Dispatch*, April 7, 1888, pg. 8.
58. *New York Sun*, April 7, 1888, pg. 1.
59. *Brooklyn Eagle*, August 14, 1888, pg. 2.
60. *Ibid.*, April 4, 1888, pg. 1.
61. *New York Evening World*, April 24, 1888, pg. 3.
62. *National Police Gazette*, May 12, 1888, pg. 11.
63. Callis, Tracy, "Joe Coburn," http://www.cyberboxingzone.com/boxing/coburn.htm.
64. *Brooklyn Eagle*, June 12, 1863.
65. Callis, Tracy, "John J. Dwyer," http://www.cyberboxingzone.com/boxing/dwyer-j.htm.
66. *New York Times*, August 10, 1876.
67. *New York Evening World*, April 24, 1888, pg. 3.
68. *Brooklyn Eagle*, April 24, 1888, pg. 1.
69. *Ibid.*
70. *New York Sun*, May 7, 1888, pg. 1.
71. *San Antonio Daily Light*, May 7, 1888, pg. 1.
72. *Boston Globe*, May 7, 1888, pg. 2.
73. *Ibid.*
74. *New York Sun*, May 24, 1888, pg. 2.
75. *New York Evening World*, May 26, 1888, pg. 1.
76. *National Police Gazette*, June 30, 1888, pg. 11.
77. *New York Evening World*, May 29, 1888, pg. 3.
78. *Ibid.*, June 28, 1888, pg. 3.
79. *St. Louis Post-Dispatch*, July 1, 1888, pg. 8.
80. *New York Sun*, July 7, 1888, pg. 4.
81. *Brooklyn Eagle*, July 6, 1888, pg. 4.
82. *Ibid.*, July 24, 1888, pg. 4.
83. *Ibid.*
84. *Ibid.*, September 1, 1890, pg. 4.
85. *Ibid.*, July 24, 1888, pg. 4.
86. *Ibid.*, July 25, 1888, pg. 2.
87. *New York Evening World*, August 1, 1888, pg. 3.

88. *Ibid.*
89. *Ibid.*, August 8, 1888, pg. 1.
90. *Omaha Daily Bee*, August 15, 1888, pg. 2.
91. *New York Evening World*, August 18, 1888, pg. 1.
92. *Omaha Daily Bee*, August 15, 1888, pg. 2.
93. *Brooklyn Eagle*, September 7, 1888, pg. 1.
94. *Ibid.*, October 8, 1888, pg. 1.
95. *Ibid.*, November 14, 1888, pg. 6.
96. *Ibid.*, September 14, 1888, pg. 5.
97. *New York Evening World*, September 15, 1888, pg. 3.
98. *Milwaukee Sentinel*, September 30, 1911, pg. 22.
99. Donovan, Michael J., *The Roosevelt That I Know*, pg. 210.
100. *Brooklyn Eagle*, August 19, 1879, pg. 4.
101. White, Charley, *Syracuse Herald*, May 24, 1911, pg. 13.
102. Donovan, Michael J., *The Roosevelt That I Know*, pg. 212.
103. *Brooklyn Eagle*, October 14, 1888, pg. 10.
104. Callis, Tracy, "Denny Butler," http://www.cyberboxingzone.com/boxing/butler-denny.htm.
105. *Boston Globe*, October 2, 1888, pg. 9.
106. *Biddeford Journal*, November 5, 1888, pg. 1.
107. *New York Evening World*, November 6, 1888, pg. 3.
108. *Boston Globe*, November 16, 1888, pg. 14.
109. Donovan, Michael J., *The Roosevelt That I Know*, pg. 213.
110. *New York Sun*, November 16, 1888, pg. 1.
111. *Brooklyn Eagle*, November 16, 1888, pg. 4.
112. *Milwaukee Sentinel*, September 30, 1911, pg. 22.
113. *Brooklyn Eagle*, November 16, 1888, pg. 4.
114. *Ibid.*
115. *Milwaukee Sentinel*, September 30, 1911, pg. 22.
116. *Brooklyn Eagle*, November 16, 1888, pg. 4.
117. Donovan, Michael J., *The Roosevelt That I Know*, pg. 220.
118. *Ibid.*, pg. 221.
119. Fox, Richard K., *The Life and Battles of Jack Dempsey*, pg. 82.
120. *National Police Gazette*, December 1, 1888, pg. 10.
121. *Ibid.*
122. *Brooklyn Eagle*, September 1, 1890, pg. 4.
123. *Ibid.*, November 21, 1888, pg. 6.
124. *New York Herald*, November 16, 1888.
125. *Los Angeles Daily Herald*, November 16, 1888, pg. 5.
126. *St. Louis Post-Dispatch*, November 20, 1888, pg. 8.
127. *Boston Globe*, November 23, 1888, pg. 5.
128. *Ibid.*, November 24, 1888, pg. 16.
129. *Brooklyn Eagle*, November 24, 1888, pg. 4.
130. *New York Evening World*, December 1, 1888, pg. 1.
131. *Chicago Tribune*, November 24, 1888, pg. 3.
132. *St. Louis Post-Dispatch*, December 2, 1888, pg. 8.
133. *Chicago Herald*, November 24, 1888, pg. 1.
134. *Daily Astorian*, December 9, 1888, pg. 3.
135. *National Police Gazette*, December 22, 1888, pg. 10.
136. *Morning Oregonian*, December 8, 1888, pg. 6.
137. *Nevada State Journal*, October 8, 1887, pg. 2.
138. *National Police Gazette*, December 22, 1888, pg. 10.
139. *Boston Globe*, December 12, 1888, pg. 10.
140. *Decatur Herald*, December 15, 1888, pg. 2.
141. *Trenton Times*, December 15, 1888, pg. 3.
142. *Brooklyn Eagle*, December 11, 1888, pg. 4.
143. *National Police Gazette*, January 5, 1889, pg. 10.
144. *New York Evening World*, December 13, 1888, pg. 1.

1889—The Nonpareil Is Brought to Earth

1. *Baltimore American*, January 10, 1889.
2. *Brooklyn Eagle*, January 14, 1889, pg. 6.
3. *Boston Globe* January 16, 1889, pg. 1.
4. *New York Sun*, January 12, 1889, pg. 7.
5. *Dunkirk Observer*, January 5, 1889, pg. 1.
6. *Daily Evening News*, February 12, 1889, pg. 1.
7. *St. Paul Globe*, February 12, 1889, pg. 8.
8. *National Police Gazette*, February 2, 1889, pg. 11.
9. *New York World*, January 14, 1889, pg. 1.
10. *New York Sun*, January 16, 1889, pg. 3.
11. *St. Louis Post-Dispatch*, January 18, 1889, pg. 5.
12. *New York Sun*, February 3, 1889, pg. 7.
13. *Ibid.*, January 6, 1889, pg. 9.
14. *National Police Gazette*, February 2, 1889, pg. 11.
15. *Ibid.*, February 9, 1889, pg. 11.
16. *New York Sun*, January 24, 1889, pg. 3.
17. *New York Times*, November 15, 1922.
18. *Deseret News*, February 1, 1889, pg. 2.
19. *Sacramento Daily Record*, January 30, 1889, pg. 1.
20. *Pittsburgh Dispatch*, February 7, 1889, pg. 6.
21. *Brooklyn Eagle*, February 16, 1889, pg. 6.
22. *New York World*, February 28, 1889, pg. 3.
23. *Fort Worth Gazette*, February 26, 1889, pg. 2.
24. *Brooklyn Eagle*, March 2, 1889, pg. 1.
25. *National Police Gazette*, March 23, 1889, pg. 11.
26. *New York Sun*, March 3, 1889, pg. 11.
27. *Pittsburgh Dispatch*, March 3, 1889, pg. 6.
28. *New York World*, March 5, 1889, pg. 3.
29. Callis, Tracy, "Mike Cushing," http://www.cyberboxingzone.com.
30. *New York World*, March 5, 1889, pg. 3.
31. *Ibid.*, March 6, 1889, pg. 4.
32. *Salem Daily News*, March 19, 1889, pg. 1.
33. *New York Sun*, March 28, 1889, pg. 3.
34. *St. Paul Globe*, March 31, 1889, pg. 3.
35. *National Police Gazette*, April 20, 1889, pg. 10.
36. *Pittsburgh Dispatch*, April 12, 1889, pg. 6.
37. *New York World*, March 28, 1889, pg. 3.
38. *Ibid.*, April 18, 1889, pg. 6.
39. *Boston Globe*, April 18, 1889, pg. 12.
40. *New York World*, April 18, 1889 (Final Edition), pg. 3.

41. *St. Paul Globe*, April 23, 1889, pg. 8.
42. Howard, William Willard, *Harper's Weekly* no. 33, May 18, 1889, pg. 391.
43. *Washington Critic*, April 29, 1889, pg. 1.
44. *Syracuse Herald*, April 28, 1889, pg. 5.
45. *National Police Gazette*, December 26, 1885, pg. 10.
46. *Brooklyn Eagle*, April 18, 1889, pg. 5.
47. *New York Sun*, May 8, 1889, pg. 5.
48. *Los Angeles Daily Herald*, May 6, 1889, pg. 2.
49. *Los Angeles Times*, May 14, 1889, pg. 5.
50. *New York Evening World*, June 11, 1889, pg. 3.
51. *Los Angeles Daily Herald*, May 13, 1889, pg. 8.
52. *Ibid.*, May 17, 1889, pg. 1.
53. *Los Angeles Times*, May 18, 1889, pg. 1.
54. *Ibid.*, May 14, 1889, pg. 5.
55. *Brooklyn Eagle*, June 9, 1889, pg. 10.
56. *Daily Record Union*, May 20, 1889, pg. 2.
57. *Oakland Tribune*, May 25, 1889, pg. 1.
58. *National Police Gazette*, June 15, 1889, pg. 2.
59. *Ibid.*, August 31, 1889, pg. 6.
60. *Daily Alta California*, September 16, 1889, pg. 8.
61. *Brooklyn Eagle*, August 27, 1889, pg. 1.
62. *National Police Gazette*, August 31, 1889, pg. 6.
63. *San Francisco Morning Call*, November 3, 1891, pg. 3.
64. *Brooklyn Eagle*, August 27, 1889, pg. 1.
65. *Ibid.*
66. Corbett, James J., *The Roar of the Crowd*, pg. 68.
67. Blady, Ken, *The Jewish Boxers Hall of Fame*, pp. 31–33.
68. *Washington Star*, September 8, 1892, pg. 6.
69. *Daily News*, June 11, 1889, pg. 1.
70. *Trenton Times*, June 22, 1889, pg. 3; *Boston Globe*, June 21, 1889, pg. 13.
71. *New York World*, June 11, 1889, pg. 3.
72. *Pittsburgh Dispatch*, April 22, 1889, pg. 6.
73. Sugar, Burt, *The Great Fights*, pg. 14.
74. *New York Evening World*, August 7, 1889, pg. 1.
75. *National Police Gazette*, September 7, 1889, pg. 10.
76. *Daily Alta California*, August 28, 1889, pg. 8.
77. *Morning Oregonian*, August 26, 1889, pg. 3.
78. *National Police Gazette*, September 7, 1889, pg. 3.
79. *Daily Alta California*, August 28, 1889, pg. 8.
80. *Ibid.*
81. *Baltimore Weekly Herald*, August 30, 1889, pg. 12.
82. *Daily Argus*, August 29, 1889, pg. 1.
83. *Baltimore Weekly Herald*, August 30, 1889, pg. 11.
84. *San Bernardino Daily Courier*, August 28, 1889, pg. 1.
85. *Daily Argus*, August 29, 1889, pg. 1.
86. *Yakima Herald*, November 7, 1895, pg. 1.
87. *Ibid.*
88. *Daily Argus*, August 29, 1889, pg. 1.
89. *Baltimore Weekly Herald*, August 30, 1889, pg. 11.
90. *Tacoma News Tribune*, July 2, 1919.
91. *Syracuse Daily Standard*, August 29, 1889, pg. 1.
92. *National Police Gazette*, September 28, 1889, pg. 11.
93. *Syracuse Daily Standard*, August 29, 1889, pg. 1.
94. *St. Petersburg Independent*, January 29, 1927, pg. 25.
95. *Ibid.*
96. *Yakima Herald*, November 7, 1895, pg. 1.
97. *Brooklyn Eagle*, August 28, 1889, pg. 6.
98. *St. Louis Post-Dispatch*, January 2, 1891, pg. 8.
99. *Brooklyn Eagle*, August 27, 1890, pg. 2.
100. *Mansfield News*, February 7, 1900, pg. 6.
101. *Brooklyn Eagle*, August 28, 1889, pg. 1.
102. *San Francisco Call*, June 22, 1913, pg. 45.
103. *National Police Gazette*, September 7, 1889, pg. 2.
104. *Syracuse Daily Standard*, August 29, 1889, pg. 1.
105. *New York Sun*, May 15, 1883, pg. 1.
106. *Mansfield News*, February 7, 1900, pg. 6.
107. *New York World*, March 1, 1897, pg. 9.
108. *St. Paul Globe*, September 26, 1898, pg. 5.
109. *Chicago Tribune*, March 30, 1892, pg. 7.
110. *National Police Gazette*, May 12, 1894, pg. 10.
111. *St. Paul Globe*, September 25, 1898, pg. 8.
112. *Ibid.*, September 26, 1898, pg. 5.
113. *Spokane Daily Chronicle*, May 3, 1918, pg. 6.
114. Lewis, Christine, "George La Blanche, The Marine, Died in Lawrence," http://fivefeetofevil.blogspot.com/2013/01/v-behaviorurldefaultvmlo_13.html, January 13, 2013.
115. *Brooklyn Daily Eagle*, October 30, 1889, pg. 1.
116. *Capital Evening Journal*, September 9, 1889.
117. *Chicago Tribune*, September 16, 1889, pg. 6.
118. *Brooklyn Eagle*, September 29, 1889, pg. 7.
119. *Ibid.*, October 6, 1889, pg. 1.
120. *Lawrence Evening Tribune*, October 21, 1889, pg. 2.
121. *Pittsburgh Dispatch*, October 9, 1889, pg. 6.
122. *Daily Alta California*, October 9, 1889, pg. 2.
123. *Wichita Eagle*, October 10, 1889, pg. 2.
124. *Janesville Daily Gazette*, October 29, 1889, pg. 3.
125. *Omaha Daily Bee*, November 7, 1889, pg. 2.
126. *St. Paul Globe*, November 8, 1889, pg. 5.
127. *Morning Oregonian*, November 8, 1889, pg. 2.
128. *Boston Globe*, November 13, 1889, pg. 10.
129.
130. *Pittsburgh Dispatch*, November 28, 1889, pg. 6.
131. *Morning Oregonian*, December 7, 1889, pg. 2.
132. *National Police Gazette*, January 4, 1890, pg. 11.
133. *Boston Globe*, December 22, 1889, pg. 6.
134. *Brooklyn Eagle*, December 29, 1889, pg. 11.

1890—In Search of the Marine

1. *Chicago Tribune*, February 23, 1890, pg. 3.
2. *New York World*, February 19, 1890, pg. 1.
3. *Daily Alta California*, January 15, 1890, pg. 8.
4. *Daily Morning Astorian*, January 19, 1890, pg. 3.
5. *Brooklyn Eagle*, January 17, 1890, pg. 6.
6. *Logansport Pharos Tribune*, January 17, 1890, pg. 3.
7. *Fort Wayne Sentinel*, February 17, 1890, pg. 5.
8. *Cincinnati Enquirer*, February 17, 1890, pg. 2.
9. *Harper's Weekly*, Volume 34, April 5, 1890, pp. 263–265.

10. *Lawrence Daily Journal*, December 15, 1889, pg. 7.
11. *Toronto Daily Mail*, January 29, 1890, pg. 2.
12. *National Police Gazette*, January 11, 1890, pg. 11.
13. *Brooklyn Eagle*, February 19, 1890, pg. 1.
14. *National Police Gazette*, March 8, 1890, pg. 10.
15. *New York World*, February 19, 1890, Sporting Edition, pg. 1.
16. *Ibid.*
17. *Los Angeles Daily Herald*, February 19, 1890, pg. 4.
18. *New York Press*, February 19, 1890, pg. 1.
19. *Providence Manufacturer's and Farm Journal*, February 20, 1890, pg. 6.
20. *Ibid.*
21. *New York World*, February 19, 1890, Sporting Edition, pg. 1.
22. *Ibid.*
23. *Providence Manufacturer's and Farm Journal*, February 20, 1890, pg. 6.
24. *New York Press*, February 19, 1890, pg. 1.
25. *Brooklyn Eagle*, February 19, 1890, pg. 1.
26. *Baltimore Morning Herald*, February 19, 1890, pg. 1.
27. *New York World*, February 19, 1890, Sporting Edition, pg. 1.
28. *Trenton Daily True American*, February 20, 1890, pg. 1.
29. *Arizona Weekly Citizen*, February 22, 1890, pg. 2.
30. *Paterson Daily Press*, February 19, 1890, pg. 2.
31. *New York World*, February 19, 1890, Sporting Edition, pg. 1.
32. *Ibid.*
33. *Daily Alta California*, February 21, 1890, pg. 8.
34. *National Police Gazette*, March 15, 1890, pg. 11.
35. *New York World*, February 19, 1890, Sporting Edition, pg. 1.
36. *Daily Morning Astorian*, March 15, 1890, pg. 1.
37. *New York Sun*, February 20, 1890, pg. 6.
38. *National Police Gazette*, March 22, 1890, pg. 11.
39. *Philadelphia Record*, February 27, 1890, pg. 2.
40. *Brooklyn Eagle*, February 22, 1890, pg. 6.
41. *Connersville Daily Examiner*, February 23, 1890, pg. 1.
42. *Daily Morning Astorian*, February 26, 1890, pg. 1.
43. *Morning Oregonian*, February 27, 1890, pg. 2.
44. *Daily Morning Astorian*, March 7, 1890, pg. 1.
45. *Morning Oregonian*, March 1, 1890, pg. 6.
46. *San Francisco Examiner*, March 1, 1890.
47. *Ibid.*
48. *Chicago Tribune*, March 1, 1890, pg. 6.
49. *National Police Gazette*, August 9, 1890, pg. 11.
50. *Ibid.*, August 16, 1890, pg. 10.
51. *Ibid.*, August 9, 1890, pg. 11.
52. Callis, Tracy, "'Professor' John Clark," http://www.cyberboxingzone.com/boxing/JohnClark.htm.
53. *Seattle Press*, March 18, 1890.
54. *St. Paul Globe*, March 22, 1890, pg. 1.
55. Weston, Stanley, *Boxing Illustrated*, "Jack Dempsey, The Nonpareil," April 1963, pg. 64.
56. *National Police Gazette*, June 21, 1890, pg. 10.
57. *Pittsburgh Dispatch*, April 6, 1890, pg. 7.
58. *Connersville Daily Examiner*, April 3, 1890, pg. 3.
59. *San Francisco Call*, May 8, 1890, pg. 7.
60. *Anaconda Standard*, June 16, 1890, pg. 4.
61. *Salt Lake Herald*, June 20, 1890, pg. 8.
62. *Ibid.*, June 22, 1890, pg. 8.
63. *Salt Lake Tribune*, June 21, 1890, pg. 5.
64. *Salt Lake Herald*, June 21, 1890, pg. 8.
65. *Ibid.*, June 22, 1890, pg. 8.
66. *Salt Lake Tribune*, June 20, 1890, pg. 5.
67. *St. Louis Post-Dispatch*, July 5, 1890, pg. 5.
68. *Ibid.*, January 12, 1891, pg. 8.
69. *Pittsburgh Dispatch*, July 4, 1890, pg. 6.
70. *Bradford Era*, July 23, 1890, pg. 1.
71. *Buffalo Courier*, July 29, 1890, pg. 8.
72. *Bradford Era*, July 28, 1890, pg. 1.
73. *Ibid.*, August 1, 1890, pg. 4.
74. *Brooklyn Eagle*, August 23, 1890, pg. 4.
75. *Ibid.*, August 24, 1890, pg. 3.
76. *Ibid.*, August 26, 1890, pg. 1.
77. *Trenton Times*, August 26, 1890, pg. 1.
78. *New York Sun*, August 26, 1890, pg. 6.
79. *Brooklyn Eagle*, August 26, 1890, pg. 1.
80. *Brooklyn Daily Standard-Union*, August 26, 1890, pg.
81. *Brooklyn Eagle*, August 26, 1890, pg. 1.
82. *Ibid.*
83. *New York World*, August 26, 1890, pg. 6.
84. *Pittsburgh Dispatch*, September 2, 1890, pg. 4.
85. *New York Sun*, August 28, 1890, pg. 3.
86. *Daily Morning Astorian*, September 11, 1890, pg. 4.
87. *Brooklyn Eagle*, September 15, 1890, pg. 6.
88. *Daily Morning Astorian*, October 12, 1890, pg. 4.
89. *Brooklyn Eagle*, September 19, 1890, pg. 2.
90. *Ibid.*, August 28, 1890, pg. 1.
91. *Ibid.*, September 1, 1890, pg. 4.
92. *Ibid.*, September 25, 1890, pg. 6.
93. *San Francisco Call*, October 13, 1890, pg. 1.
94. *San Jose Evening News*, October 30, 1890, pg. 2.
95. *Chicago Tribune*, November 12, 1890, pg. 6.
96. *National Police Gazette*, December 6, 1890, pg. 11.
97. *Ibid.*, December 20, 1890, pg. 10.
98. *Los Angeles Herald*, November 11, 1890, pg. 5.
99. *Fort Wayne Sentinel*, December 8, 1890, pg. 1.
100. *Fort Worth Daily Gazette*, December 12, 1890, pg. 2.
101. *Ibid.*, December 13, 1890, pg. 7.
102. *Brooklyn Eagle*, January 5, 1891, pg. 2.
103. *New York Sun*, December 21, 1890, pg. 5.
104. *New York Evening World*, December 23, 1891, pg. 3.
105. *San Francisco Call*, December 31, 1890, pg. 7.
106. *Brooklyn Eagle*, December 19, 1890, pg. 6.

1891—At the Hands of Ruby Robert

1. *Milwaukee Sentinel*, September 30, 1911, pg. 22.

2. *Chicago Tribune*, January 13, 1891, pg. 6.
3. *Brooklyn Eagle*, January 6, 1891, pg. 4.
4. *St. Louis Post-Dispatch*, January 13, 1891, pg. 5.
5. *Chicago Tribune*, January 13, 1891, pg. 6.
6. *San Francisco Call*, December 21, 1890, pg. 14.
7. *Brooklyn Eagle*, January 11, 1891, pg. 8.
8. *Ibid.*
9. *The Salt Lake Herald*, January 3, 1891, pg. 1.
10. *Brooklyn Eagle*, January 11, 1891, pg. 8.
11. *New York Sun*, January 14, 1891, pg. 3.
12. *Brooklyn Eagle*, January 11, 1891, pg. 8.
13. *National Police Gazette*, January 24, 1891, pg. 3.
14. *Brooklyn Eagle*, January 11, 1891, pg. 8.
15. *New York Sun*, January 14, 1891, pg. 3.
16. "The Funny Side of Fighters as Seen by Jack Skelly," *Baseball Magazine*, Vol. 8, April 6, 1912, pg. 55.
17. *Toronto Daily Mail*, January 29, 1891, pg. 8.
18. *Arizona Republican*, January 23, 1892, pg. 1.
19. *New York Sun*, January 14, 1891, pg. 3.
20. *St. Paul Globe*, January 12, 1891, pg. 6.
21. *Philadelphia Record*, January 15, 1891, pg. 1.
22. *Evening Bulletin*, January 15, 1891, pg. 1.
23. *Brooklyn Eagle*, January 14, 1891, pg. 6.
24. *Chicago Tribune*, January 15, 1891, pg. 2.
25. *New York Press*, January 15, 1891, pg. 2.
26. *Quebec Daily Telegraph*, January 15, 1891, pg. 2.
27. *Semi-Weekly Tribune*, January 17, 1891, pg. 1.
28. *Aurora Daily Express*, January 15, 1891, pg. 2.
29. *New York Press*, January 15, 1891, pg. 2.
30. *Aurora Daily Express*, January 15, 1891, pg. 2.
31. *Ibid.*
32. *San Francisco Call*, January 15, 1891, pg. 1.
33. *Sunday Oregonian*, September 17, 1905, pg. 48.
34. *Ibid.*
35. *San Francisco Call*, January 15, 1891, pg. 1.
36. *Brooklyn Eagle*, January 15, 1891, pg. 4.
37. *Ibid.*
38. *San Francisco Call*, January 15, 1891, pg. 1.
39. *Brooklyn Eagle*, January 15, 1891, pg. 4.
40. *Spokane Daily Chronicle*, January 15, 1891, pg. 2.
41. *Sunday Oregonian*, September 17, 1905, pg. 48.
42. *Montreal Herald*, January 15, 1891, pg. 1.
43. *National Police Gazette*, January 24, 1891, pg. 2.
44. *Brooklyn Eagle*, January 15, 1891, pg. 4.
45. *National Police Gazette*, January 31, 1891, pg. 10.
46. *Ibid.*, January 24, 1891, pg. 2.
47. *Sunday Oregonian*, September 17, 1905, pg. 48.
48. *Spokane Daily Chronicle*, January 15, 1891, pg. 2.
49. *The Appeal*, January 17, 1891, pg. 4.
50. *Sunday Oregonian*, October 16, 1904, pg. 32.
51. *Milwaukee Journal*, January 15, 1891, pg. 8.
52. *Aurora Daily Express*, January 15, 1891, pg. 2.
53. *Oswego Daily Times*, January 16, 1891, pg. 1.
54. *Sunday Oregonian*, September 17, 1905, pg. 48.
55. *Brooklyn Eagle*, September 1, 1892, pg. 10.
56. *Ibid.*, January 15, 1891, pg. 6.
57. *Oswego Daily Times*, January 16, 1891, pg. 1.
58. *Milwaukee Journal*, January 15, 1891, pg. 8.
59. *National Police Gazette*, January 31, 1891, pg. 10.
60. *Brooklyn Eagle*, January 15, 1891, pg. 4.
61. *National Police Gazette*, January 31, 1891, pg. 10.
62. *St. Louis Post-Gazette*, February 12, 1891, pg. 12.
63. *Ibid.*, January 23, 1891, pg. 8.
64. *Buffalo Express*, December 7, 1911, pg. 19.
65. *Anaconda Standard*, February 12, 1891, pg. 9.
66. *San Francisco Call*, February 22, 1891, pg. 2.
67. *St. Paul Globe*, February 28, 1891, pg. 4.
68. *Dalles Daily Chronicle*, February 28, 1891, pg. 1.
69. *Anaconda Standard*, March 29, 1891, pg. 9.
70. *New York Evening World*, March 24, 1891, pg. 3.
71. *New York Sun*, May 10, 1891, pg. 22.
72. *St. Paul Globe*, July 26, 1891, pg. 11.
73. Hanson, Sara Markoe, "The Hotel Leip Resort," *White Bear Lake Magazine*, August 2013.
74. *San Francisco Call*, July 10, 1891, pg. 2.
75. *Ibid.*, September 20, 1891, pg. 3.
76. *Evening Capital Journal*, September 22, 1891, pg. 2.
77. *San Francisco Call*, September 22, 1891, pg. 8.
78. *Weekly Tribune*, September 26, 1891, pg. 7.
79. *Ibid.*, pg. 8.
80. *Burlington Free Press*, October 22, 1891, pg. 1.
81. *Salt Lake Herald*, November 15, 1891, pg. 2.
82. *Record Union*, October 17, 1891, pg. 1.
83. *Ibid.*
84. *Ibid.*
85. *Ibid.*
86. *Pittsburgh Dispatch*, November 16, 1891, pg. 6.
87. *New York Sun*, November 14, 1891, pg. 4.
88. *Salt Lake Herald*, November 15, 1891, pg. 2.
89. *New York Sun*, November 22, 1891, pg. 20.
90. *Ibid.*, November 29, 1891, pg. 5.
91. *Evening Capital Journal*, November 20, 1891, pg. 2.
92. *New York Sun*, November 19, 1891, pg. 4.
93. *New York Evening World*, November 24, 1891, pg. 2.
94. *San Francisco Call*, November 30, 1891, pg. 1.
95. *New York Evening World*, November 20, 1891, pg. 2.
96. *Ibid.*
97. *Pullman Herald*, December 4, 1891, pg. 1.
98. *St. Louis Post-Dispatch*, December 5, 1891, pg. 8.
99. *Montreal Herald*, December 9, 1891, pg. 2.
100. *New York Evening World*, December 25, 1891, pg. 2.
101. *Brooklyn Eagle*, December 23, 1891, pg. 1.
102. *Wheeling Daily Intelligencer*, December 28, 1891, pg. 1.
103. *New York Sun*, December 31, 1891, pg. 3.

1892—Convalescence

1. *Brooklyn Eagle*, January 14, 1892, pg. 5.
2. *Logansport Chronicle*, January 2, 1892, pg. 4.
3. *Eau Claire News*, January 29, 1892, pg. 5.
4. Callis, Tracy, "Peter Maher," http://www.cyberboxingzone.com/boxing/maher-peter.htm.
5. *Princeton Union*, January 7, 1892, pg. 6.
6. *St. Paul Globe*, January 1, 1892, pg. 5.
7. *St. Louis Post-Dispatch*, February 20, 1892, pg. 8.
8. *New Orleans Daily Picayune*, March 3, 1892, pg. 1.
9. *Brooklyn Eagle*, January 22, 1892, pg. 1.

10. *Los Angeles Times*, December 15, 1891.
11. *Daily Optic*, February 2, 1892, pg. 2.
12. *Pittsburgh Dispatch*, January 31, 1892, pg. 6.
13. *Brooklyn Eagle*, May 13, 1892, pg. 1.
14. *San Francisco Call*, March 23, 1892, pg. 1.
15. *Boston Globe*, April 24, 1892, pg. 18.
16. *Pittsburgh Dispatch*, July 9, 1892, pg. 10.
17. *St. Paul Globe*, July 15, 1892, pg. 5.
18. *San Francisco Call*, August 17, 1892, pg. 1.
19. *Chicago Tribune*, September 2, 1892, pg. 7.
20. Fleischer, Nat, *Jack McAuliffe: The Napoleon of the Prize Ring*.
21. *San Francisco Call*, September 21, 1892, pg. 2.
22. *Arizona Republican*, September 29, 1892, pg. 1.
23. *Sacramento Record Union*, September 24, 1892, pg. 1.
24. *Arizona Republican*, November 5, 1892, pg. 1.
25. *Brooklyn Eagle*, December 3, 1892, pg. 2.
26. *Salt Lake Herald*, December 20, 1892, pg. 6.
27. *National Police Gazette*, November 26, 1892, pg. 10.
28. *Ibid.*, December 3, 1892, pg. 11.
29. *Ibid.*, December 24, 1892, pg. 11.
30. *San Francisco Call*, December 24, 1893, pg. 1.
31. *National Police Gazette*, December 31, 1892, pg. 11.
32. *Ibid.*, November 26, 1892, pg. 10.

1893—The Road Back

1. Degler, Carl M., *The Age of the Economic Revolution: 1876–1900*, pg. 121.
2. Steeples and Whitten, *Democracy in Desperation*, pgs. 17, 18.
3. Degler, Carl M., *The Age of the Economic Revolution: 1876–1900*, pg. 121.
4. Steeples and Whitten, *Democracy in Desperation*, pgs. 17, 18.
5. *St. Louis Post-Dispatch*, January 24, 1893, pg. 8.
6. *Brooklyn Eagle*, February 20, 1893, pg. 5.
7. *Ibid.*
8. *National Police Gazette*, February 25, 1893, pg. 11.
9. *Ibid.*, March 18, 1893, pg. 7.
10. *Brooklyn Eagle*, March 1, 1893, pg. 7.
11. *Ibid.*
12. *Ibid.*
13. *New York Times*, March 2, 1893.
14. *Los Angeles Herald*, March 1, 1893, pg. 1.
15. *Baltimore Morning Herald*, March 18, 1893, pg. 1.
16. *Ibid.*
17. *Austin Weekly Statesmen*, April 5, 1893, pg. 2.
18. *New York Press*, April 1, 1893, pg. 8.
19. *Brooklyn Eagle*, April 16, 1893, pg. 2.
20. *Record Union*, May 4, 1893, pg. 1.
21. *National Police Gazette*, May 20, 1893, pg. 10.
22. *Capital Journal*, May 6, 1893, pg. 1.
23. *New York Evening World*, June 14, 1893, pg. 6.
24. *Brooklyn Eagle*, May 16, 1893, pg. 8.
25. *Burlington Weekly Free Press*, May 25, 1893, pg. 7.
26. *Brooklyn Eagle*, May 17, 1893, pg. 1.
27. *St. Paul Daily Globe*, June 29, 1893, pg. 5.
28. *Chicago Tribune*, July 10, 1893, pg. 6.
29. *Brooklyn Eagle*, July 26, 1893, pg. 2.
30. *San Francisco Call*, August 11, 1893.
31. *St. Paul Daily Globe*, August 1, 1893, pg. 5.
32. *Chicago Tribune*, August 12, 1893.
33. *Daily Argus*, August 12, 1893, pg. 4.
34. *Brooklyn Eagle*, August 11, 1893, pg. 2.
35. *Ibid.*, August 15, 1893, pg. 2.
36. *St. Louis Post-Dispatch*, August 11, 1893, pg. 8.
37. *San Francisco Call*, August 12, 1893.
38. *Washington Evening Star*, August 21, 1893, pg. 3.
39. *National Police Gazette*, September 2, 1893, pg. 10.
40. *Jamestown Weekly Alert*, August 31, 1893, pg. 2.
41. *Chicago Tribune*, August 25, 1893, pg. 7.
42. *National Police Gazette*, September 9, 1893, pg. 11.
43. *Ibid.*
44. *St. Paul Daily Globe*, September 3, 1893, pg. 6.
45. *National Police Gazette*, September 16, 1893, pg. 11.
46. *St. Paul Daily Globe*, September 3, 1893, pg. 6.
47. *National Police Gazette*, September 16, 1893, pg. 11.
48. *Brooklyn Eagle*, August 29, 1893, pg. 2.
49. *New York Times*, August 30, 1893.
50. *St. Paul Daily Globe*, August 30, 1893, pg. 5.
51. *Hamilton Daily Democrat*, August 26, 1893, pg. 3.
52. *Ibid.*
53. *National Police Gazette*, September 16, 1893, pg. 11.
54. *Ibid.*
55. *New York Times*, September 18, 1893.
56. *St. Paul Daily Globe*, September 23, 1893, pg. 1.
57. *Ibid.*, September 3, 1893, pg. 6.
58. *New York Evening World* (Brooklyn Last Edition), September 5, 1893, pg. 5.
59. *New York Times*, September 5, 1893.
60. *National Police Gazette*, September 23, 1893, pg. 11.
61. *New York Press*, September 5, 1893, pg. 3.
62. *National Police Gazette*, September 23, 1893, pg. 11.
63. *New York Times*, September 10, 1893.
64. *Mower County Transcript*, October 4, 1893, pg. 4; *New York World*, September 23, 1893, pg. 5.
65. *St. Paul Daily Globe*, October 1, 1893, pg. 4.
66. *Mower County Transcript*, October 4, 1893, pg. 4.
67. *St. Paul Daily Globe*, October 4, 1893, pg. 1.
68. *Brooklyn Eagle*, October 2, 1893, pg. 8.
69. *National Police Gazette*, October 28, 1893, pg. 10.
70. *New York Times*, October 19, 1893.
71. *Brooklyn Eagle*, October 17, 1893, pg. 8.
72. *Omaha Daily Bee*, October 13, 1893, pg. 3.
73. *New York Times*, October 19, 1893.
74. *Ibid.*
75. *The Sporting Life*, February 3, 1894, pg. 8.
76. *Washington Bee*, November 11, 1893, pg. 1.
77. *Deseret News*, November 25, 1901, pg. 1.
78. *Clinton Courier*, November 23, 1893, pg. 3.
79. *Washington Times*, May 3, 1898, pg. 6.

1894—The Slowing Champion

1. *New York Evening World* (Last Edition), January 6, 1894, pg. 3.
2. *Ibid.* (Two o'clock Extra), January 9, 1894, pg. 2.
3. *Brooklyn Daily Eagle*, January 8, 1894, pg. 8.
4. *National Police Gazette*, December 9, 1893, pg. 10.
5. *St. Louis Post-Dispatch*, January 10, 1894, pg. 6.
6. *Brooklyn Daily Eagle*, January 8, 1894, pg. 8.
7. *St. Louis Post-Dispatch*, January 19, 1894, pg. 5.
8. *Newburgh Daily Journal*, January 25, 1894, pg. 1.
9. *Ibid.*
10. *Omaha Daily Bee*, February 4, 1894, pg. 16.
11. *Ibid.*, January 26, 1894, pg. 1.
12. *Great Falls Weekly Tribune*, February 2, 1894, pg. 7.
13. *St. Louis Post-Dispatch*, January 19, 1894, pg. 5.
14. *New York Evening World* (Six o'clock Extra), January 25, 1894, pg. 1.
15. *Washington Star*, January 26, 1894, pg. 2.
16. *New York Herald*, January 28, 1894, pg. 7.
17. *St. Paul Daily Globe*, January 28, 1894, pg. 5.
18. *National Police Gazette*, February 17, 1894, pg. 10.
19. *Roanoke Times*, February 7, 1894, pg. 5.
20. *Ibid.*, February 14, 1894, pg. 8.
21. *Omaha Daily Bee*, April 8, 1894, pg. 2.
22. *Buffalo Express*, April 1, 1892, pg. 8.
23. *Buffalo Courier*, April 8, 1894, pg. 8.
24. *Los Angeles Herald*, August 6, 1894, pg. 7.
25. *Lewiston Daily Sun*, August 29, 1894, pg. 4.
26. *New York Herald*, September 6, 1894, pg. 10.
27. *Baltimore Sun*, September 6, 1894, pg. 6.
28. *The Yellowstone Journal*, September 8, 1894, pg. 1.
29. *National Police Gazette*, September 22, 1894, pg. 2.
30. *Pittsburgh Press*, September 9, 1894, pg. 46.
31. *National Police Gazette*, September 22, 1894, pg. 2.
32. *San Francisco Call*, September 6, 1894, pg. 2.
33. *Brooklyn Eagle*, September 6, 1894, pg. 4.
34. *New York Evening World* (Extra), September 6, 1894, pg. 5.
35. *National Police Gazette*, September 22, 1894, pg. 10.
36. *Chicago Tribune*, September 6, 1894, pg. 8.
37. *Pittsburgh Press*, September 9, 1894, pg. 46.
38. *National Police Gazette*, October 27, 1894, pg. 10.
39. *Brooklyn Daily Eagle*, December 15, 1894, pg. 1.
40. *St. Paul Daily Globe*, December 16, 1894, pg. 1.
41. Somers, Dale A., *The Rise of Sports in New Orleans*, pg. 188.
42. *Chicago Tribune*, December 16, 1894, pg. 5.
43. *Ft. Worth Gazette*, December 18, 1894, pg. 4.
44. *New York Times*, December 16, 1894.
45. *National Police Gazette*, January 5, 1895, pg. 10.
46. *Chicago Tribune*, December 29, 1894, pg. 7.
47. *Ibid.*, December 15, 1894, pg. 2
48. *Ibid.*

1895—Tommy Ryan and the End

1. *Brooklyn Eagle*, January 2, 1895, pg. 4.
2. *Ibid.*
3. *Ibid.*, January 8, 1895, pg. 4.
4. *New York Sun*, January 6, 1895, pg. 10.
5. *Morning Oregonian*, January 10, 1895, pg. 2.
6. *Brooklyn Eagle*, January 11, 1895, pg. 4.
7. *Ibid.*, January 16, 1895, pg. 4.
8. *New York World*, January 15, 1895, pg. 3.
9. *Ibid.*, January 16, 1895, pg. 3.
10. *New York World* (Night Edition), January 15, 1895, pg. 6.
11. *Philadelphia Record*, January 19, 1895, pg. 8.
12. *San Antonio Daily Light*, January 16, 1895, pg. 5.
13. *Brooklyn Eagle*, January 13, 1895, pg. 11.
14. *National Police Gazette*, February 2, 1895, pg. 3.
15. *New York Evening World*, January 19, 1895, pg. 6.
16. *Providence Evening Telegraph*, January 19, 1895, pg. 5.
17. *Philadelphia Record*, January 19, 1895, pg. 8.
18. *New York Times*, January 19, 1895.
19. *Lewiston Daily Sun*, January 19, 1895, pg. 6.
20. *Baltimore American*, January 19, 1895, pg. 6.
21. *Ibid.*
22. *Philadelphia Record*, January 19, 1895, pg. 8.
23. *Brooklyn Eagle*, January 19, 1895, pg. 4.
24. *New York Sun*, January 19, 1895, pg. 6.
25. *Syracuse Journal*, February 5, 1907, pg. 5.
26. *New York Sun*, January 19, 1895, pg. 6.
27. *Fort Wayne News*, January 31, 1895, pg. 7.
28. *National Police Gazette*, February 16, 1895, pg. 10.
29. *New York Sun*, February 1, 1895, pg. 8.
30. *Los Angeles Herald*, February 1, 1895, pg. 2.
31. *New York Sun*, February 1, 1895, pg. 7.
32. *Ibid.*, pg. 8
33. *Brooklyn Eagle*, November 1, 1895, pg. 4.
34. *National Police Gazette*, February 16, 1895, pg. 10.
35. *New York Sun*, February 5, 1895, pg. 8.
36. *National Police Gazette*, May 11, 1895, pg. 11.
37. *Ft. Worth Gazette*, July 5, 1895, pg. 4.
38. *National Police Gazette*, June 8, 1895, pg. 11.
39. *Ibid.*, June 15, 1895, pg. 11.
40. *San Francisco Call*, June 9, 1895, pg. 3.
41. *National Police Gazette*, June 22, 1895, pg. 10.
42. *San Francisco Call*, June 9, 1895, pg. 3.
43. *National Police Gazette*, June 22, 1895, pg. 10.
44. *Ibid.*
45. *Rome Semi-Weekly Citizen*, June 11, 1895, pg. 3.
46. *National Police Gazette*, June 22, 1895, pg. 10.
47. *San Francisco Call*, June 28, 1895, pg. 9.
48. *Los Angeles Herald*, June 30, 1895, pg. 1.
49. *San Francisco Call*, July 2, 1895, pg. 4.
50. *Ibid.*
51. *New York Herald*, June 29, 1895, pg. 10.
52. *Brooklyn Eagle*, July 6, 1895, pg. 12.
53. *Ibid.*, July 12, 1895, pg. 2.
54. *Roanoke Times*, July 13, 1895, pg. 2.
55. *Salt Lake City Herald*, July 24, 1895, pg. 2.
56. *Burlington Hawk-Eye*, July 25, 1895, pg. 1.

57. Letter to the Author from Mark Dunn, June 15, 2014.
58. *Daily Morning Astorian*, December 28, 1890, pg. 4.
59. *The Islander*, October 31, 1895, pg. 1.
60. *Ibid.*
61. *Chicago Tribune*, October 28, 1895, pg. 4.
62. *Boston Globe*, October 25, 1895, pg. 8.
63. *Ibid.*
64. *Ibid.*
65. *Ibid.*
66. *Chicago Tribune*, October 28, 1895, pg. 4.
67. *Ibid.*
68. *Ibid.*
69. *Ibid.*
70. *Boston Globe*, October 25, 1895, pg. 8.
71. *Ibid.*
72. *Marion Star*, October 23, 1895, pg. 1.
73. *Alton Evening Telegraph*, October 26, 1895, pg. 8.
74. *San Francisco Call*, November 2, 1895, pg. 1.
75. *Capital Evening Journal*, November 1, 1895, pg. 1.
76. *Ibid.*
77. *San Francisco Call*, November 2, 1895, pg. 1.
78. *Ibid.*
79. *Ibid.*
80. *New York Times*, November 2, 1895, pg. 6.
81. *Anaconda Standard*, November 5, 1895, pg. 1.
82. *San Francisco Call*, November 5, 1895, pg. 5.
83. *Ibid.*, November 3, 1895, pg. 26.
84. Callis, Tracy, "'Nonpareil' Jack Dempsey ... Slick and Quick," http://www.cyberboxingzone.com.
85. *San Francisco Call*, November 2, 1895, pg. 9.
86. Isenberg, Michael T., *John L. Sullivan and His America*, pg. 52.
87. *San Francisco Call*, August 12, 1893.
88. *Wichita Daily Eagle*, September 13, 1893, pg. 6.

Immortal Nonpareil

1. *San Francisco Call*, December 4, 1895, pg. 16.
2. *Ibid.*, December 28, 1895, pg. 9.
3. *Ibid.*, January 3, 1896, pg. 11.
4. *Oak Park Vindicator*, February 21, 1896, pg. 3.
5. *Los Angeles Herald*, January 20, 1896, pg. 3.
6. *Brooklyn Eagle*, February 15, 1896, pg. 10.
7. *The Dalles Weekly Chronicle*, March 5, 1898, pg. 1.
8. *Brooklyn Eagle*, March 2, 1898, pg. 4.
9. *Eau Claire Morning Telegram*, March 8, 1896, pg. 3.
10. *Oakland Tribune*, March 4, 1896, pg. 12.
11. *Brooklyn Eagle*, December 13, 1899, pg. 14.
12. *National Police Gazette*, January 1901, pg. 10.
13. *New York Times*, "Memory of Jack Dempsey," September 4, 1910, pg. C7.
14. *Morning Oregonian*, January 15, 1902.
15. *Ibid.*
16. *Ibid.*
17. *Sunday Oregonian*, March 4, 1917, pg. 3.
18. *Morning Oregonian*, October 31, 1900, pg. 8.
19. *Ibid.*, February 14, 1902, pg. 12.
20. *Baltimore American*, July 26, 1902, pg. 2.
21. *Sunday Oregonian*, December 24, 1905, pg. 27.
22. *Morning Oregonian*, January 28, 1910, pg. 12.
23. *Ibid.*, June 10, 1914, pg. 11.
24. *Morning Oregonian*, April 17, 1919, pg. 4.
25. *New York Times*, November 19, 1907, pg.
26. *Ibid.*, November 15, 1922, pg. 1.
27. *New York Times*, August 28, 1896, pg.
28. *Ibid.*
29. *St. Paul Globe*, February 25, 1900, pg. 10.
30. McMahon, M.J., *The Nonpareil's Grave*, 1899.

BIBLIOGRAPHY

Books

Algeo, Matthew. *The President is a Sick Man*. Chicago Review Press, Inc., Chicago, IL: 2011.

Andrews, E. Benjamin. *History of the United States*, Vols. IV and V, Charles Scribner's Sons, New York, NY: 1929.

Blady, Ken. *The Jewish Boxers Hall of Fame*. Shapolsky Publishers, Inc., New York, NY: 1988.

Blinn, William. *Brian's Song*. Bantam Books, New York, NY: 1972.

Brady, William A. *The Fighting Man*. The Bobbs-Merrill Company. Indianapolis, IN: 1916.

Broughton, John. *Proposals for Erecting an Amphitheatre for the Manly Exercise of Boxing*: 1742–43.

Bullough, William A. *The Blind Boss and His City: Christopher Augustine Buckley and Nineteenth Century San Francisco*. University of California Press, Berkeley, CA: 1979.

Burgh, James. *Political Disquisitions*. Robert Bell, Philadelphia, PA: 1775.

Callis, Tracy, and Chuck Johnston. *Boxing in the Los Angeles Area: 1880–2005*. Trafford Publishing, Vancouver, BC: 2009.

Corbett, James J. *The Roar of the Crowd*. Grosset & Dunlap Publishers, New York, NY: 1925.

_____. *Scientific Boxing*. Promethean Press, Carrollton, TX: 1912, 2008.

de Saussure, Cesar. *A Foreign View of England in the Reigns of George I and George II*. John Murray, London: 1902.

Degler, Carl N. *The Age of the Economic Revolution: 1876–1900*. Scott, Foresman and Company, Glenview, IL: 1967, 1977.

Donovan, Michael Joseph. *The Roosevelt That I know: Ten Years of Boxing with the President—and Other Memories of Famous Fighting Men*. B.W. Dodge & Co., New York, NY: 1909.

Dunn, Mark T. *The Only Thing I Can Do Is to Fight*. CreateSpace Independent Publishing Platform: 2012.

Eisenberg, Michael T. *John L. Sullivan and His America*. University of Illinois Press, Urbana and Chicago, IL: 1988.

Fields, Armond. *Eddie Foy: A Biography of the Early Popular Stage Comedian*. McFarland & Co., Inc., Publishers, Jefferson, NC: 2001.

Fleischer, Nat. *Jack McAuliffe: The Napoleon of the Prize Ring*. The Ring, New York, NY: 1944.

Fox, Richard K. *Life and Battles of Jack Dempsey*. National Police Gazette Press, New York, NY: 1888.

Gee, Tony. *Up to Scratch: Bareknuckle Fighting and the Champions of the Prize-ring*. Queen Anne Press, London, UK: 1998.

Gorn, Elliott J. *The Manly Art: Bare-Knuckle Prize Fighting in America*. Cornell University Press, Ithaca, NY: 1986.

Grombach, John V. *The Saga of the Fist*. A.S. Barnes and Company, Inc., Cranbury, NJ: 1949, 1977. (Originally published as *The Saga of Sock*.)

Isenberg, Michael T. *John L. Sullivan and His America*. University of Illinois Press, Urbana and Chicago, IL: 1988.

McCallum, John. *The World Heavyweight Boxing Championship*. Chilton Book Company, Radnor, PA: 1974.

Misson, Henri de Valbourg. *M. Misson's Memoirs and Observations in His Travels Over England*. Printed for D. Browne (etc.), London, England: 1719.

Naughton, W.W. *Kings of the Queensbury Realm*. The Continental Publishing Company, Chicago, IL: 1902.

Richard Carew of Antony. *The Survey of Cornwall*, ed. F.E. Halliday. Andrew Melrose, London: 1969, pg. 44.

St. Alexis Hospital. *An Historical Sketch of St. Alexis Hospital, Cleveland*, United Printing Company, Cleveland, Ohio: 1900, pg. 50.

Smith, Kevin. *Boston's Boxing Heritage: Prizefighting from 1882 to 1955*. Arcadia Publishing, Dover, NH: 2002.

Somers, Dale A. *The Rise of Sports in New Orleans*. Vail-Ballou Press, Binghamton, NY: 1972, pg. 188.

Steeples, Douglas, and David O. Whitten. *Democracy in Desperation: The Depression of 1893*. Greenwood Press, Westport, CT: 1998.

Sugar, Bert Randolph. *The Great Fights*. The Rutledge Press, New York, NY: 1981.
Weiand, Gary K. *The First Superstar: Bareknuckles: John L. Sullivan*. Xlibris Corp., Lexington, KY: 2008.
Weinstein, Allen, and R. Jackson Wilson. *Freedom and Crisis: An American History*, Vols. I and II. Random House, New York, NY: 1974, 1978.
West, Tommy. *The Long, Long Trail in the World of Sports*. Published by the Author, Louisville, KY: 1918.

Magazines

Baseball Magazine, Vol. 8, April 6, 1912.
Boxing Illustrated, April 1963.
Buchstein, Fred, "Harry Hill—Saloon Fighting's P.T. Barnum," *New York History Review*.
Gibb, Alonzo. *Long Island Forum*, Vol. XXVIII, No. 8, August 1965, pgs. 151–152.
IBRO Journal 90, June 20, 2006, pgs. 17–18.
McKenney's Pacific Coast Directory for Businesses, Vol. 1886–87.
Pearson's Magazine, Vol. 29, No. 1, January 1913.
White Bear Lake Magazine, August 2013.

Newspapers

Alton Evening Telegraph
Amsterdam Daily Democrat
Anaconda Standard
The Appeal
Argus
Arizona Champion
Arizona Republican
Arizona Weekly Citizen
Atlanta Constitution
Atlantic Daily Telegraph
Aurora Daily Express
Austin Weekly Statesman
Baltimore American
Baltimore Herald
Baltimore Sun
Biddeford Journal
Binghamton Press
Bismarck Daily Tribune
Boston Herald
Bradford Era
Bridgeport Morning News
Brooklyn Daily Standard-Union
Brooklyn Eagle
Buffalo Courier
Buffalo Express
Burlington Hawk Eye
Burlington Weekly Free Press
Cambridge City Tribune
Capital Evening Journal
Chester Times
Chicago Herald
Chicago Tribune
Cincinnati Commercial Tribune-Gazette
Cincinnati Enquirer
Connersville Daily Examiner
Daily Alta California
Daily Argus
Daily Cairo Bulletin
Daily Capital Journal
Daily Cosmopolitan
Daily Critic
Daily Evening News
Daily Morning Astorian
Daily Northwestern
Daily Optic
Daily True American
Dalles Chronicle
Dalles Times Mountaineer
Danville-Hendricks County Republican
Davenport Gazette
The Day
Decatur Herald
Democrat Chronicle
Deseret News
Dubuque Daily Herald
Dunkirk Observer
Eau Claire Morning Telegram
Eau Claire News
Evening Bulletin
Evening Gazette
Fort Wayne News
Fort Wayne Sentinel
Fort Worth Daily Gazette
The Freeman
Galveston Daily News
Goshen Daily News
Great Falls Tribune
Hamilton Daily Democrat
Harper's Weekly
Hawaiian Gazette
Huntingdon Globe
The Islander
Jamestown Weekly Alert
Janesville Daily Gazette
Lancaster Daily Intelligencer
Lawrence Daily Journal
Lawrence Evening Tribune
Lewiston Daily Sun
Logansport Chronicle
Logansport Pharos Tribune
Los Angeles Herald
Los Angeles Times
Manitoba Daily Free Press
Mansfield News
Manufacturers and Farmers Journal
Meriden Daily Journal
Milwaukee Journal
Milwaukee Sentinel
Montreal Herald
The Morning Review
Mower County Transcript
Nashville Banner
National Police Gazette

National Republican
Nevada State Journal
New Orleans Daily Picayune
New Ulm Weekly Review
New York Clipper
New York Evening Telegram
New York Herald
New York Press
New York Sun
New York Times
New York Tribune
New York World
Newark Daily Advocate
Newburgh Daily Journal
Newburgh Daily News
Oak Park Vindicator
Oakland Tribune
Omaha Daily Bee
Oregonian
Oshkosh Daily Northwestern
Oswego Daily Times
Paterson Daily Press
Philadelphia Record
Pittsburg Dispatch
Pittsburgh Press
Princeton Union
Providence Evening Telegraph
Pullman Herald
Quebec Daily Telegraph
Reading Eagle
Reno Evening Gazette
Richmond Daily Times
Roanoke Times
Rochester Daily Republican
Sacramento Record Union
St. Louis Post-Dispatch
St. Paul Daily Globe
St. Petersburg Independent
Salem Daily News
Salt Lake Evening Democrat
Salt Lake Herald
Salt Lake Tribune
San Antonio Daily Light
San Bernardino Daily Courier
San Francisco Call
San Francisco Chronicle
San Francisco Examiner
San Jose Evening News
Santa Fe Sun
Seattle Press
Spokane Daily Chronicle
The Sporting Life
Syracuse Daily Standard
Syracuse Herald
Syracuse Journal
Tacoma News Tribune
Titusville Herald
Toronto Daily Mail
Trenton Times
Warsaw Daily Times
Washington Bee
Washington Critic
Washington Evening Star
Washington National Republican
Wellsville Daily Reporter
Western Appeal
Wheeling Daily Intelligencer
Wichita Daily Eagle
Willamette Farmer
Yakima Herald
Yellowstone Journal
Yonkers Daily News

Websites

BoxRec. http://boxrec.com/.
British Boxing Hall of Fame website, http://bbhof.info/.
Buchstein, Fred. "Harry Hill—Saloon Fighting's P.T. Barnum," *New York History Review*, 2012, http://nyhrarticles.blogspot.com/2012/07/harry-hill-saloon-fighting.
"Dan Donnelly & Donnelly's Hollow," http://www.curraghcamp.com/dan.html.
"Denny Butler," *Cyber Boxing Zone*, http://www.cyberboxingzone.com/boxing/butler-denny.htm.
"Germania Assembly Rooms," *Open Green Map*, http://www.opengreenmap.org/greenmap/east-village-eco-culture-map/germania-assembly-rooms-25554.
Good Shepherd Catholic Church, http://www.goodshepherdchurchdenver.org/about-us/history.
"Harry Hill's Infamous Dance Hall," *BPOE Elks Lodge #944*, Ashland, Oregon, http://www.ashlandelks.org/html/history/corks/environs/harry_hills.html.
"Historic Oregon Newspapers," *University of Oregon*, http://oregonnews.uoregon.edu/.
"Joe Coburn," *Cyber Boxing Zone*, http://www.cyberboxingzone.com/boxing/coburn.htm.
"John J. Dwyer," *Cyber Boxing Zone*, http://www.cyberboxingzone.com/boxing/dwyer-j.htm
"John McCormack 1884–1945," *Co. Kildare Online Electronic History Journal*, Kildare County Library & Arts Services, http://www.kildare.ie/ehistory/.
"John P. Clow," *Cyber Boxing Zone*, http://www.cyberboxingzone.com/boxing/clow-john.htm
"Pleurisy," *Mayo Clinic*, http://www.mayoclinic.com/health/pleurisy/DS00244.
Ragpala, Kenneth, "The Evolution of the Boxing Gloves," *Bleacher Report*, September 19, 2009, http://bleacherreport.com/articles/258668-the-evolution-of-the-boxing-gloves.

Index

Allen, Arly ix, 14, 23, 25
Allers, Charley 330
Ashton, Jack 155, 190, 216, 217

Bagley, J.J. 51
Baker, Billy 149, 150, 151, 176, 184, 254
Banister, Sandy 149
Banks, Johnny 82, 114, 255
Barry, Jim 52, 53, 331
Barry, Tom 89, 90, 92, 94, 104, 105, 320
Bixamos, Charlie 85, 86, 87
Boden, Mike 97, 147, 160, 192
Bosworth, Frank 160, 332
Bowen, Andy 263, 266, 269, 311, 317, 320, 321, 322, 323, 325
Bowles, Jack 59, 60
Boylan, Jack 38, 39, 40, 41, 47, 48, 174, 200
Brady, Ellen T. 11, 138, 338, 345
Brady, James F. 11, 138, 343, 344, 345
Brennan, Mike 251, 252, 253, 254, 255
Broughton, Jack 14, 15, 16, 25
Burke, Jack 72, 73, 97, 104, 106, 128, 131, 132, 133, 138, 139, 140, 141, 142, 143, 144, 145, 186, 210, 233, 259, 279

Callis, Tracy ix, x, 1, 2, 11, 61, 115, 320, 340
Campbell, Dave 97, 100, 101, 102, 103, 104, 105, 112, 115, 118, 124, 144, 225, 226, 251, 252, 253, 254, 255, 256, 289
Carr, Jim 93, 94, 96
Carroll, Jimmy (British) 226, 228, 230, 236, 239, 241, 250, 262, 264, 265, 266, 270, 274, 276, 277, 280, 281, 337, 338, 339
Carroll, Jimmy (Brooklyn) 155, 200, 218, 222, 235, 255, 256, 257, 269, 313, 325, 328, 337
Chambers, Arthur 64, 65, 69, 79, 85, 104, 106, 111, 112, 113, 114, 119, 148, 162, 191
Chambers, John Graham 19, 20
Choynski, Joe 129, 223, 226, 240, 313, 320, 322, 326, 328, 332, 342
Clark, John 70, 77, 147, 249, 261, 262, 308
Clark, Nobby 76, 77, 162, 308, 309
Cleary, Mike 70, 71, 73, 83, 88, 89, 90, 91, 92, 93, 104, 114, 116, 125, 127, 147, 192, 311
Cleary, Tom 96, 98, 104, 105, 108, 109, 112, 113, 115, 116, 118, 120, 123, 124, 128, 130, 124, 248
Clow, John 97, 98, 144, 148, 175
Coburn, Joe 33, 176, 180, 192
Collins, Father 330
Conley, Mike 97, 160, 264, 265, 270, 338
Cooper, George 27
Corbett, James J. 3, 87, 88, 91, 103, 129, 138, 145, 223, 228, 232, 267, 269, 276, 277, 280, 285, 286, 295, 305, 306, 307, 308, 309, 312, 313, 314, 315, 331, 332, 333, 335, 336, 337, 338, 345
Costigan, Dennis 31, 51, 52, 60, 71, 76, 79, 110, 128, 134, 141, 144, 145, 149, 150, 151, 153, 165, 170, 175, 176, 177, 180, 183, 184, 189, 190, 191, 193, 194, 196, 201, 208, 211, 212, 213, 214, 216, 217, 218, 221, 225, 226, 229, 231, 232, 239, 256, 262, 264, 268, 307, 308, 309, 310, 312, 313, 315, 317, 338, 346

Dacey, Billy 53, 54, 55, 56, 57, 58, 110, 159, 160, 174, 180, 226, 283
Daly, Jim 216
Davies, Charles E. "Parson" 32, 82, 84, 128, 129, 131, 132, 139, 140, 141, 144, 269, 313, 320, 322, 323, 324, 326, 328
Dempsey, Alice 138, 154, 163, 176, 187, 262, 265, 268, 335, 338, 344, 345, 346
Dempsey, Alicia Lennon Kelly 27, 28, 30, 106, 114, 123, 125, 145, 190, 195, 209, 225
Dempsey, Anne Margaret 138, 250, 257, 262, 335, 338, 344, 345, 346
Dempsey, Margaret Brady "Maggie" 11, 84, 128, 137
Dempsey, Martin (Kelly, Martin, Jr.) 27, 28, 30, 58, 80, 106, 143, 174, 200, 299, 328, 330, 331, 333, 342
Dempsey, Mike 69, 225
Dempsey, Patrick 28, 225
Dempsey, Tom 27, 28, 333
Dempsey, Wilbert Harrison "Jack" 11, 12, 348
Denning, Joe 60, 97, 117, 118, 157, 173, 174, 191, 192, 194
Donnelly, Dan 5, 27
Donovan, Mike 7, 76, 82, 87, 106, 110, 114, 116, 165, 166, 168, 170, 173, 176, 183, 192, 195, 196, 198, 199, 200, 201, 202, 203, 204, 205, 209, 216, 222, 224, 225, 248, 254, 259
Doody, Patsy 256, 268, 269
Douglas, John (Marquess of Queensbury) 19, 200
Dunn, Jere 85, 86, 106, 171, 172, 180, 182, 186, 264
Dunn, Mark T. 84, 128, 334

Edwards, Billy 49, 111, 112, 113, 192, 195, 246

Fell, Jim 52, 82, 83, 97, 104, 194
Ferguson, Tom 70, 71, 72, 73, 75, 80
Fielden, Joe 310, 311
Fitzsimmons, Bob 4, 7, 91, 232, 233, 252, 253, 254, 255, 257, 258, 259, 260, 261, 262, 263, 264, 265, 266, 268, 269, 270, 271, 272, 273, 274, 275, 276,

Index

277, 278, 279, 280, 281, 282, 284, 287, 288, 290, 291, 292, 295, 296, 297, 298, 301, 303, 307, 311, 312, 313, 317, 320, 331, 332, 333, 335, 336, 337, 339, 341, 345, 346
Fogarty, Jack 10, 106, 108, 111, 112, 113, 114, 125, 127, 128, 157, 161
Force, Harry 41, 42, 43, 44, 45, 46, 48, 53
Fox, Richard K. 5, 6, 12, 20, 32, 40, 41, 44, 46, 48, 54, 58, 59, 60, 62, 63, 65, 75, 78, 82, 103, 106, 107, 108, 110, 113, 122, 124, 126, 127, 146, 153, 155, 156, 161, 170, 171, 173, 174, 175, 182, 198, 200, 203, 213, 214, 246, 259, 267, 277, 303, 305, 306, 309, 345, 347
Frazier, Billy 48, 49, 75, 76, 77, 81, 149
Fulljames, George 5, 10, 23, 54, 55, 57, 59, 61, 62, 63, 64, 65, 66, 67, 68

Gabig, Bill 79, 160
Gallagher, Patrick "Reddy" 151, 152, 153, 154, 155, 156, 158, 254, 281, 282, 283, 292, 293, 318
Gooding, Pope 8
Gorman, Paddy 226, 240, 245, 251, 252, 253, 254, 255
Greggains, Alex 288, 342
Gunst, Mose 264, 282, 339

Harting, George 9, 226, 231
Heinrich, Father 337, 339
Heiser, Joe 52, 58, 59, 78, 83
Hennessey, Joe 52, 53
Henry, Tom 60, 61, 69, 73, 74, 75, 104, 110, 156, 173, 174, 175, 184, 216
Hill, Harry 30, 32, 33, 34, 38, 41, 46, 47, 48, 63, 75, 77, 79, 82, 114, 180, 255, 256, 347

Jackson, John (Gentleman Jack) 16
Jackson, Peter 129, 138, 145, 155, 239, 276, 282, 286, 287
Jeffries, James J. 90, 277
Joyce, Henry (Harry Force?) 41, 46

Keenan, Jack 93, 94, 95, 96, 100, 101, 102, 104, 144
Kelliher, Denny 79, 130, 160, 161, 163, 177, 178, 179, 180, 238, 239, 240, 241
Kelly, John Edward see Dempsey, Jack
Kelly, Martin 27, 28

Keogh, Billy 296, 297, 298
Killen, Denny 97, 148
Kilrain, Jake 97, 103, 116, 129, 133, 138, 155, 157, 187, 189, 190, 197, 198, 199, 205, 207, 211, 214, 215, 224, 225, 269, 305

La Blanche, George 4, 5, 9, 10, 59, 80, 96, 97, 103, 106, 108, 109, 111, 115, 116, 118, 119, 120, 121, 122, 123, 124, 125, 146, 163, 178, 196, 197, 218, 219, 220, 222, 223, 224, 225, 226, 227, 228, 229, 230, 231, 232, 233, 234, 235, 236, 237, 238, 239, 240, 241, 242, 244, 246, 247, 248, 249, 250, 251, 253, 254, 255, 259, 262, 268, 276, 279, 280, 283, 288, 292, 293, 295, 296, 311, 331, 339, 340
Lane, Harry, M.D. 8, 334, 335, 336, 337
Langdon, Jack 147, 148
Lange, Charley 144
Lucie, Mike 184, 219, 224, 284
Lusk, O.L. M.D. 333

Maber, Billy "Shadow" 289, 290, 291, 297
Madden, Billy 7, 51, 52, 53, 69, 71, 79, 81, 82, 83, 84, 149, 155, 156, 157, 161, 165, 174, 175, 176, 177, 179, 180, 187, 239, 250, 280, 285, 286, 288
Mahoney, Billy 52, 109, 216
Mallon, Mike 77, 78
Mallory, Mike 58, 60
Manning, Billy 98, 99, 100
McAlpine, Thomas "Soap" 38, 39, 41, 42, 44, 46, 47, 53, 58
McAuliffe, Con 96, 162, 184
McAuliffe, Jack 7, 9, 30, 48, 84, 109, 110, 149, 154, 155, 157, 158, 161, 162, 163, 173, 174, 184, 191, 195, 196, 209, 214, 216, 230, 236, 239, 241, 244, 250, 251, 255, 256, 257, 263, 264, 265, 268, 270, 274, 275, 278, 280, 291, 295, 307, 326, 330, 331, 332, 344, 345, 346
McCaffrey, Dominick 7, 97, 100, 104, 106, 116, 129, 133, 137, 145, 146, 147, 148, 155, 174, 175, 176, 177, 179, 180, 181, 182, 183, 186, 187, 192, 194, 205, 214, 215, 279
McCann, Ned 31, 129, 160
McCarthy, Billy "Australian" 222, 226, 236, 238, 239, 240, 241, 242, 243, 244, 245, 246, 247, 248, 250, 255, 258, 259, 288, 317, 318, 319, 320, 322
McCarthy, Charles "Bull" 129, 130

McCoy, Pete 71, 82, 101, 104, 111, 114, 115, 116, 117, 118, 123, 158, 160, 161, 163, 191, 239, 254
McDonald, Ed "Rug" 31, 33, 34, 35, 36, 37, 89, 124
McHugh, Jim 69, 83, 159
McMahon, M.J. 343, 344, 345, 348
McMahon, T.J. 342
McMahon, Tom 149
McNamee, Jim 211
Meehan, Young 52
Mitchell, Charley 60, 72, 73, 87, 91, 92, 93, 106, 107, 111, 128, 131, 132, 137, 138, 153, 156, 157, 177, 178, 179, 180, 184, 185, 186, 187, 190, 191, 192, 197, 198, 199, 200, 205, 206, 207, 208, 210, 211, 212, 213, 215, 217, 285, 308, 309, 312, 313, 314, 315
Mitchell, Young (Herget, John L.) 95, 153, 233, 235, 236, 247, 251, 278, 279, 281, 282, 283, 284, 339, 342
Moehler, Ed 135, 136
Moore, Dick 310
Moore, George "Poney" 156, 186, 190, 313
Murray, Jimmy 38, 39, 49, 61, 74, 110, 216
Murray, Professor 220

Norton, Edward see McDonald, Ed "Rug"
Norton, Jack "Paddy" 133, 134, 135
Norton, Tom 100
Nye, Bill 6

Reagan, Johnny 26, 72, 106, 115, 154, 155, 156, 157, 158, 159, 160, 161, 163, 164, 165, 166, 167, 168, 169, 170, 171, 172, 173, 176, 191, 192, 195, 196, 198, 199, 215, 217, 218, 235, 239, 248, 285, 289
Reese Eddie 158, 159
Rodda, James 94
Ryan, Jimmy 70, 81, 82, 116, 128, 130
Ryan, Paddy 33, 91, 129, 140, 141
Ryan, Tommy 4, 25, 129, 283, 302, 304, 305, 310, 316, 320, 321, 322, 323, 324, 325, 326, 327, 328, 329, 330, 331, 332, 339, 346

Sharkey, Tom 91, 342
Sheedy, Patrick F. 9, 82, 140, 141, 143, 174, 187, 201
Skelly, Jack 7, 8, 30, 268, 278, 332, 343, 344, 345, 347
Smith, Al 69, 73, 74, 112, 115, 123
Smith, Billy "Mysterious" 278,

281, 289, 290, 291, 292, 297, 298, 299, 300, 301, 302, 303, 304, 305, 316, 320, 325
Smith, Bob 34, 36, 53, 60, 71, 163, 165, 166, 173
Smith, Jem 146, 190, 212, 215
Smith, Solly 306, 341
Snelling, Nathalie A., M.D. 334
Stevens, James "Billy" 176, 192
Stevenson, Frank 53, 54, 55, 161, 162, 164, 165, 166, 167, 168, 170, 171
Sullivan, John L. 1, 3, 4, 6, 7, 8, 9, 12, 21, 22, 33, 70, 71, 72, 75, 76, 77, 78, 82, 83, 88, 91, 104, 106, 107, 109, 110, 111, 114, 116, 123, 125, 129, 132, 133, 135, 136, 138, 140, 141, 143, 144, 145, 146, 153, 155, 174, 176, 177, 179, 180, 184, 185, 186, 189, 190, 192, 193, 194, 205, 206, 207, 210, 211, 212, 214, 215, 216, 224, 232, 249, 253, 254, 276, 277, 284, 286, 295, 307, 312, 313, 331, 332, 339, 340, 343, 344
Sullivan, Tom 55
Sweeney, Jim 58

Touhey, Ed 138, 249
Turnbull, Robert "Cocky" 38, 41, 49, 71, 72, 73, 110, 226
Tuthill, Gus 41, 68, 69, 77, 80, 106, 111, 115, 116, 118, 119, 120, 123, 124, 128, 144, 148, 154, 172, 180, 201, 210, 255, 264, 265, 270, 274, 279, 285, 288, 289, 297, 298, 299, 301, 302, 304, 306, 307, 308, 309, 313, 325, 331, 342

Ward, A.J., MD 153
Ward, John E., M.D. 329, 330
Watson, Walter "Professor" 69, 73, 87, 88
White, Charley 6, 27, 31, 202
White, Frank 31, 40, 51, 52, 55, 76, 77
Wilson, George 79
Wyatt, Harry 316

www.ingramcontent.com/pod-product-compliance
Lightning Source LLC
Chambersburg PA
CBHW081534300426
44116CB00015B/2625